EUROPEAN MONETARY INTEGRATION

EUROPEAN
MONETARY
INTEGRATION

DANIEL GROS

AND

NIELS THYGESEN

LONGMAN
LONDON
ST. MARTIN'S PRESS
NEW YORK

In the U.K., published by
Longman Group UK Limited,
Longman House, Burnt Mill,
Harlow, Essex, CM20 2JE, England

In the U.S.A., published by
St. Martin's Press
175 Fifth Avenue
New York, N.Y. 10010

First published 1992

ISBN 582–079225–CSD
ISBN 582–079217–PPR

British Library Cataloguing-in-Publication Data

A catalogue record for this book is
available from the British Library

Library of Congress Cataloging in Publication Data

Gros, Daniel, 1955–
  European monetary integration / Daniel Gros and Niels Thygesen.
    p. cm.
  Includes index.
  ISBN 0–312–08045–X
  1. European Monetary System (Organization) 2. Monetary policy–
–European Economic Community countries.   I. Thygesen, Niels.
II. Title
HG930.5.G76   1992
332.4'5'094--dc20

92–6581
CIP

Set In: 10/12 pt Bembo

Printed by the Bath Press, Avon

TABLE OF CONTENTS

PART II THE EUROPEAN MONETARY SYSTEM

PART III THE ECONOMICS OF MONETARY UNION

PART IV TOWARDS MONETARY UNION

Table of Contents

INTRODUCTION

The origins of the present book go back to 1986, when the Centre for Economic Policy Studies (CEPS) set up a working group on the future of the European Monetary System (EMS). The Director of CEPS, Peter Ludlow, had perceptively identified an imbalance in the debate on the EMS of the mid-1980s: while German (and Dutch) opinion increasingly emphasized the disciplinary, anti-inflationary virtues of the EMS and the need to preserve them, officials and most academics from countries with weaker currencies appeared to favour new approaches to European monetary integration, including the introduction of a parallel currency. It was difficult to see how these divergent opinions could be reconciled.

The meetings of the CEPS working group between the Spring of 1986 and the end of 1987, helped to clarify the achievements of the EMS, challenges to the survival of the system and possible directions for its future. As rapporteur and, respectively, chairman of the group we published a preliminary analysis of these issues in March 1988 as CEPS Paper No. 35.

The subject proved to be more topical than we could have anticipated. In the spring of 1988 Economic and Monetary Union (EMU) was put on the Community's agenda by proposals from the French, Italian and German governments, and the European Council in Hanover set up a Committee for the study of concrete steps leading towards EMU, presided over by Jacques Delors. We had the invaluable opportunity to participate in the preparation of the Delors Report as Advisor to the EC Commission, and, respectively, member of the Committee. Daniel Gros subsequently was one of the principal authors of the EC Commission's study *One Market, One Money*, which addressed the costs and benefits of monetary union, a topic not addressed by the Delors Committee.

In the present book we have gone considerably beyond our earlier contributions to provide the reader with a complete analysis of European monetary integration, its history, including the achievements of the European Monetary System, its current state and the outlook for the movement towards EMU.

We thus start in Part I with a brief analysis of the history of European monetary integration in the post-war period going up to the so-called Snake (Chapter 1) and of the inspiration this experience provided for the EMS negotiations of 1978 (Chapter 2). We then proceed in Part II to examine the functioning and the achievements of the EMS, chronologically in Chapter 3, and more analytically in Chapter 4, which addresses a number of theoretical and empirical issues raised by the academic literature on the EMS. Some of the issues discussed in this chapter are: to what extent has the EMS created a zone of monetary stability as intended when it was created? How important was it in reducing inflation during the 1980s? Has it worked as an asymmetric, German dominated system? Did it impart a deflationary bias to fiscal policy?

In Chapter 5 we evaluate the challenges to the EMS that arose in 1989/90 because of the absence of realignments since 1987, capital-market liberalization (plus financial market integration under the internal market programme) and the enlargement of participation following the entry of the peseta and pound sterling. We ask whether these three developments, together with German unification, could upset the *modus operandi* of the EMS and threaten its ability to maintain price stability. As argued more fully below, the absence of realignments coupled with capital market liberalization has turned the EMS into a quasi monetary union. This chapter thus provides an analysis of the issues that arise in the transition towards EMU. Chapter 6 then discusses the role of the ecu in monetary integration in general and, in particular, its importance during the transition towards EMU.

Part III turns to the future and discusses the economics of monetary union. It starts in Chapter 7 with an analysis of the microeconomic and macroeconomic benefits of EMU which we see fundamentally in the greater predictability and transparency of prices as well as the elimination of transaction costs while the main cost comes from the loss of the exchange rate as an adjustment instrument. Chapter 8 then turns to the implications of EMU for budgetary policies. We analyse the spill-over effects of national demand policies, the need to create a Community-wide transfer system to help regions hit by adverse shocks and discuss the desirability of instituting binding guidelines for national budget deficits. Chapter 9 discusses the worldwide implications of EMU, including those of a single European currency for the international monetary system and global portfolio balance.

The final chapters, Part IV of the book, trace the public and political debate on EMU, starting from the inspirations for and the conclusions of the Delors Report (Chapter 10). Alternatives to the approach of the latter, notably the UK proposal for a 'hard ecu' as a parallel currency, are discussed in Chapter 11. Possible concrete steps towards monetary union in the first two stages envisaged by the Delors Report and currently under discussion in the Intergovernmental Conference on EMU are reviewed in Chapter 12. We devote particular attention to the idea of a Community-wide system of required reserves as a convenient instrument for the precursor of the European System of Central Banks (ESCB) to manage an increasingly common monetary policy in the transition period. Chapter 13 focuses on the ESCB in the final stage: its structure, the mandate for price stability as an overriding objective, and its relationship with the political authorities. The book concludes in Chapter 14 with our personal perspective on the outlook for achieving monetary union, its relationship with the move towards political union enlargement, and a suggested timetable.

The book is intended to offer a comprehensive perspective of the process of monetary integration in Europe. As such it is hoped that it will be of interest to readers in the academic community, in official circles, and in the wider public. We have seen a particular purpose for our book in the effort to bring together the results of theoretical and empirical research with the institutional and practical considerations which dominate in the negotiations on EMU. The focus is deliberately narrow in one sense: we devote only passing attention to non-monetary issues. But within this area we try to keep a wide focus taking into account all the arguments and forces that have shaped events and are important to understand why the Community has come so far in the process of monetary integration and why (and how) it will proceed to attain the ultimate goal of EMU.

In writing this book we have accumulated significant intellectual debts to a number of academic and official colleagues, too numerous to be listed individually. The Director of CEPS, Peter Ludlow, stimulated the initial effort and provided a fine working environment for one of us as Senior Research Fellow and for the other as Associate and part-time Senior Research Fellow. The contribution of the members of the CEPS working group on the future of the EMS was particularly important to us, as were the opportunities to present our results in restricted seminars with officials of the two central banks, Deutsche Bundesbank and Banco de España, which had helped to sponsor our group. Graduate seminars at the Katholieke Universiteit te Leuven, the University of Copenhagen, Institut d'Etudes Politiques in Paris, Servizio Studi, Banca d'Italia and the International Economics Programme at the Institut für Weltwirtschaft, Kiel, provided stimulating environments for presenting the main results. The Thyssen Foundation and Frau Lucy von Luterotti made important financial contributions to a fellowship which enabled Daniel Gros to work as a full-time research fellow at CEPS 1986–88. The contribution of the Instituto Bancario San Paolo di Torino was, however, decisive in allowing Daniel Gros to concentrate his efforts in 1990–91 on this project. Without this help the book might never have been completed.

Bart Turtelboom and Eric Jones provided excellent research assistance. Rose de Terville at CEPS prepared the long manuscript through several drafts with efficiency and cheerfulness, ably assisted by Edda Andersen at the Institute of Economics at the University of Copenhagen. Karsten Jensen read the manuscript with great care and spotted several errors. Anne Rix made a large number of editorial improvements and worked with remarkable speed. Chris Harrison of Longman showed exceptional patience with the delays incurred and great tolerance in accepting an excessively long manuscript.

Despite the devoted efforts of those listed and the kind and detailed attention given to our numerous articles and conference presentations over the past five years, we are aware that a book covering as large a topic as European monetary integration is bound to contain errors, omissions and inadequately founded conclusions, reflecting the bias of the authors. We assume sole responsibility for any such remaining deficiencies.

Brussels and Copenhagen, March 1992

Daniel Gros

Niels Thygesen

PART I

A BRIEF
HISTORY
OF EUROPEAN
MONETARY
INTEGRATION

CHAPTER 1

THE BEGINNING: FROM THE EUROPEAN PAYMENTS UNION TO THE SNAKE

The monetary history of Europe does not begin with the aftermath of the Second World War. But the early post Second World War period is a natural starting point for any description of the long-run developments in European monetary integration because that period saw both the lowest point in terms of monetary integration and the beginning of the overall integration process that led later to the creation of the European Economic Community (EEC), the European Monetary System (EMS) and finally to the present plans for an Economic and Monetary Union (EMU).

The purpose of this chapter is therefore not to analyse the monetary history of Europe in general. The main aim of this brief review of the integration process in the monetary sphere is to provide a background for the more detailed discussion of the genesis and the operation of the EMS in chapters 2 to 4. The experience of the almost thirty years (appr. 1948–78) covered in this chapter also contains some valuable lessons for the current efforts to reach EMU before the end of this century.

The unifying thread that runs through these thirty years resides in two related issues: is the process of monetary integration in Europe ultimately driven by economic or political motives? And, to what extent does the formal institutional framework affect the outcome in times of crisis?

The wider issue of the role of monetary integration in the overall integration process is not addressed here. The famous dictum 'L'Europe se fera par la monnaie ou elle ne se fera pas', attributed to Jacques Rueff, expresses a political point of view in which monetary integration is not only a goal in itself, but constitutes also a means to reach a wider goal, namely European political unification. While in this book support is given to the overall integration process, discussion is confined as objectively as possible to the economic aspects of monetary integration.

The chapter is organized as follows: section 1.1 reviews the progress made from the bilateralism in trade and payments of the early post-war years through the Organization of European Economic Cooperation (OEEC) and the European Payments Union (EPU) to convertibility by the end of 1958 for nearly all of the currencies of Western Europe. Section 1.2 then looks at the experience of the successful period for about a decade thereafter when Western Europe was part of a well-functioning global monetary system, and when the original six member states of the European Economic Community built up a customs union and some joint policies. Section 1.3 reviews the first effort at extending these policies in the direction of Economic and Monetary Union, as the Bretton Woods system unfolded – the Werner Report for EMU by 1980. Section 1.4 examines the achievements of what remained of the implementation of the first stage of that process – the 'snake'. Finally, in section 1.5 some lessons are drawn from the three decades up to 1978, which are of relevance for the creation of the European Monetary System, the subject of the following chapter.

1.1   The first step towards convertibility: the European Payments Union

The Second World War had left large parts of Europe in ruins, but the immediate consequences of the physical destruction were soon overcome and by 1948 industrial output attained again the pre-war level. Even prior to the end of the hostilities there had already been extensive planning for the post-war global economic order which led to the creation of the International Monetary Fund (IMF) and the World Bank under the Bretton Woods agreements which were concluded in 1944. The main aim of these agreements was to avoid the mistakes of the interwar period. The competitive devaluations of the 1930s and the experience with floating exchange rates in the 1920s were the main reasons why the Bretton Woods agreements created a system of fixed exchange rates which could be changed only with the consent of the IMF in cases of so-called 'fundamental disequilibrium'. Moreover, all signatories undertook to make their currencies convertible which would allow a return to a multilateral trading system. Convertibility is a sufficient (but not a necessary) condition for multilateral trade because if a currency is convertible non-residents can exchange the surplus they earn in any particular currency against another currency at the official exchange rate.

However, the Bretton Woods agreements remained for a long time irrelevant for many of the signatory countries because of another consequence of the war, which proved more difficult to overcome than the physical destruction, namely the absence of an international financial system that could form the basis for a revival of multilateral trade. This applied especially to Europe where most trade in the late 1940s was conducted through some 200 bilateral trade agreements.[1] These agreements typically contained a bilateral line of credit which determined in effect by how much the bilateral current account could deviate from zero, since deficits in excess of the specified bilateral credit line had to be settled in gold. Most European governments tried desperately to preserve their small gold holdings, using the arsenal of trade policy (quotas and high tariffs) to restrict imports from creditor countries unwilling to extend further credit. Settlement in gold was therefore avoided as much as possible.

The essence of the problem was the lack of transferability of the bilateral balances.

---

[1] The complex pattern of trade and payments restrictions is surveyed in Diebold (1952).

Deficits with one country could not be offset with surpluses against another country because there was neither an official compensating mechanism, nor foreign exchange markets, as European currencies were not convertible.

The bilateralism proved so difficult to overcome because of the famous 'dollar gap'. Most countries would have been in serious difficulties with their overall balance of payments if they had allowed unrestricted multilateral trade because in most countries the demand for imports, especially for goods from the dollar area exceeded by far the limited supply of exports. All European countries tried therefore to earn surpluses in gold, US dollars or any currency convertible into US dollars. If any individual European country had tried to make its currency convertible unilaterally it would have rendered its currency equivalent to the US dollar with the result that all the other countries would have attempted to earn a surplus in their bilateral trade with it. Any unilateral attempt to reestablish convertibility would therefore have led to even more serious balance of payments difficulties for the country that was willing to undertake such a step. The United Kingdom had this experience during an aborted attempt to reestablish the convertibility of the pound sterling in 1947. Although supported by credit lines of unprecedented magnitude, about 5 billion US dollars, the UK authorities had to suspend convertibility after only seven weeks.

In principle the continuing balance of payment difficulties were only the expression of an overvaluation of the European currencies against the US dollar. A devaluation of the European currencies would therefore have been the appropriate answer to the 'dollar gap'. However, the massive devaluations that would have been required were never seriously considered in the early post-war years. The main reason was that the 'dollar gap' was considered a structural problem: the elasticities of import demand and export supply were assumed to be so low that a depreciation would not have had a large impact on the balance of payments. Moreover, given that even in 1950 European exports to North America were less than one half of imports a devaluation would have led to a large J-curve effect and therefore, at least initially, a worsening of the European trade balance with the US dollar area.

After the failed British unilateral dash to convertibility in 1947 it became increasingly to be perceived that a return to convertibility required a joint European effort. The creation in 1948 of the Organization for European Economic Cooperation (OEEC) renamed in 1960, with an expanded membership, Organization for Economic Cooperation and Development (OECD), was the first step in this direction. The OEEC was mainly a response to the US call for a cooperative European effort to make effective use of the US aid to be provided under the Marshall Plan, extended by the US authorities to OEEC participants in the 1948–52 period. But trade liberalization, while necessary for the resumption of significant inter-European trade, was not in itself sufficient as long as payments remained severely constrained.[2]

Bilateralism therefore persisted even after the creation of the OEEC in 1948 and the

---

[2] The initiative for the creation of the European Coal and Steel Community among six European states that came in 1950, which provided the first and only step in the overall integration process prior to the signing of the Treaty of Rome by the six original member states in 1957, had little immediate impact on intra-European trade outside these two sectors.

exhaustion of the bilateral credit lines granted in 1946 and 1947 led to a complete jam in the intra-European payment system although the Marshall Plan aid alleviated the 'dollar gap' to some extent. It took a further two years until the European Payments Union (EPU) was negotiated in all necessary detail in September 1950 with retroactive implementation from 1 July 1950. All eighteen OEEC members participated in the EPU, but through the sterling and the French franc areas, the EPU in fact covered most of Africa and Asia as well. The EPU thus covered an area that accounted for about 70 per cent of world trade. Though it was more than a regional arrangement the EPU did, by its very design, imply some discrimination in trade and payments against the countries of the convertible currencies, notably the United States. It is all the more remarkable that the United States not only accepted these implications, but positively encouraged and contributed intellectually and politically to the formation of the EPU. The history of the EPU negotiations and its operations is recorded in great detail in Kaplan and Schleiminger (1989).

The EPU provided an escape from bilateralism because each month all bilateral deficits and surpluses were netted out into one overall net position *vis-à-vis* the Union. The monthly net positions were cumulated over time and only the changes in the cumulative (starting in July 1950) net position of each member country with the Union as a whole had to be settled in the end. This was the easy part of the EPU agreements. The difficult part was the way in which the net EPU position had to be settled. Countries which could expect to be EPU creditors had an interest to obtain settlement in gold, or US dollars which they could then use to finance imports from the countries with convertible currencies. Conversely, countries which could expect to have a deficit with the EPU area were interested in obtaining credit in order not to lose their precious gold or US dollars.

The success of the EPU was based on the compromise for the settlement of EPU balances that was finally obtained.[3] Each country was assigned a quota equal to 15 per cent of the sum of exports and imports in 1949, the 'turn-over'. The mix of credit and gold to be applied to the settlement of EPU positions was then a function of the size of the EPU position relative to the quota, which was divided into 5 'tranches' of 20 per cent each. A debtor position less than 20 per cent of the quota could be settled entirely with credit from the Union, but beyond that 'tranche' there was a sliding scale with an increasing proportion of gold settlement which reached 100 per cent when the quota was exhausted so that debtor positions in excess of the quota were expected to be settled entirely in gold. For debtor countries the incentive to adjust was growing with the size of the intra-union imbalance.

An important part of the EPU agreement was the asymmetry between the settlement terms for debtor and creditor positions. All creditor positions above the first, 20 per cent, 'tranche' were settled with 50 per cent gold; for creditor positions exceeding the full quota the Managing Board of the EPU had to propose special settlement terms. The asymmetry between the settlement terms for creditor and for debtor positions

---

[3] This compromise was close to the ideas developed by Robert Triffin, then an advisor to the European Cooperation Administration of the US government, see Triffin (1957) and (1966).

could in theory have led to large net liabilities for the Union, but in practice the working capital that had been established when the EPU was created was sufficient to cover the minor fluctuations in the net obligations of the Union.

This brief description of the formal rules suggests that the real test of the system could be expected if a country exhausted its quota. This happened almost immediately after the system had started to operate, since during the summer and autumn of 1950 the Federal Republic of Germany developed a large current-account deficit which soon exceeded its quota (which had been calculated using data from 1949, a year during which German foreign trade had not yet recovered to its pre-war level). Given its very low level of reserves the Federal Republic would clearly not have been able to settle its EPU deficit fully in gold as stipulated by the rules. Something had therefore to be done if Germany was to continue to participate in EPU.

The German crisis of 1950–1 was overcome quite rapidly in the course of 1951 through a combination of a tighter monetary policy in Germany, a temporary unilateral suspension of import liberalization and a special EPU credit to Germany. This package of measures had been proposed by an ad hoc expert group sent by the EPU Management Board to Germany in late 1950. Although, with hindsight, it turned out that a tightening of monetary policy would have been sufficient to eliminate the German deficit the two additional policy measures were important for the survival of the EPU because they showed that other countries were prepared to agree to policy measures that were not in their own short-term interests (and would even help a recent enemy) in order to save the system. Acceptance of temporary impediments to exports to the fastest growing economy in the area was not easy for Germany's partners. With the EPU the balance of payments position of each member country ceased to be a purely national problem and became a legitimate concern for all the other participants as well.

This first crisis, the successful resolution of which greatly strengthened the EPU, showed how the existence of an institutional framework that was valued by everybody could affect the outcome of a crisis. Member countries had to accept 'interference' in the management of their domestic policies by their partners if they wanted to remain in the system. In completely different circumstances France had to relearn the same lesson during the 1983 realignment of the EMS described in chapter 3.

The German crisis was only the first of a series of problems the EPU had to face. As the terms of trade for European countries deteriorated and inflation picked up during the Korean War, a number of different countries – the Netherlands, the United Kingdom and France – developed deficits that exceeded their quota and had to take corrective policy measures if they wanted to receive favourable terms from the EPU. The only persistent issue proved, however, to be the growing German surplus which developed after the 1950–1 crisis. Indeed Germany ran a current-account surplus almost without any interruption until 1981. This issue was never really settled. The German quota was increased several times, but the surplus continued to exceed the quota and the EPU had no real means to force a surplus country to take drastic measures. Germany, on the other hand, had to accept only partial payment in gold for its surplus as long as the EPU existed. This inability to put pressure on surplus countries was also to become a permanent feature of the international monetary system. A similar asymmetry developed thirty years later in the EMS although the rules of exchange-rate management there are, in principle, symmetric. In the EMS the more inflationary countries were the ones that had to adjust while the Bundesbank was able to pursue its stability-oriented course. It is now recognized that this asymmetry was actually an important factor for the success of the EMS.

After 1951 the German surplus became a near-permanent feature of the international monetary system until 1990 and, with the exception of 1979–81, most international crises led to calls on the Federal Republic to adopt more expansionary fiscal and/or monetary policies.

Despite the German surplus issue the EPU was able to function smoothly and over time European exports to the United States increased faster than imports, so that the 'dollar gap' became less serious. This meant that a return to full (non-resident) convertibility could be envisaged. In the mid 1950s a plan, mainly inspired by the United Kingdom, to achieve early convertibility by allowing exchange rates to fluctuate, was not pursued because the 'dollar gap' was still judged to be too serious. But by 1957–8 the cumulative EPU positions of most countries became large relative to their quota and the full gold settlement this involved meant that the EPU was no longer that important for debtor countries. The EPU was finally dissolved by a unanimous agreement at the end of 1958 and the participating countries made their currencies convertible. In a formal sense, the EPU was replaced by the European Monetary Agreement (EMA), negotiated as a successor arrangement already by 1955. The EMA was authorized to offer financial safety nets to participants, but it was clear that authority for suggesting policy adjustments and setting the terms for conditional lending would pass to the IMF Executive Board. Indeed, in 1958 the IMF staff had worked out a stabilization programme for one of the EPU members (Turkey).

In retrospect, the dissolution of the EPU was a loss to European monetary integration. The EPU Managing Board had achieved authority by its effective implementation of what much later became known as multilateral surveillance; although the weakening of the constraints on debtors in the course of its eight years of existence would in any case have diminished that authority, there were, as noted by Triffin (1966), arguments in favour of keeping the EPU in preference to moving unilaterally, though simultaneously, to global convertibility. The EPU could have continued to provide a Western European forum for policy coordination at a time when Europe fragmented into members of the EEC, signatories of the European Free Trade Area (EFTA) Agreement of 1958 and those few who did not participate in either trading arrangement. A joint multilateral commitment by the EPU participants to convertibility, but with the retention of some mechanisms for monitoring each others' performance could well have proved useful over the next decade, both in minimizing intra-European disequilibria and in engaging in a more coordinated way in the dialogue with the United States over the growing imbalance in its external accounts.

However, by 1958 European countries were anxious to remove as many vestiges of early post-war constraints as possible. They were also impressed with the increased scope for international official borrowing and lending which appeared to introduce a major new freedom of action for national economic policy. They felt they could use some more autonomy. This was not the time to propose a continuation of regional macroeconomic coordination and even less the transfer of additional authority to international bodies.

1.2 The Bretton Woods system in the 1960s: stability and crises

Only after the reestablishment of convertibility in 1958–9 did the Bretton Woods agreements become really operational. The core of the agreements establishing the International Monetary Fund (IMF) consisted of the system of fixed exchange rates which linked all currencies to the US dollar and the US dollar to gold. Changes in the 'parities' were allowed only in the case of a 'fundamental disequilibrium' of the balance of payments, temporary disequilibria could be financed through credits from the IMF.

The IMF rules allowed for a 1 per cent band of fluctuations around the central parities against the US dollar. This implied that any two European currencies could move by as much as 4 per cent against each other if they switched their relative position against the US dollar. Since this was considered excessive, the European countries agreed to limit their fluctuations *vis-à-vis* the dollar to 0.75 per cent, thus reducing the potential margin for intra-European exchange-rate fluctuations to 3 per cent. Bilateral rates were in fact much more stable than that; chapter 4 provides some evidence for the gradual success of the EMS in bringing exchange-rate variability inside Europe back towards the level observed in the 1960s.

In terms of the overall process of European integration the decisive event of the late 1950s was, of course, not the dissolution of the EPU but the signing of the Treaty of Rome which established, among the 'six' as they were then called, the European Economic Community (EEC, the official name was later abbreviated to European Communities when the Euratom and the European Coal and Steel Community Treaties were merged with the Rome Treaty of the EEC in 1967). Seven other European countries, led by the United Kingdom, preferred a looser form of integration and signed the EFTA Agreement.

The main practical elements of the Treaty of Rome were the customs union (the 'common market') and the Common Agricultural Policy. There exists a vast literature on the implementation of the customs union and the integration process in other, non-monetary, areas; these issues are therefore not discussed further in this book.[4] The only aspect of these early years of the Community that matters in this context is the extent to which the customs union and the Common Agricultural Policy did affect the monetary sphere.

The ambition of the founders of the EEC went far beyond the two, limited areas of integration that formed the heart of the life of the Community in its early years. The Treaty of Rome contains two short chapters on economic policy coordination and the balance of payments. Paragraphs 103 to 107 say explicitly that each member country considers its conjunctural policy and its exchange-rate policy a matter of common

---

[4] For surveys of the history of the EC and the full range of its policies, see Molle (1990) and Swann (1990).

concern. However, these provisions of the Treaty remained *de facto* irrelevant because exchange-rate policy and balance of payments assistance were considered the domain of the IMF. The only practical action to come from this part of the Treaty was the establishment of the Monetary Committee which comprises one representative from the central bank and one from the finance ministry of each member country plus two representatives of the EC Commission. This group provided a useful forum for the exchange of information and for preparing the meetings of the Council of Ministers of Economics and Finance (ECOFIN).

Somewhat later other Committees dealing with economic policy coordination were established. The only important one from a monetary perspective was the 'Committee of Governors of the central banks of the Member Countries of the European Community', established in 1964.[5] This Committee, which meets in the premises of the Bank for International Settlements (BIS) in Basle in conjunction with the monthly meetings of the Governors of the Central Banks in the Group of Ten countries, also provided a forum for exchange of information among the central banks of the Community. It did not develop a more operational role until the 1970s and it has only recently begun to challenge the authority of national policy-makers, see section 1.4. Nevertheless, the fact that national monetary officials have now been meeting regularly for about thirty years to exchange information and experiences and to resolve technical issues which arise in their interaction must be seen as an important cause of the present confidence that advanced monetary integration is feasible.

During the 1960s the main issue for the Community in the monetary sphere was that exchange-rate adjustments could disrupt the functioning of the customs union and the Common Agricultural Policy. This concern reinforced the IMF prescription of fixed exchange rates, but whenever member countries experienced balance of payments difficulties they turned first to the IMF and the United States for assistance. This was notably the case when Italy swung into external deficit in 1963–4.

The German surplus issue continued for most of the 1960s, but after 1961 it was overshadowed by the 'dollar overhang' created by the US current-account deficits and capital outflows. In 1961 Germany and the Netherlands revalued their currencies by 5 per cent. There was no prior consultation with other EEC members, nor with the IMF, on this occasion, but the step was generally welcomed in Europe. Although this measure did not have a large effect on their external surpluses, speculative pressure on these two currencies did abate. Moreover, since the Common Agricultural Policy was fully implemented only in 1964, this move did not directly impinge on any of the Community policies. Apart from this episode exchange rates remained fixed until 1969 among the six EC currencies.

The early 1960s was a period of low unemployment and relatively stable prices. In this environment there was little need for strong government intervention to stabilize the economy. Another reason why, despite official lip-service to the contrary, the lack

---

[5] The committee structure developed rapidly in the early 1960s: one committee for Conjunctural Policy was set up in 1960 and Committees for Medium-Term Economic Policy and Budgetary Policy followed, both in 1964. These three committees were integrated into the Economic Policy Committee as part of the 1974 overhaul of the coordination process.

of effective macroeconomic cooperation was not a real problem was that economic integration in the Community was much less intense than today. The ratio of intra-EC trade to GDP stood only at about 6 per cent in 1960, but it went up to 12 per cent in 1975; it is now at about 15 per cent.

The rather tranquil environment of the 1960s was, however, punctuated by a number of crises starting with the devaluation of the pound sterling in 1967 by nearly 15 per cent. But since the UK was at that time not a member of the EC this event did not affect the Community directly. The French devaluation of 1969 (of 11.1 per cent) was therefore the first exchange-rate adjustment in the Community since the customs union and the Common Agricultural Policy had been established. It was preceded by almost a year of speculative pressures and one aborted effort to agree on a realignment in October 1968, ultimately vetoed by France.

The French devaluation of August 1969 and the German revaluation (by nearly 10 per cent) one month later were a major test for the Community. The functioning of the customs union was not really affected by these exchange-rate changes, but the Common Agricultural Policy required policy action if intra-EC exchange rates moved because the prices of many agricultural products (especially cereals, but also dairy products) are fixed in a common unit which was then called the European Unit of Account (EUA), but has since become the ecu (see chapter 6 for a brief history of the ecu). The EUA was defined as the gold content of one US dollar, the international monetary standard at the time.

Under the Common Agricultural Policy prices for agricultural products in national currency were equal to the official Community price in EUA times the 'green' exchange rate (national currency/EUA), which was also determined by the Community. If the 'green' exchange rate were to follow simply the market rate (or, under the Bretton Woods system the official dollar parity) a depreciation of any Community currency by 10 per cent would increase agricultural prices in that country by 10 per cent as well; and vice versa for appreciations. In practice, however, this was not accepted for political reasons. The French authorities wanted to contain inflation and therefore resisted a devaluation of the 'green' French franc. In Germany producer interests were stronger (and inflation lower) so that the German government did not accept an appreciation of the 'green' mark.

In practice, exchange-rate changes did therefore endanger what was then the centrepiece of the Community, i.e., the Common Agricultural Policy. Since the French and German governments did not accept the price changes that would have followed from the exchange-rate changes the only solution was to let the common agricultural market split up and maintain different prices (for agricultural products) in different countries. In order to maintain prices at different levels a complicated system of 'Monetary Compensatory Amount' (MCAs) had to be introduced; for a recent survey of the issues involved, see Boyd (1990). France typically demanded and obtained negative MCAs which helped to keep French food prices below the Community average. Germany usually had positive MCAs to keep the prices for German producers above the Community average. Since these MCAs were really tariffs and import subsidies they effectively compartmentalized national agricultural markets. The Community recognized this and the MCAs were therefore supposed to be temporary, but since exchange rates continued to move throughout the following two decades new MCAs were created as the old ones were slowly dismantled. However, at the time they were introduced this was not foreseen since it was widely expected that the French and German moves would remain exceptional cases.

1.3   An early attempt at monetary union: the Werner Plan

At the end of the 1960s the Community had completed the customs union ahead of schedule and had established a Common Agricultural Policy. It therefore seemed time for a further move forward. The events of May 1968 had led to a wage explosion in France and had forced the French to devalue the following year and to reinforce capital controls. The continuing German surpluses (coupled with the weakness of the US dollar) had led to the revaluation of the DM. There were indications that the economies of the Community were starting to diverge. However, in most other respects the macroeconomic performance of each of the economies of the member countries was still very similar. When the European Council of December 1969 in the Hague reaffirmed the wish to move forward to Economic and Monetary Union (EMU) while opening the Community to new members – an early example of deepening and widening at the same time – the goal must have seemed to be rather close.

The initiative came primarily from then German Chancellor Willy Brandt, see Kloten (1980). He suggested that over an initial phase EC member states should jointly formulate medium-term objectives for the participants and aim to harmonize short-term policies; in a second phase a monetary union of permanantly fixed exchange rates could then be achieved. In this phase Germany would be prepared to transfer part of its international reserves to a common European institution. Proposals of France at the Hague stressed the early creation of a system of balance of payments assistance for EC member states and the formation of a uniform policy with respect to third currencies. Sufficient agreement was achieved, despite these different priorities, to commission a major study by a group of high-ranking national and EC officials.

In October 1970 this group, under the chairmanship of Pierre Werner (then Prime Minister of Luxembourg), produced a report that detailed how EMU could be attained in stages by 1980, see Werner *et al.* (1970). The Werner Report was remarkably specific with respect to the final objective of EMU, to be achieved by 1980, i.e., within a decade of the setting of the objective. Monetary union was to imply 'the total and irreversible convertibility of currencies, the elimination of fluctuation in exchange rates, the irrevocable fixing of parity rates and the complete liberation of movements of capital' (Werner Report, chapter III, p. 10). This could be accompanied by the maintenance of national monetary symbols or the establishment of a sole Community currency, though the Report voiced a preference for the latter (ibid.).

There is only a fairly brief reference to the necessary institutional framework in the Werner Report. A Community system for the central banks, based on the analogy of the US Federal Reserve System, would be established to conduct the principal elements of internal monetary policy and exchange-rate policy *vis-à-vis* third currencies. The Report, in contrast to the present efforts to define the institutional structure of EMU and of the European System of Central Banks in precise detail, was rather vague as to how the central monetary authority would be constituted and what its relationship to the political authorities would be.

The Werner Report was more prescriptive, on the other hand, with respect to joint policies in the non-monetary area. It foresaw the need for a 'Centre of decision for economic policy', politically responsible to the European Parliament, to exercise a decisive influence over EC economic policy, including national budgetary policies (ibid., p. 12):

> the essential features of the whole of the public budgets, and in particular variations in their volume, the size of balances and the methods of financing them or utilizing them, will be decided at the Community level;

> regional and structural policies will no longer be exclusively within the jurisdiction of the member countries;

> a systematic and continuous consultation between the social partners will be ensured at the Community level.

Although the Werner Report put considerable emphasis on market related processes – the free movement of goods, services, people and capital – it also stressed that factor mobility would have to be supplemented by public financial transfers to avoid regional and structural disequilibria from arising. Read in the perspective of to-day's discussion on EMU two main differences of emphasis stand out, in addition to the relative neglect of institutional features and procedures. The Werner Report paid less attention to achieving convergence and low inflation, because initial divergence in these respects among prospective participants was less visible than it is in the early 1990s, though, in retrospect, it was imminent when the Report appeared. It was, in contrast, concerned about the longer-run risk of divergence in economic performance and policies and hence made more radically constraining proposals to put into place EC authority over budgetary policies and even introduced some potential scope for a joint incomes policy.

These differences in emphasis and ambition closely reflect the rather different view of how economies work and interact which prevailed twenty years ago. The price level was seen as moving only rather sluggishly with wage negotiations and cost push playing central roles in its evolution. External imbalances were attributed primarily to differences in the stance of national demand management policies, in particular public budgets; hence the need to centralize authority over them. At that time many restrictions on capital movements were still in place and policy-makers realized only gradually that 'speculative' capital flows could provoke large currency adjustment even when the fundamentals did not seem to warrant any exchange-rate adjustment. Some further comparisons with the recent approach to EMU are made in subsequent chapters, notably in chapter 10 on the paradigm adopted by the Delors Report of 1989.

Radical as it was in its prescriptions for full EMU, the Werner Report was nevertheless endorsed at the political level and the ECOFIN Council embarked, with its Resolution on the attainment of EMU by stages of 22 March 1971, on the first of the stages designed to be completed by the end of 1973. The objective of EMU in the demanding version was also endorsed by the Heads of State and Government of the original six members and the three new entrants (Denmark, Ireland and the United Kingdom) in October 1972. The ease with which these commitments were made may have been due to two interrelated features of the whole approach which were quickly perceived by EC member states.

The first was the softness of the constraints in the first two stages which relied entirely on procedures for prior consultations on, and voluntary coordination of, national economic policies. National decisions were increasingly to be taken in the light of EC guidelines and to be monitored by EC bodies, but there were no sanctions for non-compliance. Transfer of authority was not only postponed till the final stage; there were no mechanisms or market-related incentives to give momentum to the process.

The second virtue was the apparent reconciliation achieved by the Werner Report of the so-called 'economist' and 'monetarist' approaches to European integration which had already been evident in the main proposals in the Hague the previous year. The former (in later discussion labelled 'the coronation theory') represented primarily by Germany and the Netherlands, argued that irrevocable fixing of exchange rates and centralization of monetary authority had to come at the end of a long period of voluntary coordination and convergent performance and to be underpinned by major transfers of budgetary authority towards the centre, while the second view, favoured primarily by French, Belgian and Italian officials, underlined the potential driving role of monetary integration. By adopting an intermediate position and stressing the need for parallel progress in the monetary and non-monetary areas the Werner Report achieved a compromise superficially acceptable to both sides of this elusive, but perennial debate which was resumed in the Delors Report nineteen years later. But attention was focused in the Werner Report, and in the follow up to it, more on what might constitute a balanced package of policies in the final stage than on parallelism over the process leading towards EMU. In this process monetary coordination and exchange-rate management received prime attention.

These weaknesses, which are more thoroughly analysed in Baer and Padoa-Schioppa (1989) and in Mortensen (1990), were not at the centre of the discussion of the Werner Report and the efforts at implementing its proposals for the first stage. Discussion returns to the latter in section 4 below on the snake and its constituent arrangements which left a bridgehead which proved useful in the launching of the EMS. Some of the lessons from the failure of this first attempt at EMU are taken up in section 1.5.

The Werner Report was never implemented although the objective of EMU was again unanimously endorsed by the ECOFIN Council of March 1971. The Council did not accept the need to create new institutions outside the existing framework and therefore implicitly did not see the need for a modification of the Treaty of Rome. The rejection of the 'centre of decision for economic policy' was not surprising since, at least from today's point of view as argued in chapter 8, EMU does not require the degree of centralization of fiscal policy foreseen by the Werner Report. The failure to see the need for a common monetary institution was not really compatible with the stated aim of going towards monetary union but at that time exchange rates were still thought to be in the domain of the IMF – and the Bretton Woods system had after all allowed the Community to attain almost completely fixed exchange rates during most of the 1960s without any common monetary institution.

The reason for the failure of the Werner Plan might therefore have been the implicit reliance on the Bretton Woods system which was collapsing at exactly the time the first stages of the Werner Plan were supposed to be implemented in 1973. Moreover, the exchange-rate stability of the early 1960s had been achieved in an environment in which the stabilization of exchange rates did not imply that important domestic policy targets had to be sacrificed; inflation and unemployment were low so that neither fiscal nor monetary policy needed to be used aggressively to correct major disequilibria. Moreover, at that time capital mobility was still low, which gave domestic monetary policy some leeway, at least in the short to medium run.

1.4   The 'snake' 1972–8

Some elements of the implementation of the Werner Report did survive the erosion and collapse of the Bretton Woods system. In the following three such elements are discussed: (1) intra-EC exchange-rate management, (2) the set-up of the European Monetary Cooperation Fund and (3) procedures for achieving policy coordination and convergence.

(1)   Intra-EC exchange-rate management

The Werner Report had outlined in considerable detail the desirability and mechanics of narrowing the bilateral fluctuation margins between EC currencies. The core of the Bretton Woods system was the parities declared to the IMF for currencies in terms of the (gold value of the) US dollar and the associated margins of fluctuation within which national authorities undertook to maintain their currencies. The system implied that bilateral (or cross) rates between any two European currencies could move by twice the declared fluctuation margin *vis-à-vis* the dollar, viz. if the two currencies switched position relative to the dollar. This may not have mattered greatly when the margin was 0.75 per cent, though even that preoccupied the authors of the Werner Report. They saw the greater predictability of the dollar than of intra-European exchange rates as an inherent bias in favour of perpetuating the use of the dollar as a contracting unit and a store of value to European-based firms and financial institutions. Hence the Report proposed that the bilateral fluctuation margins between EC currencies be narrowed, at first to 0.6 per cent, and subsequently gradually eliminated. Since this was one of the few specific suggestions for progressing by stages towards EMU, it was generally welcomed as a visible indicator of progress in monetary integration.[6]

---

[6] There is a close analogy in the recent EMU debate. The Delors Reports proposed a narrowing of margins of fluctuation in the EMS during stage two; the idea was under discussion in the Intergovernmental Conference but was not agreed upon, see Chapter 12. The expert group set up by the Werner Committee presided over by the Belgian Govenor, Baron Ansiaux, discussed the more radical option of eliminating in one go the margins of fluctuation, but recommended against it, because 'suppression of the margins can only be contemplated at an advanced stage of the process of economic and monetary unification', Werner et al.(1970), Annex 5, p. 15.

The first step was to have been implemented in 1971, but was given up when the German and Dutch authorities allowed their currencies to float temporarily in May 1971, only six weeks after the adoption of the ECOFIN Resolution on EMU. The two governments had originally preferred a joint float of the European currencies against the dollar. But, according to the account of Emminger (1976), France and Italy were reluctant to accept this initiative in view of the perceived underlying strength of the DM.

Whether the narrowing of intra-EC fluctuations bands would in fact have been implemented without further changes in the global system is unclear, but the Smithsonian Agreement of December 1971, which tripled the margin of fluctuation *vis-à-vis* the dollar to 2.25 per cent, greatly increased the urgency of creating a tighter intra-EC mechanism. Otherwise any two EC-currencies could move by up to 9 per cent against each other, a degree of exchange-rate flexibility perceived to be incompatible with the functioning of the common market and the Common Agricultural Policy, in particular. The six member states soon agreed to halve this margin of bilateral fluctuations to 4.5 per cent, i.e. ± 2.25, and they put this Basle Agreement – initially known as the 'snake in the (dollar) tunnel' – into operation only four months after the Smithsonian Agreement. Only one week later three of the prospective members which had signed up to join the EC on 1 January 1973 – Denmark and the United Kingdom, with Ireland as part of the UK currency area – also joined, and the fourth, Norway, followed within one month.

There was, given the experience of 1969–71, compelling logic both in the greater flexibility required of the global system and in the need for the EC member states to lean backwards rather than passively accept the implications of more global exchange-rate flexibility. The German revaluation of 1969 and the continuing speculative inflows had made it clear that narrow fluctuation margins could induce destabilizing behaviour as capital mobility increased. With the narrow margins of the Bretton Woods system, speculators expecting a further DM revaluation were faced with too comfortable a prospect: either a validation of their expectations of a gain from a jump in the exchange rate, or a small risk of a loss due to downward movements in the band. Many observers, e.g., Williamson (1977), have attributed the break-down of the Bretton Woods system primarily to the presence of such one-sided bets to speculators. Widening the fluctuation margins was a first line of defense by creating more exchange risk. Floating became the response not much later when it appeared that the realignment of the Smithsonian Agreement had been too timid to save the global system of fixed rates.

For the member states of the EC in which capital mobility was lower and the ambition was to constrain rather than to encourage use of the exchange rate as a policy instrument relative to the preceding period, the case for regional differentiation towards a tighter regime seemed obvious in 1971–2. Even the German government implicitly accepted that view when it introduced in July 1972 some controls on capital inflow, in some conflict with its generally liberal ideology. This particular move was so controversial in Germany that it led to the resignation of Finance Minister Karl Schiller.

But the cohesion did not materialize as table 1.1 of the snake's history of six and a half years shows. Within two months of the launching of the snake, sterling was set free

Table 1.1   Chronological history of the snake

1972	
24 April	Basle Agreement enters into force.
	Participants: Belgium, France, Germany, Italy, Luxembourg, the Netherlands.
1 May	The United Kingdom and Denmark join.
23 May	Norway becomes associated.
23 June	The United Kingdom withdraws.
27 June	Denmark withdraws.
10 October	Denmark returns.
1973	
13 February	Italy withdraws.
19 March	Transition to the joint float:
	Interventions to maintain fixed margins against the dollar ('tunnel') are discontinued.
19 March	Sweden becomes associated.
19 March	The DM is revalued by 3 per cent.
3 April	Establishment of a European Monetary Cooperation Fund is approved.
29 June	The DM is revalued by 5.5 per cent.
17 September	The Dutch guilder is revalued by 5 per cent.
16 November	The Norwegian krone is revalued by 5 per cent.
1974	
19 January	France withdraws.
1975	
10 July	France returns.
1976	
15 March	France withdraws again.
17 October	Agreement on exchange-rate adjustment ('Frankfurt realignment'): The Danish krone is devalued by 6 per cent, the Dutch guilder and Belgian franc by 2 per cent, and the Norwegian and Swedish kroner by 3 per cent.
1977	
1 April	The Swedish krona is devalued by 6 per cent, and the Danish and Norwegian kroner are devalued by 3 per cent.
28 August	Sweden withdraws; the Danish and Norwegian kroner are devalued by 5 per cent.
1978	
13 February	The Norwegian krone is devalued by 8 per cent.
17 October	The DM is revalued by 4 per cent, the Dutch guilder and Belgian franc by 2 per cent.
12 December	Norway announces decision to withdraw.
1979	
13 March	The European Monetary System becomes operational.

Source: Jennemann (1977), p. 245, as updated by the authors.

to float (with the Irish punt pegged to it) after a short foreign exchange crisis which quickly drove sterling to the lower intervention point and left opinion in the United Kingdom with serious doubts as to the viability of fixed-but-adjustable rate systems. The Italian lira left in February 1973. Both of these defections occurred before the floating of the dollar in March 1973 at which time the 'tunnel' disappeared, leaving the snake as a joint float for the participants, joined at the same time by a non–EC currency, the Swedish krona.

After the dollar had been set free to float, in March of 1973, it drifted down sharply until July. This created tensions in the snake, the Bundesbank having to intervene substantially in favour of weaker currencies. An initial revaluation of the DM by 3 per cent against the reference still used in the snake – the gold value of the US dollar – in March had not sufficed, and a further revaluation of 5.5. per cent was decided three months later at the height of the weakness of the dollar. Two other currencies (the Dutch guilder and the Norwegian krone) after some hesitation more or less followed the DM in separate actions in the autumn. A tendency for the snake participants to cluster into a weak and a strong currency group emerged, with the three revaluers in the latter, and the remaining four – the French franc, the Belgium – Luxembourg franc and the two remaining Scandinavian currencies of Denmark and Sweden – in the former. Divergence was accentuated by the quadrupling of the oil price in the final quarter of 1973 and the French government decided to withdraw in January 1974 and set the French franc temporarily free to float. France, however, returned to the arrangement in July 1975 at the previous central rate.

On the whole 1974–5 was a period marked by small movements in nominal exchange rates inside the snake and a modest volume of interventions but sizeable shifts in real exchange rates and a sharp acceleration of prices in most countries except Germany. The Bundesbank introduced *de facto* monetary targeting from December 1973 without making any formal announcement until December 1974 when such a move had been recommended both by the Council of Economic Experts and the German Federal Government, as recounted in Bockelmann (1979). Large wage increases in the course of 1974, as trade unions and employers apparently anticipated double-digit inflation, were not accommodated and unemployment rose sharply. Other snake participants pursued more accommodating policies towards the derived effects of the oil price hike, and inflation peaked with very high wage settlements in 1975. There was a clear inconsistency, not well perceived at the time, between exchange-rate policy and domestic actions.

Dramatic developments for some of the European currencies outside the snake, where inflation had risen even more sharply, brought home the point in early 1976. The Italian lira and the pound sterling, both subject to inflation above 20 per cent annually as against the 12–15 per cent observed in the most inflationary countries in the snake, plunged in the exchange market much further than even their worsening relative inflation could have justified. A danger of a vicious circle of spiralling prices and exchange rates became very visible. Capital flows out of the weaker currencies became large in February–March 1976 despite the tight restrictions maintained at the time. The French authorities, having themselves embarked on more expansionary fiscal policies in the autumn of 1975 as recession deepened – the 'relance Chirac' – found the pressure unsustainable by mid March, and the franc was again set free to float. Smaller non-German snake participants also experienced large outflows in the spring and again from August onwards. Bundesbank interventions in their favour rose sharply, and there was mounting political criticism of Germany importing inflation, particularly from the smaller partner in the government coalition, the Free Democrats, in the German election campaign prior to mid October.

The so-called Frankfurt realignment of October 1976, the first for nearly three years and the first in the snake which involved more than one currency, opened up a period of fairly frequent use of exchange-rate changes; a detailed account may be found in Thygesen (1979b). The Scandinavian countries, two of them only associated members of the snake, were the most active in view of the fact that they had experienced the sharpest real appreciation in the 1973–6 period. In total five realignments were undertaken in the final two years of the snake prior to the conclusion of the EMS negotiations in late 1978. The three Scandinavian currencies devalued by nearly 20 per cent over this period, and the Swedish krona left the snake to peg to a basket of its trading partners' currencies. In real effective exchange-rate terms devaluations were smaller, since inflation persisted at somewhat higher rates than in Germany; indeed, in these terms the devaluations of the Danish krone were only slightly more than what was required to keep overall Danish competitiveness stable. Norway (and Sweden) did achieve 10–12 per cent improvements in competitiveness on most measures. In contrast, the Benelux countries in this period continued to pursue a hard currency option and experienced modest real appreciation.

It may be argued that the snake developed from excessive rigidity of exchange rates in the earlier part of its existence (notably 1973–6), to a fairly permissive attitude over the final years. During the latter period the arrangements operated as a liberal version of the Bretton Woods system in its final years. Unilateral requests for realignments of individual currencies were not seriously challenged in 1977–8, although the size of the largest devaluation – of the associated Norwegian krone by 8 per cent –was slightly less than asked for. But these final years of the snake at least succeeded in putting moderate use of exchange-rate changes as an instrument of adjustment back on the policy agenda, hence avoiding the two extremes of either regarding exchange rates as untouchable, because their stability was part of a fixed-rate orthodoxy, or as market determined.

Neither the snake participants nor the EC as a whole played any significant regular role as a global actor in the 1970s. One cornerstone of the Werner approach was to establish a joint dollar policy. That failed in 1971, when some European currencies appreciated individually. On two subsequent occasions during 1973–5 the Community did try to take joint action to influence the exchange rate for the dollar.

The first was a joint action with the US authorities to stem the downswing in the dollar in July 1973. An extended swap network was established by all the EC central banks with the Federal Reserve Bank of New York. This well-publicized step was no doubt a major contributing factor to the sustained rise in the dollar which lasted into 1974.

The second was a decision taken by the Committee of Central Bank Governors in March 1975, at a time of renewed dollar weakness and volatility, to limit on an experimental basis the daily movements in the dollar rates of EC currencies, i.e., not only those of snake participants, to 0.75 or at most 1 per cent from the closing rates on the previous day. An escape clause was provided in case of a 'strong underlying market trend or exceptional circumstances'. Though this decision was never formally rescinded, it played no operational role in the subsequent exchange-market developments in 1975; nor could it apparently be invoked when the dollar began a prolonged decline from September 1977. On rare occasions some EC central banks were even net sellers of dollars when the rule should have made them buy; the rule does not seem to have influenced the concertations among the snake central banks.

This inability to develop a joint response to movements in the major third currency – or to reach common positions on international monetary reform – was a major source of concern to France, particularly during the periods when the French franc was not participating in the snake. Germany, in view of her recent experience of periodic massive interventions to sustain the dollar in 1969–3, was less ambitious. Chapter 2 traces some proposals made over the 1974–7 period to remedy the inward-looking nature of the snake and incorporate the individually floating EC currencies in a more broadly based Community exchange-rate system.

The mid 1970s marked the low point in European monetary integration. Writing in 1975, a committee of independent experts, including several members of the Werner Group (and one of the present authors) and chaired by former EC Commission Vice President and OEEC Secretary General Robert Marjolin, was asked to review the prospects for achieving EMU by 1980. They put their conclusion very bluntly, Marjolin et al. (1975), p. 1:

> Europe is no nearer to EMU than in 1969. In fact, if there has been any
> movement, it has been backward. The Europe of the 1960s represented a
> relatively harmonious economic and monetary entity which was undone in
> the course of recent years; national economic and monetary policies have
> never in 25 years been more discordant, more divergent, than they are today.

The committee attributed this 'failure' – a word which recurs frequently in their report – to three principal factors: unfavourable events in the global economy, a lack of political will to face together these difficult circumstances and insufficient analysis at the level of national governments to appreciate what would be required in terms of pooling of authority to achieve EMU. The report saw the events of the first half of the 1970s as a clear refutation of the optimistic view that European unity in the economic and monetary area could come about almost imperceptibly in a series of small steps, and it wondered (ibid. p. 5):

> if what may be required in order to create the conditions for EMU is not
> perhaps on the contrary a radical and almost instantaneous transformation,
> coming about certainly after long discussions, but giving rise at a precise point
> in time to European political institutions.

Regarding such a radical approach as unlikely, the report turned to discussing a number of more specific steps to deal with the macroeconomic imbalances and monetary disarray. A decade later the main author of the report prided himself that the report, which did not attract much attention at the time, that: 'it had its effects. There was no more talk of EMU' (Marjolin (1986), p. 364).

This assessment appears in retrospect too negative, a point which is returned to in the final chapter. Some useful habits and rules were created with the snake which proved to be extendable to other EC countries in the EMS and hence served as the first steps in the resumption of progress towards EMU in the late 1980s. It remains to look briefly at the two elements other than exchange-rate management which survived from the Werner approach and its early implementation.

(2) The European Monetary Cooperation Fund

The European Monetary Cooperation Fund (EMCF) was set up in April 1973, possibly better known under its French acronym, FECOM.

The Fund was initially charged with the monitoring of the 'Community's exchange rate system', although such a system existed at the time for only five of the nine member states, and with assuring the multilateral nature of net interventions of participating central banks in EC currencies. It was to take over the administration of existing very-short-term and short-term facilities, so far part of the agreements between the central banks. For the execution of the latter task the Bank for International Settlements was appointed as agent. The Fund was to have its temporary legal domicile in Luxembourg and to hold the meetings of its Board there. The governors of the EC national central banks were to constitute the Board, each having one vote.

There was no substance in these decisions. For the past eighteen years the Board of the Fund has met formally for a few minutes each month in Basle after the meeting of the Committee of Central Bank Governors. All issues of importance have been discussed in the Committee, not in the Board. No person has ever been employed by the Fund; the detailed work done on a personnel statute may prove useful only now in the preparations for a European System of Central Banks.

The main reason why the Fund developed only a shadowy existence was its formal subordination to the ECOFIN Council. The Werner Report had proposed that the new monetary institution should be under the control of the central bank governors, but in the 1973 decision their authority was explicitly constrained to acting in accordance with guidelines and directives adopted by the ministers. Since this was unacceptable to several governors, substantive work remained firmly with 'their' committee.[7] There may have been little risk, in retrospect, that the ECOFIN Council could, during the 1970s, have acted, in unanimity, to impose actions on the central banks which the latter would not have found acceptable, but the principle was important. As shall be seen in chapter 2, this was the main reason why the

---

[7] The President of the Bundesbank wrote in his contribution to the collected Papers annexed to the Delors Report: 'the EMCF, which is tied to directives issued by the EC Council of Ministers and hence is subject to political instructions, is not suitable as a monetary authority for the Community', Pöhl (1989), p. 149.

strengthening of the EMCF as a second stage of the EMS did not win general acceptance. It is also at the core of the issue of independence for the proposed European System of Central Banks discussed in chapter 13.

The launching of the EMCF made little difference to the course of events in the pre-1978 period. Premature creation of an institution without real authority reflected the lack of realization that by 1973 the Community was no longer on the road to EMU.

(3)   Procedures for achieving policy coordination and convergence

The other element of the Werner approach which survived to the decision stage was the efforts to coordinate monetary and other macroeconomic policies more closely. Here the results in the 1970s can only be regarded as inadequate despite the elaborate provisions for strengthening the coordination of all short-term economic policies. The starting point was two decisions taken by the ECOFIN Council on 22 March 1971.

As regards monetary policy the Committee of Central Bank Governors was asked to establish general guidelines, to be followed by each member state, for the trend of bank liquidity, the terms for supply of credit and the level of interest rates.[8] There is, however, little evidence that policy coordination extended beyond the day-to-day concertation in the foreign exchange market. The Committee of Governors did establish a Committee of Alternates and expert groups to monitor exchange market developments and trends in national money supplies and their main determinants. It also set up, jointly with the Monetary Committee, a Working Group on harmonization of Monetary Policy Instruments to follow up on the March 1971 decision. There is no published record of this work, except for a series of meticulous surveys, done by the individual central banks in the early 1970s on monetary policy instruments and on the circumstances in which they have typically been used. Money supply projections continued to be prepared nationally; although there was a gradual and impressive increase in the exchange of information about domestic aspects of monetary policy, the delegation of analytical work to national authorities made it difficult to challenge the interpretation by each of its own policies. By allowing discussion to proceed predominantly on the information volunteered – for current issues often only orally – by each interested party, the EC monetary coordination procedures fostered an attitude of defensiveness among national policy-makers. The Commission, through its two members of the Monetary Committee and its observer status in the Committee of Governors, was not in a position to challenge national representatives because its role as an initiator and as an arbiter was less developed in the monetary area than in other fields. The staff of the two main committees themselves was deliberately kept at the minimum required for preparing the more formal aspects of meetings and preparing careful minutes. It was inadequate for underpinning the initiatives that active chairmanship of the committees could have produced. It is in reality only with the

---

[8] A more detailed survey of the efforts at monetary coordination in the EC in the 1971-7 period may be found in Thygesen (1979a).

analytical capacity available in the Secretariat of the Committee of Governors since the start of stage one of the recent move towards EMU in mid 1990 that this basic handicap has been addressed though not overcome.

A couple of examples may suffice to illustrate the general point that the coordination effort for monetary policy was weak in the 1970s. The (unpublished) consultation reports of the IMF and the (published) OECD annual surveys of individual countries tended to contain more detailed analysis of policies in EC countries than documents prepared for the relevant EC committees. When the Monetary Committee had to review Italian monetary policy in 1976–7 in order to assess possible use of the EC medium-term credit facilities, the best source of information was the findings of the IMF mission, which had prepared for Italy's Letter of Intent to the IMF, rather than any analysis prepared by the Commission or the secretariats of the two main committees or other EC national authorities. And when the Monetary Committee, almost a year and a half after the introduction of the central bank money target in Germany, finally discussed this new development of the greatest importance for monetary coordination in the EC, the basis was information, largely oral, supplied by the German authorities.

The prospects looked better for coordination of budgetary policies. Detailed procedures for the examination of the economic situation in the EC and the adoption of guidelines for public budgets by the ECOFIN Council on three occasions during the year had been agreed in a March 1971 Decision, parallel to the one delegating to the Committee of Governors the task of monetary coordination. The emphasis on budgetary policy reflected the ambition of the Werner Report to move far in the direction of centralizing authority in the final stage of EMU and the prevailing view at the time that flexible use of budgetary policy was the essential and reliable tool of stabilization. As noted by Mortensen (1990) this emphasis and confidence was inspired by the recommendations of a major OECD study on the role of budgetary policy in demand management, Heller et al. (1968). This line of parentage comes through even more clearly in the Commission's review of April 1973 on progress made in the first stage of the Werner approach to EMU, and in the Decision adopted by ECOFIN in February 1974 'on the attainment of a high degree of convergence of the economic policies of member states'.

The adoption of this Decision – together with a directive on 'stability, growth and full employment' and a major simplification of the committee structure for monitoring non-monetary convergence and coordination – indicates that both the Council and the Commission had retained their belief in the need for exercising joint and discretionary authority over the stabilization function of national budgetary policies. But this affirmation came at a time, in the aftermath of the first oil price shock, when disagreements over the effects of policy and the prescriptions to follow were widening rapidly. To quote the Marjolin Report again, written one year later, (Marjolin (1986), p. 1):

> each national policy is seeking to solve problems and to overcome difficulties which arise in each individual country, without reference to Europe as an entity. The diagnosis is at national level; efforts are made at national level. The coordination of national policies is a pious wish which is hardly ever achieved in practice.

The elaborate procedures for coordination and prior consultation were not implemented, among the snake participants no more than in the EC as a whole. The machinery survived, but not in any substantive content. Hence the 1974 Decision was a prime candidate for revision in 1990 as part of preparing for the first stage in the recent move towards EMU.

1.5 Lessons from the first thirty years of European monetary integration

The three decades of Europe's post-war monetary history surveyed briefly and necessarily superficially in this chapter contain a number of lessons on which European policy-makers have been able to draw in the set-up and management of the EMS, and in the current efforts to move towards EMU. Indeed, some issues central to the establishment of EMU emerge more clearly when seen in the long perspective of the successes and failures of the three decades which preceded the EMS negotiations of 1978. Subsection 1 first identifies three such issues which have, in different guises, been present throughout the period from the late 1940s to the late 1970s, and a fourth which seemed peripheral because its resolution was regarded as either superfluous or too radical. Subsection 2 then turns to a brief discussion of the economic factors that were behind the ups and downs of the integration effort.

1.5.1 Issues in the drive towards monetary integration

(1) Global versus regional considerations

The first is the interaction of global and regional considerations. The period prior to the introduction of currency convertibility at the end of 1958 was one in which European efforts at monetary organization and policy coordination had a natural regional bias. The fragmentation of Europe's economy through the bilateralism of trade and payments, inherited from the interwar and early post-war period, and the initial lack of competitiveness *vis-à-vis* North America, strongly suggested a regional framework for trade liberalization and monetary arrangements rather than the more idealistic global system designed at Bretton Woods, but left unfinished for world trade. This regional bias was accepted and even encouraged by the United States, but it was regarded as suspect by the IMF, concerned about its role as an embryonic world monetary authority. However, the EPU never assumed authority for exchange-rate changes in the 1950s, its Board relying primarily on recommendations of domestic policy adjustments for correcting external imbalances; outright conflicts were therefore avoided.

The 1950s, and the EPU experience, in particular, provided a method for Europe to catch up with the full obligations of a global system. The years after 1958 were a period in which that system appeared to provide a sufficiently stable and satisfactory framework for the Europeans to leave aside efforts to differentiate themselves in the areas of policy coordination and monetary arrangements, while the six original EC member states built up a customs union and the Common Agricultural Policy. Until the late 1960s the main difficulties, in sustaining stable exchange rates and containing current-account imbalances, arose within Europe, rather than between Europe and the United States; major realignments among the Europeans were finally resorted to in 1967–9, but they were regarded as part of global economic management and did not lead to any institutional innovations. When the latter were proposed and received increasing attention among EC governments, in recognition that the increasing US external deficit and rising inflation could well require a European regional response, underlying divergence within Europe had already advanced too far for such initiatives to be realistic.

Paradoxically, the first project for EMU – the Werner Plan of 1970, confirmed by the ECOFIN Council in March 1971 – which was meant to open an area for tighter joint management of economic policies, and of intra-EC exchange rates in particular, instead opened up the period in which European monetary integration suffered a serious set-back, not only relative to its own past performance but also relative to the much laxer international monetary framework which evolved after the breakdown of the main pillar of the Bretton Woods system in the course of 1971–3. However serious the tensions in the exchange markets due to persistent US current-account deficits and the so-called dollar overhang, divergence in economic performance became more dramatic inside Europe where inflation accelerated sharply in a number of countries due to overly ambitious demand management policies, wage indexation in response to rising import prices and major political transformations in Southern Europe (Greece, Portugal and Spain). By the mid 1970s five of the current EC member states had inflation rates well above 20 per cent; in 1976 Italy and the United Kingdom had to negotiate stabilization programmes with the IMF. Europe had clearly failed in its effort to overtake the crumbling international monetary order or even to keep a slower pace of disintegration. The snake was only a limited, though significant exception to Europe's lapse into more divergence than at any time since the very first postwar years. Chapter 2 retraces how most EC member states nevertheless succeeded in 1978, under the threat of renewed challenges from the policies pursued in the United States, to reverse this process.

(2)   Policy coordination: rules versus discretion

The second issue is the form of policy coordination undertaken, the balance between rules and discretion and the authority of European institutions. Starting from scratch and with only the vaguest formal authority to influence national policy decisions, the EPU Managing Board was surprisingly successful in correcting most external imbalances quickly. This was due primarily to the tightness of the rules: credit lines so short that countries in overall deficit within the area soon had to begin using their scarce convertible currency and gold reserves, while – obviously weaker – incentives also operated on surplus countries to limit the accumulation of international claims.

However, occasional and decisive use of discretionary powers to influence domestic and trade policies also proved valuable, starting from the German adjustment package of the winter of 1950–1, and illustrated in a number of subsequent recommendations to debtors. Arguably discretion worked, because the rules were so constraining that action had to be taken quickly; debtor countries often undertook adjustments before seeking credits from EPU with their associated policy recommendations. Discretion and improvisation at the level of the EPU Managing Board had to be relied upon more frequently with respect to proposed measures for persistent surplus countries – extension of creditor quotas, accelerated liberalization of imports. They were effective in containing modest surpluses, but they were not designed to make a major impact on the main surplus country, Germany. The fact that the EPU Managing Board apparently did not give even private support to those officials in Germany who began to advocate revaluation of the DM from about 1956 seems attributable more to the prevailing preference for fixed exchange rates at the time than to a perception of a lack of competence to make such recommendations.

Tight rules and the assumption by the Managing Board of authority to make recommendations over a wide range of policy instruments, spanning structural policy, fiscal and monetary adjustments and international lending and borrowing, made for a powerful combination. In retrospect, the EPU was more efficient as a vehicle for policy coordination than any of its successors – the OECDs Working Party No. 3 from 1960, at the level of all industrial countries, or the EC's bodies, the Monetary Committee and the Committee of Central Bank Governors – prior to the launching of the EMS, or perhaps even beyond the early years of the latter. Coordination turned out to depend more on the objective circumstances, in particular the tightness of external constraints. The procedures for continuous coordination proved less useful than the EPU's ad hoc efforts.

(3)   Agreement on strategic policy goals

The third lesson is the need for a common policy perception of all major participants. At the time of the set up of the EPU, the combination of pressure from the US authorities, relative political weakness of Germany, and economic weakness of the United Kingdom was sufficient to obtain agreement and to operate the system efficiently. The goodwill of Germany was assured by the fact that the OEEC and the EPU were the first international organizations in which Germany was invited to participate after the War; hence she initially kept a low profile. The clear advice given by the EPU in the brief stabilization crisis of 1950–1 further consolidated the positive attitude in Germany, because the advice was seen to be disinterested. This contrasted with German perceptions of policy coordination in the 1960s and 1970s when Germany saw the international efforts as mainly self-serving on the part of others – the United States or some other Europeans – asking Germany to deviate more from her preferences than they did in return. The United Kingdom was more difficult to persuade, since the Labour Government in power in 1949–50 saw EPU as a threat to the survival of the sterling area and the longer-run role of sterling as a major international currency. Despite the unfortunate experience of the 1947 attempt at convertibility, the UK authorities remained globalist rather than regionalist in their attitude and they pushed for convertibility again from 1955 onwards despite their external deficit and speculation against sterling. But in the course of the 1950s they came to see the benefits of the regional approach in the transition.

The only country that had more permanent difficulties with the rules of the EPU was Belgium, since the permanent surplus *vis-à-vis* other union participants required special accommodation. Belgium came close to not joining in 1950, and a difficult compromise settlement had to be made in 1952, when the Belgian surplus was especially large. Opting out as one small country was, however, unattractive and the surplus dwindled in subsequent years anyway.

Policy divergence built up gradually in the second half of the 1960s, and the Community seemed to have no way of checking it. The main example was the tension between the two main EC currencies, resulting in the major realignments of 1969. The German current-account surplus rose, particularly in the aftermath of the brief 1966–7 recession. Since Germany was also subject to substantial speculative inflows, a conflict arose between internal and external stability which marked the German attitude to fixed exchange rates also within Europe for a number of years. The toughness of German demands for convergence before monetary unification reflected the critical perception of the experience of the final five years of the Bretton Woods system. The differences in perceptions might not have been irreconcilable in a less difficult environment than that of 1971–3, as the compromise on parallelism between convergence and monetary integration of the Werner Report suggested.

From 1971 divergence accelerated, as EC countries reacted in an increasingly differentiated way, first to the international boom of 1970–3 and then to the first oil price hike. Despite the recent commitment to joint monetary management and movement towards EMU, differences in policy preferences – or in the assessment of the length of the international recession of 1974–5 – overrode any formal undertaking. Even for the participants in the snake, the exchange-rate commitment was insufficient to sustain parallel inflation and compatible national budgetary policies. But by the late 1970s sufficient experience had accumulated for most EC member states to perceive a common interest in a more stable monetary relationship in Europe and their own inability to pursue divergent policies. Chapter 2 reviews in more detail the ideas that led to the EMS.

(4) Parallel currency

An issue which was almost entirely absent from the European debate over the three decades was the introduction of a common monetary standard. A common European currency was considered unrealistic in the 1950s given the aspirations of convertibility into the dominant world currency. After that had been achieved by 1958 a common currency was long considered superfluous. When the US dollar began to appear less suitable as an international anchor in the second half of the 1960s, divergence was already building up with respect to the non-inflationary qualities of the EC currencies.

Most European officials and economists were not in favour of moving towards an international multi-currency reserve system and backed the creation of the new composite asset created by the Agreement on the Special Drawing Rights in 1967. The 'dollar overhang' prompted fears that European currencies might have to assume an increasing role in international reserves.

Meanwhile the United Kingdom by the late 1960s was struggling to preserve an international role for sterling and was as unlikely as twenty years earlier to encourage any suggestions of a European common currency. Significantly the Werner Report made only a brief reference to the internal benefits of a common currency and no reference to any global role for it. An idea that would have seemed logical and almost trivial some years earlier now appeared as at best a distant objective.

After 1972 the pent-up ambition to use the exchange rate as a policy instrument, or simply as a buffer, further postponed any consideration; the Marjolin Report makes no reference to a common currency. But in the same year – 1975 – as that pessimistic assessment of the Community's prospects of ever putting EMU on the agenda again was published, there was one small practical step and a radical proposal for a new approach pointed towards strategies for monetary unification which play an important role in the recent debate on EMU.

The practical step was the introduction of the basket European unit of account (EUA). Initially the use of it was, as the name suggests, confined to some accounting functions in the EC. It had little impact on private financial markets and it took another three years for proposals for limited use of it, as an official monetary unit in settlements among central banks and a common denominator for EC currencies, to appear in the EMS negotiations. Few imagined it as a potential basis for a common currency. The long-run significance of the initial practical step is discussed in chapter 6.

The other new element was the opening of a more radical debate, initially among professional economists, on the parallel currency approach to European monetary integration. Basevi et al. (1975) – the so-called All Saints Day Manifesto – proposed the introduction of a parallel currency of constant purchasing power which would compete with national currencies in all monetary functions. This could amount to full-scale monetary reform in countries with a high inflation rate where the parallel currency could be expected to penetrate significantly into national use. A weaker version of the proposal was elaborated in the two OPTICA-reports, Commission of the European Communities (1976) and (1977). These proposals were too radical to be taken seriously by officials, though they did retain some influence among professional economists in Germany and the United Kingdom. They have recently resurfaced; such proposals are discussed in chapters 6 and 11.

The lesson of the emergence, late in the period of three decades surveyed in the present chapter, of the idea of a new unit and parallel currency foreshadowing a future single currency is that the low point of European monetary integration in the mid 1970s produced both a practical solution to some of the problems of highly unstable exchange rates in the EC and a proposed strategy for the introduction of a parallel currency designed to become dominant. Though they had little impact on the course of events in the short run, these two contributions span the range of options in the project for EMU under negotiation fifteen years later.

1.5.2 The economic factors

The discussion of the first thirty years of European monetary integration in this chapter has shown that monetary matters were for a long time dealt with outside the Community framework. One reason for this was certainly that the Bretton Woods system seemed to work reasonably well until the late 1960s. However, there has been another factor which can explain why a global approach was initially preferred and why, over time, the demand for European efforts in the monetary domain has nevertheless increased. This factor is the extraordinary increase in intra-Community trade over the last forty years. Figures 1.5.1 and 1.5.2 document this in two different ways. Figure 1.5.1 shows the percentage weight of intra-EC exports in GDP for three member countries: Germany, France and the United Kingdom. This figure, which uses a constant EC12 (i.e., its numbers are based on a Community with all the twelve current members already in by 1960), shows that the importance of intra-EC trade has grown rather steadily between 1960 and 1990. For Germany the weight of intra-EC exports almost tripled as it went from a little over 5 per cent to above 15 per cent of GDP.

There were only two short periods during which this trend was interrupted for all three countries considered. Both of them coincided with periods during which the integration effort stagnated. The first one was 1974–7, the period when the Werner Plan was not implemented and the Marjolin Report assessed the failures in the integration effort. The early 1980s are the other example of a decreasing importance of intra-Community trade. During these years the notion of 'Eurosclerosis' was invented, but this term has since been rapidly discarded as the integration effort was relaunched again and the economy of the Community started to grow anew. Figure 1.5.1 also shows that there are considerable differences in the importance of intra-EC trade among these three countries: for Germany EC trade is, and has always been, almost twice as import as for the United Kingdom and France is in an intermediate position.

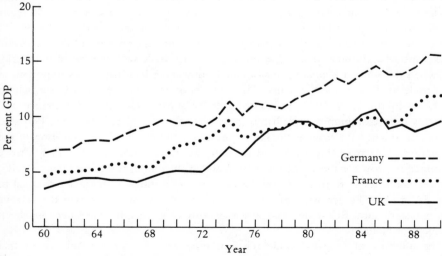

Figures 1.5.1 Intra-Community exports (share of GDP at market prices)
Source: Commission of the European Communities, 1990

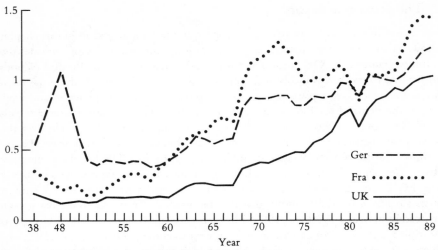

Figure 1.5.2 Intra-Community exports (ratio of intra-EC to extra-EC exports)
Source: International Monetary Fund: Direction of Trade Statistics, various issues.

The differences between member states concerning the importance of the Community become even stronger if one considers the importance of intra-EC trade relative to extra-EC trade as done in figure 1.5.2. This figure, which takes into account the changing membership of the Community goes back to 1938 to show that some differences are deeply rooted in history. This figure shows that in 1950 trade with the five partners of the Coal and Steel Community was only half as important as trade with the rest of the world for Germany. For the United Kingdom trade with the orginal 'six' was even less important, it amounted to less than one quarter of trade with the rest of the world. This situation did not change appreciably during the 1950s, which might explain why the United Kingdom was less interested in the European integration effort and did not participate in the Coal and Steel Community and the Common Market.

However, the 1960s and 1970s changed all this. Since the creation of the Common Market intra-Community trade grew much more than trade with the rest of the world, and when the United Kingdom finally joined intra trade had become as important as extra trade for France and Germany. This must have been an additional factor behind the effort in the early 1970s to go towards full EMU. However, for France and Germany intra-Community trade barely grew faster than other trade between 1970 and 1985. This might have been at the same time cause and effect of the stagnation of the integration effort over this period. In contrast, the importance of the intra-EC trade continued to grow for the United Kingdom and at the end of this period (about 1985) all three countries were in a very similar position, with intra-EC trade about equal to extra-EC trade. The accession of Spain and Portugal has since increased the relative importance of intra-EC trade. Maybe for reasons of geography this effect has been strongest for France.

The intensity of intra-EC trade relations was certainly not the only factor that determined the monetary integration process. An important further element was the cohesion (or more often the lack thereof) in terms of inflation. This is shown in figure

1.5.3 which shows for France, Italy and the United Kingdom the difference between the national inflation rate and that of Germany. This figure shows that until about 1973 inflation differentials did exist, but they were always below 5 per cent and Germany was not always the most stable country. During most of this period one of the other three countries considered in this figure had a lower inflation rate than Germany as can be seen from the fact that there is almost always one line below zero. Even the rather large French and British devaluations of the late 1960s did not lead to larger inflation differentials.

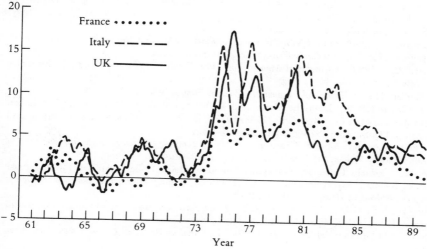

Figure 1.5.3 Inflation convergence *vis-à-vis* Germany
Source: International Financial Statistics, line 64.

This changed dramatically in 1973. For Italy and the United Kingdom the inflation differential *vis-à-vis* Germany went above 15 per cent in 1975–6 and then fluctuated widely between 15 and 5 per cent until the early 1980s. This was possible only because, as discussed above, the major member countries were not willing to use a tight exchange-rate link, for example in the snake, to contain domestic inflationary pressures. The creation of the European Monetary System (EMS) came thus at a time when inflation differentials were still very high by historical standards; this is why, as discussed more fully in the next chapter, the EMS was widely predicted to be as unstable as the snake. However, to the surprise of many, the EMS did prove to be so stable that inflation differentials are now back to the same range as during the 1960s. An analysis of how the EMS worked and the reason for its success are discussed more fully in chapters 3 and 4 below.

References

Baer, Günther and Tommaso Padoa-Schioppa (1989), 'The Werner Report revisited', in Collection of Papers annexed to Report on Economic and Monetary Union (the Delors Report).

Basevi, Giorgio, Michele Fratianni, Herbert Giersch, Pieter Korteway, Daniel O'Mahoney, Michael Parkin, Theo Peeters, Pascal Salin and Niels Thygesen (1975), 'The All Saints' Day Manifesto for European Monetary Union', *The Economist*, 1 November.

Basevi, Giorgio, Emil Classen, Pascal Salin and Niels Thygesen (1976), Towards Economic Equilibrium and Monetary Unification in Europe (OPTICA Reports '75), Commission of the European Communities, Brussels, March.

Basevi, Giorgio, Paul De Grauwe, Pascal Salin, Hans-Eckhart Scharrer and Niels Thygesen (1977), Inflation and Exchange Rates: Evidence and Policy Guidelines for the European Communities (OPTICA Report '76), Commission of the European Communities, Brussels, February.

Bockelmann, Horst (1979), 'Experience of the Deutsche Bundesbank with monetary targets', in John E. Wadsworth and François Léonard de Juvigny (eds.), *New Approaches in Monetary Policy*, Sijthoff and Noordhoff, Alphen aan den Rijn, 103–9.

Boyd, Christopher (1990), 'The EMS, the move towards EMU and the agrimonetary system', paper prepared for the Agrimoney Conference, London, October.

De Grauwe, Paul (1989), *International Money: Post-War Trends and Theories*, Oxford University Press, New York.

Diebold, William (1952), *Trade and Payments in Western Europe*, New York.

Emminger, Otmar (1976), 'Deutsche Geld- und Währungspolitik im Spannungsfeld zwischen innerem und ausseren Gleichgewicht (1948–1975)', in Deutsche Bundesbank, Währung und Wirtschaft in Deutschland 1975–6, Frankfurt-am-Main.

Giavazzi, Francesco and Alberto Giovannini (1989), *Limiting Exchange Rate Flexibility: The European Monetary System*, MIT Press, Cambridge, Massachusetts.

Heller, Walter, Cornelis Goedhart, Guillaume Guindey, Heinz Haller, Jean van Houtte, Assar Lindbeck, Richard Sayers and Sergio Steve (1968), *Fiscal Policy for a Balanced Economy: Experience, Problems and Prospects*, OECD, Paris.

Jennemann, Gerhard (1977), 'Der Europäische Wechselkursverbund', in Magnifico, Giovanni (ed.), *Eine Währung für Europa*, Nomos I, Baden-Baden.

Kaplan, Jacob, and Günther Schleiminger (1989), *The European Payments Union*, Clarendon Press, Oxford.

Kloten, Norbert (1980), 'Germany's monetary and financial policy and the European Community', in Wilfrid L. Kohl and Giorgio Basevi (eds.), *West Germany: A European and Global Power*, Lexington Books, D.C. Heath and Company, Lexington.

Marjolin, Robert (1989), *Architect of European Unity, Memoirs 1911–86*, Weidenfeld and Nicholson, London (translated from *Le travail d'une vie*, Editions Robert Laffont, Paris, 1986, by William Hall).

Marjolin, Robert *et al.* (1975), Report of the Study Group Economic and Monetary Union 1980, 'Marjolin Report', Commission of the European Communities, Brussels. (The Marjolin group was composed, like the EC Commission, of seventeen members. They were: Louis Camu (Belgium), Isi Foighel and Niels Thygesen (Denmark), Herbert Giersch and Horst Markmann (Germany), Bernard Clappier and Robert Marjolin (France), Patrick Lynch (Ireland), Franco Bobba and Francisco Forte (Italy), Georg Brouwers (The Netherlands), Donald McDougall and Andrew Shonfield (The United Kingdom).)

Molle, Willam (1990), *The Economics of European Integration (Theory, Practice, Policy)*, Dartmouth, Aldershot.

Mortensen, Jorgen (1990), 'Federalism vs. co-ordination: macroeconomic policy in the European Community', Centre for European Policy Studies, *CEPS Paper*, 47, Brussels.

Pöhl, Karl Otto (1989), 'The further development of the European Monetary System', in Collection of Papers annexed to Report on Economic and Monetary Union (the Delors Report), EC Publications Office, Luxembourg: 129–55.

Swann, Dennis (1990), *The Economics of the Common Market*, Penguin Books, London.

Thygesen, Niels (1979a), 'International coordination of monetary policies – with special reference to the European Community', in John E. Wadsworth and François Léonard de Juvigny (eds.,), *New Approaches in Monetary Policy*, Sijthoff and Noordhoff, Alphen aan den Rijn, 205–24.

(1979b), 'Exchange-rate experiences and policies of small countries: some European examples of the 1970s', *Princeton Essays in International Finance*, 136, International Finance Section, Princeton.

Triffin, Robert (1957), *Europe and the Money Muddle, From Bilateralism to Near-Convertibility, 1947–56*, Yale University Press, New Haven.

(1966), *The World Money Maze*, Yale University Press, New Haven.

Werner, Pierre, Baron Hubert Ansiaux, Georg Brouwers, Bernard Clappier, Ugo Mosca, Jean-Baptiste Schöllhorn, Giorgio Stammati (1970), Report to the Council and the Commission on the realisation by stages of Economic and Monetary Union in the Community ('Werner Report'), Supplement ·to Bulletin II–1970 of the European Communities, Brussels.

Williamson, John (1977), *The Failure of World Monetary Reform*, Nelson, London.

CHAPTER 2

THE MAKING OF THE EUROPEAN MONETARY SYSTEM

The EMS was negotiated in the course of 1978. Its origins are largely, and as viewed in this book, rightly, seen as political, rather than economic. The initiative came from the highest political level in the form of a coordinated proposal from the President of France and the German Federal Chancellor, and it was initially promoted outside the routine framework for discussing such issues in the EC: the ECOFIN Council and the two bodies which normally arrange its agenda, viz. the Monetary Committee and the Committee of Central Bank Governors. In section 2.1 the ideas are discussed that inspired the two founders, Chancellor Helmut Schmidt and President Valéry Giscard d'Estaing. A number of proposals for extending European monetary integration had been made during the turbulent period since the disintegration of the efforts to move towards Economic and Monetary Union in 1973–4 which can be said to have resurfaced in the EMS negotiations. After the European Council in Bremen in July 1978 these negotiations were carried forward in the normal committee framework and the resulting agreement reached at the European Council in Brussels in December 1978 and its implementation are reviewed in section 2.2.

The EMS agreement was much less ambitious than the Werner Plan for EMU adopted as a plan of action in March 1971; the main elements of the Werner plan and its failure were traced in chapter 1, sections 3–4 above. But the EMS agreement was also intended to contain the seeds of its own development; the Brussels agreement retained the objective of an institutional development through the set-up, within two years of the start of the EMS, of a European Monetary Fund (EMF). The functions intended for this new institution, which were never agreed among the participants, are discussd in section 2.3; plans for the EMF were quietly shelved in December 1980 and this experience evidently contained important lessons for the EC governments, causing them to adopt a different approach when further institutional steps towards closer monetary integration finally reappeared on the agenda from 1988 onwards.

2.1 The Schmidt–Giscard initiative: political and economic inspirations

Few could have predicted by late 1977 that a major new initiative to relaunch monetary integration was close. The nine EC member states at this time appeared to have settled into two groups with very different economic performances and exchange-rate regimes. One group had achieved some success in keeping inflation moderate and had maintained the outward appearance of loyalty to the intentions of the first stage of the Werner Plan by continuing to participate in the joint float *vis-à-vis* third currencies – the 'snake'. Although these countries were still firm in their oral commitments to policy coordination, there was, as the brief record in chapter 1, section 4 showed, little of the latter. The 'snake', despite the technical soundness of its operational provisions, was a lopsided system, with the German economy accounting for more than two thirds of the collective GDP of the group, and the DM as the only significant international currency. Germany, however, ran the system with a fairly light hand, leaving the choice of realignment and/or domestic adjustment very much at the discretion of her partners (the three Benelux countries and Denmark, with Norway as an associate member). Three of the remaining four EC currencies (sterling, the French franc and the lira) were floating individually and had all experienced recent high inflation, sizeable current-account deficits and substantial depreciation; the fourth (the Irish punt) was in a monetary union with sterling. It seemed difficult to find a common denominator for monetary integration that could apply to all of the floaters, and next to impossible to devise an exchange-rate policy (or system) which comprised both groups of countries.

The realities of economic divergence were not by 1977–8 as bad as they appeared in the highly critical language used by either group in characterizing the policies of the other group. This point is argued more fully below. But three political considerations were probably more decisive than any direct appraisal of the minimum prerequisites in terms of economic convergence.[1]

The first was the strengthening of the domestic political positions of the two initiators in the course of the winter of 1977–8. The most readily identifiable change was the national parliamentary election in France of March 1978. It had been widely predicted that the centre right coalition would lose its majority in the National Assembly and that, in any case, the influence of the President and his Prime Minister Raymond Barre of the centrist party (UDF) would weaken further inside the coalition. Neither of these two events occurred: the majority was comfortably maintained, and the size of the UDF representation increased while that of its Gaullist rival, the RPR, was reduced. This gave the President and his Prime Minister the political strength to follow up the long-term stabilization of the French economy, introduced with the Plan Barre eighteen months earlier, by reentering into an exchange-rate commitment with

---

[1] These political considerations are analysed in considerable detail in Ludlow (1982), chapter 3.

[2] It may be recalled that the two occasions on which France had left the snake in January 1974 and March 1976, had both been provoked by reluctance on the part of the RPR to accept the implications of such a commitment.

Germany.[2] For about three years (until the Presidential elections scheduled for May 1981) the French President would have greater freedom of manoeuvre than in the first four years of his period in office. The election results at the same time gave Germany some assurance that French economic policy would be oriented towards stability.

The political change in Germany was no less dramatic, though more dificult to pinpoint. At a time of terrorist attacks in late 1977 in Germany and on German citizens elsewhere, to which the government reacted forcefully, there was growing support for the coalition of the Social Democrats and the Liberals, and particularly for the Chancellor within his own party. This, in combination with growing signs of a conflictual relationship with the United States, prompted the Chancellor to seek a firmer and wider alliance within the EC and to resist US pressures in terms that were appealing also to France.

The second political consideration was a concern, voiced most explicitly by the German Chancellor, that political developments in Italy were taking a dangerous course. The rising clout of the Italian Communist party persuaded the leaders of the Christian Democrats, Mr Andreotti and Mr Moro, to bring the communists into the government's parliamentary majority. The efforts towards this 'historical compromise' impressed on Chancellor Schmidt the need to provide Italy, which had left the snake within the first year of its existence, with an offer of a more stable European framework for its policies.

The third political consideration, closely linked to international economics, was to prepare the ground for more independence from the United States, particularly for Germany. Chancellor Schmidt had not hidden his preference for another outcome of the US Presidential election of November 1976 – reelection of President Ford – which had brought in the Carter Administration. On foreign policy in general major differences of emphasis from traditional European perceptions of Realpolitik emerged, and on economic issues the German goverment found US domestic expansionary policies highly risky. When coupled with requests for much more stimulatory policies in the major surplus countries in the OECD area, viz. Germany and Japan, and with systematic or casual efforts on the part of leading US officials to 'talk the dollar down', German opinion resisted.[3] The London Economic Summit of July 1977 had not led to any coordinated action, but a persistant weakening of the dollar from September 1977 onwards, from a level at which the United States was already seen in Germany and elsewhere in Europe as having regained competitiveness, led to concern among German industrialists and trade unionists that any further loss of confidence in the dollar would trigger large shifts towards the DM, Europe's major international currency and at the time the only one with unregulated capital flows. This would aggravate a squeeze on profits and on employment in Germany's internationally oriented industry. Chancellor Schmidt was sensitive to these concerns and was anxious to alleviate such pressure towards 'excessive' appreciation of the DM. Undertaking any form of outright intervention obligations *vis-à-vis* the dollar – a remedy not totally absent from the thoughts of the US Administration and the Federal Reserve in 1978 – would not have

---

[3] For a thorough account of statements by US Treasury Secretary Michael Blumenthal and German reactions thereto see Putnam and Henning (1986).

been feasible in the absence of far-reaching commitments on policy coordination; the recollection in the Bundesbank and in the German financial community of events in 1971–3 when interventions to support the dollar had created major problems of excess liquidity was too vivid, particularly at a time when confidence in the US leadership was at a low point.

The Chancellor, while continuing ad hoc cooperation with the US authorities, notably in March 1978, instead developed a two-pronged strategy. One was to link the DM more firmly to as many of the individually floating major EC currencies as were willing in order to deflect pressure from the weakening dollar over a wider area. By diminishing the prospect that these other currencies could fall far and rapidly against the DM, closer monetary integration in Europe could help to achieve three objectives: (1) to stabilize the trading environment for most of Germany's trade, (2) to protect Germany against always being in the front line of attack in international organizations for being inadequately expansionary, and (3) to increase the influence of Europe on policy-making internationally. The latter objective would, however, require firmer institutional underpinnings than have yet been achieved – or might be achievable in the EMU now envisaged, as is argued in chapter 9 below.

The second element in Chancellor Schmidt's 1978 strategy was to take budgetary measures to encourage some expansion of domestic demand in Germany. This became evident at the Bonn Economic Summit of July 1978 where the Bonn government did undertake to implement a stimulation programme designed to increase German domestic demand by approximately 1 per cent in 1979 through additional Federal government expenditures and tax cuts.[4]

The combination of the two elements was appealing to France and to Germany's other potential partners in the emerging European Monetary System, since it appeared to promise both better cohesion within Europe and a satisfactory joint response to the pressure exercised by the United States in the World Economic Summits and the OECD for Europe to assume more responsibility for growth in the international economy and for the narrowing of current-account imbalances between the main regions. But there were significant differences of emphasis on the two parts of the strategy among Germany's EC partners. The United Kingdom, which had been an architect, as much as the United States, of the call for global macroeconomic coordination at the London Economic Summit of 1977, wanted Germany as the main European surplus country to undertake more of a role as an international locomotive. The top French priority was to develop a new framework for monetary cooperation in the EC, though the French did not on this occasion, or later in the 1980s, fail to emphasize the importance of such a regional system for the evolution of a more stable international monetary system. France had worked hard during the negotiations in the Committee of Twenty in 1972–4 for the formula of fixed- but-adjustable exchange rates for the global monetary system, and she had been more active than other European countries in working for the Second Amendment to the IMF Articles of Agreement of 1976 which introduced the concept of multilateral surveillance of

---

[4] Putnam and Henning (1986) provide a detailed analysis of how this package of measures was put together.

economic policies. The position of France had throughout most of the 1970s been more evenly balanced between an interest in reforming the global monetary system and in resuming European integration, than those of either Germany or the United Kingdom. But in early 1978 French and German interests appeared finally to converge on a common interpretation of the challenge posed by US policies and on the mix of initiatives required.

There are two interesting aspects in the evolution of the joint project. The first is the extent to which it built on ideas that had already been discussed in the EC in the preceeding years. The second is the way in which the initiative was developed following the initial presentation of ideas at the Copenhagen European Council in April 1978.

With respect to the ideas inherited from earlier discussions, the main challenge was whether a compromise could be found between two positions. Germany and the smaller countries participating in the snake insisted that they had implemented the original ideas of the early 1970s for the first stage of the EC's evolution towards EMU and had now been operating a well-functioning system for six years. The snake needed to be completed according to this view, simply the acceptance by the remaining EC currencies to manage their currency relationships similarly. On the other hand France, and to some extent the United Kingdom and Italy, claimed that the mechanism of the snake had a basic flaw due to the asymmetrical roles of participants which made a radically new departure desirable. With some justification the latter group regarded the snake as completely dominated by Germany.

Three approaches had been discussed at various times since 1974: the Fourcade Plan of 1974, the Duisenberg Plan of 1976 and the Commission initiative of late 1977. The substantive ideas of these approaches, and the fate they had suffered in official discussions were all instrumental in shaping the Schmidt–Giscard initiative.[5]

The French government had submitted to ECOFIN in September 1974, when reentry of the franc into a revised snake began to look feasible, the so-called Fourcade Plan, named after the then Finance Minister Jean-Pierre Fourcade. The plan proposed more use of intramarginal interventions and larger credit lines, the use of the European Unit of Account (EUA) as a pivot in the revised exchange-rate system and a joint dollar policy. All these four points subsequently became part of French proposals for launching the EMS in 1978 and in 1987–8 for revising the EMS: the most novel idea in 1974 was the role envisaged for the EUA, a unit identical to the fixed-amount basket of EC currencies and which was renamed the European Currency Unit (ecu) in 1978.

The idea of introducing an ecu pivot, instead of basing the revised and enlarged snake on a grid of bilateral parities, was fully explained already in this early memorandum. It was inspired by the discussions conducted in the Committee of Twenty to reform the intervention and settlements rules in a modified Bretton Woods system with a possible analogous function as pivot, for the Special Drawing Rights (SDR), redefined in 1974 as a basket of the sixteen internationally most important currencies, see Committee of Twenty (1974). The main advantage was seen as that of

---

[5] The following draws on Thygesen (1979), pp. 103 ff.

assigning the burden of intervention more fairly, i.e., to a country whose currency reached its margin against a Community average, whether that currency was strong or weak. The Fourcade Plan was the first explicit criticism in the European context of the asymmetry of a system of fixed exchange rates which played an important role in the EMS-negotiations. In the snake the intervention obligations were formally symmetrical – the authorities of both the strong and the weak currencies at opposite ends of the bands having to defend the margins – but the loss of reserves constitutes a more effective constraint on the weak currency country than the injection of liquidity in the country of the stronger currency – effectively making the burden of adjustment asymmetrical. That a system based on an ecu pivot would often lead to intervention in dollars, since only one currency could be expected to diverge at any one time, was openly recognized in the French memorandum. The Fourcade Plan finally suggested that, in moving to an ecu pivot, the width of the band should be enlarged.

The proposals were met with a generally unfavourable response both in the fall of 1974 and when they were resubmitted in May 1975, shortly before France in fact decided to rejoin the snake. The two other individual floaters, Italy and the United Kingdom, were both preoccupied with strongly accelerating inflation and showed no readiness to undertake even significantly modified commitments as to their exchange-rate behaviour at the time. The one idea which was put to the test in 1975 – a joint dollar policy in the limited sense of dampening day-to-day volatility – was not successful, see chapter 1, section 4.

The second initiative was the so-called Duisenberg Plan, named after the then Dutch Finance Minister, submitted in July 1976. This proposal was prompted by the sharp depreciations of the lira and sterling in the first half of 1976, as evident from the Dutch Finance Minister's letter to his colleagues:

> We are worried about the exchange rate developments in the Community. There is at present no effective Community framework for the coordination of policies in this area among all members, while recent developments have surely indicated the urgent need for common action. The large movements of exchange rates have affected our relative competitive positions, in some cases rather strongly, and have created pressures for protection. Moreover, there is danger of a growing divergence between the countries that participate in the European snake arrangement and the other countries.
>
> A weakening of the snake arrangement, which would allow these other countries to join, does not seem to us the best way to bridge the gap. Rather, we would suggest creating a general Community framework for consultation and surveillance of exchange rate policies, based on the 'guidelines for floating' which we have agreed to recommend for adoption in the context of the International Monetary Fund.
>
> As you know, these guidelines centre around the concept of agreed 'target zones' for exchange rates. I would emphasize that the guidelines do not impose any obligation on a country to keep its exchange rate within the target zone, but they do create the presumption that countries will not engage in

policy measures that are designed to push the rate away from the target zone. Periodic review of the target zones and Community surveillance of national policies on the basis of such guidelines, could provide the start of an effective framework for Community action in this area.

The main element in the Duisenberg Plan was that EC countries would declare a 'target zone' within which they would aim to contain their effective exchange rate. There would be no positive intervention obligations to defend this zone, only the negative obligation not to take action – intervention, monetary policy measures, etc. – or to move out of or away from the zone. Such movements would trigger consultation on policy coordination in the Community.[6]

It was not quite clear in the beginning whether the proposal was to apply solely to the three EC currencies then floating individually, or also to the snake as a whole, or to its largest currency, the DM. The proposal could hardly apply to the snake currencies individually, since that would have created potential conflict with the operational rules of the snake to preserve bilateral fluctuation margins – rules which the Dutch and other snake governments wished to uphold. The proposal was gradually clarified to apply only to the individual floaters. But this created an obvious assymmetry between the EC currencies – a two-tier system – which was unacceptable to the floaters and to some of the weaker members of the snake as well as difficult to defend in terms of economic logic.

The opposition of Germany to the declaration of any target zone, even in the vague sense without positive intervention obligations, either directly for the DM – thereby recognizing the DM as basically on a par with the individually floating currencies – or for the snake as a whole, finally made it necessary to shelve the Duisenberg Plan in the winter of 1976–7. But two elements survived, one procedural, the other as a substantive idea.

In shelving the plan in March 1977 ECOFIN did take one procedural step: the bodies serving it, notably the Committee of Central Bank Governors and the Monetary Committee, were encouraged to extend their consultations on exchange-rate matters. From the summer of 1977 the Commission submitted, at regular intervals, analytical papers on recent trends and prospects in exchange markets. A more satisfactory exchange of views was generated, notably on the outlook for the dollar. The central subject of the likely strains on the pattern of Community exchange rates was reintroduced on the agenda.

The substantive idea that remained in the air was the quest for some objective indicator or threshold to trigger automatically discussion of policy coordination. In the Duisenberg Plan this role was assigned to the exit of a country's effective exchange rate from its target zone. In the EMS negotiations, the role was seen to be performed by an indictor measuring the divergence of a currency from the Community average, expressed in the ECU basket. The two notions reflect the same underlying, and well-justified, concern that policy coordination is weak and unlikely to get off the

---

[6] The target zone idea had, at the time the Duisenberg Plan was put forward, only recently emerged in the academic literature, see Ethier and Bloomfield (1975).

ground without some objective indicator acting as a trigger. The role of such a trigger is to shift the burden of proof on to the country whose exchange rate has moved, thereby shifting the tone of the argument as to who should adjust to whom.

The third initiative may be labelled the Commission Plan. In January 1977 Roy (now Lord) Jenkins had assumed office as President of the EC Commission at about the most difficult point of time in the Community's history. Divergence between member states was at a peak and even modest efforts to relaunch monetary coordination beyond the snake had foundered, as the discussion of the Duisenberg Plan had demonstrated. There was no more talk of EMU. Nevertheless the new Commission President succeeded in relaunching it in the course of the second half of 1977, notably in a speech at the European University Institute in Florence in October.

Building on a careful argument which at the same time recognized (1) the strength of nation states and their resistance to EC authority in major policy areas, and (2) the benefits to be gained from a decentralized version of monetary union, Roy Jenkins provided a strong case for a more radical departure than any of the other plans, since the failure of the Werner approach, for relaunching economic and monetary integration. This vision spanned transfers to the EC level of some public finance functions along the lines proposed in the so-called McDougall Report, a major study on fiscal federalism, initiated by the Commission and completed earlier in the year, McDougall (1977), and moves towards a common currency for which the arguments were, in the light of the likely increasing instability of the US dollar, primarily international. The Florence speech provided the first comprehensive statement of subsidiarity: the Community had to persuade member states of the significant scope for better economic performance attainable by combining some enlargement of both the allocative and redistributional roles of the EC budget, but far more modest than what had been envisaged in the Werner Report, with ambitious moves towards stable exchange rates and ultimately a common currency. In advancing these ideas Roy Jenkins was influenced by advice from Robert Triffin, a main architect of the EPU of 1950 and a persistent advocate of rapid monetary integration, Jacques van Ypersele, the Belgian chairman of the EC Monetary Committee, and, above all, by Michael Emerson, a member of the Jenkins cabinet and secretary of the McDougall Report. Attitudes among his Commission colleagues were more cautious, and the official and the public reaction to the Florence speech was cool, if not hostile. Even *The Economist*, generally favourable to the Jenkins Presidency, found the relaunching of monetary union as an objective 'a bridge too far'.

The proposals actually submitted by the Commission to ECOFIN in November and subsequently to the European Council in December remained comprehensive and relatively ambitious on the monetary side; the elements of fiscal federalism of the McDougall Report were considered too radical; they may become part of the agenda for EMU, so some discussion of the case for them in the present context may be found in chapter 8. As regards exchange-rate management the main element in the Commission Plan was a revised version of the Duisenberg Plan, extending the target zone proposal for managing effective exchange rates from the three individually floating currencies to the DM, representing the snake. Several suggestions were made as to how the ECOFIN Decisions on policy coordination of 1974 could be more effectively implemented.

The Committees serving ECOFIN embarked on the new round of discussions of these proposals with considerable reluctance. Central bankers and other monetary officials had not been given new signals for the political acceptability of ideas that had on earlier occasions failed to win wide support. The external environment had apparently turned for the worse in some respects since these efforts. The dollar had started to depreciate since September 1977 and the growth performance in the Community continued to lag. Would member states be prepared to undertake new obligations, even the mild ones of the target zone variety, implying only that they would refrain from actions that could worsen divergence?

Nevertheless these discussions were overtaken by more ambitious ideas. The Schmidt–Giscard initiative, submitted to the meeting of the European Council in Copenhagen in April 1978, at the very time when the official committees were preparing to shelve the less far-reaching Commission proposals, foresaw not only a trigger mechanism for policy coordination, but outright intervention obligations for all EC member states to defend their intra-EC exchange rates. The initiative further foresaw institutional developments in the form of a successor to the EMCF, a European Monetary Fund (EMF), to be established after an initial two-year period, to manage pooled foreign exchange reserves in accordance with a joint exchange-rate policy and offer balance of payments assistance. We discuss the role of the EMF in section 2.3 below.

How did such a quantum jump in ambitions become possible? We have traced earlier in this chapter some of the political factors in the two main countries which facilitated the initiative: the domestically strengthened position of the two initiators and the change in their perception of the balance between regional and global interests for the EC. This change emerges more clearly when seen in the perspective of the ideas under discussion in 1976–7, the Duisenberg Plan and the revival of it in the Commission's proposals of November 1977.

By early 1978 the main problem had become the renewed instability of the dollar. Interventions to stem appreciation of the DM had been massive in the final quarter of 1977 and the early months of 1978; still the DM rose in effective rate terms by some 7 per cent in the six months preceeding 1 April 1978. The German authorities seemed to have increasing difficulties in avoiding the fate of some countries with individually floating currencies and relatively good inflation performance; Japan and Switzerland, for example saw their currencies rise steeply from the summer of 1977. Linkages to the smaller currencies in the snake were simply insufficient to act as a major drag on the rise of the DM, and some of these other participants were feeling the heat to such an extent that they were beginning either to devalue more frequently or withdraw. The individually floating currencies had, on the other hand, become much more stable than in 1976 when they had plunged, and divergence in terms of inflation had narrowed. What would have been totally inconceivable two years earlier, now appeared much less unrealistic. It began to look feasible – as well as politically attractive – to build on a prospective intra-European stability, rather than to retain hopes for stabilization vis-à-vis the dollar – either bilaterally through target zones for the dollar rates of individual EC currencies, or by implementing a version of the Duisenberg Plan by encouraging the four main countries to adopt a target zone for their effective exchange rates, as envisaged by the Commission. The latter would, even without positive intervention obligations, have amounted to a wide-ranging commitment to dollar stabilization, which the outlook in 1978 suggested to be both economically and politically hazardous.

The resumption of dollar instability in 1977–8 pushed the initiators of the EMS into a more regional attitude. It is arguable that, if the US authorities had acted to stabilize the dollar at the beginning of 1978 – along the lines of President Carter's package of November of that year, not to speak of the overhaul by the Federal Reserve System of monetary control procedures in October 1979 – the optimal EC strategy would have been to contribute to that stabilization through some version of the Duisenberg Plan for tight individual management of the EC currencies' effective exchange rates.

Such a more globalist approach was still favoured by the UK authorities. The two initiators of the EMS were in contact with the then UK Prime Minister, James (now Lord) Callaghan, both prior to the Copenhagen European Council and after to enlist his support in the preparation of their initiative. But James Callaghan, anxious to promote global economic coordination more successfully than had proved possible at the London Economic Summit of 1977 and concerned about the Europeans taking an initiative to promote a new international currency, did not take up the invitation. Although the United Kingdom was asked to participate actively in the preparation of the fuller EMS outline to be submitted at the Bremen European Council of July 1978, the UK representative in the three-man working party of personal representatives of the Heads of State and Governments only attended some initial meetings of the group.

This brings us to the second interesting aspect in the early evolution of the EMS project, following the Schmidt–Giscard presentation of preliminary ideas in Copenhagen. Until the Bremen European Council three months later, preparations were delegated to Bernard Clappier, then Governor of Banque de France, but acting as President Giscard d'Estaing's personal representative, and Dr Horst Schulmann of the Federal Chancellor's office. The usual committee framework was largely bypassed and was barely informed of the preparations. This was regarded as particularly objectionable by the Bundesbank; its President, Dr Otmar Emminger, publicly confirmed in May that he knew nothing about the proposals being elaborated. The Monetary Committee continued to discuss in these months primarily on the basis of the Commission's revival of the target zone proposal for the individually floating currencies, although other options and their implications were also studied in a report to the ECOFIN Council in June.[7]

The particular way in which the effort was organized may have helped to give the essential initial impetus to the project. Chancellor Helmut Schmidt has remarked on several subsequent occasions that the EMS would probably never have started if it had been proposed in the more regular and low-key fashion of asking the committees to prepare for decisions in the ECOFIN Council. But the unorthodox procedure had a cost by intensifying the sceptical attitude of many officials, in particular those of the

---

[7] The chairman of the Monetary Committee, Jacques van Ypersele, added to the agenda the idea that these currencies, instead of declaring a target zone for their separate effective exchange rates, be encouraged to declare their zones in terms of a common composite unit, defined as a simple average of the dollar and the snake; this unit was later wittily called 'the question Mark'.

Bundesbank. The cost may also have been long term in fostering the preference among officials, and of the Committee of Central Bank Governors in particular, for a return to smaller and more gradualist steps.

Different approaches for preparing important steps towards European monetary integration have been used at different times. The work of the Werner Group exemplified strong direction from the highest political levels combined with early use of all relevant committee expertise. The launching of the EMS applied the former, but relied on more informal methods of early follow-up. The EMU initiative which is analysed in some detail in chapters 10, 12 and 13 has relied on both formal and informal approaches and the unique combination of both in setting up a committee in which the central bank governors served in a personal capacity. Smaller, more gradualist steps, such as the Basle Nyborg Agreement of 1987, to be reviewed in chapter 3, have been prepared in the formal committees.

2.2   The Bremen and Brussels European Councils

Several important intentions of the EMS were already clarified in the conclusions of the Presidency of the European Council held in Bremen in early 1978; the relevant sections of the conclusions are reproduced in Annex 1 to this chapter. The EMS was to be 'a zone of monetary stability', 'a durable and effective scheme', 'at least as strict as the snake' – though 'for a limited period of time member countries currently not participating in the snake may opt for somewhat wider margins around central rates'. 'In principle, interventions will be in the currencies of the participating countries.' Changes in central rates would be 'subject to mutual consent.' A new unit, 'the European Currency Unit (ecu) will be at the centre of the System' to 'be used as a means of settlement between EC monetary authorities'. Initially ecus would be created against deposits of 20 per cent of member states' gold and dollar reserves as well as against member currencies 'in corresponding magnitudes'. Use of the latter category of ecus would be subject to conditions. There would be efforts to coordinate dollar interventions to avoid simultaneous reverse interventions. 'Not later than two years after the start of the scheme, the existing arrangements and institutions will be consolidated in a European Monetary Fund.' Finally, there would be 'concurrent studies of the action needed to be taken to strengthen the economies of the less prosperous member countries'.

With these conclusions in mind ECOFIN was asked to give guidelines for the elaboration by end October of the scheme to 'the competent Community bodies', i.e., the Monetary Committee and the Committee of Central Bank Governors. The officials soon identified the main issues and ambiguities in the Bremen conclusions as relating to (1) the choice of pivot (or numéraire) in the intervention system, (2) the limited pooling of gold and dollar reserves, (3) the settlement rules and credit mechanisms, and (4) the potential role of the EMF. Since (4) was of less pressing concern, relating only to a future stage, negotiations, though not elaboration of the main options, were postponed. The EMF is taken up in the next section, points (1)–(3) being discussed here. A tentative interpretation is given of a subject which the 'competent bodies' could not be expected to address explicitly, viz. the intended use of central-rate changes (realignments) in the system.

The Bremen conclusions had left an ambiguity as regards (1). On the one hand the ecu was to be at the centre, but on the other hand the Heads of Government of the Benelux countries, Denmark and Germany had stated that the snake 'has not been and is not under discussion . . . it will remain fully intact'. There was an evident conflict between those participants who wanted a basically reformed system and those who saw the effort as primarily directed at extending the snake to comprise as many EC member states as possible.

Read in the former perspective the Bremen conclusions looked much like the Fourcade Plan of 1974–5, and that remained the interpretation offered by French officials. Central rates and intervention limits were to be set in ecu; there would no longer be a grid of bilateral intervention limits. Such a reform would, as noted in the review of the Fourcade Plan in section 2.1, bring the system closer to symmetry by making it possible to identify divergent behaviour. Deviation of a currency from the weighted Community average as expressed by the ecu basket in either direction would trigger automatic intervention obligations for the country concerned alone. In the snake, as explained in chapter 1, section 4, divergence is not directly identified, because two currencies must be simultaneously at their upper and lower margin to trigger mandatory interventions. Proponents of the ecu as pivot attached both practical and political significance to making the average performance of Community currencies the standard of reference, rather than accepting the *de facto* asymmetry of the snake in which the strongest currency, the DM, was seen to dominate. Although the proponents of the ecu-centered system did not often put it as bluntly, they had in mind the likelihood of situations in which the DM would become divergently strong, putting the burden of adjustment on the German authorites to either revalue the DM or ease monetary policy towards the average.

For the same reasons German officials, supported by Dutch and Danish officials, were firmly against any triggering of mandatory interventions by movements in a currency's ecu rate. The Germans shared the evaluation of the French that the DM might well be prone to upward divergence against the average, so that an ecu-centered system would push the Bundesbank more often into the front line of intervention with unfortunate consequences for monetary control. Judging from subsequent experience this shared perception of the inherent strength of the DM was exaggerated, though it has materialized over some periods; but the resistance of most of the snake participants to the new pivot settled the argument in favour of retaining the bilateral grid of the snake as the basis for the intervention systems. But some concessions were made to the proponents of the alternative. One was purely formal: to denominate the central rates in ecu. These rates are calculated from the grid of bilateral central rates and play no role in the intervention system. The other – the use of a supplementary indicator of divergence calculated in terms of the ecu – was potentially more substantial; this is discussed further below. Finally the ecu was retained as a means of settlement among the participating central banks.

The role of the basket ecu in the EMS and in its transition to EMU has continued to be a subject of controversy, which will be taken up again, particularly in chapter 6. That discussion surveys issues relating to private sector use of the ecu – a purpose barely foreseen in 1978 – including the composition of the ecu basket and procedures for its regular revision. Here the review is confined to the more technical arguments against using a basket unit for setting mandatory intervention limits. These arguments were already clarified by the work of the Committee of Twenty (1974) on international monetary reform, and they played a supplementary role, in addition to the opposition by Germany to monetary use of the basket ecu in the decision of 1978 to retain the bilateral grid. They can be summarized in three points:

(1) If one or more EC member country with currencies in the basket were to withdraw from the intervention system or not to join it initially, it seemed unlikely that the remaining participants would accept to peg to the unit and hence to allow fluctuations in unconstrained currencies to determine their intervention obligations. One would then have to find a rule for freezing the value of the floating currencies in the basket. A bilateral grid system is not vulnerable in this sense to changes in participation, as is already evident from the experience with the snake.

(2) An ecu-centered system would have to agree on rules for designating which other currency was to be used when only one participant was at its ecu margin. If, say, the DM was divergently strong, the Bundesbank would have to buy some other currency; another central bank would be obliged to accept such interventions, although its own currency was not itself divergent. This could hardly be handled from case to case; rules would have to be agreed in advance, also with respect to the settlement of balances arising from such interventions. Otherwise 'involuntary' creditor or debtor positions would arise. Alternatively a currency outside the system, in practice the dollar, could be used as an intervention medium, but it was the intention of the EMS to rely, in principle, on the currencies of participating countries; outright encouragement to use of the dollar was certainly regarded as undesirable. A further, longer-run alternative would have been to develop the ecu into an intervention currency used by private market operators. That option exists today, following a decade of growth in the markets for ecu denominated financial instruments, but such a development was not foreseen in 1978.

(3) As a result of their greater weight in the ecu basket, major currencies would have scope for wider fluctuations in their bilateral exchange rates than the currencies of smaller participants. A major currency would pull the whole basket with it and might never be pushed to its margin against the ecu. A possible solution to this differential treatment would have consisted in applying narrower ecu margins for the major currencies by eliminating the weight of an individual currency in calculating its margin of fluctuation.

As is hinted at in the comments on these three points, technical solutions existed to the complications of using the basket ecu as a basis for the intervention system. Such a system could no doubt have been made operational, particularly if the participation of all EC currencies had been assured on standard terms. But the technical intricacies of an untested system, as well as the preferences of most of the snake participants for continuing with their familiar rules, combined to swing the balance of opinion against it.

At a bilateral summit meeting with the German Federal Chancellor in Aachen in September 1978 the President of France conceded that compulsory interventions in the EMS should only be triggered as two currencies reached their bilateral margins. This was significant in view of the persistent French preference for giving the ecu a central role and for taking an apparent step towards symmetry in the EMS. But as a concession to this view a subsidiary role for the ecu was found in the so-called 'Belgian compromise', devised by the chairman of the Monetary Committee: an 'indicator of divergence' was to be calculated in terms of the ecu in order to improve policy coordination, while retaining the bilateral margins as the only trigger for mandatory interventions.

The indicator of divergence is an index computed in the following way: assume that an EMS currency is simultaneously at its upper (or lower) bilateral margin against all other participating currencies. These positions will define maximum divergence, or 100 per cent of the potential margin around its ecu central rate. The calculations assume that all currencies in the basket are subject to the standard bilateral fluctuation margin of 2.25 per cent, hence solving – arbitrarily – the technical problem (1); they further eliminate the differences in weight of the individual currencies as indicated in (3). The authorities of a currency which reaches a high proportion of its maximum divergence – 75 per cent was agreed – would be presumed to – using the wording of the Resolution of the European Council in Brussels, reprinted as Annex 2 to this chapter:

> correct this situation by adequate measures, namely:
> a) diversified intervention;
> b) measures of domestic policy;
> c) changes in central rates;
> d) other measures of economic policy.

If no such measures were taken, the authorities concerned would have to justify their inaction to other participants, first in the concertations between central banks, subsequently possibly in the ECOFIN Council.

Despite the vagueness of the policy prescriptions the emergence of the divergence indicator was still seen as a potentially important innovation. It was the only example of an international monetary agreement on the use of a specific and multilateral objective indicator as a trigger for policy coordination. The Duisenberg Plan had also with its target zone proposal aimed to develop such an indicator, but only for some EC countries, and the operational questions had not been addressed. The international monetary reform discussions of 1972–4 had tried to get to grips with the definition of an objective and symmetric trigger mechanism. The US negotiators proposed that movements in countries' reserve assets be monitored with reference to an internationally agreed norm. Departures in either direction from a normal range for reserves would trigger first consultations and subsequently sanctions in the form of forfeiture of interest payments on reserves for surplus countries and charges on reserve deficiencies for deficit countries. Ultimately the proposal foresaw that even stronger sanctions might be applied to both groups of countries; a key objective for the US negotiators was to set up a system where the burden of adjustment was shared between the surplus and deficit countries.

The difficulties of defining the reserve norm made the proposal unpractical, and the European participants in the reform discussions rejected the US proposal anyway. Yet the reserve indicator proposal was a logical complement to a fixed exchange rate system and there were echoes of it in the discussions of settlements and credit arrangements in the EMS negotiations. In view of the gradualist nature of the reserve indicator proposals, notably the escalation of sanctions, the triggering of policy coordination envisaged with the ecu divergence indicator could be regarded as parallel to the first trigger in the reserve indicator structure, the so-called 'consultation points'.

It is not clear from the documents available from the EMS negotiations what division of tasks between the divergence indicator and the parity grid was envisaged. There was little explicit discussion of the selection of 75 as the percentage for defining the threshold; the percentage had to be lower than 100 to give the indicator some operational significance, and higher than some low figure, which would – if it were taken seriously – have overridden any signals from the parity grid.

This evaluation may appear interesting in retrospect, because the divergence indicator did not, contrary to anticipations in 1978, come to play any important role in the actual working of the EMS. A major reason was that several countries were not prepared to accept the degree of flexibility of their currency inside the margin which was required for the threshold to be crossed; they preferred to intervene intra-marginally instead. Other countries proved unwilling to take firm action when their currency did cross it; the wording of the Brussels Resolution was sufficiently vague to allow them to get away with inaction.

The introduction of the divergence indicator was nevertheless significant. It foreshadowed later controversies over the degree of asymmetry in the EMS. The limiting interpretation of the new element in the EMS, that of the ecu being 'at the centre' in the form of the indicator of divergence to supplement the signals from the grid of bilateral rates, was sufficient for the proponents of the ecu-centered system, notably France, to claim that the EMS was basically different and more symmetrical than the snake, hence justifying their participation in the new system. Participants in the snake on their side could claim that, since the only firm rules were those familiar from their experience in 1972–8, the EMS was basically a geographical extension of the snake.

Modest encouragement was also given to the role of the ecu as a reserve asset and means of official settlement. In the Brussels Resolution (para. 3.8) member states agreed to provide to the EMCF, through revolving three months swap arrangements, 20 per cent of their gold – revalued at six months intervals to reflect market value – and dollar reserves in return for an equivalent claim denominated in ecu. Depositing was made compulsory for participants in the exchange-rate mechanism, and voluntary for other EC member states. From July 1979 the United Kingdom joined the scheme, and Greece from January 1986. The two later entrants, Spain and Portugal, joined in 1987–8. Total deposits have fluctuated between 23 and 55 billion ecu, mainly because of swings in the market value of gold, to a lesser extent because of changes in the dollar/ecu rate.

The temporary, almost fictitious, arrangement agreed upon in 1978 did not involve reserve pooling. The depositing central banks continue to hold and manage, on behalf of the EMCF, 'their' gold and dollars and receive interest on them. This limits the role of the EMCF to a book-keeping function; hence the 1978 decision did not modify in any important way the shadowy existence of the EMCF.

The ecu credits thus created may be used in settlement of interventions at the bilateral margins. But in implementing the Brussels Resolution the central banks stipulated in their agreement of March 1979 that these ecus would not be fully usable; creditor banks would only be obliged to accept up to 50 per cent settlement in ecu, the balance being 'settled by transferring other reserve components in accordance with the composition of the debtor central bank's reserves . . .' (Art. 16.1 of the 13 March 1979 agreement).[8] This restriction was motivated by the concern in Germany that the Bundesbank would end up with most of the ecus created through the swaps. Chapter 3 reviews the protracted efforts of the Commission and some central banks to remove this acceptance limit on settlement in ecu, finally suspended in 1987.

The complex and temporary mechanism of introducing the ecu as a reserve asset and means of settlement nevertheless had the effect of potentially increasing the usable international reserves of participants. Since the early 1970s gold reserves had effectively been banned as an official means of settlement among industrial countries. The swap arrangements, which redenominated them into ecu, made them partially usable.

The core in the intervention system of the EMS was, as in the snake, the establishment of a Very-Short-Term Facility of an unlimited amount (Brussels Resolution, Art. 3.7). In short, central banks of strong currencies have an obligation not to restrict the amounts of their own currency used to defend the existing bilateral margins. But settlements would have to be made at the latest forty-five days after the end of the month of intervention; the length of the credit period in the snake had been thirty days. Any automatic extension would be limited to the size of the debtor quotas in the Short-Term Monetary Support, initially set at ecu 7,900 million; creditor quotas were set at twice this amount. The maturity of these credits would be an additional three months, extendable once. Automatic credit would be available within these limits, in other words, for a maximum of on average eight months. Beyond the debtor quotas for the two three month periods, the Committee of Central Bank Governors could, by a unanimous vote, use the so-called debtor rallonges to extend another ecu 8,800 million in credit. The total target figure for effective credits, since not all countries could in practice draw simultaneously, was put at ecu 14,000 million in the Brussels Resolution (Art. 4.2). It was to be supplemented by the Medium-Term Financial Assistance, with an effective credit ceiling, estimated similarly, of ecu 11,000 million. The latter was to be conditional lending on terms set by the ECOFIN Council, and to be financed by market borrowing. Chapter 3 reviews the actual use made of these facilities and their gradual extension in the 1980s.

---

[8] For the text of this agreement and other provisions, see, e.g., the Annexes in van Ypersele and Koeune (1985).

Both of the two additional facilities had existed already in the decisions to implement the first stage of the Werner approach to EMU in the early 1970s, but the EMS negotiations enlarged them by a factor of nearly three. Their size was still modest, only about the same size as the combined IMF quotas of participants. The Very-Short-Term Facility required repurchase by a debtor central bank, within on average two months, of the bulk of its currency accumulated by creditor central banks directly or through the EMCF. This implied that countries experiencing an outflow of reserves only gained a very limited time to adjust their policies in order to stop and reverse the flow. More generous credit lines were clearly perceived, in addition to the proposal to move to an ecu-centered system, as the second way to overcome the likely asymmetrical nature of the EMS, and much effort was spent by prospective debtors in raising them as much as possible, and by more conservative countries in limiting them.

As was the case with the proposals to put substance into the notion of giving the ecu a central role which resulted in the divergence indicator, the bargaining on the credit facilities, seen as very important at the time, yielded an outcome which turned out to have only a limited impact on the operation of the EMS and the behaviour of participants. The two enlarged credit facilities have been used only to a very limited extent. By the late 1970s EMS participants had international reserves large enough to take care of most shorter-term financing needs without recourse to special facilities. And when they experienced major imbalances they turned, in the initial period, more readily to adjustment through realignments than was anticipated in the EMS negotiations.

This brings us to the final point from the negotiations: the balance between financing and adjustment and the forms that the latter should take. These issues were not addressed explicitly in 1978. There was no hint in the official documents as to how severely the new system would constrain realignments and no ambition to eliminate them completely in any foreseeable future. The aim to create 'a zone of monetary stability' was inspired by the improving performance inside the EC where divergence had been reversed and differentials in national inflation rates reduced to single figures and much further if allowance was made for the fading-away of the effects of past movements in exchange rates. For some measures of inflation – wholesale prices for example – differentials in 1978 were down to 5–6 per cent. Only Italy had double-digit inflation (for consumer prices) and, partly for that reason she opted for the wider margin of 6 per cent which gave some freedom of manoeuvre without resorting to realignment.

Was it realistic to expect that the EMS could manage without major strain to be 'at least as strict as the snake', as the Bremen conclusions had intended? One annual realignment, rather than the two which had been observed in the final two years of the snake, of a size no larger than consistent with continuity of market exchange rates before and after the change in central rates, i.e., of no more than 4–4½ per cent, would have sufficed to keep most measures of relative national price levels in line.

Realignments were to be subject to mutual consent, a principle which had not been well observed in the increasingly unilateralist snake. In this perspective it was ominous to some that the German authorities had a different interpretation from those of other participants. The Bundesbank sought and obtained an assurance from the German government that, if a conflict between the external and internal dimensions of monetary policy were to arise, price stability should be given priority over exchange-rate stability. In short, the Bundesbank should be permitted to suspend its intervention obligations at times when they threatened domestic price stability. For obvious reasons, this assurance was only referred to in public much later, as it would have increased incentives for speculators. While the Germans were concerned that realignments would be too small and too delayed to preserve low inflation for them, most other participants were anxious to give the appearance of committing themselves to tight exchange-rate management.

Reticence to be explicit about the criteria for making use of exchange-rate changes is not surprising. By formulating clear and transparent guidelines, the officials would have created problems for themselves, as anticipations of their actions would have built up. Given that, and the very different recent experiences of participants, discretion for the major decision in exchange-rate management had to be preserved to a maximum degree. The EMS was initially to be tested on its ability to find a workable balance between elaborate rules for intervention and settlements on the one hand and constructive use of occasional and discretionary realignments by consent on the other.

The contrast to the proposals eight years earlier in the Werner Report is striking. There the destination of full EMU was explicit and the monetary prescriptions for getting there equally clear: gradually to narrow margins of fluctuations of currencies and to phase out realignments. But since the ambition was greater in 1970 than in 1978, the Werner Report also went much further in proposing a high degree of centralization of budgetary policy and major efforts for assuring convergence with respect to economic performance in a number of respects, though it was regrettably vague in explaining how that could be achieved.

The Bremen conclusions and the Brussels Resolution are conspicuously silent on policy coordination outside the monetary area. In one modest bow to the 'economist' view, so prominent in the Werner Report, the Bremen conclusions state (Art. 5):

> A system of closer monetary cooperation will only be successful if
> participating countries pursue policies conducive to greater stability at home
> and abroad; this applies to the deficit and surplus countries alike.

There is no trace of the budgetary policy coordination, partly by jointly set rules, which figure in the recent debate on moves to EMU, nor – and more significantly – of the need for a larger EC budget including some automatic transfer mechanisms which formed an important part of the package of steps proposed in the Jenkins speech a year earlier. But since that package also aimed at monetary union, there is a logic to that.

The implicit lesson of the EMS negotiations is then that, because the founders only had a looser exchange-rate arrangement in mind, where use of exchange-rate changes was far from being excluded, there was no need to propose the budgetary underpinnings, nationally and through the EC budget, which were seen as logical complements to the Werner Report proposals for monetary integration and ultimate unification and for the Jenkins approach. The EMS was seen as requiring much less effort in non-monetary areas, because it was 'only' – even in its subsequent stage after the set-up of the EMF, as shall be seen – a limited, defensive mechanism to improve monetary stability.

It seems, according to this analysis, unnecessary to ask, as does Kloten (1980), whether German interests had changed between 1970–2 and 1978. Germany, the main advocate of the 'economist' view that convergence had to precede monetary integration while implementation of the Werner Report was on the agenda, had not basically changed views or the perception of her interests. There was criticism in 1978 from the German financial community and from the Bundesbank of the risk which the government was taking in linking the DM to large and more inflationary European economies, but as long as exchange rates were not to become rigid and intervention credits had to be settled in a short period, there was little basis for using the arguments of the EMU debates in the early 1970s and reappearing today. The German resistance concentrated on the project of the EMF, see section 2.3 below.

A small concession was made to the view that the economies of the less prosperous states had to be strengthened to make them participate effectively and fully in the EMS. The Economic Policy Committee was asked to develop proposals; the European Parliament also put forward suggestions for an increase in the disbursements through the Regional and Social Funds, starting with the 1979 Budget.

Conceptually this discussion was analogous to that which prompted the enlargement of the structural funds in 1988 and has motivated proposals for their further extension in the 1990s. Market integration and constraints on the use of the exchange rate may increase the structural problems of less prosperous, often peripheral, countries or regions. As their cost levels catch up faster with those of more prosperous countries during the process of integration, while factor mobility, particularly of labour, remains more limited, unemployment may rise. Resource transfers directed at infrastructure investment and education of the labour force may then serve to soften the impact at a time when devaluation cannot be resorted to as much as in the past.

The two countries which were potential beneficiaries of the resource transfers were Ireland and Italy; the United Kingdom would also have benefited, had she decided to join the EMS. But the EPC, the ECOFIN Council and the Brussels European Council itself had great difficulties in agreeing on a proposal. The suggestion of the European Parliament was not accepted; the preference of most other governments was to offer interest-rate subsidies and delayed repayment on long-term loans extended through the European Investment Bank and a new EC Facility ('the Ortoli Facility') rather than outright grants. The Brussels European Council capped the subsidy at ecu 200 million per annum for a five-year period, with one third going to Ireland, and two thirds to Italy. These sums appear surprisingly small in view of the potential weight of the arguments for the transfers and compared to the efforts made with the structural funds in 1988–92, where disbursements to, say, Ireland reach levels at least ten times those agreed in 1978 in real terms. This is another illustration of the mood at the time, viz. that participation in the EMS was unlikely to make a major difference to the structural problems of the recipient countries. Ireland and Italy voiced disappointment in Brussels and delayed their decisions to join the EMS by a few days.

With these two decisions of mid December, participation in the EMS comprised eight of the then nine member states. Three governments that had not participated regularly in joint exchange-rate management since 1972–3 had entered; Italy used the option of wider margins already defined in the Bremen conclusions.[9] But the United Kingdom stayed outside. There are some interesting analogies to – and differences from – the current debate over UK participation in the subsequent stages of the EMU process.

The then Prime Minister, James Callaghan, having decided to hold the general election at the latest possible time in his five-year mandate (May 1979), had apparently already come to the conclusion in October 1978, after a hostile debate at the Labour Party conference, that there was no way in which he could obtain Cabinet or Parliament support for participation in the EMS during the pre-election period. Following a number of years of criticism of the Community, and only two years after the massive depreciation of sterling of 1976 which had ended half a century of often frustrating efforts to manage stable currency relationships, UK public opinion could only have been persuaded to favour EMS membership after a major investment in political persuasion. With a general election approaching the autumn of 1978 was not the time for such an effort. The issue had to be postponed until after the election. James Callaghan, whose personal evaluation of the EMS initiative appears to have been more positive than those of his Cabinet and Party colleagues and than that of the Conservative opposition, chose not to put the issue of UK participation to any formal vote. The government's Green Paper on the subject, published only one week before the Brussels European Council, took a similar low-key pragmatic approach, UK Government (1978):

> the government can not yet reach its own conclusion on whether it would be
> in the best interests of the United Kingdom to join the exchange rate regime
> of the EMS as it finally emerges from the negotiations.

It is not obvious what further clarification the UK government can have expected at this late stage. The tone of the Green Paper left little doubt that any version of the EMS would have been objectionable. Sterling was seen as different from several other European currencies about to join the EMS: greater importance in both trading and financial relationships with non-European countries, sensitive to a different degree to movements in the oil price in view of the UK's major energy resources in the North Sea, difficulties in keeping UK goods competitive if linked to the DM and less subject to domestic inflation. Jointly they imply a strong scepticism concerning the feasibility of abandoning individual management of the exchange rate.

With the decisions of eight EC countries the EMS was, in principle, ready to start on 1 January 1991. No country requested a review of the central rates at entry. The snake participants continued with the rates set at their final realignment of October 1978, while the three new entrants declared central rates at the levels established in the market towards the end of the negotiations. But actual implementation was delayed for two and a half months to 13 March 1979, in order to resolve the consequences of one provision of the Brussels Resolution, viz. that existing Monetary Compensatory

---

[9] A detailed review of the domestic political processes which produced these decisions may be found in Ludlow (1982), pp. 205–30.

Amounts (MCAs) should be progressively reduced and the creation of new MCAs avoided in order to reestablish the unity of the price system of the Common Agricultural Policy.

Chapter 1, section 2 described briefly the system of tariffs and subsidies on agricultural goods which had arisen in the late 1960s, when major changes in exchange rates inside the EC had first appeared. With the introduction of the ecu as the unit in which agricultural prices were to be fixed henceforth, a correction had to be applied to avoid an unwarranted decline in farm prices in national currencies. The European Council agreed to a proposal by the Commission to eliminate this effect, but their Ministers of Agriculture could not subsequently agree on how to implement the second and more significant part of the Brussels Resolution: to phase out the MCAs according to a pre-set timetable rather than preserve the status quo. This subject proved both technically difficult and politically sensitive, and French insistence on specific commitments could not be met; it was resisted particularly strongly by Germany where its adoption would have implied a decline in farm incomes. France accepted a fairly weak statement of principle in early March, and the EMS could finally start.

In retrospect, though exchange markets accepted the suspended intentions of the EMS and central banks behaved as they would have to do in the system, it was surprising that the initiators accepted the risk of delayed implementation after all the efforts of negotiating for many months. To some it seemed as if the new system was after all not the priority issue it had been made out to be.

2.3 The European Monetary Fund

The Brussels Resolution contains the following apocryphal reference to development beyond the initial stage of the EMS (Art. 1.4):

> We remain firmly resolved to consolidate, not later than two years after the start of the scheme, into a final system the provisions and procedures thus created. This system will entail the creation of the European Monetary Fund as announced in the conclusions of the European Council meeting at Bremen on 6 and 7 July 1978, as well as the full utilization of the ecu as a reserve asset and a means of settlement. It will be based on adequate legislation at the Community as well as the national level.

This formulation and the available records of the 1978 negotiations leave many questions open as regards the intentions of the founders. A note more than three years after the launching of the EMS, Commission (1982), lists no less than ten possible tasks for the EMF, ranging from a take-over of the accounting functions of the EMCF – which would have been uncontroversial, but without real purpose – to authority for realignments in the EMS and for formulation of a joint monetary policy. As one moves through this long list of gradually more demanding tasks, the requirements for comprehensive transfers of authority from the national to the Community level grow. One weakness of the 1978 discussion was that it did not clarify the linkage between the functional tasks and the necessary institutional structure, see Padoa-Schioppa (1980). Three factors appear to have been crucial in explaining why the EMF was not implemented as intended by March 1981 at the latest.

The first and most fundamental was that the German authorities soon made it clear that the reference to 'adequate legislation' in their view implied a revision of the Rome Treaty with its required national parliamentary ratification. The scope for extending the less formal procedures of a Resolution by the European Council, subsequently followed up by agreements among the central banks, which had been used for setting up the EMS, was exhausted. The choice was therefore between submitting a fully worked-out proposal for a transfer of authority and gaining full political support for it, or for concentrating on minor extensions of the EMS agreement – the so-called 'non-institutional' reforms. The central bankers and most governments preferred to concentrate on the latter, and chapter 3 reviews some of the modest reforms in the technical provisions of the EMS implemented in 1985 and 1987, which did not require a new institution.

The second factor which blocked the EMF was the mixture of central banking and political functions apparently assigned to it. The consolidation of the existing credit mechanism would have implied entrusting the EMF with the whole range of financing of external imbalances, from central bank interventions in the very short term to medium-term conditional balance of payments assistance. The objections of the Bundesbank were put most sharply by the President of the Bundesbank a decade later (Pöhl (1989), p. 139):

> mixing central bank functions together with areas of government
> responsibility within a single Fund bars the way to a European central bank
> with a decision-making body that is independent of governments and is thus
> to be rejected.

Nobody, least of all in the Bundesbank, would have spoken of a European central bank in 1978, but the more recent statement reflects the thinking of German and Dutch central bankers at the time of the launching of the EMS. They saw that step as already entailing risks of more inflation through excessive emphasis on exchange-rate stability. Creating an integrated and graduated mechanism for financing external imbalances in a new institution seemed to greatly increase these risks. Furthermore, experience with the EMCF had shown that, even if a new institution had only minimalist tasks, it was likely to come under the control of the ECOFIN Council, rather than a governing body of central bankers.

The third consideration weighing against the set-up of the EMF was a concern about the additional creation of international liquidity leading to monetary laxity in the participating countries. The Brussels Resolution had only spoken of the 'full utilization of the ecu as a reserve asset and a means of settlement'; and the method of creating ecus through temporary swaps against gold and dollars did not in itself imply any net creation of reserves. The 50 per cent acceptance limit on settlements in ecus was a reminder that the new asset should not be made too readily usable, but that provision was clearly targeted to be removed in the Brussels Resolution in the next stage of an institutionalized EMS. More worrisome still was the notion mentioned in the Annex to the Bremen conclusions that ecus also might be created against national currencies and 'in comparable magnitude'.

It is unclear by what method these ecus would be created. If the EMF were enabled to extend credit to participating central banks or governments, that capacity would either have to be severely circumscribed by rules or conditionality, familiar from the IMF practice, to maintain control over international reserves and avoid conflicts of interest between a regional institution and the IMF as responsible for monitoring global liquidity, see Polak (1980).

The resistance to the opening of channels by which ecus could be created against national currencies – or in the present context against private ecu – is still in evidence in the current discussions on the transition to EMU. A review of this issue is postponed to chapter 6. The perceived risk of additional liquidity creation through the EMF was enhanced by the two earlier considerations of the more cautious participants in the EMS: the lack of a firm institutional foundation and the linkage to balance of payments support. Jointly they provided a barrier to general acceptance of the institutional completion of the EMS envisaged by the founders.

The ambition to set up the EMF faltered for reasons that were in part similar to those that stopped the Werner approach to move beyond the first stage and even to prevent regression; but in part they were different. The two efforts shared the setting of arbitrary time limits which seemed generous from the start, but which were overtaken by events – the two oil price shocks – that worsened the international environment and increased divergence inside the Community. Neither project paid sufficient attention to organizational and political issues of defining the competence of a joint monetary institution. In particular, neither plan defined a balance between central banking tasks and broader macroeconomic policies. The view that the political authorities should set the priorities in both areas was as dominant in 1978 as in 1970. But the two initiatives were so different in strategy, that the causes of failure could still be seen as contrasts.

The Werner Report had set its ultimate aims so high and made such reaching demands for the transfer of decision-making from the national to the Community level that the conflict with political realities became too stark. The approach to the second, institutional stage of the EMS was, partly because of the earlier experience, deliberately more low key. It did not explicitly suggest any transfer of authority, but as the technical discussion of the possible tasks for the EMF proceded there seemed to be no institutional development of the EMS that was innovative and substantial without requiring a more basic review of long-run aims and of the framework for decision-making.

Such an institutional development became possible only after a lengthy evolution of the EMS to which the following two chapters turn.

References

Committee on Reform of the International Monetary System and related issues (Committee of Twenty) (1974), *International Monetary Reform, Documents of the Committee of Twenty*, International Monetary Fund, Washington DC.

Ethier, Wilfried and Arthur L. Bloomfield (1975), 'Managing the managed float', *Princeton Essays in International Finance*, 112, Princeton, October.

Jenkins, Roy (1977), 'Europe's present challenge and future opportunity', first Jean Monnet Lecture, European University Institute, Florence, 27 October.

Kloten, Norbert (1980), 'Germany's monetary and financial policy and the European Community', in Kohl, Wilfrid L. and Giorgio Basevi, *West Germany: A European and Global Power*, Lexington Books, D.C. Heath and Company, Lexington.

Ludlow, Peter (1982), *The Making of the EMS*, Butterworth Economic Studies, Butterworth Scientific, London.

McDougall, Sir Donald et al. (1977), *Report of the Study Group on the Role of Public Finance in European Integration* (McDougall Report), Volumes I–II, Commission of the European Communities, Brussels.

Melitz, Jacques (1988), 'Monetary discipline and cooperation in the EMS: a synthesis', in Francesco Giavazzi, Stefano Micossi and Marcus Miller (eds.) *The European Monetary System*, Banca d'Italia, Centro Interuniversitario di Studi Teorici per la Politica Economica and Centre for Economic Policy Research, Cambridge University Press, Cambridge, 51–79.

Padoa-Schioppa, Tommaso (1980), 'The EMF: topics for discussion' in *Banca Nazionale del Lavoro Quarterly Review* No. 134, Rome: 317–43.

Polak, Jacques J. (1980), 'The EMF: external relations', in *Banca Nazionale del Lavoro Quarterly Review* No. 134, Rome: 359–72.

Pöhl, Karl Otto (1989), 'The further development of the EMS', in Collection of Papers Annexed to *Delors Report*, Office for Official Publications of the European Commission, Luxembourg: 129–55.

Putnam, Robert and Randall Henning (1989), 'The Bonn Summit of 1978: how does international policy coordination actually work?' *Brookings Discussion Papers* in International Economies, No. 53, The Brookings Institution, Washington DC.

Thygesen, Niels (1979), 'The EMS: precursors, first steps and policy options', in Triffin Robert (ed.), *The Emerging EMS*, Bulletin of the National Bank of Belgium, LIVth year, vol. I, Brussels: 87–125.

United Kingdom Government (1978), 'The European Monetary System', Green Paper, HMSO, London, reprinted in *Financial Times*, 25 November.

Van Ypersele, Jacques and Jean-Claude Koeune (1985), 'The EMS, origins, operation and outlook', *European Perspectives Series*, Commission of the European Communities, Brussels.

APPENDIX I

Extract from the conclusions of the Presidency of the European Council of 6 and 7 July 1978 in Bremen and Annex

Monetary Policy

Following the discussion at Copenhagen on 7 April the European Council has discussed the attached scheme for the creation of closer monetary cooperation (European Monetary System) leading to a zone of monetary stability in Europe, which has been introduced by members of the European Council. The European Council regards such a zone as a highly desirable objective. The European Council envisages a durable and effective scheme. It agreed to instruct the Finance Ministers at their meeting on 24 July to formulate the necessary guidelines for the competent community bodies to elaborate by 31 October the provisions necessary for the functioning of such a scheme – if necessary by amendment. There will be concurrent studies of the action needed to be taken to strengthen the economies of the less prosperous member countries in the context of such a scheme; such measures will be essential if the zone of monetary stability is to succeed. Decisions can then be taken and commitments made at the European Council meeting on 4 and 5 December.

The Heads of Government of Belgium, Denmark, the Federal Republic of Germany, Luxembourg and the Netherlands state that the 'Snake' has not been and is not under discussion. They confirm that it will remain fully intact.

Annex

1   In terms of exchange-rate management the European Monetary System (EMS) will be at least as strict as the 'Snake'. In the initial stages of its operation and for a limited period of time member countries currently not participating in the snake may opt for somewhat wider margins around central rates. In principle, interventions will be in the currencies of participating countries. Changes in central rates will be subject to mutual consent. Non-member countries with particularly strong economic and financial ties with the Community may become associate members of the system. The European Currency Unit (ECU)[1] will be at the centre of the system, in particular, it will be used as a means of settlement between the EEC monetary authorities.

2   An initial supply of ECUs (for use among Community central banks) will be created against deposit of US dollars and gold on the one hand (e.g., 20 per cent of the stock currently held by member central banks) and member currencies on the other hand in an amount of a comparable order of magnitude.

The use of ECUs created against member currencies will be subject to conditions varying with the amount and the maturity; due account will be given to the need for substantial short-term facilities (up to one year).

3   Participating countries will coordinate their exchange-rate policies *vis-à-vis* third countries. To this end they will intensify the consultations in the appropriate bodies and between central banks participating in the scheme. Ways to coordinate dollar interventions should be sought which avoid simultaneous reverse interventions. Central banks buying dollars will deposit a fraction (say 20%) and receive ECUs in return; likewise, central banks selling dollars will receive a fraction (say 20%) against ECUs.

4   Not later than two years after the start of the scheme, the existing arrangements and institutions will be consolidated in a European Monetary Fund.[2]

5   A system of closer monetary cooperation will only be successful if participating countries pursue policies conducive to greater stability at home and abroad; this applies to the deficit and surplus countries alike.

[1] The ECU has the same definition as the European Unit of Account.

[2] The EMF will take the place of the EMCF.

APPENDIX 2

Resolution of the European Council of 5 December 1978 on the establishment of the European Monetary System (EMS) and related matters

A   The European Monetary System

1   Introduction

1.1   In Bremen we discussed a 'scheme for the creation of closer monetary cooperation leading to a zone of monetary stability in Europe'. We regarded such a zone 'as a highly desirable objective' and envisaged 'a durable and effective scheme'.

1.2   Today, after careful examination of the preparatory work done by the Council and other Community bodies, we are agreed as follows:

A European Monetary System (EMS) will be set up on 1 January 1979.

1.3   We are firmly resolved to ensure the lasting success of the EMS by policies conducive to greater stability at home and abroad for both deficit and surplus countries.

1.4   The following chapters deal primarily with the initial phase of the EMS.

We remain firmly resolved to consolidate, not later than two years after the start of the scheme, into a final system the provisions and procedures thus created. This system will entail the creation of the European Monetary Fund as announced in the conclusions of the European Council meeting at Bremen on 6 and 7 July 1978, as well as the full utilization of the ECU as a reserve asset and a means of settlement. It will be based on adequate legislation at the community as well as the national level.

2   The ECU and its functions

2.1   A European Currency Unit (ECU) will be at the centre of the EMS. The value and the composition of the ECU will be identical with the value of the EUA at the outset of the system.

2.2   The ECU will be used:

    (a)   as the denominator (numeraire) for the exchange-rate mechanism;
    (b)   as the basis for a divergence indicator;
    (c)   as the denominator for operations in both the intervention and the credit mechanisms;
    (d)   as a means of settlement between monetary authorities of the European Community.

2.3   The weights of currencies in the ECU will be re-examined and if necessary revised within six months of the entry into force of the system and thereafter every five years or on request, if the weight of any currency has changed by 25%.

    Revisions have to be mutually accepted; they will, by themselves, not modify the external value of the ECU. They will be made in line with underlying economic criteria.

3   The exchange rate and intervention mechanisms

3.1   Each currency will have an ECU-related central rate. These central rates will be used to establish a grid of bilateral exchange permit.

A member state which does not participate in the exchange-rate mechanism at the outset may participate at a later date.

3.2 Adjustments of central rates will be subject to mutual agreement by a common procedure which will comprise all countries participating in the exchange-rate mechanism and the Commission. There will be reciprocal consultation in the Community framework about important decisions concerning exchange-rate policy between countries participating and any country not participating in the system.

3.3 In principle, interventions will be made in participating currencies.

3.4 Intervention in participating currencies is compulsory when the intervention points defined by the fluctuation margins are reached.

3.5 An ECU basket formula will be used as an indicator to detect divergences between Community currencies. A 'threshold of divergence' will be fixed at 75% of the maximum spread for each currency.

It will be calculated in such a way as to eliminate the influence of weight on the probability of reaching the threshold.

3.6 When a currency crosses its 'threshold of divergence', this results in a presumption that the authorities concerned will correct this situation by adequate measures namely:

(a) diversified intervention;
(b) measures of domestic monetary policy;
(c) changes in central rates;
(d) other measures of economic policy.

In case such measures, on account of special circumstances, are not taken, the reasons for this shall be given to the other authorities, especially in the 'concertation between central banks'.

Consultations will, if necessary, then take place in the appropriate Community bodies including the Council of Ministers.

After six months these provisions shall be reviewed in the light of experience. At that date the questions regarding imbalances accumulated by divergent creditor or debtor countries will be studied as well.

3.7 Very Short-Term Facility of an unlimited amount will be established. Settlements will be made 45 days after the end of the month of intervention with the possibility of prolongation for another three months for amounts limited to the size of debtor quotas in the Short-Term Monetary Support.

3.8 To serve as a means of settlements, an initial supply of ECUs will be provided by the EMCF against the deposit of 20% of gold and 20% of dollar reserves currently held by central banks.

This operation will take the form of specified, revolving swap arrangements. By periodical review and by an appropriate procedure it will be ensured that each central bank will maintain a deposit of at least 20% of these reserves with the EMCF. A Member State not participating in the exchange rate mechanism may participate in this initial operation on the basis described above.

4   The credit mechanisms

4.1 The existing credit mechanisms with their present rules of application will be maintained for the initial phase of the EMS. They will be consolidated into a single fund in the final phase of the EMS.

4.2 The credit mechanisms will be extended to an amount of ECU 25 000 million of effectively available credit. The distribution of this amount will be as follows:

Short-Term Monetary Support = ECU 14 000 million;
Medium-Term Financial Assistance = ECU 11 000 million.

4.3 The duration of the Short-Term Monetary Support will be extended for another three months on the same conditions as the first extension.

4.4 The increase of the Medium-Term Financial Assistance will be completed by 30 June 1979. In the meantime, countries which still need national legislation are expected to make their extended medium-term quotas available by an interim financing agreement of the central banks concerned.

5 Third countries and international organizations

5.1 The durability of the EMS and its international implications require coordination of exchange-rate policies *vis-à-vis* third countries, and, as far as possible, a concertation with the monetary authorities of those countries.

5.2 European countries with particularly close economic and financial ties with the European Communities may participate in the exchange rate and intervention mechanisms.
    Participation will be based upon agreements between central banks; these agreements will be communicated to the Council and the Commission of the European Communities.

5.3 The EMS is and will remain fully compatible with the relevant articles of the IMF Agreement.

6 Further procedure

6.1 To implement the decisions taken under A., the European Council requests the Council to consider and to take a decision on 18 December 1978 on the following proposals of the Commission;

(a) Council Regulation modifying the unit of account used by the EMCF, which introduces the ECU in the operations of the EMCF and defines its composition;

(b) Council Regulation permitting the EMCF to receive monetary reserves and to issue ECUs to the monetary authorities of the Member States which may use them as a means of settlement;

(c) Council Regulation on the impact of the European Monetary System on the common agricultural policy. The European Council considers that the introduction of the EMS should not of itself result in any change in the situation obtaining prior to 1 January 1979 regarding the expression in national currencies of agricultural prices, monetary compensatory amounts and all other amounts fixed for the purposes of the common agricultural policy.

    The European Council stresses the importance of henceforth avoiding the creation of permanent MCAs and progressively reducing present MCAs in order to reestablish the unity of prices of the common agricultural policy, giving also due consideration to price policy.

6.2 It requests the Commission to submit in good time a proposal to amend the Council Decision of 22 March 1971 on setting up machinery for medium-term financial assistance to enable the Council (Economics and Finance Ministers) to take a decision on such a proposal at their session of 18 December 1978.

6.3 It requests the central banks of Member States to modify their Agreement of 10 April 1972 on the narrowing of margins of fluctuation between the currencies of Member States in accordance with the rules set forth above (see Section 3).

6.4 It requests the Central banks of Member States to modify as follows the rules on Short-Term Monetary Support by 1 January 1979 at the latest:

(a)   The total of debtor quotas available for drawings by the central banks of Member States shall be increased to an aggregate amount of ECU 7 900 million.

(b)   The total of creditor quotas made available by the central banks of aggregate amount of ECU 15 800 million.

(c)   The total of the additional creditor amounts as well as the total of the additional debtor amounts may not exceed ECU 8 800 million.

(d)   The duration of credit under the extended Short-Term Monetary Support may be prolonged twice for a period of three months.

B   Measures designed to strengthen the economies of the less prosperous Member States of the European Monetary System

1   We stress that, within the context of broadly based strategy aimed at improving the prospects of economic development and based on symmetrical rights and obligations of all participants, the most important concern should be to enhance the convergence of economic policies towards greater stability. We request the Council (Economic and Finance Ministers) to strengthen its procedures for cooperation in order to improve that convergence.

2   We are aware that the convergence of economic policies and of economic performance will not be easy to achieve. Therefore, steps must be taken to strengthen the economic potential of the less prosperous countries of the Community. This is primarily the responsibility of the Member States concerned. Community measures can and should serve a supporting role.

3   The European Council agrees that in the context of the European Monetary System, the following measures in favour of less prosperous Member States effectively and fully participating in the exchange rate and intervention mechanisms will be taken.

3.1 The European Council requests the Community Institutions by the utilization of the new financial instrument and the European Investment Bank to make available for a period of five years, loans of up to EUA 1000 million per year to these countries on special conditions.

3.2 The European Council requests the Commission to submit a proposal to provide interest rate subsidies of 3% for these loans, with the following element: the total cost of this measure, divided into annual tranches of EUA 200 million each over a period of five years, shall not exceed EUA 1 000 million.

3.4 The funds thus provided are to be concentrated on the financing of selected infrastructure projects and programmes, on the understanding that any direct or indirect distortion of the competitive position of specific industries within Member States will have to be avoided.

3.5 The European Council requests the Council (Economics and Finance Ministers) to take a decision on the above mentioned proposals in time so that the relevant measures can become effective on 1 April 1979 the latest. There should be a review at the end of the initial phase of the EMS.

4   The European Council requests the Commission to study the relationship between greater convergence in economic performance of the Member States and the utilization of Community instruments, in particular the funds which aim at reducing structural imbalances. The results of these studies will be discussed at the next European Council meeting.

PART II

THE
EUROPEAN
MONETARY
SYSTEM

CHAPTER 3

THE WORKING OF THE EMS

The institutional and operational set-up underpinning the EMS has not changed substantially over time although it was negotiated thirteen years ago (see chapter 2). However, the system has in some respects – well before the perspective of moving towards EMU arose – been fundamentally transformed. The changes have cumulatively gone well beyond what could initially have been foreseen. The capacity of the participants to learn from experience and develop the EMS into a framework much more ambitious and coherent than the relatively defensive mechanism which resulted from the 1978 initiative – more than any of the system's more enduring features – makes the analysis of the process of European monetary integration so interesting and challenging.

The present chapter adopts a largely chronological perspective of that process up to the present. The next three chapters in part II, and especially chapter 4, go more deeply into the analytical issues that arise in evaluating the EMS experience, while keeping in mind the rough division into subperiods suggested by the more chronological review of the present chapter and the questions raised in the 1978 negotiations. This chapter starts by providing in section 1 criteria for a chronology that suggests three distinct periods. Sections 2 to 4 then discuss in more detail each of these three periods, which consist of a turbulent start until early 1983, a calmer intermediate phase, and finally a long period without realignments starting in early 1987. Section 5 provides a summary.

3.1 Criteria for a chronology

The simplest criterion to use in evaluating the past performance of the EMS is to focus on the frequency of realignments, i.e., the external dimension of the participants' efforts to create 'a zone of monetary stability'. This is appealing because one central challenge to those who negotiated the EMS was to avoid a perpetuation, or a revival, of the violent movements in nominal exchange rates among the European currencies which marked some periods in the 1970s. The use of realignments suggests that the system responded constructively in three stages of diminishing accommodation of diverging national inflation rates to the challenge of giving substance to the vague idea embodied in Article 108 of the Treaty of Rome, viz. that EC member states should 'regard their exchange rate as a matter of common concern'. On this crucial point the EMS negotiations brought no clarification as to when realignments would be appropriate, as we discussed in chapter 2. Table 3.1.1 shows how they have in fact been used on twelve occasions since March 1979. Figure 3.1.1a & b shows the cumulative effect of these central-rate changes *vis-à-vis* the ecu. Figure 3.1.2 records the movements since 1979 of the ecu against the dollar and the yen.

Table 3.1.1. Revaluations of the Deutsche Mark against other EMS currencies (measured by bilateral central rates, in %)

Item	Belg/Lux franc	Danish krone	French franc	Dutch guilder	Irish pound	Italian lira	Total EMS[1]
Weight[2] (in %)	16.6	4.0	32.0	17.4	1.8	27.5	100
Realignment with effect from:							
September 24, 1979	+2.0	+5.0	+2.0	+2.0	+2.0	+2.0	+2.1
November 30, 1979	–	–	–	–	–	–	+0.2
March 23, 1981	–	–	–	–	–	+6.4	+1.7
October 5, 1981	+5.5	+5.5	+8.8	–	+5.5	+8.8	+6.5
February 22, 1982	+9.3	+3.1	–	–	–	–	+1.6
June 14, 1982	+4.3	+4.3	+10.6	–	+4.3	+7.2	+6.3
March 21, 1983	+3.9	+2.9	+8.2	+1.9	+9.3	+8.2	+6.7
July 22, 1985	–	–	–	–	–	+8.5	+2.3
April 7, 1986	+2.0	+2.0	+6.2	–	+3.0	+3.0	+3.8
August 4, 1986	–	–	–	–	+8.7	–	+0.2
January 12, 1987	+1.0	+3.0	+3.0	–	+3.0	+3.0	+2.6
January 8, 1990	–	–	–	–	–	+3.7	+1.0
Cumulative since the start of the EMS on March 13, 1979	+31.2	+35.2	+45.2	+4.0	+41.4	+63.5	+41.8

Notes:
1 Average revaluation of the Deutsche Mark against the other EMS currencies (geometrically weighted); excluding Spain.
2 Weights of the EMS currencies derived from the foreign trade shares between 1984 and 1986, after taking account of third market effects, and expressed in terms of the weighted external value of the Deutsche Mark.

Source: Deutsche Bundesbank (1989) and updated by the authors.

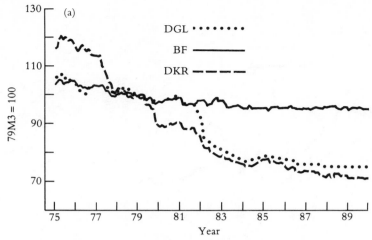

Figure 3.1.1a German Mark EMS exchange rates, 1975–90 (index of nominal bilateral exchange rates, March 1979=100)

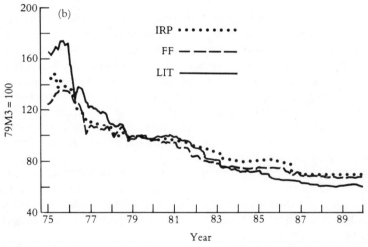

Figure 3.1.1b German Mark EMS exchange rates, 1975–90 (index of nominal bilateral exchange rates, March 1979=100)

After an initial turbulent period of four years up to and including the March 1983 realignment, during which central rates were modified at the rate of on average once every eight months and, if anything, with increasing frequency and amplitude over the second half of the period, a more tranquil phase of four years followed in which realignments were fewer and mostly smaller than in the earlier period. They were also without exception smaller than the differentials in national inflation rates between the countries concerned, thus leading to changes in real exchange rates.

The January 1987 realignment, considered by some member states as superfluous and dangerous because it was seen as a harbinger of destabilizing accommodation of external

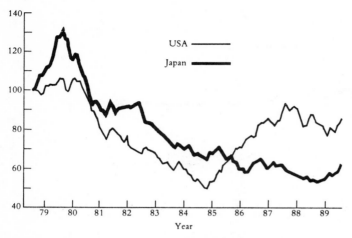

Figure 3.1.2 Nominal exchange rates of US dollar and Japanese yen versus the ecu, 1979–90 (index, March 1979=100)

financial shocks, rather than of real shocks or of differential inflation, marks the natural end to the second period. In any case, apart from the rebasing of the central rate for the Italian lira within the earlier wider band in January 1990, there have now been no realignments for more than four years. The third period has been marked by increasing awareness in financial markets that the use of nominal exchange-rate changes had been put more firmly in the background by national policy-makers, an interpretation made more compelling by the firm emphasis by several of the latter on the rigidity of the exchange-rate objective. The third period has also been marked by the first new entries into the EMS – by the Spanish peseta in June 1989 and by sterling in October 1990, both availing themselves of the wide margins.

Hence the main criterion used for describing the evolution of the EMS is the changing attitude to realignments as it emerges over three stages of roughly equal length, of four years each. But a chronology structured solely on this element, however central, would be inadequate, particularly for the second and third periods. Three other criteria should be brought into the assessment.

The first is the internal dimension of the ambition to develop a zone of monetary stability. The performance of average inflation of the participants and the dispersion around it are central to the assessment of progress and of the sustainability of the latter, since the avoidance of severe misalignments is an essential criterion for success of any exchange-rate system. That suggests a broadly similar chronology, but a less obvious trend than the first criterion. As analysed in chapter 4, the average inflation rate peaked at about 10 per cent in 1981–2; it then slowed sharply to the end of 1986, where it bottomed out not far above zero. In early 1987 there was a new take-off towards the current 3–4 per cent range for the eight original EMS participants, see figure 3.1.3 which also shows the dispersion of national inflation rates.

The second is to look at how exchange rates have actually been defended. The rules of the EMS, like those of the snake, were at the start only explicit to the extent that

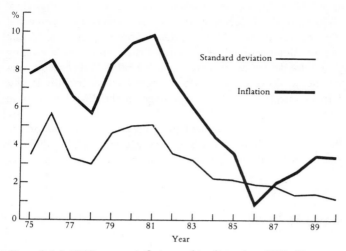

Figure 3.1.3 EMS average inflation and its dispersion, 1975–90.

they specified the margins of fluctuation at which interventions become mandatory, while leaving open the mixture of interventions, domestic monetary adjustments and intermittent capital controls. Subsequent changes have virtually eliminated the third of these options, while significantly affecting the balance between the first two, notably through the so-called Basle–Nyborg agreement of September 1987. Drawing on Godeaux (1989) it is argued that this criterion suggests a similar subdivision of periods, and that it is particularly helpful in distinguishing the transition to the third period, where the liberalization of capital flows accelerated and the national monetary authorities in the EMS decided to rely more on interest-rate changes and on exchange-rate flexibility inside the margin rather than primarily on interventions.

The third criterion is to ask what reforms were possible in the EMS or in the general framework within which the system operates. The evolution of attitudes from the defensive and minimalist which prevailed in the early years to the resumption of the process of achieving EMU by stages is evident. It is also reflected at a more pragmatic and operational level by the attitude of national officials to reforms in the March 1979 agreement among the central banks on the operating procedures of the EMS. In this perspective, there is a remarkable change as one moves from the first to the second and from the second to the third phase.

In the first four years after the start, no reforms of the EMS seemed possible, even very modest ones relating to the use of the official ecu as a means of settlement. The one important reform which had been envisaged by the EMS founders – the consolidation of the system into an EMF – was shelved. In the second four-year period some mini-reforms, under discussion since the early 1980s, finally become possible, but they had a very limited impact. At the more general political level this period, however, brought the adoption of the Single European Act to implement a unified market in goods and services, including financial services. Capital controls were eased somewhat in this period.

The fuller implications of submitting national economic performance, and monetary policy in particular, increasingly to the judgement of financial markets were perceived by the central bankers as they implemented the Basle–Nyborg agreement at the beginning of the third period. But the political authorities drew more wide-ranging conclusions, as they reopened the debate on moving towards EMU. The consequences of this new ambition for the working of the EMS lie beyond the horizon in this chapter; this is returned to in our review of the first stage of the EMU process in chapter 12.

On the whole, it is obvious that the three supplementary criteria broadly support the subdivision of the EMS experience into three phases suggested by the different approaches to realignments.[1] They will be reviewed together in the following three sections.

3.2   A turbulent start: 1979–83

The initial four-year period was very difficult in a number of respects. In the United States monetary policy was tightened and monetary control procedures significantly modified in October 1979, increasing greatly the role of interest-rate variations in achieving intermediate monetary objectives and presenting European monetary authorities with the difficult challenge of responding in a coherent way to international financial shocks. US interest rates, nominal and real, rose to unprecedented heights, leaving other countries with the unpleasant choice of finding an appropriate mixture of matching higher interest rates or accepting sharp depreciation of their currencies. With inflation again on the rise following the second oil price shock of 1979–80, the response was bound to be a mixture of the two.

The oil price shock not only raised inflation; current accounts worsened sharply, output stagnated or fell and unemployment rose sharply. Budget deficits widened initially in most member states by much more than could be explained by automatic responses. Finally, and potentially most seriously, divergence in national policy responses became more visible, notably after the election of President Mitterand in France in May 1981. French efforts at overcoming recession through budgetary expansion were met initially with sympathy in some smaller member states (Belgium, Denmark and Ireland). When German opinion turned more decisively against inflation and public deficits in 1982, leading to the replacement of Chancellor Schmidt's coalition government by the coalition of Chancellor Kohl, the consensus which had emerged in the EMS negotiations appeared to have vanished under the weight of a combination of major unfavourable external shocks and the reemergence of apparently ineradicable differences in policy preferences within Europe. It seems inconceivable, in retrospect, that, if the decision to launch the EMS had not been made in 1978, it could have been agreed at any time during this early period. Not surprisingly, discussion on its

---

[1] From this perspective it might be appropriate to label the three (or more) stages in the current EMU process, stages four, five, six, etc. since the start of the EMS. (Or five, six, seven, etc., if the snake is considered, as we believe to be justified, the initial stage of the EC's monetary integration efforts.)

further development towards a second, more institutional stage in the form of the EMF was adjourned *sine die* in December 1980.

Despite these difficult circumstances, the first four years marked progress in some respects relative to the experience of the 1970s and paved the way for the subsequent stage. Realignments – at least when they were comprehensive – became more visibly a joint responsibility; and the cumulatively large realignments that did occur were at least sufficient to prevent serious misalignments among the participants and, in some cases, to contribute to better equilibrium. To illustrate these points it is necessary to examine the seven realignments which occurred between September 1979 and March 1983.[2]

The **first** realignment of September 1979 corresponded with the pattern anticipated at the start of the EMS. The Bundesbank had been intervening on a large scale to sustain both a depreciating dollar (the realignment took place two weeks before the tightening and redesign of US monetary policy in October 1979) and two weak EMS currencies, the Belgian franc and the Danish krone. The realignment was modest and in the end involved only two countries, Germany and Denmark, in a formal change of their ecu central rates.[3]

There was no easy agreement on this first occasion, and the meeting lasted nearly to dawn, as if to underline that EMS adjustments were not going to be unilateral or voluntary acts. The problem related to the Benelux currencies. Although the Belgian franc had been under pressure, the Belgian authorities were anxious to stay at an unchanged DM rate, i.e., to move up with the DM against most of the other EMS currencies. This would not, however, have relieved tensions inside the band, where the Belgian franc had been permanently weak since March, and the move was therefore resisted by Germany and others.

The Dutch authorities, who had a stronger case for maintaining an unchanged DM rate in terms of both the guilder's position inside the band and more fundamental indicators (inflation rate and current account), were caught in the middle between their desire to underline the quality of the guilder as a close substitute for the DM and their reluctance to break up the fixity of rates among the Benelux currencies. The latter considerations prevailed, opening the way for the realignment compromise: a revaluation of the DM of 2 per cent and a devaluation of the Danish krone by nearly 3 per cent. But the course of the negotiations underlined the joint nature of the decisions, strongly suggesting that a different outcome would have been arrived at in the absence of a formal EMS agreement.

The **second** realignment was different in being largely unilateral and surrounded by a minimum of formality. In November 1979 the Danish government asked for a 5 per cent devaluation of the krone, not on the basis of urgent pressures in the exchange market (the krone was comfortably stable near the middle of the EMS band), but with

[2] The analysis draws upon Thygesen (1984), pp. 265–72; a much fuller chronological account, supplemented by extracts of realignment communiqués, may be found in Ungerer *et al.* (1983), (1986) and (1990).

[3] A more significant measure by which to judge the importance of a realignment is how market effective exchange rates moved as a result of the change in bilateral central rates; the five currencies that did not move formally still devalued by 1/2–1 per cent on this measure.

reference to the need for improving competitiveness. The devaluation was seen as part of a package which also comprised temporary and permanent modifications of indexation mechanisms.

No meeting of the Council of Ministers was held to consider the Danish request; it was approved *de facto* by telephone. The only concern voiced by other EMS members appears to have been whether the realignment would require changes in the price system of the Common Agricultural Policy, laboriously negotiated earlier in the year.

A linkage had been established during the EMS negotiations; indeed, it was this very issue that had delayed the implementation of the agreement by three months, see chapter 2, section 2.[4] But having satisfied themselves that the cumulative effect of the September realignment and the requested Danish devaluation remained below the threshold at which agricultural prices would have to be changed, there was no effort to assess whether the informality of the procedure and the absence of short-term pressures on the initiating currency would create a dangerous precedent. To most participants the case was probably seen as a parallel to the occasions during 1976–8 when the participants in the 'snake', the joint float of the Benelux and Scandinavian currencies with the DM which preceded the EMS, had reached similar decisions with a minimum of formality and essentially unilateral justifications, see chapter 1, section 4.

No further changes in EMS central rates were made over the following sixteen months. This period, by far the longest between realignments in the experience of the early phase, was marked by exceptional features favourable to intra–EMS stability, notably the prolonged weakness of the DM, as the German current account swung into unprecedented deficit. In the course of 1979, Germany had implemented the expansionary fiscal measures urged on her in successive European Councils and World Economic Summits, while most other European countries were pursuing cautious policies in view of the boost given to their already high inflation rates by the second oil-price shock. This constellation and, particularly, interest differentials favouring the weaker currencies at a time when an early EMS realignment seemed unlikely, even pushed the DM near the floor of the band for some months around the end of 1980, requiring substantial interventions at times. During this period the EMS unexpectedly protected Germany against further depreciation and inflation.

This abnormal situation came to an end in February 1981 when the Bundesbank tightened monetary policy considerably. Suspension of the Lombard facilities and a sharp rise in short-term interest rates quickly pushed the DM to the top of the band and into interventions in support of the Belgian franc, while the inherent weakness of most of the other currencies was not yet exposed.

The **third** realignment occurred in March 1981 as the Italian authorities requested a 6 per cent devaluation of the lira. As in the case of the Danish initiative, there was no urgent pressure on the lira, though the volume of intra-marginal interventions to sustain the Italian currency around the middle of the lower half of the wider band accorded to the lira was rising. Italy's request had to be seen as a defensive action to offset the wide and growing inflation differential above her EMS partners. Italy had found herself

---

[4] Giavazzi and Giovannini (1989) stress, in our view rightly, the protection of the CAP as an essential motive for the launching of the EMS and for its early operation.

unable to check the inflationary impact of the second oil-price shock, due to a mixture of institutional factors – especially the exceptionally high degree of indexation in the labour market – and relatively expansionary fiscal and monetary policies, and was experiencing a sharp deterioration of her current account.

The request was granted informally, confirming the impression that central-rate adjustments for individual currencies in the EMS might be envisaged largely on the basis of unilateral decisions by the participants – with the caveat that the lira was a currency with a special status, underlined by the wider band. The real test remained whether other significant participants could count on a similar attitude.

That was soon put to the test. Following the presidential and parliamentary elections in France in May–June 1981, attention shifted entirely to the ability of the EMS to withstand the increasing divergence of policies and performance between her two largest members. After all, the earlier effort of joint European management of exchange rates, the 'snake', had twice been set back severely by failures of Germany and France to agree on policy coordination, or rather on the exchange-rate implications of not coordinating. France had left the snake in January 1973 and March 1976; on both occasions because she was pursuing fiscal and monetary policies more expansionary than Germany's and could, or would not explore fully with Germany and the smaller participants the modalities of a comprehensive realignment. Was there any hope that such joint-management efforts would be pursued more successfully within a framework in which the new French government had not participated – the EMS was strongly associated in the French debate with the outgoing President Giscard d'Estaing – and which was known to be seen as an undesirable constraint on domestic policies by a significant part of the new majority? The answer must be in the affirmative, though some qualifications have to be added. However, the dominance of Franco-German bilateral concerns created new tensions during the rest of the early period.

The **fourth** realignment did not follow immediately upon the change of majority; the new French government chose not to request a devaluation in the EMS at any early stage, a decision that caused some subsequent soul-searching, as explained by President Mitterand and Finance Minister Delors much later. But in September 1981 after four months of an unstable French franc, kept well within the EMS band by considerable interventions, a Franco-German compromise realignment was worked out. It involved the largest bilateral change yet seen in the EMS: 8.5 per cent between the initiators (5.5 per cent revaluation of the DM, 3.0 per cent devaluation of the franc). But the two largest member states also made detailed proposals for the other EMS currencies.

When presented to the others at a meeting in early October, objections were unavoidable, in particular from Italy. She had not asked for a devaluation and found unacceptable the Franco-German proposal that the lira follow the French franc in a 3 per cent devaluation. In the end the Italian negotiators were persuaded to request the necessary authorization from Rome to devalue. The Netherlands let her currency follow the DM in a 5.5 per cent revaluation, but showed some resentment at being presented with a *fait accompli* by the two largest members, as did the other participants (Belgium–Luxembourg, Denmark and Ireland) whose currencies were technically chosen as pivots, but for whom the realignment implied devaluations of about 2 per cent in the intra-EMS effective rates.

The **fifth** realignment in February 1982 was interesting primarily as an illustration of the move away from unilateral and informal decisions. The initiative came from Belgium, who could refer both to more or less permanent pressure on her currency – the divergence indicator was touched – and to a manifest lack of competitiveness. Like Denmark in 1979, she argued that devaluation was a vital component in a package of stabilization through incomes policies, which looked like a major new policy departure. While these arguments were not unpersuasive, there were strong objections to the size of the devaluation requested – 12 per cent, far more than any previous EMS (or snake) realignment.

There were equally strong objections when Denmark unexpectedly also asked for a devaluation of sizeable proportions (7 per cent). There had been no major pressure on the krone and the scope for improving competitiveness by domestic means was not seen to have been exhausted. The other participants, all concerned with their own competitiveness and rising unemployment, were only prepared to grant substantially smaller downward adjustments to the Belgian and Danish currencies. After a full day of bargaining a compromise was finally reached to devalue the franc by 8.5 per cent and the krone by 3 per cent.

This was a clear demonstration of the constraints which at least small members could expect to feel, if they had been under the impression that realignments could accommodate them without much difficulty.

A special problem arose for Belgium because of the existence of the Belgium–Luxembourg Economic Union (BLEU). In view of the lower inflation and stronger balance of payments outlook for Luxembourg, the authorities of the smaller partner country did not agree with the Belgian request for a large devaluation. However, they were only consulted just prior to the Belgian initiative to request a meeting of the ECOFIN Council and their views had no influence on the final outcome. But the process did make it clear that future Belgian initiatives to devalue could imply the breakup of the BLEU.

In the following months the familiar pattern of a strong DM (and guilder) and a French franc fluctuating in the lower half of the band reappeared. The fact that the bilateral rate between the two currencies had not been adjusted in February 1982, despite growing divergence between the two economies, increased tension considerably and an increase of 3 percentage points in French money- market rates relative to German and US rates made little impact on the exchange market.

The **sixth** realignment came less than four months later. As the French franc drifted further towards the floor of the band, a realignment was prepared in mid June 1982, involving a revaluation of the DM and the guilder (each by 4.25 per cent) and a somewhat larger devaluation of the French franc (5.75 per cent). This brought the total bilateral change in central rates to 10 per cent, the largest realignment so far between any two currencies in the EMS (or in the snake). Detailed Franco–German discussions on the accompanying measures, notably whether a freeze of prices should be extended to salaries, as it was, preceded the realignment.

The lira was also devalued, but by 3 percentage points less than the French franc (i.e., 2.75 per cent). The two countries that had pressed for a large realignment in February – Belgium and Denmark – made no move to join in, although at least the

Belgian franc continued to be in need of supportive interventions; nor did Ireland. For these three currencies the outcome was very close to status quo, in terms of their effective intra-EMS central rates as well. Since all of them rose inside the band following the realignment, their market exchange rates rose slightly.

The **seventh** and final realignment in this phase (March 1983) followed the pattern of the preceding one, except that it was even more comprehensive and involved all participating currencies. The DM/FF adjustment was 8 per cent, bringing the cumulative change in the single most important bilateral rate in the EMS close to 30 per cent over an eighteen-month period. There was again a detailed discussion between the French Finance Minister Jacques Delors, and his German counterpart about the accompanying measures in France. Yet most of the debate centered not on the size of the total adjustment, but once more on the more cosmetic issue of the composition of upward and downward adjustment. The German authorities apparently gave ground by accepting a 5.5 per cent revaluation of the DM, leaving only a 2.5 per cent devaluation for the FF.[5] This appearance of asymmetry made it possible for France to claim that Germany had conceded to being the main cause of tension and for Germany to claim at the same time that both currencies had moved significantly. As on earlier occasions, there is no evidence that the breakdown between upward and downward adjustments had any relevance for the way in which EMS realignments affected the rates *vis-à-vis* third currencies. The DM remained the pivotal currency for these rates, and only the total size of the bilateral adjustments mattered.

Other noteworthy features about the seventh realignment were:

The separation of the guilder from the DM for the first time since September 1979. While the Dutch authorities had traditionally put great emphasis on strengthening the impression of the guilder as a close substitute for the DM, they allowed their currency to slip by 2 per cent on this occasion. This modification of policy appears to have had some effect on short-term interest differentials between the two currencies, requiring the Dutch authorities to maintain for the next five years or so their short-term rates slightly higher than comparable German rates.

The Irish punt, initially protected against a weakening of the overall competitiveness of Irish industry by the heavy weight of a strong sterling, was finally devalued after sterling had fallen against the EMS currencies.

Belgium and Denmark continued their policy of aiming for a stable position near the centre of gravity of the EMS, expressed by the ecu, whereas many observers had expected a resumption of their 1982 efforts to improve competitiveness through devaluation.

---

[5] These figures are misleading in the sense that they refer to the respective central rates *vis-à-vis* the ecu, and the value of that basket was affected for all currencies participating in the EMS exchange-rate mechanism by the recalculation of the central rate for the non-participating currency, sterling, before the new rates were announced. Since the UK currency had depreciated considerably since the previous realignment, the ecu central rates of the other currencies were due for nearly 2 per cent revaluation. In reality, therefore, there was more asymmetry than appears between the upward and downward movements of the DM and FF.

This brief outline may justify two broad conclusions with respect to the use of realignments in the EMS in this early turbulent period: (1) there was an increasingly joint element in the decisions to realign; and (2) there were no visible rules observed on the size of realignments, but broadly inflation differentials were accommodated, hence containing changes in competitiveness in this turbulent period.

The first point emerges clearly from the historical record. Some countries occasionally came away from the ECOFIN meetings where realignments were made with an outcome different from what they had asked for and in some cases had even begun to prepare their domestic opinion to expect. This is most clearly on record for some of the smaller participants, but constraints were also imposed on the size of at least the 1983 devaluation of the French franc. The precise shape of several realignments was hammered out in difficult bargaining sessions in the ECOFIN Council, following preparations in the Monetary Committee, and with central bank governors in attendance, though attention was sometimes diverted to what are from an economic viewpoint side issues: the attribution of upward and downward movements within an agreed total realignment and the implications for the Common Agricultural Policy of central-rate changes.

As regards the second point, criteria for realignments, the practice followed reveals that the seven realignments up to and including that of March 1983 compensated the non-German participants in the EMS for inflation (as measured by consumer prices) in excess of the German rate. But this average hides a considerable dispersion at the end of the period, as evident from figure 3.2.1. (The attention of the reader is drawn to the different scales used in the six panels of this figure.)

Strictly speaking the restoration of relative prices to the level of March 1979 applies only to France; the three large devaluations of the French franc in the final eighteen months compensated very closely for the entire cumulated inflation over the four years, hence removing the considerable real appreciation of the franc which had occurred prior to October 1981.

In contrast, the two countries with the highest inflation, Ireland and Italy, found themselves with a substantially higher relative price level after March 1983 than when they entered the EMS; their currencies only devalued relative to the DM by about half of their excess of inflation vis-à-vis Germany. For them, the EMS was, already in this initial period, far from fully accommodating. The loss of competitiveness they experienced inside the EMS was to some extent compensated for by improvements vis-à-vis the dollar area – more important in their trade than for other EMS participants – and for Ireland vis-à-vis the UK up to 1981. And Italy had entered the EMS at a central rate near a historical low point for the lira, which provided an initial cushion.

At the other extreme, Denmark, the Netherlands, and Belgium, in particular, had obtained some real devaluation. Belgium and Denmark had moderate inflation, but showed signs of 'fundamental disequilibrium' with large current-account deficits, i.e., signs of deficient competitiveness despite relatively low activity levels.[6]

[6] In our discussion and the associated graphs we have used bilateral changes in the DM central rate and relative rise in price level (as measured by consumer prices) *vis-à-vis* Germany. There are many possible alternative presentations: using the ecu as point of reference, taking into account the trade composition of participants, and using different price and cost indicators; for some of these alternatives, see Ungerer *et al.* (1990) charts 15–24, pp. 25–30. They give a broadly similar picture, though the impression of sharply deteriorating competitiveness for Ireland and Italy is weakened.

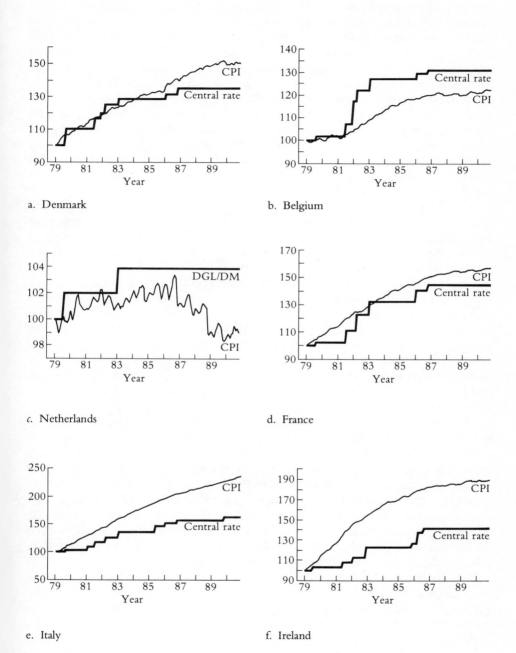

a. Denmark

b. Belgium

c. Netherlands

d. France

e. Italy

f. Ireland

Figure 3.2.1 Bilateral exchange rates (central rates for the DM) and cumulative price level differentials *vis-à-vis* Germany for six non–German EMS-currencies, March 1979–December 1990.

These observations show that the EMS had, already in this early phase, moved towards discretionary collective management of the main decision in a system of fixed-but-adjustable exchange rates: when to realign and by what criteria? The early EMS avoided both of the traps into which it could have fallen – and which had been suggested for it at the start: either to perpetuate the practice of the final stages of the Bretton Woods system or of the snake during 1976–8 in which individual participants modified their parities (or central rates) in a basically unilateral fashion, or moving to a crawling-peg system in which central rates were allowed to move steadily in small steps according to objective criteria, notably observed inflation differentials. The latter route had been suggested by the OPTICA group, see Basevi *et al.* (1976), (1977) and by Williamson (1979) as a more attractive alternative than the individual management of currencies, interspersed with periods of floating which several of the EMS participants had been following in the 1972–8 period.

A crawling-peg regime in which individual participants would be allowed in a fairly mechanical way to index their nominal exchange rate so as to eliminate emerging price level differences with Germany would, in retrospect, have been dangerous during a period when inflationary shocks, coming from rising oil prices in 1979–80 and subsequently from the rapid strengthening of the dollar from early 1981, were sizeable, and the differential impact of these shocks on individual EMS countries was highly visible. In particular, countries with initially high indexation of wages – and indexation mechanisms not excluding externally generated inflation and terms of trade changes – were far more vulnerable to the oil and dollar shocks than others. Indexing also the exchange rate in an open and transparent way would have set up a framework for rapidly increasing divergence of price trends. A similar process could have been set in motion, if EMS participants had been allowed to decide largely unilaterally the timing and size of their devaluations without showing at the same time that they had taken domestic steps to reduce inflation.

Chapter 4 reviews some of the many empirical studies that have tried to identify the contribution to lower inflation in the non-German member states of participating in the EMS. The evidence is admittedly weak that there was such a contribution. One plausible explanation of this is that it is difficult to argue convincingly what would have happened in the absence of the agreement to set up the EMS. Chapter 4 uses two possible benchmarks which both would have brought even more divergence in terms of inflation than actually observed. Merely returning average inflation to about its 1979 level by 1983 and reducing divergence (measured by the standard deviation of national inflation rates around the EMS average) somewhat, see figure 3.1.2 in the previous section, must be considered an achievement, though the full results only became visible after 1983.

The importance of participating in the EMS must also be assessed on the basis of the adjustments of domestic policies that took place in 1979–83 and their relationship to the policy of external accommodation or non-accommodation which emerges from this review of the realignments. Two countries – Denmark in 1979 and Belgium in 1982 – undertook a significant weakening of indexation mechanisms and temporary wage and price freezes at the time of their respective devaluations. This justified, also in the view of partner countries, a more liberal attitude to more aggressive use of the exchange rate, viz. going beyond what past inflation differentials would have suggested.

On the contrary, in the case of Italy, no quantifiable domestic measures were taken outside the monetary area at the time of the 4 lira devaluations of 1981–3. Hence inflationary mechanisms were only dampened through more gradual changes in the perception of the external environment on the part of price and wage setters, increasingly aware that Italian products were becoming less competitive, and on the part of policy-makers who could no longer assume that growing budget deficits and monetary financing thereof could continue unchanged. Modifications in future inflationary mechanisms were visible already in 1980–3 in the form of firmer employer resistance to wage claims and early discussion of lowering the degree of indexation, only implemented following a 1984 referendum. Of more immediate significance was the decision, embodied in the so-called 'divorce' agreement of 1981 between Banca d'Italia and the Treasury to relieve the Bank of the obligation to absorb an excess supply of government securities at issue. These examples show that participation in the EMS was not without effect on domestic policies in Italy, even though the tightening of budgetary policies that was announced at the time of some of the realignments, remained at the level of intentions rather than of actions. On the other hand, not enough progress was being made domestically to have justified requests by the Italian authorities for larger devaluations or for the EMS partner countries to have encouraged, or acceded to, such requests.

France provides the most important, but also the most questionable illustration of constructive interaction between realignments and domestic policy adjustment. The incoming socialist government had inherited a 10–15 per cent cumulative real appreciation of the franc over the first two years of the EMS; and some budgetary expansion, coupled with a major increase in the minimum wage and an initial shortening of the work week, made an early and sizeable devaluation almost inevitable. A temporary price and profit freeze was introduced at the first of the three devaluations, and the government declared an incomes policy, aiming 'only' at maintaining the purchasing power of average wages. Competitiveness worsened again until the second devaluation of June 1982, but on that occasion the domestic follow-up was much stronger; the freeze was extended to wages and future indexation practices were weakened; finally, the government restricted the 1983 budget deficit to 3 per cent of GDP, a figure that has subsequently been observed by successive French governments, hence sustaining a modest level of debt to GDP, which has put France in a comfortable position in the recent discussions of possible budgetary guidelines for EMU.

While the significant changes in domestic policy were undertaken already in 1982 and coordinated with the realignment, the most dramatic example of adjustment linked to EMS participation was that of March 1983. Since that change of policy is also regarded as a turning point for the system as a whole, it deserves additional clarification and comment.

There is no doubt that a significant part of the French government at this point found membership in the EMS too constraining and that proposals had been prepared to leave the system and possibly introduce temporary import restrictions. But Prime Minister Pierre Mauroy and Finance Minister Jacques Delors succeeded in persuading their cabinet colleagues and President Francois Mitterrand that this strategy would be too risky in terms of inflation, particularly since the international reserves of France were judged to be inadequate to defend the franc before a very sizeable depreciation had occurred. It seemed preferable to engage once more in a domestic stabilization effort, discussed with Germany as the decisive EMS partner, in return for the assurance that the franc could continue to be defended also with the resources of other EMS central banks.[7]

We have devoted most of the attention to evaluating the first four years of the EMS, the elements of the new system for which no particular rules were prescribed in 1978 – the use of realignments and the design of domestic policy measures to accompany them. The evaluation is more positive than academic or official assessments made at the time, since our account shows that a promising beginning was made in two respects: (1) in making realignments, which were probably smaller than what would have occurred without the EMS, given the inertia of inherited differential national inflation rates and the major external shocks that drove them further apart, more genuinely joint decisions; and (2) in providing linkage from realignments to domestic policy adjustments which made longer-term convergence feasible.

As the period ended, officials were clearly disillusioned with the performance, pointing out how little convergence had been achieved, and how close the system had come to a breakdown in 1983.[8] Finally, with so much attention focused on the crucial Franco-German divergence, evident from the start, but accentuated by the shift in opposite directions in France in 1981 and in Germany in 1982, insufficient attention may have been paid to domestic adjustment policies in Italy and in the smaller EMS countries particularly at the time of realignments.

The EMS was described in chapter 2 as a blend of rules and discretion: rules for the day-to-day operations, notably intervention and settlement, and discretion for realignments. In the negotiations of 1978 most of the effort was devoted to defining how exchange rates were to be defended. Considerable attention was paid to the extension of the credit mechanisms of the snake and to the role of the divergence indicator. In retrospect, these features came to play a much more limited role than expected.

The intention in 1978 was that interventions would take place primarily at the margins and in the currencies of the participants. Before the margins were reached, warning signals from the indicator of divergence were expected to have flashed and encouraged the authorities of the currency in question to take corrective action to bring it back towards the centre of the band. Central banks intervening to support a currency were expected to rely on the Very-Short-Term Financing Facility of the EMCF; credits were unlimited up to 2½ months after the end of the month of intervention, but subsequently limited to the size of the debtor quotas as explained in chapter 2.

Relative to these intentions the actual EMS experience was very different. Interventions inside the EMS remained fairly modest at the margin (approximately ecu

---

[7] A vivid account of the deliberations in the French government is given by Giesbert (1990). For an analysis of the macroeconomic perceptions in the early years after President Mitterrand's election, see Sachs and Wyplosz (1986).

[8] For a German assessment of the first four years, see, e.g., Duetsche Bundesbank (1983) Kloten (1983) and Gutowski and Scharrer (1983).

30 billion gross over the four years); only in 1981 when German monetary policy was tightened and several other currencies came under pressure did the mandatory interventions reach large proportions. But they were supplemented increasingly by intra-marginal interventions of which the bulk were in DM.

3.3   A calmer intermediate phase: March 1983–January 1987

Following the March 1983 realignment, the EMS entered a period of more stability than at any time since its foundation. There were no realignments for another twenty-eight months; when one finally came, it involved only one currency. The emphasis was increasingly on nominal convergence and coordination of monetary policies to underpin exchange-rate stability. The macroeconomic performance of the participants and the record of policy coordination, including possible indicators of symmetry (or asymmetry) inside the system, is considered in detail in chapter 4, so here discussion is limited to a summary of observable developments in the EMS as such from a chronological perspective. Reference is made to table 3.1.1 on realignments and figures 3.1.1 and 3.1.2 on movements in the participating currencies against their average in the form of the ecu and in the latter against the US dollar and the yen. Stability inside the system increased despite dollar instability; the dollar climbed to a sharp peak in February 1985, mid-way through this phase, and fell back for most of the final two years.

The **eighth** realignment was a devaluation of the Italian lira of 8 per cent against all other EMS currencies in July 1985. The Italian budget and current-account deficits both rose sharply, as inflation persisted at a rate well-above the EMS average. The lira fell to the lower half of the wide band early in the year. In view of the substantial real appreciation of the lira which had persisted from the early EMS period there were no objections to accepting Italy's request for a substantial realignment without a formal meeting of ECOFIN. The devaluation was not accompanied by major domestic policy adjustments, but the Italian government did announce efforts to raise taxes to prevent an increase in the budget deficit. They also implemented a modification of the wage indexation mechanism ('scala mobile') for which political acceptance had been won in a 1984 referendum.[9]

A **ninth** realignment with a carefully differentiated treatment of participants took place in April 1986 after the Parliamentary elections of the previous month in France had introduced 'cohabitation' between the Socialist President and a Centre-Right majority in the National Assembly. Anxious not to repeat the delay in carrying out a widely expected devaluation and facing at weekends pressures on the currency, as had happened in 1981 when the Socialist government came in, the new French government asked for a suspension of EMS margins, as a realignment was prepared over a

---

[9] There was one unusual aspect of the July 1985 devaluation: the lira was allowed to drop below the lower intervention point of its wide margin and, for one particular transaction, even below the new margin.

Thursday–Friday and negotiated in ECOFIN over the weekend. At one point no less than four currencies had moved outside the bilateral grid. A realignment was agreed to devalue the franc by 6 per cent against the DM and the guilder, somewhat less than the French goverment had requested. As was usual in the early period the realignment was presented as symmetrical, the two strong currencies revaluing by 3 per cent and the franc devaluing by a similar percentage; the other four participants remained in the middle.

The French government accompanied their initiative with some domestic policy announcements, particularly of steps to lower the budget deficit; the primary (i.e., non-interest) deficit was to be eliminated over three years. Given the rapidity of the action to devalue there was only time to inform other EMS participants, but not to discuss the measures. The policy initiated by the outgoing government to relax capital controls was confirmed.

A **tenth** realignment in August 1986 had similarities with the Italian initiative a year earlier. The Irish authorities asked for – and were granted informally – a devaluation of 8 per cent. There were strong arguments for such a step; Ireland had experienced even sharper real appreciation in their bilateral exchange rate for the DM than Italy, see figure 3.2.1f above. Initially this excess inflation had been externally sustainable, because the currency of Ireland's main trading partner, the United Kingdom, had appreciated sharply since the start of the EMS, making participation in the latter a softer option for Ireland than originally anticipated. But the subsequent weakening of sterling from 1981 had created contractionary pressures in the form of an important current-account deficit, and the major depreciation of sterling – some 20 per cent in effective rate terms in 1986 – made Ireland's position untenable. This special factor and the stabilization programme already embarked upon in Dublin made discussion of further domestic adjustments to accompany devaluation superfluous.

The **eleventh** realignment came in January 1987, only nine months after the previous general realignment of April 1986. Foreign exchange markets were in turmoil, as the US dollar resumed its rapid fall in late 1986. Outflows of funds from the dollar tended to put upward pressure on the DM inside the EMS; and the French authorities appeared unable to keep the franc away from its lower intervention margin solely by monetary means. Their situation was further aggravated by a series of public sector strikes and perceived risks of faster wage inflation. After a few days of obligatory interventions and mutual recriminations between France and Germany, agreement was reached to revalue the DM and the guilder by 3 per cent and the BLEU franc by 2 per cent against the remaining three currencies.

The official interpretation of the January 1987 realignment was that it was the first of a new type, prompted more by speculative unrest in currency markets, linked to the weakness of the dollar, than by macroeconomic divergence among the EMS participants. *Ex post* this appears to have been a correct view, since the fears of a resumption of more rapid inflation in France did not materialize. The tension in the EMS encouraged reflections on reviewing intervention policy, credit arrangements and monetary coordination so that a repetition of January 1987 would become less likely, and the ECOFIN Council asked the Monetary Committee and the Committee of Central Bank Governors to examine such measures to strengthen the operating mechanism of the EMS. The latter committee used its mandate to develop the Basle–Nyborg Agreement to be reviewed in section 3.4.

Some common elements emerge in the use of realignments in this period. First, inside the EMS all other participants appreciated in real terms *vis-à-vis* the DM and the guilder, see figure 3.2.1 above; there were no examples of permitting devaluation in excess of national inflation differentials in order to achieve real external adjustment, as had occurred for some in the early EMS period, see section 3.2. This shows the increasing emphasis of participants on nominal convergence towards the performance of the countries with lowest inflation. Second, there was less emphasis on domestic policy adjustments to accompany realignments, though this was only made explicit in the case of the January 1987 realignment, seen as motivated by financial factors. This was in contrast to the efforts made by EC bodies to discuss and monitor major domestic adjustments in the 1982–3 period. There was, in particular, next to no interest in the domestic policies in countries other than in France which initiated both general realignments.

The EMS was gradually over this period coming to be regarded as an implicit coordination mechanism through which countries which shared the broad objective of both internal and external stability could improve their performance by sticking to the rules of the system and, in particular, by observing, as best they could, stability in their exchange rates for the DM.

With realignments more infrequent and – for the two general ones – smaller than had become the pattern up to 1983, an analysis of how the system worked must, for the second period, focus more on the three supplementary criteria which were used in section 1 above to divide the evolution of the system into subperiods: (1) macroeconomic performance, particularly with respect to nominal convergence, (2) methods of defending exchange rates and (3) readiness to implement reforms which directly or indirectly affect the EMS.

With respect to the average inflation rate of participants and the dispersion around it, major improvements were achieved between 1982 and 1986, see figure 3.1.3, p. 71. The average inflation rate (consumer prices) fell from around 7 per cent to little more than 1 per cent, and the standard deviation was nearly cut in half from 4 to 2 per cent. Chapter 4 analyzes to what extent this unprecedented improvement in performance – in 1986 by the international decline in energy prices – went beyond what was achieved in other industrial countries and could hence be attributed to the EMS; and also whether it entailed higher costs in terms of output losses and unemployment than outside the EMS.

Domestic policies contributed to disinflation primarily through a gradual tightening of the budgetary stance in most participating countries over 1982–6, which reduced the average size of the deficit by about 2 percentage points, see figure 3.3.1. The process was not uniform; the countries with the largest deficits – Ireland and Italy – hardly participated in the process, though Ireland embarked on a major budgetary contraction only in 1986. On the other hand Denmark eliminated a deficit of nearly 10 per cent of GDP in the course of 1983–6. Monetary policy is more difficult to interpret; real long-term interest rates, at least when measured by *ex post* inflation, were largely constant, see figure 3.3.2, as actual inflation fell broadly in step with nominal interest rates in most countries. By any historical standard real rates remained high.

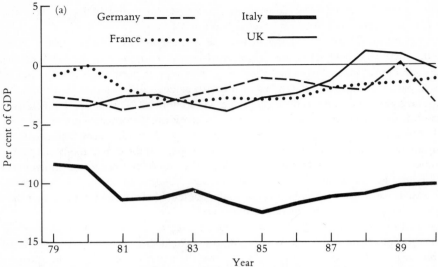

Figure 3.3.1a Surplus or deficit on government budget in Germany, France, Italy and the United Kingdom, 1979–90 (per cent of GDP)
Source: European Economy, 46, December 1990.

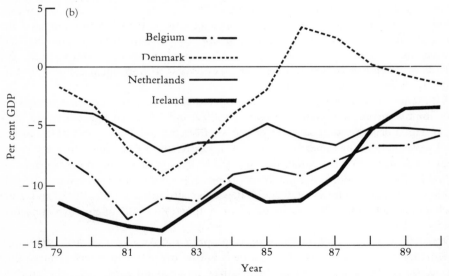

Figure 3.3.1b Surplus or deficit on government budget in Belgium, Denmark, Ireland and the Netherlands, 1979–90 (per cent of GDP)
Source: European Economy, 46, December 1990.

If one looks at nominal magnitudes, the picture is somewhat different. The decline in nominal interest rates triggered major capital gains for holders of financial and real assets, notably housing; positive wealth effects encouraged spending and borrowing. The money supply in most measures accelerated, not least in Germany, towards which

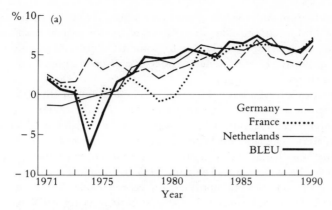

a. Germany, France, Netherlands and BLEU

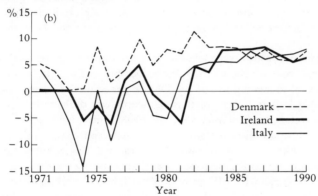

b. Denmark, Ireland and Italy

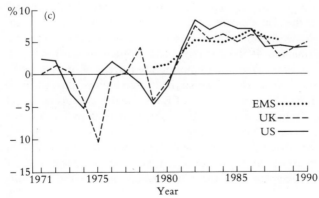

c. EMS, UK and US

Figure 3.3.2 Real interest rates 1971–90
Source: European Economy, 46, December 1990.

other EMS participants increasingly geared their policy through tighter management of their bilateral DM exchange rate; the real value of the money stock accelerated in Germany from about 1985, mainly due to domestic sources of money creation. The gradual shift in budgetary and monetary policies and in the policy-mix is analysed in more detail in chapter 4.

With respect to intervention policy, there was some shift in emphasis in this period, as already noted in this section.[10] Most participants after the March 1983 realignments used intra-marginal interventions to stay away from the margins at which interventions become mandatory. The latter declined significantly relative to the first four years in the system. On the other hand, intra-marginal interventions took on increasing importance. The strength of the dollar up to February 1985 had implied relative weakness of the DM in the EMS, and several non-German central banks had built up their DM holdings. The EMS central banks had stipulated in their March 1979 agreement on the operating procedures of the EMS (Art. 15) that central bank holdings of Community currencies should be confined to working balances within limits laid down by the Committee of Governors and only to be exceeded with the consent of the issuing central bank.

The German authorities were anxious to insist on these provisions, since they did not welcome the risks for the German money supply and for the DM's relationship to third currencies of increasing use of the DM as a medium of intervention and reserve asset in the EMS.[11] The former of these concerns was dealt with by the principle of asymmetric monetary base interventions: an EMS central bank wanting to modify its exchange rate through intra-marginal interventions purchased or sold DM in the Eurocurrency market, in which case there was no direct impact on liquidity in Germany (though obviously still on the DM exchange rate). This flexibility in administering the original EMS provisions – limited working balances and main emphasis on the multilateral settlements mechanism through the Very-Short-Term Facility – was helpful in the tighter exchange-rate management of this second EMS period. It has led gradually to major differences in reserve-holding patterns among EMS central banks; the Bundesbank, which does not itself engage in intra-marginal interventions, holds almost exclusively third currencies, while the non-German central banks hold as much as 40–60 per cent of their international reserves (excluding gold, IMF-positions and SDRs) in other Community currencies, mainly DM.

Still, the compromise on intra-marginal interventions proved inadequate. Making these interventions an admissible part of EMS practice appears to have led to more use of them than warranted, even from the perspective of the countries initiating them. One lesson of exchange-rate management in 1986 and just prior to the realignment of January 1987 was that intra-marginal interventions tended to stabilize bilateral rates too close to the centre of the fluctuation margins, and to substitute for more aggressive interest-rate management. On the other hand, some of the practitioners found the

---

[10] See also Godeaux (1989).

[11] For statements of these concerns and their modification over the first decade of the EMS, see Deutsche Bundesbank (1979) and (1989).

practice of having to seek approval by the Bundesbank of their intra-marginal interventions in DM too cumbersome. The difficulties of finding the right mixture of defensive mechanisms were illustrated by the policy conflicts and exchange-market turbulence in the build-up to the January 1987 realignment, and some lessons were subsequently drawn in the Basle–Nyborg agreement, see section 3.4.

Finally, as regards the third supplementary criterion for choosing subperiods, this intermediate phase was one in which modest reforms in the EMS became feasible, but major ones remained beyond the horizon. At the informal ECOFIN Council in Palermo in May 1985 three small steps, discussed since the early 1980s in the competent bodies, were finally taken.

The first was a 'mobilization scheme' permitting EMS central banks to acquire dollars, or another Community currency, against ecu, for two successive periods of three months. A ceiling was set initially at 1.5 times the ecus created against dollar deposits with the EMCF; in reality the increase in usable reserves is much smaller, since the dollars swapped for ecu were already available for support operations at short notice. Italy has made use of the mobilization scheme twice during 1985–7 to the extent of ecu 3–4 billion on each occasion.

The second step was to increase slightly the incentive for central banks with net creditor positions in ecu to hold them. The Palermo package increased the yield (and the interest charged to debtors) from the average of the national discount rate to the average of national money market rates, typically about one percentage point higher.

The third step was to enable non-EC central banks to acquire official ecus. This was seen as a step towards making the ecu an international reserve asset usable also outside the Community. The response has been limited; so far only four non-EC European central banks and the BIS have signed up as 'other official holders'.

The three steps taken in Palermo were modest indeed; in Community circles they are labelled the 'mini-reform'. They appear strangely unrelated to the central issues raised by the functioning of the EMS already in this intermediate phase. They focused, well in line with the original intentions of the founders of the EMS, on fostering the official ecu in which even the potential users had only a limited interest by 1985. Chapter 6 below asks whether the Community was embarking on a dead-end approach and why more ambitious ideas, notably the link-up between the private ecu market, already well developed at the time, and clearing and lending facilities in official ecu, were not considered feasible.

Yet it was in this intermediate phase that far-reaching and fundamental commitments to relaunching European integration were taken. The first Inter-governmental Conference (IGC) was concluded successfully with the signing of the Single European Act in early 1986. That Treaty revision concentrated on improving the decision-making mechanism required to achieve a unified market in goods and services, including financial services, by the end of 1992. It reaffirmed a number of longer-run objectives, amongst them to enhance the Community's monetary capacity with a view to achieve Economic and Monetary Union (EMU).

This was the first time that EMU had been explicitly confirmed as an objective by Community government since the Werner Report had faltered in the mid 1970s. There was nothing specific in the restatement and no hint of a timetable. The President of the Commission tried to push for more in the Intergovernmental Conference of 1985, but he found little support and outright hostility from several governments, notably those of Germany and the Netherlands, as well as from the 'competent bodies', to exploring what an 'enhanced monetary capacity' implied. In any case, little more than two months before the conclusion of the IGC, there was insuffcient time to explore the options.[12]

In a sense, the Single European Act of 1986 took a step back with respect to monetary integration despite the affirmation of the objective of EMU. In the new Art. 102A the member states confirmed that any institutional change in monetary integration would fall under the procedure stipulated in Art. 236, i.e., it would require a new Treaty, duly ratified by national Parliaments and/or referenda. Those critical of EMU prided themselves that henceforth EMS-like arrangements, based on agreements between the participating central banks, or the extension thereof, would not be regarded as adequate. This was always the German view, as had become evident in the debate on the EMF in 1978–80, but with the Single Act it became incontrovertible. Given the difficulties of negotiating the Single Act and having it ratified in the twelve member states, it seemed unlikely that any early move to institutional developments in Europe's monetary integration, not to speak of full EMU, would be on the agenda for the foreseeable future.

3.4   An EMS without realignments

After the January 1987 realignment there was general agreement that the monetary authorities in the EMS countries should not soon again be seen to be unable to cope efficiently and swiftly with speculative pressures. Given some considerable convergence in national inflation rates at a low level, realignments could be small and infrequent, though at least the central banks foresaw that they would still be necessary as long as national budgetary policies persisted on divergent paths. No senior official associated with the EMS would have predicted in early 1987 that the system could be managed entirely without realignments for a period of three years, and then interrupted only by a 'technical' adjustment, as the Italian authorities rebased the lira in the lower half of their wide fluctuation margin in January 1990. At the time of writing, more than four and a half years have passed since the latest general realignment; and the EMS has been joined by two additional EC-currencies, the peseta and sterling, both opting for the wide margin initially. How has it become possible to maintain this unprecedented – at least since the late 1960s – degree of exchange-rate stability inside Europe?

We see the answer in factors related to all of the three supplementary criteria which we have used to distinguish the three periods since 1979: (1) a sufficient degree of convergence was maintained, though it did not improve relative to the mid-1980s; (2) monetary coordination was strengthened and exchange rates were defended by means

---

[12] For a critical review of the 1985 IGC negotiations on this point, see Louis (1988).

of a wider range of instruments than in the past; and (3) major reforms of the EMS, including proposals for moving to EMU by stages, returned to the agenda, making participants keen to demonstrate that they were indeed ready to observe more permanently fixed exchange rates. Here (1) and (2) are dealt with primarily, since the debate of 1988–9 which relaunched the ambition of EMU is reviewed in part IV, and more specifically in chapter 10. Since the first stage of EMU began on 1 July 1990, the analysis in the present chapter, like that of chapter 4 below, only extends to mid 1990.

Average inflation in the EMS picked up from the artificially low level reached in 1986 of 1 per cent to nearly 4 per cent in 1990, but the dispersion around it, as measured by the standard deviation, was stable or declined slightly further, see figure 3.1.3. This masks, however, clearly improved convergence in the group of seven countries which had from the start of the EMS observed narrow margins, and some divergence between this group and Italy, joined by the two new entrants, Spain and the United Kingdom (the latter two not being included in this graph or in our tables and graphs in chapter 4). For the seven in the former group the range of national inflation rates had narrowed to only about 1 percentage point by 1989–90; it virtually disappeared, when the German inflation rate crept up after 1989, as the pressure on capacity utilization rose prior to and after unification. Convergence in nominal interest rates was slower, but also unmistakeable; by 1990 the differential in short-term rates was down to less than 2 percentage points in this group with the exception of Ireland, see figure 3.4.1. With both inflation and interest rates converging, long-term real interest rates had become much more uniform across this first group.

Inflation rates and interest rates offer the main criteria for assessing whether nominal convergence has progressed. Earlier in this chapter two indicators, relevant for evaluating the thrust of macroeconomic policies, were reviewed briefly: public sector deficits and real interest rates, see figures 3.3.1 and 3.3.2.

With the exception of the German surplus up to 1989, external imbalances proved more temporary than could have been expected on the basis of experience in the intermediate phase, see figure 3.4.2. The deficits of Denmark and Ireland were sharply reduced relative to earlier phases in the 1980s, swinging even into surplus at the end of the decade; the Belgian and Dutch surpluses diminished, while French accounts did not move far from balance; Italy moved into a modest deficit from 1989. With the surprisingly rapid reduction in the German surplus from 1989 onwards, at least the eight original EMS participants were moving closer to a sustainable external position.

This chapter does not comment in any detail on budget deficits, partly because the evidence is more difficult to summarize, partly because the implications for exchange-rate stability of budget imbalances and debt levels are less clear. Chapter 8 reviews various interpretations of the sustainability of national budgetary positions in connection with our review of possible entry clauses for EMU and budgetary rules thereafter. The main danger signal for the functioning of the EMS as a whole has remained the persistence of a public sector deficit of approximately 10 per cent of GDP in Italy – and very high levels of debt in Belgium and Ireland. In particular, there was often a failure of Italy and her EMS partners to link domestic policy adjustments to realignments on the occasions when the latter still occurred in 1981–7.

As regards monetary coordination, major improvements were made with the

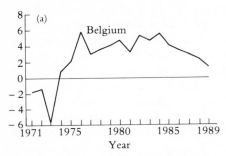

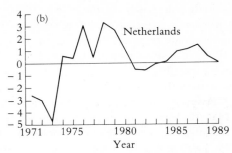

Figure 3.4.1a Nominal short–term interest differentials for Belgium *vis-à-vis* Germany, 1971–90
Source: European Economy, 46, December 1990.

Figure 3.4.1b Nominal short–term interest differentials for the Netherlands *vis-à-vis* Germany, 1971–90.
Source: European Economy, 46, December 1990

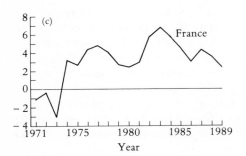

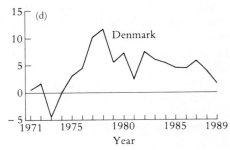

Figure 3.4.1c Nominal short–term interest differentials for France *vis-à-vis* Germany, 1971–90
Source: European Economy, 46, December 1990

Figure 3.4.1d Nominal short–term interest differentials for Denmark *vis-à-vis* Germany, 1971–90
Source: European Economy, 46, December 1990.

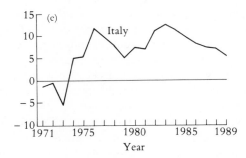

Figure 3.4.1e Nominal short–term interest differentials for Italy *vis-à-vis* Germany, 1971–90.
Source: European Economy, 46, December 1990.

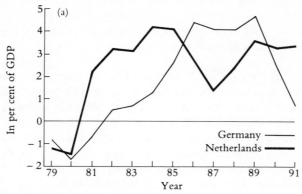

a. Germany and Netherlands

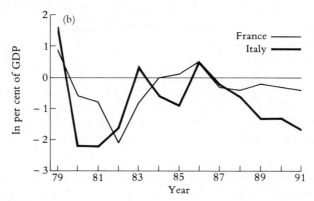

b. France and Italy

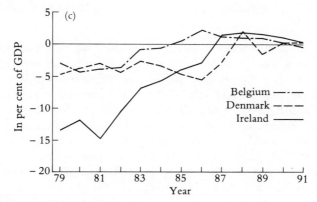

c. Belgium, Denmark and Ireland

Figure 3.4.2 Current-account imbalances 1979–91
Source: European Economy, 46, December 1990.

adoption of the Basle–Nyborg agreement of September 1987, which is reprinted as an annex to this chapter. This agreement, prepared by the Committee of Governors during the first half of 1987, made three specific changes in the operational provisions of the EMS and one general recommendation.

(1) The credit facilities of the EMCF were extended in time. Settlements of balances arising from the mandatory interventions at the margins had to take place at the latest seventy-five, rather than forty-five, days after the end of the month of intervention. The experience following the April 1986 and the January 1987 realignments had shown that the average credit period of two months could at times be too short to generate through the markets full reversal of the outflows that had preceded realignments. An extra month could give a useful respite for interest-rate differentials to operate and for the credibility of the new central rate to be fully established. At the same time the debtor quotas in the Short-Term Monetary Support Facility, which can extend part of accumulated intervention credits for another three months, renewable once, were doubled.

(2) More significantly, the possibility of using the Very-Short-Term Facility for financing intra-marginal interventions within a cumulative amount similar to the revised size of the debtor quotas in the Short-Term Facility was admitted more openly. As may be recalled from section 3.3., the use for intra-marginal intervention of an EMS currency required agreement by the issuing central bank. Now 'a presumption' was established that such agreement would be forthcoming to the extent mentioned; the creditor central bank could request repayment in its own currency.

(3) Least significant, though still important in the perspective of earlier efforts at reform in this direction, the acceptance limit for settlements in official ecus was raised from 50 to 100 per cent, initially for a period of two years. That has since been extended for another two years without formal revision of the 1979 EMS agreement (Art. 16).

(4) The general recommendation, as distinct from these specific changes in the rules, was to aim for a better balance between the three instruments for operating the EMS: exchange-rate movements within the fluctuation margin, changes in interest-rate differentials, and interventions. The implicit criticism of the past functioning of the EMS was that interventions had been relied upon excessively, relative to the other two instruments. More flexible use of currency movements inside the margin could act as a protective device by increasing the currency risk for speculators. If, say, the French authorities were prepared to see the franc move well into the lower half of the margin, speculators would be less confident of a gain in case of realignment, because the market rate after devaluation might show no discontinuity with market rates in the low end of the previous margin. At the same time the possibility that the franc could actually rise, in case of no realignment, would loom larger. More active use of changes in interest-rate differentials would also be desirable as a more basic instrument of adjustment.

The Basle–Nyborg agreement was a judicious compromise, enabling both parties in the debate on the functioning of the EMS to claim major concessions by the other. France stressed the enlargement of the credit facilities and the recognition of intra-marginal interventions which had not been part of the original intentions with the EMS. Germany stressed the strengthening of monetary policy coordination and more active use of interest rates.[13] Both were correct; the credibility of the EMS had been improved by a mixture of more visibly adequate resources for intervention and an expressed willingness to coordinate more tightly.

Both the rules and the general intentions were put to the test sooner than the participants had expected. Little more than a month after the Basle–Nyborg agreement, Wall Street experienced the Black Monday of 19 October 1987. As the Federal Reserve lowered interest rates and increased liquidity to stem the fall in stock prices, the dollar came under downward pressure against European currencies, but particularly the DM. The French franc fell sharply in the EMS, but this movement was reversed in early November by a coordinated interest-rate adjustment in the two countries. For the first, and so far only, time in the EMS the main short-term interest rates in the two largest countries were pushed simultaneously in opposite directions. Capital flows were reversed to the extent that France was able to repurchase within a couple of months its currency accumulated by the Bundesbank. Since late 1987 intra-marginal interventions have fallen back to much lower volumes than in 1986–7 and the EMS has been managed without major tension. Chapter 4 returns in some analytical detail to empirical work which tries to illustrate the evolving operations of the EMS. More flexible management of exchange rates inside the margins has indeed been practiced since 1987.

Why did the substantial reform of Basle–Nyborg become possible? This chapter has already commented on the January 1987 realignment which triggered it, since it was by common consent not an experience to be repeated. Two other general factors, characteristic of the environment of the late 1980s as opposed to earlier years, also played a role in making it stick.

The first was the Louvre Agreement of February 1987. After two years of rapid depreciation of the dollar from the peak of early 1985, the governments of the Group of Seven reached the conclusion that the dollar had reached a sustainable level and should be stabilized in a broad zone around the then current levels. This effort, published in its fairly precise details in Funabashi (1988), was successful in dampening the major swings in the dollar, though not in preventing short-term instability as became evident in October 1987. Although the EMS had withstood surprisingly well the prolonged decline of the dollar up to the Louvre Agreement, more international currency stability reduced speculation in EMS-realignments. The sensitivity of bilateral exchange rates inside the system to movements in the dollar has been sharply contained relative to earlier periods, see also chapter 4.

The second was the gradual removal of capital controls by those EMS participants which had retained them. Although commitments to a timetable were only undertaken

---

[13] Expressions of these different interpretations of the agreements may be found in Pöhl (1987), Deutsche Bundesbank (1989) and Balladur (1988).

at the Community level in June 1988, the direction of change was evident from 1985, in some cases earlier, e.g., Denmark from 1983.

Financial integration – in the double sense of removing capital controls and liberalizing financial services – had hardly progressed since the 1960s. Prior to 1983–4 countries which evoked the safeguard clauses in Arts. 73 and 108 of the Rome Treaty to retain, or temporarily tighten, capital controls were not seriously challenged. But, as a result of Commission initiatives, procedures were tightened for such derogations in 1984. In May 1986 the Commission proposed a timetable for the complete removal of capital controls; these proposals were adopted in only slightly modified form as a Council Directive in ECOFIN in June 1988 with a view to being fully implemented in the Community by mid-1990. Four countries were given derogations until 1992 (Greece, Ireland, Portugal and Spain); a further extension up to 1995 was made possible for Greece and Portugal.

By the time the Basle–Nyborg agreement was conceived, this resumption of financial integration was evident, though definitive commitments had not yet been undertaken. It was widely recognized by the central banks and Finance Ministers that the more liberal regime for capital flows would impose far greater demands on monetary coordination. An independent expert group argued that the quartet of free trade, free capital movements, fixed exchange rates and national monetary autonomy was inconsistent, and that the fourth element had to be severely circumscribed once the first three were being firmly established, and made the case for strengthening the macroeconomic policy function at the Community level in general and the EMS in particular (see Padoa-Schioppa *et al.* (1987), chapter 12). With increasing capital mobility a more explicitly external orientation of national monetary policies became more necessary than at any time since the start of the EMS.

The two factors: more stable exchange rates in the global system and greater financial openness in the Community evoked the pragmatic response of the Basle–Nyborg agreement. Most central bankers would have been content to leave the response to that and to continue to rely on realignments for more important adjustments; the Committee of Central Bank Governors explicitly took this view in submitting their proposals to ECOFIN. Since the reformed EMS appeared to work smoothly after it had passed its major test in October 1987, this pragmatic view was not difficult to defend, though a number of challenges to the post-1987 EMS are discussed in chapter 5.

Only four months after the ECOFIN meeting in Nyborg, the French Finance Minister circulated a memorandum to his colleagues in which he argued that the EMS should move much further and gradually develop into a European central bank. Chapter 10 reviews the contributions to that debate on EMU, focusing on the Delors Report of 1989. Though the inspiration for this initiative was political rather than economic, the economic reasons why the EMS, even in its reformed shape, might not be able to meet the challenges (chapter 5), and the potential benefits and costs of EMU as compared to a well-functioning EMS (chapter 7) are examined, before returning to the revival of the EMU-debate.

3.5 Summary

It has been argued that the EMS has been gradually and fundamentally transformed over the twelve years since it was launched in 1979, despite the basically unchanged institutional and organizational underpinnings of the system. Attempts have been made to illustrate with the help of one main criterion – the use of realignments – and three supplementary criteria: (1) inflation performance, (2) methods used to defend exchange rates, and (3) attitudes to reforms in the EMS and ambitions in European integration, that it may be fruitful to think in terms of three subperiods of about equal length in the working of the EMS:

The first four years up to March 1983 were a turbulent start in an international environment more difficult than anticipated. Realignments were frequent and convergence very limited. The EMS participants succeeded in holding on to the defensive mechanism they had constructed, but only just. No reforms, even of the most modest form were feasible; the project for the EMF was shelved. Policy divergence was ultimately corrected in France, Belgium and Denmark in 1982–3, but the results of these efforts were not visible for some time, and Germany (and the Netherlands) remained sceptical about the survival prospects for the EMS.

The second period was one of discipline and disinflation. Realignments became less necessary, as national inflation rates began to converge; and they were resorted to even less frequently than convergence in itself justified. Capital liberalization began and was confirmed as an objective in the Single European Act of 1986. Mini-reforms in the EMS were agreed in 1985. The system handled surprisingly well the decline in the US dollar after early 1985, but the experience of speculative pressures in the winter of 1986–7 and a general realignment only nine months after the previous one prompted even more emphasis on exchange-rate stability.

The third period which we see as beginning in early 1987 and continuing up to the beginning of the first stage of the move towards EMU took this lesson to heart. It saw the first significant, though still non-institutional, reform in the shape of the Basle–Nyborg agreement, and further major decisions to remove capital controls. The credibility of exchange-rate commitments improved as evident in narrower interest-rate differentials. Further discussion of this and other evidence of increasing symmetry in the EMS is postponed for the following two chapters.

The experience of this third period was sufficiently promising for the ambition of EMU to be rekindled in 1988. We trace in Part IV the relaunching of that debate with the nomination of the Delors Committee in June 1988 and the outcome so far in the negotiations in the IGC. Major reforms clearly beyond the horizon of the EMS negotiations in 1978, had again come to be regarded as feasible.

References

Balladur, Edouard (1988), 'The monetary construction of Europe', Memorandum from Minister of Finance to ECOFIN, Ministry of Finance and Economics, Paris, January.

Basevi, Giorgio, Emil Claassen, Pascal Salin and Niels Thygesen (1976), Towards Economic Equilibrium and Monetary Unification in Europe (OPTICA Report 1975), Commission of the European Commission, Brussels, March.

Basevi, Giorgio, Paul De Grauwe, Pascal Salin, Hans-Eckhart Scharrer and Niels Thygesen (1977), 'Inflation and Exchange Rates: Evidence and Policy Guidelines for the European Communities' (OPTICA Report 1976), Commission of the European Communities, Brussels, February.

Deutsche Bundesbank (1979), 'The EMS', Monthly Report, Frankfurt, November, pp. 178–83.

(1983), 'Memorandum', in House of Lords Select Committee on the European Communities, European Monetary System, House of Lords, Session 1983–4, London.

(1989), 'Exchange rate movements within the EMS – experience after ten years', Monthly Report, Frankfurt, November: 28–36

Dornbusch, Rüdiger (1989), 'Credibility, debt and unemployment: Ireland's failed stabilization', Economic Policy, 8, April: 173–201.

Funabashi, Yoichi (1988), Managing the Dollar: From the Plaza to the Louvre, Institute for International Economics, Washington D.C.

Giavazzi, Francesco and Alberto Giovannini (1989), Limiting Exchange Rate Flexibility: The European Monetary System, MIT Press, Cambridge, Massachusetts.

Giavazzi, Francesco and Marco Pagano (1989), 'Can severe fiscal contractions be expansionary?', in Brookings Papers on Economic Activity II, 1989.

Giesbert, Franz-Olivier (1990), Le Président, Editions du Senil, Paris.

Godeaux, Jean (1989), 'The working of the EMS: a personal assessment', in Collection of Papers Annexed to the Delors Report, Office of Publications of the European Communities, Luxembourg, pp. 191–9.

Gutowski, Armin and Hans-Eckhart Scharrer (1983), 'Das Europäische Währungssystem ein Erfolg?', in Werner Ehrlicher and Rudolf Richter (eds.), Geld und Währungsordnung, Schriften des Vereins für Sozialpolitik Neue Folge Band 138, Duncker & Humblot, Berlin, 147–80.

Kloten, Norbert (1983), 'Das Europische Währungssystem', Europa Archiv, 38, Jahr, 19 Folge, Bonn, October: 599–608.

Louis, Jean-Victor (1988), 'Monetary capacity of the Single Act', in Common Market Law Review, 25, Kluwen Academic Publishers, Dordrecht, pp. 96–134.

Padoa-Schioppa, Tommaso (1985), 'Money, Economic Policy and Europe', European Perspectives Series, Commission of the European Communities, Brussels.

Padoa-Schioppa, Tommaso et al. (1987), Equity, Efficiency and Growth, Commission of the European Communities, Brussels.

Pöhl, Karl Otto (1987), Pressegespräch mit Bundesbank Präsident Pöhl, Deutsche Bundesbank, Presse und Information, Frankfurt, 14 September.

Sachs, Jeffrey and Charles Wyplosz (1986), 'The Economic Consequences of President Mitterand', in Economic Policy, 2, 261–321.

Thygesen, Niels (1984), 'Exchange-rate policies and monetary targets in the EMS countries' in Rainer S. Masera and Robert Triffin (eds.). Europe's Money: Problems of European Monetary Coordination and Integration, Clarendon Press, Oxford.

Ungerer, Horst, Owen Evans and Peter Nyborg (1983), 'The European Monetary System: the experience 1979–82', International Monetary Fund, Washington DC, Occasional Paper, 19 December.

Ungerer, Horst, Owen Evans, Thomas Mayer and Philip Young (1986), 'The European Monetary system: recent developments', International Monetary Fund, Washington DC, Occasional Paper, 48, December.

Ungerer, Horst, Jouko Hauvonen, Augusto Lopez-Claros and Thomas Mayer (1990), 'The European Monetary System: developments and perspectives', International Monetary Fund, Washington DC, Occasional Paper, 73, November.

Williamson, John (1979), 'The failure of global fixity', in Robert Triffin (ed.), The EMS, Banque Nationale de Belgique, Brussels, April. van Ypersele, Jacques and Jean-Claude Koeune (1985), 'The EMS', European Perspectives Series, Commission of the European Communities, Brussels.

APPENDIX I

Committee of Governors of the Central Banks of the Member States of the European Economic Community

Press Communiqué 18 September 1987

At their monthly meeting on 8 September 1987, the Governors of the Central Banks of the Member States of the European Economic Community agreed on measures to strengthen the operating mechanisms of the European Monetary System, which are as follows:

1   The duration of the very short-term financing on which central banks can draw through the European Monetary Cooperation fund (EMCF) to finance interventions in EMS currencies will be extended by one month, taking the maximum duration from two and a half to three and a half months. The ceiling applied to the automatic renewal for three months of these financing operations will be doubled, i.e., it will amount to 200 per cent of the central bank's debtor quota in the short-term monetary support mechanism instead of 100 per cent as at present.

2   The Governors point out that very short-term financing through the EMCF of intra-marginal interventions in EMS currencies is already possible if the central banks directly involved concur. While there will be no automatic access to such financing, a presumption that intra-marginal interventions in EMS currencies agreed to by the central bank issuing the intervention currency will qualify for very short-term financing via the EMCF will be established under certain conditions; the cumulative amount of such financing made available to the debtor central bank shall not exceed 200 per cent of its debtor quota in the short-term monetary support mechanism, the debtor central bank is also prepared to use its holdings of the currency to be sold in amounts to be agreed and the creditor central bank may request repayment in its own currency taking into account the reserve position of the debtor central bank.

3   The usability of the official ECU will be further enhanced. The central banks will accept settlements in ecus of outstanding claims in the very short-term financing in excess of their obligation (50 per cent) and up to 100 percent as long as this does not result in an unbalanced composition of reserves and no excessive debtor and creditor positions in ecus arise. After two years of experience, the formal rules relating to the official ecu will be subject to review.

These measures form part of a comprehensive strategy to foster exchange-rate cohesion within the EMS. The Governors are convinced that greater exchange-rate stability depends on all member states achieving, through their economic and monetary policies, sufficient convergence towards internal stability. In the light of this basic understanding they have agreed in particular to exploit the scope for a more active, flexible and concerted use of the instruments available, namely, exchange-rate movements within the fluctuation band, interest rates and interventions. To promote this more effective use of the instruments, the Committee of Governors will strengthen the procedure for joint monitoring of economic and monetary developments and policies with the aim of arriving at common assessments of both the prevailing conjuncture and appropriate policy responses.

This strategy and these measures were presented by the Governors to the EC Ministers of Finance at the informal meeting in Nyborg on 12 September 1987. The changes to the operating mechanisms of the EMS will come into effect following the formal amendment of certain provisions of the central bank Agreement of 13 March 1979 which lays down the operating procedures for the EMS and consequential changes to the rules governing the operations of the European Monetary Cooperation Fund which will take place in the coming weeks.

CHAPTER 4

ANALYTICAL ISSUES: A CRITICAL APPRAISAL OF THE EMS

After the factual description of the working of the EMS in the previous chapter, this chapter provides a critical appraisal that is based on the analytical economics literature on the EMS. We do not attempt to provide a complete review of the literature on the EMS, but concentrate on the six points that constitute the headings of the following sections which we consider to be the relevant criteria under which to judge the EMS as it operated until mid–1990, i.e. up to the start of stage I of the process to move towards EMU. The issues discussed in this chapter are therefore:

Has the EMS succeeded in creating a zone of monetary stability (in its external and internal dimensions)? (Section 4.1)

How important were capital controls in assuring the stability of the EMS? (Section 4.2)

Has the EMS helped to reduce the cost of disinflation? (Section 4.3)

Has the EMS operated as a mechanism to jointly absorb shocks coming from the outside? (Section 4.4)

To what extent are these two views of the EMS reflected in an asymmetric working of the system? (Section 4.5)

Has the EMS influenced fiscal policy? (Section 4.6)

In almost all cases it is not possible to come to a definite answer, but overall the empirical and theoretical material presented in this chapter provide the basis for our positive assessment of the EMS in the last section of this chapter.

The attentive reader will note that the discussions in sections 2–5 concentrate on the impact of the EMS on macroeconomic developments in France and Italy, and to a lesser extent in Belgium and Denmark. This is a natural consequence of the widely accepted, but not uncontroversial, view that the EMS has affected macroeconomic policy much less in the centre country, Germany, than in the weaker 'peripheral' countries, Belgium, Denmark, France, Ireland and Italy.[1] In keeping with the rest of this book the emphasis of this chapter is on monetary issues.

Some of the issues discussed in this chapter will appear dated in today's perspective. They represent the challenges the EMS had to face during the first eleven years of its existence. A 'new' EMS emerged towards the end of this long period and its main characteristics are discussed more fully in chapter 5, which also reviews the experience of the two newcomers, Spain and the United Kingdom, whose currencies joined the EMS in 1989/90.[2]

4.1 A zone of monetary stability: exchange-rate stability and convergence to price stability

As discussed in chapter 2 the creation of the EMS was a response to the unprecedented inflation and exchange-rate fluctuations of the 1970s. The stated purpose of the EMS was therefore to create a zone of 'monetary stability'. This term was never precisely defined, but was clearly seen by the founders as having both an internal dimension (to promote lower inflation in each participating country) and an external dimension (to stabilize exchange rates among the participating currencies). To what extent has the EMS been instrumental in achieving these two goals? This section provides an assessment of the success of the EMS in achieving its two primary goals by discussing in some detail the effects of the EMS on exchange-rate variability and inflation.[3]

4.1.1 The external dimension of monetary stability: the EMS and exchange-rate variability

The most straightforward way to measure the impact of the EMS on exchange-rate variability is to compare the short-run variability of *intra-EMS* exchange rates before and after the formation of the EMS. This is done in figures 4.1.1–4.1.4 which indicate

---

[1] The empirical evidence on this view is discussed extensively in section 5 of this chapter. The EMS experience of the Netherlands has also attracted less attention because the Dutch guilder was linked to the DM even before the creation of the EMS.

[2] Spain joined the EMS in July 1989, the United Kingdom in October 1990.

[3] It is often taken for granted that exchange rate and price stability represent two important policy goals. However, from an economic point of view, they are important only if they increase the welfare of economic agents. This aspect is discussed in chapter 9 which deals with the costs and benefits of monetary union.

for each year since 1960 the variability (measured by the standard deviation[4]) of monthly percentage changes in nominal and real exchange rates. Figures 4.1.1 and 4.1.2 show the variability of nominal exchange rates, whereas figures 4.1.3 and 4.1.4 show the variability of real exchange rates, i.e., the nominal exchange rate adjusted for inflation measured by the consumer price index.

It is difficult to decide a priori which of these two measures is more appropriate. Since a major objective of the EMS has been to stabilize nominal exchange rates, one might argue that the variability of nominal exchange rates should be the appropriate indicator for the success or failure of the EMS. However, if inflation varies across countries, the variability of a competitiveness indicator, like the real exchange rate, might more accurately show the costs of exchange-rate variability to producers and consumers. Fortunately, it is not necessary to resolve this controversy since the results are broadly similar whether one uses nominal or real exchange rates.

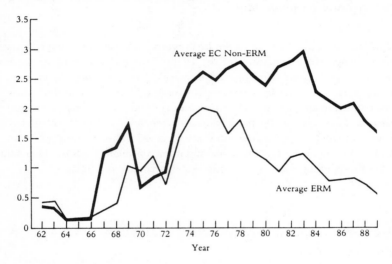

Figure 4.1.1 Nominal exchange-rate variability against ERM currencies

Note: See footnote to table 4.1.1.
Source: International Financial Statistics, line ae: end of period exchange rate.

Figure 4.1.1 shows that the average *variability of nominal exchange rates* among the currencies that participated from the beginning in the ERM has diminished greatly

---

[4] Many different measures of exchange-rate variability have been used in the empirical literature. The ideal measure would be the variability (i.e., standard deviation or variance) of unexpected exchange-rate changes. However, to measure unexpected changes requires exchange- rate predictions, which are extremely difficult to form, see Giavazzi and Giovannini (1989). The problem is fortunately less severe than might appear at first sight since there is considerable evidence (see for example Meese and Rogoff (1983)) that most changes in exchange rates cannot be predicted. This implies that the standard deviation of monthly percentage changes is close to the ideal measure. For this reason it is the most widely used measure of exchange-rate variability, see Ungerer *et al*. (1986), Emerson *et al*. (1991) and Weber (1990).

since the peak levels it attained between 1974–78. This figure shows that exchange-rate variability diminished gradually over time, confirming that the immediate impact of the EMS on exchange rates was limited as discussed in chapter 3. It is also apparent that during the decade preceding the formation of the EMS exchange-rate variability was much higher and the degree of variability changed much more from year to year than under the EMS. Figure 4.1.1 also shows that the variability of the EC currencies that have not participated in the ERM has not diminished to the same extent.

Table 4.1.1 presents averages for the data contained in figure 4.1.1 for some selected subperiods. To assess the impact of the EMS on exchange-rate variability one has to compare the pre-EMS period (1974–8) with the three EMS 'stages' outlined in the description of the workings of the EMS in chapter 3. Table 4.1.1 shows that exchange-rate variability (in terms of monthly percentage changes) in the 'mature' EMS of 1987–9 is only 0.5 per cent, about a quarter of the 1.9 per cent that constituted the average for the pre-EMS period. This table also shows that exchange-rate variability was reduced to about a quarter of its initial level in two steps: first a reduction of almost one half during the turbulent start (1979–83) followed by a further reduction of about 50 per cent over the remaining two subperiods. The overall reduction in variability achieved over the EMS period is certainly statistically 'significant' since a reduction of variability (as measured here, i.e., by the standard deviation) to one half is already statistically significant (see Ungerer et al. (1986)).

Table 4.1.1   Nominal exchange-rate variability against ERM currencies

	1960–8	1969–73	1974–8	1979–83	1984–6	1987–9
Belgium/Lux	0.42	1.30	1.44	1.29	0.71	0.41
Denmark	0.83	1.31	1.57	1.08	0.82	0.64
Germany	0.55	1.79	1.93	1.15	0.86	0.56
Greece	0.36	2.52	2.20	3.06	3.13	0.74
Spain	1.45	2.00	3.66	2.36	1.25	1.40
France	0.44	2.01	2.23	1.32	1.15	0.57
Ireland	1.39	2.11	2.61	1.09	1.51	0.75
Italy	0.42	2.25	2.83	1.18	1.18	0.70
Netherlands	0.48	1.44	1.55	0.93	0.77	0.51
Portugal	0.42	1.36	3.08	2.68	1.00	0.80
UK	1.33	2.01	2.50	3.16	2.65	2.03
USA	0.37	2.26	3.08	2.98	3.75	3.41
Japan	0.48	1.90	2.79	3.42	2.62	2.16
Average EC	0.66	1.84	2.18	1.53	1.21	0.80
Average ERM	0.47	1.66	1.87	1.09	0.89	0.52
Average EC–Non-ERM	1.28	2.00	2.83	2.92	2.22	1.76

Note: Variability is defined as the weighted sum of the standard deviations of changes in the logarithm of monthly bilateral nominal bilateral exchange rates (times 100). The average uses the trade weights of the ERM countries.
Source: International Financial Statistics, line ae.

It is also apparent from figure 4.1.1 that even in the 'mature' EMS the participating currencies fluctuated more against each other than during the Bretton Woods era of the early 1960s.[5] Although there has been some further reduction in exchange-rate variability since 1989, this implies that in this limited sense EMS currencies are even today further from the ideal of total exchange-rate stability (i.e., monetary union) than during the period of fixed exchange rates of the Bretton Woods system.

The data in table 4.1.1 show that the reduction in exchange-rate variability was broadly similar for all participating currencies. This is an important finding since four of the seven currencies participating in the EMS also participated in the arrangements of the 'snake' before 1979. It implies that the EMS is qualitatively different from the 'snake'.[6]

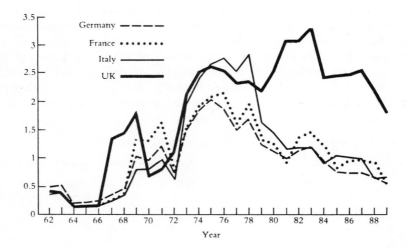

Figure 4.1.2 Nominal exchange-rate variability against ERM currencies

Note: See footnote to table 4.1.1.
Source: International Financial Statistics, line ae: end of period exchange rate.

Figure 4.1.2 allows a comparison between the major EMS currencies and the UK pound, which remained outside the system for the period of observation. This figure confirms that there are no important differences in the impact of the EMS on exchange-rate variability between the Italian lira, the French franc and the Deutsche Mark in terms of their variability against other EMS currencies. In contrast to these

[5] In the late 1960s, starting with the parity change of sterling in 1967, exchange rates became already rather unstable.

[6] See Weber (1990) for more information on bilateral exchange-rate variability which shows that only the HFL/BFR rate is an exception to the rule that the EMS reduced exchange-rate variability even for 'snake' currencies. The reason for this anomaly is that in the 'snake' there was an effort to link the BENELUX currencies, whereas in the EMS the Dutch authorities returned to their traditional policy of pegging tightly to the DM.

EMS currencies, the variability of the UK pound *vis-à-vis* EMS currencies has not gone down since the 1970s and remained clearly above that of these EMS currencies in 1987–9.[7]

The evidence that exchange-rate variability within the system has gone down after the creation of the EMS is therefore unequivocal. However, this alone could not be considered as beneficial if at the same time the variability of the EMS currencies *vis-à-vis* third currencies had increased. It has therefore been argued that the decisive criterion is whether the EMS has reduced the variability of the global average, or effective, exchange rates of the currencies participating in the ERM. The evidence on this score is more mixed since during the early 1980s the US dollar was subject to unprecedented gyrations. This is why Vaubel (1989) and Wyplosz (1989) argue that the EMS did not reduce exchange-rate variability because they find that the reduction in the variability of effective exchange rates was smaller for ERM countries than the average of other industrialized countries.[8]

Figure 4.1.3 therefore shows the average variability of EMS currencies and the US dollar against twenty industrialized countries. This figure suggests that, indeed, it is difficult to find a strong effect of the EMS on global exchange-rate variability. The reduction in variability over the entire period of observation is small and there are several years within the EMS where variability exceeds the pre–EMS level.

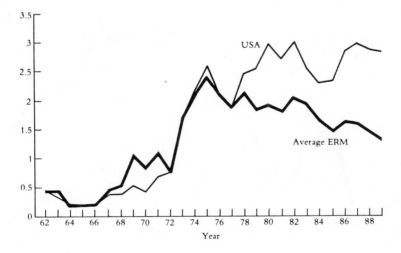

Figure 4.1.3 Nominal exchange-rate variability against 20 industrial countries

Note: Same method as for table 4.1.1 but now the average uses the trade weights of 20 industrial countries.
Source: International Financial Statistics, line ae: end of period exchange rate.

---

[7] A similar observation applies to most other Euopean non–EMS currencies, except the Austrian schilling which is tied to the DM and hence can be considered an unofficial member of the EMS.

[8] Both authors use the effective exchange rates calculated by the IMF, which are based on the Multilateral Exchange Rate Model (MERM) of the fund.

It would seem, however, unfair to judge the EMS on something it cannot and did not set out to achieve, namely the stabilization of global monetary relations. The increased instability of the US dollar in the 1980s is due on most accounts to policy measures taken in the US, such as the tight monetary policy and expansionary fiscal policy that led to the initial appreciation of the US dollar after 1980. There is also no a priori theoretical reason why the suppression of intra-European exchange-rate variability should increase global exchange-rate volatility.

Measures of *real exchange-rate variability* give almost exactly the same result as the ones based on nominal exchange-rate variability. This can be seen by comparing figures 4.1.3 and 4.1.4 and table 4.1.2 which report the variability of real exchange rates (the nominal rate adjusted for the consumer price index) for the same periods and countries as figures 4.1.1 and 4.1.2. It is apparent that the EMS has also reduced real intra-EMS exchange-rate variability. This reduction is again gradual and there is no indication that the variability of the real exchange rate of sterling has been affected by the EMS. Comparing tables 4.1.1 and 4.1.2 shows, however, one minor difference, the reduction in variability has been somewhat smaller in relative terms: real variability has been reduced by 'only' a little more than two-thirds (from 1.9 per cent to 0.6 per cent per month) if one again compares the 'mature' EMS of 1987–9 with the pre-EMS period 1974–8.

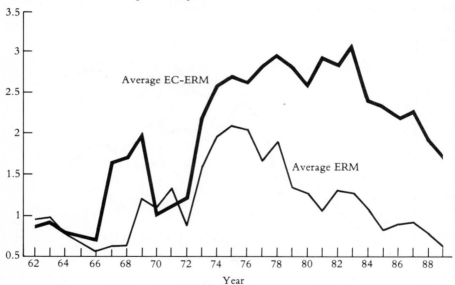

Figure 4.1.4 Real exchange-rate variability against ERM currencies

Note: Same method as for table 4.1.1. but now for real exchange rates.
Source: International Financial Statistics, line ae: end of period exchange rate.

A more substantial difference between the nominal and real measures is suggested by the fact that real exchange-rate variability in the mature EMS is already at the same level as during the Bretton Woods period of fixed exchange rates in the 1960s. According to this measure the EMS had allowed participants to return by 1989 to the level of stability achieved in the 1960s.

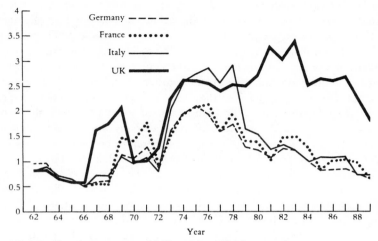

Figure 4.1.5 Real exchange-rate variability against ERM currencies

Note: Same method as explained in footnote under table 4.1.1. but for real exchange rates.
Source: International Financial Statistics, line ae: end of period exchange rate.

Table 4.1.2 Real exchange-rate variability against ERM currencies

	1960–8	1969–73	1974–78	1979–83	1984–6	1987–9
Belgium/Lux	0.76	1.36	1.53	1.39	0.79	0.50
Denmark	1.15	1.44	1.89	1.17	1.12	0.79
Germany	0.87	1.85	1.96	1.23	0.95	0.64
Greece	1.00	3.20	2.61	3.37	3.14	1.36
Spain	1.58	2.02	3.64	2.43	1.34	1.56
France	0.78	2.03	2.24	1.40	1.19	0.61
Ireland	1.51	2.13	2.63	1.27	1.54	0.79
Italy	0.84	2.30	2.87	1.27	1.23	0.73
Netherlands	1.19	1.60	1.67	1.03	0.89	0.74
Portugal	1.48	1.70	3.64	2.92	1.50	0.93
UK	1.55	2.13	2.57	3.36	2.76	2.06
USA	0.68	2.32	3.11	3.02	3.74	3.46
Japan	1.06	2.11	2.77	3.44	2.68	2.26
Average EC	1.02	1.92	2.24	1.63	1.29	0.89
Average ERM	0.82	1.72	1.92	1.18	0.96	0.60
Average EC–Non-ERM	1.53	2.12	2.91	3.08	2.33	1.84

Source: See table 4.1.1.

Note: Same methodology as in table 4.1.1.

It can be argued that the short-run variability induced by fluctuating exchange rates is not as important as the so-called misalignments, i.e., deviations of the real exchange rate from its equilibrium value which persist over a number of years and lead to persistent external and internal imbalances.[9] The prime example for a misalignment is usually the real appreciation of the US dollar during the early 1980s which was accompanied by a growing current-account deficit. This example can be used to illustrate the cost of a prolonged misalignment: the large swings in the value of the US dollar led first to a contraction, and then to an expansion of export industries in the US. Such shifts in activity are costly because they lead to plant closures and subsequently require that workers be retrained. The contraction of some internationally exposed sectors may also lead to so-called hysteresis effects as workers who remain unemployed for some time lose some of their skills and cannot therefore be easily reemployed if a readjustment of the exchange rate leads to an expansion of demand. Finally, it is also alleged that the price dampening effect of an overvalued exchange rate is weaker than the inflationary effect of an undervalued exchange rate. This 'ratchet' effect implies that exchange-rate movements up and down can, on average, increase inflation.

According to this view the EMS should therefore be judged by the extent to which it has reduced medium-term movements in real exchange rates. The creation of the EMS has led to a reduction also in this measure of exchange-rate variability as can be seen from figure 4.1.6. This figure shows the level of the real exchange rate of the DM vis-à-vis the French franc, the Italian lira, the US dollar and sterling. It is apparent that the real US dollar and sterling exchange rates fluctuate much more than the two intra-EMS rates.[10] However, the EMS has allowed sizeable trend-wise real exchange-rate movements to occur. Whether these long-run movements have led (by 1991) to a constellation of real exchange rates that should be considered as unsustainable (and thus represents misalignment) is discussed in chapter 5.

All the evidence presented so far relies on measured exchange-rate variability. However, exchange rates are thought to be determined by some fundamental factors, such as relative monetary policies, relative income growth, inflation differentials, etc. If exchange rates are volatile because the fundamentals are volatile, exchange-rate variability *per se* should be viewed just as an expression of unstable macroeconomic policies which have to be reflected in exchange rates. Another measure of exchange-rate variability is therefore the so-called '*excess volatility*', i.e., the extent to which the variability of a particular exchange rate is greater than one would expect given the behaviour of the fundamentals. Since the fundamentals are partially determined by economic policy, this measure of exchange-rate variability indicates whether the observed variability is just an outgrowth of economic policies and other events, or whether floating exchange rates add an element of uncertainty over and above the uncertainty caused by the fundamentals.

[9] For a forceful exposition of this point see Williamson (1983).

[10] Chapter 5, which presents some data about the longer-run evolution of real exchange rates in Europe, shows that intra-EMS real exchange rates also became smoother after the creation of the EMS.

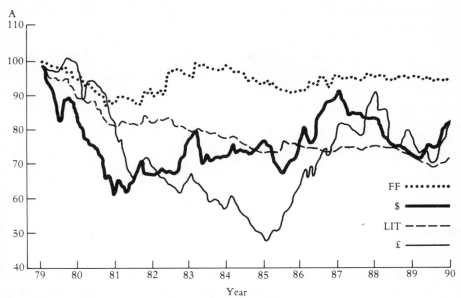

Figure 4.1.6 Real exchange rates *vis-à-vis* DM 1979=100

Source: International Financial Statistics, line ae and 64: nominal exchange rate deflated by the consumer price index.

A test of the importance of the EMS along these lines is presented in Gros (1989) where it is assumed that monetary policy is the major 'fundamental' determinant of exchange rates, and that the exchange rate is influenced not only by the present stance of monetary policy, but also by the expectations of market participants about the likely future policy stance. Taking the DM/French franc exchange rate as an example, the issue is whether the observed variability in this exchange rate is compatible with the variability that would result if market participants had perfect knowledge of the present and future stance of monetary policy.

If one applies this procedure to twelve major exchange rates *vis-à-vis* the DM for the 1973–84 period, one finds that, in general, the variability of the intra–EMS exchange rates of the DM is about as large as one would expect, given the variability in the fundamentals. For example, the value of 0.91 for France in the last column of table 4.1.3, indicates that the observed variability in the French franc exchange rate is slightly lower than one could expect, given the variability in the difference between German and French monetary policies. The values of 1.02 and 1.08 for Belgium and the Netherlands, respectively, indicate that for these countries as well, the variability in the fundamentals is an adequate explanation of the remaining variability of the exchange rate. However, the variability of the DM exchange rates for selected non-EMS currencies is much higher than one would expect, given the fundamentals. The values in excess of 2 for the United States and Switzerland in the last column of table 4.1.3, indicate that, for these floating currencies, the variability in the exchange rate is much higher than one could expect from the behaviour of the fundamentals.

Table 4.1.3   Exchange-rate volatility and fundamentals

	Variability of exchange rate justified by fundamentals★	Actual variability	Ratio of actual variability to fundamental variability
Belgium	14	14	1.02
Denmark	15	20	1.27
France	21	20	0.91
Italy	36	42	1.16
Netherlands	12	12	1.08
Japan	16	21	1.36
Sweden	20	24	1.20
Switzerland	7	15	2.04
United Kingdom	26	29	1.11
United States	11	22	1.04

Note: The variability of the exchange rate of the national currency against the DM that would be justified based on a model with sluggish price adjustment, quarterly data Q1 1973 – Q4 1984.

Source: Gros (1989).

In this context, it is also interesting to note that the measure of variability in the fundamentals – contained in the first column of table 4.1.3 – shows that, after Switzerland, the variability in the fundamentals (mainly monetary policy relative to Germany) is lowest for the United States. Even though countries like Belgium and the Netherlands are widely assumed to follow German monetary policy quite closely, it turns out that the relationship between German and US monetary policy, at least if measured by relative money supplies, was even stronger prior to the more recent EMS period.[11]

The results of this study (and others along similar lines, see for example Bini-Smaghi (1985)) thus support the finding that the EMS has reduced the variability of intra-European exchange rates to the minimum possible given the remaining differences in fundamentals. However, there is no indication that the EMS has had any impact on events in the rest of the world.

[11] Even with totally fixed exchange rates one would find some variability in the relative growth of national monetary aggregates. However, as this variability could derive only from country-specific shocks to money demand, it should not be interpreted as variability in fundamentals.

4.1.2 The internal dimension of monetary stability: the EMS and disinflation

At first sight it might appear that the EMS was also very successful with regard to the internal dimension. Average inflation within the system, about 10 per cent in 1979–80, was down to 2 per cent in 1987 (but had increased again to about 4 per cent by 1989–90). Figure 4.1.7 shows that inflation decelerated slowly but continuously until 1986–7 once the effects of the second oil shock had been overcome by 1982. However, it is not clear whether this was really a consequence of the EMS since this deceleration was, at least broadly, in line with that observable elsewhere in the Community as can be seen by comparing the EC non-EMS average to the EMS average in figure 4.1.7. This is why most empirical studies on the effect of the EMS on disinflation are inconclusive.[12] Evidence for a disinflation effect can be found only to some extent after the first EMS period, because only since 1983 has the disinflation process inside the system been faster and also more permanent than in the rest of Europe. This is another piece of evidence that suggests that the EMS became constraining only after 1983.

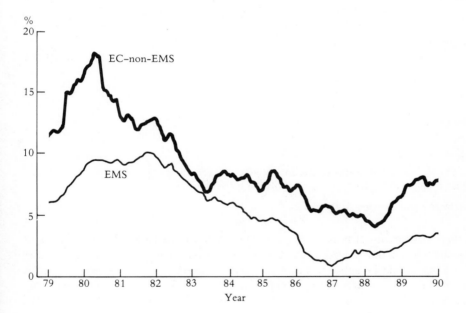

Figure 4.1.7 Disinflation in Europe

Source: International Financial Statistics, line 64: consumer price index.
Note: The graph shows average inflation (measured by the annual rate of change of the consumer price index) for EMS and EC–non-EMS countries.

[12] See for example Collins (1988).

The evidence in favour of the EMS can accordingly be brought out best by considering the three EMS subperiods. This is done in table 4.1.4 which displays the inflation rates for three groups of countries and four periods. The country groups are: EMS countries, Community countries that are not in the EMS and other European countries. The periods are: the pre-EMS period 1974–8 and the three EMS subperiods used already several times. This table shows that between the pre-EMS and the first EMS subperiod (1979–82) there is very little change in the inflation performance of all three country groups; in both periods the EMS group had the second highest average inflation rate. However, the performance of the EMS group dramatically improves during the second period (1983–6), when its inflation rate is cut to one-half and becomes the lowest of the three groups of countries. During the last EMS period (1987–9) the EMS group maintains the lowest inflation rate as its own is again cut to one-half. There is therefore some indication that since 1983 inflation has been reduced faster and more permanently than in other European countries.

Table 4.1.4: Disinflation in Europe

	1974–8	1979–82	1983–6	1987–9
Av. EMS	9.9	10.4	4.6	2.3
	(3.6)	(4.4)	(2.3)	(1.1)
Av. EC non-EMS	16.3	16.1	12.6	6.6
	(3.5)	(3.6)	(5.9)	(2.5)
Av. Europe non-EC	8.4	8.8	5.2	3.7
	(3.5)	(2.0)	(1.8)	(0.9)

Note: Europe non-EC includes Switzerland, Norway, Sweden, Finland (not Austria because its currency is linked to the DM). Standard deviations between brackets.

Source: International Financial Statistics

Given that the disinflationary impact of the EMS is usually thought to come about by the anchor function played by the German monetary policy, the disciplinary impact of the EMS should be apparent in inflation-rate *differentials vis-à-vis* Germany. This is done in figure 4.1.8 which shows the inflation differential *vis-à-vis* Germany for the big EC countries. A simple comparison between the UK and the two large EMS countries (France and Italy), all three of which had similar inflation rates when the EMS was created, suggests that the EMS did indeed have an influence on disinflation. Through a policy of sharp disinflation the UK inflation rate had come very close to the German level by 1983, but it then went up again whereas the inflation differential between Germany and the major EMS countries declined more continuously until 1989. This suggests that disinflation in the EMS might be more permanent for the reasons suggested in the next section, see also de Grauwe (1990a).

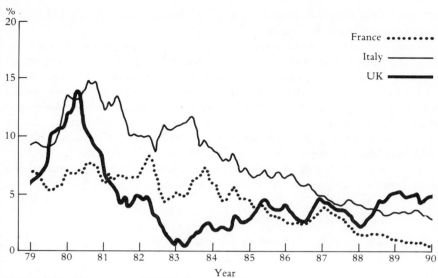

Figure 4.1.8 Inflation convergence *vis-à-vis* Germany

Source: International Financial Statistics, line 64: consumer price index, change over last 12 months.

Table 4.1.4 also measures the dispersion in inflation around the average that has been declining. This table uses the statistical measure of the standard deviation of inflation rates across countries. The data for the EMS group show that the dispersion of inflation has been cut to less than one-third (from 3.6 per cent to 1.1 per cent if one compares the first with the last EMS period). By comparison, the non-EMS control group of Community countries shows much less convergence. However, the control group of non-EC European countries shows a similar improvement in convergence in inflation, but this convergence takes place at a higher level for the average inflation rate.

Another way to measure the impact of the EMS on inflation relies on the argument that any significant change in the policy regime should change the systematic correlations among macroeconomic variables. The impact of the EMS could therefore be measured by the way it changes the evolution of inflation over time and its relationship with other macroeconomic variables. Giavazzi and Giovannini (1989) implement this approach by forming forecasts of inflation that are based on the systematic correlation between inflation and a number of macroeconomic variables (mainly output, wages, money supply, but also past inflation rates) for the pre-EMS period. These forecasts are then compared with actual inflation rates under the EMS. Their results indicate that there is no clear deterioration of the forecasts based on the pre-EMS period after 1979. Actual inflation goes below the level one would have expected based on the experience of the pre-EMS period only several years after the formation of the EMS. For France there is a clear break in 1983 and for Italy a similar, but less clear cut, shift can be observed after 1984.[13] This evidence suggests again that

---

[13] See Giavazzi and Giovannini (1989), chapter 5.

the EMS did not have an immediate impact on inflation, but that after 1983 the EMS helped to bring inflation under control.

Disinflation is almost always accompanied by a temporary increase in unemployment. This suggests that the decisive criterion by which to judge the impact of the EMS on inflation is not whether it accelerated the process of disinflation, but the extent to which it reduced the cost of disinflation. The example of the United Kingdom (up to 1983) shows that disinflation outside the EMS may – for a while – be faster than inside the EMS. However, the system could still be said to have made a contribution towards the goal of internal monetary stability if the cost of achieving disinflation was lower for participating countries. The theory behind and the evidence for the idea that the EMS was a device for weaker countries to reduce inflation at a lower cost in terms of unemployment is discussed in section 4.3.

4.2   Capital controls: necessary for stability?

Controls on international capital movements in France and Italy were an important feature of the EMS during most of the 1980s. Although these two countries had controls even before entering the EMS the controls were tightened as described in chapter 3 during the initial turbulent period of the EMS. Many observers believe that the EMS would not have survived – nor could continue to survive – without them.[14] This section therefore discusses the role of capital controls in the EMS and in particular their usefulness during turbulent periods. Whether the abolition of capital controls in 1990 threatens the stability of the EMS is discussed in chapter 5.

The analysis of the effects of capital controls will concentrate on the experience of France and Italy whose problems have dominated developments in the EMS. Ireland also had (and still has) capital controls and Belgium had, until July 1990, a two-tier exchange-rate system which is economically equivalent to capital controls.[15] However, developments in these two countries have never seriously determined events in the EMS. Spain, which also still has capital controls, joined the EMS only in July 1989. Its experience is reviewed in chapter 5 because it is less relevant for the following analysis of the effects of capital controls in the EMS up to 1990.

---

[14] See for example, Padoa-Schioppa (1987), Obstfeld (1988) and Giavazzi and Giovannini (1989).

[15] France and Italy operated similar systems in the early 1970s, but abolished them when they stopped pegging their commercial rates in 1973 and 1974, respectively.

The reason for the equivalence between capital controls and a dual exchange-rate system is that the financial rate (in the absence of interventions on the financial market) has to move in such a way that no capital outflows take place (while the commercial rate has to stay within the EMS bands). A dual exchange-rate system managed this way is equivalent to controlling capital outflows directly, but the mechanism used is different.

The experience with the Belgian two-tier exchange-rate system and its equivalence to capital controls is discussed in Gros (1988), Bhandari and Decaluwe (1987), Reding (1985) and Reding and Viaene (1990).

4.2.1 Capital controls in the EMS: 1979–90

Before analysing the effects of capital controls it is useful to consider the reasons why they were imposed in the first place. The general purpose of capital controls is to isolate domestic financial markets. With fixed exchange rates, domestic and international interest rates are linked in the absence of capital controls because investors would demand the same return whether they put their funds in the domestic or in the international market. Capital controls that introduce a wedge between domestic and international interest rates are therefore indispensable to an effective control over domestic interest rates under a fixed exchange-rate system.[16]

As national authorities in general dislike high interest rates, most capital controls have the purpose of restraining capital outflows. The effectiveness of the capital controls in France and Italy to limit capital outflows and keep domestic interest rates lower than would otherwise have been possible in the medium to long run is discussed in some detail below. However, the realignment procedures of the EMS provide another, much stronger rationale for capital controls, that is of a very short-run nature, and are therefore discussed first.

Any realignment which changes the central rates of the parity grid in excess of the width of the normal 4.5 per cent band implies, as explained in chapter 3, that the exchange rate in the market has to jump the day after the realignment. For example, in the 1981 realignment, the central rate of the French franc against the DM was increased by 8 per cent and the French franc/DM exchange rate in the market jumped by 4.4 per cent on the day following the realignment. This implies that anybody who was able to switch out of French francs just prior to the realignment would have made a gain of 4.4 per cent over one (business) day. The crucial point is that this is an extremely high return for financial markets. A return of 4.4 per cent over one (business) day corresponds to an *annual* interest rate of about 1,600 per cent.[17] This is why a *discrete* jump in the exchange rate leads to massive capital flows if it can be anticipated. Since the timing and magnitude of realignments is usually to some extent anticipated by agents in financial markets it follows that in the absence of capital controls the anticipation of a large realignment would have led to massive and potentially disruptive capital flows. This observation is the basis for the argument that the EMS would not have survived without capital controls.

However, this argument has to be qualified. First of all, it applies only to realignments that exceed the width of the band, assuming that the currency in question is already at its intervention limit before the realignment. For Italy the band was 12 per cent wide until early 1990, and since no realignment led to a change of the Italian

---

[16] In practice this international market consists of a network of banks dealing in all major currencies rather than being physically located in any particular city or country. This market is usually called the Euro-market because most of the participating institutions are in Europe. Banks participating in this market take deposits in any currency. An English bank in Luxembourg (or the UK) may therefore quote an interest rate for deposits in any currency; this interest rate is called the Euro-interest rate.

[17] For a detailed description of the exchange-rate changes that followed realignments see also Masera (1987).

lira/DM central rate of more than 12 per cent (the maximum was 6 per cent in 1981 and 8 per cent in 1985) capital controls were not necessary to deter disruptive capital flows in the case of Italy. This can also be seen in figure 4.2.1 which shows that the central rates for the lira against the DM always remained within the region covered by the 6 per cent bands which overlap during all realignments.[18]

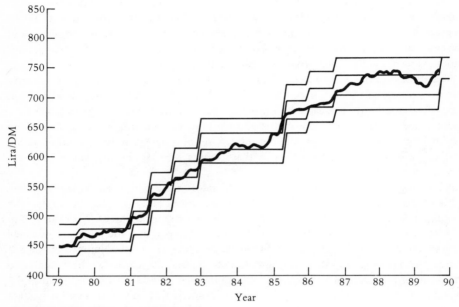

Figure 4.2.1 Lira/DM rate within bands

Note: Since January 1990, the band for the Lira narrowed from 6 per cent to 2.25 per cent. The full line is the 6 per cent band.
Source: International Financial Statistics, line ae, end of period market exhange rates.

The case of France is different as one can see from figure 4.2.2: on four occasions during the pre- and post-realignments the bands did not overlap so that the market exchange rate had to jump. This implies that only in the case of France[19] were capital controls needed to protect the EMS during the four realignments, which implied a change in the French franc/DM rate of over 4.5 per cent. However, this need arose only because the authorities chose to delay realignments until their imminence became obvious in financial markets. A policy of earlier realignments, which would not have been anticipated, would have avoided the pressure from financial markets that arose

[18] This does not imply that a realignment that is smaller than 4.5 per cent (or 12 per cent for the lira) should not have an effect on the exchange rate. A realignment is a signal that monetary policy has become lax, this alone can induce markets to devalue a currency that was realigned.

[19] Ireland and Belgium also had several realignments which exceeded 4.5 per cent; see chapter 3 for more detail on individual realignments.

when they were widely anticipated. As long as they were not anticipated it would therefore have been possible even for France to have had realignments that exceeded 4.5 per cent.

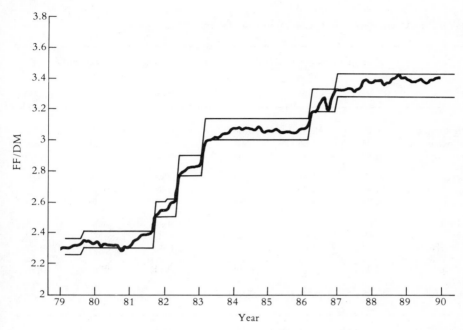

Figure 4.2.2. FF/DM rate within bands

Source: International Financial Statistics, line ae: end of period market exchange rate.

However, the importance of capital controls for the stability of the EMS must also be based on evidence that they were really effective. This point is therefore addressed first, before turning to an analytical framework (in 4.2.2) that illustrates the role of capital controls during the crisis periods that have preceded most realignments.

How effective have capital controls been? There are in principle two ways to assess their effectiveness: by looking at (i) the magnitude of actual capital flows; and, (ii) the interest-rate differential between domestic and international markets. Both measures suggest that the effectiveness of capital controls has been limited as shown below.

i) Capital controls and capital flows

The most straightforward way to measure the effectiveness of capital controls is to compare the magnitude of actual capital flows in and out of France and Italy with that of a country without any control, like Germany. This is done in tables 4.2.1 and 4.2.2 which contain data for two categories of capital flows (overall capital flows and short-term capital flows) for Community countries. These tables report the ratio of capital flows to international trade of the country concerned and the degree to which capital flows go in both directions as measured by the so-called index of intra-industry trade.

Table 4.2.1 Capital flows in the Community: overall capital

	Capital flows as per cent of trade, averages			Intra-industry index, averages		
	82–83	84–85	86–88	82–83	84–85	86–88
Belgium/Lux	11.79	58.85	55.88	0.96	0.99	0.98
Denmark	13.04	19.59	NA	0.54	0.65	NA
Germany	6.33	12.40	14.88	0.86	0.73	0.59
Greece	10.87	15.30	5.42	NA	NA	NA
Spain	8.79	6.79	6.04	0.52	0.59	0.32
France	8.79	8.59	15.38	0.70	0.90	0.93
Ireland	9.67	7.90	11.13	0.38	0.36	0.73
Italy	7.59	9.53	9.24	0.80	0.91	0.72
Netherlands	2.24	7.82	17.41	0.53	0.68	0.97
Portugal	12.05	7.16	4.34	0.11	0.42	0.96
United Kingdom	36.28	25.29	43.98	0.95	0.91	0.98

Note: The ratio of capital flows to international trade is the sum of the absolute value of asset and liability flows over the sum of imports and exports times 100. The index of intra-industry trade is 1 minus the absolute value of the difference between asset and liability flows over the sum of these assets and liabilities.

Source: EUROSTAT, Balance of Payments Statistics, various issues.

The results in table 4.2.1 suggest that the controls in Italy and France did not affect the magnitude of overall capital flows significantly. The capital flows in and out of these two countries during the period 1982–3, i.e., during a period of stringent controls, were comparable to those of Germany, at least if seen in proportion to international trade. Indeed, during this period the capital flows/trade ratio was lower for Germany than for France, Italy or even Spain. During 1984–5 (when capital controls were slightly relaxed, see chapter 3) Germany had a higher value than these three countries, but the magnitudes remained similar. In 1986–8 France and Italy further relaxed their capital controls, without, however, eliminating them completely. Maybe as a result of this France had more capital flows than Germany in this period. But the relaxation of controls can hardly explain why in this period there was a stronger difference between Italy and Spain on the one hand and Germany and France on the other hand.

Since capital controls were mainly designed to prevent short-term movements of financial capital the data concerning this category of capital movements might be more relevant. However, table 4.2.2 shows a similar pattern as for overall flows. For example, in 1986–8 the ratio of short-term capital flows to trade was higher for Spain (which also had stringent controls at the time) than for Germany. In the other two periods Italy seems to have had more capital flows than Germany and the other two countries considered here.

Table 4.2.2 Capital flows in the Community: short-term capital

	Capital flows as per cent of trade, averages			Intra-industry index, averages		
	82–83	84–85	86–88	82–83	84–85	86–88
Belgium/Lux	8.18	53.99	50.54	0.86	0.96	0.97
Denmark	6.91	12.52	9.62	0.90	0.98	0.82
Germany	1.48	4.78	5.58	0.48	0.53	0.30
Greece	1.73	5.04	1.15	NA	NA	NA
Spain	2.01	2.56	6.47	0.56	0.57	0.52
France	2.30	3.65	9.55	0.46	0.90	0.99
Ireland	5.31	2.43	5.10	0.72	0.43	0.82
Italy	6.62	7.54	3.54	0.90	0.98	0.89
Netherlands	2.09	3.58	7.06	0*	0.87	0.89
Portugal	2.09	2.05	2.85	0.43	1**	0.86
United Kingdom	26.45	15.88	30.71	0.90	0.82	0.92

Note: For the definitions of the ratio of capital flows to trade and the index of intra-industry trade see note table 4.2.1. In some cases, indicated with a *, capital inflows took place through a reduction in the assets of residents, which can lead to a negative index of intra-industry trade. In these cases the index was set equal to zero. In other cases, indicated with **, the reduction in assets was bigger than the increase in liabilities, which leads to an index bigger than one. In these cases the index was set equal to one.

Source: EUROSTAT, Balance of Payments Statistics, various issues.

Tables 4.2.1 and 4.2.2 also use the so-called intra-industry index to confirm once again the impression that capital controls were not very effective. This index is equal to one if exports and imports (in this case of capital) are equal, i.e., if there are flows of equal size in both directions. It is equal to zero if there are only imports or exports of capital, i.e., if there are capital flows only in one direction. A cursory inspection of the second half of both tables shows that for most countries there are flows in both directions since the values for the index of the intra-industry trade index are almost always above 0.5.

However, since the French and Italian controls were mainly designed to prevent capital outflows one would expect that the intra-industry index should be very low for these two countries. The two tables show that this is not the case. On the contrary, the

119

values for Italy and France (for both categories of capital movements considered) exceed often those for Germany. This implies that for these two countries with capital controls the ratio of gross to net capital flows was higher than in a country without controls. The existence of these large capital flows in both directions is not compatible with the view that the controls were effective at least one way.

ii)   Capital controls and interest-rate differentials

Another measure of the effectiveness of capital controls is their impact on interest rates.[20] Figures 4.2.3 and 4.2.4 therefore present some data on interest rates for Italy and France. These two figures show the domestic and international interest rates on three months deposits in French franc and Italian lira because this instrument is the most common vehicle to place short-term funds. The domestic interest rates refer to the interbank markets in Milan and Paris, whereas the international interest rates come from the Euro-markets. The Euro-markets, which operate mainly in London, Luxembourg and other places without controls on capital movements can, of course, not be controlled by the French and Italian authorities. This implies that if capital controls are effective domestic interest rates should be independent of Euro-interest rates. In the case of controls on capital outflows, as in France and Italy, one would expect domestic interest rates in these two countries to be below the Euro-rates in the respective two currencies.

Figures 4.2.3 and 4.2.4 show that, for most of the time, the onshore/offshore interest-rate differential is close to zero, which implies that the domestic and international interest rates are very close to each other. The only exceptions are the periods immediately preceding realignments, specially during the turbulent starting period of the EMS. This suggests that capital controls have not been effective in insulating or reducing domestic interest rates in the long run. They were effective mainly for the brief turbulent periods preceding realignments. Since there have been no protracted turbulent periods since 1986 the interest-rate differential has remained close to zero since that date.[21]

Additional, but more indirect, evidence can be obtained by analysing econometrically the intertemporal relationship between offshore and onshore interest rates. Weber (1990) finds, for example, that movements of the offshore rate seem to

---

[20] Giavazzi and Giovannini (1989), Gros (1987b) and Mayer (1990) also analyse the effects of capital controls on interest rates. Viñals (1990) analyses the Spanish experience and argues that since in 1987–9 peseta rates were higher in Spain than on the Euro-markets the controls were apparently used to limit inflows of capital.

[21] It is interesting to note that the Italian and French authorities seem to have reacted differently to the EMS. This shows up if one compares the change in the *average* yield differentials before and after the creation of the EMS. As noted by Rogoff (1985) for Italy the average yield differential declined by 1.2 per cent points (from 5.0 per cent to 3.8 per cent if one compares the first five years of the EMS to the four years preceding the creation of the EMS). However, in the case of France the average yield differential increased by 1.2 per cent (from 2.0 per cent to 3.2 per cent). In this sense the EMS led to an increased reliance on capital flows in France and the opposite in Italy.

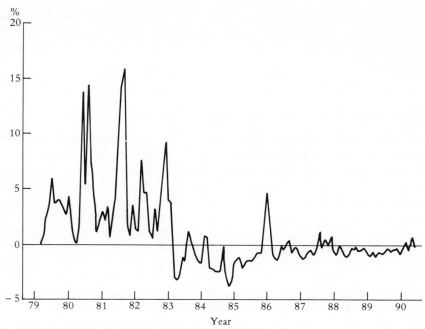

Figure 4.2.3 Offshore/onshore interest-rate differential: Italy
Source: Gros (1987) and EC Commission.

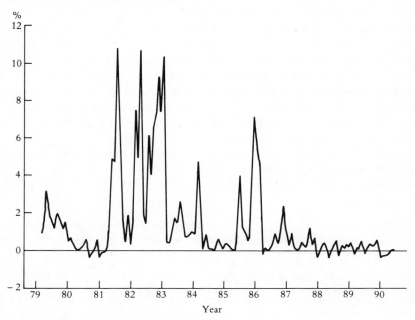

Figure 4.2.4 Offshore/onshore interest-rate differential: France
Source: Gros (1987) and EC Commission.

induce movements of the domestic rates since knowledge of past Euro-interest rates helps to predict the future evolution of domestic interest rates (but not vice versa). This confirms that capital controls have not been effective in making domestic interest rates independent of international rates.

iii) Reasons for the long-run ineffectivenss of capital controls

Why did the French and Italian capital controls have apparently such limited effects? The main reason is that France and Italy are open economies with many links to the international capital market. The existence of higher interest rates abroad constitutes an incentive for any economic agent to circumvent capital controls. With the many financial and commercial links these two countries have with the rest of the world there are many ways in which capital movements can be disguised. Newspaper reports suggest that the most important channels through which capital can be exported, in spite of the controls, are the so-called 'leads and lags', i.e., by changing the terms of payments on international trade contracts. If interest rates are higher abroad (for example when a realignment is expected) Italian and French exporters have an incentive to delay ('lag') the repatriation of their revenues in foreign currency and importers have an incentive to pay ('lead') their deliveries as early as possible.[22]

Since capital movements can be effected through 'leads and lags', capital controls have usually included provisions for the terms of payment on import and export contracts as detailed in chapter 3. Evading these provisions is costly and difficult for traders – but not impossible. Some limited capital outflows can occur through this route even in the short run. If the interest differential between domestic and international interest rates persists, traders will have more time to find new ways to evade the controls and the flows will then become more important as time goes on. These flows will go on as long as there is a yield differential between domestic and foreign capital markets. In the long run, the cumulative effect of these flows can therefore become important enough to equalize interest rates – implying that capital controls will not be effective in the long run. The fact that large capital flows did indeed take place despite the controls (as documented above) provides support for this view.

In analysing the effects of capital controls, it is important to take into account that they can only impose a cost on the cross-border transfer, that is, on the *flow* of capital abroad. Once capital has been transferred abroad, there is little the authorities can do to

[22] Gros (1987b) provides an analytical model of the costs that arise in the evasion of capital controls and argues that these costs increase with the flow of capital that is exported in spite of the controls. Giavazzi and Giovannini (1989) present a model in which the government imposes constraints on foreign trade financing that are effective so that capital flows are limited to a fraction of foreign trade. In their model firms can increase capital exports only by increasing the amount of foreign trade they are undertaking. This hypothesis appears less attractive because it is not likely that the overall amount of trade is significantly affected by interest-rate differentials. After all, any constraint on the way in which exports and imports are financed can be offset by a change in the price. Their model is also not consistent with the observation made above that capital flows were as important in France and Italy, in relation to trade, as in Germany.

affect the yield of this capital. This implies that private agents will consider capital abroad as an asset. The value of this asset compared to capital they have invested in the domestic market is determined not only by the present short-term yield differential, but by the expected future yield differentials as well, since the private agent who exported the capital can expect to earn the higher international yield for the indefinite future.

Capital outflows might therefore take place also in the presence of a small or even negative differential between domestic and international interest rates – provided this differential is expected to be sufficiently large in the future. This observation can explain why in the case of Italy the differential has been negative for extended periods. The fact that domestic Italian rates have at times been higher than international rates had been noted before (see Giavazzi and Giovannini (1989)), but had been thought to be incompatible with the fact that the Italian controls concerned only outflows.

According to this analysis, domestic interest rates in countries with capital controls should therefore move closely with international interest rates in the long run, in spite of the controls. Thus, the liberalization of capital controls does not have to lead to a difficult adjustment process in the sense that it would raise domestic interest rates on average over the long run. From this point of view, the EMS should therefore not be dramatically affected by a liberalization of capital controls. This is confirmed by the fact that the complete abolition of capital controls in July 1990 did not lead to any noticeable change in interest rates or capital flows.

Despite their long-run ineffectiveness, however, capital controls were probably effective in protecting domestic interest rates in the short run, at least prior to 1987.[23] This feature has been used by the Italian and French authorities during turbulent periods preceding realignments. However, this does not answer the question what factors caused these turbulent periods and what can be done to prevent them? The next subsection therefore analyses the role of capital controls during these turbulent periods.

4.2.2 Capital controls and tranquil versus turbulent periods in the EMS

The analysis of 'tranquility' and 'turbulence' in the exchange market for an EMS currency and the transition from one to the other requires an analytical framework which incorporates the real life features of the EMS as it operated before the late 1980s.[24] This is done in Gros (1987a) which assumes first, that there still exist some

---

[23] The same observation applies to dual exchange-rate systems. As emphasized in Gros (1988), the controls necessary to sustain a dual exchange-rate system (every foreign exchange transaction has to be classified as commercial or financial) are also usually less than fully effective. As in the case of 'leaky' capital controls there will be 'unofficial' capital flows that lead to a tendency of the official and the free rate to be equalized in the long run. The free rate should therefore be significantly above the official rate only temporarily. This is borne out by the experience of the Belgian dual exchange-rate system where the commercial and financial rates have been very close most of the time. A significant differential arose only around realignments in the EMS. The Belgian experience suggests that these forms of controls are no more effective than outright administrative ones.

[24] Chapter 5 discusses a different framework for analysing turbulent periods that assumes capital is perfectly mobile and should therefore be more relevant for the current situation.

capital controls in the weaker countries and secondly, that the authorities in these countries want to avoid high interest rates. The EMS is in a tranquil period when the commitment of the authorities to defend the parity grid is believed to be absolute, so that a realignment is held to be impossible for the near future. During such a tranquil period, shocks (for example, changes in the US dollar exchange rate) can be absorbed by small capital flows, and the commitment of the authorities is not really tested.

At some point, however, the commitment of the authorities may become less certain, and the monetary authorities in the weaker countries might then be forced to raise their domestic interest rates to prevent capital outflows. Since it is known that the authorities in the weaker countries attach a political cost to raising interest rates, this increases the uncertainty in the market of how long the authorities will be willing to defend the exchange rate. If the market believes that the willingness of the authorities to defend the exchange rate is very strong, a small increase in domestic interest rates may suffice to contain the outflows. However, if the market believes that the authorities are not willing to contemplate high domestic interest rates purely in defence of their exchange rate in the EMS, capital flows might become unstable. In such a situation any small shock – whether it be a shock to the fundamentals or just a shift in portfolio preferences – could trigger a crisis.

A crisis might start slowly with small capital outflows, but as time goes on and the pressure on domestic interest rates in the weaker countries grows, the probability of a realignment may increase and capital flows accelerate. When outflows reach a sufficiently high level, a realignment becomes inevitable although the initial shock in itself might have been too small to require such a step. After a realignment, which is perceived to be sufficient to allow the new interest rates to hold for some time, substantial reflows will normally occur and a tranquil period will follow.

This framework suggests also that whether or not a turbulent period can emerge at all depends on the perceived willingness of the authorities to defend the exchange rate and the degree of severity of capital controls. Obviously the weaker the authorities appear the more probable a turbulent period becomes. However, more severe capital controls also make a turbulent period more likely. This might appear surprising at first. The reason for this result is that tighter controls delay the capital outflows that arise for any given interest-rate differential and therefore slow down the reduction in the domestic money supply that is necessary to maintain a fixed exchange rate if there is a shock that would otherwise require a devaluation. With capital controls the increase in domestic interest rates required to bring about an inflow of reserves is larger, and hence politically more costly, than in the absence of controls.

This framework therefore suggests that a crucial element for the stability of the EMS is the perception on the part of financial markets that the authorities are committed to defend their exchange rates. A strong commitment is not even likely to be tested and can therefore ensure the stability of the EMS. The experience after 1987 confirms this point of view.

The experience with the weak commitments and frequent realignments before 1987 also illustrates, that a weak commitment is likely to be tested even if there are stringent capital controls. A weak commitment to defend the exchange rate can therefore lead to turbulent periods culminating in a crisis of substantial proportions, such as the one preceding the January 1987 realignment. In this case the realignment was preceded by a prolonged public squabble about the issue whether the DM should be revalued or the French franc be devalued. This weakened evidently the credibility of the exchange-rate commitment of the Banque de France and led to the crisis, although underlying fundamentals, in retrospect, did not justify a realignment.[25]

Once the commitment to defend the exchange rate is weakened, any small shock may trigger a crisis. It appears that minor portfolio shocks from the dollar area have often provided the trigger for turbulent periods since, as shown by Giavazzi and Giovannini (1989), most realignments were preceded by a short period of strength of the DM *vis-à-vis* the US dollar. Short-term variations in the demand for US dollar assets have indeed often caused tensions in the EMS because, as long as capital controls made the other EMS currencies unattractive for international portfolio investment, they were transmitted asymmetrically to the German money market. Giavazzi and Giovannini (1989) provide interesting anecdotal evidence from the financial press in this respect. In the light of the framework presented here, these tensions arising from the DM/US dollar exchange rate should be viewed only as a trigger, not as a cause of the ensuing realignments. This is also apparent from the fact that tensions from the dollar area were followed by a realignment only if a realignment was anyway expected in the near future. Section 4.4 on asymmetry below provides some further evidence on the DM/US dollar asymmetry.

The experience since 1987 not only confirms the implication of this framework that capital controls cannot prevent turbulent periods, but also illustrates that the controls might even have increased the vulnerability of the EMS to international portfolio movements. With capital controls in operation in most other EMS countries, the DM represented the only practical alternative for short-term capital that wanted to move out of the dollar into a low inflation currency.

This analytical framework can also be used to evaluate the steps taken by the Committee of Central Bank Governors of the European Community countries in September 1987.[26] Through the so-called Basle–Nyborg agreement the EMS central banks have signalled that the resources available for flexible currency management within the EMS are unlikely to be exhausted quickly. This agreement made the defence of the EMS parities easier since: (i) it lengthens the duration of the very short-term financing on which central banks can draw through the European Monetary Cooperation Fund; (ii) it doubled the ceiling on the automatic renewal for three months of these financing operations; and (iii) opened the possibility of financing intra-marginal interventions through the EMCF. These measures should help to deter a transition from tranquility to turbulence in the EMS and to weaken a perception by market participants that the defence of a central rate is necessarily costly and hence not certain. Developments after 1987 indicate that this is indeed the case. As discussed in chapter 3 and documented in section 4.5.2 (as well as in Bini-Smaghi and Micossi

---

[25] There was also a domestic political crisis in France, although it turned out to be less serious than it appeared.

[26] See chapter 3 for a description of these agreements.

(1989)), interventions at the margin have practically disappeared and there has been no recourse at all to the VSTF (Very-Short-Term Financing) facility.

Overall, this analysis suggests that capital controls were an essential element mainly in the case of France during a limited number of large realignments that were delayed for political reasons. Capital controls were not effective in limiting the magnitude of short-term capital flows and were not effective in insulating domestic interest rates in the long run. Moreover, capital controls did not prevent, only prolong, turbulent periods in the foreign exchange markets. This suggests, as discussed further in chapter 5, that the elimination of capital controls should not threaten the stability of the EMS.

4.3   The EMS, a disciplinary device?

The first section of this chapter documented the disinflation during the EMS period, but had to acknowledge that it is difficult to show that the EMS was instrumental in achieving or accelerating it. However, this evidence is still compatible with the widespread view that the EMS was a useful 'disciplinary device' which provided a credible framework for disinflation. According to this hypothesis, the main effect of the EMS should not be sought in the speed of disinflation but in a reduction of the cost of disinflation in terms of higher unemployment and lower growth.

The interpretation of the EMS as a disciplinary device is based on the modern view of inflation as a credibility problem. The credibility approach does not regard inflation as the result of a simple choice by the government, but emphasizes the interaction between what the government wants to achieve and what the public expects the government will do.

This 'credibility' approach is based on three assumptions:[27] (i) only *surprise* inflation affects output and therefore employment; (ii) the public has 'rational' expectations, hence inflation cannot come as a surprise on average; and (iii) the government values price stability and high employment.[28] The first two assumptions imply that the government cannot use higher inflation as a systematic tool to increase output and employment. It then follows immediately that the best policy for the government would be to aim at zero inflation since output would anyway be, on average, at the level determined by other non-monetary factors.

The crucial insight of the credibility approach is that a policy of no inflation is best in the long run, but there are incentives for the government to deviate from it in the short run. (In technical terms this is called 'time inconsistency', which means that a plan

---

[27] Barro and Gordon developed this view in a series of papers, see for example Barro and Gordon (1983).

[28] It is useful to contrast this approach with the traditional Phillips curve view of the world in which there is a simple tradeoff between unemployment and inflation, without any distinction between expected and unexpected inflation. The Phillips curve view implies that the government simply chooses the inflation rate that is optimal given its own preferences regarding unemployment and price stability.

that is optimal in the long run is not consistent with short-run incentives.) If the public believes that inflation will be equal to zero the government can improve the performance of the economy by engineering some inflation, which at this point comes as a surprise. However, the public knows about this incentive and will adjust its expectations accordingly, anticipating some inflation.

The main conclusion of this framework is, therefore, that the public has no reason to believe the government will actually follow a no-inflation policy, because once wages and other prices have been set in the private sector, the government has an incentive to produce some surprise inflation. Any promise by the government not to cause any inflation would therefore command little credibility with the public. Applied to the early 1980s this view would say that due to the second oil shock unemployment went up and, therefore, the incentive for governments to engineer some surprise inflation increased. The public correctly anticipated this and inflation was therefore higher, without any reduction in unemployment. Some countries experienced higher inflation than others just because their monetary authorities were perceived as being not very averse to inflation. In countries with 'less credible' monetary authorities inflation was therefore higher than in countries, like Germany, where the public knew that the Bundesbank would not tolerate high inflation.

Countries with monetary authorities that had only a weak anti-inflationary reputation were therefore caught in a trap of high inflationary expectations which the authorities had to ratify if they wanted to avoid the massive unemployment that would result if they were to act tough and reduce inflation below the level expected by the public. The view of the EMS as a disciplinary device most fully developed by Giavazzi and Pagano (1988) argues that by pegging the exchange rate to the DM the authorities in the weaker countries were able to convince the public of their commitment to reduce inflation. By 'tying their hands' the authorities of high inflation countries could lower the unemployment costs of disinflation. In this view, the EMS is a way to transfer some anti-inflationary credibility from Germany to the weaker member countries of the system. A similar perspective is adopted in Collins (1988).

What is the evidence for this theoretically very appealing idea? If the EMS did reduce the output cost of disinflation the most direct evidence would be a comparison of the output cost of disinflation inside and outside the EMS.[29]

The cost of disinflation is usually measured by the so-called 'sacrifice ratio', which is the ratio of the *changes* in inflation and unemployment over a given period. The sacrifice ratio measures the reduction in inflation that has been 'bought' by a one percentage point increase in unemployment.

Table 4.3.1 displays sacrifice ratios for all Community countries as well as for Japan and the US. The end period is, in both columns, the average for 1988–9. However, the first column takes the five-year period preceding the creation of the EMS (1974–8) as the base period, whereas the second column uses the average for 1978–9 as the base period. The entry for the 'EMS minus Germany' (the relevant standard of reference since the disciplinary device approach treats Germany as the anchor of the system) in

---

[29] See De Grauwe (1990a) for a more thorough attempt to measure the impact of the EMS on disinflation.

the first column of this table means therefore that each percentage point increase in unemployment inside the system 'bought' a reduction in inflation of 1.8 percentage points. The positive entry for the EC non-EMS average is a consequence of the fact that for this group of countries inflation *and* unemployment increased. Simply comparing these two numbers suggests that the EMS countries achieved a much better outcome than the rest of the Community.

Table 4.3.1: Sacrifice ratios

	88/89 – 74/78	88/89 – 78/79
Belgium/Luxembourg	– 1.2	– 0.6
Denmark	– 6.7	14.8
Germany	– 0.7	– 0.6
Greece	0.3	– 0.4
Spain	– 0.8	– 0.8
France	– 1.2	– 1.6
Ireland	– 1.1	– 0.8
Italy	– 2.4	– 2.8
Netherlands	– 1.1	– 0.6
Portugal	37.9	3.5
United Kingdom	– 2.0	– 1.7
United States	2.0	9.1
Japan	–10.5	– 7.2
EC	– 1.1	– 0.7
EMS	– 1.3	– 0.6
EC non-EMS	0.1	– 1.2
EMS minus Germany	– 1.8	– 0.6

Note: The sacrifice ratio is equal to the change in inflation over the change in unemployment for the periods indicated.

Source: Commission of the European Communities (1990), Statistical Appendix to the Annual Economic Report 1990/91.

However, this result is not robust. A horizontal comparison of the two columns shows that changing the base period leads to the opposite result. If 1978–9 is taken as the base period the average EC non-EMS group shows a 'normal' negative value of 1.2, whereas the 'EMS minus Germany' drops to (minus) 0.6, implying that the EMS countries obtained less disinflation per percentage point increase in unemployment than the rest of the Community.

This sensitivity of the sacrifice ratios to the base period is brought out more clearly in figures 4.3.1 to 4.3.3, which show the evolution of unemployment and inflation over time for three groups of European countries. The first group (figure 4.3.1) contains the EMS countries except Germany (and the Netherlands), since in the discipline view Germany is not affected by the EMS. The other two groups (figures 4.3.2 and 4.3.3) correspond to the non-EMS EC member countries and the European non-EC countries, groups already analysed for their inflation performance in the first section of this chapter.

These figures suggest that all three groups of countries have gone through a more or less complete loop since 1978. This loop started with a period of increasing inflation and unemployment (after the second oil shock), continues with a fall in inflation with further increases in unemployment (the disinflation during the early 1980s), until finally there is some reduction in unemployment during the last years of the 1980s. Depending on the base period it is therefore possible to find negative or positive sacrifice ratios. These figures do show, however, some clear differences. The 'EMS minus Germany' group shows less variation in both inflation and unemployment than the rest of the Community and the other European countries have an unemployment rate that is essentially constant. It is therefore difficult to say whether the perfomance of the 'EMS minus Germany' is better than that of the rest of the Community, but the rest of Europe (essentially Switzerland and the Scandinavian countries) seems to be better off because it has constantly much lower *unemployment*.

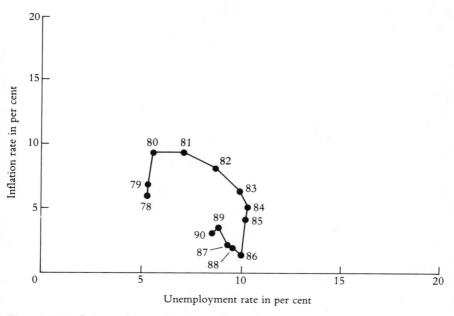

Figure 4.3.1 Inflation and unemployment in the EMS

Note: Average based on ecu weights without Germany.
Source: OECD, Economic Outlook: forecast for 1990.

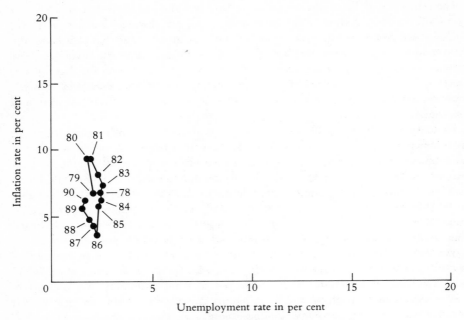

Figure 4.3.2 Inflation and unemployment in the EC non-EMS countries
Source: OECD, Economic Outlook; forecast for 1990.

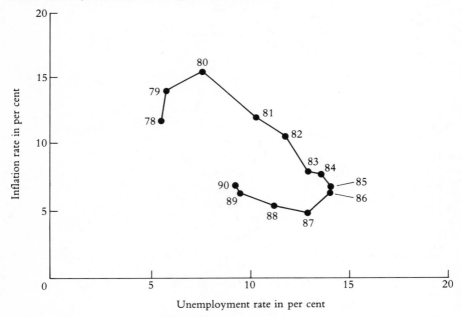

Figure 4.3.3 Inflation and unemployment in the European non-EC countries
Source: OECD, Economic Outlook; forecast for 1990.

A vertical comparison along the second (or the first) column of table 4.3.1 also does not uniformly support the discipline hypothesis, since it shows wide differences among individual countries with some positive entries.

Given these differences among individual countries it might be preferable not to look at the average of groups of countries, but compare directly the two major EMS countries, France and Italy with the United Kingdom.[30] This is especially interesting given the conscious strategy of the UK authorities to pursue a strategy of disinflation outside the EMS. (Section 4.2 showed that this strategy led to a sharper, but less permanent, reduction in inflation, than in the EMS.) A comparison of the sacrifice ratios of these three countries shows that relative to either of the base periods considered in Table 4.3.1 the UK did better than France, but worse than Italy. Spain, however, is consistently worse off (in terms of sacrifice ratios) than either France or Italy for both periods considered; this might be an explanation for the much more positive attitude of the Spanish authorities towards the EMS.

Overall the evidence does not suggest that the EMS 'follower' countries paid a lower price in terms of unemployment for each percentage point of disinflation. For some subperiods they did better than the rest of the Community, but for others they did worse. Bilateral comparisons lead to similar results: only some EMS countries did better than some countries outside the system.[31]

What could be the reason for the result that the EMS did not lower the cost of disinflation? The theory suggests that only a credible exchange-rate commitment can lower the cost of disinflation. However, much of the theoretical literature neglected the existence of the bands of fluctuations or the possibility of realignments, the two mechanisms which permit exchange-rate changes and which imply that the EMS cannot constitute a perfect exchange-rate commitment.

A recent attempt to measure the credibility of exchange-rate commitments in the EMS, Weber (1990), finds that the commitment of the weaker EMS countries to fix their exchange rate *vis-à-vis* the DM has indeed been weak, at least until 1987. Instead, the exchange rates of the lira, the Belgian franc and the Danish krone seem to have been more credibly pegged to the French franc, so that the EMS contained a 'hard currency block', which included up to 1987 only the DM and the Dutch guilder, and a 'soft currency block', which included the other currencies and was centred around the French franc. It is not surprising that in these circumstances the EMS did not increase the speed, or lower the cost of disinflation.

Given the high frequency of realignments until 1986, all of which implied an appreciation of the DM, one would anyway never have expected that the DM exchange rates of the weaker EMS countries were credibly fixed. Figure 4.3.4 depicts the continuous depreciation of the weaker EMS countries which makes it difficult to

---

[30] This is done thoroughly in De Grauwe (1990a).

[31] De Grauwe (1990a) comes to a similar, agnostic, result. Giovannini (1990) also agrees that the evidence in favour of the 'disciplinary device' hypothesis is thin. Giavazzi and Giovannini (1989) use vector autoregressions to test whether, after the formation of the EMS, inflation and unemployment were lower than one would expect based on past experience. However, these tests also led to mixed results.

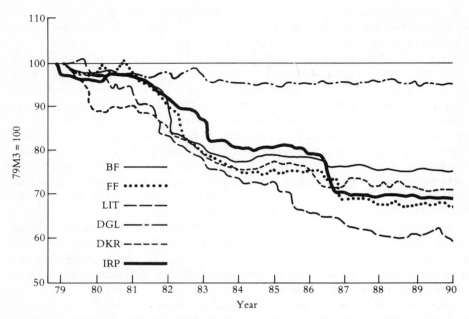

Figure 4.3.4 German mark EMS exchange rates: index of nominal bilateral exchange rates
Source: Own calculations based on IMF data.

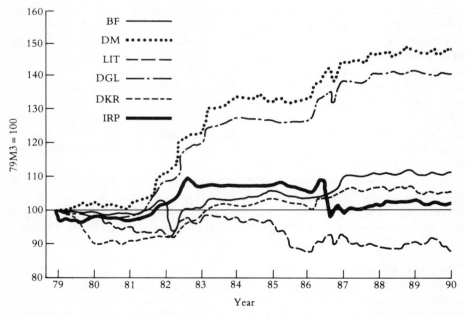

Figure 4.3.5 French franc EMS exchange rates: index of nominal bilateral exchange rates
Source: Own calculations based on IMF data.

use the assumption that the EMS represents a fixed exchange rate *vis-à-vis* the DM. The finding of a soft currency block is surprising. But the simple graph of the French franc exchange rates of the EMS currencies depicted in figure 4.3.5 already provides powerful support for this view because it shows that the exchange rates of the weaker EMS members *vis-à-vis* the French franc have not moved by more than 12 per cent over ten years.

Apart from the difficulties in showing that the EMS has indeed lowered the cost of disinflation the disciplinary device view has also two theoretical problems. First, it implies that, while the other EMS countries gain by binding themselves to the anti-inflationary reputation of the Bundesbank, Germany can only lose from this arrangement. This framework implies that under the EMS the tradeoff between (unexpected) inflation and output improves for Germany since if the other EMS countries follow German monetary policy an expansionary policy in Germany is equivalent to an expansionary policy in the entire EMS area. This implies, in turn, that, unless the commitment of the Bundesbank to price stability is absolute (and the past has shown that this is not the case), the incentive for the German authorities to create surprise inflation should have increased with the creation of the EMS. The public would anticipate this and higher inflation in Germany would be the result.[32]

In terms of this framework Germany would lose from the EMS and it becomes necessary to invoke some other compensation to explain German interest in the EMS. However, it is difficult to see why Germany should derive any special advantage from the EMS. Giavazzi and Giovannini (1989) and Melitz (1988) argue that the compensation for Germany was a stabilization of the German real exchange rate at a competitive level. However, this argument is not easy to reconcile with the theoretical framework, which implies that only unexpected monetary policy can have any real effect.

A second theoretical problem for this framework is that it is difficult to see any role for capital controls and fluctuations bands. The weaker EMS countries could only gain in credibility if they bound themselves to the DM without any margins of fluctuations and without using capital controls.[33] Indeed, as mentioned above, the credibility of DM central rates for the French franc and the lira increased as capital controls in France and Italy were dismantled after 1987.

This leads us to consider the major alternative hypothesis about the reasons for the creation and for the evolution of the EMS.

---

[32] This consideration might have been one of the factors that motivated the opposition of the Bundesbank to the EMS.

[33] See Lane and Rojas-Suarez (1989). This point has been recognized by policy-makers, especially in Germany and the Netherlands, and may have been one of the reasons why other countries agreed to liberalize capital movements. The narrowing of the fluctuations bands for the lira in January 1990 and the recent debate in the United Kingdom on the effects of narrowing the bands for pound sterling show that the implications of the credibility view are perceived by policy-makers.

4.4   The EMS, a shock absorber mechanism?

As discussed in chapter 3 the EMS was created partially as a response to the perceived instability of the US monetary policy. This has led to the 'instrumentalist' view (Fratianni and von Hagen (1990b)) that the prime purpose of the EMS was to allow its members to better absorb the shocks coming from the rest of the world by distributing their impact among the participating countries. This view of the EMS abstracts from the credibility effects that underlie the disciplinary device story discussed in the previous section. Instead, it is based on the hypothesis, that national monetary policy always has spillover effects on other countries. These external effects make a coordination of monetary policy desirable, but an explicit coordination might be difficult to achieve. In this view the EMS is a mechanism whereby such a coordination is achieved implicitly.

The formal models used to illustrate the shock absorber mechanism idea are similar to the one outlined in the previous section.[34] They also rely on the hypothesis that only unexpected monetary policy can influence output. But, in contrast to the models that emphasize the credibility issue, they assume away any incentive for the government to create excess inflation. On the contrary, in this type of model the government is led to stabilize the economy which is affected continuously by various shocks. The government has to base its monetary (and/or fiscal) policy on its imperfect knowledge of these shocks. Since it is usually impossible to evaluate the exact nature of the shocks and their magnitude, a simple rule that links monetary policy to an observable variable like the exchange rate or the interest rate would, in this type of framework, allow the authorities to at least partially stabilize the economy.

The crucial point of this approach is that stabilization policy has spillover effects on other countries. A so-called 'Nash equilibrium' in which each country just does what is in its own interest without taking into account the effects of its policy on its neighbours is therefore not an optimal solution. The optimal solution would be attained only if there is full cooperation among all countries which ensures that these spillover effects are taken into account by everybody. However, such a cooperation is difficult to achieve, because even if an agreement was reached each individual country would have an incentive to 'cheat', i.e., to conduct an independent national monetary policy while still formally participating in the coordination agreement so that it can continue to expect that the other countries take its interest into account when setting their policies.

Pegging the exchange rate is, in this view, a particular form of policy coordination that is easier to monitor, and therefore less likely to involve 'cheating', than more complicated rules because the exchange rate would signal any 'cheating' immediately and because it works without the need to take periodically new common decisions. Fixing exchange rates cannot, of course, yield exactly the same benefits as the theoretically optimal coordination agreement. How far the EMS is, in this 'shock absorber' or 'instrumentalist' view, from the theoretically optimum régime depends mainly on the nature of shocks that hit the system and the degree to which the participating economies are linked in goods and capital markets. Large asymmetric

---

[34] See Fratianni and von Hagen (1990b) and (1991), Gros and Lane (1989) and (1990).

shocks and weak links would tend to make exchange-rate changes part of theoretically optimal coordination and would therefore imply that the EMS is not a useful substitute for full cooperation.

In essence, this approach evaluates the EMS with the same criteria as the optimum currency area approach evaluates the costs and benefits of a monetary union. In the optimum currency area approach a group of countries would find it optimal to form a monetary union if the shocks are predominantly symmetric and if trade within this group is an important part of their economies. This approach is discussed more thoroughly in chapter 7 below where it is argued that the (scant) available evidence suggests that the shocks that affect the Community are predominantly symmetric.[35] To the extent that this was also the case in the early 1980s this result implies that the EMS was indeed a useful substitute for more complicated coordination exercises.

Additional empirical evidence on the 'instrumentalist' view is provided in Fratianni and von Hagen (1991). They measure the departure a simplified asymmetric version of the EMS implies from full cooperation by using an analytical model with three economies (representing two EMS participants plus the US). Since the advantages of the simple rules embodied in the EMS (relative to the cooperative scenario that would be theoretically optimal in this model) cannot be quantified they are not able to provide an analytical benchmark beyond which the EMS would be preferable to other forms of cooperation. However, this model can still be used to show what factors make the EMS less desirable. Simulations with different values for the share of intra-EMS imports indicate that increasing goods market integration does indeed tend to make the EMS optimal, however, increasing integration of financial markets does not seem to have a significant impact on the outcome. Asymmetric shocks tend, of course, to make the EMS suboptimal.

Somewhat contradictory results were obtained by Hughes-Hallet, Minford and Rastogi (1990) who compare two versions of the EMS (German-led or symmetric) to different scenarios involving flexible exchange rates. They find that the EMS is superior to uncoordinated floating only if there is a joint EMS policy that reacts optimally to disturbances from outside the system. This result, however, is entirely compatible with the initial German interest in the EMS which was motivated by the desire to construct a system that could provide a joint European response to a US policy that was perceived to be highly unstable.

The 'instrumentalist' approach does not imply that the EMS has to be symmetric, especially if the predominant shocks come from outside the system. The peripheral countries could gain from an asymmetric EMS in which they peg their currencies to the DM and in which the Bundesbank tries to stabilize the German economy against shocks coming from the dollar area. Although the Bundesbank might not take the effects of its actions on the rest of the EMS directly into account when setting its policy the outcome might still be acceptable for the rest of the EMS. It would at any rate be

---

[35] Global macroeconomic cooperation is discussed in chapter 9 where it is argued that sophisticated coordination exercises are not likely to be useful because of the weak links between the three largest economies (the EC, the US and Japan) and because of uncertainty about the nature of the spillover effects of the main policy instruments.

preferable to a system in which totally uncoordinated responses to, for example, a negative shock to overall demand from the rest of the world, led to futile attempts to obtain a competitive devaluation, or, in case of an inflationary shock, to engage in efforts of competitive monetary contraction and revaluation.

Such a system could therefore be asymmetric, but it would not imply that German monetary policy does not react to developments in the rest of the EMS. On the contrary, even if the German authorities take only their own country's interests into account it would still be appropriate for them to react to shocks in partner countries because these shocks affect Germany as well. This view of the EMS would therefore seem more compatible with the evidence of a less than totally asymmetric EMS that is presented in the following section.

4.5   Symmetry and asymmetry in the EMS

Why should the EMS be asymmetric? Section 4.3 discussed the view that the EMS could be a deflationary device in the sense that the peripheral countries peg their currencies to the DM and implicitly let the Bundesbank run their monetary policy because the domestic monetary authorities have a poor reputation in terms of inflation fighting. This theory can be tested by determining the degree of asymmetry of the EMS because it implies that the monetary policy of Germany determines that of the rest of the EMS and it also implies that German monetary policy is not influenced by events at the 'periphery' of the EMS.

The instrumentalist or 'shock absorber' view of the EMS discussed in section 4.4 implies that the system could be asymmetric, but it does not imply that German monetary policy should be totally insulated from events in the rest of the system. This view is therefore compatible with a lower degree of asymmetry.

Another, more general, motivation for asymmetry in the EMS comes from the fact that fixing exchange rates fixes only relativities, but has no implications on how the overall policy of the system is determined. This is known in economics as the N (or $N-1$) country issue. In any fixed exchange-rate system involving N currencies there are only $N-1$ exchange rates.[36] One solution to this problem is that $N-1$ countries gear their monetary policy towards defending the exchange rate, whereas the 'Nth', or centre, country determines the monetary policy of the entire system. This solution leads to an asymmetric system, with Germany as the obvious candidate for the role of the centre country in the case of the EMS. Another solution to the $N-1$ country problem is that all N countries agree collectively on the thrust of the overall policy and all are equally responsible for defending exchange rates. As discussed in chapter 3 the EMS was intended to be symmetric in this sense. The evidence on asymmetry shows to what extent this was actually the case.[37]

[36] This is apparent if N equals two, because in an exchange rate system involving two countries there is obviously only one exchange rate.

[37] Chapter 3 discussed the deep seated conviction among policy-makers that the EMS is indeed a DM zone and therefore totally asymmetric.

A central point in most assessments of the EMS is therefore the degree of asymmetry of the system. This is true not only for the economics literature. Indeed, as discussed further in chapter 10, the perceived asymmetry of the EMS has even been the main political factor in most calls for reform coming from outside Germany. A careful assessment of the actual degree of asymmetry in the EMS is thus warranted.

The empirical literature has used many different indicators for the degree of asymmetry. The main ones are:

i)   the sensitivity of the system to fluctuations in the US dollar/DM rate;

ii)   the distribution of intervention activity;

iii) the degree to which central banks sterilize the effects of interventions on their domestic monetary aggregates;

iv)   patterns in money supply correlations;

v)   interest rates linkages.

These five indicators of asymmetry are now discussed in turn. The sixth subsection pulls all the evidence together and concludes with a summary assessment of the evidence on asymmetry.

4.5.1 The US dollar/DM rate and the EMS

A first indication of the special position of the DM in the system is that tensions in the US dollar/DM market lead to tensions in the EMS. As already discussed in the preceding section there is some evidence that movements in the US dollar/DM rate precede realignments in the EMS.

This can also be seen from figure 4.5.1 which shows the US dollar/ DM rate and the dates of the realignments. It is apparent that the *level* of the US dollar/DM rate does not seem to be important since realignments occurred when the dollar was high (in 1981–6) and when the dollar was low (before and after this period). However, most realignments were preceded by a short period of DM strength.

This asymmetry might, however, have little to do with the two reasons for asymmetry discussed above. It is probably just a reflection of the fact that, as long as most EMS currencies had capital controls, short-run portfolio shifts out of dollar assets went predominantly into the DM. With capital controls the French franc and Italian lira markets were obviously less attractive and they were anyway less developed than the DM market. This source of asymmetry should therefore disappear because France and Italy have eliminated capital controls and their financial markets have become much broader and, therefore, more attractive for international investors. Indeed, Giavazzi and Giovannini (1989) find that the correlation between movements in the US dollar/DM and the DM exchange rate of the EMS countries diminishes over the course of the 1980s. Additional, and more direct, evidence for the declining importance of US dollar shocks comes from the observation that in 1989 and 1990 periods of weakness of the US dollar seem no longer to lead to tensions in the EMS.

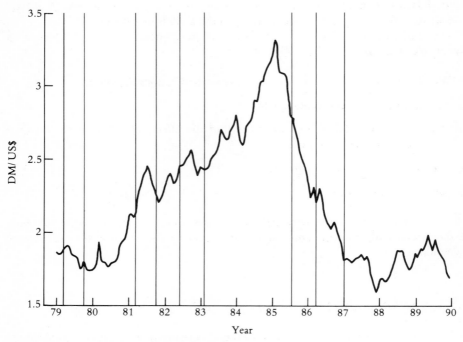

Figure 4.5.1 DM/$ rate and EMS realignments
Source: International Financial Statistics, line ae: end of period market exchange rate.

4.5.2 Asymmetry in foreign exchange market interventions

Formally, the most direct measure of the degree of asymmetry in a fixed exchange-rate system is the assignment of the obligation to intervene in the foreign exchange markets. The EMS was designed to be symmetric in this respect since, as discussed in chapter 3, both central banks have to intervene if any one bilateral exchange rate reaches the limits imposed by the parity grid.[38]

However, the data on foreign exchange market interventions in table 4.5.1 show that Germany's intervention policy is indeed quite different from that of other EMS countries. It is apparent that the Bundesbank intervenes much more in the US dollar market than in the markets for EMS currencies. Moreover, it never intervenes in EMS currencies unless the DM is at the margin. This is in contrast to the practice of other

---

[38] See also chapter 3 for the role of the so-called divergence indicator which was supposed to indicate deviations of any one currency from the average of the rest of the system.

EMS countries which intervene heavily even before their currencies have reached the margin.[39]

Table 4.5.1 Foreign exchange market interventions in the EMS (in billion of US dollars)[a]

	79–82	83–85	86–87	88–89
All ERM currencies:				
inside EMS				
– at the margin	20.5	15.4	22.3	0.9
– intramarginal:	29.2	48.6	113.7	32.4
US dollar interventions	139.4	78.4	53.7	29.5
Bundesbank:				
inside EMS				
– at the margin	3.1	1.7	3.3	0
– intramarginal	0	0	0	0
US dollar interventions	25.4	18.9	5.4	12.4
Memorandum item: Recourse to VSTF	17.1	15.3	34.3	–

Notes:
[a] Algebraic sum of purchases sales

Source: Bini-Smaghi and Micossi (1989) and Bundesbank.

The last column of table 4.5.1 is the most striking because it shows that in 1988–9 the Bundesbank did not intervene at all against ERM currencies. Even in the earlier, more turbulent periods the Bundesbank accounts for only a small part of all EMS interventions. For example during the period 1983–5, which includes the difficult realignments of 1983, the total gross EMS interventions of the Bundesbank amounted to the equivalent of 1.7 billion US dollars, out of a total of almost 65 billion. During the first four years of the EMS the interventions of the Bundesbank are also almost

---

[39] Bini-Smaghi and Micossi (1989) also report that only a very small part of all intra-EMS interventions is undertaken by the Bundesbank. Moreover, they find that EMS interventions of the other two major central banks (the Banque de France and the Banca d'Italia) are much larger than that of the Bundesbank.

insignificant since they constituted 3.1 billion out of a total of 48 billion. Somewhat surprisingly its largest EMS interventions, 3.3 billion US dollars of purchases of ERM currencies against DM, occur during the calmer period 1986–7. However, all of this was due to a short burst around the January 1987 realignment, the large size of this intervention must have been due to the process of capital market liberalization which was already quite advanced at this stage. This table also shows that the largest overall ERM interventions occurred in 1986–7, i.e. before capital controls were removed and before the Basle–Nyborg agreement. The latter extended recourse to the Very Short Term Financing (VSTF) facility of the ERM to intramarginal interventions, but, as suggested in section 4.2, once markets became confident that exchange rates would be defended, the VSTF was no longer needed.

A comparison with the data for US dollar interventions shows that the Bundesbank does intervene substantially outside the EMS. For example, in 1979–82 it accounted for about 25 billion out of a total of 138 billion for all the ERM countries combined.

The intervention data therefore suggest strongly that the Bundesbank has a special position in the EMS in the sense that most of the intervention activity inside the EMS comes from other central banks. The Bundesbank intervenes only if it is constrained to do so by the main symmetric feature of the EMS, i.e., the obligation to intervene at the margin.

Another striking indicator of asymmetry is the fact that the Bundesbank does not hold significant amounts of EMS currencies and would therefore not even be able to rely on its own reserves to support the DM in the EMS.[40] This is in contrast to the other EMS central banks that have to hold significant amounts of DM. For the other EMS central banks the share of Community currencies, i.e., mostly DM, in total foreign exchange reserves ranges from 33 per cent to 75 per cent; the average is close to 50 per cent. As table 4.5.1 shows these DM reserves were indeed used frequently.

4.5.3 Asymmetry in sterilization behaviour

The data about different intervention behaviour presented above do not have any direct implications for the relative autonomy of national monetary policy within the EMS since interventions can, in principle, always be sterilized through domestic open market operations in the opposite direction. A further indicator of the degree to which Germany occupies an asymmetric position in the EMS is therefore given by the differences in the extent to which German and other national monetary authorities sterilize the impact of foreign exchange interventions on domestic liquidity.

The available evidence in this area suggests that there is indeed some asymmetry in sterilization behaviour. Mastropasqua et al. (1988) find that whereas Germany sterilized on average (for the period 1979–87) between 60 per cent and 80 per cent of interventions within any quarter, Italy and France did so only to the extent of 30 per cent and 40 per cent, respectively, of their foreign-exchange interventions. These

[40] The Bundesbank could, however, rely on the EMCF facilities to obtain other EMS currencies.

results suggest that the Bundesbank had an ability approximately twice as great as the Italian and French authorities to sterilize the impact of external reserve flows. However, the ability to sterilize is less than complete even for the German authorities, implying that reserve flows do have some influence on German monetary aggregates even in the short run.

A major weakness of this evidence based on sterilization coefficients is, however, that the data at hand do not distinguish between EMS and US dollar interventions. It is therefore difficult to tell whether the residual influence of reserve flows on German monetary policy derives from the existence of the EMS or from the desire of the Bundesbank to take the US dollar/DM exchange rate into account when managing German monetary policy.

Moreover, most estimates of sterilization coefficients are concerned with short-run sterilization (i.e., the extent to which a given amount of foreign-exchange intervention is offset through domestic operations within a month or a quarter). This does not capture the medium- to long-run nature of the exchange-rate commitments of the ERM countries since the sizeable bands of fluctuations provide national monetary authorities with considerable leeway in the short run. In the light of the fact that these bands are used at times extensively (see chapter 3) it is not surprising that the analysis of short-run sterilization behaviour does not uncover a strong degree of asymmetry.

A related objection to the use of sterilization data is contained in Roubini (1988), who argues that differences in sterilization practices may only reflect differences in central bank optimizing behaviour that derive from the different weight accorded to interest-rate or foreign-exchange reserve smoothing. Differences in sterilization behaviour should therefore not be viewed as an indicator of asymmetry, but as the result of different short-term objectives for monetary policy.

Von Hagen (1989) provides a careful study of German monetary policy that takes into account the two aforementioned objections. This study distinguishes between short-run and long-run sterilization and between US dollar and EMS interventions. The main result of that study is that, in the short run, the Bundesbank does always sterilize foreign-exchange interventions against the US dollar, but does not always do so for EMS interventions. In the long run, however, sterilization seems to be incomplete for both types of intervention if the DM moves in the same direction against the US dollar and the other EMS currencies. This suggests that the Bundesbank does indeed take the exchange rate into account when setting its monetary policy, but developments in the EMS alone are not sufficient to lead to changes in German monetary policy in the long run. The short-run influence of EMS interventions on German monetary policy fits into this picture since EMS interventions average out over the medium to long run as DM sales during turbulent periods are usually followed by DM purchases after a realignment has taken place. However, given the small size of the EMS interventions by the Bundesbank, that were documented above, this result is compatible with the view that developments in the EMS have never substantially affected monetary policy in Germany. Another study, see Caesar (1988), which takes into account the particular definition of monetary base used by the Bundesbank and the various ways in which interventions can be sterilized in practice, substantiates the impression that EMS interventions did have some short-run influence on German monetary aggregates.

However, that study also finds that the existence of the EMS never forced the Bundesbank to change the thrust of its policy in the long run.

4.5.4 Asymmetry in monetary aggregates

The data concerning intervention and sterilization activity that have been discussed so far do not, however, address directly the fundamental issue that is at the core of the asymmetry debate, which is: who determines the overall monetary policy stance for the system?

The N–1 'theorem', that provides the most general reason for asymmetry, implies that only one country, i.e., the one at the centre, is able to conduct an independent monetary policy whereas the others have to adjust their policies to that of the centre country. This suggests that another direct way to see how the N–1 problem is solved in the EMS is to test whether German monetary policy influences policies in other countries, but is not influenced in turn by these other policies.

Most tests of this proposition use so–called 'Granger causality tests', which are based on a comparison of the forecasting qualities of two equations. A first equation forecasts, for example, Italian monetary policy on the basis of information about past Italian money supply data and contemporaneous and past German money supply data. A second equation uses only past Italian data. If the first equation predicts Italian monetary policy significantly better than the second, knowledge about German monetary policy is apparently useful in predicting Italian monetary policy. In this case it is said that German monetary policy 'causes' Italian monetary policy. The same procedure can also be used to detect any influence of Italy on Germany.

When this approach is applied to the EMS it uncovers a system of bilateral interrelationships in which Germany seems to influence most other EMS countries, but in which there is also in many cases a reverse influence of the other countries on Germany. This was found by Fratianni and von Hagen (1990a), Wyplosz (1989) and Weber (1990). For example, Fratianni and von Hagen (1990a) use quarterly data (1983 to 1988) for monetary aggregates and find that all other EMS countries together exert a significant influence on Germany.

An even stronger result emerges from table 4.5.2 which shows the results obtained by Weber (1990) based on monthly data on growth rates of the monetary base. Each star in this table indicates a statistically significant influence by the country in the corresponding column on the country in the corresponding row. (One star is used for the statistical significance level of 5 per cent, two stars for the 1 per cent level.) A dash indicates that no statistically significant influence was found. Each cell in this table has three entries. The first refers to the overall EMS period (March 1979 to July 1989), the second to the early EMS period (March 1979 to March 1983) and the third entry refers to the remaining EMS period (March 1983 to July 1989).

This table indicates that among the 'big three' EMS countries there is 'reverse' asymmetry: Germany never influences France and influences Italy only in the first subperiod. However, France influences Italy and Germany (during the second EMS period) and Italy influences Germany and France. Even more surprisingly, this table also indicates that the small EMS countries influence Germany to about the same extent to which they are influenced by Germany.

Table 4.5.2 Granger causality test results for reserve money

from	Germany	France	Italy	Holland	Belgium	Denmark
to						
Germany	—	★	—	—	—	—
	—	—	★★	—	—	★★
	★	★	—	—	★★	—
France	—		★	—	I	★
	—		I	I	★★	—
	—		★★	—	I	★★
Italy	—	—		—	—	—
	★	★★I		I	—	—
	—	★★		—	—	—
Holland	—	—	—		—	★
	—	I	I		—	—
	★	—	—		—	★
Belgium	★★	I	★	—		—
	★	—	★★	★★		I
	★	I	—	★		—
Denmark	—	—	—	—	—	
	—	★	★	—	★I	
	★	—	—	—	—	
Ireland	—	—	—	★★	—	—
	—	★★	I	—	—	—
	—	—	★	★★	—	—

Note: Stars indicate significance at 5(★) or 1(★★) per cent levels respectively; an 'I' points to instantaneous Granger causality. The top entry in each cell refers to the overall EMS period, the middle one to the early EMS (1979–83), and the bottom entry to the remaining EMS period (1983–9).

Source: Weber (1991), p. A19.

Weber (1990) extends the same methodology also to other monetary aggregates, namely M1 and M2/M3. The results based on M1 show 'normal' asymmetry since Germany influences Italy and the smaller EMS countries (but not France). They also indicate that France and Italy influence some of the smaller EMS countries, but not Germany. The results based on M2/M3 are rather inconclusive since they contain very few significant relationships.

In interpreting these results it is important to keep in mind that they refer only to the statistical significance of the relationships among monetary policies, they give no indication about the size of the impact. This is in contrast to the data about sterilization coefficients, which showed that even the peripheral EMS countries had some power to sterilize interventions, but that they did so only to a much smaller extent than Germany. When a Granger causality test finds significant reverse causality, for example from Denmark to Germany, this effect is probably much smaller than the influence that runs in the opposite direction.

A perhaps more important explanation for some of the findings of 'reverse' causality might be the fact that weaker countries have to repay the interventions that were financed with the EMS credit facilities. Since the interventions usually consisted of sales of DM to support the other currencies in the system this involves purchases of DM, which have a contractionary effect on the German monetary base. The Bundesbank would have no reason to always sterilize the effects of these operations since they support a tight monetary policy stance in Germany. In the econometric studies mentioned above this should show up in a negative sign of the coefficients that measure the 'influence' of a smaller EMS country, or even France, on monetary aggregates in Germany. The entries with an 'I' which mostly appear in entries referring to France and Italy indicate strong contemporaneous correlations – it is difficult to speak of causation in this case – within the soft currency block identified in section 4.3 above.

4.5.5 Asymmetry in interest rates

Changes in short-term interest rates are the main instrument of monetary policy. Any asymmetry in the conduct of monetary policy in the EMS should thus manifest itself in the behaviour of interest rates. This subsection therefore summarizes the considerable research that analyses asymmetry in interest rates. Most of this research has focussed on nominal interest rates, since this variable can be more directly controlled by monetary policy. The behaviour of real interest rates, which cannot be reliably controlled by monetary policy in the long run, are therefore analysed only briefly.

i) Asymmetry in nominal interest rates

The most direct evidence for asymmetry in this respect is that during the turbulent periods preceding realignments the French and Italian offshore interest rates rise dramatically, if only for short periods, whereas German interest rates do not seem to be affected by realignments. This fact was already documented in section 2 of this chapter. For example, before the large realignment in 1983 overnight interest rates on French franc deposits in the unregulated Euro-market rose in several instances above 100 per cent. The average for the month preceding the realignment was lower than these peaks, but still over 10 per cent, whereas German interest rates (both Euro-rates and domestic rates) did not move at all.

More sophisticated econometric tests have also been used to analyse the degree of asymmetry in nominal interest rates. These tests, which employ two different approaches lead to less clear-cut results.

A first approach argues that, if Germany is the dominant country in the EMS, portfolio shifts should not have any effect on German interest rates since the Bundesbank would be able to offset them.[41] The other participants of the EMS would not be able to do so and their interest rates should therefore become unstable and hence more difficult to predict.

The evidence presented in Giavazzi and Giovannini (1989) suggests that the EMS has had some asymmetric features in this respect. Using offshore interest rates they find that DM interest rates are more predictable (within the EMS period) than French franc or Italian lira interest rates in the sense that an equation which forecasts next month's interest rate on the basis of present and past interest rates and other macroeconomic variables has much lower residual errors for German interest rates. Using domestic interest rates the asymmetry is much less pronounced since Italian domestic rates are as predictable as German domestic rates. If one compares the pre-EMS period 1974–8 with the first seven years of the EMS one finds (see Giavazzi and Giovannini (1989)) that German interest rates exhibit diminished residual errors after 1978, while French franc interest rates (in the offshore markets) have become less predictable during the EMS period. However, the opposite holds true for Italian interest rates.

This, somewhat mixed, result is substantially confirmed by another study[42] which measures changes in the variability of onshore interest after March 1979, using more advanced tests. These tests suggest that short-term, nominal interest rates in all four of the domestic markets considered (Germany, Netherlands, France and Italy) became more stable after March 1979, although the reduction in the volatility of interest rates was statistically significant only in the case of Italy and the Netherlands. In this respect Germany does not seem to have a special position.

It should be noted, however, that the evidence on interest rates presented so far does not take into account that interest rates have generally become more stable since the early years of the EMS. All these studies only refer to the average prediction errors over the entire EMS period covered.

A second approach to asymmetry in interest rates again uses Granger causality tests to measure the influence of German interest rates in the determination of other interest rates in the system. As in the case of money supplies discussed above, the influence of German interest rates on, say, Italian rates is measured by comparing the residual forecast errors of two equations, both of which predict the Italian rate on the basis of its own past.[43] The first equation uses also contemporaneous and past values of the German rate, whereas the second one does not. If the information about German interest rates included in the first equation leads to a significantly lower residual forecast

---

[41] See Giavazzi and Giovannini (1989).

[42] See Artis and Taylor (1988).

[43] In some tests both equations also contain the US dollar interest rate to take into account the impact of external developments on both countries.

error, the German rate helps to predict the Italian rate and this is interpreted as meaning that the German rate 'causes' the Italian one. Vice versa, this approach can also be used to find any influence of Italian interest rates on German ones; this would be the case if knowledge about past Italian rates helps to predict German rates.

This approach was used in a number of studies. The earlier studies, see De Grauwe (1988) and Fratianni and von Hagen (1990a), found a complicated system of relationships among interest rates in which Germany did not seem to occupy a special position since other countries had some influence on Germany as well. In particular, Fratianni and von Hagen (1990a) find that all EMS countries together exert a significant influence on Germany. Paul De Grauwe (1988) also finds that there is two–way causation in the following sense: even after accounting for the US interest rate, which might influence all European rates at the same time, the German rates are influenced by movements in other EMS interest rates.

More asymmetry is found in Weber (1991), who investigates bilateral relationships and takes into account the changing nature of the EMS. This study uses monthly data for three different interest rates (on call money, three months domestic deposits and long–term government bonds) to analyse cross–country correlations of interest rate movements under the EMS for all possible combinations of EMS currencies. Table 4.5.3 reports the results concerning three months (domestic) interest rates using the same system as table 4.5.2 above (i.e., one star indicates a significant influence at the 5 per cent level, two stars a significant influence at the 1 per cent level. The top entry in each cell refers to the overall EMS period, 1979–89, the following two entries refer to the two subperiods before and after March 1983.)

Table 4.5.3 shows that German interest rates are statistically important in predicting, and therefore seem to 'cause', movements in French, Italian, Dutch and Belgian interest rates.[44] However, there is no evidence of an influence of other EMS interest rates on German rates (at least on a bilateral basis) except for the contemporanous correlation between German, Dutch and Belgian interest rates that is not surprising.

An interesting additional result emerges if one compares the pre-1983 with the post-1983 EMS periods. The impact of Germany on other countries is generally much weaker during the later EMS period. This is in sharp contrast to the general perception that the EMS became tighter and more asymmetric, at least during the period up to 1987. The contradiction can be resolved if one takes into account that these studies can detect only an influence of German monetary policy that is delayed by at least one month. If other central banks follow a move by the Bundesbank within one month these studies find only a contemporaneous relationship that cannot be used to infer about the direction of causality.

This consideration suggests that higher-frequency data, e.g., on a daily basis, would be more likely to show intertemporal causality. However, the available studies (Biltoft-Jensen and Boersch (1990) and Gros and Weber (1991)) indicate that even using daily data there is some two-way causality and there remains a very strong contemporaneous 'causality'. Higher frequency data can also be used to analyse whether

---

[44] This evidence is very strong for short-term (call money and three months) interest rates, weaker for interest rates on longer-term government bonds.

Table 4.5.3: Granger causality test results for 3-month interest rates

from	Germany	France	Italy	Holland	Belgium	Ireland
to						
Germany	–	–	I	I	–	
	–	–	–	I	–	
	–	–	I	I	–	
France	★★		★★	★★I	–	–
	★★		★	★	–	–
	–		–	I	I	–
Italy	★	–		I	–	–
	★	–		I	–	I
	–	–		I	–	–
Holland	★★I	★★I	I		★★	–
	★★	★★	I		★★	–
	I	I	–		–	–
Belgium	★★	–	–	–		–
	★★	–	–	–		–
	–	–	–	–		–
Ireland	–	–	–	–	★	
	–	–	I	–	–	
	–	–	–	–	★	

Note: Stars indicate significance at 5(★) or 1(★★) per cent levels respectively. An 'I' points to instantaneous Granger causality. The top entry in each cell refers to the overall EMS period, the middle one to the early EMS (1979–83), and the bottom entry to the remaining EMS period (1983–9). No data were available for Denmark.

Source: Weber (1991), p. A19.

there has been any change in the working of the system over the more recent past. Biltoft-Jensen and Boersch (1990) find that the EMS has become more asymmetric since the Basle–Nyborg agreement of 1987. This is somewhat surprising since this agreement could be interpreted as constituting a step towards a more symmetric system. Gros and Weber (1991) find that the use of daily data is indeed appropriate because most cross-country influences occur within one week. But even with daily data the contemporanous causality reaches a high level in the period after 1987. They also find that the relative size of the influence of an innovation in German interest rates (compared to the influence of French rates on German ones) diminishes rapidly over time. In the earlier periods the influence of Germany on France was about ten times as strong as the one the other way round; after 1987 this is no longer the case as the German influence remains only somewhat stronger than the French one. These results are suggestive because casual experience suggests that central banks discuss their policy continuously among themselves and react increasingly in a uniform manner to unforeseen developments. However, more research is needed before any definite conclusions can be drawn from high-frequency data.

ii)   Asymmetry in real interest rates

Much less research effort has gone into determining the degree of asymmetry in real interest rates, mainly because real interest rates have to be considered a more long-run phenomenon. In the short run the behaviour of real interest rates is anyway dominated by movements in nominal rates since inflation changes much less in the short run. This subsection therefore discusses only the medium- to long-run evolution of real interest rates.

Table 4.5.4 shows that Italian and French real interest rates (crudely measured by the difference between short-term interest rates and inflation rates over the following year) increased strongly during the EMS period compared with the pre-EMS period. Moreover, they increased also in relation to Germany. Before the creation of the EMS there was a real interest-rate differential in favour of Germany of around 5 per cent with respect to Italy and of around 3 per cent with respect to France. This real interest-rate differential was eroded during the first years of the EMS and, more recently, even changed sign with French and Italian real interest rates (at 5.2 and 7.0 per cent, respectively) now being higher than the German ones. In contrast, before the creation of the EMS real interest rates were on average negative in Italy (−3.3 per cent) and France (−1.5 per cent) in the period 1974–9, but positive in Germany (+1.2 per cent).

Table 4.5.4   Real[a] Short Term Interest Rates

	Germany	France	Italy
1974–78	1.2	−1.5	−3.3
1979–83	3.7	1.2	−0.1
1984–88	3.8	5.2	7.0

Note:
a) Three months interest rate minus actual inflation (consumer prices).

Source: Commission of the European Communities (1990).

Figure 4.5.2 also shows the more short-run movements in real interest rates in which some asymmetry is again apparent since German real interest rates have moved much less than those of the other EMS countries. However, there is little evidence that movements in German real rates caused movements in other countries. The econometric tests that were applied to nominal interest rates have not yet been used to analyse the behaviour of real interest rates. However, since, as mentioned above, inflation rates are more stable than interest rates an econometric investigation of the short-run interdependences in real interest rates is likely to come to the same result as the studies employing nominal rates that were discussed above.

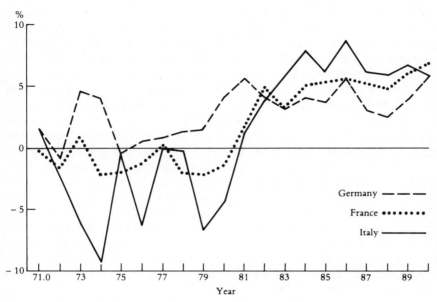

Figure 4.5.2 Real short-term interest rates
Source: European Economy, no. 42, table 48, p. 259: nominal interest rate deflated with the consumer price index as recorded in International Financial Statistics, line 64.

4.5.6 Summary assessment of asymmetry

The empirical evidence on asymmetry discussed somewhat extensively in this section presents a mixed picture. On the one hand, some indicators, such as foreign exchange interventions, sterilization coefficients and the behaviour of interest rates during realignments suggest that Germany has a special position in the system. On the other hand, the results regarding the short-run links in interest rates and money supplies do not support the hypothesis if Germany's monetary policy is insulated and completely independent from developments in the EMS.

The contradiction between these two sets of results is, however, more apparent than real, since formal asymmetry tests based on the Granger causality approach can only reject an extreme form of asymmetry in the form of the so-called German dominance hypothesis (which holds that Germany's policy should be completely unaffected by other countries). The other indicators which do not have this limitation would also reject the extreme form of asymmetry, since the data on sterilization coefficients indicate that even Italy and France retain some autonomy, which, however, is much lower than that of Germany. The overall picture that emerges is therefore that Germany has a strong influence on the other EMS countries, but there is also some weak influence the other way round.

What could be the reasons why German monetary policy was influenced by its EMS partners after all? One reason might be that the Bundesbank has become increasingly perceived by the outside world, notably by the monetary authorities in the United States, Japan and the United Kingdom, as setting monetary policy for the entire EMS. Pressure might well then build up from outside the EMS on the Bundesbank to take into account the interests of its EMS 'followers' in the adjustment of global economic imbalances because the outside world realized that the adjustment of global imbalances affects other EMS countries, given their weaker initial position, more strongly than Germany. A second reason might be that other EMS members more readily accepted the discipline imposed by an increasingly tighter EMS if they perceived that the decisions by the Bundesbank took into account their interests and priorities as well.

All in all the empirical evidence is more favourable to the view that the EMS constituted a mechanism to absorb shocks coming from outside the system than to the view that it was a disciplinary device. One would never expect German monetary policy to be completely insulated. It will always be in the interest of Germany to take into account developments in the economies of the other EMS members, which constitute after all its main trading partners. Some of the measures of asymmetry also confirm a point repeatedly emphasized in this study, namely that the nature of the EMS has changed over time. Formal tests of asymmetry fare best in the 1983–6 period when the EMS might indeed have functioned primarily as a disciplinary device.

4.6   Fiscal policy in the EMS

The resumption of rapid economic growth in 1988–90 pushed the issue of how the EMS affects fiscal policy into the background. This was different during much of the period prior to 1987–8, when it appeared that the European economy needed some demand stimulus to get it out of a low growth and high unemployment trap. At that time it was argued[45] that the EMS had introduced a deflationary bias in the conduct of the fiscal policy of its members.

The argument that, in a fixed exchange-rate system with decentralized fiscal policy, some coordination is necessary applies to the entire EMS experience as well as to the emerging monetary union.

The basis for this argument is that, given the openness of all European economies and the fact that the EMS limits changes in exchange rates, no country alone has an incentive to expand demand using fiscal policy. This disincentive arises from the fact that a large part of the benefits, in terms of increased employment, would accrue to its

---

[45] See, in particular, De Grauwe (1990b). A similar line of reasoning has been followed by the CEPS Macroeconomic Policy Group; see Drèze et al. (1987).

neighbours and most of the costs, in terms of a deterioration of its balance of payments, would fall squarely on the country itself. However, all the economies participating in the EMS together represent a much more closed system and have floating exchange rates *vis-à-vis* the rest of the world. A coordinated expansion by all the countries together would therefore have a much bigger impact on employment.

This implies that a coordinated response to a negative shock to demand, such as the second oil shock, would be an expansionary fiscal policy. In the absence of coordination, i.e., if every country decides on its fiscal policy, taking into account only its own interests, fiscal policy would be on average deflationary. It was therefore argued that the EMS, like any fixed exchange-rate system, might contain a deflationary bias.

The empirical support for this argument came from the observation that during the first half of the 1980s the growth performance of the EMS countries had been disappointing (especially when compared with other European and non-European industrialized countries) and that fiscal policy had been more restrictive in the EMS countries.[46]

Closer inspection of the theoretical and empirical arguments will show, however, that the alleged deflationary bias cannot be held responsible for the unsatisfactory growth performance of the economy of the Community during the early 1980s.[47] The theoretical arguments will be analysed first.

The theoretical argument that the EMS causes a deflationary bias in fiscal policy needs to be qualified on two accounts because it is based on two assumptions that are questionable: (i) capital is not mobile internationally and (ii) countries are concerned about their external position.

i)   Limited capital mobility. This assumption was largely correct for the Bretton Woods system when this line of analysis of strategic interdependence was first developed; and it may have applied to the early years of the EMS. However, given the high capital mobility in the EMS after its turbulent beginnings that were documented in section 2 of this chapter, the assumption of limited capital mobility does not offer a good description of how the EMS has worked most of the time (and certainly not after July 1990).

With increasing capital mobility and nominal exchange-rate rigidity, fiscal expansion in one country has a diminishing impact on domestic interest rates, which are increasingly determined at the EMS level. There will accordingly be less crowding out of private domestic, interest-sensitive expenditure, notably investment. The larger consequent effects of fiscal policy on domestic output and employment increase the incentive for national authorities to use fiscal policy more actively. However, there is an offsetting disincentive in that the deterioration of the current account also increases in the absence of induced higher domestic interest rates. The overall impact of capital mobility in this framework is therefore

---

[46] See de Grauwe (1990b).

[47] This bad growth performance was one of the causes of 'Euro-pessimism', which was fashionable until 1988.

ambiguous, but De Grauwe (1990b) shows that, for an interesting special case, full capital mobility can easily lead to an expansionary bias in the EMS.

The available macroeconomic models support the view that a fiscal expansion in one country does not, in fact, benefit other member countries. In the simulations reported in Masson and Melitz (1990) and Emerson *et al.* (1991), both of which assumed full capital mobility, fiscal policy is a 'beggar-thy-neighbour' policy. Chapter 8 returns to the empirical evidence on fiscal transmission effects in the EMS and their likely modification in an EMU.

ii) Importance of the external constraint. *De facto* capital mobility has a further effect which would make one of the basic assumptions of this framework obsolete since it may induce the authorities to pay less attention to the current-account position of the economy. Indeed, in a world of mobile capital there is no particular reason why the authorities should be concerned with the current-account position of the private sector. A current-account deficit of the domestic private sector represents an excess of domestic (private) investment over domestic (private) savings which is financed by capital imports from abroad. The traditional concern of public authorities with current-account deficits was a consequence of the fact that international financial markets were not as developed as today and access to them could be limited if doubts about the creditworthiness of the country as a whole arose. The debt crises of LDCs in the early 1980s illustrates this concern. However, the authorities of member countries of the EC realize that they can rely on the international capital market to finance private sector current-account deficits for quite some time since within the EC private as well as public sector debtors can be forced to service debt as long as they are solvent. Moreover, in contrast to many sovereign debtors among the LDCs, EC member states participating in the ERM are perceived to have to conduct sound macroeconomic policies which is a further guarantee for regular debt service. To a degree that varies from country to country the importance of the so-called current-account constraint was therefore diminishing in the late 1980s. The position of the UK authorities, which profess a 'benign neglect' of the current account, offers an illustration of how far this process has advanced in some countries.

The simple deflationary bias view must also be modified if one accepts the view that the EMS is an asymmetric system. The effects of fiscal policy and therefore the spillover effects that arise in the use of this instrument then become different for Germany than for the rest of the EMS.[48] If the Bundesbank sets its own monetary stance independently, a domestic fiscal expansion in Germany will lead to some increase in German, and hence EMS-wide interest rates. This implies that an expansion in Germany might actually depress overall demand in the other EMS countries so that German fiscal expansion may become a 'beggar-thy-neighbour' policy that hurts the rest of the EMS area. However, a fiscal expansion by the peripheral EMS countries leads to a much smaller increase in German, and hence

---

[48] See Van der Ploeg (1990) for more details.

system-wide, interest rates that can at most choke off part of the additional demand directly created in the non–German EMS area. Fiscal expansion by the peripheral countries is therefore always beneficial for Germany. If German fiscal policy has actually a negative spillover effect this framework would imply that German fiscal policy could be too expansionary which is not taken into account by the German authorities when setting their policy.

The view that the EMS contains an inherent deflationary bias has, therefore, to be qualified in several respects even on purely theoretical grounds. But what is the empirical validity of this idea?

A first, and fundamental, point suggested by the experience of the mid–1980s is that it cannot be taken for granted as assumed in this discussion, that a fiscal expansion always increases demand at home. This point was made on a theoretical basis in Blanchard (1984), but the experiences of Germany, Denmark and Ireland probably provide a more convincing illustration.

In Germany a new government came into power in 1982 with a programme of fiscal consolidation.[49] It was widely believed at the time, that the policy of demand stimulation through a widening of the federal deficit initiated during the Bonn Economic Summit of 1978 had gone beyond the limits of its effectiveness and that a reversal would prove not only prudent in public finance terms, but might well be expansionary. The effects of lower anticipated future deficits over a number of years would operate via lower interest rates to offset the short-term effects of fiscal consolidation. This view may well have had some merit initially, and to the extent that fiscal consolidation had a positive impact on expectations, German fiscal policy cannot be said to have been deflationary over this period. On the contrary, part of the disappointing growth performance of the EMS economies prior to the recent past may, on this line of reasoning, be attributable to the unsatisfactory progress made in several other EMS countries in fiscal consolidation.

It is therefore arguable that significant reductions in the public sector deficits of, for example, Belgium and Italy would have stimulated, rather than impeded, the growth of output and employment. The experience of Denmark which enjoyed growth well above the European Community average in the period 1983–6, while fully eliminating a large public sector deficit, as well as the more recent experience of Ireland, provides further evidence for this view.[50]

In all three countries (Germany, Denmark and Ireland) fiscal retrenchment was not followed by a fall in demand. However, it would seem premature to conclude from this that a restrictive fiscal policy does not reduce demand because in each case other things were not equal. In Germany the rise of the US dollar stimulated export demand, in Ireland a large devaluation improved competitiveness, and in Denmark capital market liberalization led to sharply lower interest rates.

However, despite this qualification it can be argued that, even in 1986–7, when

---

[49] See Fels and Fröhlich (1987).

[50] See chapter 5 for further references and an analysis of the experience of these countries.

sluggish growth and persistent unemployment seemed to call for a more expansionary fiscal policy, a redistribution of the stance of fiscal policy within the EMS rather than a general easing in most of the member countries would have been appropriate as analysed in more detail by Dréze et al. (1987). In those EMS countries where the stock of public debt had grown to more than 100 per cent of GDP, consolidation of deficits had to take precedence over fiscal expansion.

The evidence for the 'deflationary bias' view was based on the average difference in economic performance between the EMS and a control group of non-EMS countries. This more systematic evidence that does not take into account the specific circumstances of the countries mentioned above needs therefore to be examined. This is done in figures 4.6.1 and 4.6.2.

Figure 4.6.1 displays the growth rates of real GDP for the EMS and non-EMS EC member countries. This figure indicates that there was indeed a slowdown in growth in the EMS countries compared with the other two groups of countries, at least if one compares the early EMS years with the pre-EMS period. During the pre-EMS and the early EMS period, i.e., from 1975 to 1981, the EMS group had a higher real growth rate than the non-EMS control group, although both groups experienced a slowdown after the second oil shock. But after 1982 growth in the EMS recovers more slowly than outside, so that real growth in the EMS slips below the non-EMS group. These developments provide the evidence for the 'deflationary bias' view.

However, figure 4.6.1 also shows that since 1987 the gap has started to narrow and that since 1989 growth inside the EMS is higher than outside. Could this change in performance be attributed to differences in the path of fiscal policy?

Figure 4.6.2 provides some evidence by measuring the stance of fiscal policy by the cyclically adjusted budget balance (as a percentage of GDP) which represents the discretionary element of fiscal policy.[51] This figure suggests that fiscal policy reacted indeed quite differently to the second oil shock of 1979–80. In the EMS group a substantial deficit remains until 1981, but is followed in 1982 by a sudden fiscal tightening of more than 1.5 per cent of GDP. In contrast, in the non-EMS groups there is an expansion of almost 1 per cent of GDP in the same year. This divergence in fiscal policy coincides with the relative slowdown of real growth in the EMS and is thus compatible with the view that the EMS led to deflationary fiscal policies, but it precedes by about two years the change in the management of the EMS which came only in 1983.

However, developments since 1984 are hardly compatible with the 'deflationary bias' view since there has been a gradual convergence in the fiscal stance between these two groups, although the room for exchange-rate movements has been increasingly restricted. Moreover, as shown in figure 4.6.1, growth in the EMS remains initially sluggish and then picks up again in 1987–8 despite the convergence in fiscal policy.[52]

---

[51] Other simple measures, such as the primary budget deficit (i.e., the actual deficit adjusted for interest payments) yield similar results. More complicated measures, for example the index of fiscal impact developed by the OECD show little movement over this period and are more difficult to interpret.

[52] The convergence in fiscal policy is complete by 1986, it therefore comes too early to be due to capital market liberalization.

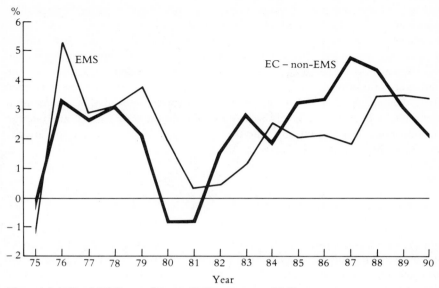

Figure 4.6.1: Real GDP growth rates: EMS versus non-EMS

Note: The growth rates were averaged using ECU weights.
Source: Commission of the European Communities (1990).

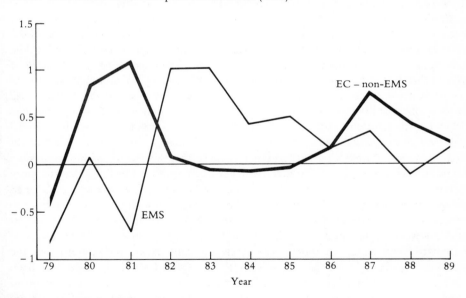

Figure 4.6.2: Fiscal Policy: EMS versus non-EMS

Note: Cyclically adjusted budget balance (a plus sign indicates a surplus and thus a fiscal tightening).
Source: See table 4.6.1

This lack of a close association of growth and fiscal policy could well be explained by the positive effects of fiscal consolidation that were discussed above.

In summary, the view of an inherent deflationary bias in the EMS seems questionable. Since capital controls in the past were less effective than generally believed (this was documented in section 2) the theoretical reasons to expect that the EMS did exert a deflationary influence must have been weak. Moreover, there is some indication that an expansionary fiscal policy may depress demand if it threatens to increase public debt above the level that is sustainable in the long run. At any rate the path of fiscal policy and growth over the later part of the 1980s does not confirm the impression that arose in the early 1980s.

4.7 A summary assessment of the EMS

Any summary assessment of the EMS has to start by acknowledging that the nature of the system has changed considerably over time. This was already clear from the narrative account given in chapter 3, but it is confirmed by the more analytical indicators discussed in this chapter which concur in indicating 1983 and 1986–7 as two likely watersheds. The interest-rate differential maintained by capital controls almost vanishes after 1983. The credibility of the central rates increases after 1983 (and 1986) and the degree of asymmetry of the system also changes around these dates.

Although the *modus operandi* of the system has changed over time one aspect has not changed. This constant feature of the EMS is the quest for stability. The creation of the EMS was indeed a successful response to external and internal monetary instability. The increasingly tight management of the exchange-rate mechanism led to a reduction of the external element of instability (intra-EMS exchange-rate variability) to about one quarter by 1990. Internal monetary instability (inflation) was reduced at the same time; however, there is little evidence that the EMS was instrumental in achieving this. The EMS seems therefore not to have worked primarily as a disciplinary device. In its initial phase realignments were used quite frequently and there seems to have been a 'soft currency' block centred around the French franc so that disinflation within the system was not faster than outside. Only after 1983, and even more so after 1987, has the more limited recourse to realignments forced member countries to follow the German example more closely and has thus allowed them to lock in the disinflationary gains.

A less widely recognized achievement of the EMS is that it has been an important shock absorber mechanism. It would not have been a useful instrument in this respect if asymmetric intra-European shocks had been dominant during its existence but the available evidence indicates that this was not the case. The EMS might even have been particularly important in providing a stable framework for a coordinated response to outside shocks, e.g., swings in the US dollar or in the price of oil. The EMS period provides a striking contrast to the 1970s since these shocks, which were important in both periods, no longer provoked divergent policy responses within the Community.

Capital controls were often assumed to be necessary for the stability of the system. However, there is considerable evidence that they were never fully effective in insulating domestic financial markets in the long run. Their short-run effectiveness was useful before realignments, but indispensable only when the French franc was devalued *vis-à-vis* the DM by more than 4.5 per cent. The controls could therefore not prevent, only prolong turbulent periods. The EMS has been more stable since capital controls were increasingly relaxed starting in 1987.

The EMS, as a European mechanism, was doubtless originally designed to be as symmetric as possible. The desire for symmetry conflicts, however, with the basic $N-1$ problem, which implies that in a fixed exchange-rate regime only one country can, in the long run, determine its own monetary policy. This policy then constitutes the anchor that ties down the price level and money supply in the other countries as well. This basic proposition implies that a system like the EMS has to be asymmetric if exchange rates are really to be kept fixed.

The empirical research reviewed in this chapter tends to show that the EMS has been less asymmetric than is often assumed and the degree of asymmetry seems to have changed considerably over time. A low degree of asymmetry during the initial phase is not too surprising in view of the frequent recourse to realignments prior to 1983. The following period, 1983–6, was characterized by a high degree of asymmetry. Indeed, the experience of this period may have determined many overall assessments of the EMS. Since 1987 the degree of asymmetry has again diminished, indicating that in the short run the Bundesbank did take developments in its partner countries into account when setting its own policy. However, there is no indication that German monetary policy was influenced in the long run. The system was therefore never totally asymmetric, but the available indicators suggest that German monetary policy was more important for France and Italy than vice-versa.

The renewed momentum towards monetary integration starting in 1988 was largely a consequence of the realization that the only practical alternative to an asymmetric system anchored by the German monetary policy would be to formulate a common European monetary policy, i.e., a move towards monetary union. The decisions taken since 1988 have therefore tended to transform the EMS into a 'quasi monetary union'. The issues that this 'new EMS' has to face are quite different from the ones facing the 'old EMS' that were analysed in this chapter. They stem from the larger size of the system (through the full participation of sterling and the peseta), from the economic impact of German unification and from the increasing degree of financial market integration. These issues are discussed in the following chapter. The costs and benefits of a full monetary union are addressed in chapter 7.

References

Artis, Michael and Mark Taylor (1988), 'Exchange rates, interest rates, capital controls and the European Monetary System: assessing the track record', chapter 7 in Francesco Giavazzi, Stefano Micossi and Marcus Miller (eds.), *The European Monetary System*, Banca d'Italia, Centro Interuniversitario di Studi Teorici per la Politica Economica and Centre for Economic Policy Research, Cambridge University Press, Cambridge, 185–203.

Barro, Robert and David Gordon (1983), 'A positive theory of monetary policy in a natural rate model', *Journal of Political Economy*, 91, 4: 589–610.

Bhandari, Jagdeep and Bernard Decaluwe (1987), 'A stochastic model of incomplete separation between commercial and financial exchange markets', *Journal of International Economics*, Amsterdam, 22, February: 22–5.

Biltoft-Jensen, Karsten and Christian Boersch (1990), 'Interest rate causality and asymmetry in the EMS', manuscript, Copenhagen, National Bank of Denmark.

Bini-Smaghi, Lorenzo (1985), 'Have exchange rates varied too much with respect to market fundamentals', *Giornale degli Economisti e Annali di Economia*, 1: 45–54.

Bini-Smaghi, Lorenzo and Stefano Micossi (1989), 'Managing exchange markets in the EMS with free capital', *Banca Nazionale del Lavoro Quarterly Review*, 171, December: 395–430.

Blanchard, Olivier (1984), 'Current and anticipated deficits, interest rates and economic activity', *European Economic Review*, 25: 7–27.

Caesar, Rolf (1988), 'German monetary policy and the EMS', in David Fair and Christian de Boissieu (eds.), *International Monetary and Financial Integration – The European Dimension*, Kluwer, Dordrecht, 103–25.

Collins, Susan (1988), 'Inflation and the European Monetary System' chapter 5 in Francesco Giavazzi, Stefano Micossi and Marcus Miller (eds.), *The European Monetary System*, Banca d'Italia, Centro Interuniversitario di Studi Teorici per la Politica Economica and Centre for Economic Policy Research, Cambridge University Press, Cambridge, 112–33.

Commission of the European Communities (1990), 'Annual Economic Report 1990/91', *European Economy*, 46, December.

De Grauwe, Paul (1988), 'Is the European Monetary System a DM-zone?', Centre for European Policy Studies, Brussels, *CEPS Working Paper*, 39.

(1990a,) 'The cost of disinflation in the European Monetary System', *Open Economies Review*, 1, 2, March: 147–75

(1990b), 'Fiscal policies in the EMS – a strategic analysis', chapter 7 in Emil Claasen (ed.) *International and European Monetary Systems*, Praeger, 121–40.

De Grauwe, Paul and Wim Vanhaverbecke (1990), 'Exchange-rate experiences of small EMS-countries: the cases of Belgium, Denmark and the Netherlands', chapter 3 in Victor Argy and Paul De Grauwe (eds.), *Choosing an Exchange Rate Regime: The Challenge for Smaller Industrial Countries*, International Monetary Fund, Macquarie University and Katholieke Universiteit Leuven, 135–55.

Drèze, Jacques, Charles Wyplosz, Charles Bean, Francesco Giavazzi and Herbert Giersch (1987), 'The two-handed growth strategy for Europe: autonomy through flexible cooperation', Centre for European Policy Studies, Brussels, *CEPS Paper*, 34.

Emerson, Michael, Daniel Gros, Jean Pisani-Ferry, Alexander Italianer and Horst Reichenbach (1991), *One market, one money*, Oxford University Press, Oxford.

Fels, Gerhard and Hans Peter Fröhlich (1987), 'Germany and the world economy: a German view', *Economic Policy*, 4, April: 177–95.

Fratianni, Michele and Jürgen von Hagen (1990a), 'The European Monetary System ten years after', Carnegie Rochester conference on public policy, supplement to *Journal of Monetary Economics*, 32, Spring: 173–242.

(1990b), 'Asymmetries and realignments in the EMS', chapter 5 in Paul De Grauwe and Lucas Papademos (eds.), *The European Monetary System in the 1990's*, Longman, 86–113.

(1991), '*The European Monetary System and European Monetary Union*', Westview Press, San Francisco.

Giavazzi, Francesco and Alberto Giovannini (1989), *Limiting Exchange Rate Flexibility: The European Monetary System*, MIT Press, Cambridge, Massachusetts.

Giavazzi, Francesco and Marco Pagano (1988), 'Capital controls and the European Monetary System', *Capital Controls and Foreign Exchange Legislation, Occasional Paper*, Euromobiliare, Milano.

Giovannini, Alberto (1990), 'European monetary reform: progress and prospects', *Brookings Papers on Economic Activity* 1990: 2, Washington, DC. Brookings Institution, 217–74.

Gros, Daniel (1987a), 'Tranquil and turbulent periods in the EMS and the possibility of self-fulfilling crises', Centre for European Policy Studies, Brussels, *CEPS Working Document (Economic)*, 30, June. To appear in *European Economic Review*, 35 (1992).

(1987b), 'The effectiveness of capital controls: implications for monetary autonomy in the presence of incomplete market separation', International Monetary Fund, Washington, DC, *Staff Papers*, 34, 4, December: 621–42.

(1988), 'Dual exchange rates in the presence of incomplete market separation: long run ineffectiveness and implications for monetary policy', International Monetary Fund, Washington, DC, *Staff Papers*, 35, 3, September: 437–60.

(1989), 'On the volatility of exchange rates – tests of monetary and portfolio balance models of exchange rate determination', *Weltwirtschaftliches Archiv*, Band 125, Heft 2: 273–94.

Gros, Daniel and Timothy Lane (1989), 'Monetary policy interaction in the EMS', International Monetary Fund, Washington, DC, *IMF/WP/89/8*, January.

(1990), 'Asymmetry in a fixed exchange rate system: who gains from the EMS?', paper contributed to the Konstanz Seminar on *Monetary Theory and Policy*, Reichenau, June: 13–15.

Gros, Daniel and Niels Thygesen (1988), 'The EMS: achievements, current issues and directions for the future', Centre for European Policy Studies, Brussels, *CEPS Paper*, 35.

Gros, Daniel and Axel A. Weber (1991), 'Changing asymmetries in the EMS – what does the high-frequency data tell us?', manuscript, University of Siegen, August.

Hughes-Hallett, Alexander, Patrick Minford and A. Rastogi (1991), 'The European Monetary System: achievements and survival', *CEPR Discussion Paper*, 502.

International Financial Statistics, various issues.

Lane, Timothy and Liliana Rojas-Suarez (1989), 'Credibility, capital controls and the EMS', International Monetary Fund, Washington, DC, *IMF WP/89/9*, January.

Mastropasqua, Christina, Stefan Micossi and Roberto Rinaldi (1988), 'Interventions, sterilization and monetary policy in European Monetary System countries, 1979–1987', chapter 10 in Francesco Giavazzi, Stefano Micossi and Marcus Miller (eds.), *The European Monetary System*, Banca d'Italia, Centro Interuniversitario di Studi Teorici par la Politica Economica and Centre for Economic Policy Research, Cambridge University Press, Cambridge, 252–81.

Masera, Rainer (1987), *L'Unificazion Monetaria e lo SME*, Il Mulino, Bologna.

Masson, Paul and Jacques Melitz (1990), 'Fiscal policy independences in a European Monetary Union', *CEPR Discussion Paper*, 414, April.

Mayer, Jörg (1990), 'Capital Controls in the EMS: a survey', Centre for European Policy Studies, Brussels, *CEPS Working Document (Economics)*, 43.

Meese, Richard, and Kenneth Rogoff (1983), 'Empirical exchange rate models of the seventies: do they fit out of sample?' *Journal of International Economics*, 16: 3–24.

Melitz, Jacques (1988), 'Monetary discipline and cooperation in the European Monetary System: a synthesis', chapter 3 in Francesco Giavazzi, Stefano Micossi and Marcus Miller (eds.), *The European Monetary System*, Banca d'Italia, Centro Interuniversitario di Studi Teorici per la Politica Economica and Centre for Economic Policy Research, Cambridge University Press, Cambridge, 51–79.

(1990), 'Comment on Fratianni and von Hagen', chapter 5 in Paul de Grauwe and Lucas Papademos (eds.), *The European Monetary System in the 1990's*, Longman, 116–19.

Obstfeld, Maurice (1988), 'Competitiveness, realignment, and speculation: the role of financial markets', chapter 9 in Francesco Giavazzi, Stefano Micossi and Marcus Miller (eds.), *The European Monetary System*, Banca d'Italia, Centro Interuniversitario di Studi Teorici per la Politica Economica and Centre for Economic Policy Research, Cambridge University Press, Cambridge, 232–43.

Padoa-Schioppa, Tommaso (1987), 'Efficiency, stability and equity: a strategy for the evolution of the Economic System of the European Community', Commission of the European Communities, Brussels, April.

Reding, Paul (1985), 'Interest parity in a two-tier exchange rate regime: the case of Belgium 1975–84', Cahiers de la Faculté Des Sciences Economiques et Sociales de Namur, *Série Recherche*, 65, March.

Reding, Paul and Jean-Marie Viaene (1990), 'Leads and lags and capital controls on the official market of a dual exchange rate regime', Facultés Universitaires Notre-Dame de la Paix Namur.

Rogoff, Kenneth (1985), 'Can exchange rate predictability be achieved without monetary convergence? Evidence from the EMS', *European Economic Review*, 28: 93–115.

Roubini, Nouriel (1988), 'Offset and sterilization under fixed exchange rates with an optimizing central bank', *NBER Working Paper*, 2777, November.

Ungerer, Horst, Owen Evans, Thomas Mayer and Peter Young (1986), 'The European Monetary System: recent developments', International Monetary Fund, Washington, DC, *Occasional Paper*, 48, December.

Ungerer, Horst, Jouko Houvonen, Augusto Lopez-Claros and Thomas Mayer (1990), 'The European Monetary System: developments and perspectives', International Monetary Fund, Washington, DC, *Occasional Paper*, 73, November.

Van der Ploeg, Frederick (1991), 'Macroeconomic policy coordination during the various phases of economic and monetary integration in Europe'. *European Economy*, special edition No 1, Commission of the European Communities, Brussels, 136–64

Vaubel, Roland (1989), 'A critical assessment of the EMS', paper presented at the Financial Times conference on World Banking 'Europe after the Delors Report', 30 November–1 December.

Viñals, Josè (1990), 'The EMS, Spain and macroeconomic policy', *CEPR Discussion Paper*, 389, March.

Von Hagen, Jürgen (1989), 'Monetary targeting with exchange rate constraints: the Bundesbank in the 1980s', Federal Reserve Bank of St. Louis, September–October.

Weber, Axel A. (1991), 'European economic and monetary union and asymmetries and adjustment problems in the European Monetary System: some empirical evidence'. *European Economy*, special edition No 1, Commission of the European Communities, Brussels, 187–207.

Williamson, John (1983), 'The exchange rate system', Institute for International Economics, *Policy Analyses in International Economics*, 5, September.

Wyplosz, Charles (1989), 'EMS puzzles', paper presented at the Simposio de analisis economico, Barcelona, December 18–20.

CHAPTER 5

CURRENT ISSUES FOR THE EMS
THE TRANSITION TOWARDS MONETARY UNION

The previous chapter has provided a critical appraisal of the EMS as it has worked up to July 1990, i.e., before complete capital market liberalization was achieved and with only eight currencies participating for most of the time. The present chapter analyses the issues that arise as the EMS enters its fourth phase.[1] This new phase can be described as a combination of full capital mobility, increasing financial market integration under the 1992 programme, an increased membership plus a high degree of price stability by a core group whose members have demonstrated that they will resort to realignments only under exceptional circumstances.

This mixture of elements is seen by many as unstable because it raises a number of issues:

Will capital market liberalization expose the EMS to speculative attacks? (Section 5.1)

Will financial market integration within a tighter EMS lead to currency substitution? (Section 5.2)

Is it possible that a credible commitment not to realign can increase inflationary pressures in the short run and thus slow down convergence? (Section 5.3)

Is the loss of the inflation tax that will come with price stability important for the fiscally weak members of the system? And can they reduce their accumulation of public debt? (Section 5.4)

Is the present constellation of real exchange rates tenable in the long run and is it therefore appropriate to avoid realignments for the foreseeable future? (Section 5.5)

Does German unification pose a threat to exchange-rate stability? (Section 5.6)

What particular issues are raised by the participation of the peseta and the pound? (Section 5.7)

---

[1] The first three phases were 1979–83, 1983–6 and 1987–90, see chapters 3 and 4 for more details.

These issues are discussed one by one below. The last section of the chapter then provides an overall evaluation of this 'new' EMS. July 1990 was, of course, not only the date for full capital market liberalization, but also the starting date for stage I of the Delors plan for EMU (see chapter 10 for a description of the Delors Report). Although the present chapter does not adopt the view that the EMS is only a transitional stage towards EMU, it contains in fact an analysis of most of the issues that arise during the transition towards EMU, especially in sections 1, 2 and 4.

Full capital market liberalization plus the intention to minimize the recourse to realignments makes the 'new' EMS akin to a 'quasi' monetary union. The discussion in sections 3, 5 and 6 can therefore be regarded as specific examples of the general point that the formation of a monetary union involves a cost, i.e., the loss of the exchange rate as an adjustment instrument. However, the general analysis of the costs and benefits of full EMU is left for chapter 7; the present chapter concentrates on the specific situation of the EMS in the early 1990s.

5.1 The EMS without capital controls: a potential for speculative attacks?

The EMS after 1990 can be described as a system of 'fixed-but-adjustable' exchange rates with fully mobile capital. Can such a system be stable? In the discussion about capital controls in chapter 4 it was argued that capital controls were not effective in the long run so that they could play only a minor role in assuring the stability of the system. Their main effect was to allow the authorities to delay realignments and to prolong, not prevent, the occurrence of turbulent periods. This view implies that as long as realignments are smaller than 4.5 per cent, so as to ensure that market rates do not have to jump on the day of the realignment, the abolition of capital controls should not lead to instability. Given the small residual inflation differentials that remain, this analysis suggests that capital market liberalization should not represent a major problem.

However, this might be an excessively optimistic view if one takes into account that after full capital market liberalization the reserves held by the monetary authorities would be much smaller than the liquid assets that the public could use to buy foreign exchange almost instantly as shown in table 5.1.1.

This table compares foreign exchange reserves to M1 because M1 consists essentially of sight deposits, which could be converted into foreign exchange at a moment's notice if the public decided that there was immediate danger of a devaluation. It is apparent that in all member countries the foreign exchange reserves of the authorities are much smaller than M1.

Central banks could, of course mobilize additional reserves if a crisis did occur, but this process takes some time. Even if it takes only days to arrange the necessary credit lines this would not be sufficient to enable a central bank to convert a substantial proportion of M1 into foreign currency at the EMS intervention rates. An extreme example is France, where the foreign exchange reserves of the central bank would just

Table 5.1.1: M1 and foreign exchange reserves in the EC

	Foreign exchange reserves (1)	Money (M1) (2)	Money/reserves (2) / (1)
Belgium	8 152	27 916	3.4
Denmark	6 545	33 397	5.1
Germany	46 826	195 841	4.2
Greece	2 269	5 136	2.3
Spain	32 220	91 119	2.8
France	18 803	223 818	11.9
Ireland	2 895	3 846	1.3
Italy	40 101	264 863	6.6
Netherlands	12 757	49 934	3.9
Portugal	5 856	10 529	1.8
United Kingdom	26 118	270 893	10.4
Total EC12	205 167	1 177 291	5.7

Note: All data in million of Ecu. First quarter of 1990, except Greece 2nd quarter of 1988 and Portugal 2nd quarter of 1989.

Source: International Monetary Fund, International Financial Statistics, various issues.

be sufficient to cover about 10 per cent of M1. It is therefore clear that a really massive speculative attack could not be stopped by relying on foreign exchange reserves alone. The crucial question is therefore whether there would ever be any reason for the holders of liquid assets to believe that it is in their interest to convert domestic assets into foreign assets.

Obstfeld (1988) provides a framework in which this might be the case. His basic observation is that any fixed exchange-rate system with full capital mobility is inherently vulnerable because the mere suspicion in financial markets that the exchange rate might be changed can trigger a speculative attack. Given that, as documented above, the authorities have only limited reserves whereas speculators in the foreign exchange markets can demand to convert instantaneously almost unlimited amounts of assets into foreign currency, a speculative attack will force the authorities to abandon the fixed exchange-rate commitment. (In this view it is irrelevant whether or not the authorities intend to keep realignments small since the entire system could break down under speculative attacks.) Such a self-fulfilling attack might start if agents in financial markets have doubts about the current exchange rate. Every single operator in these markets knows that if enough speculators demand foreign exchange for their assets they can exhaust the foreign exchange reserves of the central bank, thus forcing the authorities to abandon the fixed exchange rate and to let the currency float. If most operators believe that the others will act likewise it will be in the interest of everybody to participate in a run on the currency to avoid the windfall loss they will suffer if they keep a depreciating currency. This is why many speculators might act together in exchanging assets denominated in the currency under 'attack', presumably one of the weaker EMS currencies, for a more secure currency, perhaps the DM.[2]

The crucial element of this framework is, however, the question of what happens the day after the speculative attack, since speculation will only be profitable if the exchange rate is actually devalued. A crucial assumption of this framework is that the monetary authorities would increase the money supply after the speculative attack so that the exchange rate would settle at a lower level than the previously fixed rate. It is this policy of 'validation' that ensures profits for speculators and ratifies the doubts about the solidity of the exchange-rate commitment if it is really tested.

It is therefore apparent that a policy of full accommodation is essential for this to happen. If the authorities were to react to the speculative attack with a restrictive monetary policy, the floating exchange rate that results after the speculative attack would be above the pre-attack level. In this case the initial expectations of a devaluation would not be confirmed and speculators would lose money in participating in the attack. Since this would be anticipated in the markets no speculative attacks of this sort could therefore arise if the authorities are known not to accommodate them. In practice a tough monetary policy after a speculative attack could just consist of a policy of non-sterilization. The loss of foreign exchange reserves would then be sufficient on its own to reduce liquidity, thus increasing domestic interest rates and providing a check on speculative outflows.

Two further elements that make speculative attacks of this sort unlikely in reality are that, even after capital market liberalization, speculative movements still involve transactions costs and that the 4.5 per cent bands of fluctuations of the EMS imply that there is considerable downside risk for speculators. The main motive for keeping margins of this size has indeed been the experience of the breakdown of the Bretton Woods system when speculators were offered a 'one-sided bet'. The experience with the EMS has shown repeatedly that a strong reaction to speculative pressures can move the exchange rate from the bottom to the middle, or even the top, of the band, implying losses for speculators who were hoping for a devaluation. All in all, it is therefore extremely unlikely that the EMS would be subject to random and self-fulfilling speculative attacks of this type in the future.

Another line of arguments maintains that a potential for speculative attacks might also arise in the absence of an accommodating monetary policy stance. This might be the case for countries with a very large public debt. The authorities of these countries might be perceived as not being willing to raise interest rates to defend their currency because this would have undesirable consequences for their public finances via higher

---

[2] Two further important assumptions of this framework are that there is absolutely no cost for speculators to convert their holdings into DM and that there is no downside risk because an appreciation of the weak currency is ruled out.

interest payments. As argued in Giavazzi and Pagano (1989) the mere perception of this reluctance in financial markets might induce many speculators to exchange their domestic currency assets into foreign currency. Similarly as in the description of turbulent periods in the EMS this capital flight would require the domestic central bank to intervene to support its own currency. In doing so it would lose reserves and this loss of reserves might worsen the confidence crisis. Without capital controls the capital flight could then rapidly increase and become so large that the amounts converted by speculators exceed the foreign exchange reserves the domestic authorities have at hand. The latter would then no longer be able to maintain the exchange rates at the intervention margin and the entire system might collapse.

It is apparent that speculative attacks of this type can be set in motion only if a large proportion of the public debt needs to be refinanced at a time when doubts about the willingness of the authorities to pay higher interest rates arise because interest rates on the remainder that is outstanding are not affected by current developments. This implies that crises of this type are unlikely if public debt has, on average, a long maturity. The longer the maturity, the smaller the proportion of the debt that can be affected by turbulences in financial markets.

It is important to keep in mind that a basic element in both scenarios of speculative attacks is that financial markets have some reason to doubt the commitment of the authorities to defend the exchange rates. If no such doubts exist a fixed exchange–rate system like the EMS·might be stable even without capital controls. There are indeed several examples of fixed exchange rates that have been maintained without capital controls.

A good example is given by the Dutch guilder which has usually been pegged much more closely to the DM than required by the EMS rules, that allow for margins of +/– 2.25 per cent. Indeed, since 1983 it has never moved outside a corridor of about 1 per cent, i.e., it has behaved as if the allowed margins were +/– 0.5 per cent. Despite full capital mobility, continuing large public deficits and a growing public debt that is now close to 80 per cent of GDP (similar to the level of Portugal or Greece), there have never been any speculative attacks on the Dutch guilder/DM exchange rate nor has the potential for such an attack been noted by the Dutch authorities.

The Dutch–German experience (as also the linkage of the Austrian schilling to the DM outside the EMS) represents, of course, a special case since these two countries are even more highly integrated in terms of trade and financial flows than the members of the Community in general. The differences in their approaches to economic policy-making are also smaller than among Community members in general. Moreover, the Dutch–German relationship is much more 'asymmetric' than that of Germany vis-à-vis the rest of the EMS as documented in chapter 4. Other real world cases have been similarly 'asymmetric', for example the pegging of the Irish pound to that of the UK until the creation of the EMS, and currently the pegging of the Hong Kong dollar to the US dollar. Indeed some observers have argued that historically symmetric fixed exchange-rate systems have not been stable.[3] In many instances countries have preferred

---

[3] For example Carli (1989).

to reimpose capital controls or to devalue rather than accept the discipline coming from a fixed exchange rate and open capital markets. It is therefore difficult to decide whether the Dutch experience can be taken as representative for the EMS in the early 1990s.

A related argument to why the EMS might not be stable in the near future relates to the observation that most fixed exchange-rate systems contain a country that provides effective leadership, either because of its economic weight or because of its superior price stability record.[4] Up to now Germany has provided this leadership because it had a superior price stability record and the DM was the only major international reserve currency in the system. However, as the price stability record of some other currencies gets close to that of the DM and as capital market liberalization gives the other currencies a potentially bigger international role the predominant position of the Bundesbank in the system may indeed be weakened.[5]

Despite the lack of historical experience with fixed exchange-rate systems without capital controls there is reason to be optimistic about the stability of the EMS. The main reason for optimism is that governments in Europe are aware of the fundamental importance of acquiring a credible exchange-rate commitment. The Basle–Nyborg agreement described in chapter 3 may be viewed as a further reason for optimism since both frameworks for speculative attacks rely on the assumption that the foreign exchange reserves of central banks are limited. Since this agreement increases the availability of the 'Very-Short-Term Facility' it may be viewed as an attempt to lower the probability that a speculative attack could not be contained. A factor that could further reduce the danger of speculative attacks in the intermediate stages is the binding rules for budgetary policy that were proposed for stages II and III of the Delors report.[6] These may require or induce member governments to take corrective action well before their financial situation becomes unsustainable in the eyes of the markets.

Overall there is therefore little reason to believe that the EMS would be destabilized by random self-fulfilling attacks in the early 1990s. There is therefore no need to construct special safeguards against turbulences in financial markets.[7] Technical safeguards would be difficult to put into practice and would anyway be only a poor substitute for what experience has shown to be the basic ingredient for exchange-rate stability: a firm and credible commitment to subordinate domestic policy goals to the defence of the exchange rate.

[4] See Matthes (1988).

[5] Recent events in eastern Europe and German unification have further complicated the issue of the leadership inside the EMS. This issue is discussed further in section 4 below. Chapter 12 discusses whether the tighter voluntary cooperation in stage I and the establishment of a European monetary institution in stage II might overcome a potential leadership vacuum.

[6] The Commission has subsequently advocated binding 'procedures' instead of binding 'rules'.

[7] Giovannini (1990a) argues that in the case of a crisis in the foreign exchange markets governments should react by accelerating the move towards monetary union.

5.2 The EMS and financial market integration: a potential for currency substitution?

The removal of controls on capital flows is only one aspect of the overall programme of the integration of financial markets, which in turn is part of the overall 1992 internal market programme. Financial market integration goes beyond the lifting of all controls on cross-border and foreign exchange transactions. Full financial market integration would lead to a point where there is no longer any difference between domestic and international financial transactions because the various national financial systems have been completely integrated. This is quite different from the situation created by the mere removal of capital controls which preserves the identity of national financial markets. As will become clearer below, this is why currency substitution might arise because of financial market integration and not only through the abolition of capital controls.[8]

What is currency substitution and why is it generally held to represent a threat to the stability of the EMS? In general the term currency substitution refers to a process whereby one (or several) international currencies displace national currencies even for purely domestic transactions.[9] (In the specific context of the EMS it is usually assumed that the main alternative to the domestic currency is the DM.[10]) Currency substitution is generally held to be destabilizing because it might show up in large shifts in money demand. Such shifts would make it more difficult for national central banks to interpret their own national aggregates and would pose a problem for national monetary policies.

Some currency substitution is already occurring as documented by Kremers and Lane (1990) who find that the aggregate demand for money of the EMS countries was more stable than the national money demands taken individually even during the late 1980s, when there were still some capital controls. However, the extent of the phenomenon is still limited since national money demands have not become more unstable in absolute terms. The issue for the EMS in the coming years is whether financial market integration will increase currency substitution to the point of destabilizing national monetary aggregates.

In many discussions of currency substitution it is taken for granted that a change in the currency of denomination of bank deposits does affect national monetary aggregates. However, this assumption is not warranted because most central banks include in their monetary aggregates all deposits by residents with the domestic banking sector,

---

[8] Chapter 11 deals with the question whether currency substitution could be used as a mechanism to achieve monetary union.

[9] For international transactions foreign currencies are, of course, always used extensively.

[10] For recent contributions see Giovannini (1990a) and Bini-Smaghi and Vori (1990). The alternative plan for EMU prepared at one point by the UK Treasury that is analysed in more detail in chapter 11 is based on the potential for currency substitution (see HM Treasury (1989)).

irrespective of the currency of denomination.[11] For example, if a corporation outside Germany decides to keep its working balances in DM instead of its national currency this would not lead to a reduction of the measured money supply (M1 if it is a current deposit, M2 if the balances are kept in time deposits), nor would it show up in German monetary statistics.[12] In most cases currency substitution would therefore affect national monetary statistics only if it is accompanied by a cross-border shift in the account.[13] A priori it is unclear to what extent this would happen. It is therefore not clear whether currency substitution in the narrow sense (i.e., the use of a different currency) would lead to cross-border movements of deposits and would therefore affect monetary aggregates.

Even if it is granted that currency substitution might under certain circumstances destabilize national monetary aggregates, this would represent a problem mainly for those countries that still pursue an independent monetary policy based on national intermediate targets. Countries that do not pursue an independent national monetary policy, but instead use monetary policy only to maintain a fixed exchange rate, have less to fear from currency substitution. As long as they keep the exchange rate fixed, currency substitution will just lead to shifts in their national monetary aggregates that will, however, not influence interest rates and liquidity which will continue to be determined by the country to which they are pegging.

For those who think that the EMS is a DM zone (see chapter 4 for the evidence) this implies that currency substitution poses a threat only if it destabilizes German monetary aggregates, i.e., if it destabilises the anchor for the entire system. Currency substitution between two 'peripheral' currencies, e.g., the French franc and the Italian lira might show up in French and Italian monetary aggregates. But as long as both currencies are tightly pegged to the DM this would not affect interest rates in either country. However, currency substitution into the DM, which would lead to an increase in German monetary aggregates, might induce the Bundesbank to tighten its policy (for example by increasing interest rates), although this increase in the demand for DM balances would not represent a threat to price stability. Currency substitution into the DM (or rather: into the German banking system) would therefore pose a problem for the EMS. It is apparent that currency substitution into the ecu would not pose these problems unless the ecu balances were concentrated with a particular national banking system.

---

[11] The UK is an exception to this rule since its main target aggregate is sterling M4, which contains only balances in national currency. The UK adopted this target because of the importance of international bank deposits in London, which are in many different currencies. Italy is another partial exception since treasury bills in lire (BOT) are included in M3, but treasury bills indexed on the ecu (BTE) are not.

[12] In the case of cash, currency substitution obviously affects directly the monetary aggregates. If Italians use DM banknotes instead of lira notes the item 'currency in circulation' of the Bundesbank statistics would increase and the same item would fall in the accounts of the Banca d'Italia. It is unlikely, however, that currency substitution would affect cash for the reasons discussed below.

[13] This is why financial market integration is more important for currency substitution than just the possibility to have foreign currency deposits with a domestic bank that comes with the abolition of capital controls. Only under financial market integration could it ever become interesting to use accounts held in a foreign banking system for national transactions.

It is not clear, however, why the fixing of exchange rates would increase the potential for currency substitution. For bank deposits that are remunerated at market rates of interest, expectations of moderate exchange-rate movements do not constitute an incentive for currency substitution since the expected rate of depreciation of the weaker currency is offset by a higher interest rate. It follows that exchange-rate expectations should not be a factor that determines currency substitution for the wider monetary aggregates because most of the deposits that make up the wider aggregates are remunerated at market rates of interest.[14] Exchange-rate expectations should therefore play a role mainly in influencing the holding of cash (and sight deposits in those countries where no interest is paid on this type of deposits). For example, in countries with very high inflation rates the public often uses a foreign currency for larger cash transactions.[15] However, the residual small inflation differentials in the EMS are too small to trigger this type of currency substitution. At any rate these considerations suggest that abandoning the use of realignments in the EMS should only reduce the incentive for currency substitution.

This is also the reason why the empirical literature on currency substitution is not very useful in determining the potential for currency substitution within the EMS. This literature usually just tries to determine whether foreign interest rates or expected exchange-rate changes affect domestic money demand. A significant influence of, e.g., the foreign interest rate is taken as evidence of currency substitution.[16] Since a more stable EMS implies more convergence in interest rates and smaller expected exchange-rate changes the result that currency substitution is significant also implies that it should be reduced by a tighter EMS. However, this literature has usually found that currency substitution, even where it can be detected statistically, is not an important factor in money demand.

Currency substitution has therefore little to do with the EMS, but might arise as a consequence of the increasing integration of European markets in general and the integration of financial markets in particular. This increasing integration makes it more attractive and easier to use foreign currencies even for local transactions. The commitment not to realign that is part of this new phase of the EMS should therefore not be a decisive factor and the danger of currency substitution should therefore be viewed as a side effect of the internal market programme in financial services.

---

[14] In countries where banks pay competitive interest rates on sight deposits (this is the case in most Community countries, Belgium and Germany are the main exceptions) only cash would be affected by exchange-rate changes. See tables 5.2.1 and 5.2.2 for data about the composition of the main monetary aggregates.

[15] This process is usually called 'dollarization'. It rarely starts before inflation exceeds 100 per cent per annum. When inflation reached several hundred per cent per annum (and even went above 1,000 per cent) in Argentina and Israel in the late 1980s many domestic transactions were carried out in dollars. A similar process occurred in Yugoslavia where the DM was used instead. In all these cases the use of the foreign currency for domestic transactions stopped when the domestic currency was stabilized.

[16] For recent examples of econometric estimates of currency substitution see von Hagen and Neumann (1990) or Thomas and Wickens (1991).

How important is the potential for currency substitution in an environment of stable exchange rates? The crucial factor is the cost of converting currencies. As documented in Emerson *et al.* (1991), bid–ask spreads, which constitute the main element of the cost of exchanging currencies, are in the range of 2–5 per cent for cash, about 1 per cent to 2 per cent for small bank transfers, but less than 0.1 per cent for large transactions.[17] For the small transactions that are typical for individuals, the conversion costs seem therefore large enough to make large-scale currency substitution highly improbable. However, for corporations, which are responsible for the bulk of international transactions, this is not the case since the currency conversion costs on large transactions are 10 to 50 times lower than the costs on the small transactions typically undertaken by individuals.

Corporations do not only face much lower costs, they also have stronger incentives to use several currencies since they are much more involved in international operations than households. With the increasing integration in the Community through the internal market programme the use of one vehicle currency for all wholesale trading might become increasingly common. At this point corporations might substitute balances in national currencies with balances in this vehicle currency, which might be the DM or the ecu.

Since individuals are much less likely to engage in large-scale currency substitution than corporations the potential for currency substitution depends on the proportions of the overall monetary aggregates that are held by these two sectors. Tables 5.2.1 and 5.2.2 therefore report some data about the distribution of the usual monetary aggregates (M1, M2 and M3) for Italy and Germany (the only countries for which data are easily available). These tables show that in both countries the corporate sector holds only between 16 per cent and 32 per cent of the aggregates considered. Since Germany and Italy have two rather different financial systems but the proportions held by corporations are rather similar, it can be assumed that this situation is typical for the rest of the Community as well. The potential for currency substitution should therefore be limited to a fraction of the total balances that are actually held.

Another reason why currency substitution should be limited is that a large share of all transactions in most member countries is with the government, and therefore has to be made in the domestic currency.[18] The share of government receipts and expenditures in most member countries is close to 50 per cent, this would also seem to limit currency substitution to only part of the overall balances held for transactions purposes.

There is, however, one factor that would tend to make currency substitution a serious issue even if it affects only a small fraction of the overall monetary aggregates held in the Community.[19] Since the German monetary aggregates represents only a fraction of the total EC aggregates any small percentage shift into the DM has a

---

[17] For more details see appendix A in Emerson *et al.* (1991).

[18] See Giovannini (1990b).

[19] In non–member countries without capital controls, like Switzerland and Austria, currency substitution is not perceived as a problem. This is another indication that currency substitution does not arise because of fixed exchange rates or the abolition of capital controls.

Table 5.2.1 Sectoral breakdown of the main monetary aggregates
(In billion of DM)

			Germany[a]	
M3	1.112,4			
–	466,8	Saving deposits★ held by :	corp. sector households public sector	4,2 458,8 3,8
= M2	645,6			
–	260,5	Time deposits★★ held by :	corp. sector households public sector	79,8 141,0 39,7
= M1	385,1			
–	261.1	Sight deposits held by :	corp. sector households public sector discrepancy	91,6 152,4 16.2 (0.9)
= Cash	124,0			

Part held by: (in %)	households	corporate sector★★★
M1	72	24
M2	65	27
M3	79	16

Notes:
★ Domestic non banks saving deposits at statutory notice.
★★ Domestic non banks time deposits and funds borrowed for less than 4 years.
★★★ Assuming all cash is held by households.
[a]Own elaborations on 1987 data.

considerable impact in proportional terms on the corresponding German aggregate. Germany accounts for 18 per cent of total M3 held in the Community, and for 31 per cent of M1. Since this corresponds roughly to the part held by the corporate sector it follows that a 1 per cent shift of corporate balances out of the other EC currencies into the DM would result also in an increase of roughly 1 per cent in the corresponding

Table 5.2.2 Sectoral breakdown of the main monetary aggregates
(In thousands billion of Lire)

				Italy[a]	
M3	829				
–	163	Treasury notes*	corp. sector	12	
		held by :	households	149	
			public sector	1	
= M2	666				
–	305	Time deposits**	corp. sector	46	
		held by :	households	259	
			public sector	0	
= M1	361				
–	310	Sight deposits	corp. sector	114	
		held by :	households	175	
			public sector	31	
			discrepancy	(10)	
= Cash	51				

Part (in %) held by:		households		corporate sector***
	M1	63		32
	M2	73		24
	M3	76		21

Notes:
*'Buoni ordinari di Tesoro (BOT)' and 'Accettazioni'.
** Mainly savings accounts with banks and the post office, passport savings accounts and certificates of deposit.
*** Assuming all cash is held by households.
[a] Own elaborations on 1987 data.

German aggregate.[20] Currency subsitution, even if limited to a fraction of overall balances, could still pose a significant threat to the stability of German monetary policy.

This section has mainly discussed the widespread concern with currency substitution as a factor that destabilizes money demand. Another view of currency substitution (see Canzoneri (1990)) emphasizes a more positive aspect of currency substitution. This

[20] A shift of this magnitude would imply a reduction of only one fourth to one third of 1 per cent in the corresponding aggregates in the rest of the Community.

view says that currency substitution should be viewed as a factor that increases the elasticity of the demand for money with respect to exchange-rate changes. This implies that the higher the degree of currency substitution the smaller is the required adjustment in exchange rates for any given disturbance. In this view currency substitution is therefore a *stabilizing* factor since it makes it easier to offset changes in money demand through small adjustments in relative interest rates or small exchange-rate movements.

This positive view of currency substitution is not necessarily incompatible with the more conventional negative one. Currency substitution might have indeed two effects: it increases the uncertainty in money demand and it increases the sensitivity of money demand to relative yield differentials.

Overall, however, the decisive factor that might limit large-scale currency substitution in the short run is the transactions costs that still remain. The factors that might induce the corporate sector to substitute national currencies by the DM are anyway of a more long-run nature so that the view of currency substitution as a destabilizing factor in the short run seems to exaggerate the negative aspects of this issue.

5.3 Can too much exchange-rate stability delay convergence in inflation?

The essence of the EMS is the idea that convergence towards a low level of inflation can be achieved by progressively tightening the management of the weaker currencies. For a core group of countries consisting of France, Denmark and the Benelux countries this strategy has worked. However, for Italy and Spain it appears that inflation has stopped converging to the German level as can be seen from figure 5.3.1.[21] This phenomenon is not only surprising since it comes at a time when the EMS becomes tighter, but it is also worrisome because if it were to continue sizeable realignments would become unavoidable in the near future.

What is the reason for this apparent failure of the EMS strategy to work? A recent interpretation of this development argues that it does not indicate a failure of the EMS strategy. A temporary halt in the convergence process might be the result of an exchange-rate commitment that is more effective in financial than in labour markets.[22]

This analysis starts from the idea that a credible exchange-rate commitment has an immediate effect on financial markets. If the national currency is no longer expected to devalue against the DM, domestic interest rates (in the absence of capital controls) will immediately fall to the German level. However, a commitment not to devalue against the DM does not necessarily have the same immediate impact on the wage-setting

---

[21] Since the UK joined only in October 1990 it is not surprising that its inflation increased relative to German inflation between 1984 and 1990.

[22] See Miller and Sutherland (1990).

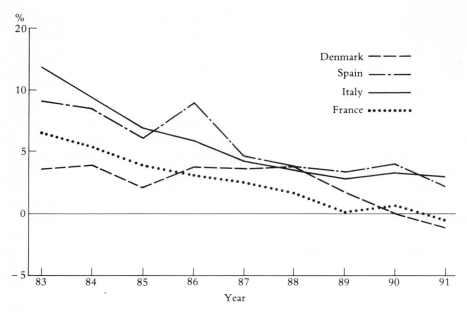

Figure 5.3.1 Incomplete convergence in inflation (inflation differential *vis-à-vis* Germany)

Note: Inflation measure by CPI (consumer price index).
Source: Commission of the European Communities (1990).

process, which is subject to many other factors. Out of inertia or because of previous long-term contracts, wages, and hence prices, might continue to increase for some time after the exchange-rate commitment has been taken.

These two effects together imply that the real interest rate has to fall (the nominal rate falls immediately, inflation falls only slowly). A credible exchange-rate commitment could therefore lead, initially, to an increase in demand, and hence additional upward pressure on prices due to the fall in real interest rates. It is possible in this framework that the impact of this (temporary) increase on demand is strong enough to lead, at least initially, to an *increase* in inflation.[23]

The crucial point of this analysis is, of course that the impact on financial markets is stronger than the impact on the wage-setting process. In Miller and Sutherland (1990) this follows from differences in the expectations of participants in financial and labour markets. In Giavazzi and Spaventa (1990b) this follows from the fact that inflation is determined by its own past. The precise reason for this differential effect of the exchange-rate commitment on financial and labour markets is not crucial, however, since in both models initially domestic demand will increase because of the immediate reduction in the real interest rate. Given that the reason for this 'perverse' effect lies in

[23] Sometimes this is also called the 'Walters critique' because this analysis reflects the criticism of the EMS by Sir Alan Walters, an advisor to the former British Prime Minister Margaret Thatcher, see Walters (1986) and (1990).

the asymmetry between financial and labour markets, it follows that it is stronger the higher the degree of financial market integration and the stronger is the credibility of the exchange-rate commitment.

Since the initial boost to domestic demand increases inflation on impact, are there any forces that can lead back to a low inflation equilibrium? They exist, but they work only after some time. The main factor that should eventually reduce inflation is the fact that, if inflation continues for some time but the exchange rate stays fixed, external demand will fall because of the loss in competitiveness. The fall in external demand will put pressure on prices until a long-run equilibrium is attained in which inflation has fully converged to the German level. In Giavazzi and Spaventa (1990b) the same two factors that produce the initial increase in inflation should also accelerate the eventual convergence to the inflation equilibrium.

This framework does therefore not suggest that the EMS strategy would not work in the medium to long run, but it does suggest that fixing exchange rates might not lead immediately to convergence in inflation.

Since this interpretation of the slowdown of convergence in the EMS was inspired by the experience of Spain and Italy it is useful to compare these two countries with Denmark, which provides an example of complete convergence to the German inflation performance.

The Danish disinflation process started after the stabilization programme of 1982, which included a sharp reduction in the fiscal deficit, the abolition of capital controls and a commitment to peg the krone more closely to the DM.[24] The Danish stabilization package was followed by a sharp fall in interest rates (both nominal and real), large capital inflows and by a prolonged increase in domestic demand. Inflation fell gradually and by the end of 1990 it was even below the German rate.

Are Italy and Spain on a similar adjustment path? Neither country had a similar radical adjustment programme. However, both have liberalized capital controls (not completely in the case of Spain) and their currencies have been pegged closely to the DM; since 1989 in the case of Spain, since about 1987 in the case of Italy. In this sense both can be considered to provide an example of a high inflation country that entered an exchange-rate commitment with a low inflation partner.

The decisive evidence as to whether Italy and Spain fall indeed into the pattern suggested by the framework discussed here should come from real interest rates and domestic demand. The evidence in favour of the hypothesis that stable exchange rates have led to a temporary stop in convergence in inflation was based on the observation that domestic demand in these two countries had increased relative to Germany.[25] Figure 5.3.2 therefore shows domestic demand in Italy, Spain and Denmark relative to Germany.

However, this figure shows that most of the difference in the level of domestic demand between Italy and Germany that has arisen between 1979 and 1989 dates from the early years of the EMS and can therefore not be attributed to capital-market liberalization and a tighter management of the lira, both of which are more recent.

---

[24] For a thorough analysis of the Danish experience see Giavazzi and Pagano (1990).

[25] This is emphasized in particular in Giavazzi and Spaventa (1990).

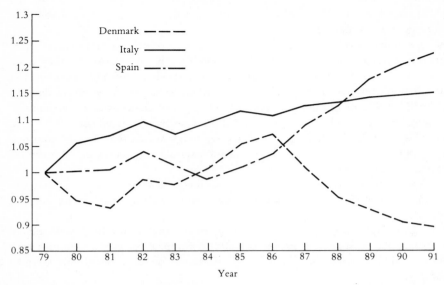

Figure 5.3.2 Real total domestic demand (1979 = 1: relative to Germany)

In the case of Spain the divergence in domestic demand is more recent, but most of it still occurred before the entry of the peseta into the EMS.[26] However, one could argue that the peseta was 'shadowing' the DM even before it formally joined the EMS in June 1989. The experience of Denmark seems to conform better with this theory since the stabilization package was followed by an increase in demand for three years, but subsequently there was a sharp fall (always relative to Germany). The evidence from the behaviour of domestic demand is therefore mixed.

More decisive evidence can be obtained from the behaviour of interest-rate differentials. The central point of the framework discussed here is that a credible exchange-rate commitment leads to an immediate convergence in (nominal) interest rates even if inflation stays initially high. However, the (nominal) interest-rate differentials displayed in figure 5.3.3 do not suggest that this effect has been strong in Italy and Spain: between 1985 and 1990 the nominal long-term interest-rate differential *vis-à-vis* Germany has actually slightly widened in the case of Spain. In the case of Italy the differential did diminish after 1982, but only slowly.[27]

Moreover, as shown in chapter 4, *real* interest rates in Italy have increased during the EMS period (both in absolute terms and relative to German rates) and are now higher than in Germany. This is difficult to reconcile with the idea that convergence in inflation is only delayed because low real interest rates stimulate domestic demand.

[26] Moreover, Spain still has some capital controls, but it seems that the residual capital controls in Spain have not prevented large capital inflows.

[27] In the case of Italy there was a substantial decline in the short-term interest differential over this period. But long-term rates should be more relevant for major investment and savings decisions.

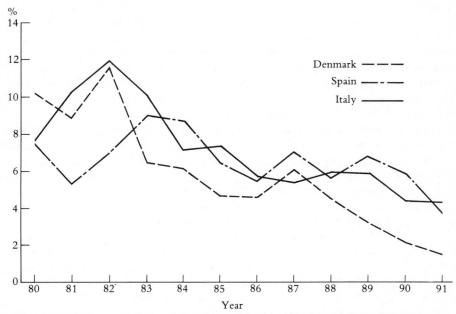

Figure 5.3.3 Convergence in long-term interest rates (interest differential *vis-à-vis* Germany)
Source: Commission of the European Communities (1990).

The persistence of large nominal interest-rate differentials can, on the contrary, be taken as evidence that financial markets expect sizeable realignments of the lira and the peseta in the near future. This would indicate that the slowdown in the convergence process is not a temporary consequence of credibly fixing exchange rates, but that participants in both financial and labour markets have not yet been convinced of the commitment of the Italian and Spanish authorities to avoid realignments.

5.4   The fiscal implications of price stability

The twin commitment to minimize the occurrence of realignments and to abolish capital controls is likely to present a challenge for those member countries that have relied so far on monetary means to finance large public deficits, i.e., the inflation tax. A related implication of this is that in some EMS countries the public debt/GDP ratio may soon reach an upper limit; this implies that these countries will have to run a surplus on the non-interest part of the budget. These two points are discussed separately below.

5.4.1 The EMS and the revenue from seigniorage

Price stability has a cost in fiscal terms because it reduces the inflation tax (also called seigniorage in technical terms). This raises the question whether countries with large deficits and a rising public debt/GDP ratio can manage without this source of revenue. Dornbusch (1988) and Giavazzi and Giovannini (1989) argue that fiscally weak countries may need the inflation tax because their tax collection systems are inherently weak and for political reasons it is not possible to reduce expenditures. The loss of the inflation tax revenue might therefore be an important cost of participating in the zone of monetary stability the EMS is finally becoming.

Whether or not the inflation tax is part of the ordinary array of taxes to be used by the government under ordinary circumstances is debated in the literature (see Spaventa (1989) for a summary). Given this uncertainty about the welfare-theoretic justification for the use of the inflation tax it is best to leave the theoretical arguments aside and simply measure the importance of the inflation tax at present and thus determine the loss of revenue that would come through price stability.

Measuring the importance of the inflation tax requires, first of all, a proper definition of the concept. The government obtains the inflation tax when it sells to the private sector assets on which it does not pay interest. The most important source of seigniorage revenue is usually the printing press for cash, since for each DM or French franc note the government prints it can buy goods and services from the private sector. However, in some EMS countries required reserves imposed on commercial banks constitute another important source of seigniorage since, as in the case of bank notes, usually no, or below market, interest is paid on these reserves. The tax base for seigniorage is therefore currency in circulation and required reserves.

The revenue the government obtains from its monopoly of issuing zero interest debt in the form of cash or required reserves on banks can be measured in two ways:[28]

A first approach emphasizes flows and looks at the additional money balances the public demands each year because the increase in the price level has reduced the real value of the balances it holds.[29] This approach measures therefore literally the money the government prints each year and can use to buy goods and services, it can therefore be called the *cash flow measure of seigniorage*. This measure of seigniorage is, however, unstable, because the demand for money can vary for many reasons. (The data below confirm this.) For example, if the public economizes on its *real* money balances, e.g. by using cash dispensing machines, it might not demand any additional *nominal* balances in a given year because the erosion of the real value of the existing balances through inflation is approximately equal to the savings in transactions balances due to technological progress. This approach could therefore find that seigniorage revenue goes up and down (and even becomes negative) although inflation stays constant.

---

[28] See Gros (1989a) for a further discussion of these two approaches.

[29] Similarly when prices go up the public has to acquire new bank deposits to keep the real value of these balances constant. A rising price level therefore leads to an increase in the demand for bank deposits (in nominal, not in real terms), and therefore, via the required reserve coefficients to an increased demand for required reserves which commercial banks have to acquire from the central bank.

A second approach emphasizes a stock concept. It is based on the idea that cash (and required reserves) constitutes a liability to the government on which it does not pay interest. The government saves the interest it would have to pay on public debt on each DM or French franc that is held by the private sector in the form of cash or required reserves. This measure might therefore be called the *opportunity cost measure of seigniorage*. This measure is equal to the interest rate on public debt times the total amount of cash and required reserves outstanding. Since these stocks are much more stable than the flows this measure is also much more reliable than the first one.

Despite its shortcomings the first, cash flow, measure has been widely used in the literature (see for example Dornbusch (1988), Giavazzi and Giovannini (1989)). Table 5.4.1 therefore shows the cash flow measure of seigniorage revenues as a per cent of GDP for the four EC member countries that had the highest seigniorage revenues plus Germany and the US for comparison.[30] This table shows that the inflation tax has been most important in the two non-EMS members Portugal and Greece. Among the EMS members it is important mainly for Spain and Italy; however, even in these two cases seigniorage revenues have already declined to less than 1 per cent of GDP in 1988–9.

Table 5.4.1 Seigniorage in EC, 1979–93[a]
(Cash flow definition of seigniorage)

	Averages			Projected
	1979–81	82–85	86–89	1993
Portugal	5.29	2.57	1.90	− 0.02
Greece	2.28	1.85	1.09	0.24
Italy	1.37	1.56	0.37	− 0.62
Spain	1.32	3.00	0.31	− 0.05
Germany	0.00	0.41	0.72	0.58
US	0.32	0.38	0.51	n.a

Note: [a] In percent of GDP

Somewhat surprisingly this table indicates that over the four-year period 1986–9 Italy had on average a lower revenue from seigniorage than Germany, although its inflation rate was still considerably above that of Germany during this period.[31] This is a result of shifts in the demand for money. An increase in the demand for DM (i.e., a fall

---

[30] These data take into account the interest payments on required reserves that are important in Italy and Spain. This is why these estimates of seigniorage revenue are lower than those provided by the two authors cited above.

[31] The accounts of the Bundesbank contain a line with the title 'seigniorage', but this item has nothing to do with the concept of seigniorage as used by economists. For an account of how seigniorage revenue is distributed in Germany, see Klein and Neumann (1990).

in the velocity of circulation in Germany) increased the flow of seigniorage revenue in that country whereas the opposite happened in Italy.

The second, 'opportunity cost', measure of seigniorage is much more stable, as can be seen by inspection of table 5.4.2. However, this measure is always very close to the medium-run average of the cash flow measure. The main exception is Italy for which this measure indicates a considerably higher revenue, thus reversing the previously mentioned result that over the period 1986–9 Italy had a higher seigniorage revenue than Germany.

Table 5.4.2 Seigniorage in EC[a]
(opportunity cost definition of seioniorage)

		Averages		Projected
	1979–81	82–85	86–89	1993
Portugal	3.83	4.42	1.97	0.63
Greece	2.30	2.24	2.18	0.69
Italy	2.12	2.01	0.94	0.47
Spain	1.77	1.67	1.13	0.62
Germany	0.87	0.75	0.58	0.54
US	0.70	0.67	0.50	n.a.

Note: [a] In percent of GDP.

Taking this second measure of seigniorage as the more appropriate measure it appears that during the EMS period seigniorage revenues were reduced by about 1–1.5 per cent of GDP in Italy and about 0.5 per cent in Spain. No reduction is apparent in Greece, but the other high-inflation non-EMS country, Portugal experienced a reduction of about 1.5 per cent of GDP.

Gros (1989a) also considers other countries and shows that, in the early years of the EMS when inflation was higher in northern Europe, countries like Belgium, Ireland and France did obtain about as much seigniorage revenues as Spain and Italy at present. Seigniorage was never really important in the UK despite the at times very high British inflation rates because the tax base is very small, which, in turn, is due to the absence of required reserves and a low ratio of cash to GDP.

To estimate the revenue loss that can result from participation in a tight anti–inflationary EMS it is necessary to estimate the evolution of the tax base (currency in circulation and required reserves) and the tax rate (i.e., inflation) over a medium-term horizon, say up to four years. The results of this exercise are also contained in tables 5.4.1 and 5.4.2. The assumptions underlying these projections are (i) that inflation in all member countries will be reduced to about 2–3 per cent over a period of four years, and (ii) that financial market integration will force countries with very high required reserve ratios to lower them to the present Community average. See Gros (1989a) for more details.

The projections for the early 1990s contained in tables 5.4.1 and 5.4.2 show the loss of seigniorage revenue that can be expected from continuing deflation and an eventual move to economic and monetary union. The two definitions yield strikingly different results for the two current EMS members, Spain and Italy. The cash flow is projected to be negative until the end of the adjustment period it turns, of course, positive thereafter – while the opportunity costs measure remains positive throughout and declines along with inflation in a continuous manner. The reason for this difference is, that the tax base has to shrink in both countries since they both impose required reserve ratios that are well above the Community average. This has a stronger impact on the flow concept. However, since by assumption the tax base would have adjusted to the EC average by 1994, the flow of seigniorage revenues would become positive again from that date. Indeed from 1994 onwards all member states would have a similar flow of seigniorage revenues equal to about 0.3–0.6 per cent of GDP.

The stock, or opportunity cost, measure of seigniorage declines much more continuously in the transition; according to this measure the revenue loss would be only about 0.5 per cent of GDP for Spain and Italy. The (currently) non-EMS members Portugal and Greece would lose much more on both accounts since their inflation rates are still considerably above the level of Spain or Italy.

5.4.2 Debt limits and the need for fiscal consolidation

The discussion so far shares with most of the seigniorage literature the defect of neglecting other effects of inflation on government revenues and expenditures than those related to revenue from money creation. For example, the unavoidable lags in tax collection imply that an increase in inflation leads to a fall in the real value of tax revenues. As shown in Sinn (1983), this and other effects that arise because tax systems are not indexed, make it likely – at least in Germany – that higher inflation will reduce, *ceteris paribus*, government revenue. Although this specific result has so far only been demonstrated for Germany and may not generalize to all EC member states with different tax systems, it does suggest that the calculations of loss of seigniorage as inflation recedes give only a partial view of the public finance implications of moving towards an EMU with a high degree of price stability.

The long-run commitment to price stability has other, more indirect implications for fiscal policy. In the short run there is no direct link between monetary and fiscal policy since it is possible to finance deficits by non-monetary means, i.e., by issuing public debt. This is why it has been possible to achieve a large reduction in inflation in recent years in spite of continuing large deficits in some countries, such as Italy and Belgium. However, the present situation – of large deficits financed by non-monetary means – cannot persist indefinitely. The situation will become unsustainable at some point if the stock of public debt continues to grow because of persistent large fiscal deficits and if real growth continues to be too sluggish to prevent the public debt/GNP ratio from rising under the impact of interest payments. Fiscal deficits in the order of magnitude of 8–10 per cent of GNP, as currently observed in some member countries, are in the long run not compatible with EMS commitments, since sooner or later these deficits would have to be at least partly monetized.

An analysis of the government budget constraint shows under what circumstances there is a tight link between monetary and fiscal policy in the long run. For a simple analytical framework see Sargent and Wallace (1986) or Blanchard (1984). According to this analysis the limit for the indebtedness of the government lies in the ratio of public debt/GNP which cannot grow without bounds; at some point the debt/GNP ratio has to be stabilized. This is not difficult if the growth rate of (real) GNP exceeds the real rate of interest the government has to pay on its debt. Indeed, if the growth rate of GNP exceeds the real interest rate, it would be sufficient to balance the non-interest part of the public sector deficit. The stock of debt would then continue to grow at a rate equal to the interest rate, but the debt/GNP ratio would slowly fall. However, for some years, the growth rates of GNP have been below the real interest rate in most EMS member countries (and nominal interest rates have exceeded the rate of increase in nominal GNP). If this combination of rates of growth and real interest rates persists, as has to be expected given the recent increase in interest rates following German unification, this implies that the debt/GNP ratio can be stabilized only by achieving a surplus on the non-interest part of the budget. (Given that, as shown above, the contribution from seigniorage will be limited to about 0.5 per cent of GDP.)

The continuing deficits in some countries are therefore compatible with a stable EMS only if these countries attain significant surpluses on the non-interest part of the budget in the near future. The problem will, of course, be most acute for those countries that have the highest debt/GNP ratios. Tables 5.4.3 and 5.4.4 provide some data about deficits, interest rates and growth rates plus the resulting estimates of the fiscal adjustment required in the fiscally weak countries. Table 5.4.3 is based on the 1990 survey of the OECD and calculates the adjustment that would be necessary given *current* interest rates and growth rates. Table 5.4.4 is taken from Emerson *et al.* (1991) and shows the adjustment required in some countries in a longer-run perspective, under which it is assumed that interest rates in the Community have to converge to the same level and that real growth has also settled at a common level (with some allowance for faster growth in the four poorest member countries). The last but one column in each table shows the adjustment that would be required in the country in question by comparing the present primary budget balance (i.e., the balance net of interest payments, which for most member countries is in surplus) to the surplus that would be required to stabilize the debt to income ratio. A positive value implies that the current primary surplus is *not* sufficient to cover the impact the high real interest rates have on debt growth so that on present policies debt will explode. A negative value in the last column indicates that the actual balance (in terms of the non-interest surplus) is so high that the debt to GDP ratio will decline over time.

A comparison of the results of the two tables shows that it is not possible to measure the 'sustainability' of fiscal policy with great precision. However, both tables support the conclusion that of the current EMS members mainly Italy and the Netherlands need to reduce their deficits significantly to attain a fiscal position that is sustainable in the

Table 5.4.3   Sustainability indicator (OECD) data (All data in % of GDP)

| | net debt/ GDP | i–n[a] | primary balance | Gap between actual primary surplus and the surplus required to: | |
				stabilize debt/GDP ratio	achieve convergence in debt/GDP ratio in 10 years
Belgium	122	3.2	4.2	-0.28	6.96
Denmark	23	6.4	3.8	-2.32	-5.01
Germany	21	2.0	1.4	-0.96	-3.77
Greece	79	2.4	-5.8	7.70	10.60
Spain	29	3.4	1.6	-0.60	-2.67
France	25	3.7	1.0	-0.60	-2.52
Ireland	122	4.1	5.8	-0.77	6.49
Italy	94	3.7	-1.1	4.59	9.02
Luxembourg					
Netherland	57	2.9	-0.2	1.86	2.58
Portugal					
United Kingdom	32	4.5	2.4	-0.92	-2.63

Note:
[a] Difference between interest rate and growth rate of GDP.

Source: OECD, Economic Outlook 1990.

long run. For Spain, and to some degree Belgium, the two results point in opposite directions. However, for Belgium the adjustment indicated by the second table is rather small and for Spain the need for immediate adjustment is less obvious since the current debt/GDP ratio (however measured) is below the Community average.

Both tables indicate that Greece is the country most in need of a fiscal adjustment, which is estimated at between 7.7 per cent and 11.8 per cent of GDP. However, since Greece is not a member of the EMS this situation does not represent a danger for the EMS, rather it shows the adjustment this country has to undertake before it can join the system. Portugal and Italy seem to be in a similar position with an adjustment that is estimated with less dispersion in the case of Italy: 4.6 per cent and 4.3 per cent of GDP according to the OECD and the Commission data respectively. For the Netherlands the required adjustment is much smaller: the two sources estimate it at between 0.5 per cent and 1.9 per cent of GDP.

The remaining member countries seem to be in a sustainable fiscal position although the size of the margin by which this is estimated to be the case varies considerably between the two estimates. For example for Ireland one source indicates that the actual

Table 5.4.4 Sustainability indicator (EC) (All data in % of GDP)

	Debt/ GDP	i–na	primary balance	Gap between actual primary surplus and the surplus required to:	
				stabilize debt/GDP ratio	achieve convergence in debt/GDP ratio in 10 years
Belgium	128	2.0	2.4	0.17	7.17
Denmark	63	2.0	4.7	-3.43	-2.93
Germany	43	2.0	1.6	-0.74	-2.29
Greece	86	2.0	-10.0	11.82	14.59
Spain	43	1.5	-0.9	1.56	0.09
France	35	2.0	0.8	-0.09	-2.39
Ireland	104	1.5	7.7	-6.13	-1.49
Italy	98	1.5	-2.3	3.78	7.82
Luxembourg	9	2.0	1.2	-1.02	-5.97
Netherlands	78	2.0	1.1	0.47	2.46
Portugal	73	1.5	-3.2	4.30	5.76
United Kingdom	44	2.0	4.3	-3.41	-4.83

Note:
[a] Difference between interest rate and growth rate of GDP.

Source: Commission of the European Communities, 'One market, one money', *European Economy*, 44, November 1990.

primary surplus exceeds the one required for a stable debt/GDP ratio by only 0.7 per cent of GDP whereas the other source gives a margin of 6.1 per cent of GDP.

The results in these two tables differ not only because of the differing assumptions about growth and interest rates, but also because of discrepancies in the underlying data concerning the actual deficits and debt levels. The importance of these measurement problems will be analysed further in chapter 9 in the context of the discussion of the need for binding guidelines as proposed by the Delors Report.

The arguments for the use of the inflation tax referred to above have also been used to argue that the adjustment necessary to stabilize debt/GDP ratios would be facilitated if the countries in need of this adjustment could rely on seigniorage revenues.[32] However, the high public debt/GNP ratios already reached in some countries can also be seen as an additional rationale for their governments to bind themselves to a rigid

[32] See Dornbusch (1988).

non-inflationary regime through the EMS.[33] The reason for this is that a high public debt represents an incentive for any government not bound by EMS obligations to try to reduce the real burden of servicing this debt by devaluing the currency. Devaluation would lead to inflation and would thus reduce the real interest rate paid on public debt if it is not anticipated. However, the public will perceive this incentive and will therefore expect higher inflation rates. It will prove impossible for the government to surprise it. Consequently, even a government not bound by EMS obligations would not be able to reduce the real burden of the public debt. At the same time the absence of EMS obligations would have the undesirable effect that the public would expect higher inflation rates. Countries with high public debt/GNP ratios might therefore have an additional incentive to adhere to a low-inflation EMS, rather than a disincentive as is sometimes argued.[34] There is no escape route through inflation and devaluation from real adjustment through a strengthening of public finances and a check on interest payments facilitated by a credible attachment to the EMS.

Overall the fiscal implications of the 'new' EMS do not seem to harbour a risk for the system. Only two of its current members (Italy and Spain) face a reduction in seigniorage revenue of minor importance.[35] Two members (the Netherlands and, again, Italy) also need to implement an overall fiscal adjustment to stop the debt/GDP ratio from rising above its high present level.[36] This overall fiscal adjustment is much more important than the seigniorage revenue loss.

5.5   Is there a need for a maxi realignment?

The cumulative effects of realignments over the entire EMS period have in the cases of Italy and Spain been insufficient to compensate for the accumulated inflation differentials. As documented in chapters 3 and 4 this implies that some countries have experienced a considerable real appreciation if one compares present real exchange rates to their levels before the formation of the EMS. These shifts in real exchange rates or competitiveness are seen sometimes as the root cause of the large current-account deficit of Spain and the relatively high unemployment in both Italy and Spain. It has therefore been argued that before totally abandoning the use of realignments it would be useful to have a last but large realignment that creates a sustainable constellation of real exchange rates.[37] The adjustments that are required according to this view – 10 to

---

[33] See Gros (1990) for a formal analysis of this point.

[34] See Padoa-Schioppa et al. (1988) and Dornbusch (1988).

[35] Moreover, taking the other indirect effects into account (p. 181), lower inflation might increase tax revenues. This applies, a fortiori, to Portugal and Greece with their inflation rates well above those of Italy and Spain.

[36] For Spain some fiscal adjustment might also be needed, but since the current debt/GDP ratio is below the average for the Community, the adjustment is not that urgent.

[37] See, e.g., Cline (1989) and De Grauwe et al. (1991).

20 per cent – can be effected only by a jump in nominal exchange rates. To achieve the same effect via movements in relative prices would require countries like Italy or Spain to have an inflation rate that remains for some time several percentage points below the German rate, which seems very difficult to achieve.[38]

The argument that a maxi-realignment is needed has to be based on the observation that the real exchange rate of the lira and the peseta appreciated by 15–20 per cent over the EMS period.[39] France experienced a much smaller real appreciation over the same period and the real exchange rates of the smaller EMS countries were in 1989–90 generally within 5–10 per cent of the level of the late 1970s. This data alone would indicate that the only adjustment that is needed is a steep depreciation of the lira and the peseta.

However, a maxi-realignment cannot be justified only by the observation that real exchange rates have moved, it needs also to be demonstrated that the current constellation of real exchange rates is unsustainable or leads to prolonged unemployment in some countries. What is the evidence for such a position? The following discussion concentrates on Italy (which now has narrow margins) because Spain could realign by over 10 per cent without necessarily creating a discontinuity in market exchange rates.

One way to judge the current (1991) constellation of real exchange rates within the Community is to analyse the longer-run evolution of real exchanges. This can be done by looking at figures 5.5.1 to 5.5.4 which show the real exchange rate of four major currencies (the lira, the French franc, the peseta and sterling) against the DM.[40] This bilateral point of view is appropriate because the EMS can affect only exchange rates within the system and a realignment would probably have to involve a depreciation against the DM. Each figure shows the real exchange rate, as measured by the nominal exchange rate adjusted by changes in the consumer price index of the country concerned relative to Germany.[41]

The graph for France shows that the French franc has depreciated in real terms vis-à-vis the DM by almost 25 per cent if one compares the 1960s with the EMS period. However, this depreciation was not uniform. Most of the overall depreciation came through a jump in 1969; after 1969–70 there was a further depreciation, which was, however, already corrected before the creation of the EMS. This suggests that there is no need for a correction in the French franc/DM exchange rate.

The graph of the real exchange rate of the lira also shows some long-run swings. As in the case of the French franc there was a sharp real depreciation at the beginning of

---

[38] Such a maxi-realignment would, however, need to take financial markets by surprise. In an environment of capital mobility the system would break down if such an event were to be anticipated by financial markets, see section 5.1 above.

[39] See De Grauwe et al. (1991) .

[40] The real exchange rates of the smaller EMS countries are analysed in De Grauwe and Vanhaverbecke (1990).

[41] Various competitiveness indicators are compared by De Grauwe et al. (1991), who come to the result that there are significant differences between different indicators, but on average most indicators show a similar real appreciation of the lira and peseta.

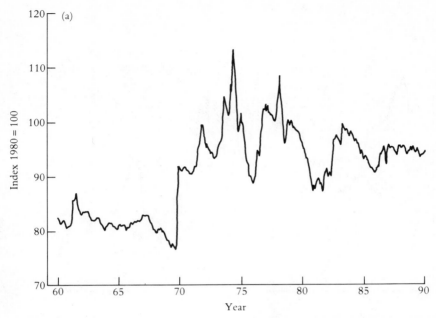

Figure 5.5.1 France: long-run real exchange-rate movements (the bilateral real exchange rate FF/DEM based on the CPI)

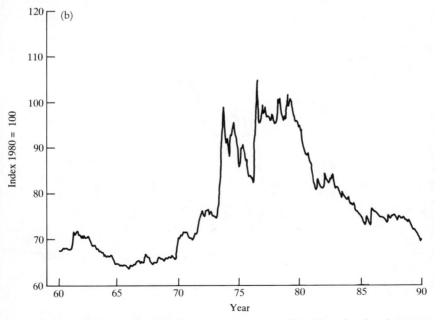

Figure 5.5.2 Italy: long-run real exchange-rate movements (the bilateral real exchange rate LIT/DEM based on the CPI)

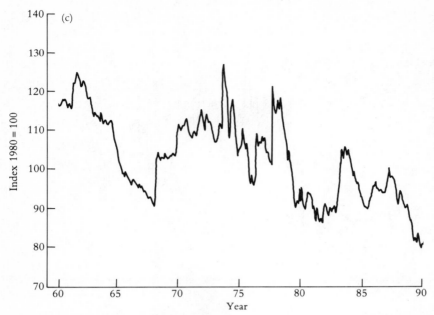

Figure 5.5.3 Spain: long-run real exchange-rate movements (the bilateral real exchange-rate PTA/DEM based on the CPI)

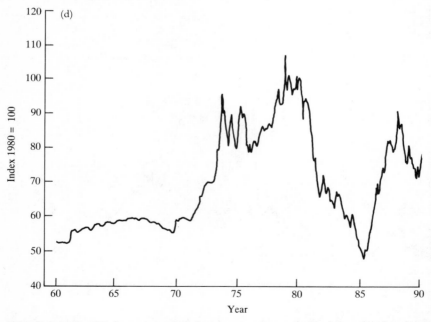

Figure 5.5.4 The UK: long-run real exchange-rate movements (the bilateral real exchange rate GBP/DEM based on the CPI)

the 1970s, but the depreciation was smaller and was subsequently totally reversed during the EMS period. One could therefore argue that the real exchange rate of the lira is now only returning to a level it stood at during the 1960s, when Italy enjoyed healthy growth and an external surplus. Taking this longer run into account suggests that the real appreciation of the lira in the EMS period represents only a correction of the undervaluation that developed during the 1970s.

The real exchange rates of the peseta and sterling show more short-term variability. Compared to the long-run average sterling was depreciated by over 40 per cent between 1973 and 1979 (an example of a misalignment?); compared to the pre-EMS period sterling has therefore appreciated by almost 30 per cent. However, these exchange rate movements occurred outside the EMS and few are arguing now (see section 5.7 below) that the rate at which sterling entered the EMS is clearly unsustainable. The real value of the peseta was also subject to some short-run variability, but there seems to be an overall trend towards a real appreciation of the peseta. The level reached by 1990 was unprecedented even in the longer-run perspective of these figures which would indicate therefore that the peseta is the most likely candidate for a large devaluation.[42]

However, as mentioned above it is not sufficient to rely only on observed shifts in the real exchange rate. To justify a maxi-realignment one would have to show that the present constellation of real exchange rate leads to imbalances, i.e. that the current real exchange rate represents an overvaluation in the sense that it causes an external deficit and unemployment. On this account the evidence is difficult to interpret. The Italian current account deficit in 1989/90 is rather small, i.e., about 1 per cent of GDP, the situation is therefore not unsustainable from the external side, especially if one takes into account the increase in external financing that will be forthcoming through capital market integration.[43] In the case of Spain the external deficit is more important, about 3 per cent of GDP at present. However, a large part of this deficit is covered by direct investment and could therefore be viewed as an expression of an investment boom which is necessary to allow Spain to catch up with the more advanced members of the Community. Moreover, since Spain did grow faster than Italy over the last forty years (including also the EMS period) a real appreciation of the peseta could be expected from the so-called Balassa effect. If productivity in Spain continues to grow faster than in the rest of the Community, a continuing real appreciation of the peseta is justified by these real factors. The external deficit of the UK is also much larger than that of Italy, but this does not seem to have created much concern about the appropriate level of sterling in the EMS.

On the internal side the judgement on the lira has to be less optimistic since unemployment in Italy has not fallen over the last five years. This is in sharp contrast to the other big EC countries were unemployment has fallen considerably over the same period. Closer inspection of the Italian unemployment data reveals, however, that it is

---

[42] The Spanish EMS experience is briefly discussed in section 5.7 below.

[43] However, De Grauwe et al. (1991) uses the fact that the ratio of exports to GDP has fallen in Italy over the 1980s to argue that there is indeed an external disequilibrium.

very unevenly distributed inside Italy. Table 5.5.1 shows that in 1988 the unemployment rate for the northern part of Italy was 6.4 per cent, only one third of the level in the south, which stood at 20.6 per cent.[44] Since the northern part of Italy is the part where the economy is the most integrated internationally (only 15 per cent of total employment in industry is in the south) it is difficult to argue that a loss of international competitiveness is the root cause of high unemployment in Italy.

Table 5.5.1 Unemployment in Italy by regions*

	1951	1961	1973	1980	1988
North**		3.0	4.0	5.8	6.4
Centre	8.8	3.9	6.5		9.8
South	9.1	4.9	9.4	12.1	20.6
Average	8.9	3.9	6.4	7.9	12.2

Note:
* In per cent of regional labour force.
** North/centre for 1951 and 1980.

Source: OECD (1990)

This table shows that the increase in overall unemployment in Italy came almost exclusively from a large increase in the south, whereas unemployment in the north was much more stable. This is again difficult to reconcile with the thesis that an EMS induced real appreciation caused the increase in unemployment between 1980 and 1988. Table 5.5.1 also suggests that this regional problem cannot be ascribed to the EMS. Southern and northern unemployment rates were very similar in the 1950s, but they have diverged continuously throughout the last forty years, not only since the creation of the EMS.

In 1990 unemployment was still higher in Spain (15.8 per cent) than in Italy (10.2 per cent), but Spanish unemployment had already come down from 20.4 per cent since 1987 whereas there had been no improvement in Italy. One could therefore argue that a temporary period of high unemployment in Spain is the consequence of the real integration of the Spanish economy into the Community that started only in 1985. In the case of Spain there are therefore structural factors at work that would tend to justify the expectation of a continued fall in unemployment (assuming, of course, that the adjustment is successful).[45]

However, even if one accepts the hypothesis that the present distribution of current

---

[44] The unemployment rate of the northern part of Italy was also lower than that of Germany.

[45] Moreover, Spain seems to be facing a regional unemployment problem that is similar in some respects to the Italian one. See OECD (1990) for an international comparison of regional disparities in incomes and unemployment.

accounts and unemployment rates is not sustainable or undesirable a realignment would be the best answer only if the following two conditions are met.[46]

1) The necessary real adjustments require a change in real exchange rates and not adjustments of other policies. For example, the existing current-account imbalances inside the EMS might also be corrected by some change in fiscal policy, with a reduction of the deficit in the weaker countries and maybe some expansion in the stronger countries.

   Whether the existing current-account imbalances can best be dealt with by demand policies or by changes in the real exchange rates depends on the relative effectiveness of these two policies. The relative impact of changes in demand and the real exchange rates is evaluated by Vona and Bini-Smaghi (1988). This paper suggests that there are important asymmetries between the price and income elasticities of these three countries and that the price elasticities are very small relative to income elasticities. This implies, as shown by some simulations, that even small corrections in current-account imbalances would require large changes in the intra-EMS exchange rates, whereas small changes in demand would have much stronger effects on the current account. This result suggests that the most effective means to deal with current-account imbalances are demand policies and not the exchange-rate changes.

   There is little formal evidence in the econometric literature about a link between exchange rates and employment. It is therefore uncertain (even abstracting from the regional problems in Italy and Spain) that a real depreciation of the lira or the peseta would alleviate unemployment in these countries.

2) Even if changes in real intra-EMS exchange rates are deemed necessary, it is not clear why these should be brought about mainly by changes in the nominal exchange rate as opposed to adjustments in domestic prices and wages. This issue is discussed further in chapter 8 where it is argued that in general it would be preferable to rely on wage and price flexibility. However, if one accepts the thesis, that the present situation represents a large disequilibrium which accumulated over a number of years a once-and-for-all large realignment would be justified to start a period of stable intra-EMS exchange rates 'with a clean slate' (De Grauwe *et al.* (1991)).

   The history of the EMS, however, is a warning against excessive reliance on realignments to achieve changes in real exchange rates, because realignments that are not accompanied by changes in domestic demand policies are likely to be ineffective. Renewed inflationary pressures would quickly offset the gains in competitiveness initially achieved through the realignment. This is why some of the major realignments within the EMS in the turbulent 1981–3 period were accompanied by major domestic efforts by the devaluing countries. This suggests that a 'maxi-realignment' would be useful only if accompanied by a determined

---

[46] The following discussion has to be based on essentially the same arguments as the evaluation of the cost of foregoing the exchange-rate instrument in chapter 7.

effort of the devaluing countries to adjust domestic policies. In the case of Italy this adjustment would certainly have to start with a reduction in the fiscal deficit. But given the regional problems in both Italy and Spain it appears that some structural policy measures are also called for to make a maxi-realignment a sensible policy option.

5.6 The effects of German unification on exchange rates in Europe

German unification has important implications for the EMS because the need to finance public and private investment in the territory of the ex-GDR is determining all macro-economic variables in Germany. In particular German unification changes three variables that had almost become fixed points for the EMS: the fiscal budget deficit, the rate of growth of real growth of the German economy and the external current account.

The first consequence of unification, i.e. the large fiscal deficit, should be welcomed by the other EMS participants, but it has nevertheless caused some tensions in the EMS because it also led to an increase in German interest rates which forced the other EMS countries to raise their interest rates as well. However, interest-rate differentials (vis-à-vis the DM) have also narrowed so that the pass-through effect was only partial. This is an illustration of the result already discussed in chapter 4, namely that the spillover effects of fiscal policy can be negative if the direct demand effects (through increased German imports from the rest of the EMS) are smaller than the indirect effects coming from higher interest rates. However, since, as shown below, the increase in German imports is very substantial the net effect of the German fiscal expansion caused by unification on the other EMS members might be positive and certainly cannot be very large if it is negative. This implies that the fiscal deficit is mainly a problem for Germany.

The second consequence of German unification, i.e., faster real growth, is not a source of tensions. On the contrary, since it has often been argued that the slow growth of the German economy until 1989 was a cause for slow growth for the entire area, faster growth in Germany should improve the growth prospects in other member countries as well.

However, the third effect of German unification (which is mainly a consequence of the other two) is often alleged to constitute a challenge for the EMS because, it is argued, a large shift in the German current account requires a large appreciation of the DM, and hence possibly a realignment.

The crucial question for the EMS is therefore whether the economic consequences of unification require a real appreciation of the DM. If it does a realignment would be desirable to forestall the tensions that would otherwise arise inside the EMS.[47] This is the issue discussed in the remainder of this section.

---

[47] A real appreciation of the DM could also be achieved without a realignment if inflation in Germany increases considerably, but we assume that the Bundesbank will not let this happen.

In doing so it will be convenient to distinguish between the demand effects that arise in the short run and the supply effects from factor movements that might take longer to occur. Finally this section will also speculate about the effects of German unification on the leadership position of the Bundesbank in the EMS.

5.6.1 The short to medium run: demand effects

The crucial point to be kept in mind in the ensuing analysis is that, at given West German wages, the exchange rate of the DM (against, say the French franc) determines the price of West German goods relative to French goods. It is therefore essential to distinguish between the effects German unification will have on the demand for goods produced in East and in West Germany. The relative price of these two goods can change through changes in wages in East Germany, which, at least for the coming few years, will be negotiated independently from wages in West Germany.

The widespread hypothesis that GEMU requires a real appreciation of the DM is based on the conventional tradables versus non-tradables framework. In this framework an increase in overall demand goes partly towards tradables, thus reducing the external surplus, but it also goes partly towards non-tradables, the supply of which is not infinitely elastic (or at least much less elastic than that of tradables) thus requiring an increase in the relative price of *non-tradables*. At given nominal wages an increase in the relative price of non-tradables requires then an appreciation of the nominal exchange rate.

If this standard model is applied to the problem at hand, however, it does not lead to the conclusion that a real appreciation of the DM is required. A real appreciation of the DM would be required only if the demand for West German non-tradables goes up, which can happen only if *West Germans* spend more. However, this is not a necessary consequence of unification since West Germans have not become richer; they just lend or transfer large accounts of purchasing power to East Germans. There is therefore no reason why the relative price of, say French and German non-tradables should change.

On the contrary, one could even argue that citizens in the western part of Germany must expect to pay higher taxes: either now to reduce the deficit, or later to service the debt that has been incurred in the meantime. This should reduce the consumption demand of West Germans, part of which would fall on non-tradables requiring a real *depreciation* of the DM. The decision of the federal government to increase taxes that was taken in early 1991 only confirmed something that had been evident for some time. Moreover, recent econometric estimates (see Lipschitz and McDonald (1990)) suggest that in general the expectations of future taxes cause (West) Germans to save more in response to higher fiscal deficits. In the short run savings increase by approximately 30 per cent of the increase in the deficit; in the long run the increase in private savings is about equal to the rise in public dissaving.

The thesis that German unification might actually depress consumption demand in the western part of the country is entirely compatible with the fact that (in 1990–1) the West German economy was continuing to expand, whereas industrial production was collapsing in the East. The boom in West Germany appears to be based to a large extent on orders (of tradables goods) from the East and not on a large increase in consumption expenditure by West German households.

The relative price of East German non-tradables (goods that cannot be traded between say Germany and France can presumably be considered also as non-tradables between East and West Germany) may of course have to change, but a large jump already occurred through conversion at 1 : 1 for wages and further adjustments can and already have taken place through large wage increases in the territory of the ex-GDR.

Another framework that is often used to argue that German unification requires a real appreciation of the DM is one in which there are nationally differentiated tradables goods. In this framework there would also be a need for a real appreciation of the DM only if East Germans (they are the ones who receive the additional purchasing power) spend most of their additional income on West German tradables. This does not seem to be the case. With the possible exception of West German investment goods, most of the spending seems to go towards goods that can also be supplied by other members of the EC or the newly industrializing countries in East Asia. Only to the extent that East German demand goes towards goods imported from the rest of the world can there be a reduction in the current-account surplus. If East Germans were to concentrate their demand on West German goods the German current account would not be affected. In this framework there is therefore either a large impact on the German current account (and little impact on the equilibrium real exchange rate) or the German current account is not affected and the real exchange rate of the DM has to move instead.

Other European economies of a size comparable to the ex-GDR (e.g., Holland, Belgium) receive about one fourth of all their imports from the Federal Republic. Applying the same percentage to the ex-GDR implies that even if the GDR region runs a current-account deficit with the old Federal Republic of 80 billion DM per annum (about 30 per cent of the GDP of the ex-GDR) the additional demand for West German exportables would be only about 20 billion DM (and the reduction in the German current-account surplus would be 60 billion DM).[48] This represents only about 3 per cent of the overall exports of the Federal Republic (in 1989, i.e., prior to unification) which total 600 billion DM and is not likely to require a large price change.

Events up to early 1991 indicate that there is indeed no need for a realignment. The German current account has swung into deficit because of a surge in import demand that has taken place without any large change in relative prices. Indeed the increase in German imports, over 20 per cent if one compares the last quarter of 1990 to the last quarter of 1989, is much larger than one would expect from the increase in the size of the German economy through unification, which is only about 10 per cent because income in the East is only one half of that in the West (and the population of the ex-GDR was equal to about 25 per cent of that of the old Federal Republic). Figure

---

[48] These crude calculations do not take into account the import content of West German deliveries to East Germany, which have been estimated to be as high as 40 per cent, implying that each DM of exports from West to East Germany reduces the current-account surplus by 0.4 DM. However, preliminary calculations suggest that this effect is more or less offset by the fact that exports from the rest of the Community (and EFTA) have a West German component.

5.6.1 below illustrates this point by showing the demand for imports (for West Germany alone and for all of Germany) that one could expect based on the past relationship between imports and domestic demand and the real exchange rate. Up to July 1990 there is a close correpondence between the predicted and the actual values, but after that date actual imports (both those for West Germany and for all of Germany) increase much more than one would expect given the behaviour of domestic demand and the DM exchange rate (see Gros and Steinherr (1991) for more detail).

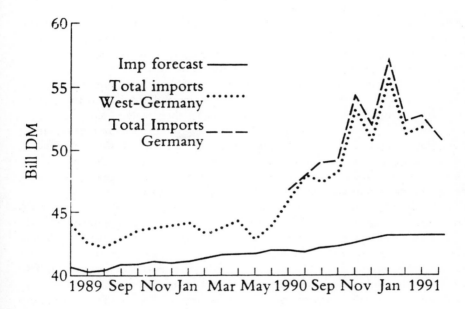

Figure 5.6.1 German imports, 1989–91

5.6.2 The long run: factor movements

A different way to look at the implications of German unification for the EMS is to take into account not only its effects on demand, but to use the standard Heckscher–Ohlin framework, which takes into account factor endowments and movements.[49] The crucial point in this framework is that East Germany starts out with a much lower capital/labour ratio. This should lead to capital flows into East Germany and should also be reflected in the capital intensity of the goods traded by East Germany.[50] However, given that the German capital market is open to the rest of the world, most of the

---

[49] The demand-side story takes implicitly at given factor endowments.

[50] Perfect, i.e., instantaneous, mobility of both factors would, of course, lead to instant equalization of the capital/labour ratio. However, since movements of both factors involve adjustment costs the capital/labour ratio will not be equalized immediately.

capital will come from the rest of the world (hence the lower external surpluses). As long as the East German economy is in the factor price equalization region movements of goods and factors can equalize prices and consequently there is again no need for a change in the relative price of (West) German exports relative to its imports.

5.6.3 Systemic implications

It has been argued so far that German unification might not really imply a need for a large exchange-rate adjustment, basically because it represents an interregional shock inside Germany. However, it might still have considerable systemic implications if it affects the leadership position of the Bundesbank within the system.

German unification brought with it a large financial shock because it implied a considerable increase in the uncertainty about the demand for DM balances. For example, East German households have been reducing their savings deposits because they now have access for the first time to a whole range of investment opportunities. This uncertainty about the German money demand relationship makes it more difficult for the Bundesbank to control inflation through the monetary targets it has used so far and thus reduces the usefulness of the anchor function of the DM. Arguably this makes a more symmetric system more desirable. However, the uncertainty concerning money demand in Eastern Germany should not persist too long since the West German banking system is already implanted in the East. After an initial adjustment period, during which the East German public learns about this system, its demand should become as predictable as those of the West German public before unification.

A more serious reason why the leadership of the Bundesbank might become less strong is that, at least in the eyes of some, its anti-inflationary credibility has been reduced. The decision by the German government early in 1990 to offer to introduce the DM into the GDR clearly showed the limits of the independence of the Bundesbank. Moreover, it is widely perceived that if the shock treatment administered to the GDR economy leads to politically unacceptable unemployment in the territory of the ex-GDR the Bundesbank might not be in a position to resist the pressure for an easier policy stance in the form of lower interest rates and/or debt relief for enterprises in East Germany.

However, there are also offsetting factors. If the process of integration of the East German economy proceeds smoothly after a necessarily difficult initial transition period, the relative economic weight of Germany and therefore that of the Bundesbank should increase. Moreover, it can be expected that some of the Eastern European countries (Czechoslovakia, Hungary, perhaps Poland) will use the DM extensively in their foreign trade, a large part of which will be with Germany. This will reinforce the dominant position of the DM in the system. However, these factors might become important only after an initial adjustment period of several years. At that time the current EMS should have been superseded by full EMU and a joint monetary authority, the European Central Bank, that can substitute for the leadership role of the Bundesbank.

5.7   A widening of membership: Spain and the United Kingdom

The previous sections of this chapter have reviewed a number of challenges facing the current EMS. Some of these challenges have been accentuated by the successful ambition of extending participation in the exchange-rate mechanism of the EMS to as many EC member states as possible. Spain joined in June 1989 and the UK in October 1990; the decision of both countries was regarded in political terms as a significant advance in European integration. It could hardly be otherwise; the EMS was from the start conceived to be an open system and participation in monetary integration by two additional large member states adds potentially major benefits to all participants in the form of greater assurance of stable trading relationships without the dramatic fluctuations implied by the swings in the exchange rates of the peseta and of sterling prior to entry. However, in terms of the issues discussed in this chapter, the widening of membership has brought increasing risks: the scope for disruptive capital movements has become much larger (section 5.1); incomplete convergence of inflation rates could become temporarily self-reinforcing if nominal interest rates are more quickly aligned than inflation rates (section 5.3); and the perception that realignments and the conflicts that surround them may have become harder to avoid causes discomfort to both the older and the two new members (section 5.5).

The present section does not, therefore, raise new issues but asks to what extent the entry of the two additional currencies has already provided illustrations of these fears of instability.

A priori the starting positions of Spain and the UK had some important similarities. Both entered with inflation rates well above the EMS average, sizeable and growing current-account deficits and interest rates – both nominal and (probably) real – higher than elsewhere in the EMS. Both currencies entered at central rates which were considered ambitious in terms of their level of competitiveness, their external positions and their underlying inflation rates. Both aimed to achieve the credibility effects of pegging their inflation rates and looked forward to their nominal interest rates being arbitraged down towards the level of Germany.

Despite these initial similarities the experience of the two new participants has been strikingly different. Ever since entry the peseta has typically been the strongest EMS currency; the Spanish authorities have had difficulties in keeping the peseta within the wide band as the high interest rates required to dampen strong domestic demand tended to cause capital inflows. Sterling, in contrast, after a short period of strength fell to the lower half of the band. The UK authorities had anticipated a positive confidence shock upon entry and lowered short-term interest rates immediately. Subsequent experience in the band did not leave much room for further monetary ease and required coordination with the monetary authorities of the currency at the other end of the band. The peseta was often in that position, as illustrated in figure 5.7.1 (a). The most direct constraint on British monetary policy thus did not come from a strong DM, but from the strong peseta. However, movements of sterling against the DM have also, at times, in 1991–2 imposed constraints on the capacity of the UK authorities to reduce interest rates; from October 1991 sterling dropped out of the narrow band against the

DM which the UK had hoped to informally observe (see figure 5.7.1 (b)). Despite the weaker EMS performance of the pound nominal convergence has proceeded faster in the UK than in Spain, but this may be temporary since the fall in the UK inflation rate may be due more to the domestic business cycle than to credibility effects of EMS membership.

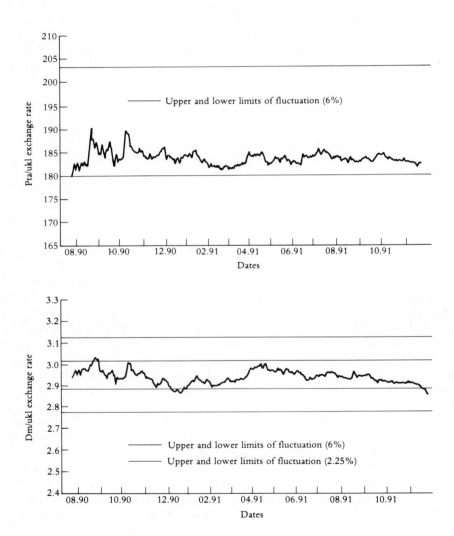

Figure 5.7.1 (a) and (b) The position of sterling against the peseta (a) and the DM (b), August 1990 – November 1991
Source: Commission of the European Communities

Both countries have undoubtedly been temporarily constrained by entry in their conduct on monetary policy – given the initial conditions and the difficulties of using budgetary policies for stabilization purposes. Their examples illustrate different versions of the dilemma between external and domestic considerations which arise for a country which enters an area of stable exchange rates with initial conditions different from those of other participants. Spain was unable to let its interest rates rise even higher to choke off some of the rapid rise in demand in 1989–90 as long as the peseta was near the top of the band, and the UK was unable to allow interest rates to fall sharply as the clear signs of domestic recession may have warranted. Even in a wide band, limits to divergent monetary policy soon emerge. There is no evidence yet that EMS entry had any major impact on the rate of increase of prices and wages; it seems possible so far to explain observed developments in terms of inertia and changes in domestic demand. In this sense the experience of both countries illustrates the different speeds of adjustment of financial variables on the one hand and the price level on the other hand, prominent in the international macroeconomics literature. By the end of 1991 it was not yet possible to judge whether the pace of adjustment of prices and wages was sufficiently rapid to lead to a durable equilibrium in the exchange rates initially chosen.

But it is also understandable why a conflict is emerging between the relatively high degree of preparation of the earlier EMS participants for rapid moves towards EMU and the doubts in the two new members whether a longer transition is required for them. Both the Spanish and the UK governments envisage a lengthy transition during which the option of realignments is to be retained. However, it is not obvious that such a lengthy transition – up to the late 1990s – would be in the interest of either the two new participants or the older members, since that would retain the prospect of realignments. Inevitably that prospect will have some contagion effect throughout the EMS, as financial market agents ask themselves whether an opportunity to realign will be seized by several members, if one or both of the new participants take an initiative. Resorting to a small realignment, say in connection with a narrowing of the bands, after some years of membership could damage credibility, as it could trigger expectations that more were to follow; this would reverse the narrowing of interest-rate differentials between markets in EMS currencies. A maxi realignment, the pros and cons of which we discussed in section 5.5 above, could delay monetary integration, because there would need to be assurances through domestic adjustments in the devaluing countries that it would not lead to renewed divergences in national inflation rates.

The implications of wider membership in the EMS and doubts as to the speed of convergence of new members thus poses a dilemma in a sharper form than it would have done in the earlier incarnations of the EMS. The system now has less flexibility to deal with divergence than before. The older EMS members have increasingly come to be regarded as stable in terms of each other. They have a stake – shared by the UK and Spain, of course – that this credibility be extended to the recent participants, particularly in a period where the scope for destabilizing capital flows has widened so much. If the new members are not prepared to give up the option of realigning and envisage using it at some point, it would seem advisable to exercise it sooner rather than later and then participate fully in a short transition to EMU.

5.8   A new EMS?

This chapter has addressed a number of issues that arise for the EMS as it enters the transition towards monetary union in the early 1990s. This 'new' EMS is characterized by complete capital market liberalization, the high degree of price stability achieved by a core group of countries, a commitment to limit the use of realignments to exceptional circumstances and a wider membership. In the view of this chapter this new environment does not pose a threat to the stability of the system.

Speculative attacks are unlikely if the commitment to defend the parity grid is maintained and currency substitution is likely to remain limited. A more serious issue is represented by the fiscal implications of price stability, not so much in the form of lost seigniorage revenues, but because a stabilization of public debts requires substantial adjustment in some countries. At present (1990–1) the Netherlands and Italy are the only EMS members to have unsustainable fiscal policies. In the case of the Netherlands the adjustment required to stabilize the debt/GDP ratio is minor, but a much more significant effort (a reduction in the deficit of about 4.5 per cent of GDP) is needed in Italy.

The question whether the current exchange-rate grid contains any serious misalignments that require a major realignment in the EMS is difficult to answer on the basis of the available evidence. The main candidate for a large realignment is Italy, but even in this case the need for an exchange-rate adjustment is not beyond doubt.

It is certain, however, that a realignment without accompanying policy measures would be useless. The general rule should be that existing imbalances should be addressed first by domestic policy measures. Moreover, in the new environment, external current-account imbalances become much less important since capital mobility implies that it is possible to finance larger external deficits for some time. Provided the external deficits come from the private sector and represent an increase in productive investment they should not be a concern for policy-makers because the purpose of capital market liberalization was exactly to provide financing mechanisms for this type of deficit.

Overall, however, the decisive factor in assuring the stability of the EMS in the early 1990s will be the perspective of full EMU scheduled for 1996–7, or, at the latest, 1999 (see chapter 12). In financial and labour markets the overall macroeconomic policies of member countries will increasingly be judged by their compatibility with participation in an EMU that aims at price stability. Inflationary risk premia in interest rates and wage settlements will arise only in those countries where the commitment of the government to take the necessary action is not beyond doubt. Chapter 7 discusses the benefits and costs of full EMU, while the institutional aspects of the transition are analyzed in chapter 12.

References

Bini-Smaghi, Lorenzo (1989), 'Fiscal prerequisites for further monetary convergence in the EMS', Banca Nazionale del Lavoro, *Quarterly Review*, 169, June: 165–89.

Bini-Smaghi, Lorenzo and Silvia Vori (1990), 'Concorrenza, Egemonia e Unificazione Monetaria', mimeo, April.

Blanchard, Olivier (1984), 'Current and anticipated deficits, interest rates and economic activity', *European Economic Review*, 25: 7–27.

Canzoneri, Matthew (1990), 'Currency substitution in the European Community', International Monetary Fund, Washington, DC, mimeo, July.

Carli, Guido (1989), 'The evolution towards economic and monetary union: a response to HM Treasury paper', Ministero del Tesoro, Rome, mimeo, December.

CEPR (1990), 'The impact of Eastern Europe', *Monitoring European Integration*, 2.

Cline, William R. (1989), 'The global impact of US trade adjustment', Institute for International Economics, Washington, DC.

Cohen, Daniel (1989), 'The costs and benefits of a European currency', chapter 7 in M. de Cecco and A. Giovannini (eds.), *A European Central Bank?*, Centre for Economic Policy Research, Cambridge University Press, Cambridge, 195–209.

De Grauwe, Paul, Niels Thygesen, Jean-Pierre Danthine and Louka Katseli (1991), 'North/South in the EMS: convergence and divergence in inflation and real exchange rates', Centre for European Policy Studies, Brussels, *CEPS Paper*, 50, March.

De Grauwe, Paul and Wim Vanhaverbecke (1990), 'Exchange-rate experiences of small EMS-countries: the cases of Belgium, Denmark and the Netherlands', chapter 3 in Victor Argy and Paul De Grauwe (eds.), *Choosing an Exchange Rate Regime: The Challenge for Smaller Industrial Countries*, International Monetary Fund, Macquarie University and Katholieke Universiteit Leuven, 135–55.

Dornbusch, Rüdiger (1988), 'The EMS, the dollar and the yen', chapter 2 in Francesco Giavazzi, Stefano Micossi and Marcus Miller (eds.), *The European Monetary System*, Banca d'Italia, Centro Interuniversitario di Studi Teorici per la Politica Economica and Centre for Economic Policy Research, Cambridge University Press, Cambridge, 23–41.

Dornbusch, Rüdiger (1989), 'Credibility, debt and unemployment: Ireland's failed stabilization', *Economic Policy* 8, April: 173–210.

Emerson, Michael, Daniel Gros, Jean Pisani-Ferry, Alexander Italianer and Horst Reichenbach (1991), *One Market, One Money*, Oxford University Press, Oxford.

Giavazzi, Francesco and Alberto Giovannini (1989), *Limiting Exchange Rate Flexibility: The European Monetary System*, MIT Press, Cambridge, Massachusetts.

Giavazzi, Francesco and Marco Pagano (1989), 'Confidence crises and public debt management', *CEPR Working Paper*, 2926, April.

——— (1990), 'Can severe fiscal contractions be expansionary? Tales of two small European countries', *NBER Working Paper*, 3372, May.

Giavazzi, Francesco and Luigi Spaventa (1989), 'Italy: the real effects of inflation and disinflation', *Economic Policy*, 8, April: 133–172.

——— (1990), 'The 'new' EMS', chapter 4 in Paul De Grauwe and Lucas Papademos (eds.), *The European Monetary System in the 1990's*, Longman, 65–84.

Giovannini, Alberto (1989), 'How do fixed-exchange-rate regimes work? Evidence from the gold standard, Bretton Woods and the EMS', in Marcus Miller, Barry Eichengreen and Richard Portes (eds), *Blueprints for Exchange Rate Management*, Academic Press, New York, 13–41.

——— (1990a), 'The transition towards monetary union', *CEPR Occasional Paper*, 2, March.

——— (1990b), 'Currency substitution and monetary control', paper prepared for the conference on 'Financial Regulation and Monetary Arrangements after 1992', Gothenburg University and Marstrand, May.

Gros, Daniel (1988), 'The EMS and the determination of the European price level', Centre for European Policy Studies, Brussels, *CEPS Working Document (Economic)*, 34.

——— (1989a), 'Seigniorage in the EC: the effects of the EMS and financial market integration', International Monetary Fund, Washington, DC, *IMF/WP/89/7*.

——— (1989b), 'On the volatility of exchange rates – tests of monetary and portfolio balance models of exchange rate determination', *Weltwirtschaftliches Archiv*, Band 125 Heft 2: 273–94

(1990), 'Seigniorage and EMS discipline', chapter 7 in Paul De Grauwe and Lucas Papademos (eds.), *The European Monetary System in the 1990's*, Longman, 162–77.

Gros, Daniel and Alfred Steinherr (1991), 'Einigkeit macht stark: The Deutsche Mark also?', chapter 4 in Richard O'Brien (ed) *Finance and the International Economy: 5. The Amex Bank Review Prize Essays*, Oxford University Press, Oxford, 52–67.

Gros, Daniel and Niels Thygesen (1988), 'The EMS: achievements, current issues and directions for the future', Centre for European Policy Studies, Brussels, *CEPS Paper*, 35.

HM Treasury (1989), 'An evolutionary approach to economic and monetary union', London, November.

Klein, Martin and Manfred Neumann (1990), 'Seigniorage: What is it and who gets it?', *Weltwirtschaftliches Archiv*, 126, Heft 2: 205–21.

Kremers, Jeroen and Timothy Lane (1990), 'Economic and monetary integration and the aggregate demand for money in the EMS', International Monetary Fund, Washington DC, WP/90/23, March.

Krugman, Paul (1989), 'Differences in income elasticities and trends in real exchange rates', *European Economic Review*, 33: 1031–54.

Lipschitz, Lelie and Donough McDonald (1990), 'German unification: economic issues', *Occasional Paper* 75, International Monetary Fund, Washington, DC, December

Matthes, Heinrich (1988), 'Entwicklung des EWS mit Blick Auf 1992', in D. Duwendag (ed.), *Europa Banking*, Baden-Baden.

Miller, Marcus and Alan Sutherland (1990), 'The "Walters Critique" of the EMS: a case of inconsistent expectations', *CEPR Discussion Paper*, 480.

Obstfeld, Maurice (1988), 'Competitiveness, realignment and speculation: the role of financial markets', chapter 9 in Francesco Giavazzi, Stefano Micossi and Marcus Miller (eds.), *The European Monetary System*, Banca d'Italia, Centro Interuniversitario di Studi Teorici per la Politica Economica and Centre for Economic Policy Research, Cambridge University Press, Cambridge, 232–43.

OECD (1990), *Economic Outlook*, July.

Padoa-Schioppa, Tommaso *et al.* (1988), 'Efficiency, stability and equity', Commission of the European Communities, Brussels, April.

Romer, Paul (1989), 'Increasing returns and new development in the theory of growth', *NBER Working Paper*, 3098, September.

Sargent, Thomas and Neil Wallace (1986), 'Some unpleasant monetarist arithmetic', chapter 5 in Thomas Sargent, *Rational Expectations and Inflation*, Harper and Row.

Sinn, Hans-Werner (1983), 'Die Inflationsgewinne des Staats', in Eberhard Wille (ed.), *Beiträge zur Gesamtwirtschaftichen Allokation,* Peter Lang, Frankfurt.

Spaventa, Luigi (1989), 'On seigniorage: old and new policy issues: introduction', *European Economic Review*, 33: 2–3, March: 557–63.

Thomas, Steve and Michael Wickens (1991), 'Currency substitution and vehicle currencies: tests of alternative hypotheses for the dollar, DM and yen', *CEPR Discussion Paper*, 507, January.

Vinals, José (1990), 'The EMS, Spain and macroeconomic policy', *CEPR Discussion Paper*, 389, London, March.

Vona, Stefano and Lorenzo Bini-Smaghi (1988), 'Economic growth and exchange rates in the EMS: their trade effects in a changing external environment', chapter 6 in Francesco Giavazzi, Stefano Micossi and Marcus Miller (eds.), *The European Monetary System*, Banca d'Italia, Centro Interuniversitario di Studi Teorici par la Politica Economica and Centre for Economic Policy Research, Cambridge University Press, Cambridge, 140–78.

von Hagen, Jürgen and Manfred Neumann (1990), 'Currency substitution and the demand for money, further international evidence', Discussion Paper B–150, Sonderforschungsbereich 303, May.

Walters, Alan (1986), *Britain's economic renaissance: Margaret Thatcher's reforms 1979–1984*, Oxford University Press, Oxford.

Walters, Alan (1990), *Sterling in danger*, Fontana, London.

CHAPTER 6

THE ECU: MOTOR OR EXPRESSION OF EUROPEAN MONETARY INTEGRATION?

This chapter discusses the development of the ecu up to the end of 1991. Although the ecu never played an important role in the EMS (see chapter 3) the unexpected emergence of a widespread use of the ecu in private international financial markets has helped to make the ecu the natural choice for the future common currency. The success of the ecu in international financial markets has also led to proposals that the ecu be used as a vehicle for further progress in monetary integration. These ideas are discussed in chapter 11 when the so-called parallel currency approach is dealt with. The global role for the ecu that will arise with EMU is discussed in chapter 9.

The present chapter therefore concentrates on an analysis of the ecu markets that have developed so far. It starts in section 1 with a brief description of the origins and the definition of the ecu. This is followed in section 2 by an appraisal of the limited role of the ecu in the official sector. The main focus of the chapter is then, in section 3, a description of the success of the ecu in the private sector, especially in international financial markets, and an analysis of the reasons for this development. Section 4 deals with a more recent phenomenon, i.e., the independence of the ecu basket from the actual ecu in terms of interest rates and exchange rates. Finally, section 5 concludes with a reflection about the broader role of the ecu in European monetary integration as well as a discussion of the practical steps that could be taken to encourage further use of the ecu.

6.1 Origins and definition of the ecu

The ecu was born in 1974 as the European Unit of Account (EUA) which was used at the official level when it was adopted in 1975 as the accounting unit for the European Development Fund (see Thygesen (1980)). This unit was defined as a basket of specified amounts of the currencies of the (then) nine member countries of the Community. The EUA became subsequently also the unit of account for the European Investment Bank and for the budget of the Community itself. Such a European accounting unit was clearly needed in the early 1970s, when currencies began to diverge considerably. It would not have been acceptable to use a national currency for the accounting and the budgets of the Community's institutions.[1]

Before the creation of the EUA different parts of the Community had used different units of account which were all based on the Bretton Woods definition of the gold content of the US dollar.[2] At the global level the International Monetary Fund had faced similar problems and had already in 1967 introduced the Special Drawing Right (SDR) which was initially defined as the gold value of the US dollar, but was subsequently (1974) revised as a basket consisting of fixed amounts of the sixteen internationally most important currencies.

The European unit was also defined as a basket of fixed amounts and initially (28 June 1974) one SDR was equal to one EUA.[3] Subsequently, however, the two units developed along different paths. The SDR was never widely used in financial markets, was redefined later and now serves mainly as the accounting unit for the International Monetary Fund and the World Bank. The EUA, however, took off in private financial markets some time after it was renamed ecu when the EMS was created in 1979. This new name, ecu, can be interpreted as standing for European Currency Unit or as the name of a medieval coin used in France and England.

The ecu (or EUA as it was called initially) was from the beginning an effort to represent a European average. All Community currencies were included and the amounts were chosen so as to give each currency a weight that would reflect the relative economic size of the country. This concern is also evident in the provision that the composition of the basket could be revised by the ECOFIN council every five years or, on request, if a change in weight exceeded 25 per cent. This provision was not used in 1979 although by that time some imbalances had emerged; for example the steep devaluation of the Italian lira had reduced its weight to less than one third of the DM. However, in 1984, when the drachma was added to the basket, and in 1989, when the escudo and the peseta were added, some judgemental adjustments were made which offset some of the increase in the weight of the stronger currencies that had occurred.

The weights of the component currencies are determined, at the time of recomposition, by a combination of economic criteria and other more subjective considerations. The official economic criteria are: the share of the country in the GDP of the Community, its share in intra-Community trade and its share in the EMS financial support system. These objective criteria were used in 1974 to determine the initial composition of the ecu basket. However, since 1979 they serve only as broad

---

[1] To use the US dollar, or another existing basket, such as the Special Drawing Right (SDR), was also not attractive from practical and political points of view.

[2] The unit of account of the Coal and Steel Community, the unit of account of the general budget of the Community, the agricultural unit of account and the monetary unit of account of the Community were all defined on the basis of the gold content of the US dollar, i.e., about 0.89 ounces of gold. Since the SDR had officially the same gold content as the US dollar this implied that these units of account were on a par with the SDR.

[3] Initially one EUA was also equal to about 1.2 US dollars. Both the ecu and the SDR have subsequently appreciated to about 1.4 US dollars (December 1991).

indicators as can be seen from table 6.1.1 which displays the initial amounts, the weights according to economic criteria[4] and the actual weights at the beginning of the EMS.

Table 6.1.1 The initial composition of the ecu

	Amounts in national currency	Percentage shares based on:		
		economic criteria	market exchange rates	
			09/1974	03/1979
B/LUX	3.8	10.1	8.2	9.7
DKR	0.2	3.0	3.0	3.1
FF	1.15	20.2	20.5	19.8
DM	0.83	25.0	26.4	33.0
IRL	0.0076	1.5	1.5	1.2
LIT	109.0	13.0	14.0	9.5
HFL	0.286	7.9	9.0	10.5
UKL	0.088	17.9	17.4	13.3

Source: Ungerer *et al.* (1986)

It is apparent that in 1979 the actual shares of the two strong currencies, the DM and the Dutch guilder, exceeded their economic weight (and correspondingly the shares of the weaker currencies are lower than their economic weights). According to the economic criteria the share of the DM should have been 25 per cent (in 1979), but its actual share in 1979 was 33 per cent; conversely the economic criteria gave the lira a share of 13 per cent, but its actual share in 1979 was only 9.5 per cent. The recompositions in 1984 and 1989 followed a similar pattern in that the shares of the DM and the Dutch guilder always remained well above their weights according to the official economic criteria.

Figure 6.1.1 gives a picture of the evolution of the shares over time between 1974 and the first basket revision in 1984. This figure shows how the continuing depreciation of the lira reduced its weight from initially 14 per cent to below 8 per cent in 1984. Conversely, the weight of the two strong currencies (the DM and the Dutch guilder) increased from 35.4 per cent to almost 50 per cent in 1984. These changes in the relative weights were partially corrected during the 1984 basket revision which, aside from adding the drachma with a weight of 1.3 per cent, reduced the combined Dutch guilder and DM share by over 6 percentage points but increased the shares of the French franc and the Italian lire, each by about 2 percentage points. Figure 6.1.1 shows that the 1984 basket revision corrected in most cases about one half of the changes in weight that had occurred over the preceding decade.

---

[4] Using the simply average of the three criteria calculated over the period 1979–84.

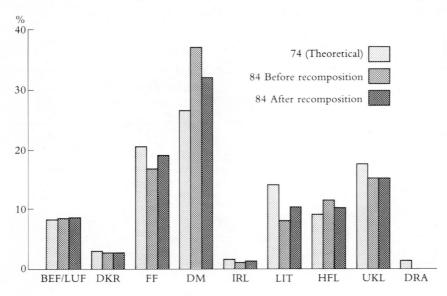

%

74 (Theoretical)

84 Before recomposition

84 After recomposition

BEF/LUF DKR FF DM IRL LIT HFL UKL DRA

Figure 6.1.1 The ecu weights (an historic overview)

The fixed-amount basket definition thus has the drawback that, in times of high inflation, it creates a need for periodic revisions if the basket is to continue to reflect some representative average performance. It would have been possible to avoid this problem by adopting another basket definition, for example the fixed-weight basket. There are several different ways in which a fixed-weight basket can be achieved in practice. One solution would be to increase automatically the amounts of the depreciating currencies and to reduce automatically the amounts of the appreciating currencies. Under this option the average exchange rate of the fixed-weight basket could be close to that of the actual ecu basket in the short run.

A further option that was not retained at the time was an 'asymmetrical' basket with a no-devaluation guarantee. A basket that would not depreciate against even the strongest currency could be obtained if quantities of the weaker currencies were added automatically in the same proportion as they depreciated whereas the amounts of the appreciating currencies remain unchanged. The hard ecu proposed by the UK as an alternative to the Delors plan is a variant of this approach (see chapter 11 for more details on the hard ecu plan). These options were rejected because they would be too cumbersome for potential private market participants.[5]

After 1984 inflation rates declined substantially so that the relative shares remained more stable, the basket revision of 1989 therefore did not have to correct for changes

[5] A third option, the average constant purchasing power unit proposed first in the All Saints Day Manifesto (see Basevi *et al.* (1975)), was not considered seriously in official circles. For a summary of early views on the potential use of the ecu in the private sector see Thygesen (1980).

that had occurred since 1984. As shown in table 6.1.2 the 1989 basket revision, which fixes the composition of the ecu until 1994, made room for the peseta and the escudo by reducing the weight of the strongest currencies in the previous basket (DM, guilder and Belgian franc), while also increasing the weight of the French franc and, in particular, the lira.

Table 6.1.2   The current composition of the ecu

	Amounts in national currency	Percentage shares based on:		
		economic criteria	market exchange rates:	
			18/09/89	21/09/89
B/LUX	3.43	6.9	8.9	7.9
DKR	0.198	2.5	2.7	2.5
FF	1.332	18.4	18.7	19.0
DM	0.624	23.8	34.8	30.3
IRL	0.0085	1.3	1.1	1.1
LIT	151.8	13.7	9.3	10.7
HFL	0.2198	8.7	11.0	9.4
UKL	0.0878	16.3	12.9	12.9
DRA	1.44	1.3	0.6	0.8
PTA	6.885	6.1		5.3
ESC	1.393	1.1		0.8

Source: Ungerer *et al.* (1990)

6.2   The official ecu: a dead end?

Although convenience of use for the private sector played a significant role in the definition of the ecu the main purpose of its creation was to provide an accounting unit for the official sector. After the creation of the EMS the ecu was supposed to be 'at the centre of the system'. It was the numéraire for the exchange-rate mechanism, the basis for the divergence indicator, the unit of account for the operations of the European Monetary Cooperation Fund (EMCF) and the means of settlement for operations arising through the system (see chapter 2). However, as described in chapter 3, in reality the use of the ecu in the EMS was limited to the operations of the EMCF so that the official ecu was effectively used only to settle transactions among EMS central banks.

Chapter 3 also describes more fully another part of the EMS agreement: that national central banks had to deposit (through automatically renewable three-months swaps) 20 per cent of the (approximate) market value of their gold and dollar reserves with the EMCF and received corresponding amounts in ecu. This is the origin of the 'official ecu'. These official ecus could be held only by EC central banks and, since 1985, by other official 'designated' institutions. The way in which these official ecus are created shows that they should not really be regarded as a currency or a reserve asset, but primarily as a book-keeping device for exchanges of the underlying US dollar and gold reserves.

The official ecu was never widely used. Holdings by non-EC official institutions (mainly the BIS and some smaller European central banks) always remained minimal. The main contribution of the official ecu was to make the large gold reserves of some member central banks more usable. However, given the large amounts of foreign exchange reserves accumulated by member central banks in the meantime, this aspect is no longer of any importance. Holdings of DM or US dollars, or, in recent years increasingly the private ecu as well as other EC currencies, remain the only usable reserves and can be more easily used in foreign exchange market interventions.

Until 1985 the official ecu had the additional disadvantage, from the point of view of the creditor central banks in the system, that balances in official ecu were not remunerated at full market rates. Holding official ecus did therefore involve a higher cost than holding other reserve assets. The central banks of the stronger EMS currencies were understandably reluctant to extend large credits in official ecu through the Very-Short-Term Facility of the EMCF when these were remunerated at an interest rate which was, at a time when capital controls kept domestic interest rates artificially low, between 3 and 4 percentage points below the rates that were paid for similar maturities in the private ecu market.

However, even after the interest rate of the official ecu was brought close to market rates in 1985, use of the official ecu did not expand because the availability of short-term financial resources on the international capital market had increased in the meantime. The official financial support system of the EMS thus became less important and was used less and less.[6]

The official ecu circulates only among central banks and cannot be exchanged against ecu held by private agents; there are thus two separate ecu circuits. This somewhat anomalous situation led to proposals to connect the two circuits.

Masera (1987b) proposed to link the private and the official ecu via an intermediary, e.g., the Bank for International Settlements (BIS). Commercial and central banks could then hold ecu deposits with this intermediary, central banks would deposit (or withdraw) official ecus whereas commercial banks would deposit (or withdraw) private ecus. This would allow central banks to use their official ecu reserves for intervention purposes by exchanging them first against private ecus via the intermediary.[7] This scheme would thus allow central banks to use their official ecus for intervention purposes without using the official financing mechanisms of the EMS. However, it did

---

[6] See chapter 4 for a discussion of intervention policy in the EMS.

[7] In a typical operation a central bank wishing to support its currency would deposit official ecus with the intermediary and would receive a deposit of private ecus with a commercial bank instead. Commercial banks would acquire a deposit from a central bank (a liability) and deposit with the intermediary (an asset). They would be willing to do this as long as the interest offered by the intermediary was just above market rates since deposits with the BIS (the intermediary) would be riskless.

not receive wide support because EMS central banks were able to accumulate large amounts of international reserves so that there was no pressing need to mobilize holdings of the official ecu. Moreover, there was strong opposition from some central banks which feared that linking the private and official ecu would lead to the creation of additional liquidity. The idea to merge the two circuits of the private and the official ecu has not been revived in the more recent debate about EMU (see part IV) because it is widely recognized that the financial support mechanism of the EMS will not need to be used as exchange rates are credibly fixed. On the contrary, some proposals have even gone as far as advocating a major reduction of the financing facilities of the EMS.[8] With EMU the two ecus will in any case be merged.

6.3   The private ecu

What is the private – as opposed to the official – ecu? It is simply a contract in which the contracting parties have denominated payment obligations in ecu and have accepted its official definition. This is the so-called 'open basket' ecu which changes composition when the official composition changes. In practice private markets have almost always used this 'open basket', instead of the 'closed basket' under which the ecu is defined as the sum of the amounts of the currencies in the basket at the time the contract is concluded. This implies that a ten-year ecu bond which was concluded before 1989, when neither the peseta nor the escudo were in the basket, has to be repaid with ecus that contain at least two new currencies.

The fact that the ecu used in financial markets is just a private contract that uses an official basket definition illustrates the interaction of the two most important determinants of the demand for the ecu, namely transactions costs and economies of scale. In a world without transactions costs there is no reason for the private sector to use the official definition of the ecu since each private contract could be based on a different, tailor made, currency basket. However, in reality this is not even taken into consideration because of the transactions costs that would arise if the basket had to be negotiated separately for each contract. Moreover, once a large number of private agents use the same unit of account, i.e. the open basket definition of the ecu, transactions costs decline as regular markets in ecu denominated instruments begin to appear.[9] The purpose of this section is to describe how this process took place.

6.3.1 The ecu in international financial markets

The ecu was not immediately a success in private financial markets when it was created as the EUA in 1975. Private use of the ecu took off only after the creation of the EMS.

---

[8] See, e.g., Ciampi (1989), p. 228.

[9] Chapter 11 provides further arguments underlining the importance of economies of scale in the use of money.

The first ecu bond issues and bank deposits came in 1981 and the amounts involved were modest. Figure 6.3.1 shows the evolution of international ecu bond issues since 1981.[10] Starting from almost nothing (213 million ecu issued in 1981) the market exploded as new ecu bond issues increased by a factor of 60 to 12.2 billion in 1985. Since 1985 growth has been more irregular and less spectacular in relative terms. More recently there has again been an expansion in overall issues, mainly led by EC governments. Figure 6.3.1 also shows that most of the issuers of ecu denominated bonds have come from the Community.

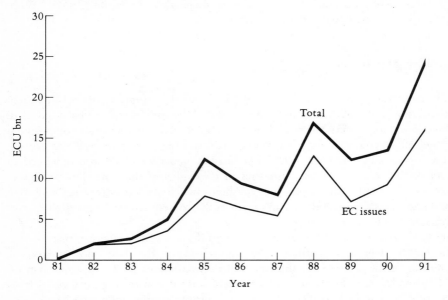

Figure 6.3.1 Evolution of the ecu bond market (international issues only)
Source: Ecu Newsletter, Instituto Bancario, San Paolo di Torino.

The sharp growth at the beginning and the subsequent slowdown can be explained if one assumes that investors desire to hold a certain proportion of their portfolio in ecus. An initial period of substantial new issues is necessary to create a certain stock of bonds. However, once this stock exists, the flow of new issues can fall to the level necessary to replace previously issued bonds that have reached maturity, while allowing for some growth in the overall size of portfolios. This interpretation is consistent with the data for the share of the ecu in the *stock* of international[11] bonds outstanding, which initially

[10] There were some bond issues in the EUA even before the ecu bond market took off; however, the available statistics start with the ecu issues.

[11] Since the ecu is a currency basket an ecu bond should always be treated as an international investment. For this reason, most discussions of the ecu use international bonds as the reference portfolio. An international (or Euro-) bond is a bond that is issued in currency that is not the currency of the country where it is issued.

also grew rapidly to reach 5 per cent in 1985, and did not decline after 1987 (see figure 6.3.2).

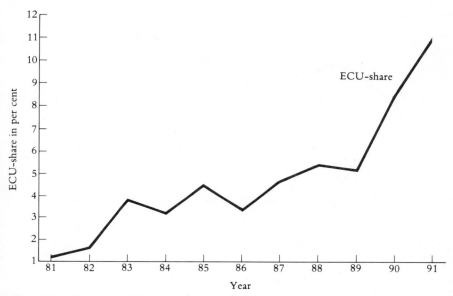

Figure 6.3.2 The share of the ecu in the international bond market
Source: J.M.M. Schofield (1991) and *European Economy*, 46, December 1990.

The use of the ecu in the banking sector follows a similar pattern. The share of the ecu in international banking (measured by the share of the ecu in foreign currency positions of banks) jumped from near zero in early 1984 to about 3 per cent in 1985. As shown in figure 6.3.3 it then continued to increase more slowly, but continuously, reaching about 4 per cent in 1990.

An interesting feature of the ecu banking market is the imbalance between assets and liabilities that is apparent in this figure. Banks can have open positions in ecu because they can cover themselves by taking the opposite position in the individual currencies that constitute the basket.[12] Since 1984–5 the share of ecu assets in total assets has continuously declined relative to the share of ecu liabilities in total liabilities. However, in absolute values banks always had more assets than liabilities in ecu (the shares behave differently because total international assets exceed total international liabilities).

This brief survey suggests that the use of the ecu in private international financial markets, which started only in 1981, increased very rapidly until 1985. By that time the ecu had become a 'significant minor Euro-currency' (Lomax (1989)). Once this base had been established growth slowed down considerably but it picked up again during

---

[12] The open positions in other currencies that are apparent from the international banking statistics are not interesting because banks presumably have offsetting positions on the national markets.

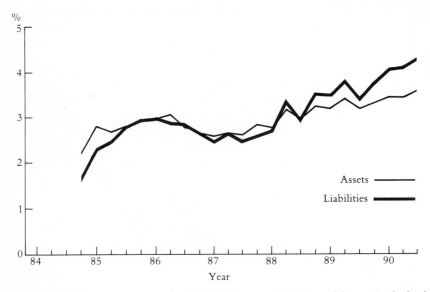

Figure 6.3.3 The ecu and the international banking market (share of the ecu in the banks' foreign currency positions *vis-à-vis* residents)

Source: BIS, Monetary and Economics Department, International Banking and Financial Market Developments, various issues (quarterly data).

1990. The ecu has therefore not yet become a major currency at the global level. In the international bond market it ranks sixth (in terms of the volume outstanding), behind the US dollar, the Swiss franc, the Japanese yen, the Deutsche Mark and the pound sterling.[13] However, if compared only to national EC currencies, the ecu already occupies third place.

Even as a Eurocurrency the ecu is 'a currency not like any other' (Girard and Steinherr (1989) and (1991)), since its yield curve is not just a simple weighted average of the yield curves of the component currencies. Because the ecu is a basket the interest rate, at a given maturity, is a weighted average of the interest rates for the component currencies. However, it is not widely recognized that the implicit weights change with the maturity of the asset considered.

Girard and Steinherr (1989) provide an exhaustive technical analysis of this point. The intuition behind it can best be illustrated by considering zero coupon bonds (i.e., bonds that do not yield any current interest payments, but just one lump-sum payment at maturity). This type of bond is equivalent to the promise to pay a certain amount of ecus at maturity. What is the value of this promise today? It is the sum of the present value of the payments in the component currencies. The crucial point is that the weak currencies depreciate more rapidly than the strong currencies; the shares of the weaker

---

[13] For more details see the contributions by Schofield and Steinherr in Johnson (ed.) (1991) and Gros (1991a).

currencies at this present value are therefore lower than their shares in the ecu measured at today's exchange rates. In the case of a short-term bond, say of three months maturity, this effect is so weak that the three months ecu rate is equal to the weighted average of the component short rates, with weights equal to the weights measured at current exchange rates. However, in the case of a long bond, say of ten years, this effect can be strong. An example (unrealistic today) may illustrate this point: if there is a 10 per cent interest differential between the DM and another currency, say the lira, the present value of the DM component is more than twice as high (per unit of the two currencies) as that of the lira component (unless a recomposition is expected to reduce the weight of the DM in the ecu). It follows that for a long bond the weight of the DM interest rate is much higher than the weight of the DM in the basket measured at current exchange rates. This is not just a technical point because it implies that in a certain sense the ecu is better than the average, the stronger currencies having more influence on long-term interest rates than the weaker currencies.

While the ecu is widely used in financial markets it has never become important as a vehicle for current transactions, notably the invoicing of international trade.[14] There exists a clearing system in ecu, which operates through the Bank for International Settlements (BIS), but it is mainly used to clear the transactions connected with the use of the ecu as a financial instrument. As a unit of account the ecu is not widely used in the private sector. This explains why most of the ecu bank activity constitutes interbank business, for example, in 1990 ecu denominated cross border bank assets were equal to 144 billion, of which only 31 billion were with non-banks.[15] However, the predominance of interbank business is a general feature of the international banking market since a similar ratio between inter-bank and non-bank business applies to all currencies.

Since 1985 there has also been considerable development in a number of derivative markets which enhance the usefulness of the basic instruments denominated in ecu. For example, it is now possible to take forward positions in the ecu, to cover interest-rate exposure. Moreover, the ecu markets have become more liquid and technically more complete attracting different classes of investors.[16] Although less spectacular than the initial growth of the ecu in the bond and banking markets, this widening and deepening of the ecu markets since 1985 might be no less important since it is crucial for the future development of the ecu as exchange-rate variability becomes less important. One sign that the ecu is overcoming the barrier of low transactions volumes and therefore high costs is that the turnover in ecu securities has increased constantly over the last few years until in 1990 the ecu accounted for over 10 per cent of the total turnover in the Euromarkets.

---

[14] The share of the ecu in foreign trade invoicing is less than 1 per cent for most member countries.

[15] For the liabilities of banks the predominance of interbank business was even more pronounced since cross border ecu deposits totalled 147 billion ecu, of which less than one tenth, i.e., 13 billion, were held by non-banks.

[16] For a survey see, for example Girard and Steinherr (1991) and Steinherr (1991).

6.3.2 The determinants of the demand for the ecu

The ecu was at first mainly used as a convenient hedge against exchange-rate variability since the diversification effect inherent in the basket nature of the ecu was especially important during the first half of the eighties, when exchange rates were much more variable than today. A number of studies (see, for example, Masera (1987a) and Jorion (1987)) therefore estimated the demand for the ecu using the standard model of the theory of finance which explains the shares of short-term assets denominated in different currencies (in a given overall portfolio) by the relative combinations of risk and return offered by the different currencies.

The riskiness of an investment in a given currency depends, of course, on the 'habitat' of the investors. For example, the risk of an investment in DM is likely to be greater for an Italian than for a German. The results of this approach depend therefore to some extent on the assumed 'habitat' of the investor. However, for most European 'habitats' the results are similar. The ecu usually emerges as an efficient financial instrument in the sense that there are no other national currencies that offer a higher return for the same risk (or a lower risk for the same return). This approach also suggests that in most Community countries the ecu should occupy a significant share in the so-called minimum variance portfolio. Masera (1987a) reports that for French residents the ecu would constitute 90 per cent of the minimum variance portfolio and for German residents the share would still be almost 25 per cent.

Most portfolio demand studies measure the risk/return combination of the ecu from the point of view of different national habitats. From this point of view the ecu is, of course, always more risky than the national currency. Girard and Steinherr (1990) take the opposite approach by analysing the demand for national currencies and the ecu from the point of view of a 'European habitat', i.e., from the point of view of an investor whose consumption basket corresponds to the ecu basket. For such an investor the ecu is, of course, less risky than any national currency. For a European investor the ecu is thus a very attractive investment vehicle.

The results of these portfolio studies, which tend to show a high weight for the ecu, cannot be taken literally since they derive from a number of restrictive assumptions and are clearly at odds with the relatively small weight of the ecu in international portfolios that was documented above. However, the portfolio approach does suggest that the ecu was a useful instrument to diversify exchange-rate risk.

While important, the diversification argument should not be overestimated. The data presented above document that despite the reduction of exchange-rate variability among the component currencies to less than one half since the early 1980s (see chapter 4) the ecu has apparently maintained its attractiveness in financial markets. Other factors must therefore have played a role as well.

One factor that tended to favour the ecu in the past was that it received preferential treatment from the French and Italian authorities because certain transactions that were prohibited under the French and Italian capital controls could be carried out if the ecu was used. In Italy, for example, forward cover of import bills could be done only via the ecu. Moreover, the public authorities and state-owned financial institutions encouraged the private ecu market by favouring the unit in their issuance of debt because they saw in the ecu a politically more acceptable alternative to the DM. In this light it does not seem surprising that the ecu markets were initially concentrated in France, Italy and the Benelux countries.

It was even argued, e.g., Kloten (1987), that these factors were the main causes for the initial success of the ecu. However, the use of the ecu in these (and other) countries actually increased even after capital markets were fully liberalized in France and Italy. In a similar vein, it appears that the German prohibition on denominating bank accounts in ecu, which was lifted only in 1987, was also not very important, as the use of the ecu in the banking sector in Germany has remained very limited even after this obstacle was eliminated.[17]

Another factor that might have been important in the beginning was the official support from the European Communities and the efforts of some private financial institutions, such as the Istituto Bancario San Paolo di Turino which recognized its potential early on. Indeed the first issues all came from institutions, whether public or private, that had an overall commitment to the European integration process. However, the fact that the European Communities use the ecu for accounting purposes and that the European Investment Bank makes regular large bond issues in ecu cannot explain the success of the ecu with private investors.

Most studies of the diversification aspect of the ecu tend to concentrate on the demand for ecu denominated instruments by investors. However, a similar diversification aspect is also operating on the supply side in the sense that firms with sales dispersed over the entire Community will also be interested in using the ecu because this allows them to reduce their exposure to exchange-rate changes. Viewed from this angle the supply of ecu denominated investments should depend on two factors: the degree of exchange-rate variability and the importance of intra-EC trade. The first factor should have the same effect on the supply and demand of ecu denominated assets, and it can therefore not explain the recent resumption of growth in the ecu market. However, the second factor might help to explain the broad pattern in the ecu markets because intra-EC trade as a proportion of GDP grew rapidly until 1985 when it fell sharply (by historical standards) for about two years. Growth resumed after this interruption, but it was initially slow (the 1985 level was overtaken only in 1989), but more recently intra-EC trade is again growing strongly.[18] This suggests that the internal market programme which should boost intra-EC trade considerably might offset in part the reduction in exchange-rate variability.[19] However, the share of

---

[17] The German currency law of 1948 prohibits the use of indexation clauses in private contracts except if the Bundesbank grants an exception. According to some interpretations of the law the ecu cannot be considered a (foreign) currency, but constitutes an indexation clause. This interpretation implies that the opening of a private bank account in ecu would have required permission by the Bundesbank. The problem did not arise for bonds because a sale of an ecu denominated bond, if it was issued abroad, did not constitute a contract between two German residents. Since June 1987, however, the Bundesbank has given a general authorization to use the ecu in domestic transactions.

[18] Intra-EC imports increased between 1981 and 1984 from 12.2 to 14.0 per cent of GDP. This ratio fell then to 13.0 in 1985 but has since increased to 14.4 per cent in 1990.

[19] Allen (1990) also stresses the point that the ecu is a standard product whose usefulness increases with the degree of integration and homogeneity of the market.

intra-EC trade in the GDP of the Community has not expanded as fast as has the share of the ecu in the international bond market.

The decisive factor favouring the ecu might, however, be the prospect that full EMU with the ecu as the single currency will come towards the end of the decade. This idea has been stressed in particular by Padoa-Schioppa (1988) who argues that switching to a new currency or a new financial instrument involves costs. Operators in private financial markets will be willing to sustain this cost only if they are convinced that there will be a return from this investment. If the ecu becomes the common currency they will have to bear this cost, which is one of the minor costs of EMU as discussed in chapter 7, at any rate. But financial institutions that start to use the ecu earlier would have the advantage of being already established in the market when the switchover to the ecu comes. This suggests that the prospect of EMU could spark off a dynamic process which leads to an increased use of the ecu well ahead of the official schedule even though the initial *reason d'être* of the ecu is disappearing.

6.4   The ecu versus the basket

In this process the ecu is gradually being transformed from a 'basket of currencies' to a 'currency basket'.[20] The most recent sign of this development is that the actual ecu interest and exchange rates do at times deviate considerably from the rate that can be obtained by investing in the bundle of currencies that constitute the ecu. Until 1990 it was always assumed that arbitrage through bundling and unbundling would limit the movements of the ecu exchange and interest rates relative to the theoretical rates. However, the more recent experience suggests that this is no longer the case. Subsection 6.4.1 documents the surprising developments in the relationship between the ecu and the basket in 1989–90 and subsection 6.4.2 speculates about the causes.

6.4.1 The ecu and the basket: recent developments

Figure 6.4.1 shows the percentage difference between the value of the ecu on the spot foreign exchange markets and the value of the basket of the component currencies. This differential will henceforth be called the *spot* differential. Each point on this figure represents the percentage difference between the cost of the basket and the ecu.[21]

Until early 1989 this spot differential was almost always below 20 basis points, which is within the range permitted by the costs that arise for banks if they 'bundle' the ecu, i.e., buy the component currencies one by one on the foreign exchange markets. However, starting in mid 1989 the ecu became cheaper than the basket by almost 50

---

[20] Padoa-Schioppa (1988) and Allen (1986).

[21] The cost is measured here in terms of the Danish krone. The choice of this currency as the numiraire is, however, irrelevant since exactly the same differential would emerge if the DM or the US dollar were taken as the unit of measurement.

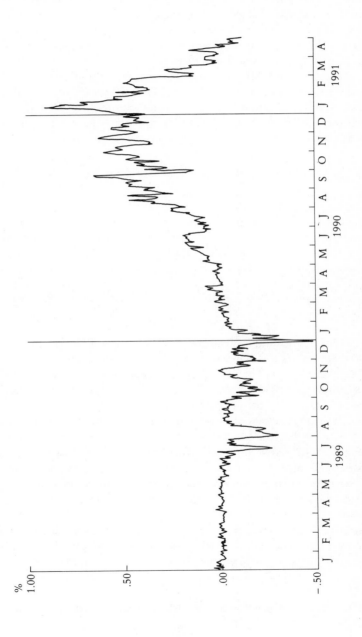

Figure 6.4.1 Foreign exchange percentage spread (market ecu minus theoretical ecu)

basis points. In the course of 1990 the situation reversed and the ecu became increasingly more expensive than the basket until the divergence reached almost 1 full percentage point in January 1991. Since then the situation has again changed and later in 1991 the value of the basket was again close to the value of the ecu. The maximum premium of the ecu relative to the basket was achieved in January 1991, and the highest discount of the ecu relative to the basket occurred in December 1989.

Figure 6.4.1 shows that the spread on the (spot) exchange-rate market is rather volatile. This impression is confirmed in table 6.4.1 which uses the standard statistical indicators of volatility and shows that the spot differential, ecu/basket, is actually twice as volatile as the DM/HFL exchange rate and about as volatile as some other intra-EMS exchange rates, such as the BF/FF or the DM/BF rates. The ecu spot differential is also almost as volatile as the FF/ECU exchange rate (but the DM/ECU exchange rate is much more volatile). At present, attempts to arbitrage the ecu *vis-à-vis* the basket are thus as risky as speculation in the foreign exchange markets.

Table 6.4.1   Volatility* of the ecu spot differential and exchange rate volatility in the EMS

ecu spot differential	DM/BF	FF/BF	DM/HFL	DM/FF	FF/ECU
12.0	14.5	14.5	5.5	19.8	16.0

Note:
* Volatility measured by the standard deviation of weekly changes. Dates: Week 46 of 1990 to week 17, 1991.

Moreover, statistical analysis (for details see Gros (1991b)) also shows that until early 1990 there was a strong tendency for the value of the ecu to go back to the value of the basket. After early 1990 this tendency becomes very weak and it finally disappears during the year. However, this divergence now appears to have been temporary; it may have been caused by the prospect that some version of the proposals to harden the ecu might be endorsed officially and implemented in the transition towards EMU. This result suggests that in 1990 the ecu did indeed become independent from the basket.

Figure 6.4.2 shows the ecu/basket *interest-rate* differential which is the difference between the interest rate on three months ecu deposits and a weighted average of the interest rates on three months deposits in the component currencies. For short-term deposits the problem in finding equivalent securities in all twelve component currencies is probably smaller than for long-term bonds; hence the three months deposit interest-rate differential might be more revealing than the data on bond interest rates that are most often used.[22] Figure 6.4.2 shows two, partially overlapping series. The series that starts in January 1989 is based on the pre-1989 basket, which does not

[22] However, the bond data show that large differences have arisen throughout the entire maturity spectrum.

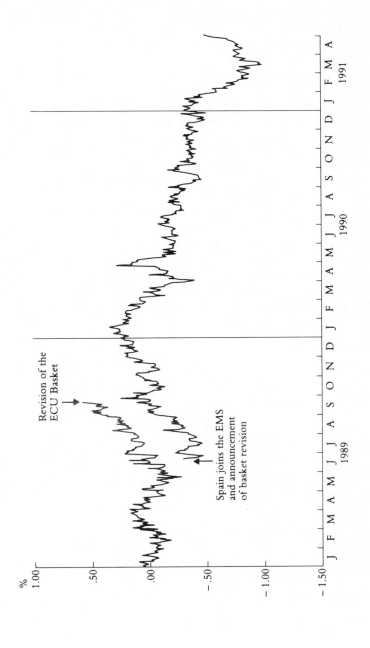

Figure 6.4.2 Short–term interest-rate spread (3 month market rate minus 3 month theoretical rate)

include the peseta and the escudo. The series that starts in September 1989 is based on the current ecu basket, which includes all twelve EC currencies.

In the case of the interest-rate differential between the ecu and the basket (i.e., between actual and theoretical ecu interest rates) it is more difficult to determine exactly at what time the differential changed behaviour because there was a large differential in 1989 that was due to the revision of the ecu basket in September of that year which was obviously anticipated by the market; before June 1989 (the earliest time for expectations about the basket revision to affect the interest rate on three months deposits) the differential was usually in the 20 basis points range. After the basket revision the differential fluctuated for some time within 20 to 30 basis points, but in early 1991 it went down to minus 1 per cent, i.e., at that time an investment in a basket of three months deposits denominated in the component currencies would have yielded almost 100 basis points more than an investment in a three months deposit in ecu.

A statistical analysis of the interest-rate differential (actual minus theoretical ecu) also suggests a growing independence for the ecu. Before early 1990 there was a strong tendency for it to return to zero, but after late 1990 this changes and in statistical terms the interest-rate differential becomes also a random walk.

Table 6.4.2 displays some comparisons of volatility. This table shows that the differential between the actual ecu and the ecu–basket on three months rates is actually more volatile than the interest-rate differential between the DM and the Dutch guilder. The volatility of the other differentials reported in that table are also of the same order of magnitude. Attempts to arbitrage the ecu versus the basket should therefore be considered as risky as speculation on these national interest-rate differentials. The second row of table 6.4.2 shows also that the variability of the ecu differential is almost as large as the variability of some of the national interest rates.

Table 6.4.2 Volatility★ of the interest differential actual ecu – basket and interest rate volatility in the EMS currencies

ecu–basket	DM–BF	FF–BF	DM–HFL	DM–FF	
6.8	7.0	9.4	5.5	8.0	
Volatility of national rates:	DM	BF	HFL	FF	ecu
	7.1	6.4	6.7	8.3	8.3

Note:
★ Volatility measured by the standard deviation of daily changes. Dates: 20/12/1989 to 16/05/1990

Some of the various hypothesis that have been advanced to explain why the ecu could become independent of the basket are based on expectations about interest rates. This implies that one would expect to find some correlation between the differential on the spot exchange market and the differentials on the different maturities on the deposit and bond markets. However, statistical analysis reveals that there is no correlation between the spot exchange-market differential and the three months deposit differential.[23]

6.4.2 Explanations for the independence of the ecu

What is the reason for this independence of the ecu from the basket? The traditional explanation was based on the transactions costs that arise in the bundling and unbundling operations, which indeed are large enough to create some independence for the ecu *interest* rate. Some simple calculations can show that the independence of the ecu interest rate from the theoretical rate (i.e., the properly weighted average of the component rates) can indeed be substantial, at least for some maturities. The direct cost of bundling (i.e., transactions cost involved in buying (or selling) the component currencies on the spot market) is estimated to be about 0.25 per cent. This implies that for three month instruments the difference between the theoretical and the actual ecu rate would have to exceed 1 per cent (per annum, obviously) before arbitrage involving the bundling and unbundling becomes profitable. This reasoning would imply that for one year instruments, arbitrage could set in as soon as the interest-rate differential reached 0.25 per cent. However, for this type of maturity other problems arise which increase the independence of the ecu rate from the theoretical rate.

Arbitrage through bundling is more difficult for longer maturities (one year and above) because there are no Euro-markets in some of the minor component currencies of the ecu. An arbitrageur wishing to replicate the ecu because the actual ecu rate is below the theoretical rate would have to invest in domestic capital market instruments which are of a different quality, have higher transactions costs and might involve a different tax regime (Euro-instruments are always free of taxation at source). This is why a substantial neutral band for the ecu interest rate remains even for the longer maturities for which the direct cost of bundling is proportionally less important.

Explanations based on the cost of bundling and unbundling operations can thus explain to some extent why there can be substantial differences between the *interest* rate of the theoretical basket and that of the ecu. However, since this reasoning assumes that the ecu is always equivalent to the basket it cannot explain why the *exchange rate* of the ecu has deviated so strongly from that of the basket. The behaviour of the spot differential can therefore be explained only if the ecu and the basket are no longer equivalent.

If private agents use the ecu in a contract they implicitly (and often also explicitly) accept the official definition of the ecu, and both parties probably assume that the value

[23] Gros (1991b) shows that there is also no evidence of any link between the differentials that have arisen in the one year, three to five years and the ten years bond markets.

of the ecu would always be the same as the value of the basket. Most private contracts provide for payment in 'ecu', which seems to exclude that the debtor could deliver the component currencies of the basket (the debtor would prefer to settle in the basket if it is cheaper than the ecu, and vice-versa for the creditor). The existing bond covenants refer to the official definition of the ecu, but do not seem even to consider the possibility that the value of the ecu could be substantially different from the value of the basket. It is therefore not clear whether or not bond holders could demand to be paid in the basket in case the basket was worth more than the ecu when the bond matured.

However, until 1988–9 the equivalence of the ecu and the basket was assured in practice since inside the ecu clearing system it was possible to deliver the basket instead of the ecu to settle outstanding liabilities that were denominated in ecu. The commercial banks that organize the ecu clearing system through the Ecu Banking Association were thus, in effect, operating a currency board. A substantial difference between the exchange rate of the ecu and that of the basket became therefore possible only once the basket and the ecu were no longer interchangeable on the interbank market. As noted first by Bishop (1991) this started to be the case in 1988–9 when the Ecu Banking Association decided, for purely technical reasons, that in the ecu clearing system payments in the basket would no longer be accepted to settle liabilities denominated in ecu. From this point onwards the ecu and the basket ceased to be interchangeable and a substantial spot differential, exceeding by far the cost of bundling, could arise.

The fact that the ecu and the basket are no longer interchangeable implies only that large differentials can arise. However, this does not explain what factors account for the actual behaviour of the spot differential since 1989, i.e., why the ecu became at first cheaper and subsequently more expensive than the basket. Bishop (1991) argues that the large supply of ecu bonds and an increased demand of ecu deposits by central banks in late 1990 might have been the key; however, this explanation is difficult to reconcile with the fact that the differential has become positive although the boom in ecu bonds continues. Further explanations are discussed in Steinherr et al. (1991), but at present it does not seem possible to find a single factor that could account for the developments of the differential since 1989.

Despite the statistical evidence that suggests that the ecu has become independent from the basket it is not likely that a very large differential can arise in practice as long as EMU remains a reasonably close prospect. The ecu is the only candidate for the common currency and when it actually achieves this status existing claims in national currencies will presumably be converted into ecu at the current market exchange rate of the basket (which is, after all, the official definition). If financial market participants expect this to happen in a not too distant future they would certainly intervene in the markets if the value of the ecu went too far from the value of the basket.

6.5   The future of the ecu

The emergence of the ecu in international financial markets came as a surprise even for the institutions that had created the unit and the precise reasons for this development are difficult to determine as discussed above.[24] The risk diversification argument cannot provide a full explanation because the fate of the ecu seems linked to the evolution of the EMS. The unit existed even before the creation of the EMS, but it took off only several years after the EMS was created. For some observers the ecu should therefore be considered just one of the financial innovations of the early 1980s; in that view it was a convenient instrument to diversify intra-EC exchange-rate risk.[25] However, the fact that the use of the ecu has not diminished, but, on the contrary, rather increased with the decline in exchange-rate variability brought about by the EMS suggests that the ecu is not only a hedge against exchange-rate risk.

Indeed in the long run the importance of the ecu can only increase since in the final stage of EMU one common currency will simply replace national currencies and because it is both now certain that this common currency will be the ecu and that the amounts of national currencies in the ecu have been frozen (i.e. there will be no further recomposition in 1994). What does this timetable imply for the spontaneous development of the ecu?[26]

Starting from the observation that the share of the ecu in more 'monetary', i.e., short-term assets held in the Community, is less than 5 per cent today, Bishop (1991) argues that this implies that the share of the ecu has to increase by a factor of twenty in the run-up to EMU. This simple point implies that some of the longer-term bonds, mortgages or other long-term contracts that are concluded at present in national currencies might in the end have to be settled in ecu. Any European who takes out a twenty-year mortgage can be almost certain to have to repay part of it in ecu. The British objections to EMU notwithstanding, it is also certain that the famous consols of the UK government will eventually be denominated in ecu.

However, the movement towards EMU will affect the ecu market well before the introduction of the ecu as the common currency. The creation of a single market in financial services will be an occasion to eliminate many of the restrictions that impose the use of the national currency for large investors, such as pensions funds or life insurance companies. These restrictions are no longer appropriate as intra-EC exchange-rate fluctuations are slowly being eliminated by the EMS making the ecu a low risk investment. A huge new market, estimated by some at 800 billion ecu (Bishop (1990)) will therefore open for the ecu when certain regulations that impose the use of the national currency for the investments of insurance companies and pension funds can also be fulfilled by an investment in ecu as proposed in a recent framework directive on non-life insurance.

A second growth phase for the ecu could therefore start well before EMU is achieved. During this phase exchange-rate variability will be progressively eliminated so

---

[24] Indeed, as shown by Bordo and Schwartz (1989) there is no precedent in history for the emergence of the ecu as a currency.

[25] See Levich and Sommariva (eds.) (1987).

[26] EMU will not only affect the domestic (European) role of the ecu. EMU will also make the ecu a major global currency, presumably on a par with the US dollar since the economic potential of the Community exceeds that of the US. The global role of the ecu that arises with EMU is discussed in chapter 9.

that the ecu will not be used because of its hedging qualities, but because it will become a convenient instrument to tap a truly European-wide capital market.

The prospect of a rapidly expanding use of the ecu and a substantial independence of the ecu interest rate raises two issues:

i)   Does this transformation of a 'basket of currencies' into a 'currency basket' imply that the ecu needs a central bank; i.e., an institution that acts as lender of last resort, organizes the payment mechanism and oversees the ecu market in the same way as national central banks do for their currencies?

ii) Should Community institutions and EC governments take measures to promote actively the use of the ecu?

The first issue, i.e., the need for a central bank for the ecu, has been debated for some time (see, e.g., Allen (1989)). The central consideration in this debate is that the microeconomic central banking functions that are lacking for the ecu (i.e., lender of last resort, assuring orderly market conditions, etc.) arise because of market failures in the commercial banking system and are therefore not specific to any particular currency. From this point of view there is therefore no need for an institution that specifically oversees the ecu market. This would be needed only if the ecu market becomes so large that shifts in the demand for ecus can affect overall national money market conditions significantly.

However, as reported in chapter 11 the size of the balances in ecu that can be considered money is at present so small (ecu deposits are equivalent to about 3 per cent of the total money supply of the Community) that this is not yet the case. This will change if the importance of the ecu in the money (as opposed to the capital) markets increases for the reasons outlined above. The need for some oversight of the ecu market will arise in the transition to EMU and is specifically foreseen as a task for the European Monetary Institute (EMI) to be set up as a temporary insitution on 1 January 1994, see chapter 12. There is therefore no need to create an institution whose sole responsibility is to be a lender of last resort for the ecu market.

The second issue involves similar considerations. Chapter 11 is skeptical of the view that a wider role for the ecu could be achieved by favouring the ecu in its competition with national currencies. However, measures to promote the ecu are nevertheless desirable because in the absence of such measures the DM might become the object of currency substitution which would endanger the anchor function of the DM in the EMS and thus endanger price stability for the entire Community, as discussed further in chapter 5. Moreover, it is anyway desirable that private operators become acquainted with the ecu as the date of the introduction of the common currency comes close.

Official measures to promote the ecu can be limited to disseminating information about the ecu and creating the legal and institutional framework for ecu markets to operate smoothly, because these are the areas where the official sector has a general role to play. The most potent measure to promote the ecu remains a speedy implementation of the timetable for EMU agreed in Maastricht. If private operators perceive that the introduction of the ecu as the common currency is certain and only a few years away currency substitution towards the DM should be limited as private operators will use the ecu to an increasing extent if the necessary markets exist.

The clarification brought by Maastricht is also reflected in financial markets. Since it is now clear that the definition of the ecu will not be changed before stage III, and since private operators can anticipate that there will be no jump in the market value of the ecu when it loses its basket character on the first day of EMU, the relationship between the ecu and the basket has now settled down. The foreign exchange spread between the ecu and the basket discussed above has almost disappeared and the short-term interest rate spread has also narrowed down considerably. However, a more substantial difference between long-term ecu interest rates and the theoretical rate based on the basket remains. The theoretical rate has been about 50 basis points below the actual ecu rate since late 1991. The fact that the theoretical rate is higher than the actual ecu rate is understandable for long-term bonds since it reflects the expectation that the ecu will lose its basket definition on the first day of the third stage. At that point the interest rate of the ecu will be determined by the anticipated policy of the European Central Bank and the inherited inflation of the full participants; it will no longer matter that some of the present component currencies which can not immediately participate in stage III retain higher interest rates.

The EMU treaty has thus in a certain sense sealed the fate of the ecu. It began in the early 1980s as a basket which was useful to insure against intra-Community exchange rate fluctuations. With the stability achieved through the EMS this aspect is now redundant. But the ecu now has a new role as the fully fledged currency of the Community under EMU.

References

Allen, Polly Reynolds (1986), 'The ecu: birth of a new currency', *Occasional Papers*, 20, Group of Thirty, New York.
(1989), 'The Ecu and monetary management in Europe', in Paul De Grauwe and Theo Peeters (eds.), *The Ecu and European Monetary Integration*, Macmillan, London, 25–55.
(1990), 'The private ecu markets: what they are, why they exist, and where they may go', *Journal of Banking and Finance*, 14 (5), November.
Bank for International Settlements, *International Banking and Financial Market Developments*, Monetary and Economic Department, Basle, various issues.
Basevi, Giorgio, Michele Fratianni, Herbert Giersch, Pieter Korteweg, Daniel O'Mahoney, Michael Parkin, Theo Peeters, Pascal Salin and Niels Thygesen (1975), 'The All Saints' Day Manifesto for European Monetary Union', *The Economist*, 1 November.
Bishop, Graham (1990), *Toughening the ecu–practical steps to promote its use*, Salomon Brothers, London, October.
(1991), *Eculand–the thirteenth member of the EC?*, Salomon Brothers, London, April p. 223.
Bishop Graham, Paolo Kind, Daniel Gros, Tim Liund, Eric Perée and Giorgio Spriano (1991), 'The ecu–to be or not to be a basket–that is the Question', a report by the macrofinancial study group of the Ecu Banking Association, Paris.
Bordo, Michael and Anna Schwartz (1989), 'The ecu–an imaginary or embryonic form of money: what can we learn from history', in Paul de Grauwe and Theo Peeters (eds.), *The Ecu and European Monetary Integration*, Macmillan, London, 1–21.

Ciampi, Carlo Azeglio (1989), 'An operational framework for an integrated monetary policy in Europe', in Collection of Papers annexed to the Delors Report, 225–32.

Girard, Jacques and Alfred Steinherr (1989), 'The Ecu: a currency unlike any other', *EIB Papers*, 10, European Investment Bank, Luxembourg, June.

(1990), 'In what sense is the ecu a low risk currency?', working document, European Bank for Investment.

(1991), 'Ecu financial markets: recent evolution and perspectives', in Alfred Steinherr and Daniel Weiserbs (eds.), *Evolution of the International and Regional Monetary Systems*, Macmillan, London.

Gros, Daniel (1991a), 'The Development of the Ecu', in Johnson, Christopher (ed.), *Ecu–The Currency of Europe*, Euromoney, London.

(1991b), 'The ecu and the basket', manuscript, Centre for European Policy Studies, Brussels.

Istituto Bancario San Paolo di Torino, *Ecu Newsletter*, Turin, various issues.

Jorion, Philipp (1987), 'The ECU and efficient portfolio choice', chapter 8 in Richard Levich and Andrea Sommariva (eds.), *The ECU Market: Current Developments and Future Prospects of the European Currency Unit*, Lexington Books, New York.

Kloten, Norbert (1987), 'Die ECU: Perspectiven monetärer Integration in Europa', *Zeitschrift für Internationale Politik*, vol. 15: 451–66.

Levich, Richard and Andrea Sommariva (eds.) (1987), *The ECU market: current developments and future prospects of the European Currency Unit*, Lexington Books, New York.

Lomax, David (1989), 'The Ecu as an Investment Currency', in Paul de Grauwe and Theo Peeters (eds.), *The Ecu and European Monetary Integration*, Macmillan, London, 119–39.

Masera, Rainer S. (1987a), *L'Unificazione Monetaria e lo SME*, Il Mulino, Bologna.

(1987b), 'An increasing role for the ecu: a character in search of a script', *Essays in International Finance*, 167, International Finance Section, Princeton, October.

Padoa-Schioppa, Tommaso (1988), 'The ecu's coming of age', in M. Nighoff (ed.), *The Quest for National and Global Economic Stability*, Kluwer Academic Publishers, Dordrecht.

Schofield, Jennifer (1991), 'Ecu bond markets and their operation', in Christopher Johnson (ed.), *Ecu–The Currency of Europe*, Euromoney, London, 1991.

Steinherr, Alfred (1990), 'Roles for the ecu in the process of achieving European Monetary Union', *The Journal of International Securities Markets*, Winter: 359–70.

(1991), 'Investing in ecu ', in Christopher Johnson (ed.), *Ecu – The Currency of Europe*, Euromoney, London.

Thygesen, Niels (1980), 'Problems for the European currency unit in the private sector', *The World Economy*, 235–64

Ungerer, Horst, Owen Evans, Thomas Mayer and Philip Young (1986), 'The European Monetary System: recent developments', International Monetary fund, Washington, DC, *Occasional Paper*, 48, December.

Ungerer, Horst, Jouko Hauvonen, Augusto Lopez-Claros and Thomas Mayer (1990), 'The European Monetary System: developments and perspectives', International Monetary Fund, Washington, DC, *Occasional Paper*, 73, November.

PART III

THE ECONOMICS OF MONETARY UNION

CHAPTER 7

WHY MONETARY UNION? COSTS AND BENEFITS

This chapter discusses the economics of monetary union to determine whether a monetary union for the Community would be beneficial on purely economic grounds. However, before analysing the costs and benefits of monetary union this chapter discusses the meaning of the term 'monetary union'. This is necessary because the two current definitions of this term (irrevocably fixed exchange rates and common currency) imply different costs and benefits. The costs and benefits of irrevocably fixing exchange rates are therefore discussed first, in section 2, whereas the additional benefits from a common currency are evaluated in section 3.

The regional distribution of costs and benefits is discussed in section 4. Finally, section 5 concludes with our personal assessment of the net overall benefits of monetary union. This assessment cannot be totally objective because, as shown in sections 2 and 3, the different costs and benefits differ so much in their nature that they cannot be aggregated into one figure.

Monetary union (however defined) implies an almost total convergence in inflation. But the concept of monetary union has no implications as to what the common inflation rate will be. Since there is now wide agreement that the future European central bank should aim at price stability it is implicitly assumed throughout this chapter that the performance of EMU in terms of price stability will be as good as that of the best in the Community at present. Chapter 13 analyses how this can be achieved and argues that this is the appropriate policy target on economic grounds. This assumption has the important implication that EMU will yield for most countries an additional benefit, namely price stability. However, since this benefit depends entirely on future policy of the European central bank it is not further taken into account in this chapter.

The collapse of the East German industry following the German monetary union is sometimes used as an argument against EMU. This particular case of an immediate economic and monetary union is analysed separately in the appendix to this chapter where we argue that the circumstances were so special that this experience cannot be used to make inferences about the consequences of EMU.

7.1 What is the meaning of monetary union? Irrevocably fixed exchange rates versus a common currency

The Delors Committee defined a monetary union as 'a currency area in which policies are managed jointly with a view to attaining common macroeconomic objectives'.[1] However, for most non-economists the meaning of 'monetary union' might be more straightforward. A European monetary union would mean a common currency. This is somewhat in contrast to the view of the Delors Committee (and that of the 1970 Werner plan) for which a common currency was not essential: indeed, for the Delors Report the principal features of a monetary union were:[2]

i)   the complete liberalization of capital transactions and full integration of banking and other financial markets; and

ii) the elimination of margins of currency fluctuation and the irrevocable locking of exchange-rate parities.

The 1970 Werner plan stated explicitly that this would make national monies perfect substitutes and therefore be equivalent to the creation of a common currency. A similar view seems to underlie the Delors Report, but is not made explicit. However, there is very little evidence for this view.

The purpose of this section is therefore to show that a system of irrevocably fixed exchange rates would behave differently from a full monetary union with a common currency.[3] This does not imply that a monetary union without a common currency could not survive with more than one monetary policy. From a macroeconomic point of view it is clear that a system of fixed exchange rates (and full capital mobility) implies that there is only one system-wide monetary policy. The arguments of this section concentrate on the microeconomic implications, or the 'fine print' of the notion 'monetary union' (which will be shown to be crucial in assuring the most important benefits).

National monies would become perfect substitutes through the irrevocable fixing of exchange rates if they became equally convenient for the three classical functions of money, namely: unit of account, store of value and transaction medium. To what extent will that be the case?

---

[1] Committee for the Study of Economic and Monetary Union, (1989) 'Report on economic and monetary union in the European Community', para. 22. To some extent this is already true of the EMS; this is why the EMS can now be considered a 'quasi-monetary union'. It is not surprising that a Committee composed mainly of central bankers should adopt such a policy-oriented definition.

[2] *Ibid.*, para. 22. An additional feature mentioned was 'the assurance of total and irreversible convertibility of currencies'. However, convertibility has not been an issue since the early 1960s when the remaining restrictions of the post-war period were eliminated.

[3] The remainder of this section draws heavily on Gros (1989c).

Unit of account

As long as national currencies continue to exist, prices in the retail trade will presumably continue to be quoted in national currencies. Consumers who are used to thinking of and comparing prices in one national currency will find it inconvenient to translate prices quoted in one currency into another at any exchange rate, if this is not a convenient round number. For consumers in, e.g., Germany, the Italian lira, or even the Dutch guilder, would therefore not be a close substitute for the DM as a unit of account.

Store of value

Financial assets denominated in different national currencies would be perfect substitutes as stores of value if interest rates were perfectly equalized across currencies. However, this is not certain to happen. As long as national currencies continue to exist, exchange-rate changes can never be ruled out even if rates are supposed to be irrevocably fixed. The credibility of the exchange-rate commitment will therefore determine the degree to which interest rates are equalized across national currencies.

The potential for interest differentials that remains, even in an environment of fixed exchange rates and free capital mobility, can be illustrated by the interest-rate differentials between the Dutch guilder and the DM. Over a period of eight years, from March 1983 to end-1990, the Dutch guilder depreciated by a total of only one-half per cent against the DM and the DM/HFL exchange rate never moved outside a corridor less than 1 per cent wide. The Dutch guilder therefore behaved, de facto, as if the allowed band of fluctuations had been less than 0.5 per cent. This might be considered a good approximation to a monetary union between these two countries. However, despite the absence of capital controls, short-term Dutch guilder interest rates were over the same period on average almost 50 basis points (and at times almost 100 basis points) higher than German mark interest rates.[4]

In the absence of complete interest-rate equalization, for example because of some doubts about the irrevocable nature of exchange-rate commitments, national currencies would therefore not become perfect substitutes as a store of value.

Transaction medium

This is the most important barrier to making national currencies perfect substitutes, even with irrevocably fixed exchange rates. For a person doing his shopping in Germany the Italian lira will not be a close substitute for the mark if he has to exchange

---

[4] This is true for assets with exactly the same risk characteristics, since the two interest rates compared here are three-month Euro rates. It is also interesting to note that, despite the existence of the Belgium–Luxembourg Economic Union, an exchange-rate guarantee for the Belgian–Luxembourg franc exchange rate costs about 25 basis points. See Giovannini (1990b) for a discussion of alternative explanations for large interest-rate differentials in the context of, ex post, stable exchange rates.

them prior to every transaction. Exchanging currency involves a cost in the form of the bid–ask spread, which would continue to exist since financial institutions would still have to use them (or foreign exchange commissions) to cover the costs they incur by holding bank notes in different currencies and having to set up several accounting systems. These costs of exchanging currencies plus the fact that over two thirds of all money is held by individuals make it improbable that large-scale currency substitution will take place.[5] Section 3 in this chapter gives more detail on these costs and shows that they can reach 2–3 per cent for small cash transactions.

The transaction costs that exist at present are unlikely to be significantly reduced through the irrevocable fixing of exchange rates since all the available evidence indicates that exchange-rate variability has only a minor effect on bid–ask spreads.[6] Market size seems to be a more important determinant of the spread, since in most European countries the spread on the US dollar is lower than on other European currencies.

Maintaining separate currencies has the additional disadvantage that it makes it practically impossible to integrate national transfer and clearing systems. A large part of the very high costs of transferring funds internationally outside the established interbank systems derives from the fact that transactions across national clearing systems have to be executed manually.[7]

These large costs of exchanging currencies would probably deter individuals from using more than one currency contemporaneously for everyday retail transactions. The Dutch case is again a useful example since, even with the very low exchange-rate variability and the large degree of commercial and financial integration between the Netherlands and Germany, there is no indication that a significant process of currency substitution has taken place in the Netherlands so far.

The evidence for the thesis that irrevocably fixing exchange rates makes national monies perfect substitutes is that there are examples of fixed exchange-rate systems in which this seems to be the case. The examples usually offered in this respect are the Belgium–Luxembourg exchange-rate union and the linkage of the Panamanian currency to the US dollar (also at 1:1). However, in these, as in other similar systems, there is always one currency that dominates the other, smaller one, which is used only locally. Moreover, the union (however unequal) consists of only two currencies, and not of the dozen that would subsist in Europe and the exchange rate is a convenient round number, i.e., one. These examples are therefore not a useful guide to what would happen after the irrevocable fixing of exchange rates in Europe.

An important practical aspect of existing unions, like the BLEU, is that they have one integrated payment system because the smaller country has adopted that of the dominant one. Since a large part of the costs of making international payments is due to the existence of different payments systems this also contributes decisively to making the

---

[5] See chapter 5 for more detail.

[6] See Boyd, Gielens and Gros (1990), Glassman (1987) or Black (1989).

[7] For a survey of the costs of making international payments for retail customers see Commission of the European Communities (1990).

two currencies equivalent for most transactions. Since it is unlikely that the existing national payment systems would be integrated in the Community before the introduction of a common currency, this obstacle to perfect substitutability will probably remain as long as national currencies exist. It would therefore be difficult to achieve the economic equivalent of a common currency by forcing banks to exchange all Community currencies at 'par', i.e., at the central rate without any allowance for bid-ask spreads or commissions as proposed in Dornbusch (1990).[8]

For all these reasons it is unlikely that the fixing (even if it is supposed to be irrevocable) of exchange rates in Europe will make national monies perfect substitutes. This result matters because it has two consequences that are economically and politically important.

i) As long as national monies remain imperfect substitutes, national money demands should remain broadly stable. This implies that there is no economically compelling reason for creating a common monetary institution. As long as there is agreement as to which national central bank is the leader, the system could work much like the present EMS: the leader, or anchor, national central bank would set its monetary stance (presumably geared to the objective of price stability, if it is the Bundesbank) and the other national central banks would just react. The stance of the leading national central bank would then be transmitted through the foreign exchange markets to the entire system.[9] The degree to which national currencies become substitutes has therefore important implications for the economic arguments for a European central bank.

ii) Most of the benefits from a monetary union will come from savings in transaction costs. (This is discussed in more detail in section 3, which discusses the benefits of going from a system of irrevocably fixed exchange rates to a common currency.) It is evident from the nature of these benefits that they could at best be only partially obtained in a system of irrevocably fixed exchange rates. But the main cost associated with a monetary union, namely the loss of the exchange rate as a policy instrument, would arise even in a fixed exchange-rate system. A system of irrevocably fixed exchange rates might therefore yield only some of the economic benefits of a monetary union while implying most of the costs.

7.2   Costs and benefits of irrevocably fixed exchange rates

In evaluating the costs and benefits of irrevocably fixing exchange rates it is crucial to define precisely the alternative or benchmark. The most natural benchmark is the EMS

---

[8] The only practical way to achieve the economic equivalent of a common currency would be to 'rebase' all currencies so that the exchange rate(s) between the new lira, mark, pound, etc. is equal to one, see Giovannini (1990a). However, it is difficult to see why this should be preferable to the introduction of a common currency. The only advantage would be that national monetary symbols could be retained.

[9] See Gros (1988) for a further elaboration of this idea.

as it has recently operated because it represents the starting point for steps towards monetary union and is a more realistic alternative than floating exchange rates which have long ceased to be regarded as desirable inside the Community.[10] The alternative to irrevocably fixing exchange rates is therefore not freely floating exchange rates, but a situation in which for most participants realignments of central rates might still occur if warranted by exceptional circumstances. This section therefore analyses the costs and benefits of formally renouncing the future use of realignments between participating currencies which member countries would have to do at the beginning of the final stage of EMU[11]

The most important implications of irrevocably fixing exchange rates are of a macroeconomic nature. This section therefore begins with an analysis of the macroeconomic implications. The first subsection deals with the general issues raised by the traditional literature on optimum currency areas and the credibility issue raised by the more recent literature on incentives for policy-makers to behave in a time-consistent manner. The second subsection deals with a number of more specific issues often raised in more policy-oriented discussions in Europe. The last subsection discusses briefly the microeconomic benefits that can be expected from a suppression of exchange-rate variability.

7.2.1 General considerations: optimum currency area and time inconsistency

Traditional macroeconomic theory suggests a general answer to the question of why realignments represent a useful policy option. If a nationally differentiated shock hits the economy the real exchange rate may have to adjust and this adjustment might be easier to achieve through a change in the nominal exchange rate than through a change in domestic wages and/or prices because the exchange rate can be moved instantaneously at the discretion of the authorities whereas domestic prices and wages adjust only slowly and under pressure from unemployment.[12]

The importance of the exchange rate as an adjustment instrument relies therefore on three elements: (i) the magnitude and nature of nationally differentiated shocks, (ii) the sluggishness of domestic prices and wages and (iii) the degree of labour mobility. However, in evaluating the exchange rate it is also necessary to consider whether other policies, especially fiscal policy, might provide an alternative adjustment mechanism.

---

[10] Since EMU would, ideally, encompass the entire Community the real benchmark would be an EMS with twelve participants and the same limited degree of exchange-rate variability as already achieved by the core of the EMS at present.

[11] Even when realignments are excluded one might envisage a limited flexibility in market exchange rates within narrow fluctuation bands such as in the present EMS. The benefits of eliminating this residual flexibility too are best seen as being of a similar nature to the introduction of a common currency. These benefits are discussed in the following section.

[12] For a survey of the literature on optimal currency areas see for example Cohen (1989).

These four points, which constitute the core of the traditional optimum currency area criterion, are now discussed in turn. The more recent time inconsistency literature is considered only at the end of this subsection.

i) Sources for nationally differentiated shocks

The traditional optimum currency area literature has never put much emphasis on the real life sources for such shocks. Usually it just assumed as an example that there was an exogenous downward shift in the demand schedule for the goods exported by the country in question (see for example Mundell (1961)). It is clear that once such a shock has occurred a real depreciation would be required to reestablish external equilibrium. But it is less clear how such a shock could materialize in the modern environment where all member countries export and import predominantly a large number of industrial products, only slightly differentiated from those of their trading partners.

It was natural for the traditional optimum currency area literature to assume that there might be shocks to the overall demand for the exports of a given country because as long as the dominant model of international trade implied that each country exports only one product (or one type of product). In this so-called Heckscher–Ohlin model imports and exports are two distinct products that differ in their respective capital/labour intensities. In contrast, the modern view of international trade (see Helpman and Krugman (1985) for a survey) stresses the importance of economies of scale and product differentiation. In this view trade develops even between countries with identical capital/labour ratios. However, this trade consists of the two-way exchange of slightly differentiated goods produced under economies of scale so that each country simultaneously exports and imports very similar goods.

The view that most trade between industrialized countries, which by definition have all similar capital/labour ratios, is based on economies of scale and product differentiation is by now widely accepted because it offers a convincing description of the huge two-way trade in manufacturing products within this group of countries.[13] Most intra-Community trade is of this 'intra-industry' type which implies that most member countries export more or less the same 'product', namely a basket of manufacturing goods coming from a large number of different industries.[14] Shocks affecting individual industries (e.g., cars or consumer electronics) are, of course, easy to imagine, but there is no reason why these shocks should be correlated across industries. To the extent that they are independent across industries they tend to cancel out in the aggregate and do not constitute an important source of shocks to the entire economy of a member country.

Unfortunately little research effort has gone into measuring the importance of country-specific versus industry-specific shocks. The scant evidence that is available, see Stockman (1988), Baxter and Stockman (1989), Emerson et al. (1991), indicates that for

---

[13] The seminal contribution on 'optimal currency areas' Mundell (1961), uses indeed an example of two regions producing two distinct products.

[14] The Heckscher–Ohlin view, based on differences in capital/labour ratios retains some relevance, however, for the trade of Greece and Portugal with the North of the Community.

most member countries the industry-specific shocks are more important than the country-specific ones. It would indeed be difficult to imagine a reason why there should be shift in demand from, say, German cars, German investment goods, German chemicals, etc. to the French (or other) versions of these same products.

Furthermore, Emerson *et al.* (1991) presents some evidence that the degree of asymmetry in industry-specific shocks is related to an index of the remaining intra-EC trade barriers. This suggests that the abolition of these remaining barriers under the internal market programme that is part of EMU, should further reduce the degree to which industries in different member countries are subject to differentiated shocks.

The view that economic integration leads to a more uniform industrial structure has recently been questioned on the basis of models in which there are agglomeration effects (see Krugman (1991)). In this view a total elimination of trade barriers can lead to more regional specialization in the sense that industries that use intensively a certain type of specialized skilled labour would tend to concentrate in one small region. This implies that increasing integration can increase the likelihood of shocks that affect an entire region. However, since this agglomeration would take place at the regional and not the national level most countries would presumably contain a number of different regions. Moreover, while there is some evidence for this view from the United States (where for example most of the automobile industry used to be concentrated around Detroit) it appears that in the Community no such process of industrial concentration has taken place so far.

Since the pattern of regional specialization is different in the Community De Grauwe and Vanhaverbeke (1991) analyse the adjustment process at the regional level in the larger member countries. They find that the dispersion of regional growth rates within member countries is considerably larger than the dispersion of national growth rates within the Community. This suggests that the primary source of shocks is regional. It follows that, since each country represents a diversified 'portfolio' of regions, the net effect of many different regional shocks at the national level is likely to be relatively minor.

The main source of nationally-differentiated (as opposed to regional or industry-wide) shocks must therefore be of domestic origin. A domestic wage explosion is an example that comes readily to mind. Having experienced such a shock, a government would come to regret an earlier commitment to a fixed exchange rate, since accommodation of the shock through realignment may entail lower costs of adjustment than the alternative of a much more gradual correction through unemployment which forces a reduction in the excessive wage level. The likelihood of such a development is difficult to assess *a priori*, but it is evident that it cannot be independent of the exchange-rate regime. Participation in EMU would be a clear signal to all participants in the labour market that excessive wage increases would have serious consequences and hence should reduce the likelihood of wage explosions for purely domestic reasons.

It is impossible to determine *a priori* to what extent participation in EMU increases domestic wage discipline. The only directly relevant evidence is the observation that, in the countries belonging to the hard core of the EMS, labour markets participants seem to have accepted this constraint. This is further evidence for the thesis that the frequency and magnitude of domestic shocks is not policy independent and especially not independent of the exchange-rate regime. The importance of domestic shocks should therefore be decisively reduced through EMU.

Shocks that affect all member countries at the same time do not constitute a rationale for exchange-rate changes unless their impact differs across countries because of differences in the structure of the different economies. Giavazzi and Giovannini (1987) estimate the extent to which this might be the case in reality, taking as an example an oil price hike. Using 1980 input–output data they find that a 10 per cent increase in oil prices raises domestic prices by between 0.3 per cent and 0.6 per cent more in the energy–importing countries than in the oil–producing countries (the Netherlands and the UK). This is a substantial difference should the oil price change (up or down) be much more than 10 per cent. However, it does not seem to be so large that it could not be overcome by wage moderation in the oil-importing countries.

The temporary increase in the price of oil that followed the occupation of Kuwait has shown that this commodity remains a major source of shocks. However, this episode did not strengthen the position of the pound, which despite its recent entry into the ERM could have appreciated considerably within the wider bands. This is an indication that the relative importance of oil (and gas) to the two Community energy exporters (the United Kingdom and the Netherlands) has been steadily declining. Future oil price changes should therefore have a much more symmetric impact. Apart from oil there are no other obvious sources of major international shocks that could affect member countries differentially.

All in all, there is no obvious source of nationally differentiated shocks requiring adjustment in real exchanges that is independent of the exchange-rate regime and of the ongoing progress of integration.[15]

ii) Nominal versus real exchange-rate adjustment

The second condition for making realignments a useful policy option is that changes in nominal exchange rates lead to changes in competitiveness and are not offset by domestic inflation. The extent to which changes in nominal exchange rates lead to changes in real exchange rates is analysed in Emerson et al. (1991), where it is found that the correlation is strong in the short run, but weakens considerably over longer time spans. This result is entirely compatible with modern macroeconomic theory which emphasizes that changes in the nominal exchange rate should have only temporary effects. It implies that a devaluation can only accelerate the adjustment in response to a shock if the private sector accepts the need for a real depreciation or a reduction in real wages. If the reduction in real wages is resisted, domestic inflation quickly offsets the initial gain in competitiveness.

---

[15] So far the discussion has assessed the importance of the exchange rate as an adjustment mechanism with the implicit assumption that the benchmark is an idealized EMS, inside which exchange rates move only because of realignments (and realignments take place only if justified by real shocks). However, if freely floating exchange rates were to be taken as the benchmark, locking exchange rates irrevocably would have the benefit of eliminating the macroeconomic shocks caused by unwarranted exchange-rate movements, i.e., the so-called misalignments.

The crucial question is therefore whether the adjustment to a negative shock is hindered because real wages are not allowed to fall or because there is 'money illusion' that allows a reduction in real wages only through an increase in prices at unchanged nominal wages, but not directly through a reduction in nominal wages. In the case of 'real wage' rigidity there is little point in using the exchange rate as a policy instrument.

It is widely assumed that wages and prices are slow to adjust because they are often fixed in nominal terms. But this casual evidence is not conclusive because wage indexation can also lead to rigidity in real wages. Italy (and other countries) discovered this after the two oil shocks, when the Italian wage indexation scheme did not allow real wages to fall. Successive devaluations did little to restore competitiveness until the indexation mechanism was finally reformed in the mid 1980s. Once this was done real wages did show some flexibility in Italy as reported in Giavazzi and Spaventa (1989).

All that can be said in confidence is therefore that wages and prices change more slowly than exchange rates. From a theoretical point of view it is clear that the slower adjustment speed through movements in prices and wages is more important in the case of temporary shocks. In the case of permanent shocks adjustment takes place anyway after some time and the disadvantage of a slower adjustment is somewhat offset by a lower variability in domestic inflation. In reality, however, the advantage of realignments over adjustments in domestic prices and wages is offset even in the case of temporary shocks by the unavoidable time lag between the occurrence of the shock and the appropriate policy reaction.

Moreover, modern macroeconomic theory points out that, since monetary expansion and devaluation are at their most effective when least expected, the short-term rewards of breaking the fixed exchange-rate commitment would actually increase after the declaration of an intention to keep the rate irrevocably fixed.[16] This suggests that governments may have, or discover, incentives to opt out of the exchange-rate commitment in order to pursue macroeconomic objectives. Governments that see *a priori* the remaining scope of action as too narrow will perceive a likely cost in joining EMU. However, that cost can be offset by benefits through the mechanism described under point (v) below.

The effectiveness of the nominal exchange rate in producing changes in competitiveness depends also on the degree of openness of the economy as emphasized by McKinnon (1963). If trade constitutes a large fraction of GDP, changes in the exchange rate become less powerful in affecting competitiveness because imported goods, whose prices change directly with the exchange rate, make up a large part of the overall price index. McKinnon (1963) argues therefore that for a small country frequent use of the exchange rate as an adjustment tool would destabilize the domestic price level. In this sense small countries might prefer to use alternative adjustment policies, such as fiscal policy to which the discussion will return after reviewing an adjustment mechanism that in some cases might work automatically.

There is little systematic evidence on the effectiveness of changes in the nominal exchange rate to accelerate the adjustment to shocks (as opposed to being an additional

---

[16] See Wihlborg and Willett (1990).

source of shocks). It is often argued (e.g., Eichengreen (1989)) that the fact that the variability of real exchange rates among EC member countries (or even among the EMS participants) is higher than that of 'real exchange rates' among regions of the United States shows that adjustments in nominal exchange rates are still needed in the Community. However, the greater variability of real exchange rates within the Community could also be interpreted as the result of a greater variability of nominal exchange rates (which are fixed among regions of the United States). De Grauwe and Vanhaverbeke (1991) come closer to measuring the importance of nominal exchange rates for the adjustment process by looking at the correlation coefficients between regional growth rates and regional real exchange rates within member countries. They find, somewhat surprisingly, that this correlation is significant which suggests that inside member countries prices and wages can react at the regional level to facilitate adjustment to the regional shocks which were discussed above. An even more surprising result is that the correlation between national growth rates and real exchange rates is much weaker than that at the regional level. It would, of course, be going too far to argue that this particular result suggests that the exchange rate is less important as an adjustment instrument among countries than among regions, but the evidence from the regional data shows that adjustments of prices and wages at the regional level can be an important adjustment mechanism in a monetary union.

iii)   Labour mobility

The traditional literature on optimum currency areas also stressed that if domestic prices and wages were slow to adjust workers could leave the regions hit by adverse shocks. Labour mobility could thus mitigate the unemployment problems that are caused by the limited flexibility of wages. Although we have argued in the preceding two sections that there is little evidence for wage stickiness in the long run and that there are reasons to believe that country specific shocks are much less important than industry or region specific shocks it might still be useful to discuss to what extent the Community satisfies this criterion for an optimal currency area.

Most studies agree that labour mobility among the member states of the Community is much lower than the mobility of labour across regions of the United States. This is used by some authors (see for example Eichengreen (1991)) as evidence for the view that the Community is not an optimum currency area unless EMU is supplemented by an important fiscal transfer mechanism that can alleviate the political problems that would arise from high unemployment in member countries that are hit by adverse shocks. The issue of a Community fiscal 'shock absorber' is discussed in chapter 8; at this point it is sufficient to come back to the observation that regional shocks are more important than national shocks. This suggests that regional labour mobility should be more important than mobility across member countries. De Grauwe and Vanhaverbeke show that this is indeed the case since they find that movements of labour between regions (but inside countries) are more than ten times as important as migration between member countries. They also note that interregional labour mobility is strongest in the Northern member countries which also have the lowest dispersion of regional unemployment rates. This suggests that regional labour mobility can indeed be an important adjustment mechanism, but it does not seem to operate with the same strength in all member countries.

iv) Fiscal policy as an alternative adjustment tool

The overall fiscal policy issues raised by EMU are surveyed in chapter 8. This brief subsection is therefore limited to the discussion of whether fiscal policy represents an alternative to exchange-rate adjustments in the face of temporary shocks because a fiscal stimulus could alleviate the fall in demand that results if domestic prices do not fall fast enough.[17] Theoretically it should always be possible to maintain full employment through the proper use of fiscal policy; however, this would have side effects and therefore involve other costs. For example, an expansionary fiscal policy in a country hit by an adverse shock to its export earnings would create a current-account deficit for that country and would also have spill-over effects on demand in the other EMU member countries, as well as the rest of the world.

It seems impossible to determine *a priori* to what extent fiscal policy could be used to offset the loss of the exchange rate as a policy instrument because the international spill-over effects of fiscal policy and its effects on the current account depend on a number of other factors. As shown by Frenkel and Razin (1987) it matters a lot whether additional expenditure falls on tradables or non-tradables, whether an increase in expenditure is bond or tax financed and whether it is temporary or permanent.

A quantitative assessment of the effectiveness of fiscal policy has therefore to be based on existing macroeconomic models. Such assessments have been attempted by Emerson *et al.* (1991) and Masson and Melitz (1990). The result of these simulations is that fiscal policy can indeed eliminate output losses that result from wage rigidity, but it would also lead to larger current-account imbalances within EMU. However, since one of the advantages of EMU is to make current accounts less visible it is not clear to what extent the latter effect can be regarded a real cost. Even under EMU fiscal policy would thus remain effective enough to offset potentially the effects of adverse shocks on national economies.

v) Time inconsistency considerations

The benefits of irrevocably fixing exchange rates are the same as those underlying the 'disciplinary device' view of the EMS (see chapter 4), only more unambiguous. Modern macroeconomic theory implies that a government which explicitly wants to retain freedom to realign its exchange rate (or a government whose commitment to fix the

---

[17] In welfare theoretic terms, however, fiscal policy can only be a second-best adjustment tool becuase it can only alleviate, but not remove the distortion in relative prices that arises when wages are slow to adjust. This is only partially reflected in the results referred to above which show that fiscal policy can produce the same outcome, in terms of inflation and unemployment, as a devaluation if the government is willing to tolerate a higher deficit.

rate remains subject to some doubt) pays a price. Agents in the national markets for goods, labour and financial assets will assume that such a freedom of manoeuvre will occasionally be used. They will tend, in an economy whose currency could become subject to devaluation, to set a more rapid rate of increase of prices and costs and to add a risk premium to the required yield on assets denominated in the national currency. Higher inflationary expectations would raise actual inflation and nominal interest rates.

If the exchange rate in fact remains fixed, there will be temporarily higher inflation and lower output than in the situation where the commitment to fixity has been seen as truly irrevocable. If the currency is in fact devalued, the critical perceptions of private economic agents will have been borne out and a non-inflationary reputation will be that much harder to build up in the future.[18] As the EMS experience has shown, markets have a very long memory. For EMS member countries the irrevocable fixing of exchange rates would thus still yield a benefit because it would eliminate the residual uncertainty that is evident in the substantial interest-rate differentials that persist even between currencies that have long been managed in a stable way, like the DM and the French and Belgian francs.

For a country in which the anti-inflationary reputation continues to be questioned there is therefore no substitute for the irrevocable locking of the exchange rate in achieving full convergence in interest rate and inflationary expectations. In the parlance of the time inconsistency literature, irrevocably fixing exchange rates signals a change in the regime which can eliminate the doubts of financial and other markets about the anti-inflationary credibility of the government and can therefore drastically accelerate convergence, especially in financial markets.

vi) *Summary of the general considerations*

The discussion of this section suggests that in general macroeconomic terms the basic cost-benefit assessment of irrevocably fixing exchange rates has to weigh (1) the cost of giving up the possibility of accommodating exogenous[19] nationally differentiated, major and non-transitory shocks, against (2) the benefit of more definitively strengthening confidence in the long-run predictability and stability of the price level. Moreover, one has to take into account that fiscal policy can provide an important, but somewhat imperfect, adjustment mechanism. The verdict on how the balance between (1) and (2) comes out for any particular participant must necessarily be subjective, since it depends on the likelihood of future shocks and the degree of credibility of national political

---

[18] This was recognized by the Delors Report when it says, in para. 22 that the pace with which convergence in inflationary expectations and interest rates takes place will 'depend critically on the extent to which firms, households, labour unions and other economic agents were convinced that the decision to lock exchange rates would not be reversed'.

[19] For one major category of shocks to a participating economy, changes in domestic economic policy that make the fixed exchange rate unsustainable, there is clearly no independence of the exchange-rate regime. In EMU policy shocks would be limited to those that do not threaten to upset fixity.

institutions.[20] All that can be said in confidence is that the balance between costs and benefits must have shifted significantly in favour of the latter as the likelihood of nationally differentiated shocks within the Community is reduced while the benefits of full convergence of interest rates and of inflationary expectations at a low level become more clearly perceived.

7.2.2 European policy issues

Against the general background of the previous subsection it may be useful to examine some of the more specific arguments advanced for retaining the exchange rate as a policy instrument. They draw largely on the macroeconomic theory of the 1960s and 1970s, on the relative merits of fixed versus flexible exchange rates and on criteria for delimiting optimal currency areas. Though they may all be regarded as variants of the above general principle for deciding upon the exchange-rate regime, they still need to be addressed since they are bound to appear in the national debate on EMU in several of the prospective participating countries. They also tend to place the debate on EMU more squarely in the environment facing the European economies in the 1990s than in the more general and ahistorical context of the discussion so far in this chapter. Realignments of central rates have been seen as desirable on the following grounds:

i)   to accommodate residual differences in the *autonomous* elements affecting national inflation rates
ii) to modify the real exchange rate as part of a current-account adjustment;
iii) to accommodate international portfolio shifts that affect participating currencies differentially; and/or
iv) to enable some participants to continue to make use of an inflation tax.

We examine each of these propositions below:

i)   As documented in chapters 3 and 4 inflation differentials have narrowed sharply between EMS participants since the early 1980s. Most notably, disinflationary policies in France and, to a lesser degree, Italy have reduced the rate of increase in unit labour costs to nearly the rates observed in Germany and the Netherlands.[21]

   While it was accepted in the early 1980s as an inevitable legacy of the turbulent decade of 1973–82 that inflation rates were likely to remain trend-wise higher in Italy and France than in Germany regardless of major policy efforts to reduce them (and had to be accommodated by occasional and rather sizeable realignments) there

---

[20] Obviously the level at which exchange rates are set initially would also have to be appropriate, see chapter 5 for a discussion of the current constellation of exchange rates in the EMS.

[21] The arguments here have adopted the perspective of EMS participants with insufficient anti-inflationary credentials. Since EMU aims to be consistent with the best past price behaviour, there should in principle be no cost in terms of higher average inflation for the lead group in price performance. Whether that assumption is likely to prove correct, and what could be done to make its achievement more likely, is discussed in chapter 11.

is in retrospect today a realization that observed inflation differentials over that decade were largely the result of divergent policy responses. In some cases this was a clear policy choice, in others a consequence of wage indexation, that imparted a strong inflationary bias to some European economies following the global inflationary boom of the early 1970s and the first oil-price shock. Differences in vulnerability to external price shocks due to different production structures and energy input requirements, or to the composition of foreign trade, appear to have been much less important than the secondary effects for which policies were largely responsible. Observed divergences in inflation should therefore not be considered as an autonomous force, but as phenomena that could have been avoided with a different policy response.

Could the divergence in permissiveness with respect to domestic inflationary mechanisms be attributed to different degrees of aversion to inflation or to differences in the perception by national policy-makers of the attainable unemployment–inflation trade-off? These views, too, have been weakened by the experience of the 1980s. The trade-off turned out to be less unfavourable than expected in the high–inflation countries; and the reduction of inflation has been given higher priority in economic policy in all EMS countries after the absorption of the second oil-price shock. The argument that nominal exchange-rate changes are required to accommodate residual, small but cumulatively important inflation differentials which are largely unavoidable is accordingly today of much less significance than earlier assumed.

ii) The experience of 1982–7, when the German economy tended to grow more slowly than the rest of the Community, led to the fear that some trend changes in real exchange rates might be necessary even in the long run to accommodate differences in growth rates of capacity outputs. It was also observed that, even with identical trend growth rates in productive capacity, differences in income elasticities in the foreign trade of participants are potential sources of external and/or internal imbalances in the long term. If, say, France and Italy want to grow faster than Germany, for demographic or other reasons, *or* if the income elasticity in the world demand for German-produced goods is above those for French- and Italian-produced goods, some trend-wise real appreciation of the DM against the other two currencies might be warranted.

Empirical evidence supporting this view can be found, e.g., in Vona and Bini-Smaghi (1988). This study finds systematic differences in income elasticities in foreign trade within the EC, suggesting that France would face trend-wise deterioration of its trade balance at growth rates of domestic demand equal to Germany's. Furthermore, differences in labour-force growth between, on the one hand, France, Italy and Spain (which, in addition, presently have relatively high unemployment), and, on the other hand, Germany suggest that the former three would need to grow faster than Germany. According to the usual models of international trade this would require a continuous real appreciation of the DM *vis-à-vis* these other currencies.

German unification has eliminated the concern that the German economy is bound to grow more slowly than the rest of the Community.[22] This event, coupled with the other developments in the eastern part of Europe, has now encouraged the perception that Germany might grow faster than the rest of the Community for an extended period. But since it is widely assumed that Germany will profit more from the expected overall increase in the demand for investment goods induced by the reconstruction of Eastern European economies, the fear of the need for a trend-wise real appreciation remains, albeit for a different reason.[23]

The strongest evidence against this view is that there is no persistent correlation between trends in real exchange rates and trend growth rates[24] as implied by the above reasoning on relative demand growth and income elasticities.

Theoretical models of intra-industry trade, which more adequately describe the nature of the trade between member countries, imply that differences in trend growth rates can be accommodated without any need for changes in the real exchange rate.[25] In trade between the potential members of an EMU there are no permanently acquired comparative advantages; the pattern of specialization is marked primarily by increasing returns in the production of a wide range of industrial goods. Faster growth in output and exports can therefore be achieved at unchanged exchange rates through the creation of new products, rather than through higher sales of existing products as assumed in the models of international trade used in most macroeconomic forecasts.

This view implies that changes in nominal and real exchange rates are not needed to reach a long-run equilibrium. Empirically this shows up, as the work of Krugman (1989) demonstrates, in a long-run positive correlation between these two determinants of the trade balance: countries with above average growth also tend to face high income elasticities in the world demand for their products, creating some automatic offset in the long run between the two.

In a similar vein, but focusing on the medium run, it has been argued that when the participants collectively adjust their external position *vis-à-vis* the United States some intra-European exchange-rate adjustments are unavoidable, given the very different starting positions. Although the US external current-account deficit has already started to fall it may still have to be reduced further, by about $100 billion over a fairly short span of years, to make the US external debt position sustainable.[26] A substantial part of the counterpart to this adjustment will have to

[22] See chapter 5 for a brief analysis of the likely impact of German unification on the EMS.

[23] See Begg *et al.* (1990).

[24] See Emerson *et al.* (1991), chapter 6 for further evidence.

[25] See Gros (1986) and Krugman (1989).

[26] To eliminate the US current deficit fully, a swing of about US dollars 200 billion would actually be required, but a modest deficit may be sustainable. Cline (1989) has, using a model of world trade and macroeconomic interaction, calculated a so-called 'Feasible Adjustment Package', consisting of fiscal tightening in the US, faster growth in Europe, Japan and the East Asian economies, and real depreciation for the dollar differentiated by country, which would achieve an apparently sustainable constellation of current-account imbalances. The package envisages substantial intra-European realignments, e.g., a 17 per cent devaluation of the French franc *vis à vis* the DM and even larger adjustments for the Italian lira and for sterling (from their end 1989 levels).

show up as a deterioration of the current accounts of potential EMU participants. Could this large adjustment – even though it may lead only to a small collective deficit by the early to mid 1990s – be made without realignments? If not, should the decision to fix exchange rates irrevocably at least wait for this adjustment to be completed?

These arguments are all specific examples of the generic 'real shocks' referred to in the previous subsection. It was argued there that a realignment does not always present the best policy option in the case of real shocks. These arguments apply in these specific examples as well and need therefore not be repeated here in detail. But there are also two specific 'European' reasons for the position that neither the trend-wise arguments on imbalances, nor the more transitory need for adjustment to a reduced US deficit, justify continued reliance on nominal exchange-rate changes within Europe.

The first, and most important is that the price elasticities in the foreign trade of European countries – though large enough to meet the minimum stability conditions – appear simply to be too low to be relied upon to bring about a major part of the projected adjustment. If they were to be used with that purpose in mind, realignments would have to be so large (estimates go up to 20 per cent, see note 26) that they would more permanently upset the results of inflationary convergence and monetary cohesion which have been laboriously achieved in the EMS since 1983. The bulk of the adjustment will have to come from other policy instruments and from the more indirect impact on imbalances of long-run market-oriented processes. Furthermore, in an EMU, temporarily large external imbalances will be more readily financeable.

The second reason is that the experience of some EMS countries suggests that real effective exchange rates do change to some extent independently of the policy of pegging to other EMS currencies (see De Grauwe and Vanhaverbecke, (1990)). For example, Belgium has improved its competitive position (measured by relative unit labour costs) by approximately 10 per cent in the 1983–9 period while the Belgian franc was broadly stable in the EMS. In contrast the competitiveness of Denmark has deteriorated by 10 per cent over a similar period and in spite of a similar nominal exchange-rate policy.

In summary, the cost of not being able to facilitate through realignments the real exchange-rate changes that might become necessary in the foreseeable future cannot be dismissed as insignificant, but it is smaller than the traditional literature assumes. Furthermore, much of it has already been incurred in the current EMS with gradually diminishing recourse to realignments since 1983.

iii) The experience of the EMS is sometimes used to warn that international portfolio shocks may affect national currencies differentially, because the latter do not have a similar degree of international acceptability. Initially in the EMS the role of the DM as the only internationally used currency in the system was seen as justifying occasional realignments, as the global demand for DM assets appeared to grow faster than the demand for assets in other EMS currencies. Historically portfolio shifts out of the dollar on several occasions determined the timing of EMS realignments (see chapter 4).

This historical asymmetry, though clearly weakening with time as financial markets developed outside Germany, capital controls were removed and economic convergence improved, may have persisted in a mild form until recently (see Giavazzi and Giovannini (1989)). However, with the total elimination of capital controls in July 1990 and the growing sophistication of national capital markets in France and Italy there is no reason to expect that this asymmetry will continue. The improved competitiveness of newer financial centres in Europe has rectified much of any initial imbalances and the experience in 1990-1 suggests that movements in the value of the US dollar do no longer produce tensions in the EMS.

At any rate, locking exchange rates permanently would bring benefits rather than costs in this respect. Under irrevocably fixed exchange rates assets denominated in the participating currencies would become much closer substitutes than in the past, thus removing major incentives to shifting between them; and they would become fully substitutable by definition after the introduction of a common currency. It was never an optimal response to financial disturbances to adjust exchange rates within the EMS, though it was occasionally seen as necessary or as providing a useful occasion for triggering realignments which were basically justified by other factors. Accommodating portfolio shifts through coordinated intervention and stabilization policies is a superior method of adjustment because it distributes the impact of the shock over the entire area.[27] And in the final stages of EMU this source of shock would be absorbed more efficiently than in any intermediate stage in which national currencies are still in existence.

iv) As already mentioned in chapter 5 several economists, in particular Dornbusch (1988), have argued that there are important public finance arguments for allowing significant differentials in national inflation rates. Within an EMU, governments in Italy, Spain, Portugal and Greece would find it hard to compensate, through increases in other taxes and/or by cutting expenditures, for the seigniorage gains they have made in the past decade and a half of relatively high inflation.

This argument was already analysed in more detail in chapter 5 where it was found that on closer examination much of the alleged cost of exchange-rate fixity turns out to be of secondary importance. Seigniorage was exceptionally large in the decade of 1975–85. It has already been very significantly reduced and the remaining potential loss is of the order of ½ per cent to 1 per cent of GDP for Italy and Spain and about twice that for Portugal and Greece.

Moreover, it should be kept in mind that, regardless of whether exchange rates are irrevocably fixed or not, the scope for extracting seigniorage would be narrow, as financial integration forced those countries that operate relatively high reserve requirements (and/or pay low interest on such reserves) to reduce this tax on their

---

[27] Advocacy of tighter management of the global exchange-rate system, is also primarily motivated by the observation that in today's world financial disturbances tend to be more important than real disturbances. As argued above it is primarily with respect to the latter that preservation of exchange-rate flexibility can be justified.

banking systems. Gros (1989a) and Emerson *et al.* (1991) provide estimates of the effects of financial market integration on seigniorage revenues. These estimates indicate that only about one half of the overall reduction in seigniorage revenue through EMU can be ascribed to the reduction in inflation, which is the only direct consequence of irrevocably fixing exchange rates. The other half has to be imputed to economic factors, i.e., the 1992 programme to which these countries are committed independently of the progress towards monetary union.

On the whole, the issue of the need for revenue from seigniorage does not provide a justification for high and differentiated inflation rates.

The four specific arguments advanced in favour of retaining use of realignments as a policy instrument for macroeconomic adjustment do not appear to be decisive. One of them (portfolio shifts) in fact points to benefits from locking exchange rates. Two others carry limited weight (accommodation of residual autonomous inflation differentials, seigniorage gains) given the convergence that has already taken place in inflation rates among those who have participated in the EMS for some time and the pressures from integrated financial markets.

Only the loss of the potential to influence competitiveness through changes in the nominal exchange rate may qualify as a potentially major cost in the historical context of the adjustment of the European economies in the 1990s. But in this context realignments would in any case have to play a minor role relative to other methods of adjustment, while financing of external imbalances would be more easily sustainable.

7.2.3 Microeconomic benefits from fixing exchange rates

The discussion in this section so far has examined the (macroeconomic) costs of irrevocably locking exchange rates while arguing that these costs have already to some extent been incurred by participants in the present EMS and that time is working to reduce them. However, locking exchange rates yields also microeconomic benefits.[28]

The expectation of important microeconomic benefits from a reduction in exchange-rate variability is based on the idea that more exchange-rate variability makes trade more risky. Stabilizing exchange rates should therefore increase trade and hence the standard gains from trade. This idea is explored in a large empirical and theoretical literature that analyses the effects of exchange-rate uncertainty on trade and on direct investment.

The theoretical literature indicates that exchange-rate variability has a negative impact on trade only if the risk generated by unstable exchange rates cannot be hedged or at least priced in efficient financial markets. If exchange-rate risk can be hedged increased exchange-rate variability could even increase trade.[29] This suggests that the

---

[28] No effort seems to have been made so far to integrate the results of the more macroeconomic literature that show that exchange rates tend to be more volatile than justified by the fundamentals (see for example, Gros (1989b)) with the more microeconomic literature discussed in this subsection.

growing sophistication of international financial markets, especially in those EMS countries that had capital controls, should gradually lessen and perhaps eventually eliminate any influence of exchange-rate variability on trade.

The empirical literature also does not find a strong influence of exchange-rate uncertainty on trade. Most of this literature uses US dollar exchange rates and might therefore not be directly applicable to the European experience where exchange-rate fluctuations never had the same amplitude. A survey by the IMF (see International Monetary Fund (1984)) reports that the empirical results are not conclusive. The only studies which report a significant impact of exchange-rate variability on intra-EMS trade are Bini-Smaghi (1987) and De Grauwe (1987).[30] Since the EMS has reduced exchange-rate variability of the intra-EMS exchange rates, the results of these studies would imply that the EMS has indeed had a positive impact on the volume of intra-EMS trade.

This result is somewhat surprising in view of the fact that the trendwise growth in intra-EMS (and in general intra-EC) trade slowed down for a number of years in the early 1980s, despite a large observed reduction in exchange-rate variability.[31] The slower growth of intra-EMS trade in the 1980s, relative to the 1960s and 1970s, would then have to be explained by the fact that, during the earlier period, the creation of the Common Market had a strong positive impact on intra-European Community trade, which has been absent in the 1980s. This represents a qualitative change in the trading environment that is not explicitly accounted for in empirical studies that are only concerned with the impact of exchange-rate changes, relative income trends and exchange-rate variability on trade flows. This might explain why a more recent study, see Sapir and Sekkat (1990), does not find evidence for the view that the EMS did stimulate trade.

Moreover, the positive effects of the EMS implicit in the results of the studies that do report a significant effect, are small in absolute terms. Eliminating the remaining intra- EMS exchange-rate variability would lead to an increase in intra-EMS trade of less than 1 per cent. Chapter 4 showed that exchange-rate variability in the EMS has already been reduced to one fourth of the level of the late 1970s. This implies that the effect of suppressing the residual degree of exchange-rate uncertainty can be expected to be much smaller than 1 per cent, if the above estimates are taken at face value. Fixing rates irrevocably should increase intra-EMS trade only by less than 0.25 per cent. This suggests that steps other than exchange-rate stabilization *per se*, notably the internal market programme, may be more important to the promotion of intra-European trade.

Nevertheless it may be misleading to take the estimated impact of exchange-rate stabilization as a reliable indication of the likely effects of full monetary union. Such a step would imply a qualitative difference in the environment within which intra-European trade and investment takes place. Effective minimization of both shorter-term

---

[29] For an explanation of this seemingly counterintuitive result see Gros (1987) and Emerson *et al.* (1991), chapter 3.

[30] Bini-Smaghi (1987) analyses trade between Italy, France and Germany. De Grauwe (1987) analyses trade among EMS members and trade of the latter with third countries.

[31] See chapter 4 and the discussion in Jacquemin and Sapir (1987).

variability and longer-term misalignment within a European currency area is likely to have effects that go well beyond what is measurable on the basis of past experience with a gradual tightening of the EMS. We return to this subject in section 7.3.2 below.

These benefits of irrevocably fixed exchange rates are still – despite the absence of realignments in the EMS since 1987 – some way from being realized. Nor is it obvious that they could be realized fully without the additional step of introducing a common currency to underline the definitive nature of EMU and eliminate the inconveniences that would remain in managing an economically and financially integrated area with separate national currencies. The benefits of irrevocably fixing exchange rates may in themselves already be sufficiently substantial to offset the costs outlined above. But the move to a common currency would more decisively shift the balance of costs and benefits in favour of the latter. Hence these benefits are reviewed in the following section.

7.3 Additional benefits from a common currency

The irrevocable locking of exchange rates eliminates exchange-rate variability, so what additional benefits can one expect from a common currency? The introductory section about the meaning of the term 'monetary union' has already discussed in what respects a system of irrevocably fixed exchange rates differs from an area with a common currency. That section argued that transaction costs and the impossibility of making the 'irrevocable' commitment to fixed exchange rates totally credible constitute the main difference between irrevocably fixed exchange rates and a common currency. This section shows that this difference implies that the introduction of a common currency yields significant additional benefits. Since these benefits come from a variety of different effects it is convenient to deal separately with the following five sources of benefits from a common currency.

7.3.1 Elimination of transaction costs

The most obvious reason for expecting significant economic gains from the introduction of a common currency is that this is the only way to totally eliminate all exchange-rate related transaction costs. Since exchange-rate variability has only a small impact on bid-ask spreads (see above) merely fixing exchange rates is not sufficient to significantly reduce these transaction costs. These direct benefits from a common currency can be estimated by calculating the sum of all the transaction costs (i.e., bid-ask spreads and other commissions on foreign exchange-rate transactions) that arise in intra-Community transactions.

In practice it is not straightforward to determine the transaction costs savings because foreign exchange transaction costs vary greatly with the size of the transaction. Most readers of this book will have experienced for themselves the large costs involved in retail transactions: for banknotes the bid-ask spread is seldom below 2 per cent, often around 5 per cent and it may go up to 10 per cent if the exchange involves two minor currencies. However, since banknote exchanges and other retail transactions (eurocheques, credit cards, etc.,) do not account for a large share of the GDP of the Community, their total is small. An estimate by the Commission arrives at about 2 billion ecu per annum.

Most of the savings in transaction costs come therefore from intra-EC trade which involves mostly the corporate sector. Although the cost per transaction is much smaller in percentage terms (about 0.5 per cent) at the wholesale level at which the corporate section operates, the total is much higher because intra-Community trade is equal to about 530 billion ecu, or about 13 per cent of the GDP of the Community. There are two sources of potential savings regarding intra-Community trade: (i) bid-ask spreads and other commissions, and, (ii) the in-house costs that arise because enterprises have to keep separate foreign exchange departments. Finally enterprises located in smaller countries can also expect to save in their external trade because transaction costs using the ecu, which under EMU would be a major international currency, should be lower than the costs they have to bear at present when using the national currency.

Table 7.3.1 summarizes the transaction cost savings that can be expected from a common currency.

Table 7.3.1 Transaction cost savings from a common currency
(in billion of ecu per annum)

	lower bound	upper bound
Financial transaction costs:		
Wholesale: bank transfers	6.4	10.6
Retail: Banknotes,		
eurocheques, etc.	1.8	2.5
Corporate in-house costs	3.6	4.8
Economies of scale in external		
transactions	1.2	2.0
Total	13.0	17.9

Source: Emerson *et al.*, table A. 14 and box 7.1.

The direct savings in transaction costs should therefore be around one fourth to one half of 1 per cent of the GDP of the Community (which was equal to 4,020 billion ecu in 1988, the base year for this data). This estimate can be confirmed by looking at the revenues banks obtain from intra-Community foreign exchange operations. Surveys in several member countries show that about 5 per cent of all revenues come from this source; given that the banking sector accounts for about 6 per cent of GDP this implies a transaction cost saving of about 0.3 per cent of GDP.

It should be clear that this elimination of exchange-rate related transaction costs represents a net gain to society only if the resources (mainly personnel) previously engaged in executing foreign exchange transactions can be usefully employed somewhere else. Given the overall expansion in the banking industry that is likely to continue for some time this is likely to be the case.

A more important qualification to these estimates of the transaction cost savings is that they can be reaped in full only if cross-border transaction costs in the common currency cost as little as domestic transactions because there is a Community-wide transactions and clearing system. However, since the banking sector will have a strong incentive to establish such a system it is likely that this will be the case once a common currency has been introduced.[32]

It is interesting to note that these direct savings from the introduction of a common currency are of about the same size as the direct savings from the abolition of frontier controls as estimated in the study that evaluated the benefits of the internal market programme.[33] This suggests that the indirect effects of a common currency could very well be of the same order of magnitude as the indirect benefits that are expected from an important part of the internal market programme.

7.3.2 Elimination of information costs and price discrimination

Even small transaction costs can sometimes lead to considerable distortions. This was found to be the case in the 'Cost of Non-Europe' study, but it could also be true for the issue at hand. For example, the continuing existence of national currencies can lead to large indirect costs if it allows firms to engage in price discrimination between national markets. For consumers, used to evaluating prices in their own national currency, it is inconvenient and difficult to compare prices in different currencies, even if exchange rates are fixed. The practice of retailers in border areas, using approximate 'round' exchange rates several per cent away from the true rates, indicates that this implicit information cost can be quite high. These information costs allow firms to obtain some local monopoly power and to charge higher prices in the markets where demand is inelastic. Such artificial differences in prices imply losses of economic welfare because they give a signal that is not related to the true scarcity of the good.

Since the transaction cost savings through the common currency are of about the same size as the direct border cost savings through the abolition of frontier controls the indirect effects of EMU should be comparable in size to that of the internal market programme. An order of magnitude for the welfare gains from the suppression of exchange rates can therefore be obtained from the 'Cost of Non-Europe' study which

[32] First steps in this direction are the ecu clearing system run on a private basis and the exploratory discussions in the Committee of Governors on payments systems which have started in 1991.

[33] That study is commonly referred to as the 'Cost of Non-Europe' study. See Emerson (1988).

argues that the suppression of all residual barriers to intra-EC trade could raise the GDP of the Community by 4.5–6.5 per cent.[34] The higher value would result from a complete elimination of price discrimination, whereas the lower value still leaves room for some price differences.

Given that exchange-rate conversion costs will continue to exist as long as national currencies are there one could argue that the full elimination of price discrimination might come about only with a common currency. If full market integration can yield additional benefits of about 2 per cent of the GDP of the Community (i.e., the difference between 4.5 per cent and 6.5 per cent of GDP, about 80 billion ecu per annum in absolute terms) it is clear that there is a potential for additional indirect benefits from the introduction of a common currency that go well beyond the direct savings in transactions costs.

This is not to suggest that the introduction of a common currency should yield benefits of the same size as the internal market programme. But the similarity between the currency exchange transaction costs and the costs of frontier controls suggests that only a common currency leads to all the benefits that can be expected from a truly common market.

7.3.3 Dynamic efficiency gains

The two sources of efficiency gains considered so far do not take into account the time dimension and the accumulation of capital. However, the increase in overall efficiency that comes through the common currency translates also into an increase in the (marginal) productivity of capital. This, in turn, should raise investment, and thus lead, over time, to a higher capital stock until the (marginal) productivity of capital has returned to its original level. Since a higher capital stock means more output with the same labour force this mechanism multiplies the output effect of the initial increase in efficiency. Baldwin (1989) and (1991) estimates that the multiplier through induced capital formation is about 2. This implies that the overall increase in output that can be expected from a common currency, after enough time has passed to allow the capital stock to adjust, should be about one half to two thirds of 1 per cent of the GDP of the Community. Taking into account that the capital stock adjusts in response to an increase in economic efficiency therefore doubles the gains in terms of output that can be expected from a common currency.

However, this dynamic effect does not double the welfare gains since the increase in the capital stock has to be paid for by a reduction in consumption. The welfare effect of the dynamic gain is the difference between the value of the consumption foregone and the additional output produced by the additional capital. In a competitive system which is close to its equilibrium point this difference will be small. The indirect dynamic effect should therefore imply only a small additional increase in welfare. This is in contrast to the savings in direct transaction costs, which come 'for free'.

---

[34] *Ibid.*

It has been argued that an additional dynamic effect arises if EMU reduces the risk premium attached to investment because it reduces uncertainty about exchange rates and national monetary policies.[35] A reduction in the risk premium would stimulate investment and increase output over time as the capital stock increases in the same way as the indirect dynamic effects of the transaction cost savings discussed so far. As shown in Baldwin (1991) a reduction in the risk premium of 10 per cent, for example if the risk premium goes from 5.0 per cent to 4.5 per cent, could lead to an increase in output of 10 per cent in the long run. This effect could potentially dwarf the direct savings in transaction costs.

However, it is not clear why EMU should lead to a fall in the risk premium. As discussed in the previous section, there is little evidence that past reductions in exchange-rate variability have affected trade or investment in a major way. It is therefore difficult to see why the fixing of exchange rates should affect investment so strongly that it leads to a considerable increase in output. A common currency would eliminate any residual uncertainty about exchange rates, but this effect cannot be stronger than that of fixing exchange rates. It is therefore unlikely that a common currency would lead to the sustained increase in investment of over 10 per cent that would be required to achieve an increase in output of 10 per cent.

Most evaluations of the benefits of EMU concentrate on the effects it can have on the level of output instead of its growth rate. The reason for this focus on the level effects is that until recently there was no adequate theoretical framework to explain continuing growth other than that simply resulting from exogenous technological progress. Recently, however, a number of models have been developed to explain what other factors could lead to continuing growth in the long run. These models are still in an early stage and can therefore not yet be used to assess quantitatively the impact of the introduction of a common currency on growth in the long run.[36] But it is clear that these dynamic growth effects could have a cumulative effect larger than the once-and-for-all efficiency gains whose magnitude can be more easily assessed. Even a very small increase in the growth potential has a cumulatively significant, exponentially increasing effect on the level of income over time. For example, an increase in the growth rate of only 0.1 percentage point (e.g., from 2.0–2.1 per cent per annum) implies a cumulative difference in the level of income of over 2 per cent after twenty years. Even a minute increase in the growth rate would therefore be more important than the direct gains in terms of transaction costs savings.[37]

Most of the newer models that explain the sources of continuing growth stress the importance of the economies of scale and spill-overs that arise in the accumulation of knowledge. Rivera and Romer (1990) thus show that trade in goods is sufficient to generate the gains from economic integration in terms of higher growth only to the extent that goods embody new knowledge. This approach would therefore imply that in the long run the most important source of gains might not be the transaction cost

---

[35] See Emerson *et al.* (1991), chapter 3.

[36] For a survey of these new theories see Romer (1989).

[37] Taking into account that future income gains are worth less than present ones would not lead to a substantially different result.

savings that should affect primarily trade in goods, but the integration in the market of knowledge that can be achieved through other aspects of the EMU (and the internal market) programme that increase the exchange of knowledge inside the Community.

7.3.4 Savings through lower official international reserves

As long as national currencies subsist national monetary authorities have to keep large foreign exchange reserves to be seen to be able to defend exchange rates. The European central bank overseeing a common currency would no longer need to hold reserves to defend intra–Community exchange rates, reserves would be needed only to the extent that the exchange rate of the ecu has to be managed against other currencies, i.e., primarily the US dollar.

In 1990 the monetary authorities of the twelve Community members held the equivalent of about 200 billion ecu in international reserves, of which about one half, i.e., the equivalent of about 90 billion ecu, was in non–Community currencies (mainly US dollars). This exceeds by far the amount held by the United States, which was equal to only about 40 billion ecu. If the US were the benchmark a common currency could therefore lead to savings in international reserves of about 160 billion ecu. The large holdings of foreign exchange reserves in Community currencies (essentially in DM) would, of course, cease to be useful and could be put at the disposal of national treasuries. From an economic point of view it does not matter how these former foreign exchange reserves are used. The net worth of the government (aggregating central bank and treasury) does not change when, for example, foreign exchange reserves are used to retire public debt[38].

However, the cost of holding reserves is small since they are invested in interest-bearing assets. The overall savings that are available because the central monetary authority of EMU needs less international reserves than the sum of the holdings of member countries should therefore be small. The magnitude of the savings is difficult to estimate since little is known about the liquidity premium central banks are prepared to pay when investing their reserves. Moreover, as foreign exchange reserves fluctuate widely over time it is therefore difficult to estimate both the foreign exchange needs of a European EMU and the amount that might have been accumulated in the meantime by national central banks. Chapter 9 provides some illustrative calculations about the global distribution of foreign exchange reserves after EMU.

7.3.5 Global effects: stronger European presence in the international monetary system and in global financial markets

The effects of the creation of EMU on the global economy are discussed in chapter 9. This short section deals only with the benefits that might stem from the fact that a

---

[38] For a discussion of the size and use of 'excess' foreign exchange reserves in EMU see chapter 13.

common European currency would be a strong competitor for the US dollar in the international financial system and can therefore be expected to partially replace the US dollar in global financial investments. In Emerson *et al.* (1991) it is estimated that the increase in the weight of the ecu in the global financial portfolio will be limited to about 5 per cent since diversification away from the US dollar has already taken place to a large extent. However, given the large size of the world portfolio of financial assets, even this small proportional change still implies that assets worth about 200 billion US dollars will be converted into ecus.

However, portfolio substitution towards the ecu does not, *per se*, produce any benefits for the Community. It would benefit the Community only to the extent that it lowers ecu interest rates because global financial markets are willing to hold a given supply of ecu assets at a lower interest rate. The size of the benefits from this effect depends therefore crucially on the elasticity of substitution between assets denominated in ecu and other currencies (principally the dollar).

Large-scale international portfolio substitution away from the US dollar into the European currency might even have adverse consequences. Unless the supply of ecu assets is very elastic it could have an undesirable effect on the exchange rates of the European currency against the dollar, causing the ecu to go above its longer-run sustainable level.

Economic benefits for the Community can be expected from the international dimension of EMU only to the extent that the ecu bills replace the US dollar in retail transactions around the world. The direct seigniorage gains for the European central bank that would result from this effect have been estimated to be about 30 billion ecu. However, this is a once-and-for-all gain, as opposed to the efficiency gains which would be available year after year. Only the interest rate gain on this sum is comparable to the efficiency gain, at an interest rate of 8 per cent the seigniorage gain would be about 2.4 billion, only one eighth of the transaction cost gains.[39]

7.3.6 The cost of introducing a common currency

The main cost of a monetary union, i.e., the loss of the exchange rate as an adjustment instrument was discussed at some length in section 7.2 above. Since the additional costs from the introduction of a common currency are minor the present subsection can be brief.

The main costs of introducing a common currency would be the initial change in accounting units and the cost of converting outstanding financial and other long-term contracts into the single currency. The introduction of the common currency will come after a period of stable exchange rates and all the conversion rates applied to existing contracts in order to convert payment obligations from national currency into

---

[39] See Emerson *et al.* (1991). The figure of 30 billion in ecu notes used outside the Community is based on estimates that about 130 billion US dollar notes are used outside the US (presumably most of it in Latin America), one third to one fourth of which might be converted into ecu.

ecu will presumably be equal to the market rates of exchange. The introduction of the common currency would therefore not lead to any wealth redistribution. It would be just a redenomination, but it would not make anybody richer or poorer.

However, experience shows that the introduction of a new unit of account is a lengthy process. The difficulty of adopting even very simple changes in the unit of account is illustrated by the French experience of taking two zeros off the French franc in 1958. Thirty years later some people continue to use the 'old' franc as a unit of account. Given its much more complicated matrix of exchange rates the introduction of the common European currency would therefore have to be carefully prepared to allow the general public to familiarize itself with this new unit of account. If this is done the replacement of national currencies by the ecu might even become a popular event.

A more serious problem can arise with respect to the determination of interest rates in long-term financial contracts denominated in national currencies if the interest is not fixed, but set with reference to some market rate. For example, a mortgage contract under which the interest rate is set at a certain premium above the rate prevailing in the domestic interbank market (which would constitute the new reference rate) will be affected to the extent that the ecu interest rate might be slightly different from the rate on the domestic market just prior to the introduction of the common currency. Similar problems could arise also for large international bank loans because the interest rate is often just set with reference to LIBOR (London Interbank Offered Rate). But these problems can be much reduced to the extent that contracts have the appropriate clauses that stipulate what to do when the ecu becomes the common currency (which is still five years or more away).

The main point is, however, that all these costs would be of a–once-and-for-all nature whereas the benefits would be available continuously. The costs of introducing a common currency can therefore be considered negligible in the long run relative to the benefits discussed above.

7.4 Regional distribution of costs and benefits

The Community does not constitute a homogenous economic area. The differences in economic structure, income per capita, unemployment, etc. are even larger than those inside the United States. This implies that the costs and benefits will be distributed unevenly across member countries. The overall balance of costs and benefits cannot therefore be used to assess the economic arguments for and against participation in EMU for any particular member country.

A detailed country-by-country assessment of the costs and benefits is, however, beyond the scope of this paper. Given the nature of the costs and benefits it would anyway be impossible to provide a precise quantitative assessment of the net benefit (or cost) of EMU for any given member country. The purpose of this section is therefore merely to provide two indicators that indicate the approximate strength of the main costs and benefits for each member country.

The first indicator is simply the importance of intra-EC trade measured as a percentage of GDP. A high value of this indicator implies that the transaction cost savings as well as all the other indirect benefits of a common currency discussed above are important.[40] Figure 7.4.1 shows that intra–EC trade accounts for more than 20 per cent of GDP in four member countries: Belgium, Ireland, the Netherlands and Portugal. These countries are therefore the ones that would benefit most from the direct and indirect microeconomic benefits of a full monetary union. For all the remaining member countries intra–EC trade is much less important, but it never falls below 10 per cent of GDP.

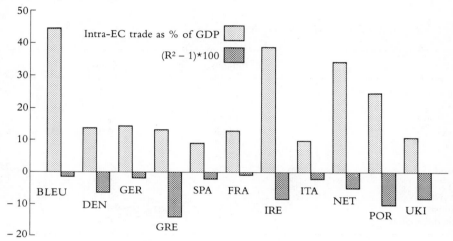

Figure 7.4.1 Costs and benefits by member country based on intra–EC trade and differences in economic structure

Note: Intra–EC trade = (exports+imports)/2.
Source: European Commission. The R has been taken from a regression of each country's economic structure over a weighted EC average (using ecu weights).

The second indicator is a statistical measure of the difference between the economic structure (the distribution of value added over thirty different branches of the economy) of the country considered and the structure of the economy of the Community on average.[41] Differences in economic structure indicate the likelihood of country-specific shocks for which the exchange rate would be a useful adjustment instrument, and this indicator therefore represents the importance of the main cost of a monetary union, namely the loss of the exchange rate as an adjustment instrument. Since it measures a cost this indicator is reported as a negative value. The more a country's economic

---

[40] Furthermore, as argued above, a high degree of openness also implies that use of the exchange rate destabilizes the domestic price level.

[41] The statistical measure used here is the adjusted correlation coefficient between the national values and the Community averages of the shares of about thirty economic sectors in total value added. Table 7.4.1 reports the value of this coefficient minus one.

structure differs from that of the Community the lower (the more negative) becomes this indicator.

Table 7.4.1 shows, not surprisingly, that the poorer member countries have a different economic structure. Greece, Ireland and Portugal have the highest cost indicators. But for two of these (Ireland and Portugal) the benefits indicators are also very high, so that the overall balance should still be positive. Greece stands out as the country with the worst balance since it has the highest value for the costs indicator and only a moderate value for benefits.

Table 7.4.1   Costs and benefits by member country.

	Benefits	Costs
Belgium–Luxembourg	44.5	−1.39
Denmark	13.65	−6.47
Germany	14.35	−1.81
Greece	13.25	−14.01
Spain	8.95	−2.07
France	12.95	−0.71
Ireland	38.85	−8.48
Italy	9.7	−2.02
Netherlands	34.2	−5.14
Portugal	24.55	−10.31
United Kingdom	10.7	−8.40

Note: Benefits = intra-EC trade as % of GDP.
   Costs = $(R2 - 1) \star 100$, see note to figure 7.4.1.

The results for the other countries are also interesting because they correspond almost exactly to the political attitudes towards EMU. Belgium and Holland, two very open economies with a structure very similar to that of the Community, on average stand to gain most from EMU. This group (it also includes Luxembourg which already is in a monetary union with Belgium[42]) constitutes also the part of the Community where EMU receives most political support.

The four large continental member countries (France, Germany, Italy and Spain) have also little to lose from no longer being able to use the exchange rate because their structure is also very close to the Community average. However, their gains are somewhat smaller than those of smaller countries, such as Belgium, because their economies are less open. In the case of Spain the result is somewhat surprising because this country is often put into the same category as Portugal and Greece. In all these countries EMU is accepted, but the commitment is somewhat weaker than in the previous group of countries.

The United Kingdom and Denmark are the countries, next to Greece, for which the

---

[42] For Luxembourg data on the industrial structure were not available.

balance of costs and benefits is more uncertain since both countries do not trade very intensively with the rest of the Community and their industrial structure differs more from the Community average. This last factor has perhaps been overlooked in discussions about EMU when it is often just assumed that all countries with a similar income per capita also have a similar economic structure. These economic factors are certainly not the sole or even the main determinants of the British hostility towards EMU, but they might explain why the economic benefits of EMU are less widely perceived in the United Kingdom.

Overall this brief discussion suggests that for most member countries the benefits should clearly outweigh the costs. On the basis of the two simple indicators used here this does not appear to be the case for Greece, but that country would surely benefit from another aspect of EMU, namely a high degree of price stability that has eluded Greece so far, but that can be expected from the policy of the European central bank.

7.5   Summary evaluation of the economic costs and benefits of monetary union

This chapter has attempted to state the main costs and benefits of moving from the present EMS to full monetary union. The latter was defined as the irrevocable fixing of exchange rates, followed by the introduction of a common currency. Nevertheless, the following two sections separated the cost-benefit analysis of those two steps. With the irrevocable fixing of exchange rates exchange-rate changes permanently disappear as an instrument for macroeconomic policy adjustment. Though this is indeed a cost, much of it has been incurred already by the present members of the EMS who have used the instrument to a diminishing extent over the past decade. Moreover, given the broad similarity in industrial structures that is apparent in the increasing importance of two-way trade in intra-EC trade, the likelihood of nationally differentiated shocks that are not caused by policy and that are large enough to require an exchange-rate adjustment is already low and should be further reduced by the ongoing process of integration.

Some of the traditional arguments used for relying on exchange-rate adjustment in the European context have weakened considerably (accommodation of residual, autonomous inflation differentials and the public finance arguments for not removing seigniorage) while one could be reversed: portfolio shifts are better accommodated within a fixed rate system than by letting the exchange rate move. The main argument to which one must continue to attach importance is that there is still some risk in discarding an instrument that may reduce, however limited the scope for a significant contribution from it may be, the initial external imbalances of the prospective participants.

Against these costs one would have to set the, mainly microeconomic, benefits. One point of separating the irrevocable fixing of rates from the subsequent step of introducing a common currency is that only the latter step assures that all these benefits will be fully reaped: full convergence of inflationary expectations, disappearance of transaction costs and greater transparency in the environment for the internal market in goods and in financial services.

Opponents of EMU often stress that the transaction cost savings are minor, only 0.3 per cent of GDP. However, this misses the essential point that the benefits of a common currency are like an iceberg: transaction cost savings constitute the small part that is visible because it emerges from the water. The other benefits which derive from the complete integration of markets which can only be reached with a common currency are potentially much more important, but they are hidden under the water. It is said that in the case of an iceberg only one eighth of the total is visible. A similar proportion might be appropriate in the case of EMU, the overall benefits of a common currency could therefore be substantial even if they are not apparent at first sight.

References

Baldwin, Richard (1989), 'On the growth effects of 1992', *Economic Policy 9*, October: 248–81.
(1991), 'On the microeconomics of European Monetary Union', in *European Economy*, special issue, October.

Baxter, Marianne and Alan Stockman (1989), 'Business cycles and the exchange rate regime: some international evidence', *Journal of Monetary Economics*, 23, 3: 377–400.

Begg, David, *et al.* (1990), 'The impact of Eastern Europe', Centre for Economic Policy Research, London.

Bini-Smaghi, Lorenzo (1987), 'Exchange rate variability and trade flows', mimeo, University of Chicago and Banca d'Italia.

Black, Stanley (1989), 'Transactions costs and vehicle currencies', International Monetary Fund, *IMF WP/89/96*, November.

Boyd, Chris, Geert Gielens and Daniel Gros (1990), 'Bid-ask spreads in the foreign exchange markets', mimeo, Brussels, February.

Cline, William R. (1989), 'The global impact of US trade adjustment', Institute for International Economics, Washington, DC.

Cohen, Daniel (1989), 'The costs and benefits of a European currency', chapter 7 in Marcello de Cecco and Alberto Giovannini (eds.), *A European Central Bank?*, Italian Macroeconomic Policy Group and Centre for Economic Policy Research, Cambridge University Press, Cambridge, 195–209.

Commission of the European Communities (1989), *European Economy*, 42, special edition, October.
(1990), 'Making payments in the internal market', *Discussion Paper*, COM(90) 447, September.

Committee for the Study of Economic and Monetary Union (1989), 'Report on Economic and Monetary Union in the European Community' (the Delors Report), Office of Publications of the European Communities, Luxembourg.

De Grauwe, Paul (1987), 'International trade and economic growth in the European Monetary System', *European Economic Review*, 31: 389–98.

De Grauwe, Paul and Wim Vanhaverbecke (1990), 'Exchange-rate experiences of small EMS-countries: the cases of Belgium, Denmark and the Netherlands', chapter 3 in Victor Argy and Paul De Grauwe (eds.), *Choosing an Exchange Rate Regime: The Challenge for Smaller Industrial Countries*, International Monetary Fund, MacQuarie University and Katholieke Universiteit Leuven, 135–55.
(1991), 'Is Europe an optimum currency area? Evidence from regional data', manuscript, Catholic University of Leuven.

Dornbusch, Rüdiger (1988), 'The EMS, the dollar and the yen', chapter 2 in Francesco Giavazzi, Stefano Micossi and Marcus Miller (eds.), *The European Monetary System*, Banca d'Italia, Centro Interuniversitario di Studi Teorici per la Politica Economica and Centre for Economic Policy Research, Cambridge University Press, Cambridge, 23–41.

(1990), 'Problems of European monetary unification', chapter 11 in Alberto Giovannini and Colin Mayer (eds.) *European Financial Integration*, Cambridge University Press, Cambridge, 306–40,

Eichengreen, Barry (1990), 'One money for Europe? Lessons from the US Currency Union', *Economic Policy*, 10: 117- 87.

(1991), 'Is Europe an optimum currency area?', NBER Working Paper No. 3579, January.

Emerson, Michael (1988), 'The economics of 1992', Commission of the European Communities, *European Economy*, 35.

Emerson, Michael, Daniel Gros, Alexander Italianer, Jean Pisani-Ferry and Horst Reichenbach (1991), *One market, one money*, Oxford University Press, Oxford.

Frenkel, Jacob and Assaf Razin (1987), *Fiscal policies and the world economy*, MIT Press, Cambridge, Massachusetts.

Giavazzi, Francesco and Alberto Giovannini (1987), 'Exchange rates and prices in Europe', *Weltwirtschafliches Archiv*, 183: 592–605.

(1989), *Limiting Exchange Rate Flexibility: The European Monetary System*, MIT Press, Cambridge, Massachusetts.

Giavazzi, Francesco and Luigi Spaventa (1989), 'Italy: the real effect of inflation and disinflation', *Economic Policy*, 8, April: 133–71

Giovannini, Alberto (1990a) 'The transition towards monetary union' *CEPR Occasional Paper*, 2, March.

(1990b), 'European monetary reform: progress and prospects', forthcoming in Brookings papers on Economic Activity, Washington DC, November.

Glassman, Debra (1987), 'Exchange rate risk and transactions costs: evidence from bid-ask spreads', *Journal of International Money and Finance*, 6: 479–90.

Gros, Daniel (1986), 'The determinants of competitiveness and profitability', International Monetary Fund, Washington, DC, *DM/86/21*.

(1987), 'Exchange rate variability and foreign trade in the presence of adjustment costs', Department of Economics, Catholic University of Louvain, Louvain-la-Neuve, *Working paper*, 8704.

(1988), 'The EMS and the Determination of the European Price Level', Centre for European Policy Studies, Working Documents, No. 34, February.

(1989a), 'Seigniorage in the EC: the effects of the EMS and financial market integration', International Monetary Fund, Washington, DC, *IMF/WP/89/7*.

(1989b), 'On the volatility of exchange rates – tests of monetary and portfolio balance models of exchange rate determination', *Weltwirtschaftliches Archiv*, Band 125 Heft 2: 273–94.

(1989c), 'Paradigms for the monetary union of Europe', *Journal of Common Market Studies*, 27, 3, March: 219–30.

Helpman, Elhanan and Paul Krugman (1985), *Market structure and foreign trade: increasing returns, imperfect competition, and the international economy*, MIT Press, Cambridge, Massachusetts.

International Monetary Fund (1984), 'Exchange rate variability and world trade', *Occasional Paper*, 28.

Jacquemin, Alexis and André Sapir (1987), 'Intra-EC trade: a sectoral analysis', Centre for European Policy Studies, Brussels, *CEPS Working Documents (Economic)*, 24, January.

Krugman, Paul (1989), 'Differences in income elasticities and trends in real exchange rates', *European Economic Review*, 33: 1031–54.

(1991 forthcoming), 'Increasing returns and economic geography', *Journal of Political Economy*.

Masson, Paul and Jacques Meltiz (1990), 'Fiscal policy independence in a European Monetary Union', Centre for Economic Policy Research, *Discussion paper*, 414, April.

McKinnon, Ronald (1963), 'Optimum currency areas', *American Economic Review*, 53, September: 717–25.

Mundell, Robert (1961), 'A theory of optimum currency areas', *American Economic Review*, 51, September: 657–65.

Rivera, Luis and Paul Romer (1990), 'Economic integration and endogenous growth', NBER Working Paper No. 3528, December.

Romer, Paul (1989), 'Increasing returns and new development in the theory of growth', NBER Working Paper, 3098: September.

Sapir, André and Khalid Sekkat (1990), 'Exchange rate volatility and international trade', chapter 8 in Paul De Grauwe and Lucas Papademos (eds.), *The European Monetary System in the 1990's*, Longman, 182–98

Stockman, Alan (1988), 'Sectoral and national aggregates disturbances to industrial output in seven European countries', *Journal of Monetary Economics*, 21: 387–409.

Vona, Stefano and Lorenzo Bini-Smaghi (1988), 'Economic growth and exchange rates in the EMS: their trade effects in a changing external environment', chapter 6 in Francesco Giavazzi, Stefano Micossi and Marcus Miller (eds.), *The European Monetary System*, Banca d'Italia, Centro Interuniversitario di Studi Teorici per la Politica Economica and Centre for Economic Policy Research, Cambridge University Press, Cambridge, 140–78.

Wihlborg, Clas and Thomas Willett (1990), 'The instability of half-way measures in the transition to a common currency', *Gothenburg Studies in Financial Economics*, 1990: 13.

APPENDIX

EMU and German Unification: Any Lessons for Europe?[1]

German unification, in particular the German monetary and economic union that preceded political unification, is often compared to EMU for the Community. Some observers stress the differences, whereas others warn that the experience gained in the German case has important lessons for Europe. The purpose of this appendix is therefore to analyse the similarities and differences between the German monetary and economic union and EMU. The likely impact of German unification on the EMS has already been discussed in chapter 5.

Section 1 starts by providing some background information about the formation of the German economic, monetary and social union (henceforth GEMSU) and the ensuing political unification. This is then followed by a comparison of the main economic effects of GEMSU along the lines of the analysis of the costs and benefits of EMU in chapter 9. This appendix concludes with some discussion of different speeds in the transition, and the lessons GEMSU might have for EMU.

1 Background[2]

Preparations for an economic, monetary and social union started after the first democratic elections in the now defunct GDR on 18 March 1990 and the modalities were fixed in a 'state treaty' (the first *Staatsvertrag*) between the two German governments. The treaty took effect on 1 July 1990 and starting from that day the Deutsche Mark became the sole legal tender in the territory of the ex-GDR. All current payments (wages, rents, etc.) formerly expressed in East German Marks were converted at the rate of 1 : 1, whereas assets and liabilities were converted in

---

[1] This appendix is based on the contribution of one of the authors to Emerson *et al.* (1991).

[2] For a description and an analysis of German unification see, for example, Siebert (1990), Institute for World Economics (1990) provides numerous references.

general at the rate of 2:1 (except a lump sum of 4,000 per adult, 2,000 per child and 6,000 for persons over fifty-nine years).

The first *Staatsvertrag* also specified that all dispositions of the Bundesbank and the West German banking law were to apply to the ex-GDR as well. Since the major banks of the Federal Republic took over immediately a large part of the existing banking network, this implied that the West German banking system was practically extended in one stroke to East Germany.

At the same time, i.e., also on 1 July 1990, the government of the ex-GDR adopted a large number of laws and other legal dispositions of the FRG that freed economic activity from the constraints imposed by the previous régime, thus creating the legal framework for a market economy. Furthermore, starting 2 July trade between the FRG and the ex-GDR was also totally liberalized.

An important part of GEMSU as it was implemented in July of 1990 was the social union aspect, under which most aspects of the social security system in the ex-GDR were remodelled according to the West German system. Pensions were increased substantially, unemployment insurance was introduced and the health care system of the Federal Republic was extended to the territory of the ex-GDR.

These measures created an economic, monetary and social union between the two parts of Germany without any transition period.

It should not be overlooked that GEMSU was in reality not an exclusively internal German afffair. The West German economy, as other member countries, is already integrated into the Community to such an extent that the conditions inside the Community are already close to being equivalent to an economic union (the free movement of goods and services and factors of production). In a certain sense one could say what had happened was that the ex-GDR participated in the economic union that has already formed to a large extent in the Community. The fact that Germany is a member of the Community also limits the kind of economic policy measures the German government can take. For example any restrictions on the free movement of goods inside Germany would have to be approved by the Community.

The unification process continued after July 1990 and ended in October with formal, political unification. This was achieved under Article 23 of the German basic law by which the ex-GDR declared its accession to the Federal Republic. The choice of this procedure implied that the entire legal and institutional framework of the Federal Republic was not affected by unification and that the territory of the ex-GDR became part of the Community without the need for an enlargement treaty. A second 'state treaty' (Staatsvertrag) was concluded, but it contained only a number of transitional clauses, some which were anyway made obsolete by subsequent events.

After one year it is too early to assess the full consequences of the German monetary and economic union. However, the developments during 1991 suggest that the adjustment process will be more difficult than initially hoped for. Massive unemployment, in about 20 per cent of the workforce in the new *Länder* (much of it hidden and subsidized under the German 'part time' working scheme) and the lack of private investment produced a crisis atmosphere that led the government to increase taxes in order to be able to finance a package of investment incentives and financial support for the new regional governments in the ex-GDR. These direct and indirect consequences of German unification are expected to lead to a budget deficit for the federal authorities of about 5 per cent of GDP in 1991 (after approximate balance in 1989).

2 GEMSU and EMU: a comparison

It is difficult to compare GEMSU to EMU because the former created also overnight a market economy (through the elimination of price controls, recognition of private property of capital, etc.). The jump to a market economy is interesting in its own right, and might constitute a useful reference point for the more gradual transition process that is currently taking place in other central and eastern European countries.[3] However, given that all member countries already have market economies, this aspect is not relevant for the comparison with EMU.

A further difficulty in evaluating the effects of GEMSU comes from the difficulty of constructing a hypothetical alternative scenario, i.e., a useful benchmark. In the case of the Community one might argue, as done in chapter 7, that the status quo (including the internal market programme) provides a useful benchmark. However, in the German case the status quo was certainly not a stable alternative. Political considerations made a rapid unification process imperative once the Berlin wall had come down in November 1989.

This brief comparison is therefore limited to an analysis of the main economic effects of GEMSU as it was executed in reality. It concentrates on the two main components of the costs and benefits of EMU already discussed in chapter 7, i.e., the gains from market integration and the loss of the exchange rate as an adjustment instrument. The fiscal aspects and the issues arising from the different speed in the transition are discussed separately.

2.1 Efficiency gains from market integration

The most important effect of GEMSU was the complete integration of markets for goods, services and capital that was made possible by the introduction of the DM in the ex-GDR.[4] In contrast to EMU this gain cannot be measured through the gain in terms of transactions costs made possible by the common currency, since market integration consisted of creating new markets that did not exist or were completely isolated from the world economy.[5]

The most important market that was created overnight was the capital market since the ex-GDR did not have a capital market prior to GEMSU. After this event savers and investors in the ex-GDR could immediately use the efficient West German capital market and financial system. The introduction of the DM thus reduced the cost and increased the availability of credit and risk capital allowing existing enterprises to finance the huge investment needed to modernize the capital stock of the East German economy and facilitate the creation of new enterprises, especially small to medium ones. Without access to this capital market, investment and employment creation through new enterprises would be much more difficult and the catching up process much slower.

Moreover, introducing the DM also eliminated for the ex-GDR the current-account constraint. The reduction in the German current-account surplus documented in chapter 5 indicates that the eastern part of the country is presently running a large current-account deficit which could be as large as 50 per cent of the GDP of the *Länder* on the territory of the ex-GDR.[6] This would have been impossible without GEMSU since the ex-GDR would certainly have been forced to maintain capital controls had a separate GDR currency been maintained. This benefit of a common currency should therefore be much more important for the ex-GDR than in the context of EMU.

---

[3] See Gros and Steinherr (1991) for an evaluation of the economic transformation in Eastern Europe.

[4] By adopting the DM, the ex-GDR also immediately gained all the advantages of a stable currency and of the credible anti-inflationary policy of the Bundesbank. Although overt inflation had not been high under the previous regime this can be considered an important economic benefit for the people in the ex-GDR since experience has shown that periods of liberalization often bring high inflation. Moreover, it would have been impossible for the authorities in the ex-GDR to quickly establish the reputation for price stability the Bundesbank has acquired over the last four decades.

[5] Emerson *et al.* report that the cost of a transfer from East to West Germany was reduced by almost two orders of magnitude (from about 100 DM per transfer before GEMU to the cost of an transfer within the German banking system, i.e., about one DM).

[6] This estimate results from the fact that the reduction in the current-account surplus of all of Germany is equivalent to about 5 per cent of German GDP and that East Germany accounts only for about 10 per cent of the total German GDP.

The creation of an efficient capital market and access to foreign savings are, of course, particularly important if the demand for investment is strong. The extent to which this will be the case is difficult to judge. The confusion surrounding property rights for real estate (unresolved legal claims for restitution are estimated to affect about one third of the entire territory of the new Länder) was an important brake on investment. But it is certain that in the absence of GEMSU investment by West German (and other western) firms would have been even lower.

The liberalization of trade (i.e., the external economic aspect of GEMSU) also had an importance that is absent in the case of EMU since the internal market programme will already eliminate all barriers to trade inside the Community. In the case of Germany, however, the starting point was totally different in that, before GEMSU, the ex-GDR economy traded very little with market economies and trade with the COMECON partners was conducted at artificial prices and distorted by political considerations. Opening an economy as closed as that of the ex-GDR must lead to all the well-known gains from trade through increased specialization and economies of scale.

Because of the different starting point the efficiency gains from both the economic and the monetary union aspects should therefore be several orders of magnitude higher in the case of GEMSU, compared to EMU. However, as recent events have shown, this applies to the adjustment costs as well.

2.2 Adjustment costs

As argued in chapter 6 the main cost of a monetary union is the loss of the exchange rate as an adjustment instrument in the face of asymmetric regional shocks. This idea was also the main argument used by many German academics in early 1990 against the introduction of the DM in the ex-GDR since the economy of the ex-GDR will go through a period of profound adjustment whose success and speed cannot be predicted *a priori*. The changes in the product mix produced in the ex-GDR and the rapid growth of income that can be expected during the catching-up process imply that the real exchange rate between the two parts of Germany has to change significantly in the near future. During a transition period the need for real exchange-rate adjustments will therefore be much greater between the two parts of Germany, than inside the Community. One could, therefore, argue that in this respect the potential cost of a monetary union could be higher in the German case.

However, as emphasized in chapter 7, governments can directly affect only the nominal exhange rate which is therefore a useful adjustment instrument only if nominal wages are somewhat rigid. Had the ex-GDR maintained a separate currency to be able to adjust the exchange rate during the transition period, exchange-rate changes would have been effective only if wages could be relied upon not to react immediately. Given the high degree of integration of the German labour market (and of most other markets as well) it is, however, likely that workers would have been able to 'see through' the effects of exchange-rate adjustments. Exchange-rate changes would hardly have been a more useful policy tool for the ex-GDR than for other Community countries which have realized that exchange-rate changes on their own cannot correct major external or internal imbalances.

An important factor that would tend to reduce the importance of the exchange rate as an adjustment instrument in the German case is the fact that the mobility of labour and capital inside Germany is much higher than between member countries and actual movements of labour, although not costless, are more acceptable in social terms. This implies that labour mobility can provide a more acceptable adjustment channel than in the case of EMU.

The crucial element in reducing the costs associated with the loss of the exchange rate as an adjustment instrument is, however, the extent to which the exceptional nature of the situation is recognized by the social partners, and wages are allowed to react (in both directions) to unforeseen developments. The wage agreements that have been concluded so far indicate that this is not the case since most of these agreements stipulate that East German wages should match the West German level by about 1994. It is widely estimated that in 1989 productivity in the ex-GDR reached only about one third of the FRG level. A full catching up of the wage level would therefore be appropriate only if productivity in East German industry were to triple in five years; wages are thus clearly outstripping productivity.

The appropriate conversion rate for the East German Mark was extensively debated before GEMSU and the rate finally chosen; 1 : 1 for current payments, was widely regarded a political decision. The issue of the initial level of the exchange rate is, of course, specific to GEMSU. In the case of EMU, market exchange rates provide a reliable guide to the appropriate level at which to fix rates for the monetary union. Only for countries with large imbalances would it be appropriate not to fix exchange rates at the level at which they trade in the markets. However, in the case of GEMSU no such indicator existed and the conversion of wages aand other current payments had been chosen only on the basis of some rough calculations regarding productivity. The subsequent explosion of wages even from the level attained with the 1 : 1 conversion indicates, however, that the initial conversion rate cannot have been important.

2.3 Fiscal aspects

In terms of fiscal policy it is necessary to make a distinction between GEMSU and political unification. For example, as long as the state ex-GDR existed with its own government it was bound by the dispositions in the first *Staatsvertrag* that stipulated that it could not finance any deficit without the approval of the FRG. In this sense the first *Staatsvertrag* implied very strict 'binding guidelines'. However, after political unification these issues no longer arise.

Most of the fiscal consequences of GEMSU derived from the social aspect, i.e., the need to provide initial financing for a new social security system. After unification the social aspects continue to be the most important reason for the approximately 5 per cent of GDP the federal government spends in the new Länder. Only part of these expenditures come in a form that could be compared to the regional efforts of the Community, i.e., in the form of transfers to the new Länder on the territory of the ex-GDR.[7]

The economic rationale for the different size of these transfers (as compared to what is planned inside the Community) can be found in the much higher degree of labour mobility that exists between these parts of Germany. The mobility of labour between member countries of the EC is much lower so that much larger differences in income can persist without leading to unacceptable migration flows. Political factors are certainly very important since a common citizenship and the clause in the German basic law which instructs the federal government to achieve 'uniform living conditions' do not leave the federal government any choice. However, to some extent these political considerations can also be understood as a reaction to a different economic environment, i.e., a different degree of labour mobility. The massive migration flows that followed the fall of the Berlin wall were after all one of the main factors that pushed the federal government to offer GEMSU to the ex-GDR in early 1990 and that made early unification unavoidable.

2.4 Differences in the speed of the transition

The German economic and monetary union went into effect literally almost overnight. In contrast, in the case of the Community it took over a decade to eliminate tariffs and the internal market programme will have taken a number of years to be completed since it was launched in 1985. In the monetary field it took several years of operation of the EMS to reduce exchange-rate variability and achieve some convergence in inflation. The introduction of a common currency for the Community is also expected to take a number of years. Political factors certainly were the main reason for this difference in the speed of the transition. However, there are also economic aspects to this choice.

---

[7] These transfers are not passing through the *'Finanzausgleich'*, which provides for horizontal transfers from richer to poorer Länders in the FRG, but directly from the federal government because the *Finanzausgleich* was designed for the rather small differences in income between the Länder in the old Federal Republic. The *Finanzausgleich* is not due to include the new Länder until 1994.

In the case of the ex-GDR the need to create a market economy as quickly as possible dominated the decision concerning the speed of the transition. Theoretically it would have been possible to create first a distinct East German market economy and then integrate that economy with the West German one in a second stage. However, the crucial problem in the transition to a market economy is how to create not only a host of new laws, but also institutions that can credibly implement these new laws. The experience of the Eastern European countries that are still in the transition process illustrates this point vividly. In the case of the ex-GDR this problem was solved by the immediate adoption of the West German system.

For the Community the main reason for a gradual transition to EMU is that convergence of inflation usually takes some time. In the German case the jump to the common currency eliminated this consideration. Another reason for not going immediately to full EMU is that the institution that will manage the common monetary policy needs to establish its credibility and needs to learn how to operate on a Community-wide financial market. This consideration does not apply to GEMSU since in this case the Bundesbank, which is an experienced institution with a well-established reputation for price stability, will be in charge of the joint monetary policy.

In summary it appears that the main arguments for a gradual transition towards EMU that can be made at the level of the Community do not apply in the case of Germany.

3. GEMSU and EMU: any lessons for the Community?

The discussion of this appendix has shown that a number of the economic effects that determine the costs and benefits of EMU work in the case of GEMSU as well. However, the relative magnitude and importance of these effects are so different that the GEMSU experience cannot be used in the discussion about EMU.[8] The most important differences which lead to this conclusion are:

> GEMSU did not lead to any pooling of monetary authority. The territory of the DM and the authority of the Bundesbank were simply extended. However, once political unification was achieved the creation of new Landeszentralbanken in the territory of the former GDR ensured that representatives from the new Länder were participating in the Council of the Bundesbank. One interesting lesson that emerges from the German experience in this respect is, however, that the increase in the number of Länder representatives to a total of seventeen was regarded as excessive since even without a corresponding increase in the number of members of the Direktorium the Bundesbank Council would have had over twenty members. Since this was regarded as excessive, a proposal to restructure the Bundesbank so as to reduce the membership of the Bundesbank Council to around fifteen is currently under discussion in Germany. In the case of the European Central Bank, discussed in chapter 12 and 13 a similar need to reduce the membership will certainly also arise once the numerous applicants from Central and Northern Europe have joined the Community. This is discussed further in chapter 13.

> The extraordinary size of the fiscal transfers that are taking place is possible only because Germany constitutes one nation and therefore also a 'social union' and they are necessary on this scale only because the economy of the ex-GDR was in such a dire state after almost forty years of communist rule. As will be argued more fully in chapter 8, in the case of EMU there is no similar need for large fiscal transfers to poorer regions.

---

[8] Similarily in physics the experience from the 'macro' world cannot be used to describe events at the subatomic level although the laws of nature are valid everywhere. The differences in the relative importance of the different forces (gravity, electro-magnetic, etc.) are such that at the subatomic level a different approach is needed.

The speed of the transition in the German case was dictated by the need to create a market economy as quickly as possible and by the extraordinary migration flows that took place immediately once the border had fallen. This argument does also not apply to the Community.

The one useful lesson the German experience might hold for the Community is that a common currency could constitute a temptation for trade unions to call for an equalization of wages. If this were to happen in the Community the less productive regions would certainly suffer immensely. However, it is not likely that this will happen in the Community because wage bargaining takes place at the national level and both trade unions and employers associations are therefore organized along national lines. All this was different in the German case where western trade unions quickly extended their organization eastward. Moreover, due to full political union public sector employees had anyway to be paid the same all over Germany.

References

Emerson, Michael, Daniel Gros, Jean Pisani-Ferry, Alexander Italianer and Horst Reichenbach (1991), *One Market, One Money*, Oxford University Press, Oxford.

Gros, Daniel and Alfred Steinherr (1991), 'From centrally-planned to market economies: issues for the transition in Central Europe and the Soviet Union', Centre for European Policy Studies, Brussels, *CEPS Paper*, 51, April.

Institute for World Economics (1990), 'Bibliographie zur deutsch-deutschen Wirtschafts-, Währungs-und Sozialunion', Kiel, October.

Siebert, Horst (1990), 'The economic integration of Germany – an update', Kiel Institute of World Economics, Kiel Discussion Paper, 160a, September.

CHAPTER 8

THE RELATIONSHIP BETWEEN ECONOMIC AND MONETARY INTEGRATION: EMU AND NATIONAL FISCAL POLICY

As emphasized repeatedly, this book concentrates on monetary integration in spite of the fact that *economic and monetary* union is on the agenda of the Community. The focus on monetary union is justified by the fact that there is much less debate about the implications of economic union (in its narrow sense of a unified market). The creation of the Community in 1957 already had the aim of creating 'a common market'. In this sense the movement towards economic union predates the movement towards monetary union.

The wide agreement on the desirability of an economic union derives from the microeconomic gains a wider and truly unified market yields. However, there is much less agreement on the implications of EMU for fiscal policy in general although EMU will affect almost all aspects of fiscal policy.[1] For example, as already emphasized in chapter 7, the loss of the exchange-rate instrument implies that national governments might have to turn to a more active use of fiscal policy. Moreover, as discussed in chapter 5, an EMU committed to price stability has further implications for national budgets since inflation affects tax revenues and the value of expenditures. Finally, EMU will also increase the mobility of the tax base in a number of areas (e.g., capital income taxation and corporate taxation) and will therefore raise the issue of tax competition.

The purpose of this chapter is not to provide a survey of all the fiscal issues raised by EMU. Instead it concentrates on the issues that are closely related to the monetary and macroeconomic aspects that are the overall subject of investigation of this book. There are two broad issues in this area, both of which have become an integral part of the debate on EMU: the need for 'binding guidelines' for national fiscal policy and the desirability of some fiscal shock absorber at the Community level.

This chapter is therefore organized as follows: before going into the discussion about fiscal policy in EMU it first introduces briefly, in section 1, the concept of economic union and discusses the issue of 'parallelism', i.e., the desirability of parallel progress between the monetary and non-monetary aspects of the process of unification. Section 2 then discusses the most contentious issue in the entire EMU debate, i.e., the alleged

---

[1] For surveys on fiscal policy and EMU see Emerson *et al.* (1991), Gros (1991) and Wyplosz (1991).

need for binding guidelines for national fiscal policy in EMU that was sparked off by the Delors Report. Section 3 continues with an aspect of this issue that is often neglected, namely the practical difficulties that arise in the implementation of the guidelines. Section 4 then turns to the issue of whether a fiscal shock absorber mechanism is needed at the Community level to offset the effects of country specific shocks.

Since chapter 5 has already addressed the issues that arise in the transition towards EMU, this chapter concentrates on EMU in its final form,[2] assuming throughout that for political reasons the Community remains at the 'pre-federal' stage (McDougall (1977)), i.e., that the budget of the Community will not exceed 2–2.5 per cent of GDP and that most competences in the fiscal area will remain at the national level. This limit on the size of the EC budget is a further reason why we do not discuss fiscal mechanisms to redistribute income. Moreover, the politically motivated limit on Community competences in the fiscal area means that there is no need to discuss the vast literature on fiscal federalism which analyses the optimal distribution of economic policy competencies between the federal and sub-federal (i.e., national) level in a variety of fields (regulation of industry and labour markets, provision of public goods, etc.).[3]

8.1   What is economic union?

There is no precise and universally agreed definition of economic union. However, since the publication of the Delors Report its definition has been widely used. Paragraph 25 of the Delors Report lists, somewhat arbitrarily, four basic components that form the core of the economic dimension of unification:

(1) the single market within which persons, goods, services and capital can move freely;

(2) competition policy and other measures aimed at strengthening market mechanisms;

(3) common policies aimed at structural change and regional development; and

(4) macroeconomic policy coordination including binding rules for budgetary policies.

The first two components are part of the definition of economic union generally accepted by economists. Progress in these two areas seems assured since the internal market programme is well on schedule. It is also beyond doubt that the creation of a single market with an authority to enforce competitive structures yields economic benefits.

---

[2] The issues related to the transition, e.g., the idea that there should be a 'no-entry' clause in the EMU Treaty, as proposed by Giovannini and Spaventa (1991), are taken up in chapter 12.

[3] See Van Rompuy, Abrahams and Heremans (1990) for a survey.

It is also becoming increasingly accepted that the initial legislative programme for 1992 is not sufficient to ensure the aim of a perfectly integrated market.[4] The original internal market programme did not contain provisions for common policies in those areas where an intervention by the Community is justified by the existence of important international external effects. Examples of these additional areas for common policy-making are network infrastructures or research and development, see Emerson *et al.* (1991), chapter 3 for more detail. EMU should make it easier to perfect the original internal market programme in this way. However, these elements are uncontroversial and of only limited significance relative to the other components of economic union.

The third component of the Delors Report's definition of economic union is difficult to assess purely on efficiency grounds. It must be based on considerations such as income distribution that relate more to equity than efficiency. These issues are dealt with in the literature on fiscal federalism, see Van Rompuy, Abrahams and Heremans (1990) for a survey.[5] These issues are not discussed here, mainly because they are not linked to the primary focus of this book, namely monetary integration.

The fourth component required to achieve an economic union in the vision of the Delors Report is coordination of national budgetary policies, going well beyond voluntary efforts on the part of each participant. While it is apparent that irrevocably fixed exchange rates (or a common currency) require a common institutional framework to manage the common monetary policy, there is a wide divergence of views as to whether that needs to be paralleled in the fiscal sphere by giving a collective body the authority to intervene in national budgetary policies in a binding way. Both economic and political objections can be raised to this interpretation of parallelism.[6] The economic ones are discussed in some detail below.

As will be described in chapter 10, the Delors Report stresses that 'economic and monetary union form two integral parts of a single whole and would therefore have to be implemented in parallel'.[7] This view has been widely accepted, and, if it is interpreted as a statement about the final stage, it can be defended on the ground that the benefits from a monetary union discussed in the previous chapter can be reaped only if there are no non-monetary barriers to trade within the area.

However, since it is impossible to measure and compare precisely the degree of monetary and economic integration, it is very difficult to assess whether the progress that will actually be taking place can be regarded as parallel or not. In contrast, the endpoints of both areas of unification, namely monetary union and economic union can be more readily defined. Parallelism should therefore be mainly understood as the idea that the economic benefits of economic and monetary integration reinforce each other

---

[4] See, for example, Pelkmans (1991), who provides an exhaustive survey of the concept of economic union.

[5] The way the Structural Funds are allocated by the Community is described in the 1990–1 Annual Economic Report of the Commission. The commission will publish in the first half of 1992 a thorough review of the experience since the decision to enlarge regional transfers in 1988.

[6] See Thygesen (1990). For a survey of macroeconomic policy-making in the Community see Mortensen (1990).

[7] Delors Report para. 42, see Committee for the Study of Economic and Monetary Union (1989).

so that the full benefits of monetary *and* economic union exceed the benefits that derive from integration in only one of these two areas.

There is, however, one controversial issue, which should not be included in this broad interpretation of parallelism although it links directly the economic and monetary aspects of integration. This is the issue of binding guidelines for national fiscal policy to which we now turn.

8.2 Does a stable monetary union require binding guidelines for fiscal policy?

The economic rationale for binding guidelines for fiscal policy is that, whatever the exchange-rate regime, there are international externalities to a country's budgetary policies. In a regime where exchange rates are either flexible or where governments occasionally resort to realignments, important elements of those externalities are deflected into movements in the currency of the initiating country. To this extent the consequences of budgetary expansion fall primarily on the country itself as domestic investment is in part crowded out by a mixture of higher interest rates at home and an appreciation of the currency.[8] However, as exchange rates are increasingly fixed these external effects become potentially more important.

The general economic[9] objection is that this sort of intervention in national policy-making would be superfluous in an EMU, since the fixed exchange-rate system, underpinned by a common monetary policy, would adequately constrain budgetary policies. There are therefore serious economic arguments on both sides.[10]

In the lively academic (and political) debate that has developed since the publication of the Delors Report three broad sets of arguments for imposing binding guidelines can be distinguished which are now discussed in turn.

In the following discussion it is assumed throughout that the guidelines would in practice be asymmetric, i.e., that there would only be upper limits for deficits. Although this is not always explicitly stated in the Delors Report it seems natural to assume since it is difficult to see how the Community could bring effective pressure on a country to spend more and thus to increase its deficit.

8.2.1 The EC needs to achieve a proper policy mix in the EMU

This argument is based on the view that national demand management via fiscal policy has spill-over effects because a fiscal stimulus in one member country leads to an

---

[8] Some externalities remain even under flexible exchange rates: shifts in competitive conditions (if devaluations occur and are subsequently eroded) and direct demand spill-over from budgetary policy.

[9] The political ones are outside the scope of this book, see also chapter 10 for an account of the politics of this aspect of the Delors Report.

[10] For a thoughtful survey see Bredenkamp and Deppler (1990).

increase in demand for the products of other countries as well. Chapter 4 discussed one variant of the widespread view that in the absence of proper coordination these spill-over effects lead to a deflationary bias in a fixed exchange-rate system if countries are concerned about their current-account position and/or capital mobility is limited. Under EMU national current accounts should no longer be a cause for concern so that this particular issue should not arise.[11]

However, chapter 4 also emphasized that the magnitude and sign of the spill-over effects are very difficult to determine because there are other effects (besides the direct demand spill-over) that go in the opposite direction (see Van der Ploeg (1991) for a survey). The extraordinary swing in German fiscal policy (from approximate balance in 1989 to a deficit of 5 per cent of GDP starting with the second half of 1990) is a good illustration of this problem. It has been estimated that the direct demand impulse coming from German unification led to additional imports from the Community of about 30 billion ecu per annum (almost 1 per cent of the GDP of the EC minus Germany). At the same time the increase in German interest rates spread throughout the EMS and led to higher interest rates in the Community which tended to depress demand. It is therefore not clear whether all of Germany's partners in the EC actually benefit from this expansionary German fiscal policy.

This particular example illustrates the theoretical difficulties in determining the magnitude and even the sign of the spill-over effects. In many cases it is therefore impossible to determine *a priori* whether the appropriate response in a given situation is one of fiscal expansion or the contrary. In principle one could use macroeconomic models to solve this theoretical indeterminacy. However, the existing models differ considerably in their estimates of the spill-over effects. In general they suggest that they are rather small in absolute terms, i.e., less than one tenth of the home country effects, and are often negative. Table 8.2.1, adapted from Emerson *et al.* (1991) illustrates this point:

This table shows that the demand spill-overs are often close or equal to zero and that spill-overs in terms of inflation might be more important. However, even the latter appear to vary in sign; French fiscal expansion leads to lower inflation in Italy and the United Kingdom, whereas the opposite is true for German fiscal policy.

These results cannot constitute a reliable guide because they are based on models that were estimated with data from the 1970s and 1980s. The common currency and other constraints on national policy implicit in EMU will alter radically some fundamental macroeconomic relationships, e.g., the wage–price link or the elasticity of the demand for (intra-EMU) exports. It will therefore remain very difficult for some time to come to estimate reliably the spill-over effects of national fiscal policy under EMU.

Uncertainty about the sign and magnitude of the cross-country spillovers can have serious consequences. Indeed, some calculations of the welfare gains from international policy coordination based on the major existing macroeconomic models of international

---

[11] The remainder of this section is based, in part, on Gros (1991).

Table 8.2.1   Spillover effect of a rise in government expenditure by 2 % of GDP

	Country originating the policy:	
	Germany	France
GDP:		
Germany	1.6	− 0.16
France	0	1.6
Italy	0	− 0.08
United Kingdom	− 0.02	− 0.1
Inflation:		
Germany	2.0	0
France	0.16	3.66
Italy	0.1	− 0.34
United Kingdom	0.1	− 0.14

Source: Emerson *et al.* (1991), table 5.5.

interaction show that the gains from policy coordination are ambiguous.[12] The basic point of this research is that coordination based on the wrong model can be welfare-reducing. Given that the true model will never be found this implies that the welfare gains from fiscal policy coordination predicted by many models will always remain elusive.

For those that regard these conceptual problems as solvable the case for fiscal policy coordination rests on the fact that the European Community is very different from large federal states. The EC budget, presently little more than 1 per cent of the combined GDP of member states, is too small to exert any significant stabilization function. For the foreseeable future, influence over the aggregate budgetary stance can come only via decisions on national budgets.[13] Large federal states permit themselves to be more relaxed about budgetary policies of regional governments because a federal budget of typically 20–30 per cent of GDP provides ample potential leverage. When imbalances in the policy mix appear, they are not due to insufficient centralization of budgetary authority. Recent experience in the United States provides a striking illustration of this point. The US Federal government has run a large deficit throughout much of the 1980s, while the aggregate position of the fifty states has been in small surplus.

Even if the central EC budget is too small to achieve the proper policy mix, there are two practical objections to the alleged need for a central EC authority to impose

[12] See Frankel and Rockett (1988) on coordination between the US and the rest of the world. Less modelling effort has gone into the intra-Community transmission of demand effects.

[13] At a more political level one could argue that an EMU whose members have preached to other major industrial countries the virtue of a correct mix of monetary and fiscal policy can not leave itself with no effective means to influence that policy mix. This issue is discussed further in chapter 9.

'effective upper limits on budget deficits of individual member countries of the Community'[14] in order get the right aggregate policy mix: (a) there is no logical reason for its influence to be asymmetrical, i.e., directed only at excessive deficits, and (b) it is not obvious that binding rules are required.[15]

(a) The policy mix may become inappropriate because national budgetary policies are in the aggregate too restrictive. Such a situation would be characterized by a rising current-account surplus for the EMU area as a whole (or by a reduction of an area deficit regarded as globally appropriate). Another illustration of national fiscal policies becoming too restrictive in the aggregate could be upward pressure on the exchange rate of the union through a rising current-account surplus, which is then countered by monetary expansion, considered inappropriate in a perspective of long-term price stability. It was often argued that there were distortions of this type in the policy mix in the EMS during the mid 1980s, when most member countries pursued budgetary consolidation while monetary growth accelerated. Situations of this type cannot be ruled out in the future and could not be addressed by asymmetric rules that limit only deficits.

(b) Across-the-board proportional adjustments of budgetary balances would be difficult to justify solely with reference to the argument on the appropriate policy mix. They might well be recommended as appropriate and they will become increasingly logical as EMU deepens integration. But, given the major differences between national budget positions that can be expected to persist for any foreseeable time, they would be difficult to justify.[16] A differentiated judgement would be required that takes into account the position of individual member states with regard to their public debt and internal conjunctural position.

There are further arguments against the view that Community-led joint demand management through national budgetary balances is desirable. For example, one might actually see a virtue in the capacity of EMU to reduce the need for discretionary coordination of non-monetary policies. That would be desirable, both because of past failures to get to grips with such coordination between the EMS countries and at the global level, and because of the inherent difficulties and arbitrariness of the exercise.

Finally it should not be overlooked that EMU will provide a reason for more divergence in national fiscal policy since, as discussed in chapter 7, fiscal policy will be the only remaining major policy tool for reacting to nationally differentiated shocks. In the case of major shocks exceptions to the guidelines may have to be made on a discretionary basis. This cautions against writing any specific norms into the Treaty framework for EMU.

---

[14] Delors Report, para. 30.

[15] Chapter 10 shows that the Delors Committee was aware of both points.

[16] See De Grauwe (1990) for more details concerning the present fiscal position of member countries and the reasons for divergent developments.

8.2.2 Union-wide interest-rate effects of national deficits

The economic basis for this argument are spill-over effects of a different nature from those deriving from the demand management aspects discussed above. Excessive budget deficits in any one country have often led in the past to a risk premium required by investors to hold assets denominated in the currency in question because of the anticipation that it would become more attractive for politicians to monetize large deficits and allow the currency to depreciate than to undertake the difficult task of fiscal consolidation. With exchange rates at least potentially flexible, the risk premium and the wealth losses imposed on domestic asset holders and on those (including the government) who have borrowed in foreign currencies would be borne by the country itself.[17] However, with credibly fixed exchange rates, investors might require a risk premium on assets denominated in any of the currencies of the entire area or in the single currency when that has been introduced.[18] These union-wide interest-rate effects are undesirable because even a country with a sound fiscal position would have to pay the higher interest rate.

Economic integration and monetary unification increase the transmission of the interest-rate effects of national budgetary policies. It follows that in order to discourage free-riding on partner countries the imposition of some central authority becomes more necessary under EMU than in the present, more decentralized system.

This issue can be important in practice because some individual member states have budget deficits that are large relative to the entire economy of the EMU area (and much larger than those of single states in most existing federations, such as the United States or Switzerland). A deficit of 10 per cent of GDP in a large member state corresponds to more than 1 per cent of collective GDP and to more than 5 per cent of EC net savings. Borrowing by a large member state, as recently observed in Italy, is in a different category from that of even the biggest private firms or public enterprises. The absorption of a substantial part of EC savings by large and persistent public deficits would raise political pressures for correction of undesired externalities that affect other member states. While this line of reasoning may apply only to the actions of large member states, 'binding rules' would have to apply potentially to all. Though the international system and the EC has traditionally been more tolerant of imbalances in small than in large industrial countries, there could hardly be positive discrimination in favour of the former in a new mandatory system.

In this view the authority to set 'binding rules' could therefore serve to prevent more improvised and brutal pressures for adjustments coming from financial markets or political pressures by other member states late in a process of divergence.

---

[17] We do not discuss a related argument for binding rules, namely that large budget deficits, particularly if they come on top of already large debt/income ratios, may threaten the fixity of exchange rates until the credibility of EMU has been firmly established. This is an argument for insisting on better budgetary convergence in the transitory stages, but not necessarily for binding rules once EMU has been set up.

[18] For a thoughtful discussion which reaches a more agnostic conclusion, see Bredenkamp and Deepler (1990).

8.2.3 EMU could bring fiscal laxity

This argument for binding guidelines is based on the fear that launching an EMU without any mandatory budgetary coordination could encourage an excessively lax aggregate fiscal stance. Some who favour the rigid locking of exchange rates in EMU over the present arrangements do so because the financing of external deficits becomes more automatic and the potential effects of fiscal policy more predictable and possibly larger within the borders of the initiating country. This is the counterpart to the argument discussed in the previous sub-section: there will be less crowding out of fiscal expansion through higher interest rates at home and less need for concern with external imbalance. A policy-adviser could find good arguments for concluding that ambitions in fiscal policy can be raised once exchange rates are fully fixed. A policy-maker, no longer confronted with pressures on the currency or from large reserve flows, might more readily follow the advice.

This attitude, if widespread (and if consciously adopted by several member states) would, indeed, create a bias towards budgetary laxity. Such a bias may anyway be observable in the transitory stages, as greater homogeneity of national tax régimes is approached through lower indirect and direct taxes in high-tax countries rather than by tax increases elsewhere. Given the starting point of major differences in national budgetary stance and the likely further sources of divergence in the 1990s, there is no scope for encouraging licence in budgetary policy. Furthermore, if fiscal laxity did follow EMU, the other two arguments above would both be reinforced.

This argument would not be conclusive if alternative disciplining mechanisms were to emerge so as to prevent an excessively lax aggregate fiscal stance. Participation in EMU would eliminate the escape route of devaluation and surprise inflation which has in the past occasionally reduced the real value of public debt. Participation in a fully integrated European financial area opens captive national markets for public debt where governments have been able in the past to finance deficits at below-market interest rates through high reserve requirements on bank deposits and compulsory minimum holdings of government debt. With these privileges gone, financial markets would be in a position to undertake a straight professional evaluation of the varying degrees of creditworthiness of national governments. Those persisting in rapid issues of debt would face rising borrowing costs and some outright rationing of credit, possibly linked to a downgrading of their credit rating.[19]

There is little evidence, however, that such mechanisms, even if they are allowed to develop fully, would provide adequate constraints on budgetary divergence. The experience of large federal states suggests that the sanction of an inferior credit rating is of minor importance. Within Canada, where the divergence in budgetary stance and in indebtedness is wider than in other federations, the range of borrowing costs spans less than 50 basis points. Within the United States borrowing costs show a similar lack of

---

[19] It is apparent that this mechanism can only work if the European Central Bank does not use open market operations to narrow interest-rate differentials on public debt issued by different national governments, but in fact allows risk premia to emerge reflecting the market's perception of differences in creditworthiness. See chapter 13 for more details.

sensitivity to the budgetary policies of states which tend anyway to be fairly uniform. And global financial markets at first had difficulties in assessing properly the credit risks attached to Third World sovereign borrowers, then in 1982 reacted sharply and almost indiscriminately as the prospects for debtors worsened. Even New York city, which almost went bankrupt in the mid 1970s, did not have to pay a large premium until its credit was cut off almost completely.

This episode, as well as the experience with bank lending to LDCs suggests that financial markets do not operate with smoothly increasing risk premia. The fundamental reason for this *modus operandi* of financial markets lies in the adverse selection effect of higher interest rates as suggested by Stiglitz and Weiss (1981). The crucial point of this analysis is that borrowers always have better information about their own financial position. Banks (or creditors in general) will therefore be reluctant to lend to borrowers offering to pay very high interest rates since they can expect that only borrowers who are in fact very bad risks accept high interest rates. This is why credit (especially bank loan) markets are not characterized by smooth supply curves of credit that are only a function of the interest rate. The spread between bad and good borrowers is usually rather low and, beyond a certain interest rate, credit is just cut off. Financial markets might therefore exercise very little discipline until a certain threshold has been reached. Beyond this point the unavailability of any further funds would precipitate at least a liquidity crisis for the government concerned.

Stiglitz and Weiss (1981) also show that a small reduction in the quantity of credit available can in some cases cause extensive credit rationing. A small tightening of credit conditions by the European Central Bank could thus, at times, push a member country into a liquidity crisis. Under these circumstances the ECB would probably not be able to refuse to provide some 'temporary' financing. The absence of a more graduated discipline means therefore that it is likely that a funding crisis can undermine a tight monetary stance.

Could financial markets be induced to apply a more graduated discipline to the borrowing by member states in an EMU? That is possible as some observers have argued, see, e.g., Bishop *et al.* (1989). One would expect financial markets to discriminate more between member countries than between Canadian provinces which for more than a century have been part of a monetary union. But financial markets might still primarily interpret the formation of EMU as an upgrading of the creditworthiness of weak members; Bishop (1991) reports that already the differences between the interest rates paid by different member governments appear to be insufficient to account for the differences in risk that arise from the different debt burdens. If this is the case now it is difficult to see how the situation could change radically with EMU, even if the central authorities of the EMU were to state explicitly, as they appear determined to do, that they would not provide bail-out facilities (an 'umbrella') for member states. Participation in the EMU could therefore effectively protect deficit spending from market pressures. Binding guidelines could be viewed as a necessary correction to 'free-riding' that would be difficult to avoid through a mere statement of the Community that it would not bail out member states.

The evidence reported in Grilli, Masciandro and Tabellini (1991), which shows that an independent central bank can produce, on average, lower inflation even in the context of lax fiscal behaviour, is not conclusive evidence to the contrary since this result only indicates that an independent central bank can mitigate, not eliminate, the inflationary impact of excessive fiscal deficits. Recent research indicates, moreover, that even if financial markets provide adequate discipline there might be external effects of national budgetary policies. In Alogoskoufis and van der Ploeg (1990) it is argued that the level of public debt in one country can influence the rate of growth in other countries because there are international economies of scale. A high debt abroad would tend to reduce the amount of domestic savings available for domestic investment and hence domestic growth. This implies that member countries would have the right, even on purely economic grounds, to be concerned about excessive debts in their partner countries in EMU. It is apparent that this line of reasoning would provide an argument for guidelines on public debts, rather than deficits.

8.3   Practical problems in implementing binding guidelines

Even those who accept the arguments in favour of mandatory budgetary coordination and share the view that financial markets will not provide a substitute discipline have doubts about how the proposal would be implemented and enforced. In principle, the 1974 Decision on convergence, which was revised in 1990, provides the Community with a tool to organize macroeconomic coordination if this is deemed desirable. Although the 1974 Decision was never used to achieve effective coordination this implies that in principle there is no need for further legislative action to ensure the proper amount of coordination of fiscal policy in short-run demand management terms.

However, the 1974 Decision would not be useful in addressing the more long-run issues discussed above that provide the more urgent reason for imposing the 'upper limits on budget deficits' mentioned in the Delors Report. The challenge is therefore to provide an operational guideline for budgetary policy for some Community oversight over national fiscal policy.

During the transition towards EMU the most logical approach would be to intervene in a country's policy only if it became a threat to the fixed exchange-rate system. That will not, however, provide a clear operational criterion: the ECOFIN Council would be guided by its collective concern whether a government could fulfil its commitment to fully fixed exchange rates without recourse to monetary financing, which would, in principle, be excluded in an EMU – but the Council will be reluctant to voice such doubts explicitly in public.

Any permanent guidelines would therefore have to be as objective as possible so that there is little room for interpretation and for political pressures to relax them in specific cases. Especially if they are to be backed up by sanctions they would have to be as justifiable as possible. Four related operational concepts have been proposed to solve this problem.

8.3.1 Ceilings on the deficit relative to GDP

The simplest type of rule, hinted at in the Delors Report, is to relate the maximum permissible deficit directly to GDP. However, that could be too crude a measure, as one would want to relate the ceiling also to the private savings-investment balance of the country; for this reason alone it would be impossible to apply uniformly. The Delors Report itself hints at this in saying (para. 30) that 'the situation of each country might have to be taken into consideration'. Could other generally applicable rules be envisaged?

References to the absence of federally imposed constraints on state deficits in the United States often omit to point out that a large number of states have adopted 'balanced budget amendments'.[20] This is just a particular version of a uniform ceiling on the deficit. It would be too rigorous in a Community with wide differences in budgetary positions and public debt/GDP ratios ranging from 35 per cent in France to 128 per cent in Belgium (disregarding Luxembourg with only 9 per cent), see table 5.4.4 in chapter 5. Allowance would, at a minimum, have to be made for the equally wide differences in the net costs of debt servicing which these differences in debt impose on national governments.

Reference to the US experience might be particularly misleading if one takes into account that there the problem is that the federal administration and Congress have tended not to follow their own guidelines (i.e., the Gramm–Rudman–Hollings Act of 1985 which aims at reducing the federal deficit) whereas the states in general adhere to their own restrictions and run mostly balanced budgets over the medium run. In contrast, in the Community the federal level (i.e., the Commission, Parliament and the Council) has always adhered to the provision in the Treaty for the EC budget to be balanced. The problem for the Community is therefore in some sense the opposite of that of the US, namely excessive state (national) deficits instead of an excessive federal deficit.[21]

8.3.2 Ceilings on the primary deficit (relative to GDP)

The simplest way of making an allowance for differences in national situations would be to set *a rule for the primary deficit*, i.e., the deficit net of interest payments. If monetary financing is excluded (see chapter 5 for estimates of the residual amount available under a financially integrated, low-inflation EMU) and nominal interest rates correspond approximately to the growth of nominal incomes in the participating countries, the

---

[20] Some research indicates, however, that the importance of these legal provisions should not be exaggerated. See for instance Von Hagen (1991), who finds little systematic relationship between actual state deficits or debts and the severity of the formal constraints.

[21] The starting point for EMU resembles more that of the thirteen states which formed the United States in 1789. But, in that historical example, the new Federation took over a major share of the debt of its component states, which was to a large extent due to their part in a joint war effort.

primary deficit relative to GDP would fully determine public debt accumulation relative to GDP. A conceivable formulation of a rule, provided these (rather strong) assumptions are roughly met, would be to aim for a primary deficit of zero, implying a stable level of debt relative to GDP.[22]

8.3.3 Ceilings based on an assessment of long-run sustainability

However, at present interest rates exceed growth rates of GDP and even a primary deficit of zero would therefore not be sufficient to stop the debt/GDP ratio from rising. Chapter 5 provided some estimates of the primary *surplus* needed in member countries to achieve a stable debt level relative to GDP.

In principle, one could therefore determine analytically a sustainable trend of public debt and derive the implications for the maximum primary deficit compatible with such a trend.[23] But there are two objections to such a procedure:

1   The rule would appear to be too lax. In 1988 most member countries had a primary surplus large enough to imply a gradual reduction in the debt burden relative to GDP (see table 8.3.1 below and chapter 5 for more detail). Only four problem countries have to undertake a fiscal adjustment to stabilize their debt ratio. An EMU would not want to be seen to encourage relaxation of the efforts of the majority, efforts that are certainly necessary in those countries where debt amounts to more than 100 per cent of GDP.

2   The estimates would be surrounded by a very considerable margin of uncertainty, leaving much room for divergent interpretations by EC and national authorities. Chapter 5 provided two estimates of the adjustment needed to stabilize debt to GDP ratios that come from two respected international institutions, the OECD and the Commission. Table 8.3.1 uses these data, but shows only the *differences* between the data provided by these two institutions. This table shows that it is indeed very difficult to judge whether fiscal policy is sustainable or not because this judgement has to rely on a number of assumptions.

Table 8.3.1 shows that all the factors that are used to calculate the usual indicator of sustainability are difficult to determine with any precision. Even the debt/GDP ratio, that is the basic ingredient in these calculations, is measured differently by these two international organizations because the OECD data refer to net public debt whereas the

---

[22] In the early phases of the transition towards EMU governments that are large debtors might still have to pay a premium on outstanding debt which is not offset by faster growth in their nominal GDP, so that their debt/income ratio would rise even with a zero primary deficit.

[23] For an effort along the lines developed by Blanchard (1984) see chapter 5 in Emerson *et al.* (1991). EMU resembles more that of the thirteen states which formed the United States in 1789. But, in that historical example, the new Federation took over a major share of the debt of its component states, which was a large extent due to their part in a joint war effort.

EC data refer to the gross debt of general government. As can be seen from the first column of the table this leads to the result that the EC estimates of the debt/GDP ratios for Denmark and Germany are 40 and 21 percentage points higher than the estimates provided by the OECD. Given that it is not clear *a priori* whether the sustainability criterion should be based on net or gross debt it is difficult to determine objectively even the starting point for any subsequent assessment of the sustainability of a particular fiscal situation.

Table 8.3.1 The need for fiscal adjustment: discrepancies between OECD and EC data

			Adjustment in Fiscal Deficit needed to:		
	debt/GDP	*Interest rate minus growth rate*	*Primary balance*	*Stabilize debt/GDP*	*Achieve convergence in debt/ GDP in 10 yrs*
	(1)	(2)	(3)	(4)	(5)
Belgium	6.1	−1.2	−1.8	0.45	0.21
Denmark	40.4	−4.4	0.9	−1.11	2.08
Germany	21.1	0.0	0.2	0.22	1.48
Greece	7.2	−0.4	−4.3	4.13	4.00
Spain	14.5	−1.9	−2.5	2.16	2.76
France	8.1	−1.7	−0.2	−0.03	0.13
Ireland	−17.7	−2.6	1.9	−5.35	−7.97
Italy	4.6	−2.2	−1.2	−0.81	−1.20
Netherlands	21.2	−0.9	1.3	−1.39	−0.12
United Kingdom	11.40	−2.50	1.9	−2.49	−2.20

Note: No entries for Luxembourg and Portugal because they are not covered by the OECD.

Source: OECD (1990) and table 5.3 in Emerson *et al.* (1991)

A further important factor in assessing sustainability is the difference between the interest rate and the growth rate of GDP. The OECD uses growth rates and actual long-term market rates of interest whereas the EC just assumes that real interest rates will exceed real growth rates by 2 percentage points for most member countries in the long run. This leads to further important differences as can be seen from column (2) of the table. To some extent these differences in underlying assumptions offset each other, but columns (4) and (5) of the table show that very large differences remain regarding the magnitude of the fiscal adjustment needed to attain a sustainable fiscal position. In the case of Ireland the OECD estimate of the necessary adjustment is 5.35 per cent of GDP larger than that of the EC. Conversely, in the case of Greece, the OECD estimate of the necessary fiscal adjustment is 4 per cent of GDP lower than that of the EC.

An even more serious problem arises if one considers only the deficits and debts reported by the EC. In theory the reported deficits should account for the observed changes in debt levels, at least over the long run. However, this is not the whole case as shown in table 8.3.2 below.

Table 8.3.2   Discrepancy between reported deficits and changes in debt levels

	Averages over 1981–1989:		
	theoretical change in debt/GDP	actual change in debt/GDP	discrepancy[a]
Belgium	2.0	5.2	3.2
Denmark	− 2.0	2.4	4.4
Germany	0.1	1.1	1.0
Greece	3.6	6.1	2.5
Spain	0.3	2.7	2.4
France	− 0.1	1.2	1.3
Ireland	0.3	2.5	2.2
Italy	2.5	4.2	1.7
Netherlands	3.2	3.2	− 0.0
UK	− 2.9	− 1.1	1.8

Note :
[a] Difference between actual reported changes in debt levels and the change in debt that would have resulted from the reported deficits.

Source: Commission of the European Communities (1990).

This table shows that public debts can increase substantially more than one would expect from the reported deficits. For example, between 1981 and 1989 the Belgian public debt/GDP ratio increased by more than 50 percentage points (i.e., 5.2 times ten) but this was over 30 percentage points (3.2 times ten) more than one would expect given the deficits reported over these ten years. Discrepancies on a similar scale are reported for Greece and, somewhat surprisingly, Denmark. The Netherlands apppear to be the only country where there is no discrepancy, on average, between the reported deficit and the actual behaviour of the debt to GDP ratio.

These data suggest that, assuming the published data about public debt are credible, the official fiscal accounts data are of little value since the debt/GDP ratio can increase considerably even if the officially reported deficits would suggest that it should be stable (this is the case of Spain) or even fall (this is the case of Denmark). Temporary deviations from the accounting relationship that links debts to deficits are certainly understandable, but the discrepancies over the ten-year averages found here suggest that the problem is more fundamental.

Except for extreme cases it would therefore always be difficult to find an objective indicator of sustainability that would eliminate the need for discretionary judgement and would therefore also minimize the room for political interference.

8.3.4 Ceilings on the current balance: the 'golden rule'

Finally it has also been suggested that the so-called 'golden rule' might be used as a guideline. Under this approach the overall public deficit would not be allowed to exceed investment expenditures which is equivalent to the prescription that current receipts (taxes and social security contributions) have to match fully current expenditures.[24] This approach would have to distinguish between current public expenditure (e.g., salaries to civil servants or social security transfers) and public investment (e.g., infrastructure investment or capital transfers) along the lines of the German constitution that rules out any deficit on current expenditure by forbidding deficits that exceed public investment.

While such a rule might have some theoretical appeal it would be even more difficult to implement than the ones discussed so far since the distinction between current and capital expenditure is always to a large extent arbitrary. Moreover, since not all public investment can be assumed to increase future tax revenues (for example investment to protect the environment), the theoretical case for constraining only the current deficit is weak.

The distinction between current and investment expenditure is crucial for one important part of total expenditure, namely interest payments on the public debt, which amount to over 10 per cent of GDP in some member countries. At present the accounting practices of all member countries classify interest payments as current expenditure. However, this classification becomes particularly doubtful when inflation is high because high inflation leads to high nominal interest rates, which compensate for the loss of purchasing power of the principal. It follows that under high inflation rates a large part of interest payments really represent capital transfers.

From an economic point of view it would be preferable to correct for this artificial increase in current expenditure by splitting total interest payments into two parts: one part represents the inflation capital adjustment (which is equal to the inflation rate times the value of the debt), and the remainder represents the true current interest expenditures, i.e., real interest payments. Only with zero inflation would all interest expenditures consist of the latter, current part.

Table 8.3.3 shows therefore two measures of public gross savings (i.e., current income minus current expenditure). The first column contains the uncorrected measure obtained with the usual accounting procedures. According to this measure six member countries do not obey the golden rule. The second column shows the inflation adjustment to current expenditures. The third column in this table then shows gross

---

[24] See for example the Annual Economic Report 1990–1 of the Commission.

savings adjusted for the effect of inflation on current expenditures. It is striking that once this adjustment is made all member countries appear to follow the golden rule.

Since the last column represents (approximately) the gross savings that would be measured with zero inflation under current accounting practices it follows that the golden rule cannot be expected to become very stringent once an EMU with stable prices has been established.

Table 8.3.3 Alternative measures of government savings

	Gross savings	Inflation adjustment	Inflation adjusted savings
Belgium	− 3.8	4.3	0.5
Denmark	0.9	1.9	2.8
Germany	0.3	1.6	1.9
Greece	−14.7	18.6	3.9
Spain	2.8	3.3	6.1
France	2.3	1.3	3.6
Ireland	− 1.2	2.1	0.9
Italy	− 5.6	7.2	1.6
Luxembourg	8.3	0.2	8.5
Netherlands	− 1.4	2.3	0.9
Portugal	− 2.4	9.4	7.4
UK	2.5	3.3	5.8
EC12 average	− 0.2	3.4	3.2

Source: Commission of the European Communities (1990). All data refers to 1990 and is in per cent of GDP. The inflation adjustment is equal to the inflation rate times the debt/GDP ratio.

The decisive objection against the golden rule is therefore that it would simply be too lax. Even some of the countries that are clearly in a fiscal position that is not sustainable in the long run would at present not be affected by such a rule. It might, however, still be useful to retain the basic idea underlying the golden rule, i.e., that it matters whether the government has a deficit because it spends on public investment or whether the deficit is caused by excessive public consumption and transfer payments.

Concern about the 'quality' of government expenditure is justified by the fact that in many cases fiscal adjustment efforts start by cutting public investment, which does not have the same powerful political constituencies as transfer payments. Figure 8.3.1 illustrates this by displaying the inflation–adjusted public sector balance (as per cent of GDP) against spending on public investment (also as per cent of GDP). If all member countries were to obey strictly the golden rule all observations should be on line with a slope equal to minus one. However, the data clearly show that the association between the overall public sector balance and spending on public investment is not negative as required by the golden rule. The data suggest, on the contrary, that, for the political economy reasons outlined above, countries that have less budgetary difficulties invest more.

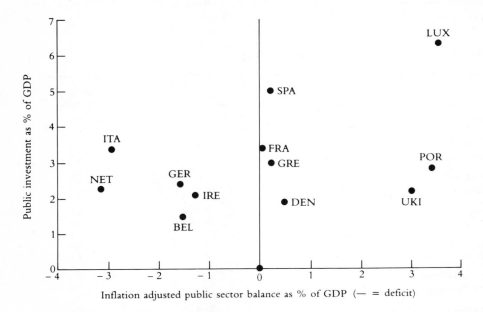

Figure 8.3.1 A Golden Rule? (Inflation adjusted public sector deficits and public investment.)

The need to take the 'quality' of public spending into account provides therefore another reason to be sceptical about the usefulness of general guidelines for fiscal policy.

8.4 Fiscal shock absorbers

As discussed in chapter 7 national fiscal policy might become more important under EMU because it remains the only policy instrument that can be used by national authorities to react to outside shocks especially if labour mobility is too low to mitigate unemployment. As long as these shocks are temporary and therefore average out over the long run this would appear to pose no problem since national governments should be able to rely on the capital market to finance temporary deficits. However, it has been argued, e.g., Eichengreen (1990), that even national governments sometimes do not have sufficient access to financial markets (especially when they already have a large debt outstanding) implying that the Community should help member countries to weather the impact of adverse shocks. Although this could be done in principle through assistance to member governments (along the lines of the German *Finanzausgleich*) the debate has focused on ways by which the Community aid could be channelled directly to individuals.

Proponents of the point of view that some 'fiscal shock absorber' is needed agree that any Community mechanism would have to be as automatic and 'invisible' as possible and that its purpose would not be to equalize income levels, but to provide insurance against country-specific shocks. Assistance that involves a large discretionary element would be subject to 'bureaucratic capture' and would pose obvious moral hazard problems. This is why it has been suggested (Eichengreen (1990), Bean *et al.* (1990)) that the Community should finance a part of national unemployment insurance schemes and receive also a corresponding part of the contributions. Countries with above-average unemployment would then receive a transfer from countries with below-average unemployment. Payments to the unemployed in the former would in effect be financed by contributions from those employed in the latter. Such a scheme would be automatic in the sense that no specific decisions concerning the direction and the magnitude of the transfers need to be taken once the system has been established.

The argument for a Community unemployment insurance scheme has often been made with reference to the United States where there is some reinsurance at the federal level. However, as reported by Von Hagen (1991), in practice, the federal reinsurance scheme has not been used for some time, so that *de facto* in the United States unemployment insurance is organized and financed exclusively at the state level.

Other proposals for some Community fiscal shock absorber mechanism refer to the MacDougall report which documented that in most existing federations the federal budget redistributes income across regions and thus offsets at least part of the interregional differences in income. For the United States, MacDougall (1977) and Sachs and Sala-i-Martin (1989) estimate that the federal budget offsets about 30 to 40 per cent of the differences in income per capita across states because poorer states contribute on average lower income tax and receive higher social security payments. It has therefore been argued (Eichengreen (1990)) that because labour markets seem to be less flexible in the Community the need for a fiscal shock absorber is even greater in the Community than in the United States where migration in response to unfavourable economic shocks can be quite substantial.

However, the argument that a stable EMU needs such an automatic fiscal equalization scheme seems to be based on a misreading of the US experience. The results referred to above imply that federal fiscal systems offset about 30 to 40 per cent of the difference in the *level* of income per capita. However, this does not automatically imply that these mechanisms also provide an insurance against *shocks*, i.e., changes in income. The level effect found by Sachs and Sala-i-Martin (1989) implies that, at each point in time, individuals in a state with an income per capita 1,000 dollars lower than the average, pay about 300 dollars less in income taxes and receive about 100 dollars more in direct payments.

Von Hagen (1991) obtains different results by looking at changes in income. He finds that a fall in income per capita by 1 per cent reduces federal income tax also by 1 per cent. Since the federal income tax accounts only for 8 per cent of income this implies that if income per capita goes up from 1,000 to 1,010 dollars the federal income tax goes from 80 to 80.8 dollars; the offset is thus only 80 cents over 10 dollars, or 8 per cent.[25] Moreover, in the regressions reported by Von Hagen (1991), direct federal payments to households do not react at all significantly to *variations* in state income per capita. Gros and Jones (1991) find a level effect in the sense that inviduals in a state with a per capital income of 1 000 dollar above the average pay about 240 dollar more in federal income tax and federal social security contributions. However, year-on-year changes in income do not seem to cause significant changes in taxes or social security contributions. Moreover, neither the level nor the changes in federal transfers are correlated with income. These results suggest that the automatic insurance provided by the US tax and social security system is much more limited than sometimes claimed.

All in all, it is therefore difficult to rest the case for some Community shock absorber on the US experience. For those favouring such a policy on efficiency (as opposed to equity) grounds it would therefore be imperative to spell out in more detail why capital markets do not allow national governments to weather temporary adverse shocks by borrowing on the capital market. The distinction between transitory and permanent shocks is crucial in this area because permanent shocks could, of course, not be financed forever and would thus require adjustment in real wages and/or migration. However, it is difficult to see how the Community could provide insurance against permanent country-specific shocks without addressing directly the issue of income redistribution.

8.5 Binding guidelines in the Intergovernmental Conference on EMU

We have dealt more superficially with the economic aspects of integration, in part because it is more difficult to determine what they imply. Our discussion of budgetary rules in an EMU, the most controversial part of the recommendations in the Delors Report, concluded that while there are spill-over effects of national budgetary policies in an EMU it would be difficult to formulate and implement rules regarding short-run demand management. However, concerns about the systemic stability of EMU can justify more interference in budgetary policies, especially when public debt or deficits threaten to become unsustainable or 'excessive'.

The considerations about the practical difficulties in implementing binding guidelines suggest that substantial allowances for differences in initial national situations have to be made to make general rules a useful tool for improving the average quality of budgetary policies in the Community. One is led, inevitably, towards the consideration of more discretionary methods of formulating the collectively agreed budgetary guidelines. This implies that a recommendation which a qualified majority in the ECOFIN Council could agree to address to a participant would constitute a 'rule' in the sense that non-compliance with it would trigger some form of sanction on the part of the Community. Such a procedure is envisaged in the Treaty revision relating to EMU (Art. 104C).

---

[25] Von Hagen (1990) seems to overstate his case by comparing (page 9) the *change* in federal income tax to the *level* of income per capita.

However, there is little reason to think that the ECOFIN Council would use such authority frequently and vigorously; the past history of the Community clearly suggests that this is more than unlikely. The Council has never been demanding, for example, in administering its medium-term financial support system. Nor has the EC Commission, with which the initiative to implement the guidelines would rest, shown any eagerness in the past to use the authority which it has had since 1974 to issue recommendations to a member state; in nearly sixteen years it has only acted once.[26] The challenge in EMU is to encourage the Council and the Commission to be less cautious in confronting national policy-making than they have been in the past.

Whatever the form of binding rules adopted, one element to keep under observation is that the binding guidelines should not apply to budget forecasts. They would have to trigger corrective actions as a function not only of planned, but primarily of *actual budget out-turns*. Although this may seem self-evident it needs to be emphasized because this was not the case in the US.[27]

Finally, as regards the time horizon for the budgetary rules, their purpose would not be to serve short-term, activist aims, but to keep participants on a medium-term course of debt accumulation (or reduction) which is sustainable in terms of maintaining the cohesion of EMU. Binding guidelines would accordingly be formulated for a period of several years, though mandatory for each budget year within that period. One difficulty in using the (non-binding) authority under the 1974 Decision may have been that its premise was an ambition to pursue more activist stabilization policies than was either economically desirable or politically realistic.

The revised Treaty now submitted for ratification in the member states does appear to meet the criteria discussed in this chapter. It requests member states to avoid 'excessive government deficits' and it defines in a separate protocol the reference values for the evaluation by ECOFIN as 3 per cent of GDP for the deficit and 60 per cent of GDP for government debt. The text of the relevant Article 104C is reproduced in Appendix 1 to Chapter 13. Article 104C also lists the procedure to be followed by ECOFIN: the Commission is to prepare a report and submit it to the Economic and Financial Committee, the successor to the present Monetary Committee after the transition to the final state of EMU. The ECOFIN Council will then 'decide after an overall assessment whether an excessive deficit exists' and make recommendations to the member state concerned, at first in private, but if there is no effective follow-up, in public. If a member state persists in failing to put into practice the recommendations, the ECOFIN Council may ask for specific measures to reduce the excessive deficit. If

---

[26] Against Belgium, on the issue of wage indexation. Article 17 of the 1974 Decision on convergence entrusts the Commission with this task, if a member state is 'pursuing economic, monetary and budgetary policies departing from the guidelines laid down by the Council or entailing risks for the Community as a whole'.

[27] In the United States, Congress adopted constraints on the *forecast* budget balance through the Gramm–Rudman–Hollings Act, which prescribed proportional cuts in a range of specified expenditures if the deficit forecast for the coming year exceed a prescribed downward trend. There was no subsequent sanction if the actual budget deficit was excessive. This procedure has generated disputes about the economic assumptions underlying the budget forecasts and incentives to push some expenditures off budget.

the member state concerned still fails to comply, the ECOFIN Council may (1) require additional information to be published before any issue of bonds and securities, (2) invite the European Investment Bank to reconsider its lending policy towards the member state, (3) ask for non-interest bearing deposits, or (4) impose outright fines.

This tough gradualist procedure will no doubt bring considerable pressure to bear on a participant in EMU which persists in pursuing a divergent budgetary policy. In the light of the discussion in the present chapter the concern must be that the reference values proposed are arbitrary and so demanding that they go beyond what is required for EMU rather than that they are too loose. But arbitrariness cannot be avoided, if discussion of containment of excessive deficits is to begin. Chapter 12 returns to the application of some of the procedure already in the transition to EMU; much of the discussion in the Intergovernmental Conference centered on the suitability of the reference values as the underpinnings for a qualification system to EMU. Taken literally, they would appear to constitute a no-entry clause for some member states, an issue which is also addressed in Chapter 14.

References

Alogoskoufis, George and Frederick van der Ploeg, (1990) 'Endogenous growth and overlapping generations' Tilburg University, Center, *Discussion Paper*, 9072.

Bean, Charles, Edmond Malinvaud, Peter Bernholz, Francesco Giavazzi and Charles Wyplosz, (1990), 'Policies for 1992: The Transition and After', in 'The Macroeconomics of 1992', *CEPS Paper* No. 42, Centre for European Policy Studies, Brussels.

Bishop, Graham (1990), 'Separating Fiscal from Monetary Sovereignty in EMU – A United States of Europe is not necessary', London, Salomon Brothers, November.
(1991), 'The EC's Public Debt Disease: Discipline with Credit Spreads and Cure with Price Stability', London, Salomon Brothers, May.

Bishop, Graham, Dirk Damrau and Michelle Miller, (1989), 'Market discipline can work in the EC monetary union', London, Salomon Brothers, November.

Blanchard, Olivier, Jean-Claude Chouraqui, Robert Hagemann and Nicola Sartor (1991), 'The Sustainability of Fiscal Policy: New Answers to an Old Question', *OECD Economic Studies*, No. 15, Autumn.

Bredenkamp, Hugh and Michael Deppler (1990), 'Fiscal constraints of a hard-currency regime', chapter 7 in Victor Argy and Paul De Grauwe (eds.), *Choosing an Exchange Rate Regime: The Challenge for Smaller Industrial Countries*, International Monetary Fund, MacQuarie University and Katholieke Universiteit Leuven, 35–73.

Committee for the Study of Economic and Monetary Union (1989), 'Report on Economic and Monetary Union in the European Community' (the Delors Report), Office of Publications of the European Communities, Luxembourg.

Commission of the European Communities (1990), 'Annual Economic Report', *European Economy*, 46, December.

De Grauwe, Paul (1990) 'Fiscal Discipline in Monetary Unions', Centre for European Policy Studies, Brussels, *CEPS Working Document*, 50.

Dornbusch, Rüdiger, and Mario Draghi (1990), *Public Debt Management: Theory and Evidence*, Cambridge University Press, Cambridge.

Eichengreen, Barry, (1990), 'One Money for Europe? Lessons from the US Currency Union', *Economic Policy* No. 10, April, pp. 117–87.

Emerson, Michael, Daniel Gros, Alexander Italianer, Jean Pisani-Ferry and Horst Reichenbach (1991) *One market, one money*, Oxford University Press, Oxford.

Frankel, Jeffrey and Katharine Rockett (1988), 'International macroeconomic policy coordination when policymakers do not agree on the true model', *American Economic Review*, 78, 3, June: 318–40.

Giovannini, Alberto and Luigi Spaventa (1991), 'Fiscal Rules in the European Monetary Union: A No-Entry Clause', CEPR Discussion Paper No. 516, January.

Grilli, Vittorio, Donato Masciandro and Guido Tabellini (1991), 'Political and Monetary Institutions and Public Financial Policies in Industrial Countries', *Economic Policy*, 13 October, 342–92.

Gros, Daniel (1991), 'Fiscal Issues in EMU', *Moneda y Credito*, forthcoming.

Gros, Daniel and Erik Jones (1991), 'Fiscal Shock Absorbers in the US', manuscript, Centre for European Policy Studies, Brussels, July.

MacDougall, Sir Donald, Dieter Biche, Arthur Brown, Francesco Forte, Yves Fréville, Martin O'Donoghue and Theo Peeters (1977) 'Public Finance in European Integration', Commission of the European Communities, Brussels.

Mortensen, Jrgen (1990), 'Federalism vs. Co-ordination: Macroeconomic Policy in the European Community', Centre for European Policy Studies, *CEPS Paper*, 47.

OECD (1990), 'Annual Economic Outlook', Organization for Economic Cooperation and Development, Paris, May.

Pelkmans, Jacques (1991), 'Towards Economic Union', in *Setting EC Priorities*, Brasseys for the Centre for European Policy Studies (CEPS), November.

Sachs, Jeffrey and Xavier Sala-i-Martin (1989), 'Federal Fiscal Policy and Optimum Currency Areas', Working Paper, Harvard University.

Stiglitz, Joseph and Weiss, Andrew (1981), 'Credit Rationing in Markets with Imperfect Information', *American Economic Review*, Vol. 71, No.3, June: 393 – 410.

Thygesen, Niels (1990), 'The benefits and costs of currency unification', in Horst Siebert (ed.) *The Completion of the Internal Market*, Kiel Institute of World Economics and J.C.B. Mohr, Tübingen.

Van der Ploeg, Frederic (1991), 'Macroeconomic policy cooordination during the various phases of economic and monetary union', *European Economy*, special issue, October, 136–64.

Van Rompuy, Paul, Filip Abraham and Dirk Heremans (1991), 'Economic federalism and the EMU.', *European Economy*, special issue, October, 107–35.

Von Hagen, Jürgen, (1991), 'Fiscal Arrangements in a Monetary Union: Evidence from the US', Discussion Paper # 58, Centre for Global Business, Indiana University, May.

Wyplosz, Charles (1991), 'Monetary union and fiscal policy discipline', *European Economy*, special issue, October, 165–84.

CHAPTER 9

EMU AND THE GLOBAL
MONETARY SYSTEM

Most of the academic and political debate about EMU has centred on its implications for the Community itself. International considerations have figured in the European debate about EMU mainly through the argument that EMU would increase the influence of the Community in international monetary relations. For the outside world the situation is obviously different. The United States and Japan, which constitute the main non-European participants in international macroeconomic coordination, are mainly concerned with the impact of EMU on the global monetary system.[1]

This chapter begins by providing some indicators of the economic size of the Community (in relation to the US and the global economy). In terms of GDP and trade the Community is somewhat larger than the US and represents about a third of global economic activity. EMU would therefore definitely be a large economy, in the same league as the United States.

Section 2 then turns to the main effect of EMU, namely the emergence of a single European currency, the ecu, as a competitor to the US dollar as the global currency. If the ecu does partially replace the US dollar in some of its international functions, large portfolio shift can be expected. However, although the portfolio shifts could be quite large in absolute terms (several hundreds of billions of ecu), they should not have any disruptive effects on exchange rates or capital flows because they will be distributed over time and because financial markets have become so sophisticated that the currency of denomination of international assets and liabilities can be changed quickly and at a low cost.

The impact of EMU on global macroeconomic coordination, which is discussed in the third section, should also not be exaggerated. There is anyway, at least at present, little effective macroeconomic coordination. Once EMU has been achieved global cooperation in the monetary field would involve only three participants and would thus

---

[1] The smaller European countries that are not (yet?) part of the Community are concerned that their economies and therefore also their economic policy-making might be dominated by the Community. This has already prompted several of them to apply for membership.

become easier. However cooperation in the fiscal field will remain difficult because EMU will probably not lead to a coordination of fiscal policies in the Community.[2]

9.1 EMU and the weight of the Community in the world economy

Before discussing the effects of EMU on the world economy it is useful to provide some data that show that the Community is indeed large enough in economic terms to affect global economic relations.

The two measures of economic size that are most often used are gross domestic product (GDP) and external trade. Table 9.1.1 therefore presents some data about GDP and international trade for the three major world economies (the Community, the US and Japan).[3] Moreover, further progress towards EMU (including the completion of the internal market) should lead to higher growth in the Community than in the United States over the next few years.

Table 9.1.1 The Community in the world economy

	GDP		Trade★	
	billion ecu	% of OECD total	billion ecu	% of world total
EC12	4 700	34.4	430.7	16.1
US	4 300	31.5	386.9	14.5
Japan	2 550	18.7	218.5	8.2

Note:
★ Trade is measured by (imports + exports)/2, excluding intra-EC exports and imports for the Community.
Trade: 1989 data; GDP: 1990 data.

Source: Annual economic report of the Commission 1990/91 and OECD

This table suggests that the Community is large enough to affect the world economy. Both in terms of total GDP and in terms of foreign trade the Community is

[2] The issue of fiscal policy coordination within the Community is discussed in chapter 8.

[3] Although the weakness of the US dollar in 1990 might distort the GDP figures, these figures are more likely to represent an understatement of the relative size of the Community in the late 1990s since by then the economy of the ex-GDR will have been integrated fully into the Community and some smaller countries might have joined as additional members. See chapter 14 for an outlook and our guess about the future size of the Community.

of the same size as the United States. The Community is also a significant part of the global economy since its external trade accounts for nearly one sixth of world trade; it accounts for more than a third of the total GDP of the OECD (whose member countries represent all of the important market economies).

In terms of financial indicators the Community would appear to be much bigger than the United States as suggested by table 9.1.2 below. Member countries hold about 200 billion ecu in foreign exchange reserves, which represents more than a third of the world total and is more than five times the amount held by the United States and about four times the amount held by Japan.[4]

Table 9.1.2 The Community in international finance

	Foreign exchange reserves		Capital flows*
	billion ecu	% of world total	billion ecu
EC	222.7	37.1	231.0
US	37.4	6.2	123.0
Japan	51.6	8.6	237.4

Source: International Monetary Fund, International Financial Statistics, December 1990 and Eurostat, Foreign trade statistics. Foreign exchange reserves: September 1990; capital flows: 1988.
* Capital flows are measured by the average of inflows and outflows of all types of capital.

However, this measure clearly overstates the global weight of a European EMU since a large part of the overall capital flows of Community member countries consists of intra-EC flows which would become domestic flows under EMU. Moreover, a large part of the foreign exchange reserves were accumulated to allow member countries to manage their national currencies in the EMS where increasing capital mobility required high levels of reserves. Under EMU the foreign exchange reserves of the Community to be pooled in the European central bank would be much smaller than at present.[5] Chapter 13 below discusses the possibility that such pooled reserves may be only one third of present levels. But these data do suggest that if the similarity in economic size between the United States and the Community leads to a similar behaviour in terms of

[4] Foreign exchange reserves fluctuate widely from year to year because of interventions in the foreign exchange markets and the valuation effects of exchange-rate changes. The data should therefore be taken only as an approximate indicator.

[5] It is sometimes argued that this effect is one important benefit of EMU. However, since reserves yield interest the net cost of holding reserves is small and the reduction does not lead to significant savings (see chapter 7).

foreign exchange reserve holdings the US will have to increase its reserve holdings considerably.

The weight of the Community in a number of international economic organizations (such as the International Monetary Fund (IMF), the Bank for International Settlements (BIS) and the World Bank) is larger than that of the United States if one just adds the quotas of individual member countries. For example, the sum of the national quotas of member countries in the IMF is 28.2 per cent compared to a US quota of 19.1 per cent. However, even after EMU, individual member countries may well wish to continue to be represented in these organizations, as any independent political entity is entitled to representation in the IMF and the World Bank. Full political union, not EMU, would therefore be a condition for the Community to participate as one entity in the management of the international economic institutions.[6]

At present, the quotas or voting rights of individual Community member countries are based in part on the size of their overall international trade and financial relations. With a common currency a large part of the trade (whether in goods, services or capital) of member countries would no longer be regarded as 'international' and the basis for assessing the quota of member countries would be correspondingly smaller. In this sense EMU necessarily implies a reduction of the aggregate representation of European countries in some international economic institutions.

Overall this discussion suggests that EMU will create an economic unit which will be of the same size as the United States. However, it is doubtful whether this automatically implies an increase in the European influence in the management of the global economy since the representation of European (i.e., Community) countries in international organizations might be reduced.

9.2   The ecu as the new global currency

The most visible effect of EMU at the global level will be the emergence of second global currency once the ecu becomes the common currency. The previous section has shown that the economy of the Community is large enough to make the ecu a serious competitor to the US dollar for the position as the key international reference and vehicle currency.

However, this does not imply that the introduction of the ecu as the common currency will cause sudden large shifts in international financial relations. History has shown that the international role of currencies changes only slowly because new financial markets and instruments develop only gradually over time. For example, it took serveral decades until the US dollar fully replaced the pound sterling as the dominant international currency although the US economy was clearly in a dominant position after the First World War.[7]

---

[6] For a further discussion of the impact of EMU on international institutions see Alogoskoufis and Portes (1991).

[7] Eichengreen (1989).

Another reason why the US dollar might retain its dominant position in some areas comes from the economies of scale in international transactions that make it to a large extent arbitrary what currency becomes the vehicle currency. Once a certain currency is widely used as a 'vehicle', transactions costs decline and that currency becomes more convenient to use even if some other currency has a larger domestic potential.[8]

The effect of these economies of scale can best be seen in the interbank foreign exchange market where the share of the US dollar exceeds by far the weight of the US economy in the world economy. Emerson et al. (1991) report that the dollar is used in almost 90 per cent of all foreign exchange transactions. Even in the European markets the dollar is still on one side of the transaction in over three quarters of all foreign exchange transactions. Moreover, the share of the US dollar has remained steady over the last decade although its share in other uses, such as invoicing and international bond issues, has declined substantially.[9]

It is therefore likely that the erosion of the dominant international position of the US dollar will be gradual. But given the size of the Community some substitution in international invoicing, foreign exchange reserves and the currency of denomination for international financial transactions can be expected.

One factor that will cause at least some currency substitution away from the US dollar stems from the practices in the invoicing of international trade. In general, trade among the major industrialized countries is invoiced in the currency of the exporter. However, a significant part of the trade of the smaller EC and other European countries and nearly all of world trade in oil and in a number of other important commodities, regardless of exporting country, is still denominated in US dollars. The share of the US dollar in trade invoicing therefore exceeds the US share of world trade. With EMU this should change since most of the exports of the Community may then be invoiced in ecu. The Community will also then become more influential than its member states have been individually in persuading exporters of oil and other commodities to enter into contracts denominated in the currency of the importer. The share of the ecu in trade invoicing could then become about equal to the share of the US dollar.[10]

Some currency substitution towards the ecu is therefore likely. However, there are a number of reasons why this will be less important for the Community than is often believed.

First of all, expectations are sometimes voiced that the Community would earn large seigniorage revenues if the ecu becomes an international currency. This point was already discussed as one of the minor side benefits of EMU in chapter 7 where it was found that the seigniorage gains for the Community would be limited because they can be made only on ecu assets that bear no interest or are remunerated at below market

---

[8] See Krugman (1980) and chapter 11 for a further discussion of the economies of scale in the use of money as a transactions medium.

[9] See Black (1989) for more detail about the international role of the US dollar.

[10] The external trade of the Community is actually somewhat larger than that of the US as shown above. Both the US and the EC would also dominate trade within their regions (Latin America and the rest of Europe) so that the shares of the ecu and the US dollar in trade invoicing would both exceed the respective trade weights.

rates. In the international context this is the case only for cash (i.e., bank notes and coins in circulation) since foreign exchange reserves are always held in the form of interest-bearing money market instruments. As reported in chapter 7, the equivalent of about 30 billion ecu in US dollar bank notes might be converted into ecu bank notes.[11] The potential for seigniorage gains for the Community may therefore seem to be important. However, this is a once-and-for-all effect and since this substitution can be expected to take some time the seigniorage gain would be minor as a flow over time. If full adjustment takes ten years the benefit to the Community would be about 3 billion ecu annually, less than one tenth of one per cent of its GDP.

A second effect that is often thought to be important is that portfolio demand shifts could have an effect on the ecu/dollar exchange rate. The reasoning behind this is that (at given asset supplies) only a change in the ecu/dollar exchange rate can change the proportion of assets denominated in US dollars and relative to the assets denominated in ecu. Assuming these assets are only imperfect substitutes, it follows that a sudden shift in portfolio preferences from US dollar assets into ecu assets requires an appreciation of the ecu (relative to the US dollar). However, it is crucial to keep in mind that this effect works only if the supply of ecu assets does not increase along with the demand. If both demand and supply increase at the same time there is no reason for the exchange rate to move. In order to estimate the impact of portfolio shifts towards the ecu on its exchange rate it is therefore necessary to discuss both the supply and the demand effects.

Since the determinants of the supply and demand of ecu assets differ considerably between the official and the private sector it is necessary to discuss the effects of portfolio shifts for official and private portfolios separately.

i)   The ecu in foreign exchange reserves

Given the weight of the Community in international trade it can be expected that EMU will lead to a shift in the composition of the foreign currency reserves held by monetary authorities worldwide. In 1988 the share of the US dollar in these reserve holdings was equal to 63 per cent, almost three times the combined share of the major EC currencies, which together accounted for 22 per cent.[12] Given that the economy of the Community is about the same size as that of the US it is likely that the share of the ecu will increase considerably. By exactly how much is difficult to predict.

An upper limit for the shift towards ecu reserves can, however, be calculated by assuming that the shares of the other currencies do not change with EMU and that after EMU the ecu and the US dollar become equally important. As shown in table 9.1.3

---

[11] For details see Emerson et al. (1991), chapter 7.

[12] Ibid. The issue of gold reserves which are anyway no longer actively utilized by central banks are not discussed in this book. The part of the gold reserves of member countries (which total about 370 million ounces versus 260 million ounces for the US) that is not transferred to the European central bank might be retained by national treasuries and in some cases be used to pay off a part of the national debt. Chapter 13 discusses some issues that might arise in the pooling of foreign exchange reserves.

this implies a share of 42.5 per cent for the ecu.[13] Under this hypothesis the ecu share would have to rise by more than 20 percentage points (from the present 22 to 42.5 per cent).

Table 9.1.3 EMU and the currency composition of foreign exchange reserves

	Percentage shares:		
	US dollar	Ecu	Other
Current: 1990	63	22	15
EMU	42.5	42.5	15

Since total foreign exchange reserves amounted to about 600 billion ecu in 1990 this would imply an increase in the demand for ecu assets of about 120 billion ecu. Since there is no *a priori* reason for Community governments to increase their external liabilities in ecu by a similar amount this adjustment in the currency composition of international reserves should represent a net increase in the demand for ecu-denominated assets and could therefore have an effect on exchange rates. In other words this portfolio shift of the official sector is equivalent to official foreign exchange market intervention of about 120 billion ecu.

However, even an increase in the demand for ecu assets in the order of 120 billion is not likely to have large exchange-rate effects if it is spread over a number of years. A certain diversification out of the US dollar has already taken place in the past since between 1976 and 1988 the share of the Community currencies increased from about 10 per cent to 22 per cent. Even a considerable acceleration of this process is not likely to put large pressures on foreign exchange markets where gross turnover amounts to over 100 billion dollars *daily*.[14] The ecu will not become the common currency much before the end of the century, and the process of portfolio adjustment can therefore be expected to take about ten years. This would imply an annual shift of only 12 billion ecu which should not have a large impact on exchange rates since this amounts only to about 2 per cent of total foreign exchange reserves.[15]

[13] The share of the other currencies is at present 15 per cent (100 minus 63 for the US dollar minus 22 for the EC currencies). The dollar and the ecu are therefore assumed to retain one half of their joint share of 85 per cent. This is an upper limit because the Japanese yen is currently underrepresented in world official currency reserves relative to economic and financial indicators for Japan.

[14] See Bordo and Schwarz (1991) for a survey of foreign exchange market intervention.

[15] The actual shift towards the ecu might anyway be smaller than the estimate of 120 billion which represents an upper limit that does not allow the share of other currencies, especially that of the Japanese yen, to increase as they have done in the past.

ii)   The ecu in private international portfolios

Shifts in the preferences of private investors should have a more important effect on the exchange rate of the ecu because private international portfolios, which are estimated to have reached over 4,000 billion US dollars in 1989, are six to seven times larger than the official foreign exchange reserves.[16] Emerson et al. (1991) estimate that EMU is likely to lead to a shift towards ecu assets of about 5–10 per cent in a so-called world reference portfolio of about 4,000 billion US dollars in 1988. The range for the potential shift in private portfolios towards ecu denominated assets would therefore be about 150 to 300 billion ecu.[17]

However, this estimate does not take into account that under EMU all cross–border claims and deposits inside the Community (e.g., claims of Germans on French residents, or deposits held by Community residents in London) will no longer be part of the 'international' portfolio. The reference portfolio should thus exclude all international claims between Community residents. However, available data on international financial transactions do not always allow one to identify the nationality of both the borrower and the lender. The only sector where this is possible is the banking market; data for this sector show that intra–Community business constitutes about one third of all international transactions (if measured by the value of cross–border and foreign currency deposits).

For obvious reasons a large share (about 60 per cent in 1990) of the intra–Community business is conducted in Community currencies. This implies that the share of the US dollar in the remaining 'non-EC' international business is higher than its share in the overall international banking market. For example, in 1990 in the overall international banking market the share of the US dollar was about 50 per cent and that of all Community currencies combined about 30 per cent, but in the international banking market outside the Community the share of the US dollar was about 60 per cent and that of Community currencies less than 20 per cent.

If the structure of other international financial markets is similar to that of the banking market this means that Community currencies (including the ecu) are still mainly used in Europe and that the US dollar remains in a dominant position in the rest of the world. It follows that, under the assumption that EMU allows the ecu to compete on an equal footing with the US dollar even in the markets that do not have any direct link with the Community, the shift out of the US dollar might be much larger than one would assume from the data that include intra–Community business. The above-mentioned estimate of a portfolio shift of 150 to 300 billion ecu is based on a US dollar share of 50 per cent in the global reference portfolio. If one assumes that the world portfolio outside the Community has the same currency distribution as the banking market (i.e., that the share of the US dollar is 60 per cent) the portfolio shift out of the US dollar would be much larger.[18]

---

[16] See, for example, chapter 7 in Emerson et al. (1991).

[17] At the end–1991 ecu/US dollar exchange rate of 1.3 dollars per ecu.

[18] Since this share is equal to the US dollar in the banking market this sector should be broadly representative of the overall international portfolio.

Table 9.1.4 shows that if the non-EC portfolio is taken as the benchmark the US dollar share might have to fall by 23 percentage points (from 61.1 to 38.6), instead of the 11.7 (from 50.3 to 38.6) that would result if the overall world portfolio is used. Table 9.1.4 also shows that between 1985 and 1990 the share of the Community currencies in non-EC business has not greatly increased, the fall in the US dollar share is due rather to an increase of the role of other currencies, notably the yen. This is in contrast with the data on the overall portfolio which show a much larger increase in the share of Community currencies because the volume of capital flows inside the Community, which contains a large share of Community currencies, has increased considerably.

Table 9.1.4 EMU and the shift in international portfolios

Shares in %:	US dollar	EC currencies	Other
Overall portfolio	50.3	26.6	15.2
Non-EC portfolio:			
1985	73.3	12.2	14.5
1990	61.6	15.6	22.8
EMU (hypothetical)	38.6	38.6	22.8

Source: Emerson *et al.* (1991) for the first row and own calculations based on Bank for International Settlements data.

A shift of the full 23 percentage points, which would be equivalent to 700 billion ecu, is not likely since this value represents certainly an upper bound. One reason is that, as explained in Emerson *et al.* (1991), Community residents that at present have foreign currency claims in Community currencies inside the Community might want to go out of the ecu once EMU is achieved, since they might have held these positions in order to diversify their national portfolios. Moreover, as shown in detail by Barenco (1990), all the data about the currency composition of private international portfolios are subject to large margins of errors. However, these illustrative calculations show that the potential for a portfolio shift towards the ecu is large. Even if only half of the potential were to materialize this would imply that private agents want to exchange 350 billion of bonds and bank deposits from US dollars into ecu.

Does this imply that EMU will lead to a large appreciation of the ecu *vis-à-vis* the dollar? Not necessarily, since, as argued above, exchange-rate effects can be expected only if the shift in demand (towards ecu-denominated assets in private portfolios) is so fast that the supply cannot adjust in time. If the ecu becomes more attractive than the US dollar at the same time for borrowers and investors (in the private sector) they can just denominate new contracts in ecu and there would be no effect on the exchange rate or on other macroeconomic variables. If the ecu grows gradually in its international role there is little reason to believe that it should become more attractive only for investors and not for borrowers. A more liquid market, an increased acceptability of the currency and a wider array of financial instruments are all factors that affect equally lenders and borrowers.

Moreover, sophisticated financial market techniques, such as interest-rate or currency swaps, allow financial intermediaries to change the currency of denomination of bonds and bank loans at very low cost. For example, if investors continue to demand bonds in US dollars, but borrowers prefer the ecu, banks would sell US dollar bonds to private investors, exchange the receipts into ecu and arrange swaps for the future US dollar payments in terms of principal and interest. In this way the borrower would have only ecu obligations. These techniques are not limited to a small segment of the overall market: in 1989 interest-rate and currency swaps were arranged for a total of over 2,000 billion US dollars of different international financial instruments.[19]

A last argument why EMU should not lead to large exchange-rate effects is that the introduction of the ecu as the single European currency will not come as a surprise to financial markets. If there are any exchange-rate effects they should therefore arise gradually, well before EMU is reached and also well before the portfolio shifts actually take place.

Full EMU is sufficiently far away to make it impossible to make any projection for the current account of the Community and the ecu/dollar exchange rate. At present it seems likely that the Community will run a modest aggregate current-account deficit during the transition to EMU. Such a deficit would represent a net supply of claims on the Community. However, since these claims would not all be expressed in Community currencies, only a part of this deficit constitutes an additional supply of ecu assets. Moreover, since gross capital flows are always a multiple of the net flows (which represent the counterpart to the current account) the overall current-account position of the Community should not be an important factor in accommodating the portfolio shifts that can be expected to result from EMU.

In sum, pressures for appreciation of the ecu might result from a growing financial role for the European currency in official and private portfolios. But there is no need for a large appreciation of the ecu, especially if the Community proves willing to accept a collective current-account deficit in the transitory period.

We have not discussed whether the suppression of exchange-rate changes within the Community could lead to an increase in the volatility of the exchange rate of the ecu. The idea underlying this concern is that the variability that is suppressed within the Community appears somewhere else, i.e., in the exchange rate of the ecu against the US dollar. However, this argument does not fully apply to EMU since EMU will not only suppress the symptoms of some underlying source of variability, i.e., shocks coming from national monetary policies or disturbances to national financial markets, but will suppress the source by establishing a common monetary policy and by creating one Community-wide financial market. Within this larger financial market shocks coming from different regions of the EMU should to a large extent offset each other. Whether or not EMU leads to a more stable international monetary system will depend mainly on the degree of coordination that can be achieved between the three global

---

[19] See Bank for International Settlements (1990).

economies. This is the subject of the following section. *A priori*, however, there is no reason to believe that the creation of EMU *per se* would either threaten, or, on the contrary, increase the stability of the international monetary system.[20]

9.3 Global macroeconomic policy coordination in a tri-polar system

At present global macroeconomic policy coordination issues are discussed at the annual economic summits of the heads of state and of governments and the regular meetings of finance ministers and central banks' governors of the so-called group of seven (which consists of the US, Japan, Canada, plus the four largest EC member countries: Germany, France, Italy and the UK). However, since these meetings rarely produce agreements about specific policy actions to be taken by individual countries, there is in reality little effective international macroeconomic policy coordination.

The lack of coordination is most visible for fiscal policies because budgetary 'contributions' have to come from national parliaments. Agreements between finance ministers on fiscal policy coordination are of little practical value because national parliaments often do not ratify measures that are required from an international point of view, if those measures are not perceived to serve domestic political interests. The main illustration of this lack of fiscal policy coordination is represented by the repeated promises during the late 1980s of the US administration to cut the US budget deficit, which were never fulfilled because of the stalemate resulting from the different political priorities of the Administration and Congress. Monetary policy coordination is in principle much easier to achieve since central bank governors do not face similar permanent difficulties in implementing agreements. The most visible episodes of effective global monetary cooperation are the so-called Plaza agreement of September 1985 and the Louvre accord of February 1987 to keep the US dollar exchange rate 'around current levels'. However, apart from these episodes, the three major central banks (the Bundesbank, the Bank of Japan and the Federal Reserve) have mostly been guided by domestic considerations when setting their national monetary policies and have cooperated visibly only in the face of major disturbances on the foreign exchange markets.[21]

Given that the US economy is twice as large as that of Japan and three to four times as large as the larger European economies that participate in the G-7, the current international (global) monetary system can therefore best be described as a 'game' with one large and several medium to small 'players'. The asymmetry resulting from the difference in economic size, between Germany and the US, has, however, already

---

[20] The scant evidence that can be obtained from the experience with EMS is also mixed as discussed in chapter 4.

[21] For an account of exchange-rate policy in the 1990s from a US point of view see Frankel (1990). Funabashi (1988) offers a vivid account of how the Plaza and Louvre agreements come about and of different national interpretations – also among the European participants – of their substance and implications.

been tempered by the existence of the EMS. As shown in chapters 4 and 5 a common monetary policy is already emerging through a mixture of the *de facto* leadership of the Bundesbank in the EMS and the informal coordination among central bank governors. This implies that EMU might change the environment for international macro-economic coordination less radically than is sometimes believed.

However, EMU will still have a substantial impact on the nature of the global monetary system because a *de facto* common monetary policy has only existed so far for the core of the EMS, which represents little more than half of the economic potential of the Community. Moreover, even among the participants in the core of the EMS there is not always agreement on how to react to disturbances in the foreign exchange markets and the coordination of national monetary policies achieved by the EMS is of a different nature than the complete unification imposed by EMU.

EMU should therefore lead to a more symmetric global monetary system. General game-theoretic considerations suggest that a coalition among a sub-group of players can only improve their welfare (at the expense of all other players). This suggests that the Community could only gain from a more symmetric international monetary system. However, there are several reasons for doubting that there will actually be more cooperation and that any cooperation actually achieved will bring substantial benefits.

First of all, history suggests that the international monetary system was more stable when it was dominated by one power, such as the Bretton Woods system until 1970 which was dominated by the US. In this line of thought the instability of the period between the two World Wars is ascribed to the lack of a dominant power that was willing and able to provide the leadership for the reestablishment of the gold standard. The economic mechanisms that underly this 'hegemonic stability' are discussed for example in Eichengreen (1989) who argues that a 'hegemon' has an incentive to provide stability if it is so large that its own actions affect the global equilibrium significantly. Policy-makers in a dominant economy will therefore be more inclined to take into account the international spillover effects of domestic policy actions than policy-makers from small countries who realize that their actions cannot affect the overall equilibrium. Moreover, arranging for international cooperation always involves a political cost which should be independent of the size of the country. Since a large country should gain more, in absolute terms, from a system that ensures international cooperation than a small country, a large country might be more willing to bear the political cost of arranging for international cooperation.

Even if one does not accept the 'hegemonic stability' idea it is not clear that it will be easier to achieve cooperation among three similar players than among seven where there is at least a natural candidate for the leadership position. It has even been shown that (in the context of a specific example concerning trade policy) a system consisting of three players could be the worst of all (i.e., in the absence of cooperation a system with two, or more than three participants leads to a superior outcome).[22] The only apparent

---

[22] See Krugman (1989). This should only be taken as a theoretical possibility, not a general statement that policy coordination is always most difficult with three participants. Bergsten (1990) advances some more specific arguments why a tripolar system of the US, Japan and Europe could be unstable: on several issues two of the three players appear to have an interest in ganging up on the third.

beneficial effect of a smaller number of participants is that it becomes easier to ensure that all participants are at least fully informed about each others positions and intentions.

A second reason for not expecting large economic benefits from better cooperation in monetary policy is that the three blocs that will dominate the global monetary system after EMU constitute the rather closed economies since their external trade amounts only to 10–12 per cent of their respective GDP; the bilateral trade links between them are even weaker as shown in table 9.3.1.

Table 9.3.1   Trade between the three major world economies

	*Overall trade as % of GDP	Bilateral trade (as % of total) with:		
		EC12	US	Japan
EC12	9.6	–	18.4	8.0
US	10.6	20.5	–	16.5
Japan	13.2	15.7	29.3	–

Note:
* Trade measured by (exports + imports)/2, goods and services for the first column, goods only for the matrix of bilateral flows; for the EC the percentages refer to external trade.

Source: Annual Economic Report of the European Commission 1990/1991 and International Monetary Fund, Directions of Trade, yearbook 1990.

For example, the overall external trade of the Community accounts only for about 10 per cent of its GDP and only about one fourth (18.4 plus 8.0 per cent) of this trade was with the US and Japan, so that the direct trade links with these two other economies account only for about 2.5 per cent of the GDP of the Community. For the Community, trade with the other small European countries is more important than trade with the US since it accounts for over 26 per cent of the external trade of the Community.[23] The Community depends less on trade with the other two global economies than do the US and Japan.[24] These numbers suggest that, even taking into account third-market effects, direct demand spill-over effects among these three economies are very small and that in a certain sense the Community has less stake in global macroeconomic coordination than the other two major economies.

Large econometric models that take into account third-country effects and differences in elasticities of demand also suggest that the economic links are not very

[23] Likewise, Canada is almost as important in trade terms for the US as the entire Community.

[24] Trade with the EC and Japan accounts for 3.8 per cent of US GDP and trade with the EC and the US accounts for over 5 per cent of Japan's GDP. The corresponding figure for the EC is only 2.5 per cent as mentioned in the main text.

important. For example, Masson *et al.* (1990) report that the impact of an increase in the US federal deficit on the US economy is 6 to 7 times larger than the impact on the major European countries. A fiscal expansion of about 10 per cent of GDP would be required in the US to increase demand in the Community by only 1 per cent of GDP. For monetary policy the cross-country multipliers are even smaller and of an uncertain sign as discussed below.[25]

The third, and possibly most important, obstacle to effective coordination is that policy-makers are assumed to agree on a view of how their own and their partners' economies work and that their view corresponds to reality. However, this is not the case, especially not for monetary policy. There is as much disagreement among policy-makers about the nature of international economic interactions as there is among professional economists. While there is broad agreement about the effects of fiscal policy and the approximate size of the cross-country multipliers when fiscal instruments are applied, there is more uncertainty as to the cross-border impact of monetary policy changes and even to the sign of the impact, which may differ between partner countries. For example, Masson *et al.* (1990) report – on the basis of extensive simulations with the econometric model of the international economy used by the IMF – that a monetary expansion in the US would reduce demand in Japan and the US, but increase it in the UK, France and Italy. In the monetary field it is therefore very difficult to evaluate the international spill-over effects even within the framework of one model. It follows that precise policy prescriptions that could form the basis for coordination are hazardous.

These problems are compounded by model uncertainty, see Frankel and Rockett (1988), who analyse the welfare implications of full international cooperation under different assumptions about the true model of the international economy and the beliefs of policy-makers in the United States and in the rest of the world about what the true model is. Using the ten most important international macroeconomic models they examine 1,000 different combinations of assumptions about the true model and the policy-makers' beliefs and find that cooperation improves welfare for the United States or for other countries in only about half of these possible cases. This implies that in about one half of all the cases considered cooperation leads to a loss of welfare. Ghosh and Masson (1991) arrive at a somewhat similar, but less radical, result by taking into account the possibility that policy makers learn gradually about the 'true' model. Their main conclusion is that coordination might make the global system dynamically unstable if it is not based on the correct view of the world. Learning about the way the international economy works diminishes the scope for instability and makes coordination more desirable. However, the structure of the world economy can change (it will certainly change with EMU) and learning about these structural changes requires time. The overall lesson to be drawn from this literature is thus that international macroeconomic coordination should not be overly ambitious.

A fourth and final reason for not expecting large economic benefits from monetary policy coordination under a more symmetric global system is that coordination limited

---

[25] This type of result can be obtained for a large number of different econometric models, see Frankel (1988) for a survey.

to one policy area can be counterproductive in the absence of coordination in other areas. This might be the case for the Community since EMU will not lead to a common fiscal policy (we discuss the fiscal policy issues raised by EMU in chapter 8). Cooperation at the global level might thus effectively be restricted to the monetary area. The experience of the 1980s, when the root cause of the problem was an expansionary fiscal policy in the United States, shows that coordination that is restricted to monetary or exchange-rate policies cannot offset the effects that arise from a lack of coordination in other areas.

Under these circumstances one can hardly be surprised that global coordination of monetary policies in the regime of floating exchange rates has been and is likely to remain largely *ad hoc* and designed to modify only the most obvious imbalances. All in all there is therefore little reason to believe that the emergence of a more symmetric global monetary system will lead to more effective macroeconomic coordination on a systematic basis and to significant benefits for the Community or its two main partners. This implies that EMU would not necessarily lead to a more stable global environment. With only one European counterpart it might appear that it should be easier to stabilize the US dollar, but the size of capital flows between EMU and the US dollar area will also multiply so that it will not become easier to stabilize exchange rates through official intervention. Moreover, EMU reduces by definition one important motivation for stabilizing the dollar, namely the desire to prevent individual Community currencies from moving in a divergent manner after shocks to the US dollar exchange rate. Under EMU individual member countries might therefore be less concerned with global policy coordination and exchange-rate management.

9.4 EMU and the global monetary system: an overall assessment

The present chapter has offered a rather critical view of the past achievements of global policy coordination and has also argued that it is unlikely that the set-up of EMU would make a major difference by unifying responsibility for a European contribution to the workings of the global monetary system. Our critical view was based primarily on the difficulties of making any reliable assessment of the empirical linkages between the main economies. The knowledge available about how policy changes are transmitted internationally appears simply insufficient to permit any permanent efforts at welfare improvements in terms of the main macroeconomic objectives of the participants. The best one can hope for is the occasional correction through joint efforts of the more glaring disequilibria as they find expression in major exchange-rate misalignments and large current-account imbalances.

In a way the European experience with the EMS looks the most encouraging when compared to the global difficulties in policy coordination. The inspiration for the EMS came, as was argued in chapter 2, in part from a desire to avoid the consequences of non-coordination already observable globally at the time the system was negotiated in

1978. The founders of the EMS perceived that they would put at risk many of the achievements of the Community if they failed to develop some simple framework for policy coordination. There is no evidence that they had an ambitious objective such as permanent optimization of macroeconomic policies in mind. By focusing on a defensive mechanism to limit recourse to exchange-rate changes among the participants they could not achieve that; but the system which resulted saved participants from some potentially large mistakes and gave the process of policy coordination a start by making the transmission of policy effects within Europe more transparent.

The major question that EMU would raise for the global system is why the case for regime preservation[26] and evolution has appeared so much more evident to the member states in the Community than to the participants in the group of seven. The main reason is that EC members are much more open to international trade than the US, Japan, or the EC seen as a block, as our tables earlier in this chapter illustrated. Moreover, the Europeans also have developed some joint policies, notably in agriculture, the survival of which was conditional on some minimal exchange-rate stability within the region.[27] These factors created a bias favourable to putting exchange-rate stabilization at the forefront of joint efforts to improve policies. Though these factors are much less visible at the global level, some of the arguments in favour of managing exchange rates still apply at this level. For all major participants in the world economy the costs of putting international adjustment burdens as heavily on the sectors producing tradeable goods as has happened in the 1980s, are significant. The Europeans, having steadily reduced these burdens of large swings in competitive conditions inside their area, may become a force for a similar effort at the global level. With more stable exchange rates globally, it will become more evident than has been the case since 1973 which contributions of national economic policies are welfare-improving for the other participants. This would at least create a firmer basis for policy coordination; but whether the occasion for more policy coordination will be used still depends on the readiness of the three main actors to take into account the international repercussions of their actions also with respect to budgetary policies.

References

Alogoskoufis, George, and Richard Portes (1991), 'International costs and benefits from EMU', in *European Economy*, special issue, 231–45.

Bank for International Settlements (1990), 'International banking and financial markets developments', Basle, December.

Barenco, Bixio (1990), 'The dollar position of the non-US private sector, portfolio effects and the exchange rate of the dollar', OECD, *Economic Studies*, 15, Paris, Autumn.

Bergsten, Fred (1990), 'The world economy after the Cold War', *Foreign Affairs*, 3, 69, Summer: 96–112.

[26] This is the term used by one leading advocate of global exchange-rate management, see Kenen (1988), particularly pp. 91–2.

[27] Giavazzi and Giovannini (1990) stress this point in particular.

Black, Stanley (1989), 'Transactions costs and vehicle currencies', International Monetary Fund, Washington, DC WP/89/96, November.

Bordo, Michael, and Anna Schwartz (1991), 'What has foreign exchange market intervention since the Plaza agreement accomplished?', *Open Economies Review*, 2, March: 39–64.

Eichengreen, Barry (1989), 'Hegemonic stability theories of the international monetary system', in Richard Cooper, Barry Eichengreen, Chris Randall Henning, Gerald Holtham and Robert Putman (eds.), *Can Nations Agree?*, Brookings Institution, Washington, DC 255–98.

Emerson, Michael, Daniel Gros, Jean Pisani-Ferry, Alexander Italianer and Horst Reichenbach (1991), *One Market, One Money*, Oxford University Press, Oxford.

Frankel, Jefrey (1990), 'The making of exchange rate policy in the 1980's', *NBER Working Paper*, 3539, Cambridge, December.

Frankel, Jeffrey, and Katharine Rockett (1988), 'International macroeconomic policy coordination when policy makers do not agree on the true model', *American Economic Review*, 78, June: 318–40.

Frankel, Jeffrey (1988), 'Obstacles to international macroeconomic policy coordination', *Princeton Studies in International Finance*, 64, Princeton.

Funabashi, Yoichi (1988), *Managing the dollar: from the Plaza to the Louvre*, Institute for International Economics, Washington, DC.

Ghosh, Atish and Paul Masson, 'Model uncertainty, learning and the gains from coordination', *American Economic Review*, 81, 3, June: 465–79.

Giavazzi, Francesco and Alberto Giovannini (1990), 'Can the EMS be exported', chapter 6 in William H. Branson, Jacob A. Frenhil and Morris Goldstein (eds.), *International Policy Coordination and Exchange Rate Fluctuations*, National Bureau of Economic Research and University of Chicago Press, Chicago, 247–69.

Kenen, Peter (1988), *Managing exchange rates*, Royal Institute for International Affairs and Routledge, London.

Krugman, Paul (1980) 'Vehicle currencies and the structure of international exchange', *Journal of Money, Credit and Banking*, August: 513–26.

Krugman, Paul (1989), 'Is bilateralism bad?', *NBER Working Paper*, 2972, Cambridge, May.

Masson, Paul, Steven Symansky and Guy Meredith (1990), 'Multimod Mark II: a revised and extended model', International Monetary Fund, *Occasional Paper*, 71, Washington, DC, July.

PART IV

TOWARDS
MONETARY
UNION

CHAPTER 10

THE MAKING OF THE DELORS REPORT AND BEYOND

In the early months of 1988 the debate on EMU and the set-up of a European central bank got underway through initiatives of the governments of France, Italy and Germany. The most novel element in this process was the readiness of the German government, particularly through a memorandum of the Foreign Minister, Hans-Dietrich Genscher, to engage in this debate.

This chapter interprets the views of the three governments and the course of the debate which led, at the Hanover European Council of June 1988, to the nomination of a Committee for the Study of Economic and Monetary Union in the European Community, presided over by the President of the EC Commission (the 'Delors Committee'). The Report of the Delors Committee proposed to move towards EMU through three stages, a proposal that has, at least in form, been retained in the preparatory work for the Intergovernmental Conference (IGC) on EMU which started in December 1990 and was concluded in December 1991 in Maastricht. The present state of this work is analysed in chapter 12 with respect to the transitional stages and in chapter 13 to full EMU, with particular emphasis on the structure and functions of the proposed European System of Central Banks. Before that chapter 11 examines alternatives to the approach of the Delors Report.

The present chapter is in three sections. The first examines the debate prior to the Hanover European Council; section 2 reviews the work of the Delors Committee and section 3 the follow-up ending with the conclusions of the Rome European Council in October 1990.

10.1 Political initiatives to relaunch EMU: January–June 1988

The French government had been active at the ECOFIN meeting which decided on the January 1987 realignment in prompting reflections on a strengthening of the EMS. These efforts had been successful in bringing about the Basle–Nyborg agreement. But less than four months later the French Finance Minister, Edouard Balladur, in a memorandum to his ECOFIN colleagues made it clear that French ideas went well beyond non-institutional reform of the operating mechanism of the EMS.[1]

Balladur's memorandum began with a restatement of familiar French criticisms of the EMS, though the language was unusually strong. The various credit mechanisms could only temporarily spread the costs of intervention:

> ultimately it is the central bank whose currency is at the lower end of the permitted range which has to bear the cost. However, it is not necessarily the currency at the lower end of the range which is the source of the tension. The discipline imposed by the exchange-rate mechanism may, for its part, have good effects when it serves to put a constraint on economic and monetary policies which are insufficiently rigorous. It produces an abnormal situation when its effect is to exempt any countries whose policies are too restrictive from the necessary adjustment. Thus the fact that some countries have piled up current account surpluses for several years equal to between 2 and 3 per cent of their GDPs constitutes a grave anomaly. This asymmetry is one of the reasons for the present tendency of European currencies to rise against the dollar and the currencies tied to it. This rise is contrary to the fundamental interest of Europe and of its constituent economies. We must therefore find a new system under which this problem cannot arise.

The memorandum went on to argue that 'rapid pursuit of the monetary construction of Europe is the only possible solution'.

Balladur is quoted here at length because the implicit criticism of German policy – Germany is not mentioned by name – is so strong that the memorandum seemed an unlikely starting point for the debate on EMU. Germany could hardly be expected to respond favourably to a plea for sharing the leadership attributed to her, when the view of her partners of the present EMS was so critical and had so often before been rejected.

The Italian Minister of the Treasury, Giuliano Amato, followed up his French colleague the following month.[2] He was even more blunt in his criticism. The problem with the EMS was that an engine for growth was missing. The German external surplus had become structural so as to 'remove growth potential from other nations', and the DM was 'fundamentally undervalued'. Italy had taken risks in these circumstances by committing herself to reducing exchange controls; she would have to insist on escape clauses in the proposed EC directive on complete liberalization of capital movements and to press for 'a minimum degree of convergence in the sectors of taxation, supervision and other forms of regulation'. Italy further proposed the creation through the EMCF of 'a recycling mechanism which could borrow funds on the market and reallocate them in such a way as to compensate the inflow and outflow of capital . . .'; and she favoured 'enlarging somewhat the normal band of fluctuation within the EMS'

---

[1] The memorandum, Balladur (1988), is dated 8 January 1988. Quotes in this chapter are from the English translation for the EC Monetary Committee of 29 April 1988.

[2] Amato (1988). The Italian memorandum to ECOFIN, dated 23 February, was published under the title 'Un motore per lo SME' in the Italian business paper *Il Sole 24 Ore* two days later.

in order to facilitate the entrance of sterling and to establish uniform conditions of membership in the system. The Italian memorandum fully concurred with the French insistence on developing procedures for 'identifying divergent countries – whatever the direction of imbalance – from whom to require a greater effort of adjustment'. In total, the Italian memorandum, no more than the French, seemed to offer a likely starting point for a fundamental reform of Europe's monetary construction.

The most surprising element in the history of the 1988 relaunching of EMU was that Germany nevertheless responded favourably and aggressively, rather than defensively as had been the pattern in earlier discussions in ECOFIN; a defensive attitude had been encouraged by the Monetary Committee and the Committee of Governors – the 'competent bodies' advising ECOFIN. There were, according to the view presented here, two main reasons why the critical contributions by France and Italy evoked a German response, or rather two responses, since both the German Foreign and Finance Ministers responded.[3] The French and Italian memoranda, specific as they were in their somewhat similar criticisms of the EMS, left the institutional implications of moving towards monetary union and much closer economic policy coordination rather vague. They accordingly left room for German initiative and assertiveness. Balladur raised a number of questions about moving to a single currency zone and a European central bank but he professed no particular views; his questions seemed genuinely open. Amato did not focus specifically on the central bank or on the single currency. He underlined that, in the longer perspective, the participants had to look beyond the issue of symmetry; 'without a common and homogeneous attitude towards inflation', as expressed in a monetary rule of some form, a fixed exchange-rate system could become biased towards monetary instability. 'A common identification of the objectives of economic policy which include the stability of prices, but also growth' was required. This raised the debate on monetary unification well beyond technical issues to the most general political level.

Genscher seized this initiative by making proposals about a European central bank with well-defined characteristics – and a procedure for bringing it into existence, Genscher (1988). His memorandum had the ambitious title, 'A European Currency Area and a European Central Bank', and it stated firmly in the introduction that they both should be seen as an 'economically necessary completion of the European Internal Market'. He saw the single currency and the central bank as catalysts in the efforts to achieve the necessary convergence of economic policies in the member states without which monetary union could not exist. This formulation was quite close to what had earlier been termed 'monetarist' views.

Genscher's memorandum also appeared to accept two other elements in traditional French and Italian views. An important motive for the creation of a European currency area was to reduce Europe's dependence on the dollar and facilitate generally 'the management of exchange rates to third currencies closer to equilibrium'. And he had surprisingly favourable comments on the ecu:

---

[3] Germany held the Presidency in the EC in the first half of 1988, so it was perhaps natural that the Presidents of the General Affairs and the ECOFIN Council should both want to put Europe's monetary construction on their agenda.

Among possible alternatives (i.e., for the single currency) the use of the ecu first as parallel and later as common currency should have the best prospects of realization. The set-up of a European central bank and the extension to the ecu of legal tender status, would make the unit more attractive and, after a transitory period of several years, develop it into the general means of payments in Europe.

This was an unusually conciliatory statement, closer to the views of critics of the EMS than had been seen earlier from a leading German official. It attracted strong criticism in Germany, particularly from the Bundesbank, for not showing sufficient caution. But in the characterization of the functions and the structure of the European central bank, Genscher's memorandum had a more familiar ring.

A European central bank was to be autonomous in relation to both national and Community political authorities. Money creation had to be clearly separate from the financing of public sector deficits; a European central bank could not be obliged to finance national or EC deficits. Price stability should be a priority objective for the joint monetary policy, as it had been for the Bundesbank in Germany. But the German lessons were more comprehensive and constructive than that.

As Genscher pointed out, economic policy in Germany is based not only on the Bundesbank Act of 1957, but also on the Stability Act of 1967 in which the German Federal government undertook to further, through its budgetary and other economic policies, four macroeconomic objectives: price stability, high employment, external equilibrium and economic growth. The German Foreign Minister proposed that two such pillars of economic policy should also be integral and mutually supportive elements in EMU and embodied in a 'European Magna Carta of Stability'.

In short, as already argued above, the French and Italian memoranda had, by leaving the structure and function of the European central bank open, in the French case, or by underlining the need for a comprehensive agreement on economic policy, in the Italian case, offered Genscher the opportunity to point to the dual nature of policy-making in Germany in general and to underline the virtues of the Bundesbank's autonomy and structure within it. By his remarks on the ecu, Genscher at the same time showed recognition that, while the institutional model for EMU might well be found in Germany, the flavour would be different at the European level; no take-over by the DM was intended.

The element that attracted the most attention in Genscher's memorandum was, however, the urgency with which he clearly viewed the European monetary construction. He proposed that the forthcoming European Council at Hanover in June nominate a group of 5–7 independent experts with 'professional and political authority' with a mandate to clarify the principles for the development of a European currency area, including a statute for a European central bank and transitory measures. The group was to submit its report within a year.

The other reason why a genuine dialogue could start in these early months of 1988 may be found in the second German memorandum, circulated to ECOFIN by Finance Minister Gerhard Stoltenberg on 15 March, Stoltenberg (1988). As President of ECOFIN Stoltenberg was particularly keen on securing the adoption, before the middle of the year, of the proposed directive for capital liberalization, which had been put forward by the Commission two years earlier. He underlined the strategic importance of taking this step in an irrevocable manner, distancing himself from the Italian request for safeguard clauses and for prior harmonization of capital taxation and of the national frameworks for financial regulation. Once this crucial step had been taken, the German government would not block discussion of adopting the existing mechanism for temporary balance-of-payments support assistance and, in particular, it would be prepared to discuss the 'far-reaching political and institutional reorganisation of the Community' required for the creation of EMU. The Finance Minister's memorandum restated the main criteria on which the desirability of a European central bank should be judged: commitment to price stability, independence of political instructions and proper balance between central and federative elements in its decision-making.

The Finance Minister's memorandum differed from Genscher's in making no procedural suggestions for the subsequent debate and in showing more awareness of the risks of instability in transitory arrangements. Independence of central banks in all member states, enabling them to give priority to price stability, might be a prerequisite for embarking on intermediate steps. This second memorandum was also more openly critical of the analysis of asymmetry in the French and Italian memoranda. Nevertheless, by insisting so much on full capital liberalization as the prerequisite for any movement on the German side, Stoltenberg's memorandum kept the door open to significant and even early movement, if other countries would drop their residual objections to liberalization and submit their policies to the judgement of financial markets. This duly happened in ECOFIN in June. A number of other EC governments and the EC Commission were anxious to test how far the new-found German readiness to consider anything more than modest, non-institutional reforms would go.

While the four major statements referred to above were the significant ones in launching the subsequent initiative to nominate the Delors Committee in June, some non-official initiatives went further than the fairly general statements by Ministers. The two founders of the EMS, former Chancellor Helmut Schmidt and former President Valery Giscard d'Estaing had set up in late 1986 a Committee for the Monetary Union in Europe with a mixed membership of former politicians, central bankers and some private bankers and academics. That committee published in April 1988 a fairly detailed blueprint for monetary union and a European central bank, including the politically sensitive issues of the composition of the governing bodies of a European central bank and their relationship to the political authorities.[4] The Schmidt–Giscard Committee also encouraged the formation in 1987 of the Association for Monetary Union in Europe (AMUE), with a number of Europe's main industrial companies as members. This Association began in 1987–8 to publicize statements and the results of questionnaire studies in European enterprises which were generally favourable to the introduction of a single currency. These expressions of political and business support for EMU as a complement to the integration of the EC's economies through the

---

[4] Committee for the Monetary Union in Europe (1988).

completion of the Internal Market were no doubt helpful in bringing forth more rapid initiatives from governments.

At a more technical and academic level efforts to develop ideas for EMU in general, and a European central bank in particular, were intensified in 1987–8. The two present authors had organized from 1986 onwards a working group of central bankers and economists to evaluate the EMS and discuss directions for the future. A report (Gros and Thygesen (1988)) was published in March 1988 and gave rise to several discussions with policy-makers in European central banks and Treasuries. Suggestions to explore carefully the analogy to the US Federal Reserve System in designing a European System of Central Banks, made in more detail in a separate article, initially presented in May 1987 (Thygesen (1989a)), were discussed with particular attention on these occasions. At academic conferences, which in the area of monetary and international economics have a long tradition of bringing together economists from universities and central banks, papers on the welfare economics of monetary unification and various approaches to it began to mix with empirical studies of the working of the EMS.[5] Monetary officials were far from unfamiliar with more radical approaches to monetary unification than those on the regular agenda of the 'competent EC bodies' and the expert groups serving them.

The 'competent bodies' themselves were not in these early months actively involved in the discussion of the longer-run initiatives submitted by the three governments. The Genscher proposals, being largely procedural, were put on the agenda of the European Council at Hanover by Genscher. The initiatives were so far-reaching that technical work could not begin without a confirmation at the highest political level of the objectives of EMU.

As was recorded at the end of chapter 3, most monetary officials would have been content to adopt a pragmatic attitude. The Basle–Nyborg agreement had only recently been implemented, and most EC central bankers had a preference for developing its full potential within a system of voluntary coordination. Some of them considered the proposals for a European central bank divisive and dangerous, because they diverted attention from more immediate matters in operating the EMS and were likely to bring to the surface differences in policy objectives which the Committee of Governors did not have to address in the regular operations of the EMS.[6] But once it became clear that the proposals were likely to be sent for detailed study to some group after Hanover, either of independent experts as proposed by Genscher or the 'competent EC bodies', the Governors were anxious not to be left out, as had happened in the initial stages of the EMS negotiations in 1978.

In the end a compromise was reached, mainly as a result of an understanding between Chancellor Helmut Kohl and President Jacques Delors. In confirming the

---

[5] Two major conferences in Perugia, October 1987, and in Castelgandolfo, June 1988, both organized by the Centre for Economic Policy Research (CEPR), are prime illustrations, see Giavazzi *et al.* (eds.)(1988) and de Cecco and Giovannini (eds.) (1989). Extensive use has been made in earlier chapters of these volumes.

[6] This view was reflected in early reactions by the Bundesbank to the Genscher initiative, e.g. at a Press conference in May. For an explicitly sceptical view of institutional design, see Hoffmeyer (1988).

objective of progressive realization of economic and monetary union, the European Council 'decided to entrust to a committee the task of studying and proposing concrete stages leading towards this union'. This committee would be chaired by President Delors and consist of the twelve governors of the EC national central banks 'in a personal capacity', one additional member of the EC Commission, and three independent persons. In an Annex to this chapter the conclusions of the German Presidency are reproduced. The Committee was asked, as Genscher had proposed, to complete its work sufficiently well ahead of the meeting of the European Council scheduled for end June 1989 in Madrid in order to enable the ECOFIN Council to examine its results.

The work of the Committee was seen above all as providing recommendations for the actions required to move to EMU. The mandate was wider, but also less detailed than that proposed initially by Genscher. The emphasis was to be on both economic and monetary aspects of unification and on the transition, and the Committee was not asked to go as far as to propose a draft statute for a European central bank.

This task was reserved for subsequent work by the Committee of Governors during 1990, but preliminary work got underway in parallel to the Delors Committee through an unofficial group sponsored by several central banks financially and through participation – obviously again in a 'personal capacity' which included legal experts of several EMS central banks and other experts in constitutional and administrative law. The work of this group chaired by Professor Jean-Victor Louis, was published shortly after the Delors Report and provided a useful blueprint for the draft statute.[7]

10.2   The Delors Report

The Delors Committee held eight meetings between September 1988 and April 1989 when its Report was submitted to a meeting of ECOFIN.[8] The summary of its conclusions can be short, since most of the specific recommendations have survived to the Intergovernmental Conference (IGC) and the proposed Treaty revisions and hence form the basis for our review in later chapters. The Report itself is brief; within the time constraint and recalling that the central bank governors were nominated personally – many of them did not involve the staff of their banks in the drafting of the Report – it could hardly be otherwise.

The Report is in three chapters: (1) a brief overview of the past record of economic and monetary integration in the Community, (2) a more detailed analysis of the implications of the final stage of EMU, including institutional arrangements and (3) proposals for the approach by stages. Here the focus is on (2) and (3) using in part the Werner Report of 1970 as a reference point.

---

[7] Louis *et al.* (1989). This source was drawn on in preparing chapter 13.

[8] There was immediate publication of the Report itself in April. A volume including the Collected Papers contributed by members and rapporteurs was published in August. This and other chapters refer to this fuller version, Committee for the Study of Economic and Monetary Union (1989).

The Delors Report made its main contribution through its analysis of the stringent requirements for achieving EMU. Although the 'principle of subsidiarity', according to which the functions of higher levels of government should be as limited as possible and subsidiary to lower levels, should be respected, EMU would require a transfer of decision-making from Member States to the Community in macroeconomic management generally, but particularly in monetary policy, where responsibility would have to be vested in a new EC institution, the European System of Central Banks (ESCB). Centralized and collective decisions on the instruments of monetary policy would be required from the time, at the start of the final stage, when participants committed themselves to maintaining permanently – or 'irrevocably fixed' – exchange rates inside the union.

There are interesting differences of emphasis relative to the Werner Report although both claim to adhere to the principle of parallelism between economic and monetary elements in the union. The Werner Report had proposed a high degree of centralization of budgetary policies at the community level, in part through a major increase in the EC budget, in part through a transfer of authority over national tax and expenditure instruments, in order to assure a flexible and discretionary stabilization policy. By contrast, the Delors Report does not envisage any radical increase in the EC budget, though the possibility that regional and structural policies might have to be strengthened after 1993, beyond the doubling of the size of transfers to less favoured regions agreed upon in 1988, was kept open. There is no recognition that an automatic transfer mechanism to even out the effects of exogenous shocks affecting Member States differentially may become necessary. On the whole the Delors Report takes a more positive view of the capacity of price flexibility and factor mobility – in conjunction with judicious and modest use of national budgetary policies, including automatic stabilizers – to take care of the adjustment problems in EMU than did the Werner Report. Nor was the confidence of the latter in the virtues of activist and discretionary use of budgetary policy shared by the authors of the Delors Report, which stressed instead the need for strengthening convergence through medium-term guidelines for budgetary policies.

But the Delors Report went beyond this in proposing to give to an EC body – the ECOFIN Council in cooperation with the European Parliament – the authority to apply binding rules in the form of upper limits to national budget deficits. The arguments for this recommendation are based on the view that individually divergent behaviour of one or more member states towards large deficits and high debt levels may endanger the country's participation in EMU, put pressure on the collective monetary policy and be unacceptable politically to other member states. The possibility that such divergent behaviour may be sufficiently constrained in EMU by the need to observe permanently fixed exchange rates (and hence a common low inflation rate) and by credit risk premia applied by financial markets to sovereign borrowers, was considered, but found too remote.

Despite the softening of the centralized approach taken by the Werner Report, the Delors Report recommendations on mandatory guidelines for national budget deficits proved the most controversial in the Report. There was less than full agreement on them in the Committee; President Delors was to remove himself to some extent from these recommendations later, notably in the EC Commission's paper to the informal ECOFIN meeting at Ashford Castle in March 1990, Commission (1990). They have nevertheless survived in only slightly softer form as proposals for Treaty revision.

The attitude towards 'binding guidelines' for national fiscal policy may have changed since the Delors Report was written in the winter of 1988/9. Persistently very large budget deficits in some countries (Greece and Italy) are seen more clearly by the early 1990s as a potential risk to any effective participation by these countries in EMU, and the sudden shift in the budgetary position in Germany in 1990–1 has strengthened the view that externalities of national policies may at times become sufficiently important to justify EC authority to constrain them. The analytical arguments for mandatory budgetary coordination are reviewed in some detail in chapter 8, including possible indicators for monitoring; here it is just noted that the recommendations in the Delors Report cannot simply be dismissed as an effort by a group, consisting largely of central bankers, to raise the prerequisites for EMU so high that national policy-makers would never agree to the transfer of authority required.

Because the tasks of the EC authority in budgetary matters were seen primarily as those of (1) monitoring medium-term plans for budgetary policies prepared nationally for their mutual consistency and compatibility with EMU, and (2) applying generally agreed rules to constrain divergent behaviour, the Delors Report did not repeat the proposal of the Werner Report to create a new decision-making body, the 'Centre of decision for economic policy'. It saw the existing ECOFIN Council as adequate for the less activist and discretionary operations it had in mind. In this sense the political implications of the Delors Report are less far-reaching; EMU in the more recent vision does not require as much of a political union as did the Werner Report.

The Delors Report is, quite naturally, at its most explicit on monetary union and the joint institution required to run the single policy. It adopts the definition of monetary union of the Werner Report; the necessary conditions are (para. 22):

the assurance of total and irreversible convertibility of currencies;

the complete liberalization of capital transactions and full integration of banking and other financial markets; and

the elimination of margins of fluctuations and the irrevocable locking of exchange-rate parities.

The first was seen as already achieved, and the second was in sight, given the ECOFIN Decision of June 1988 to liberalize capital movements fully for most EMS members by July 1990 and by 1992–5 for the remaining four member states, and the progress in financial integration in general under the 1992 programme. The crucial remaining step was the locking of exchange rates.

There was one difference of emphasis in the Delors Report relative to its predecessor: the introduction of a single currency should take place as soon as possible after entering the final stage, because that would (para. 23):

clearly demonstrate the irreversibility of the move to monetary union, considerably facilitate the monetary management of the Community, and avoid the transactions costs of converting currencies.

The arguments for a single currency are examined in chapter 7, so the substance of the pros and cons are not entered into here. Despite the resistance of some countries, notably the United Kingdom, to seeing the single currency as an integral part of the final stage of EMU, its early introduction has moved higher up on the agenda of priorities than was evident in the Delors Report. There the drafting still bears the mark of those with long experience of a gradually tightening EMS, to whom the further narrowing of margins of fluctuation and their elimination in the final stage seemed to constitute a momentous and sufficient series of commitments.

The Delors Report proposals on the ESCB are virtually identical to those found in the draft statute, elaborated on in the second half of 1990 by the Committee of Governors, and annexed in its final form to the proposed new Treaty as a Protocol, which are reviewed in chapter 13. As regards the mandate and functions, structure and organization, and status, all major points were clarified in the Delors Report. The ESCB would be committed to the objective of price stability – the adjective 'primary' has been added in the draft statute and in Art. 105 of the proposed Treaty revision to clarify the nature of the objective – and, 'subject to the foregoing, the System should support the general economic policy set at the Community level'. The System would have a federative structure and be governed by a Council, consisting of the governors of the national central banks and the members of the Board, the latter to be appointed by the European Council. The Delors Report did not make precise proposals with respect to voting procedures. Members of the Council should be independent of instructions from national governments and Community authorities; they would be subject to substantial reporting requirements vis-à-vis the European Parliament and the European Council to facilitate their accountability.

The provisions are clear and far-reaching. They incorporate the main principles advanced in the two German memoranda of early 1988 and the more detailed views submitted by the President of the Bundesbank at the beginning of the work of the Delors Committee, see Pöhl (1989). Opinions were clearly converging among the governors that the experience of the Bundesbank was useful as a model of mandate, structure and relationship with political authorities, but there was no careful review of this experience or of that of the United States, the other main industrial country with a federal structure and a tradition of central bank independence. It is, in retrospect, not surprising that the central bankers found the German model appealing, particularly with respect to the Bundesbank's autonomy in monetary policy formulation and implementation. It is more surprising that the political authorities, initially the participants in the ECOFIN Council of whom most followed the evolution of the Delors Report at close range, did not object to a proposal to give the ESCB more independence than they had been prepared to give their own central banks within their respective national systems. There was no important disagreement on any of the main provisions for the ESCB.

Consensus was more difficult to achieve with respect to the description of the stages by which EMU was to be achieved, and there was no consensus at all on a timetable.

It is arguable that had there not been a clear request in the mandate to the Delors Committee to 'propose concrete stages', an important proportion of the members would have expressed a preference for continuing with the existing EMS until sufficient convergence was deemed to have been achieved to move to permanently fixed rates. They might then have proceeded to define a set of objective criteria for such a judgement to be made; efforts along these lines were made in the IGC to establish such criteria for the transition to EMU. In particular, Karl-Otto Pöhl, President of the Bundesbank until August 1991, who has since been explicit on this subject in public statements, was highly critical of the notion of passing through an intermediate stage in which monetary authority was somehow shared between the national level and an emerging ESCB. A crucial paragraph in chapter III, section 1, of the Delors Report discussing this issue under the heading of 'gradualism and indivisibility' had to be skipped, because differences of opinion could not be bridged. It was obvious that there should be no doubts in financial markets as to who was responsible for any particular decision, but did this exclude the attribution of some clearly defined policy functions to the ESCB already in the transition? Some members of the Committee did not think so, as is evident from the nature of individual contributions to the preparation of the Delors Report, but others did. The substance of the proposals are discussed in chapter 12; none of them won wide support and they were relegated to the annexes for which the Committee as such was not responsible.

In the end the Delors Report confined itself to a brief description of two transitory stages, of which the first was basically a continuation of the EMS, though with some reinforcement of the authority of the Committee of Governors and of its secretariat (see chapter 12), and a second stage about which little more could be said than that (1) the ESCB would be set up and absorb the functions of the existing monetary arrangements, (2) realignments would be made 'only in exceptional circumstances', and (3) the margins of fluctuations would be narrowed as a move towards the final stage. Ultimate responsibility for monetary policy decisions would remain with national authorities, but (para. 57):

> The key task for the ESCB during this stage would be to begin the transition from the coordination of independent national monetary policies by the Committee of Central Bank Governors in stage one to the formulation and implementation of a common monetary policy by the ESCB itself, scheduled to take place in the final stage.

This vagueness was a key weakness of the Delors Report, further aggravated by the failure to set any timetable for the beginning of stage two. Agreement could not be reached that stage one, which was to begin on 1 July 1990, should end by the end of 1992, to coincide with the target date for full implementation of the internal market. At the Rome European Council of October 1990 this date was postponed by one year to 1 January 1994, but without a more specific content having been defined for stage two. There was no agreement at all about the duration of this stage. Some argued in favour of a long span of years, to be assured of convergence, while others thought of the transition as a fairly short rehearsal period, maybe a couple of years, in which the new institution would get ready to assume full monetary authority.[9]

Disagreements were also evident in the brief attention given in the Delors Report to the role that the ecu might play in the process of economic and monetary integration (paras. 45–49).

The Delors Report made four specific points:

(1) The ecu has the potential to be developed into a common currency.

(2) A parallel currency strategy for the ecu can not be recommended.

(3) The official ecu might be used as an instrument in the conduct of a common monetary policy.

(4) There should be no discrimination against and no administrative obstacles to, the private use of the ecu.

These short and in appearance conflicting points reflect a compromise between two rather different concepts. The first starts from a concern that any parallel currency could bring inflationary risks, since an additional source of money creation without a precise link to economic activity could jeopardize price stability; moreover the addition of a new currency would further complicate the coordination of national monetary policies.[10] The other takes as its starting point the responsibility of EC monetary authorities for the existing private ecu market – at the time of the preparation of the Delors Report already of more than ecu 100 billion in the banking sector, see chapter 6 – and the need to confirm users of the unit, in the belief that, if there were to be a single currency in EMU, it would be defined in continuity with the existing unit. The former group felt vindicated by (2) above, whereas the second could take comfort in (1).

The merits of the parallel-currency approach are discussed in more detail in chapter 11, since it has been seen by some as an alternative approach to monetary integration by institutional design and timetables associated with the Delors Report. Here it is just noted that the mention in the Delors Report of the ecu – and only that unit – as the potential basis for a common currency has given market participants the assurance that the present ecu will shade over into a common currency unit with fixed exchange rates *vis-à-vis* the component currencies, and subsequently into the single currency. This assurance is an important cause behind the take-off of the longer-term ecu bond market in 1990–1. The apparently modest statement in the Delors Report was also a prerequisite for the endorsement at the Rome European Council in October 1990 of 'a single currency – a strong and stable ecu' as an integral part of the final stage of EMU.

The Delors Report last, but not least, made procedural suggestions (para. 64–6). Subject to acceptance by the European Council of the Report as a basis for further development towards EMU, it recommended that the decisions necessary to implement

[9] The EC Commission in 1990 explicitly proposed a two-year transitional stage, see Commission (1990).

10 These different views with the Delors Committee are discussed more fully in Thygesen (1989b).

the first stage not later than 1 July 1990, be taken, and that preparatory work for the negotiations on the new Treaty should start 'immediately' as a basis for an Intergovernmental Conference to revise the EC Treaty.

10.3 The political follow-up to the Delors Report – June 1989–October 1990

The European Council in Madrid in June 1989 accepted both of the main procedural proposals of the Delors Report. It agreed to start the first stage – for which it accepted the outline given in the Report – on 1 July 1990, and to convene an Intergovernmental Conference to consider the Treaty changes necessary for moving beyond the first stage. It did not set a date for the IGC, since the Madrid Conclusions stated that 'full and adequate preparations' had to precede the setting of dates.

The impression that this formulation, introduced at the insistence of the United Kingdom, left scope for considerable delay, and that the highest levels of governments were still only committed to the gradualist steps of stage one, was corrected in the course of the second half of 1989. Following an informal ECOFIN Council meeting in Antibes in September, the French Presidency constituted a high-level group of officials from national Ministries of Finance and Foreign Ministers to prepare the questions for the IGC. This group, presided over by Mme. Elisabeth Guigou, produced already by the end of October a report – the 'Guigou Report' – which raised in the form of questions rather than even preliminary answers, most of the issues for the IGC agenda. In retrospect, it may seem puzzling why the questions already addressed in the Delors Report had to be reopened in the relatively agnostic tone of the Guigou Report, but the explanation is simple: the Delors Report had only involved central bankers or others who had no national political responsibilities. The framework of the high-level group permitted an immediate rehearsal of the themes of the IGC among the national decision-makers who would subsequently be participating in the negotiations. The Madrid Conclusions had referred to a role for both the ECOFIN and the General Affairs Councils in preparing for the IGC and there was acceptance for the view that 'full and adequate preparations' could consist of formulating adequate questions rather than going into the substance of the answers.

While the Guigou Report concealed, rather than clarified future disagreements, on one central point it did illustrate the growing unease of the United Kingdom with respect to the EMU process. The UK representatives disassociated themselves strongly from the need for a European central bank to operate a single monetary policy. Indeed, the day after the submission of the Guigou Report, the UK Treasury circulated a paper on an evolutionary alternative approach to EMU through competition among currencies and national monetary policies, which is discussed in detail in chapter 11.

The December 1989 European Council at Strasbourg agreed to convene the IGC on EMU 'before the end of 1990', but no date was initially set for its completion. The Dublin European Council of April 1990 decided that the IGC – and a parallel conference on European Political Union – should end in time for their results to be ratified by member states before the end of 1992. Initially this was thought to imply that the second stage proposed in the Delors Report could then begin on 1 January 1993, to coincide with the implementation date for the Internal Market, but it became clear in the following months that opinions were strongly divided on the advisability of setting in advance the dates for the transition period, including the move to the final stage of EMU. A compromise on this issue was reached at the October 1990 European Council in Rome, which set the date of 1 January 1994, as the starting point for stage two; the United Kingdom did not associate herself with this compromise. Since the Rome European Council also added some conditions to the transition, it requires a more careful interpretation whether a clear political guideline was in fact given to the IGC. This subject is discussed in chapter 12.

For the purposes of the present chapter the above summary of the factual follow-up of the Delors Report at the highest political level may suffice to demonstrate that the momentum to implement the Report built up in the first eighteen months after its publication. The political support for the EMU process proved initially to be stronger than the authors of the Delors Report, including the President of the EC Commission, could have anticipated. That ambition was rising became clear both from the setting of dates for the IGC and the efforts to provide a timetable for the stages, subjects understandably left open by the Delors Report. An even more unmistakeable signal was the adoption by the Rome European Council of the single currency – 'a strong and stable ecu' – as an integral and early element in the final stage; the language in the Delors Report was less unequivocal on this point.

Two developments may have facilitated the higher political priority given to the single currency. The strong interest expressed by major European industrial enterprises in a single currency has already been referred to. The EC Commission also, starting with its preliminary paper to the ECOFIN council in March 1990, and followed up in great analytical detail in the report 'One Market, One Money' of October 1990,[11] brought out with greater clarity than before the superiority of a single currency over a system of national currencies with fixed exchange rates between them.

That political momentum to proceed towards EMU was building up in 1989–90 was surprising in view of the explicit opposition of the United Kingdom. It was even more surprising given the urgency of challenges facing the European Community due to Geman unification, political and economic reforms in Eastern Europe and the Soviet Union and – from the summer of 1990 – the build-up towards military conflict in the Gulf. While these events were not in themselves causes for eroding or delaying the EMU, the project might well have been temporarily pushed into the background and political energies focused entirely on the new challenges. The final chapter comes back to the linkages between EMU and political union in the Community. The almost exclusive focus in this book on monetary unification would not make sense to someone who believes these linkages to be strong and immediate. That these views are not shared in this book should, however, emerge more than implicitly in chapter 14.

---

[11] Subsequently published under the names of the main authors, Emerson *et al.* (1991).

It is interesting to reflect, in concluding the present chapter, on how fast the debate on EMU has moved since the start in early 1988. As was documented in the review of French, Italian and German positions, there was some common ground, but there were also obvious differences in the approaches of these three countries. The common ground was that, while the EMS had worked well and fostered convergence towards lower inflation, it might not be up to the challenges of full capital mobility and increasingly rigid exchange rates; institutional steps leading to a common monetary policy and a European central bank were thus advisable.

The differences in emphasis were, however, even more evident. The initial French and Italian positions were critical of asymmetry in the EMS and of the way in which German leadership in the system had been exercised with low growth and a large German current-account surplus as results.

The French and Italian memoranda had accordingly emphasized the need for a sharing of monetary authority and a basic reassessment of macroeconomic coordination with an effort to set joint objectives. The German contributions put more exclusive emphasis on the emergence of a stable joint monetary policy and the institutional prerequisites; they were clearly more interested in the final outcome than in the process of gradual transfer of authority. Genscher's memorandum also extended to macroeconomic policies in general.

These differences of approach, though still visible in 1991, have narrowed considerably over the past three to four years. In part that may be explained by the relatively rapid growth in the EC since 1987; France and Italy no longer perceive, as was the case in the mid 1980s, the EMS as a straitjacket. German economic policy would for a time no longer be criticized for being too cautious. Indeed, the main criticism in 1989–91 has been that fiscal policy has become too expansionary. The German current-account surplus has been replaced by a small deficit.[12]

Another element of an explanation of the greater consensus may be found in a growing acceptance by policy-makers in countries other than Germany (and the Netherlands) that the long-term institutional arrangements of EMU provide a more solid foundation for managing the transition than the more pragmatic approach, favoured notably by the United Kingdom. By defining the final stage clearly and getting wide political support for it, a constructive feed-back is assured on how the EMS is managed and changed into a European monetary authority. This approach was already visible in the Delors Report, and it has become even more so in the course of the years that have followed its publication, and most clearly in the draft statute for a European System of Central Banks, submitted initially by the Committee of Governors in November 1990. The main provisions of this statute are reviewed in chapter 13.

References

Amato, Giuliano (1988), 'Un motore per lo SME', *Il Sole 24 Ore*, Rome, 25 February, reprint of Memorandum to ECOFIN Council, 23 February.

[12] For a discussion of the effects of German unification on the EMS see chapter 5.

Balladur, Edouard (1988), 'Europe's monetary construction', Memorandum to ECOFIN Council, Ministry of Finance and Economics, Paris, 8 January.

Commission of the European Communities (1990), 'Economic and monetary union', Paper for informal ECOFIN Council at Ashford Castle, Brussels, March.

Committee for the Monetary Union of Europe (1988), *A Programme for Action*, Crédit National, Paris.

Committee for the Study of Economic and Monetary Union (1989), 'Report on economic and monetary union in the European Community' (the Delors Report), Office of Publications of the European Communities, Luxembourg, August.

de Cecco, Marcello and Alberto Giovannini (eds.) (1989), *A European Central Bank?*, Italian Macroeconomic Group and Centre for European Policy Research, Cambridge University Press, Cambridge.

Emerson, Michael, Daniel Gros, Jean Pisani-Ferry, Alexander Italianer and Horst Reichenbach (1991), *One Market, One Money*, Oxford University Press, Oxford.

Genscher, Hans-Dietrich (1988), 'A European currency area and a European central bank', Memorandum to General Affairs Council, Ministry of Foreign Affairs, Bonn, 26 February.

Giavazzi, Francesco, Stefano Micossi and Marcus Miller (eds.) (1988), *The European Monetary System*, Banca d'Italia, Centro Interuniversitario di Studi Teorici per la Politica Economica and Centre for Economic Policy Research, Cambridge University Press, Cambridge.

Gros, Daniel and Niels Thygesen (1988), 'The EMS: achievements, current issues and directions for the future', Centre for European Policy Studies, Brussels, *CEPS Paper*, 35.

High-Level Group of Representatives of Governments of the EC Member States (1989), *Report on Economic and Monetary Union* (the Guigou Report), Paris, 31 October.

Hoffmeyer, Erik (1988), 'Speech to annual meeting of Danish Savings Banks' (in Danish), Danmarks Nationalbank Kvartalsoversigt, Copenhagen, August: 20–2.

Louis, Jean-Victor *et al.* (1989), *Vers un système Européen de banques centrales*, Collection Etudes Européennes, Editions de l'Université de Bruxelles.

Pöhl, Karl Otto (1989), 'The further development of the European Monetary System', in collection of papers annexed to Delors Report, Office of Publications of the European Communities, Luxembourg, 131–55.

Stoltenberg, Gerhard (1988), 'The further development of monetary cooperation in Europe', Memorandum to ECOFIN Council, Ministry of Finance, Bonn, 15 March.

Thygesen, Niels (1989a), 'Decentralization and accountability within the central bank: any lessons from the US experience for the potential organization of a European central banking institution?', in Paul De Grauwe and Theo Peeters (eds.), *The Ecu and European Monetary Integration*, Macmillan Press, London, 91–114.

Thygesen, Niels (1989b), 'The role of the ecu in the process to EMU', Bulletin of the Ecu Banking Association, Paris, September.

APPENDIX

Excerpts from the conclusions of the Presidency presented after the meeting of the European Council in Hanover on 27 and 28 June 1988

Monetary union

The European Council recalls that, in adopting the Single Act, the Member States confirmed the objective of progressive realization of economic and monetary union.

They therefore decided to examine at the European Council meeting in Madrid in June 1989 the means of achieving this union.

To that end they decided to entrust to a Committee the task of studying and proposing concrete stages leading towards this union. The Committee will be chaired by Mr. Jacques Delors, President of the European Commission.

The Heads of State of Government agreed to invite the President or Governor of their central banks to take part in a personal capacity in the proceedings of the Committee, which will also include one other member of the Commission and three personalities designated by common agreement by the Heads of State or Government. They have agreed to invite:

Mr. Niels Thygesen, Professor of Economics, Copenhagen;

Mr. Lamfalussy, General Manager of the Bank for International Settlements in Basle, Professor of Monetary Economics at the Catholic University of Louvain-la-Neuve;

Mr. Miguel Boyer, President of Banco Exterior de España.

The Committee should have completed its proceedings in good time to enable the Ministers for Economic Affairs and for Finance to examine its results before the European Council meeting in Madrid.

CHAPTER 11

ALTERNATIVES AND COMPLEMENTS TO THE DELORS REPORT

This chapter discusses two related alternative approaches to monetary union that were not retained by the Delors Report. The most radical approach which holds that no institutional steps are needed is discussed first. According to this so-called competing currencies approach competition is always the best market structure. Governments should therefore let currencies compete in the market until the best one wins. Monetary union would, or rather could, therefore be the outcome of a purely market determined process.

A more nuanced variant of this approach, called the parallel currency approach, is based on the premise that the Community should create a currency which would circulate in parallel to the existing national currencies. Monetary union could then again be reached with little official action if the parallel currency crowded out national currencies. The only official action necessary would be to manage the parallel currency in such a way as to ensure that it would indeed be used increasingly by the private sector.

The two alternatives to the Delors Report presented by the government of the United Kingdom in 1989 and 1990 are discussed in this chapter since they can be considered special cases of the competing and parallel currency approaches. The first proposal, which put the emphasis on the role of competition between national monetary policies, is discussed under the general heading of market-led versus institutional approaches in the first section of this chapter. The second UK proposal, based on the so-called 'hard ecu', is discussed in the second section because it is really a specific variant of the parallel currency approach.

11.1 Institutional versus market-led approaches to monetary union[1]

The Delors Report is based on the premise that a new monetary institution is needed to

---

[1] This section draws heavily on Gros (1991).

manage the transition towards EMU and to manage the common monetary policy once stage III has been reached. This approach has been contested by some economists, who argued that competition should also extend to the choice of currencies, and by the UK government, which argued that only competition between national monetary policies can ensure lasting price stability.[2] These two points of view are discussed in the following two subsections.

11.1.1 Currency competition and economies of scale in the choice of money

The most radical objection to the Delors Report comes from a school of thought which maintains that if the gains from currency unification are real they will lead markets to move spontaneously towards the adoption of a single currency. The only official action required would be to eliminate all legal restrictions that impose the use of national currency. It would not be necessary to fix exchange rates and coordinate national policies.

The economic logic behind the general idea is quite straightforward: in general competition is the best market structure; it should therefore also be applied to the choice of money. At its logical extreme this line of thought would imply that there should be free private issuance of money.[3] The public would then choose the best money, presumably the one that is the most convenient because it offers the most stable purchasing power.

This approach therefore raises the fundamental issue of the optimal monetary constitution. This issue has been debated at great length in the economic profession; it is, in principle, completely independent of the process of European monetary integration. Hence this book cannot do justice to the fundamental nature of this controversy. Instead, the purpose of this brief section is merely to outline the economic objections to currency competition

At first sight, the logic of the call for currency competition seems undeniable. But it implies that the monetary constitutions of almost all countries of this era are fundamentally flawed because they give the government a monopoly on the issuance of money. For the proponents of this approach the reason for this discrepancy between theoretical optimum and reality can be found in political considerations, in the sense that governments want to keep the monopoly of issuing money to keep a source of potentially large seigniorage gains under their control.

However, even from a purely economic point of view one could argue that this approach is flawed because there are important economies of scale in the choice of money. The benefits from a common currency discussed below are an indirect

---

[2] A forceful plea for currency competition is found in Von Hayek (1984). The UK alternative was outlined in HM Treasury (1989). The economists of the so-called Bruges group generally support this idea, see Salin (1990).

[3] See Von Hayek (1984).

expression of these economies of scale, and the estimates of the order of magnitude of the potential benefits imply that they can be quite important. Free competition is in general not the optimal market structure if there are external[4] economies of scale. It is therefore possible to make a strictly economic case for a government monopoly of money and for institutional steps towards monetary union.

The economies of scale that arise in the use of money can be illustrated by an analogy: just as a telephone is useful only if there are other users of telephones that can be reached, a particular money can be used for transactions only if other economic agents accept it. This point is not disputed by the proponents of the competing currencies approach, see for example Vaubel (1984).[5] These economies of scale that arise in the use of money as a medium of exchange are apparent at an intuitive level. Even ordinary daily shopping would become very cumbersome if every store or every customer used a different currency. At a more sophisticated level and in an international context these economies of scale manifest themselves in the fact that the transactions costs (mainly bid-ask spreads) in the foreign exchange markets diminish with the size of the market. This leads to the emergence of 'vehicle currencies' as shown by Krugman (1980). The choice of the vehicle currency is therefore to a large extent arbitrary but, once a currency has been chosen as a vehicle it becomes the most convenient currency to use because transactions costs decline. There is no inherent economic mechanisms that would ensure that the currency that becomes the vehicle is superior (in terms of a stable purchasing power, for example) to other currencies.

Another manifestation of these economies of scale is embodied in the standard Baumol–Tobin money demand functions. Swoboda (1968) generalizes this standard approach to the case of several currencies to explain the predominance of the US dollar in the Euro-markets.

There are therefore theoretical reasons to doubt the claim that currency substitution would automatically lead the private sector to choose a money with a stable purchasing power. The experience with the US dollar which did not lose its pre-eminent position as the global currency, despite the fact that other currencies had much more stable purchasing power, shows that currency competition cannot be relied upon to ensure low inflation. Another piece of empirical evidence is that, as recognized by Vaubel (1990), currency competition is particularly restricted in Germany through the currency law (Währungsgesetz) of 1948, but this fact did not prevent the DM from becoming one of the most stable currencies of the world.

The argument that currency competition could help to ensure price stability seemed particularly important during the high inflation period of the 1970s. As inflation has now been brought down in Europe there seems to be less need for the disciplinary influence of currency competition. However, the present low and converging inflation

---

[4] It is crucial that the economies of scale be external. If they could be internalized by each private provider of money, competition would break down as one money would displace others and remain without competition.

[5] From a welfare-theoretic point of view, however, the crucial question is whether these indisputable external effects are Pareto-relevant, i.e., whether they lead to a difference between private and social costs. Vaubel (1984) argues that this is not the case in the particular analytical framework used by him.

rates could also be seen as the result of a system (the EMS) that has encouraged competition between stability-oriented national monetary policies (as opposed to competition between currencies). This argument is the basis of the first alternative plan put forward by the UK government which is discussed in the next section.

11.1.2 The UK proposal mark I: competing monetary policies

According to the first of the two UK proposals only stage I of the Delors plan should be implemented.[6] After stage I competition among currencies would become operational and increasingly effective because capital market liberalization and the single market for financial services would widen the range and currency denominations of available financial instruments and services. Increased competition through the single market in financial services would also contribute to currency competition by reducing the cost and inconvenience of switching between Community currencies. In such an environment an inflationary monetary policy by any central bank would reduce the international and perhaps also the domestic use of that currency. Since central banks realize this and since they dislike seeing the domain for their own currency shrink they would have an incentive to follow less inflationary policies.

According to this version of the UK approach, the only policy action to be taken beyond stage I would therefore be to eliminate all restrictions on the use of Community currencies and to tackle the remaining barriers between currencies, for example by promoting cheaper European cheque-clearing systems and eliminating anti-competitive practices by banks in charging for foreign exchange services.

It is apparent that these elements of the UK proposal could and should be part of the internal market programme on financial services. However, it is not clear from the UK document whether and how competition between monetary policies would lead to a monetary union, in the conventional definition of a single currency. As argued in the preceding section it is unlikely that, in the environment of low inflation and low exchange-rate variability which would be created by stage I, existing national currencies would be replaced either by a parallel currency or by the strongest Community currency. It is therefore highly unlikely that any further progress towards monetary union could be achieved by relying exclusively on competition among monetary policies caused by market forces.

The UK position argues implicitly that the present low and converging inflation rates are the result of a system (the EMS) that has encouraged competition between stability-oriented monetary policies. According to this argument it would be dangerous to create a new Community institution to coordinate national monetary policies because that would limit the extent of this competition. A Community institution might encourage an overall monetary policy stance closer to the average performance than to the best, progress towards price stability might therefore stop or even be reversed if competition between currencies (or more precisely between national

[6] HM Treasury (1989).

monetary policies) were eliminated or reduced. This is the main reason why it would be preferable, according to the UK position (of November 1989), not to take the institutional steps towards a common monetary institution foreseen in stage II of the Delors Report, and not to exclude the possibility of realignments.[7]

However, the argument that only competition between national monetary policies ensures price stability exaggerates the influence of currency competition and overlooks the difficulties in determining a stable anchor for prices and expectations that would arise in a stage I environment. Private markets do not always adopt the currency with the most stable purchasing power. That quality is only one of the determinants of the 'success' of a currency; economies of scale are more important as long as inflation remains moderate.

The most fundamental objection against the notion that only currency competition, at fixed exchange rates, ensures price stability is, however, that a fixed exchange-rate system needs an anchor for prices and expectations. In the EMS this anchor was, for much of the period since 1983, provided by the monetary policy of the Bundesbank. The Bundesbank was able to perform this role mainly because it was able to sterilize intra-EMS reserve flows and stick to a domestic monetary objective. Up to 1989–90 these flows were limited because the UK and Spain did not participate in the ERM and because capital controls dampened capital flows in the short run. However, in an extended stage I environment, with all major European currencies participating in the ERM, with capital controls eliminated and financial markets everywhere more sophisticated and liquid, the potential for reserve flows could exceed the sterilization potential of the Bundesbank. This might jeopardize the anchor function of the Bundesbank. The increasing integration of financial markets and wider ERM membership therefore represent no guarantee of a good price stability record; on the contrary, they might endanger it, as was already argued in the discussion of current issues for the EMS in chapter 5.

A related problem inherent in the UK approach is that it explicitly aims at making Community currencies increasingly substitutable. Progress towards monetary union may come through currency substitution, but widespread currency substitution would also make national monetary policies less reliable and threaten the anchor role of the DM in the EMS. If widespread currency substitution were to occur, a common monetary institution would definitely be needed. In this sense significant progress under the market-led approach, whether under the original UK proposal or the parallel currency approach focussing on the ecu (which is discussed next), would create a need for institutional steps.

---

[7] This line of reasoning is close to that of Rogoff (1985): monetary coordination among national central banks can become 'counterproductive' by removing the incentives and the sanctions inherent in a system of competitive monetary policies. A similar argument may be found in Jaans (1989) who also extols the virtues of such competition.

11.2 The parallel currency approach

The competing currencies approach was and is defended mainly by academic economists who have stressed, in the tradition of von Hayek, the importance of the market as a 'discovery device'.

A more popular alternative to institutional steps has focused on the so-called *parallel currency approach*.[8] Monetary unification might be achieved with little official action if private agents in a group of countries were increasingly induced to adopt a common parallel currency of high monetary quality, that gradually crowded out national currencies until it became *de facto* the single currency. This approach would also not rely on exchange rates being fixed; instead, through the increasing use of the parallel currency, a single currency area could be created without any need for the difficult process of convergence in national policies.[9] This approach might best be thought of as substituting only for stage II of the Delors Report since its proponents would agree that, if currency substitution did lead to a common currency, a common monetary institution would be needed to formulate and execute the monetary policies for this common currency.[10]

As described in chapter 10, the Delors Report rejected the parallel currency approach which it defined as the creation of a new currency which would be created autonomously and issued in addition to existing Community currencies.[11] It is apparent that the creation of an additional currency could jeopardize price stability and complicate monetary policy as argued in the Delors Report. Hence the authors of that report were anxious to discourage the idea that the present ecu – or a different version of a parallel common currency – could be relied upon to advance monetary integration.

However, the parallel currency approach does not necessarily rely on the creation of a new currency by an official authority. Except for notes and coins all forms of 'money' can be created by the private sector. In the case of the ecu, credit cards, traveller cheques, bank accounts, etc. already exist. The discussion of this section therefore concentrates on the (private) ecu in its present basket form which does not involve the creation of a new currency and assesses whether the ecu is likely to become a parallel currency.

Currency substitution, could, of course, represent a problem for national monetary policies. However, whether or not currency substitution is likely depends on the degree

---

[8] For an early and very thorough contribution see Vaubel (1978).

[9] Bini-Smaghi (1990) labels the demand for a parallel currency a 'demand' for monetary integration. Accordingly he distinguishes between the demand and supply of integration, the latter being given by institutional developments.

[10] It could also be seen as a complement to stage 1 of the Delors Report, since an essential element of stage I is capital-market liberalization, which is also an indispensable ingredient of all market-led approaches.

[11] Committee for the Study of Economic and Monetary Union (1989), para.47. Pöhl (1989) takes a similar position.

of integration of financial markets, not on the strategy for monetary integration: chapter 5 discusses this point in more detail. Moreover, currency substitution towards the ecu would create less problems than currency substitution towards the DM. As argued in chapter 5, the latter might under certain circumstances weaken the link between the money supply and nominal variables in Germany, thus jeopardizing the anchor role of the Bundesbank in the EMS.[12] In contrast, currency substitution towards the ecu would not destabilize German monetary policy and would not affect the overall European monetary aggregates (provided ecu balances are included). Currency substitution towards the ecu is preferable to substitution towards the DM.

The proposal of the UK government to create a 'hard ecu' to be managed by a European Monetary Fund would fall in with the definition of the Delors Report. At the same time the objection of the Delors Report, that a new currency might create additional liquidity, does not apply in this case either since the 'hard ecu' would be issued only in exchange for national currencies.

11.2.1 The ecu as a parallel currency.

This subsection concentrates on the ecu in its present form of a basket of fixed amounts of national currencies. There are numerous academic proposals based on a different, 'inflation-proof', ecu,[13] but these proposals seem less relevant in the present environment of low and converging inflation rates. Such an abstract parallel currency, even if 'inflation-proof' because of some purchasing power guarantee, would not benefit from the diversification element underpinning the ecu and can therefore not be expected to be successful when inflation rates are around 2–4 per cent as in the core of the EMS at present. This point is analysed in more detail in the separate discussion of the 'hard ecu' proposal of the UK government, see section 11.2.2.

Given that the purpose of the parallel currency approach is to avoid the need for fixing exchange rates this section discusses the factors that would determine the success of a parallel currency in an environment of moderate exchange-rate flexibility, roughly equivalent to the situation in the Community at present. In addition it will also be assumed that there are no capital controls, no legal restrictions on the use of a particular currency, but it will also be assumed that national financial markets and payments systems are only in the process of full integration, and will therefore conserve some national characteristics.

As in the discussion about the meaning of monetary union (see chapter 7) it is convenient to organize the discussion around the three classical functions of money: unit of account, store of value and transaction medium. Since in most modern economies one currency fulfils all three functions of money, a parallel currency could out-compete national currencies only if it had advantages substantial enough to

---

[12] For a formal analysis see Gros (1988).

[13] Starting with the 'All Saints Day Manifesto', see Basevi et al. (1975).

outweigh these economies of scale. A marginal advantage in one of the functions of money would not be enough.

The ecu as a unit of account

For large corporations with widely dispersed sales and plants the ecu might become convenient for accounting purposes if such corporations could pay taxes on the basis of their accounts in ecu or if they felt that consolidated accounts in this currency were used by the markets to determine the evaluation of the firm. The latter effect might arise only once corporations no longer had a distinct nationality.[14] However, in dealing with the general public, the ecu (or any other parallel currency) would become a convenient way to quote one European price only for the small segment of the market that is sophisticated enough to be familiar with this currency.[15]

This use of the ecu depends on the extent to which the Community can be viewed as one market. The 1992 internal market programme should therefore boost the demand for a supranational parallel currency as a convenient unit of account for the unified European market. However there is little prospect that the ecu could be widely used by corporations that mainly operate in the domestic market and by households which will always do most of their shopping domestically.

The ecu as a store of value

An important element of the parallel currency approach is that a high degree of exchange-rate variability would increase the usefulness of a parallel currency as a store of value or as a financial asset. A high degree of exchange-rate variability would make financial instruments denominated in a basket currency useful because it would allow issuers and investors who seek to reduce exchange-rate risk to save on the transaction costs that would arise if they had to construct a new basket each time and take out positions in each of the components. However, as the experience with the ecu shows, this type of demand for a parallel currency would be restricted mainly to international corporations exposed to exchange-rate variability and to wealthy individuals who can contemplate investing in several currencies. Moreover, the low degree of exchange-rate variability (between EC currencies) that can be expected by 1992 would further reduce

[14] The most elaborate proposals for advancing the parallel-currency role of the ecu put much emphasis on these two aspects. Association for Monetary Union in Europe (1990) proposes that initially companies incorporated under the European Statute, and subsequently all companies, should be allowed to pay their taxes in ecu, and that company reports and accounts should include ecu denominations.

[15] Quoting one price in the parallel currency to consumers throughout the entire Community would be difficult as long as national VAT rates differ since in most member countries prices are quoted tax inclusive. A price quotation in the parallel currency net of local taxes, as is the practice in the United States, would therefore not be accepted easily in retail markets though it might facilitate sales through mail order.

the usefulness of a basket currency as an instrument for risk diversification. Chapter 4 showed that by 1989 exchange-rate variability had already been reduced to around one fourth relative to the situation in 1979–80.

The remaining predictable, or expected, changes in exchange rates (as opposed to the unexpected changes that constitute exchange-rate variability) should be an even less important factor in the environment of moderate inflation rates that can be expected for the 1990s. Given its basket nature this element cannot increase the demand for the ecu on average. Any positive effect that would operate in countries whose currencies are expected to depreciate against the ecu would be offset by countries with stronger currencies.

Section 11.2.2 below pursues this argument in the discussion of the importance of the limited purchasing-power guarantee offered by the 'hard ecu'.

The ecu as a transactions medium

The most important obstacles to widespread use of a parallel currency as a transaction medium are again the bid-ask spreads and the similar conversion costs that arise when more than one currency is in circulation and used for daily transactions. For purely domestic transactions in the retail and corporate sector there seems in general to be no reason to incur the additional cost of using a parallel currency. The only area where a parallel currency might be used for transaction purposes is therefore that of international commercial transactions where it would be convenient to use the parallel currency only if it constituted a convenient *vehicle currency*, that is if it is cheaper to make two transactions (national currency into parallel currency and parallel currency into other national currency) in the market for the parallel currency than one transaction in the market for national currencies.[16] This applies to transactions with agents from outside the Community as well.

It is often claimed that it would be enough to give *legal tender* status to the potential parallel currency to ensure its success as a transaction medium.[17] This idea therefore deserves some further discussion. Legal tender is defined as 'the mode of offering payment of a debt which a creditor is entitled to demand and in which a debtor alone is entitled to make payment'.[18] There is more than one way in which the parallel currency could become legal tender that would be compatible with this definition. The influence of this factor on the demand for the potential parallel currency would

---

[16] A vehicle currency arises because the interbank market for foreign exchange concentrates on a few major vehicle currencies; it is not active for all possible bilateral exchange-rate combinations. However, it is to a certain extent arbitrary which currency becomes a vehicle currency since, once it has been chosen as such, it will also be cheaper to use because it will have a large market, see Krugman (1980). This is just an expression of the economies of scale that arise in the use of money as argued above.

[17] At present only the national currency is legal tender in all Community countries with the exception of Luxembourg where the Belgian franc is also legal tender.

[18] See Walker (1980).

therefore depend on the details of how the legal tender status of the currency is organized.

One solution might be that the parallel currency becomes legal tender for all contracts in which it is used to denominate payment obligations. It would thus be on the same legal footing as the domestic currency, obtaining a sort of 'most favoured currency' status. Compared to the current practice, which allows enforceable contracts in any currency for international transactions, this implies that the only effect of such a legal tender status would be to permit the use of the parallel currency also for purely domestic transactions.[19] Since for domestic transactions there seems to be no advantage to the use of a parallel currency, such a limited legal tender status would have no effect on the incentives to use the parallel currency.

A more effective legal tender status for the parallel currency would therefore be *preferential* legal tender, which would imply that the debtor could choose to settle obligations denominated in any national (Community) currency in the parallel currency (presumably the ecu) but not vice versa.[20] However, as long as exchange rates are not irrevocably fixed and fluctuation bands eliminated a preferential legal tender status would introduce an important element of uncertainty in all contracts denominated in a national currency.

A crucial point is the rate at which the parallel currency could be used to fulfil obligations denominated in a national currency. To ensure that there was a unified conversion rate between the parallel currency and national currencies it would be necessary for the authorities of the Community to publish each day a conversion table which would determine how many units of the parallel currency would be equivalent to one unit of the national currencies for legal tender purposes.[21] However, in this case differences between the legal conversion rate and market exchange rates would arise. This implies that the incentive to use the parallel currency would vary from day to day and from currency to currency. Whenever the legal conversion rate undervalues the parallel currency with respect to the market exchange rate all debtors would prefer to pay in the parallel currency, and vice versa if the legal conversion rate overvalues the parallel currency.

As long as exchange rates are not fixed it would therefore be practically impossible to give any parallel currency a meaningful legal tender status that goes beyond the freedom to contract in any Community currency that will anyway exist in the European Community by 1992.

---

[19] Even at present it is possible to use balances denominated in one currency to pay contractual obligations denominated in another simply by exchanging the two national currencies on the market; the only difference a non-preferential legal tender status for a presumably supranational currency would make is that there would be no transaction cost (e.g., the bid-ask spread) for the agent making the payment.

[20] A historical example for a preferential legal tender status is the Vereinsmünze created by the Vienna Coin Treaty of 1857, see Holtfrerich (1989).

[21] If this rate is valid for the entire day, it is clear that there would be incentives for debtors to take advantage of intra-day exchange-rate changes by paying in the currency that is cheaper on the market than for legal tender purposes.

This chapter has repeatedly emphasized that economies of scale are an important determinant of the demand for money and therefore of currency competition. In assessing the prospects for the ecu it is therefore useful to compare the market share of the ecu to that of its main competitor, the DM. This is done in table 11.1.1:

Table 11.1.1 The ecu and the DM in financial markets

	Market share (in per cent)		EC total (in billion ecu)
	ecu	*DM*	
Money market*	3.5	22.5	3,243
Capital Market	3.3	n.a.	2,294

Note:
* Defined as the sum of bank liabilities and bonds with a maturity under four years, the capital market comprises all other bonds.
Source: Bishop (1991) and Salomon Brothers (1990)

It is apparent that the economies of scale factor favours the DM even in financial markets since its share is several times larger than that of the ecu. In other areas the advantage of the DM is even greater since the use of the ecu for transactions purposes is much more limited than its use in financial markets. This suggests that the ecu would have to have significant other advantages in order to overcome its disadvantage in terms of initial market size. However, it is difficult to see what those might be given that its main past attraction, i.e., risk diversification through its basket definition, should diminish over time as exchange-rate movements become smaller and smaller.

Despite the limited prospects of success for any strategy based on the parallel currency approach, the United Kingdom proposed in June 1990, an alternative strategy is based on a so-called 'hard ecu'.[22] Since this proposal has received much attention in official circles it is discussed separately in the following subsection.

11.2.2 The UK proposal Mark II: The 'hard ecu'

The second UK proposal is based on the idea that a 'hard ecu' should be created which would be defined in a similar way as the present ecu, but with the additional element that the new unit would not be allowed to depreciate against any national currency in a realignment. The new currency unit would therefore be distinct from the existing ecu,

[22] See Bank of England (1990).

and unlike the existing ecu it would be issued by an official institution, the European Monetary Fund, against national currencies.

The UK proposal sees the set up of a new institution as necessary to manage the 'hard ecu' from the start of stage II, and to provide some sort of a common monetary policy. This institutional aspect of the second UK proposal is not analysed here since the main point of the UK position is that the success of the 'hard ecu' in the market would decide whether or not a common currency is desirable.[23] This brief section therefore only analyses the importance of a purchasing power guarantee – or a no-devaluation clause – for the success of a parallel currency in general and then turns to a discussion of the prospects for the 'hard ecu'.[24]

How important is the strength of a currency, i.e., its advantage as a store of value, for its potential as a parallel currency? A fundamental point in this context is that in efficient international capital markets expected changes in the exchange rate are reflected in the rate paid on interest-bearing assets. This implies that, if a particular national currency is expected to depreciate against the parallel currency, this would only be an incentive to use less cash (and other non-interest-bearing instruments) in that currency. However, a parallel currency would still be attractive as a store of value for these instruments only if the increased transaction costs from the frequent exchanges between national and parallel currency, that are necessary if both are to circulate side by side, do not outweigh the gain in terms of a more stable purchasing power.

An order of magnitude of the minimum gains in purchasing power required to make a parallel currency attractive can be calculated easily from the observed costs of exchanging currencies, i.e., bid-ask spreads. Among the major Community currencies these spreads amount at present to about 3–5 per cent for cash. The velocity of circulation of currency exceeds ten in most member countries, which implies that each bank note or coin is used at least ten times per year. It follows that in the domestic retail sector, where most of the cash is used, a parallel currency could displace national currencies only if expectations of exchange rate changes of over 3 per cent per month, i.e., 40 per cent on an annual basis, persist. Expected exchange-rate changes of this size can be ruled out for the 1990s; they would be incompatible with the aim of moving towards a monetary union. For the foreseeable future it is therefore highly unlikely that a parallel currency would be used by households.

For other non-interest-bearing transaction balances, such as sight or checking deposits with commercial banks, bid-ask spreads and other exchange costs are sometimes much lower. For retail transactions the conversion costs are similar as for cash; but for large transactions the conversion costs can be as low as 0.1 per cent. This type of balance might therefore more easily be converted into the parallel currency. For firms large enough to have treasury departments that can switch between currencies at a low cost, small interest differentials or exchange-rate expectations might therefore be sufficient to lead to large shifts in transaction balances. However, the size of non-

---

[23] The institutional aspects, particularly how the issue of a new currency would fit into the perception to avoid sharing monetary responsibility between the national and the European level, are discussed in chapter 12.

[24] For a more thorough analysis of the hard ecu proposal see Bofinger (1990).

interest-bearing transaction balances held by the corporate sector is small relative to total transaction balances, since in the corporate sector most balances can be held in an interest-bearing form (e.g., overnight deposits).[25] Expected exchange-rate changes would therefore provide only a limited incentive for corporations to shift their transaction balances across currencies.

This implies that an advantage in terms of a more stable purchasing power has to be large in order to lead to significant currency substitution. The question is therefore whether the no devaluation guarantee of the 'hard ecu' is large enough to have an impact on the market.

Since expected exchange-rate changes are reflected in interest-rate differentials an answer to this question requires therefore an assessment of the interest rate advantage of the 'hard ecu'. At present, and for the foreseeable future, interest rates on the DM are the lowest of all EC currencies, which indicates that the DM is expected to appreciate against all other EC currencies. The 'hard ecu' would therefore compete mainly against the DM. It would be stronger, i.e., carry an even lower interest rate than the latter to the extent that market participants perceive that the DM could be devalued during a realignment. While such an event seems remote at present it cannot be ruled out. But it is clear that this element can never give the 'hard ecu' a decisive advantage allowing it to out-compete the DM.

It is possible to provide an estimate of the order of magnitude of the interest-rate advantage of the 'hard ecu' by making some deliberately extreme assumptions about the likelihood and size of a devaluation of the DM.[26] For example, the assumption that during the next ten years the DM will be devalued by 10 per cent (given the 2.25 per cent bands this would require more than one realignment) against another Community currency (say, the French franc) must certainly be considered extreme given the past performance of the DM. However, even in this case the interest-rate advantage of the 'hard ecu' would be only one tenth of one percentage point (i.e., if German long-term interest rates were equal to 8 per cent the long-term interest rate on the 'hard ecu' would be 7.9 per cent).[27] Even under such a pessimistic scenario for the DM, the advantage of the 'hard ecu' would be much lower than the advantage the DM has at present *vis-à-vis* many other EC currencies. Such a small interest-rate advantage would certainly not be enough to overcome the transaction costs that would arise through the use of an additional, fourteenth, currency besides the existing 12 national currencies and the basket ecu.

---

[25] For example, in Germany the corporate sector holds about one quarter of total M1. See chapter 5 for more details.

[26] In economic terms the hard ecu is equivalent to the existing basket ecu plus an option to buy the strongest currency during each realignment. The following simple calculation should be viewed as a crude attempt to measure the value of this option.

[27] If the devaluation of the DM were the only expected change during this period the French franc would be as strong as the hard ecu. It must therefore be assumed that over the same period the French franc is also expected to devalue against the DM. This is theoretically possible; for example the French franc could for an initial period be devalued against the DM and subsequently be revalued by the amount indicated in the example used here.

There has never been substantial currency substitution towards the DM even when German interest rates were ten percentage points lower than Italian or French interest rates. It is therefore highly unlikely that the minute interest rate advantage the 'hard ecu' might have would be sufficient to make it an attractive alternative to the DM.

11.3 Summary assessment of the main alternatives and complements to the Delors Report

The discussion in this chapter shows that neither the competing currencies nor the parallel currency approach represent a practical alternative to the institutional steps outlined in the Delors Report. Economies of scale in money demand favour existing currencies, so that the ecu cannot be expected to gradually crowd out national currencies. From this point of view it also does not make sense to create an additional currency, such as the 'hard ecu' proposed by the UK government. In practice the 'no devaluation' guarantee of the 'hard ecu' would be insignificant since a substantial devaluation of the DM is highly unlikely. The 'hard ecu' would therefore not be widely used even in financial markets.

The fact that the ecu cannot be expected to replace national currencies under a pure parallel currency strategy does not imply, however, that the market share of the ecu will not substantially increase in the near future. On the contrary, as it becomes more likely that the ecu (in something like its present definition) will one day become the common currency its market share should increase since markets will try to anticipate this event and get acquainted with the future European currency. In this sense credible progress along the lines of the Delors Report might actually ensure that the ecu does become a parallel currency during the transition to full monetary union.

References

Association for Monetary Union in Europe *et al.* (1990), *A strategy for the ecu,* Kogan Page, London.

Bank of England (1990), 'The hard ecu in stage 2: operational requirements', mimeo, Bank of England, London, December.

Basevi, Giorgio, *et al.* (1975), 'The "All Saints Day" Manifesto for European Monetary Union', *The Economist,* 1 November.

Bini-Smaghi, Lorenzo (1990), 'Progressing towards European monetary unification: selected issues and proposals', Banca d'Italia, Rome, *Temi di discussion del Servizio Studi,* 113, April.

Bishop, Graham, (1991) 'Die ECU: Korbwährung ohne Zukunft oder Keimzelle einer Euro-währung', chapter 3 in Manfred Weber (ed.), *Auf dem Weg zur Europäischen Währungsunion,* Wissenschaftliche Buchgesellschaft, Darmstadt.

Bofinger, Peter (1990), 'The political economy of the hard-ecu proposal', paper prepared for the CEPR and Banco de Espana Workshop on *Financial and Monetary Integration in Europe,* Madrid, 15 December.

Committee for the Study of Economic and Monetary Union (1989), 'Report on Economic and

Monetary Union in the European Community' (the Delors Report), Office of Publications of the European Communities, Luxembourg.

Emerson, Michael, Daniel Gros, Alexander Italianer, Jean Pisani-Ferry and Horst Reichenbach (1991), *One Market, One Money*, Oxford University Press, Oxford.

Gros, Daniel (1988), 'The EMS and the determination of the European Price Level', Centre for European Policy Studies, Brussels, *CEPS Working Document (Economic)*, 34.

—— (1989), 'Paradigms for the monetary union of Europe', *Journal of Common Market Studies*, 27, 3, March: 219–30.

—— (1991), 'Parallelwährungskonzepte – eine alternative?', chapter 3 in Manfred Weber (ed.), *Auf dem Weg zur Europäischen Währungsunion*, Wissenchaftliche Buchgesellschaft, Darmstadt.

HM Treasury (1989), 'An evolutionary approach to economic and monetary union', London, November.

Holtfrerich, Karl-Ludwig (1989), 'The monetary unification process in nineteen-century Germany: relevance and lessons for Europe today', chapter 8 in M. de Cecco and A. Giovannini (eds.), *A European Central Bank?*, Italian Macroeconomic Policy Group and Centre for Economic Policy Research, Cambridge University Press, Cambridge, 216–41.

Jaans, Pierre (1989), 'The basic difference between the framework for policy decision-making provided by the EMS and EMU', in Annex to Delors Report, office for Official Publications of the European Communities, Luxembourg, 221–3.

Krugman, Paul (1980), 'Vehicle Currencies and the Structure of International Exchange', *Journal of Money Credit and Banking*, 12, 3: 513–26.

Pöhl, Karl Otto (1989), 'The further development of the European Monetary System', in collection of papers annexed to Delors Report, September: 131–55.

Rogoff, Kenneth (1985), 'Can international monetary policy co-operation be counter-productive?', *Journal of International Economics*, 18: 199–217.

Salin, Pascal (1990), 'European monetary integration: monopoly or competition', speech given at the launching of the Bruges Group, Bruges, April.

Salomon Brothers (1990), 'How big is the world bond market – 1990 update', Salomon Brothers Inc., August.

Swoboda, Alexandre (1968), 'The Eurodollar market: an interpretation', *Princeton Essays in International Finance*, 64.

Vaubel, Roland (1978), *Strategies for currency unification*, Tübingen, J.C.B. Mohr, Kieler Studien, 156.

Vaubel, Roland (1984), 'The government's money monopoly: externalities or natural monopoly?' *Kyklos*, 37, Fasc. 1: 27–58.

Vaubel, Roland (1990), 'Currency competition and European monetary integration', *Economic Journal*, 100: 936–46.

Von Hayek, Friedrich (1978), *Denationalization of money*, Institute of Economic Affairs, London.

Von Hayek, Friedrich (1984), 'The theory of currency competition', chapter 1 in P. Salin (ed.), *Currency Competition and Monetary Union*, Martinus Nijhoff Publishers, The Hague, 29–42.

Walker, D.M. (1980), 'Oxford Companion to Law', Oxford, Clarendon Press, 755.

CHAPTER 12

CONCRETE STEPS TOWARDS MONETARY UNION

This chapter discusses the practical and institutional measures that will be taken – or should be taken – during the transition towards EMU. The economic implications of full EMU were already analysed in chapters 7 through 9 and the structure of the European System of Central Banks (ESCB) in the final stage is discussed in the following chapter 13. This chapter therefore starts, in section 1, with a discussion of stage I, which marks an effort to go as far as possible in policy coordination without introducing Treaty changes, while producing the necessary proposals for such changes. A brief review of the main features of stage I as an evolution of the present EMS serves as an introduction to a discussion of the limits of voluntary coordination.

Section 2 then introduces the discussion of stage II which constitutes the core of this chapter. The Maastricht Treaty has clarified a number of provisions for the transition: when will it start, what will be its substantive content, and when and how will it end? Having reviewed the results of the IGC which preposed the EMU Treaty, the section turns to the monetary content of stage II which presents challenging analytical issues for the design and implementation of policy, as this stage marks a transition between two systems – the present EMS and full EMU – the economics of both of which are now better understood.

The main issue for the transition is to manage a system in which ultimate responsibility for monetary policy remains in national hands while preparing for full EMU and the high degree of centralization foreseen for the final stage. Different ways to overcome the implications of the 'indivisibility' of monetary policy which has been the main inspiration for the proposed provisions for the transition are discussed in section 3. One particular monetary instrument, namely a European reserve requirement, is discussed in more detail in section 4 as it could provide the core of a more substantive stage II then the proposals embodied in the Treaty.

Section 5 focuses on the transition to stage III and offers interpretations of the criteria proposed for the convergence required to qualify for full EMU. A major breakthrough was achieved in Maastricht with a carefully designed compromise on the procedure for ending Stage II. The Treaty proposals now contain both fairly demanding criteria for entry by each prospective Member State into the final stage and a firm timetable for taking the decisions required. This unique and complex procedure is evaluated in some detail.

Throughout this chapter and the next a number of references are made to the proposed EMU Treaty (henceforth the Treaty). The full text of the latter, and the relevant parts of the separate Protocols on the ESCB and on the new monetary institution, the European Monetary Institute (EMI) annexed to it, have been reproduced in Appendices I–III to Chapter 13.

12.1 Stage I: tighter voluntary coordination

Stage I was approved by the European Council in Madrid in June 1989 in the form proposed in the Delors Report. It began on 1 July 1990, while no date was initially agreed for its completion.

The European Council in Rome in October 1990 set the date of 1 January 1994, for the start of stage II, but it also attached some conditions to the transition. The date has since been confirmed in the Treaty without conditions (Art. 109e). Hence there is no longer any ambiguity about the duration of stage I. The following subsections ask how (1) improvements in coordination, (2) participation of additional currencies and (3) spill-over effects from the emerging agreement about the longer-term features may affect the challenges to the EMS identified in chapter 5 over the remainder of stage I.

12.1.1 The new coordination procedures

New procedures for coordination were put into place by the Decisions of the Council of the Economics and Finance Ministers (the so-called ECOFIN) in March 1990 to replace the 1964 Council Decision (defining the mandate of the Committee of Central Bank Governors) and the 1974 Council Decision (on economic convergence). The new Decisions guide the form and substance of the efforts at policy coordination by central banks and in the ECOFIN Council.

The new Decisions follow closely the proposals in the Delors Report (paras. 51–2). However, they are difficult to evaluate, because it is still too early to determine how the two EC bodies will make use of their mandate; those of 1964 and 1974 were never used fully, see chapter 3. The new Decisions implied that the Governors' Committee could develop a more visible public profile, having strengthened its analytical capacity (and its sub-committee structure) with a view to developing an *ex ante* approach to, rather than an *ex post* analysis of monetary coordination. This would be a significant change, but it remains to be seen to what extent the Governors will wish to speak up in their new reports to the European Council and to the European Parliament, or to give collective opinions on policies of individual countries or of the EMS participants as a whole.[1] (Committees of central bankers are traditionally reluctant to comment publicly on policies in individual countries in any critical way, since considerations of collegiality and concerns about upsetting financial markets suggest prudence.) An important new proviso is that the chairman of the Committee may decide to make the deliberations of the Committee public, thus having a potentially significant influence on countries that come up for criticism. But discussions in the Delors Committee suggested that the scope for moving voluntarily, i.e., without institutional change, towards genuine *ex ante* coordination is likely to be severely circumscribed.

The Delors Committee conducted a questionnaire study among EC central banks to clarify the scope for moving ahead without Treaty changes. Crudely summarized, the smaller participants did not see major problems in going further in the direction of submitting the policy formulations and decisions for *ex ante* coordination to the Committee of Governors; the smaller countries have few illusions of monetary autonomy left. But several of the larger countries did not see any possibility of moving significantly further without important changes in national monetary legislation and in the Treaty. The reason is either that in some countries (France and the United Kingdom) national monetary authority is divided between the central bank and the political authorities, with the latter unwilling to delegate some of its prerogatives to an unspecified process of central bank coordination, while in others (notably Germany) the central bank itself has an elaborate decision-making structure which makes it difficult to conceive that it could delegate, through its Governor, or other participants in the coordination procedures, even non-binding competence to a European body. Hence the problem of achieving some *ex ante* coordination is not only that of making the participating national central banks independent of their political authorities. From the perspective of either of these situations there is a need for something more well-defined than voluntary cooperation to be put at the centre before genuine change can be expected.

This conclusion is reinforced if one looks at recent trends in the EMS. As argued in chapter 4 it became conventional wisdom in the mid and late 1980s that the EMS operates as an asymmetrical system. In this system the Bundesbank exercised to a large extent the residual degree of freedom available to a group of countries within a fixed exchange-rate system, by pursuing a domestic monetary objective without regard to the exchange rate. Chapters 3 and 4 showed that such an evolution was inevitable in the 1983–7 period as anti-inflationary preferences intensified throughout Europe, and that it would be beneficial for other participants to maintain it as long as the anti-inflationary credentials of the Bundesbank remain stronger than those of other participants and governments in the system. While this condition may still be met, at least over a longer-term horizon, it is increasingly open to question whether the EMS still functions as an asymmetric system with German leadership. The observation that it is visibly the Bundesbank which operates as a price leader in interest-rate adjustments, readily

---

[1] The Chairman of the Governors' Committee has appeared before the Economic and Monetary Committee of the European Parliament, but no written report has yet been submitted. A first report, covering the first 18 months of stage I up to the end of 1991, was to be published in April 1992.

followed by most other participants with minimal delay, is not in itself evidence of preservation of the status quo. We restate here briefly our reasons, discussed at greater length in chapters 4 and 5, why this view of the EMS must now be critically examined and replaced by the perspective of a more symmetric EMS.

The emerging alternative view would say that monetary leadership was already becoming widely shared in the course of 1987–90, and during stage I when exchange rates have become rigid and markets have developed confidence in their perpetuation.[2] Some currencies that used to be considered weak have experienced massive inflows of funds, as market participants take advantage of the large interest differentials in their favour. Countries with so-called weak currencies have reacted with some appreciation of their currency inside the EMS-band, while trying to sterilize most of the inflows in order not to stimulate demand in their already rapidly expanding economies. The Bundesbank, on its side, has been trying to sterilize the outflows from Germany while occasionally raising short-term interest rates. The latter move serves to dampen domestic demand and inflation – traditional concerns of the Bundesbank – but they may also be seen as steps to ease tensions in the EMS. To the extent that they substitute for restrictive policy actions, notably on budgetary policy, in some of the partner countries (Italy, Spain, UK), these increases in short-term interest rates cannot be interpreted solely as evidence of traditional German leadership. In particular, the nominal anchor function of German monetary policy had become less prominent even before the strong pressures on capacity utilization in the former Federal Republic appeared in 1989–90. Since German unification in mid-1990 the strong expansion in public expenditure has continued the erosion of the nominal anchor function.

In summary, the initial *modus operandi* characterized by a low-inflation centre country that pursues a domestic monetary target, while partners peg to its currency and sterilize outflows only moderately, did impart a disinflationary trend to the system as a whole. The recent workings of the system in which flows have often been in the direction towards countries with relatively high inflation and interest rates, and all countries have sterilized their interventions more fully, imply some inflationary bias and require more explicit coordination, preferably ranging beyond the monetary area. This is particularly essential if, as observation of behaviour since January 1987 suggests, most participants are not prepared to make use of realignments.[3] The present EMS, even with the procedures put into operation in stage I, appears too weak and informal to tackle the required rethinking of adjustment mechanisms in a more symmetrical system.

One illustration of the inherent weakness of stage I procedures was provided by the inability of the Committee of Central Bank Governors to arrive at any announceable conclusion to their first effort in the winter of 1990–91 at setting coordinated intermediate monetary targets. Prior to the start of stage I and in the first months thereafter the intention was to develop, through a careful surveillance exercise of

---

[2] See chapter 5 for a discussion of this view which was first expressed by Giavazzi and Spaventa (1990).

[3] The President of the Bundesbank and some leading politicians in Germany openly suggested in the autumn of 1989 that realignments would be appropriate but this was strongly resisted by some other EMS participants, notably France.

national monetary projections or intentions, a consistent set of projections for 1991. Few may have expected this exercise to lead to joint monetary targeting at the first attempt; a more realistic expectation was that the Governors would have been able to present early in 1991 some form of quantitative assessment of the monetary objectives of the participants, rationalizing, at a minimum, how already announced objectives for countries that make such announcements – the Bundesbank's annual target for M3 being the prime example – fitted into a coherent picture. No such result was achieved for several reasons: (1) the difficulty of agreeing to joint assumptions about external shocks, (2) differences in monetary or credit aggregates used by the participants and (3) misgivings by some as to the role that such aggregates can play in fostering coordination.

The first of these factors may be temporary. Uncertainty about the oil price and the dollar was at a peak as the exercise was undertaken in the autumn of 1990 and individual participants were basing their monetary and inflation projections on assumptions that were far from uniform. In the established macroeconomic forecasting exercises of international organizations such as the IMF and the OECD (or in the EC) joint assumptions with respect to largely exogenous factors are imposed by the Secretariat, following discussions with national representatives. This procedure which helps to assure consistency proved more difficult to apply in the monetary framework where the impact of the assumptions on intermediate objectives had to be explicitly addressed. This problem will be of less significance in a less turbulent international environment than that of 1990–1.

Even then the second difficulty will remain, though work is now under way in national central banks and in the Economic Unit set up to serve the Committee of Governors on the statistical compatibility of the different aggregates used by the participants. Efforts at harmonizing concepts of broad monetary aggregates and of the sources of money creation will have to be intensified to make future exercises more productive. Once this has been achieved, the Committee of Governors will be expected to express a view as to the consistency of national targets expressed in terms of harmonized aggregates. It is obvious from the report of the first eighteen months of stage I that the Governors will need at least another year to get this far.

The third difficulty is the most basic: the suspicion that the linkage of even the most refined and appropriately harmonized measure of money creation to changes in nominal income and to the inflation rate is too uncertain or too imperfectly understood to justify putting the main emphasis in the coordination effort on joint target setting for money and credit aggregates. The United Kingdom has de-emphasized the information content of such targets in the light of observed instability in the demand for the various potential aggregates, and only broad illustrative ranges for them are provided in the annual budget statements in March. Several smaller countries convey their intention of a non-accommodating monetary stance only through a firm exchange-rate policy and publish no domestic monetary objectives. Even in Germany, where the targeting of first central bank money and then M3 has a more successful record than elsewhere, doubts as to the reliability of the information contained in monetary aggregates are strengthened greatly by the effects of the integration of the former German Democratic Republic into the economy.

The difficulties experienced in the first *ex ante* coordination exercise may have been exceptional. They still illustrate the long distance one would have to travel to implement the logically appealing scheme proposed for the EMS, notably by Russo and Tullio (1988), for decentralized implementation of a joint monetary policy in a system of fixed exchange rates, i.e., to achieve control over aggregate money creation for the area as a whole by allocating to participants targets for domestic credit expansion (DCE) which add up to the aggregate objective, if reserve flows between participants are not sterilized.

Does it matter if participants in stage I continue to manifest a reluctance to underpin their cooperation with quantitative objectives for money and credit aggregates, as long as they stick to stable exchange rates in the EMS? The latter in themselves will give some assurance that inflation rates are kept from diverging and that they will, on average, be moderate. But the nominal anchor function is eroding as the system becomes more symmetric without being explicitly recognized as such. In this sense stage I without intermediate monetary objectives could prove incapable of developing a sufficient analytical basis for a truly coordinated policy except in a short-run *ad hoc* sense. Upward drift in money creation then becomes a likely outcome.

Whatever the methodological approach adopted by the Committee of Governors in monitoring the consistency of national monetary policies and the overall thrust they produce for the EMS participants as a whole, it is important that the Committee already begins to develop some publicly visible profile in stage I. In the past competent management of the exchange rate mechanism in comparative secrecy may have been enough. When Member States have ratified a new Treaty conferring very major powers on the future central banking institution, public visibility and accountability of its precursor, the Committee of Governors, have to develop. In a formal sense these new qualities are encouraged by publication of an annual report and hearing-like appearances of the Chairman of the Committee before the Economic and Monetary Committee of the European Parliament, but these formal steps have to be accompanied by substance in the form of a higher profile in the analysis of monetary trends. There is yet little evidence that this is emerging.

12.1.2 Participation of additional currencies in the EMS.

The participation of additional currencies in the EMS has intensified the need for procedures going beyond voluntary coordination. We argued in chapter 5 that the entry of the Spanish peseta in June 1989 already provided illustration of the need for more explicit coordination as the EMS moves towards a more symmetrical system. The participation of sterling from October 1990 may have improved long-run confidence in the UK currency and implied – while sterling interest rates were well above DM interest rates – outflows from Germany and other countries with lower interest rates to the UK in the process of arbitrating away part of the interest-rate premium on sterling assets. This process has come to an end and occasional anticipations of a realignment have arisen. The UK reservations about joining full EMU tend to prolong this uncertainty.

Markets may therefore be justified in assuming that the EMS is in for a rougher ride in the next few years than, say, in the 1987–9 period; especially given the long British tradition of using monetary policies in an activist way for domestic stabilization, and the precarious state of the UK current account. Although we argued in chapter 5 that there is no immediate danger for the stability of the EMS one cannot exclude the possibility that the system could come to look more like the view first presented in Walters (1986) or in other unstable models of economic interaction between countries where inflation and nominal interest rates have not converged closely, or do so at different speeds, and discrete realignments could still occur.

In such a world capital flows can be destabilizing, by flowing towards the higher inflation (and interest-rate) country, hence perpetuating inflation differentials, and by generating large outflows prior to a realignment followed by a reversal after it. We have in the past regarded such a view as unduly pessimistic, and we found little evidence of it in the recent EMS experience as surveyed in chapter 5. During the second half of the 1980s this view offered a somewhat caricatural perspective of the EMS, because the present members have tended to orient their monetary policies strongly towards cohesion in the system, and have managed the realignments of 1986–7 relatively smoothly. Repetition of this successful experience cannot be taken for granted in a stage I with enlarged membership, but without efforts to go beyond voluntary coordination.

In short, the enlargement of membership has made it more, not less, urgent to move beyond stage I towards an EMU with irrevocably fixed exchange rates, virtually complete convergence of interest rates and centralization of monetary management.[4] Labelling the system 'a half-baked house', to use Sir Alan Walters's expression, prompts relevant reflection on how the EMS might be strengthened. Improving coordination beyond the voluntary should also be a British priority, though the UK official view is, understandably, that EMS membership (as it is at present) has already been such an economically and politically demanding step that nothing more is required in the short term.[5]

The EMS now has eleven of the twelve member-state currencies participating in the exchange-rate mechanism. Though the Delors Report (para. 52) had the ambition that all should participate in stage I – and follow the same rules – it seems currently doubtful that the remaining currency, the Greek drachma, could accede fully within the time horizon of up to the end of 1993. That ambition has been explicitly modified recently by the European Council also. Nor is it likely that applicants for EC membership will be permitted by a majority of the present members to associate their currencies with the exchange-rate mechanism as foreseen in the 1978 Articles of Agreement for the EMS. Norway opted in October 1990 for unilateral pegging to the ecu, and Austria has long observed narrow margins for the schilling *vis-à-vis* the DM. Sweden and Finland followed the Norwegian example in the spring of 1991 by pegging to the ecu, but the number of outright participants in the exchange-rate mechanism may now be regarded

[4] This point is also made forcefully in Matthes (1988).

[5] For an expression of this view, see H.M. Treasury (1989). Some UK observers, however, broadly share the concern of the present paper of instability in the first stage, see, e.g., Goodhart (1989).

as virtually fixed for the length of stage I up to the end of 1993. (Accession negotiations with Austria, Sweden and Finland may permit their entry into the EC by 1 January 1995 at the earliest, but, if the negotiations have advanced sufficiently, it is conceivable that the applicants could join the monetary arrangements from the start of stage II.) Whether they will all be subject to the same rules in terms of the width of the band is more uncertain; as Spain, the UK and Portugal consider when it may become appropriate for them to narrow the band to the usual 2.25 per cent, the Netherlands and Belgium have unilaterally imposed tighter margins on the fluctuations of their currencies.

12.1.3 Spill-over effects on stage I from the Intergovernmental Conference on EMU

The third new feature of stage I was the Intergovernmental Conferences on EMU and on political union, started in December 1990 and completed in Maastricht one year later, which discussed the revisions of the Treaty required to move beyond the first stage and succeeded in clarifying the contents and the timing of the process towards full EMU.

The process set in motion by these two Intergovernmental Conferences (IGCs) could provide a constructive feedback on the first stage. Those countries least ready to envisage early moves to full EMU (Germany and the Netherlands) may become the most anxious to demonstrate that voluntary coordination replicating the mandatory procedures proposed for subsequent stages can do as well as a reformed system.[6] A constructive feedback process may start which was absent in the past EMS as long as there was no prospect (or threat) of institutional change. Such a projection into the practices of stage I for later full and mandatory coordination would obviously be unobjectionable. If successful, the process would contradict the prediction made above that the first two features of stage I – growing *de facto* symmetry and a risk of increasing instability upon enlargement – make it unlikely that the system could qualitatively improve or even retain its stability without institutional change.

12.1.4 Conditions for moving to stage II?

At its meeting in Rome on 27–8 October 1990, the European Council discussed the timing and content of stage II and set 1 January 1994 as the starting date for this transitional period. The Council also, however, listed several results which were to have been achieved by that date and one more general prerequisite for moving on to stage II. This appeared to leave some ambiguity as to whether the date could be regarded as

---

[6] Some statements by officials of the Bundesbank and the Netherlands Bank comment on the first stage in this spirit, see, e.g., Pöhl (1989), pp. 146 ff, and Szasz (1990).

definitive – quite apart from the general reservation by the United Kingdom to any pre-set timetable.

The first two conditions listed by the Council were the completion of the Single Market, and the ratification of the revised Treaty.[7] Both of these conditions should be fulfilled by 1994; this is apparent for the Single Market programme whose deadline is in 1992 and the European Council has on earlier occasions set the end of 1992 as the target date for the ratification of the revised Treaty.

However, the Conclusions added that the passage to stage II required that:

the Member States shall have started the process with a view to the independence of their central bank being achieved not later than at the date of transition to the final stage of EMU;

effective arrangements are in place to prevent, in each Member State, the monetary financing of public-sector budget deficits and to ensure that the Community or the Member States are not liable for the debts of another Member State (no bail out);

all restrictions of capital movements shall have been removed; and

all Member States shall take the measures necessary to enable them to take part in the exchange-rate mechanism of the EMS.

At the request of the German Chancellor the following general prerequisite for the transition to stage II was added to the Rome Conclusions:

The European Council recalls that in order to enter stage II other satisfactory and durable progress towards real and monetary convergence, in particular price stability and the consolidation of public finances should have been made.

With the exception of this general prerequisite which left substantial room for differing interpretations and hence ambiguity about the date for entering stage II, most of the more specific achievements listed did not appear to place difficult barriers to the transition. The wording on participation in the EMS signalled some softening relative to the position taken in the Delors Report which required participation by all EC currencies within the normal margins of the EMS before any move to stage II could be envisaged; the Rome Council only asked that all Member States had taken the measure necessary to enable them to take part.

Whatever the interpretation of the Rome Conclusions, the new Treaty – the ratification of which obviously remains the central prerequisite for moving beyond stage I – has removed any lingering doubt as to the finality of the date for this move. Art. 109e flatly states that this will occur on 1 January 1994. It then proceeds to add that before that date each Member State shall have abolished capital controls – though Greece and Portugal retain the possibility of obtaining derogations until the end of 1995

---

[7] See Conclusions of the Presidency (1990). The text of some of the points has been incorporated in the Draft Treaty on the Union agreed in Maastricht, see below and Appendix I to chapter 13.

– and monetary financing of public deficits. These points repeat elements of the Rome Conclusions. Two other prerequisites will no longer apply prior to the end of stage I: the no-bail out rule will only apply from the start of stage II, and the move to make national central banks independent only has to start some time during stage II.

The main new element in the Treaty relates to convergence, i.e. to the implementation of the German point of view as expressed in the Rome Conclusions. Before 1 January 1994 each Member State shall adopt 'multiannual programmes intended to ensure the lasting convergence necessary for the achievement of economic and monetary union, in particular with regard to price stability and sound public finances'. The Council shall then, on the basis of a report from the Commission, assess progress in convergence.

The emphasis in the wording of the Treaty has clearly shifted from substance towards procedure. The responsibility is placed on the individual Member State to present a coherent, longer-term perspective on their adjustments towards EMU, but no specific quantitative results are required for passing to stage II. Given the shortness of time prior to 1 January 1994 the latter would hardly have been realistic. There is therefore no doubt that all twelve Member States – and possibly those additional countries that have applied for EC membership and whose accession negotiations are well advanced by the end of 1993 – will embark on stage II on the date set. The softening of the criteria for entry which occurred over the year prior to Maastricht was obtained at the cost of some considerable erosion of the substantive monetary content of stage II relative to the vision in the Delors Report and in the Rome Conclusions. But on the other hand the criteria for convergence in terms of price stability and public finances have been clarified and tightened and there is now a relatively firm timetable for stage II. It is therefore not obvious whether the retention of a firm date for moving beyond stage I has entailed costs in terms of a loss of momentum for the EMU process in later stages. This question is taken up again in the final chapter 14.

12.2   Stage II: 'soft' union and an emerging central bank

Having decided on a date for moving on to stage II one might have expected the European Council to have set guidelines for the substance of this transitional stage. But the Conclusions of the Presidency from the Rome Council confined themselves to stating that the new monetary institution (the ESCB) will be set up at the start of stage II in order to strengthen the coordination of monetary policies, introduce the instruments and procedures required for the conduct of a common policy in the future and monitor the evolution of the ecu. The EC Commission and several governments subsequently made more specific, though still fairly general, proposals for stage II, elaborating some ideas mentioned in the Delors Report. By contrast, the Committee of Central Bank Governors in their November 1990 Draft Statute for the ESCB left the transitional stage unspecified. The President of the Committee then indicated that provisions for the transitional arrangements would be submitted by the Committee in the course of the IGC. This was provided in the form of a Draft Statute for a temporary institution, the European Monetary Institute (EMI), submitted to the IGC at the end of October 1991, and now annexed, in virtually unchanged form, to the Treaty as a separate Protocol (see Appendix 3 to chapter 13).

The evolution of the discussions in the IGC reflected well the basic difficulties of designing monetary arrangements for a transitional stage in which ultimate monetary responsibility remains in national hands, while intensifying preparations for a fully joint monetary policy in the final stage. The Rome European Council of October 1990 had foreseen the set-up at the start of stage II of '*the* new monetary institution', i.e. an early embodiment of the future ESCB. To some countries (Germany and the Netherlands), anxious to emphasize the voluntary and decentralized aspects of monetary policy in the transition, associating the name and prestige of the future monetary authority with its much more feeble predecessor was misleading; hence these two countries preferred a minimalist, almost cosmetic institutional reform of relabelling the Committee of Governors the Council of Governors.

The Luxembourg Presidency of the first half of 1991 attempted compromise by dividing stage II into two subperiods: (1) 1994–5 and (2) 1996 until the, as yet undefined, start of stage III. During the former of these subperiods, a Board of Governors would take over all functions of the present Committee of Governors and of the Board of the EMCF. With its unchanged composition and a mandate very similar to those of the bodies it was to replace, the real significance of this institutional step remained obscure. In particular, the Board of Governors would have had no special mandate to prepare for stage III. This second task would only have been addressed in the more substantive second subperiod, starting on 1 January 1996 (or earlier, should the ECOFIN Council decide unanimously to advance the date). On that date the ESCB would be set up to prepare the instruments and procedures necessary for carrying out the single monetary policy required in full EMU. It was this second subperiod only which resembled stage II as outlined in the Delors Report. The Luxembourg Draft, however, was optimistic as to the time required for completing these preparations, because it proposed that a decision to move to stage III and to set a date for its start could be taken by the end of 1996. This procedure would, however, have implied that the introduction of the single currency, which requires much longer preparation than a single year, could not have taken place earlier than two to three years after the locking of the parities, assuming that a decision to move to full EMU could in fact have been taken by the end of 1996.

When the Netherlands took over the EC Presidency in mid-1991 the two subperiods were again merged into one. A temporary institution, the EMI, would be set up on 1 January 1994 with the double task of reinforcing voluntary coordination and of preparing for the final stage (Art. 109 f, restating Art. 4 f of the EMI Statute). Instead of the chronological separation of these two functions envisaged in the Luxembourg Draft, they were now to be exercised in parallel from the start of stage II. This assures that there will be adequate time for preparing the future, but it also raises the question whether the two tasks can or should be regarded as separate.

As regards the EMI's role in policy coordination – Article 109 f (2 and 4) and Article 4.1 of the EMI Statute – it is difficult to see any significant changes of mandate relative to the tasks performed up to now by the Committee of Governors and the Board of the

EMCF, both of which will be replaced by the EMI Council on 1 January 1994. The latter may, by qualified majority, formulate opinions or recommendations on monetary and exchange rate policy in the Member States and convey these views confidentially. It may publish unanimously adopted opinions or recommendations. It will take over all tasks of the Board of the EMCF and facilitate the use of the ecu. This does not go beyond what could be done by the present Committee of Governors through its chairman. The role of the EMI in policy coordination hence closely reflects the concern of a majority of EC countries that monetary authority should remain in national hands until it can be fully transferred to the European level in the final stage of EMU – the so-called 'indivisibility doctrine' discussed below.

The Treaty introduces three potentially important institutional innovations relative to stage I. The first is that the European Council will appoint – on a recommendation from the Committee of Governors, and after consulting the ECOFIN Council and the European Parliament – the President of the EMI Council, initially for a period of three years, the likely life-time of the Institute. This was the one important point on which the final outcome at Maastricht differed from the Draft EMI Statute submitted by the Committee of Governors which had proposed that, as in stage I, one of their midst would be elected to preside. The Governors will now elect one such colleague as Vice President, also for three years.

It is difficult to evaluate *a priori* to what extent the appointment of an external President – presumably a senior political figure or a former central bank governor – will raise the profile of the EMI in a way that otherwise appears to elude a pure collegiate body. The President will have only one vote in a Council of initially thirteen, but possibly as many as eighteen members, if, as currently seems likely, accession negotiations with Austria, Sweden and Finland, who have already applied for EC membership, and possibly Switzerland and Norway, who may apply, are successfully completed for them to join the EC early in stage II. The presence of the central bank governors from all Member States in the EMI Council, each with one vote, is itself a symptom that the role of the EMI is limited and primarily consultative, although voting is foreseen both on current monetary policy issues and on the design of the policy framework for stage III. Anyway, the EMI President will have a relative influence somewhat similar to that of the Bundesbank President in the Council of that Bank. The special appointment procedure and the status as the only full-time member of the EMI Council should strengthen the internal position of the EMI President. On the other hand, the impression of having an outsider imposed may invite challenges to the President's authority at a time when some of his colleagues on the Council are still anxious to prove the point that responsibility for monetary policy has not yet shifted to the European level. One likely effect of the external Presidency will be to increase the visibility of the position vis-à-vis the national and EC political authorities, the participants in financial markets – some of the authority of successful national central bank governors derives from their ability to express and to influence views held in financial markets – and the public in general, hence preparing the ground for the position of authority with accountability which the President of the future ECB will have.

Two additional points throw some light on the position of the EMI Council relative to that of the present Committee of Governors. Whether national central banks have become more independent or not – in some countries decisive steps are unlikely to be taken before the end of stage II – Art. 107 of the Treaty and Article 8 of the EMI Statute state that members of the EMI Council may not, in that capacity, 'seek or take any instructions from Community institutions or bodies or Governments of Member States'. Collectively at least the members of the EMI Council will begin to work independently from the beginning of stage II.

A final new element is that the EMI is intended from its start to have a seat separate from the Bank of International Settlements in Basle which currently accommodates the nineteen-member secretariat of the Committee of Governors. No decision has yet been taken on the seat of the EMI which is also expected to be that of the ECB in the final stage; Article 13 of the EMI Statute stipulates that a decision should be taken before the end of 1992, following ratification of the Treaty in all Member States, presumably at the European Council meeting in Edinburgh in December 1992. Whether that will, in fact, be possible then depends, however, more on the resolution of the present conflicts over the seat for the European Parliament and some new EC agencies than on the relative merits of the numerous European cities presented as candidates for hosting the EMI/ECB.

The appointment of an external President, the signs of increasing independence for the EMI Council as a body, and the move to a more permanent location can hardly fail to give more authority to the new institution in stage II in the execution of its second main task besides reinforcing the coordination of monetary policy: to prepare fully for the final stage (Article 109f(3) and Article 4.2 of the EMI Statute). The preparation of instruments, procedures and operational rules, including the sensitive issue of the degree of centralization in the ECB in full EMU to be discussed in more detail in chapter 13 and, finally, of a more efficient system of cross-border payments, is likely – barring major crises in current monetary management – to provide the bulk of the agenda for the EMI Council and its, no doubt somewhat enlarged, staff. This forward-looking part of the EMI's mandate is interpreted in the following subsections.

A final monetary provision for the transition is the decision to fix (or freeze) the currency composition of the ecu (Article 109g). This implies that, once the Treaty proposals are ratified, there will be no more recompositions of the ecu basket; the amounts of the twelve component national currencies will remain as agreed in the September 1989 recomposition, see chapter 6. This removes one significant source of uncertainty for users of the unit, as the quinquennial recomposition otherwise foreseen in 1994 is henceforth excluded. Potentially more important, a subsequent recomposition of 1999 which could have brought the currencies of additional Member States into the basket, is also excluded. The freezing of the basket, though a very modest step as long as realignments are likely to remain small and infrequent, implies a slight hardening of the ecu. Alternative and more radical formulas for hardening, including the asymmetrical basket and the devaluation-proof 'hard ecu' proposed by the UK government in 1990 (discussed in chapter 11) would have gone further towards hardening the ecu and making it a very close substitute for the strongest currency in the EMS, but at the cost of complicating the use of the unit to private market operators for the reasons referred to in chapter 6.

A residual, but irreducible, uncertainty remains for private ecu users. From the start of stage III, the ecu will become 'a currency in its own right', effectively the common denominator of the currencies of those Member States who are both ready for and willing to join full EMU and hence to adopt permanently fixed exchange rates (Article 109g and 1(4)). While the external value of the ecu will not be modified at the time of this qualitative change – indeed, the continuity of the external value of the new with the old ecu is the central element in assuring confidence in the unit for personal users[8] – the evolution, after the start of stage III of the exchange rate of the ecu, and of the interest rate attached to it, will be determined by the joint monetary policy through the ECB and by the initial inflation and interest rates of the participants in full EMU. For some-one entering into a long-term ecu–denominated contract today, an evaluation of this particular constellation of factors in the second half of the 1990s when stage III is likely to start cannot now be made with any high degree of certainty. Such certainty could not have been provided by any revision of the ecu applicable to the transition, given that a quantitative change in the ecu must necessarily take place at the start of stage III.

Far more important for the evolution of the use of the ecu than this residual uncertainty is the prospect that stage II will be limited to a duration of three, or at most five, years for a large group of Member States, the major result of Maastricht with respect to the transition. In the view of most private market operators, a definitive commitment to the ecu as the single currency in the late 1990s, is bound to give a major impetus to the growth of the ecu markets for securities and other financial assets. The EMI – and before 1 January 1994 even the Committee of Governors – will be faced with challenges in the ecu market more quickly than could have been imagined under a slower and less definite timetable for EMU. The innocuous wording of Article 109g (2), entrusting to the EMI the task to 'facilitate the use of the ecu and oversee its development, including the smooth functioning of the ecu clearing system' would then take on a more substantive meaning than may have been imagined. For instance, the EMI Council would have to take a more explicit view on the fluctuations in the exchange rate and in the interest rate of the ecu relative to the basket average than the fairly detached attitude the central banks have permitted themselves in the past, as evident from the experience in 1989–91 analyzed in chapter 6.

The EMI Council has not been asked to 'promote the ecu' – a term which figured in early Treaty drafts on the transition, but was removed at the insistence of Germany. However, this should no longer be necessary, since preparation to make the ecu the single currency in a not very distant future has become part of the decisions of Maastricht. That, indeed, is the most effective type of 'promotion' which could be imagined. In this new environment the EMI Council will find it difficult to distinguish between the current and the forward-looking parts of its assignments. The more efficiently it prepares for a stage III with early replacement of the national currencies by the ecu, the more it will find itself confronted with market participants who take seriously that the near future is telescoped into the present and hence has increasingly strong implications for current monetary management.

---

[8] The importance of this point was recognized in the Delors Report, see the discussion in chapter 10, p. 322.

The parallel currency approach did not win favour with most European governments for the reasons discussed in chapter 11, and the EMI will not issue ecu as was envisaged in some earlier suggestions advanced in the spirit of this agreement. Yet it may well enter the stage in the transition, as market participants seize the opportunity of investing in advanced use of the ecu, now made more attractive by the decisions of Maastricht. This is one of the two major challenges posed by the new Treaty.

The second challenge is one that is not referred to explicitly in the new Treaty. It is related to the use of realignments in stage II and the related issue of the width of the fluctuation margins. The present section ends with a discussion of these two issues.

Realignments can still be resorted to in 'exceptional circumstances' in stage II, to use the formulation of the Delors Report. But the new Treaty has added incentives for making use, if any, of this instrument either early in the transition or, possibly, at the very end and in connection with the adoption of the permanently fixed rates at the start of stage III. The incentive for the former arises from the inclusion among the prerequisites for participation in full EMU that a country must, at the time of the decision to be taken by the European Council before the end of 1996, have observed 'the normal fluctuation margins provided for by the Exchange Rate Mechanism of the European Monetary System, for at least two years, without devaluing against the currency of any other Member State' (Article 109j(1)).[9] With the decision to move to stage III coming up at the latest at the end of 1996, a country that foresees a need to devalue will have to do so not much later than mid-1994. This implicit deadline of the final date for a realignment might increase speculative activity in the EMS up until 1994 and widen risk premia in interest rates which have recently been declining steadily.

Chapter 5 argued that there was no obvious need for a major ('maxi') EMS realignment, given the present constellation of real exchange rates, but the persistence of recent inflation differentials for a few more years in Italy and Spain, in particular, could make this constellation unsustainable, even if full convergence as a result of EMU were then to come quickly. Projected long-term difficulties of reconciling external and internal balance in the UK economy at the present level of sterling, even if the UK inflation rate were to have converged in a satisfactory way, put another question mark at the scenario of simply moving all the way to full EMU without realignments. Whether one still believes this scenario to be realistic (as do the present authors) or not, a significant number of market participants are bound to try to test the resolve of the national authorities more actively than in the recent past. This underlines the judgement of chapter 5 that the EMS may well be in for a rougher ride over the next few years than in the recent past.

The remaining possibility of a realignment can be dated to the very end of stage II. Unfortunately the Treaty as agreed as Maastricht does not rule out such a last minute

---

[9] The Protocol elaborating the convergence criteria clarifies this point by stating: '... the Member State shall not have devalued its currency's bilateral contral rate against any other Member State's currency on its own initiative for the same (i.e. two year) period' (Article 3 of the said Protocol). It has not been easy in some earlier EMS realignments to determine who took the initiative to realign and the balance between re- and devaluations has often been a source of controversy. The criterion is therfore less clearcut than it sounds; in particular a DM revaluation in, say, 1995 might still disqualify all countries that did not follow the DM from being considered ready for EMU in 1996.

realignment, though the language of Article 109 l(4) – '... the council shall ... adopt the conversion rates at which ... currencies shall be irrevocably fixed ...' – suggests continuity with the exchange rates prevailing at the end of stage II as the most likely outcome. Some economists have argued that, in order to facilitate the eventual introduction of the ecu as the single currency, a realignment which rounded off the highly complex exchange rates for the ecu in national currencies might be desirable.[10] It is not obvious, however, why the existence of 'broken' exchange rates for the ecu would greatly complicate the conversion into ecu of existing contracts and prices in modern societies with advanced information systems, given that some time for preparation would inevitably lapse between the freezing of exchange rates and the introduction of the ecu as the single currency. It would seem preferable to avoid this source of uncertainty and incentive for speculation by taking care of any perceived rounding-off problems early in stage II – or even better, as we suggest in chapter 14 below, to agree on any final realignment before the end of stage I, hence relieving the transition of the additional burden of dealing with occasional speculative pressures.

In the light of the still open possibility of realignments in the course of stage II it may have been wise of the IGC not to have included a narrowing of the fluctuation margins in the agenda for stage II. A narrowing of the margins has traditionally been regarded as an essential part of the transition to monetary union. The Werner Report advocated a gradual narrowing; and the Delors Report repeated that suggestion as a means of reinforcing coordination on the participants during the transition (para. 57):

> As circumstances permitted and in the light of progress made in the process of economic convergence, the margins of fluctuations within the exchange rate mechanism would be narrowed as a move towards the final stage of monetary union, in which they would be reduced to zero.

A narrowing of the margins was also a central element in the recommendations of the Committee for Monetary Union for Europe over the 1988–91 period and of the European Parliament. Yet, when the Danish government proposed in the IGC that the margins should be narrowed from ± 2.25 per cent to ±1.5 per cent on 1 January 1994 there was no support for the proposal from other governments. Some referred to the Basle-Nyborg agreement of September 1987, a central provision of which was that the national monetary authorities should make fuller use of the margins than they had done prior to the agreement; they felt that they still needed the cushioning effect of the 'normal' margins of ± 2.25 per cent.

A narrowing to ± 1.5 or 1.0 per cent would eliminate much of the residual freedom in interest rate policy still enjoyed by central banks in the EMS. Two countries have

---

[10] Giovannini (1991) discusses such a final realignment in some detail and presents illustrative calculations of how it could be done. Since it would be difficult at this late stage to make significant corrections of relative price level distortions among the participants Giovannini proposes the publication well in advance – say, two years before the date for deciding on EMU – of an announcement of the permanent conversion rates. Such a procedure would minimize disruptions at the time of moving to the single currency. The problem was discussed by some members of the Delors Committee in 1989, but this type of discussion for obvious reasons did not find its way into an official report.

already indicated that they have unilaterally moved in this direction: the Netherlands has for many years managed the guilder within a band of ± 0.5 per cent of the central rate for the DM at the cost as we saw in chapter 4 of having to shadow German interest rates very closely. Since mid-1990 Belgium has taken a similar step. In these two cases, unilateral narrowing of the margins has tended to build confidence and has enabled the two countries to virtually eliminate any interest rate differential with Germany. A different strategy has been followed by France and Denmark who have similarly been able to squeeze their interest rate differential with Germany over the past year or so while managing their currencies near the bottom of the normal ± 2.25 per cent margins. As these two currencies have gradually been seen as increasingly unlikely to devalue, market participants will in normal circumstances see a return towards the centre of the margins as more probable than a move further away (which could imply a realignment of the central rate); hence a small negative risk premium can gradually develop. The constraints on enlarging it by not following interest rate increases in Germany, or on attempting unilateral cuts in interest rates remain – as the frustrated efforts of France in late 1991 illustrates. German nominal interest rates appear to continue to set a floor under the rates in other EMS countries. France and Denmark would probably find their ability to maintain short-term rates virtually identical to Germany's somewhat curtailed if the margins were narrowed. Similarly Spain would find her ability to maintain the high nominal interest rates seen as appropriate for the Spanish economy reduced by a narrowing of the margins from the current ±6 per cent to the normal ± 2.25 per cent, because such a step would limit the size of the depreciation of the peseta which could take place inside the margins.

These examples illustrate why countries in different positions in the EMS provided unwilling to reduce the residual freedom they retain in their present margins and commit to a narrowing in stage II. They may also feel that margins no narrower than those presently in use may be required to minimize discontinuities in market exchange rates surrounding realignments, if the latter are still to occur in stage II.

The logic would be different, if convergence were to proceed further and the 'deadline' for realignments among currencies which are obvious candidates for full EMU by end-1996 has been passed. The case for formally narrowing margins could then have strengthened as a preparation for monetary union. Given the different starting points of potential EMU participants, it now seems more likely that actions to narrow will be individual and unilateral rather than an integral part of stage II. If there are clear indications, say in connection with a final realignment in 1992, that no further realignments are intended in stage II, a formal and general narrowing of the margins could still be part of the agenda for stage II. This is the course of action recommended in the timetable for EMU presented in chapter 14.

This completes the discussion of the provisions in the new Treaty as regards the entry into, and the substantive monetary content of, stage II. A review of the criteria by which the performance of Member States with respect to government deficits and debt will be judged in the evaluation of their degree of preparedness for entering stage III and adopting the single currency is postponed until section 5 below dealing with the procedures for ending stage II in the second half of the 1990s.

It is obvious that the monetary content of stage II as it appears after Maastricht represents a minimalist approach to institutional developments that go clearly beyond stage I. The seriousness of this deficiency is, however, to a large degree compensated by the shortness of stage II. Although the Delors Report did not specify the duration envisaged for the transition, the nature of some of its proposals, aiming at a gradual transfer of monetary authority to the new central banking institution, reveals that it had a longer time frame in mind than the three to five years provided at Maastricht. Gradualism is not very meaningful over such a short time span. The central result of Maastricht with respect to stage II is to have designed a transition primarily as an extension of stage I, but with the task of preparing for stage III in the near future. In combination with the clarification of the non-monetary prerequisites for moving to full EMU this apparently meagre result could still make stage II substantially more ambitious than stage I.

It is necessary to reflect, nevertheless, on a transition more ambitious than the new Treaty in the monetary area, while respecting the now dominant view that ultimate monetary authority will have to be retained in national hands until the start of stage III. The rest of this section and the following two therefore explore the limits of the 'indivisibility doctrine' and takes as its point of departure some of the ideas discussed in the Delors Committee which had not subsequently gained support. The reader should be warned that these ideas are discussed not because the authors believe that they are likely to be adopted subsequently, but rather to illustrate what could have been achieved in addition to improve monetary policy coordination and to prepare efficiently for stage III.

12.2.1 The role of stage II: essentials of the learning process

The role of the institutional developments that define this stage was initially formulated in the following passage in the Delors Report (para. 55), often referred to approvingly by individual governments and central banks:

> stage II must be seen as a period of transition to the final stage and would thus constitute a training process leading to collective decision-making, while the ultimate responsibility for policy decisions would remain at this stage with national authorities.

The foundation for this view of monetary authority as 'indivisible' is that there should never be any doubts as to where authority is vested and that, as long as national governments have the possibility to resort to realignments, though only 'in exceptional circumstances', and national central banks have not become fully independent, it would not make sense to pretend that there is any genuine sharing of responsibility between the national and European levels. The new EMI should in this perspective do no more than to prepare the formulation and the execution of policy for which its successor will be given full responsibility in the final stage.

Is it possible to reconcile this restrictive view with the ideas which have been developed for stage II? Is there an area of actions which the new institution could move into constructively without undermining the 'ultimate responsibility' of national authorities? If this area is narrow, would it not have been preferable simply to extend stage I until the final steps of irrevocable locking of exchange rates and, as soon as possible thereafter, the introduction of a single currency can be taken?

There must be some sympathy for this view. The problem associated with it is whether the final steps could emerge without an intermediate stage which prepares three elements:

(i)   a consensus on the specific formulation of the ultimate objective(s);

(ii) a common analytical framework for intermediate objectives and for the design of monetary policy; and

(iii) a sufficient degree of experience with common operations.

These three elements are all part of a learning process in the absence of which it seems doubtful whether the final steps could be taken without major risk. The view of the Delors Report that an intermediate, but not necessarily long, stage is required, seems correct. In particular, experimentation with some forms of genuinely joint decision-making is desirable before monetary authority is fully centralized in the final stage. But a clear attribution of responsibilities assuring the cohesiveness of the system would then be essential between the national central banks and the EMI.

The Delors Report refrained from presenting a detailed blueprint of the intermediate stage, 'as this (transition) would depend on the effectiveness of the policy coordination achieved during the first stage, on the provisions of the Treaty, and on the decisions to be taken by the new institutions' (para. 57). Nevertheless, some preliminary ideas were offered in the Report, and some of them are elaborated on in papers contributed to the work of the Committee by members in their individual capacity. How could the intermediate stage provide a framework for the learning process?[11]

It is evident that, once exchange rates have been irrevocably locked at the transition to the final stage of EMU, a common monetary policy is required and will have to be formulated collectively by the ECB Council and Board. In contrast, during stage II when realignments and fluctuations inside the bands may still occur, national authorities will retain the final word concerning their exchange rates and hence their monetary policies. But the same considerations that lead to the conclusion that the final locking of parities requires a common monetary policy also imply that to the extent that exchange rates become *de facto* stabilized, and recognized to be unlikely to change, national monetary policies will become ever more severely constrained. It follows that the competence for monetary policy is not an 'all or nothing' choice. The more explicit the degree of exchange-rate fixity, and the higher the degree of financial market integration, the closer must be the coordination and the extent to which the overall policy stance of the participants has to be decided in common.

How could the need for a strengthening of common element in monetary policy be organized during stage II? A taxonomy of the different solutions is offered in the

---

[11] The following draws on Thygesen (1989), which is the contribution of one of the authors to the collection of papers annexed to the Delors Report.

collection of Papers annexed to the Delors Report. Lamfalussy (1989) refers to three possible approaches in stage II. The first is for the participating central banks to set up a jointly owned subsidiary in the EMI, whose facilities they would share in performing certain of their operations in domestic money and foreign exchange markets without requiring any formal transfer of authority. The second is to assign a small number of monetary instruments to the EMI while leaving others for national decisions or non-binding coordination. The third is to implement a gradual but formal transfer of decision-making power from the national to the collective level. The three approaches may perhaps be labelled pooling of (1) operations, (2) instruments and (3) authority.

The three approaches have been presented by their respective proponents to be complementary rather than mutually exclusive. Indeed, (2) and (3) are difficult to distinguish, since both, in order to be effective, would require the introduction of some hierarchical order in the relations of the governing bodies at the European level and the constituent national monetary authorities. They will be treated as a combined approach in the following. However, pooling of operations is different in kind by requiring no formal transfer of authority; in that sense it might even have been experimented with or prepared already in stage I.

The pooling of operations as proposed in Lamfalussy (1989) would consist in the establishment of a common operations facility incorporating all of the foreign exchange and domestic money market activities of participating national central banks in a jointly owned subsidiary. Each central bank would staff its own operations; later the national staffs could be merged into a single unit. The use of common facilities would make the operations of each individual participant fully transparent to other participants. Perhaps surprisingly to most outside observers, this is not the case today with respect to domestic money market operations or with respect to the management of foreign exchange reserves, apart from interventions proper. Pooling of operations would at the same time present a common appearance in the markets. Private market participants would be unable to determine the source of instructions for operations from the jointly owned agency. There could no longer be occasionally conflicting signals to the markets.

Centralization of operations would furthermore provide a more efficient training ground for national foreign exchange and money market operators than the *ad hoc* concertations by telephone in today's system. The approach would facilitate efforts to develop a more convergent framework for the design and implementation of monetary policy, including the domestic aspects of the latter. This would provide efficient preparation for fully joint management in the final stage. Centralization may also offer some potential for cost savings. Chapter 13 returns to the desirable degree of operational centralization in the fully operational ESCB. It is noted there that the central banks show some reluctance, even in the final stage, to centralize operations to the degree envisaged in the Lamfalussy proposals.

A small step in the direction of opening the possibility of joint operations in one of the two main areas suggested by Lamfalussy has been taken with the new Treaty. The EMI Statute (see Appendix 3 to chapter 13) foresees that some centralization of foreign exchange operations can take place on a voluntary and bilateral basis in stage II. Article 6.4 of the EMI Statute states:

> The EMI shall be entitled to hold and manage foreign exchange reserves as an agent for and at the request of national central banks ... The EMI shall perform this function on the basis of bilateral contracts ... Transactions with these reserves shall not interfere with the monetary policy of the competent authorities of any Member State ...

This is a limited and strictly voluntary arrangement and it is currently not clear how many central banks will wish to avail themselves of this opportunity for pooling foreign exchange operations, though it is certain that the Bundesbank will not be one of them. Despite these severe limitations the additional capacity of the EMI to operate as an agent is at least a beginning along the lines suggested by Lamfalussy.

Pooling of operations has potential virtues and is clearly not in conflict with the 'indivisibility doctrine'. Yet the very virtues of the idea which make it attractive to some and grudgingly accepted by others also point to its limitations. Operations would be merely an aggregate of the instructions received with no one visibly in charge of the consistency of policy over time or of preventing actions at cross purposes within any period of time. The approach should ideally be complemented by the two other approaches in the course of stage II. To implement either of them would, however, require some consensus about:

(i)   ultimate and intermediate objectives,

(ii) the design of monetary policy, and

(iii) use of instruments.

Such a consensus cannot be said to exist today in any explicit form, as shown by the review of coordination efforts in stage I.

The following subsection addresses the first of these three issues in a preliminary way, mindful that the formulation of monetary objectives requires substantial efforts of macroeconomic analysis, study of empirical regularities and assessment of practical feasibility. The remaining two issues form the core of section 12.3 below.

12.2.2 Ultimate and intermediate objectives for stage II

In the final stage of EMU it is now clear that price stability will be a priority objective for monetary policy; the rationale for this mandate as well as its implementation is discussed in chapter 13. The long-term mandate is the clearest example of an area where the spillover effects from successful completion of the IGC and ratification of Treaty changes could have a positive influence on the transition. That might not, however, be sufficient to assure continuity in the nominal anchor function. Attention will have to be paid explicitly from at the latest the start of stage II to the specification of the ultimate and intermediate nominal objectives. A collective price objective, underpinned by national targets for nominal income and monetary aggregates, would greatly assist the monitoring of both the aggregate thrust of policy and the compatibility of national developments.

The final EMU average consumer prices in the Community may have a strong claim on the attention of policy-makers as the measure most suitable for overall welfare. (See also the discussion of the objective of price stability in chapter 13, section 3.1 below; this is also the index singled out for monitoring in the convergence criteria, see section 5 below). A natural candidate for the collective price objective might be to aim for stability in average producer prices in the internal market, see also chapter 13. A price index of this kind would, as the process of integration and competition advances significantly over the next few years, provide an increasingly reliable indication of a common price trend. Such an objective could be said to be a logical complement to the construction of the unified market. If it were seen as desirable that external price shocks, such as major changes in the prices of energy or other important imported inputs, should be, in part, accommodated through monetary policy adjustments, one could focus on the sources of inflation internal to the EC. A deflator of value added in manufacturing industry, calculated as a weighted average for the internal market, would leave out externally generated price shocks and the participants would implicitly accommodate such shocks. This would in practice not be far from policies followed in the least inflationary EMS countries in response to the 1979–80 oil price shock and in Germany in 1974, but explicit agreement of it would be important.

Would such a collective objective need to be underpinned by national nominal objectives, such as nominal income or final demand, and by intermediate objectives? It could be hazardous to gear the setting of the monetary instruments exclusively to a relatively remote objective such as average price stability. For a lengthy initial period there will be uncertainty as to what degree of national dispersion around the average inflation rate is compatible with the emerging fixed exchange-rate system, and it may become increasingly difficult to give a precise interpretation of national intermediate objectives in the form of domestic credit expansion (DCE) in each participating country as financial integration progresses. As shown in Russo and Tullio (1988) there is a solid analytical basis for developing a framework in which national DCEs, coupled with a general presumption against sterilization of interventions *vis-à-vis* other participating currencies, provide the main underpinning for monitoring national contributions to the collective monetary policy. The setting of national DCE targets could in turn be guided by nominal income (or final demand) objectives compatible with the average price target.

Such an emphasis on quantities will seem outdated to many central banks at a time when most national monetary aggregates are becoming blurred. Monetary institutions committed to price stability are always faced with a choice between a supply rule, under which additional money is issued only at a slow, non-inflationary rate, see, e.g., Leijonhufvud (1983), and a convertibility rule which assures holders of money that they can acquire at a fixed rate an asset with attractive qualities in future exchanges against goods.

The regime here envisaged for the increasingly joint-monetary policy during stage II would contain elements of both systems. There is today no external reserve asset, such as gold in the pre-1914 period and the US dollar in the Bretton Woods period convertibility into which could assure a high degree of confidence in the future purchasing power of national monies; hence reliance on a quantitative supply rule at the collective level seems unavoidable. However, a supply rule alone could prove too weak in the framework of stage II, marked by a growing commitment to EMU and to full financial integration. It would be hard to know *a priori*, i.e., until some experience has been gained within the new framework as to the demand for money and credit, whether a particular DCE-target (or target range) is the appropriate one. Hence there is a strong case for experimentation with an explicit price objective, in combination with DCE supply rules.

The Delors Report did not envisage any significant commitment for the participants in the process towards EMU to stabilize participating currencies against third currencies. If net interventions in dollars or in other third currencies are undertaken by the participants, total money creation will diverge from the sum of national DCEs. This would have to be taken into account in setting objectives for the subsequent periods. If interventions in dollars or in other third currencies are indeed modest, because the participants are prepared to live with a system of floating exchange rates among the major currencies, this external source of money creation should not greatly upset control over aggregate money creation through the sum of DCEs in the participating economies. If, however, such interventions were to be substantial in any one period they should be subject to commonly agreed guidelines and allowed for in setting the DCE targets for the subsequent period (see the discussion of instrument pooling below).

For the individual central banks the main operational objective in stage II would be to continue to maintain in a credible way stable exchange rates *vis-à-vis* other participating currencies. *Ex ante* coordination of DCE objectives should make that task easier on average; in practice, the DCE objective may, in particular situations, have to be overridden to maintain shorter-term exchange-rate stability.

Collective formulation of ultimate and intermediate monetary objectives would in itself constitute a major step towards *ex ante* coordination. The participating central banks would deepen the exchange of information on their respective formulations of monetary policy by giving the reports prepared for them a more explicitly common analytical framework and by formulating joint intervention strategies and guidelines for DCE rather than primarily reviewing the past record as in stage I. Closer coordination could begin in stage II, while the guidelines emerging from it are not yet mandatory, to replicate the effects of a more advanced stage. In principle, this process should be getting underway already during stage I through the exercise of joint target-setting now attempted by the Committee of Governors (see section 12.1.4).

Yet it is unlikely that anything resembling a common monetary policy could be conducted merely through discussions but without vesting in the EMI any explicit functions with respect to some significant instrument(s) of monetary policy. Indeed, that is the rationale for suggesting a reinforced institutional framework from the start of stage II, some years before the irrevocable locking of parities which makes a common monetary policy a simple necessity. The central issue is then whether monetary authority could operate as if it were effectively shared from 1 January 1994 onwards between a centre and the participating national central banks. As noted already, the efficiency of operations requires that there must never be any doubt in the financial markets, or among national policy-makers as to which body has the responsibility for taking particular decisions. Monetary authority is less easily divisible than budgetary authority where elements of decentralization and even of competitive behaviour between different levels of government, or within the same level, may be observed in national states. For those who want to give real substance to the monetary content of the transition, it becomes imperative to be specific as to the role of the EMI Council in strengthening monetary coordination in stage II.

12.3 Possible monetary instruments/decisions for stage II

Five types of policy decisions might be considered in the design of a workable pooling of instruments or responsibilities in stage II:

(1) adjustment of short-term interest differentials,

(2) intervention policy *vis-à-vis* third currencies,

(3) a Community-wide reserve requirement,

(4) realignments, and

(5) issue of a parallel currency (the ecu).

These possibilities are examined in turn, although it must be recognized that they were not given attention as proposals for stage II in the IGC. The third element, a Community-wide reserve requirement is in our view important enough to merit more detailed discussion in section 4. Subsection 12.3.6 concludes by arguing that, if none of these five instruments are used because attribution of one or more of them to the EMI would violate the principle of 'indivisibility' of monetary policy, it is difficult to see a meaningful role for stage II as distinct from stage I − except for its functions in preparing for final EMU in a more decisive way.

12.3.1 Adjustment of short-term interest differentials

Adjustments of relative short-term interest rates constitute the central instrument in managing the present EMS and the main candidate for gradual pooling of authority. A high degree of coordination and occasionally *de facto* joint, or at least bilateral, decisions are already observable.

As discussed in chapter 3, participants have, since the so-called Basle–Nyborg Agreement of September 1987, relied on a flexible set of instruments for containing incipient exchange-market tensions: intramarginal intervention, wider use of the fluctuation band, and changes in short-term interest-rate differentials. This combination has proved fairly robust in most periods of tension since September 1987. But a risk remains that periods of tension will be repeated. In the past mutual recriminations between Ministers of Finance occasionally intensified tensions and made monetary management difficult. The main examples of such episodes are December 1986–January 1987, November 1987, April 1989 and February 1991, the latter prompted by strongly rising demand in Germany at a time when other EMS economies had become much less buoyant.[12]

The participation of additional currencies in the EMS in the course of stage I, notably sterling, which has traditionally been managed with considerable involvement on the part of the UK Treasury and even of the Prime Minister, makes it urgent to strengthen further procedures for a more joint element in adjustment of interest rates in stage II.

Decision-making in this sensitive area would remain in national hands in stage II, but the launching of the EMI would imply that national governments become less likely than in the past to involve themselves directly in the management of exchange crises. In the course of stage I the Committee of Central Bank Governors has already begun to perform more efficiently the role of multilateral arbitrator, which was missing occasionally in the past. A common analytical framework for intermediate objectives as outlined above would give more explicit guidance as to who should adjust to whom. If the proposal to develop a joint operational facility for foreign exchange (and money market) operations were to be pursued in something like the form proposed by Lamfalussy, participating central banks would be pushed into more continuous contact also with respect to their transactions in their domestic financial markets, facilitating coordinated action on interest rates.

Upgrading of decision-making on *relative* interest-rate adjustments from the purely national level to the EMI will not in itself assure that the *average* level of interest rates in the participating countries is appropriate, though it should make occasional inefficiencies of interest-rate escalations and tensions less likely. To get a firmer grip on the average level of rates, the attribution to the EMI of an instrument which would permit a collective influence on domestic sources of money creation would have been desirable. Such an instrument could be reserve requirements on domestic money creation and the consequent evolution of a market for a European reserve base – a Federal funds market – with its own lending rate.

12.3.2 Intervention policy *vis-à-vis* third currencies

A second instrument for which some degree of joint management could be envisaged is foreign exchange interventions in third currencies. There are two potential arguments for developing a joint policy: containment of major misalignments, and smoothing-out of short-term volatility.

The former argument can hardly be assessed without making a judgement on the feasibility of a more managed global exchange-rate system. Could other major monetary authorities, notably in the United States, commit themselves to support,

---

[12] This challenge to the EMS is discussed in chapter 5. The increase in German short-term interest rates in December 1991, followed by a number of other EMS participants, while subject to much criticism in other countries, did not lead to similar recriminations at the political level as in 1986–7.

through intervention and domestic monetary adjustment, any understanding reached on the appropriate levels of the main bilateral exchange rates?[13] Given the experience throughout the period since 1977 and the persistence of major current-account imbalances for the United States and Japan, an emerging joint dollar policy of the EMS countries could hardly be anything more than *ad hoc* guidelines for managing an approximately stable rate against the dollar. Given the current (end 1991) level of the US dollar *vis-à-vis* the ecu and the overall current-account deficit of the EC, EMS members appear to have in the aggregate completed the reduction required of them to assume an important share of the adjustment of the US current deficit to a sustainable low level. This adjustment put the cohesion of the EMS currencies to a test which the system passed well. It has also provided for the early 1990s an opportunity, as in 1985–7, during the prolonged fall in the dollar, for a broadly satisfactory price performance in Europe.

As regards the task of smoothing out short-term exchange-rate volatility, we noted in chapter 4 that tensions between EMS currencies have often in the past decade been triggered off by external financial disturbances, notably movements in the dollar. The currencies participating in the EMS were seen by the markets as being sensitive to different degrees to such disturbances. Such perceived differences had their origins in varying degrees of controls on capital movements and in expectations of the likelihood of divergent policy reactions to external financial disturbances.

For example, a depreciation of the dollar was normally expected to strengthen the DM relative to most other EMS currencies, because the DM had a far larger domestic financial base, the most liberal regime for capital flows and the non-German authorities in the EMS were seen as more prone than the Bundesbank to try to avoid the contractionary effects of the appreciation of their currencies. The tensions to which these real or perceived differences in structure and/or behaviour gave rise were occasionally mitigated by an EMS realignment. Conversely, in periods of an appreciating dollar, outflows from Europe were observed to be particularly strong from the DM area, reflecting closer substitutability between the US dollar and the DM than that prevailing for other EMS currencies, but presumably also a perception of decreasing probability of a realignment within the system.

In recent years the liberalization of capital movements in France and Italy and in some smaller EMS-countries, the deepening of continental European financial markets and the improved cohesion of the EMS economies have all contributed to a weakening of the earlier negative correlation between movements in the US dollar (in effective exchange-rate terms) and movements in non-DM currencies in the EMS *vis-à-vis* the DM. In chapter 5 the weakening of this asymmetry between the DM and the other EMS currencies was reviewed (together with other evidence of more symmetry). Yet a tendency for dollar movements to affect the EMS currencies differentially may be expected to persist in moderate form into stage II. The task remains in that case to avoid the persistence of such tensions (if unwarranted by more fundamental economic divergence) and to contain their ability to force realignments.

This task could in principle be achieved through joint guidelines for essentially

---

[13] The implications of EMU for the global monetary system are discused in chapter 9.

decentralized interventions by the participating national central banks, but a visible capacity to intervene jointly in third currencies, and to do so in ways that further the cohesion of the EMS, is potentially a superior method. Presence in the major exchange markets would give an emerging European institution the capacity to check the impact of external financial disturbances on EMS stability at source. Hence 'a certain amount of reserve pooling' (Delors Report, para. 57) as well as ample working balances in EMS currencies would become desirable in stage II. Such pooling was reproposed by France and Spain in their respective contributions to the IGC, but it survived into the Treaty text only in the weak form already referred to, i.e. by enabling the EMI to operate as agent for and at the request of national central banks in their foreign exchange management. The voluntary and bilateral nature of the arrangements envisaged make them more akin to pooling of operations then to pooling of the instrument of interventions.

It is impossible to determine *a priori* what percentage of external official reserves should be pooled in order to create a credibility effect in the financial markets for an emerging joint intervention policy. Leaving the percentage low, say 10–20 per cent, as proposed by some members of the Delors Committee as a possible step in stage I (para. 53), runs the risk of complicating existing cooperative procedures without making a qualitative difference. Even limited pooling would provide some beneficial effects from the learning experience of coordinating interventions through the same trading floor (de Larosière, 1989). Pooling reserves would have the clear advantage over pooling operations in that it would push the participants to formulate guidelines for intervention to reinforce their daily telephonic concertation at the operational level.

Joint intervention in third currencies by means of pooling of part of exchange reserves did not win general favour in the Delors Report as a proposal for stage I; 'too much emphasis might be put on external considerations relative to the correction of imbalances within the Community' (para. 54). This argument would not necessarily apply to a capacity to undertake joint intervention in stage II if the voluntary pooling of part of international reserves were to be accompanied by experimentation with at least one significant monetary instrument with direct implications for domestic money creation by the participants as proposed in the following subsection.

12.3.3 Reserve requirements

Such an instrument, which could be specifically assigned to the EMI from the start of its operations, is the ability to impose (potentially variable) reserve requirements on domestic money creation. This instrument is discussed more thoroughly in section 4 below; the present subsection concentrates on the general principle and the relationship with the other instruments.

Coordination of interest-rate policy and pooling of reserves/joint interventions (and realignments to be discussed below) are directed primarily at relative adjustments within the EMS. Changes in required reserve ratios would affect the aggregate thrust of monetary policy. International monetary agreements, notably the Bretton Woods system, have been more explicit on relative than on aggregate adjustment in the participating countries. The EMS is no exception; more attention has been given to procedures for correcting policy differences than to discussion of whether monetary policy was, in the aggregate, appropriate.

The Bretton Woods system and the early EMS did not have to face up to this issue directly, because both systems were protected by a mixture of capital controls for the short term and some scope for changing the exchange rate in the longer term. The post-1983 EMS has had more difficulty in avoiding the issue. In the absence of some aggregate monetary target for the whole system, an implicit rule emerged: monetary policy in most participating countries has tended to be determined via the ambition to hold more rigidly fixed nominal exchange rates *vis-à-vis* the currency of its largest and, normally, least-inflationary participant. The practice in the EMS (i.e., that reserves used for intervention in defending a weak currency have to be reconstituted within the span of a few months) implies, as realignments are phased out, that convergence will be towards low inflation and not towards some average as would be the case if intervention credits provided a more permanent safety net. In the latter event, efforts at 'sterilization' would have become more widespread in the weaker currency countries, and aggregate money creation would have drifted upwards.

By using the degree of freedom of aggregate monetary policy for implicitly attaching policies to the domestic monetary target in Germany, the EMS succeeded for a number of years after March 1983 in becoming 'a zone of monetary stability' in the double sense of promoting both exchange rate and price stability, as explained in chapters 4 and 5. The more symmetric operation of the recent EMS has begun to endanger this achievement. The challenge for stage II (and stage III) is to design intermediate objectives and monetary instruments so as to make a strengthening of these stability features likely. The pooling of an instrument to influence domestic sources of money creation in all participating countries could be the prime example of the third approach referred to above.

If the ability of the Bundesbank to keep a preferred domestic monetary target close to a desired path diminishes, financial integration increases the risk of policy errors due to misperceptions in the setting of intermediate targets and creates an incentive for all participants, including Germany, to modify the present paradigm. The increasing ease, as the credibility of fixed exchange rates improves, with which any participant can attract inflows of capital by raising short-term rates is another illustration of the same basic point. Recognition thereof should push the thinking of all monetary authorities in the direction of aggregate money creation in the area, to the formulation of intermediate objectives for domestic money creation consistent with such an aggregate target and, finally, to designing procedures whereby the latter can be kept close to an agreed course. Ciampi (1989) and Thygesen (1989) provide an analysis of how the system could be implemented.

According to these early proposals made in the context of the Delors Report the EMI might from the start of its operations attempt to orchestrate uniform or differentiated reserve requirements on either the increase in the monetary liabilities of each participating national central bank or on the credit extended by these banks to their respective domestic sectors. This requirement could be met only by holding reserves with the EMI; and the supply of reserves would be entirely controlled by the latter through allocations of a reserve asset (official ecu) to each central bank corresponding to the demand for reserves which would arise, if agreed targets for money creation or DCE were observed. Both cost and availability considerations would provide each national central bank with an incentive to stay close to declared objectives. The EMI would have to be given some discretion in extending or withdrawing reserves to provide marginal accommodation. The new system could replace the present method of creating official ecu through temporary swaps of one fifth of gold and dollar reserves as well as the credits extended through the Very Short-Term Facility of the EMCF.

The system would create a monetary control mechanism analogous to that through which national central banks, who use reserve requirements, influence money and credit creation through their banking systems. It would introduce a certain hierarchy into the relationship between the EMI and the participating national central banks, while leaving freedom for each national central bank in designing its domestic instruments for ensuring compliance with the jointly formulated guidelines.

The reserve requirements might alternatively, as proposed in Thygesen (1989) be applied directly to DCE in the total national banking system, i.e., to the domestic sources of broad money creation. The advantage of this method would be to assign the collective monetary instrument more directly to a national intermediate objective (DCE) underpinning fixed exchange rates. But it might introduce more slack into the control mechanism, as it would no longer apply to items that appear on the balance sheet of the central banks for which the latter could be regarded as more directly responsible.

In a certain sense, proposals along these lines would take monetary policy in stage II closer to relying on a parallel currency (the official ecu) for improving coordination, an approach that was apparently rejected by the Delors Committee as a whole. However, use of the parallel currency would be restricted to the voluntarily participating central banks, and the proposals would not imply any linkage between the private and the official ecu which has traditionally been resisted by most EC central banks. The official ecu would simply become a common monetary base through which the recommendations of the emerging monetary authority impinge on the average rate of money creation of the participants. The latter would then tend to become national currency boards, dependent on the rate at which the system as a whole created a monetary base relative to the demand for a monetary base enforced through the reserve requirements.

In this sense the proposals of Ciampi and Thygesen do not go as far as the UK proposal, see H.M. Treasury (1991), to set up a monetary institution, the European Monetary Fund in stage II authorized to issue a new parallel currency, the so-called 'hard ecu' described in chapter 11, to non-official holders in exchange for national currencies, though they could be extended in this direction.

A different approach, discussed in section 4 below, would allow the new European monetary authority to have some direct impact on conditions in the financial markets more broadly in stage II. It would be implemented by a uniform European reserve requirement on commercial bank deposits or on increases thereof.[14] Under this variant all Community commercial banks would hold a certain small fraction of their deposits (say 1–2 per cent) as reserves with the EMI. The only asset that could be used to satisfy this reserve requirement would be 'federal funds' which could be denominated in ecu.

The aggregate supply of these federal funds would be strictly under central control, since only the EMI could issue them. The distribution of the total across countries and banks would be left to a federal funds market where commercial banks could trade among themselves the deposits, with the central monetary institution, which they need to satisfy the European reserve requirement. This scheme would therefore work like national reserve requirements, but on a European scale.

The European reserve requirement should be in addition to and independent of national reserve requirements; it would therefore not interfere directly with national monetary policy.

This approach would imply that the EMI would intervene directly in a market that reflects system–wide liquidity conditions. This is preferable, if the task of the EMI is to be concerned with overall conditions as opposed to the specific conditions in national markets. In order to ensure a gradual transfer of authority from the national to the Community level initial limits would be imposed on the total amount of open market transactions the EMI would be allowed to undertake within a given period.

Critical questions arise with reserve requirements as the major instrument for an emerging joint policy to influence the domestic sources of money creation, as a complement to the control over the external sources which a joint exchange rate and intervention policy vis-à-vis third currencies would provide. Reserve requirements have historically been the prime method by which central banks have achieved monetary control in most countries, but reliance on that instrument is more limited in the Community today (see, e.g., the surveys by Kneeshaw and van den Bergh, (1989) and Deutsche Bundesbank (1990), and in the main industrial countries more generally, see Batten et al. (1990)).

In most industrial countries the banking system has become indebted to the central bank to an extent that makes it dependent on the terms on which marginal accommodation of reserve needs is provided. The mechanisms suggested illustrate ways in which an analogous influence may be brought to bear through a reserve requirement system either on the relationship between a central monetary authority and the participating central banks or more directly on commercial banks and financial markets in general. A direct contact between the central institution and financial markets would provide a smooth passage to the final stage when the ECB will manage a single currency defined in continuation with the ecu used for the reserve requirement system and the Federal funds market in the transition.

In summary, the three instruments discussed so far constitute a comprehensive package which would have enabled the EMI Council to exert significant monetary authority, while leaving ultimate decisions on adjustments in relative national interest rates as well as realignments in the hands of national authorities, in the latter case subject to agreement with partner countries in the ECOFIN Council.

[14] See Gros (1991) for more details.

The three instruments provide examples of all three types of pooling referred to above. The arbitration function on national interest rates would imply some pooling of authority, though the collective recommendations would not be binding in stage II. The pooling of international reserves would imply early partial pooling of an important instrument and, by definition, some pooling of operations. Finally, the assignment to the joint monetary institution in the transition of the power to coordinate reserve requirements would be an exercise in the voluntary pooling both of important instruments and of a significant degree of monetary decision-making authority.

12.3.4 Realignments

One major decision in the EMS is today subject to *de facto* joint decision-making, *viz.* realignments of central rates. Might there be a case for vesting authority over this – exceptional – decision with the EMI as part of monetary management rather than leaving it as in the present EMS with the ECOFIN Council? There are arguments for and against such a transfer, while keeping in mind that realignments will only be resorted to in 'exceptional circumstances' (even though this wording was not explicitly retained in the Treaty).

One purpose of setting up a collective monetary institution before the irrevocable locking of parities in the final stage of EMU is to constrain realignments and phase out the need for them. A more specific objective would be to ensure that exceptional recourse to them will be made in sufficiently small steps to preserve continuity of market exchange rates around realignments. This has been an important feature in the containment of speculative pressures in the recent EMS experience; and it could become even more important, if stage II is introduced by a narrowing of margins as discussed above. If financial market participants interpret a transfer of authority for making residual small realignments to the EMI as a signal of an intended tightening of the EMS in the transition, such a transfer could prove stabilizing and hence desirable.

Putting the question in this way, however, suggests the counter-argument, *viz.* that governments might not succeed in conveying such a signal. They might instead feel relief at not having, as in the present EMS, to bear the political burden of initiating a realignment – and without the new, more hidden, discipline inherent in membership of a union with irrevocably fixed exchange rates. The Council of the EMI might be faced with *fait accompli* situations in which only a realignment could ease tensions, and with national policy-makers blaming either private speculators or the central bankers themselves for the outcome. This would imply a deterioration relative to the recent performance of the EMS.

On balance, these arguments suggest that the decisive consideration in assigning the authority to undertake realignments is how close participants have come to meeting the prerequisites for full union. It would be dangerous, if feasible, to shift the responsibility for deciding on realignments to the EMI in stage II, if major divergence of economic performance has persisted among the participants in the exchange-rate mechanism into that stage. It could be desirable to shift that responsibility, if the need for realignments were generally accepted as truly exceptional – as is, indeed, the intention for stage II – and if adequate monetary instruments for underpinning fixed rates had been assigned to the EMI along the lines proposed above.[15]

A tentative conclusion is that the authority to decide on realignments could become part of the mandate of a new monetary authority in stage II, but that this is less of a priority than the attribution of the day-to-day instruments of an increasingly collective monetary policy. If realignments are virtually banned in stage II there is, of course, no need to consider changes in present procedures for deciding upon them. Anyway, while some central bankers have shown sympathy for the idea no government proposed in the IGC that the EMI should exercise authority in this area. Whatever the pros and cons in economic terms, any move in this direction in stage II is unlikely for political reasons. An important part of the approach underlying the Treaty as agreed at Maastricht is indeed that individual Member States should themselves bear the main responsibility for preparing for full EMU.

12.3.5 Issue of a parallel currency

Finally, there is the possibility of authorizing the issue of a parallel currency in stage II. This idea, dismissed in the Delors Report, was first put forward in June 1990 in the form of the so-called 'hard-ecu' proposal of the UK government, see chapter 11. It has subsequently been elaborated on and to some extent clarified in draft Treaty amendments submitted to the IGC, and a memorandum from the Spanish government, submitted in January 1991 to the IGC, brought further refinements.[16]

We have discussed the parallel currency approach in chapter 11 as an alternative to the institutional approach, involving gradual centralization of policy-making, which was favoured by the Delors Report and of which the pooling of operations, authority and specific instruments may be regarded as representative illustrations. It is therefore possible to be brief at this point – even though many observers, including some that are hostile to the parallel currency approach, at times have regarded the proposals in this area as the most concrete among the possible steps that may be taken in stage II. The precise definition of the ecu and alternatives (present basket, fixed-amount basket, fixed-weight basket, asymmetrical basket or 'abstract') were reviewed in chapter 6; the proposed Treaty revision has opted for the fixed-amount ecu (Art. 109g). Here the question addressed is simply to what extent the attribution to the EMI Council of responsibility not only for monitoring the private ecu market, already a function of the Committee of Governors in stage I, but also for issuing a parallel currency might have enhanced monetary convergence in stage II by giving additional operational content to the activities of the new monetary institution in the transition.

According to the proposals made in the IGC by the UK and Spain the new monetary authority in the transition would issue ecu in exchange for national currencies

---

[15] In chapter 14 it is argued that participants should, if at all necessary, have a final realignment no later than the end of stage I.

[16] See HM Treasury (1991) and Ministerio de Economica y Hacienda (1991).

like a currency board; no net creation of outside money would be involved. If the firms and households in a country were to find it attractive — because of overissue of their own currency and/or convenience and low transactions costs of using the ecu — to switch massively into the ecu, the EMI would apply increasingly onerous terms to its further accumulation of the national currency held as counterpart to the ecus issued. Beyond certain pre-set thresholds a country would be obliged to buy back its own currency against international reserves. Further down the road it might face suspension of the convertibility into ecu for its currency. This type of disciplining mechanism exists already today in the EMS: a country which issues its own currency faster than warranted by the demand for it will initially accumulate debt to another central bank or to the Very Short-Term Facility, but after three and a half months it will have to repurchase its own currency or make sure that foreign holdings of it remain below a modest threshold (the debtor quota in the Short-Term Facility). To this extent the mechanism of the proposed stage II is a re-invention of what already exists. It reinforces discipline only to the extent that substitution out of the national currencies is enhanced by the evolution of the ecu as an alternative besides the other foreign currencies already available.

For the reasons elaborated in chapters 5 and 11 we believe that currency substitution is unlikely to be observed on any sizeable scale in a non-inflationary environment; this applies also if the ecu is moderately hardened to make it more competitive, as implied by the decision to freeze the currency amounts in the basket. The emergence of the ecu as a publicly encouraged parallel currency, even in the perspective of foreshadowing its future role as the single currency, will speed up that process especially if accompanied by measures to reduce the transactions costs of using the ecu towards those prevailing for domestic currencies. A number of such favours may be technically conceivable extending all the way to making the ecu legal tender for a number of purposes within individual Member States — a step left strictly at the discretion of national governments in the UK and Spanish proposals — but are unlikely to be taken in a fairly short transitional stage. A government that went further in this direction than others might find itself penalized as it transgresses the thresholds set collectively for 'excess' accumulation of its currency — not because of reckless issue of the latter but, on the contrary, because it had succeeded better than others in Europeanizing its monetary system. Some discretion would have to be left to the new monetary authority in managing the transitional phase to allow for distinctions between such different sources of ecu creation.

The tasks of issuer of ecu would obviously be enhanced if the new institution could also lend. A possible role as lender to EC commercial banks active in the private ecu market would be a logical extension of the EMI's role in the clearing system foreseen in the revised Treaty 1986 (Art. 109 d).[17] By accepting to provide short-term overdraft facilities within pre-set limits the EMI would help to balance the private ecu market and reduce costs, since commercial banks would be relieved of the costly task of

---

[17] The Spanish memorandum (see Ministerio de Economia y Hacienda (1991)) refers to this possibility for stage II — 'but not necessarily since its beginning'.

rebundling in the component currencies, if the growth of privately held ecu deposits does not match the growth in bank ecu assets, as has sometimes been the case in the past.[18] That would, however, resuscitate the plans for linking the private and the official ecu markets discarded in the mid 1980s (see chapter 6), requiring strict upper limits to the credit facilities of the EMI. It would also raise the question of the terms on which the institution would lend – in short whether the EMI should, through its terms for marginal accommodation in the ecu market, be allowed to exert some influence on national interest rates.

The conclusion from this discussion of the potential contribution to stage II of giving the EMI the right to issue ecu appears to be the following: it is possible to devise methods of issue sufficiently bound by rules to say that 'ultimate responsibility' for monetary policy remains firmly in national hands in stage II. A scenario with an EMI operating much like a currency board matching its issues of ecu closely with withdrawals of national currencies, but with substitution proceeding slowly relative to the thresholds set for accumulation, and possibly supplemented by limited (and overnight) credit facilities for the ecu market could be regarded as safe in this sense. But the issue of ecu would then make only a marginal contribution to monetary convergence and discipline and it would not visibly offer incentives for participants to risk steps that could shrink their own monetary turf.

12.3.6 'Undivided responsibility' for monetary policy in stage II?

It is possible, however, to think of more ambitious variants in which the role of ecu issuer is combined with one or more of the other proposals for stage II of an institutional nature. Pooling of operational activities could begin, but need not end, with transactions involving the ecu. Pooling of instruments likewise: the EMI could be authorized through a network of bilateral contracts to undertake operations in third currencies against ecu and, if the need arises, to maintain a substitution account for official holders of ecu wishing to diversify into the asset. Enabling rules exist now in the EMI Statute to make these additional tasks with the EMI as agent feasible. The operation of a reserve requirement scheme based on a federal funds market in ecu would be truly complementary to the role as an issuer of ecu. Management of short-term interest-rate differentials might be facilitated by an emerging role of the institution as a lender in the ecu market because the signals given through changes in the lending rate with increasing scope for departure of the ecu rate from the rates on the component national currencies which could give indications of who should adjust to whom.

The more one moves towards considering these combinations of the institutional and the parallel currency approaches, the further stage II would move towards *de facto*

---

[18] Recently a substantial accumulation of private ecu deposits by the EMS central banks has, as discussed in chapter 6, tended to remove the imbalance between assets and liabilities of the private non-bank sector.

sharing of responsibilities for monetary policies in the transition. Governments that have subscribed to more than simply pooling operational activities and issuing ecu on currency board principles appear to us to have implicitly rejected the ambition to keep monetary responsibility firmly in national hands. Monetary authority would, in fact, be divided between national authorities and the new institution. National governments would retain an essential authority as long as realignments could still take place.

It would have clarified the substantive content of stage II if governments and national central banks were more ready to accept that insistence by some on the indivisibility of monetary authority implies inability to design a stage II which is a meaningful improvement over stage I. Monetary responsibility is today *de facto* shared: between the political authorities and the central banks in all EMS countries, and between the central banks participating in the tight exchange-rate mechanism of the EMS. Even the authorities of countries which have opted for the wider band (Spain and the United Kingdom) are now well aware of the severe constraints on their ability to conduct monetary policy according to their domestic needs. Chapters 4 and 5 examined the high degree of interdependence which has developed in the EMS in recent years and the further challenges posed by deepening financial integration. Monetary responsibility is today more fragmented and held less firmly in national hands than the debate among officials suggests.

If the options were either to preserve a German-led system or to replace it by a joint monetary institution with a high degree of autonomous decision-making it would make good sense to seek to avoid an unclear transition phase lacking the virtues of either system. But more careful analysis of the present functioning of the EMS and its likely evolution during stage I suggests a more pragmatic attitude to proposals for stage II implying that some explicit division of responsibility between the new monetary institution and the participating central banks would have been appropriate for the transition. The proposals discussed in this section seem more likely to check than to accelerate the diffusion of responsibility anticipated in stage II.

12.4 European reserve requirements: a potentially decisive element

The previous section argued that some 'division' of monetary policy is necessary to produce a meaningful stage II in which the average thrust of monetary policy is determined at the Community level. The purpose of this section is to discuss the instrument that seems the most appropriate to fulfil this function because it would minimize interference with national monetary policies, while guaranteeing an anti-inflationary bias because it could be used only to impose a more restrictive monetary policy.

As mentioned above this potentially crucial instrument would be a Community-wide reserve requirement, which could take two forms that are discussed separately.

12.4.1 The three-tier system: reserve requirements on national central banks

Imposing reserve requirements on the liquidity creation by national central banks implies, as proposed by Ciampi (1989),[19] that the emerging joint monetary authority[20] would assume a position *vis-à-vis* national central banks similar to those of the latter *vis-à-vis* commercial banks. This would lead to a three-tier system under which national central banks would maintain reserve accounts in a special account with the ECB. Figure 12.4.1 shows the organizational structure of this scheme.

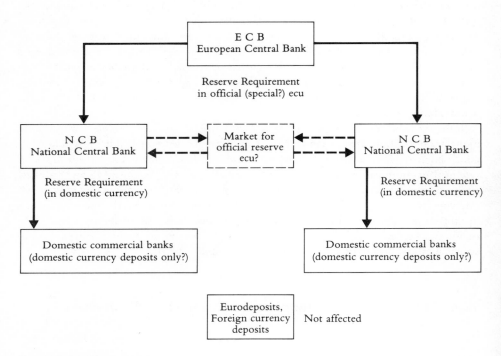

Figure 12.4.1 The 3-tier system

The reserves to be held by national central banks with the ECB would be equal to a proportion of certain national monetary aggregates (or the increase thereof) and would

[19] Padoa-Schioppa (1988) also alludes to such a system.

[20] In the following discussion this institution is labelled the European Central Bank (ECB) in order to recall that the proposed scheme is seen as applicable also to the final stage as long as national currencies continue to exist.

be denominated in 'official' ecus. The latter requires that the automatic credit facilities of the EMS would have to be discontinued (unless the circuit for the new 'reserve ecu' was isolated from the existing official ecu).

Ciampi (1989) also mentions that the reserve requirement could be based on the liabilities of national central banks (i.e., the monetary base) or part of their assets (i.e., credit extended to the government or the domestic banking sector). The former option would allow the ECB to control indirectly the overall monetary base in the Community. The latter option would require the ECB to coordinate interventions *vis-à-vis* third currencies if it wants to retain control over all sources of monetary base expansion. However, this latter option will not be considered any further in this paper because the role of domestic sources in the creation of a monetary base varies too much across countries. In the case of the UK, applying a reserve requirement on the domestic assets of the Bank of England would not make sense because this item is negative.

12.4.2 The two-tier system: reserve requirements on commercial banks

As mentioned above, an alternative, analysed in more detail in Gros (1990) and (1991), would be to allow the ECB to impose a uniform Community reserve requirement on commercial banks. This possibility is already foreseen in Art. 19 of the draft statute for the ECB reprinted in Appendix 1 to chapter 13.[21]

Under this approach all commercial banks located in the Community would have to hold an account with the ECB whose balance would have to be equal to a certain fraction of all the deposits received from Community residents.

It is crucial that the European reserve requirement be independent of national reserve requirements, because only in this case would it constitute an independent policy instrument for the ECB.

Commercial banks would be able to satisfy this reserve requirement only by acquiring deposits with the ECB. These deposits might be called 'ecu federal funds' in analogy with the federal funds market in the US on which US banks trade the deposit they need to satisfy the reserve requirement imposed by the Fed.[22] Since the ECB can always control its liabilities it would then be able to control the overall rate of monetary expansion in the Community in the same way a national central bank can control

---

[21] This does not imply that the governors endorse the idea of using reserves on commercial banks during the transition; the governors had only the final stage in mind for which they wanted to keep the option of using this instrument. Art. 19 of the draft statute mentions that these reserves might have to be held with national central banks. However, it is not important where commercial banks would have to hold their reserves. This is just a question of accounting as long as all decisions regarding the reserve requirement are taken by the ECB Council.

[22] To give banks access to deposits with the ECB the latter could initially buy the appropriate amount of securities in the market. These securities could be denominated either in ecu, or in national currencies, provided the proportions of the different national currencies correspond to the ecu weights. Once the initial amount of federal funds has been created the ECB could regulate the total amount of federal funds in the system simply by additional open market purchases or sales.

monetary expansion in the domestic banking system by limiting the supply of reserve money. Figure 12.4.2 shows the organizational structure of such a system.

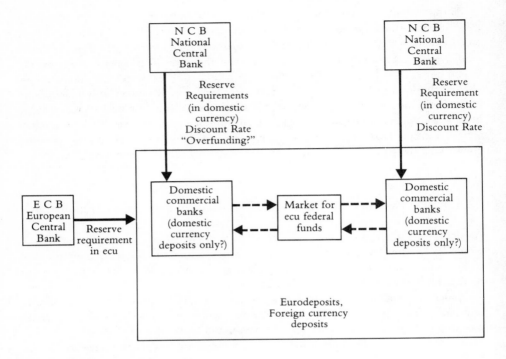

Figure 12.4.2. The 2-tier system

The reserve coefficient could be kept very low to minimize the tax it imposes on deposits within the Community. If the example of the US is a good guide a flat (average equal to marginal) reserve requirement of 1 per cent should not lead to a significant displacement of deposits (it would involve an interest rate loss of only 8 basis points at an interest rate of 8 per cent). But at the same time, given that the total commercial bank deposits in the Community amount to over 2,600 billion ecu, a 1 per cent reserve requirement would lead to total reserves of over 26 billion ecu, enough to provide a solid basis for a common monetary policy.[23]

Through its open market operations the ECB would be able to directly influence overall liquidity conditions in the system. If it makes an open market sale, reducing the

[23] The seigniorage the ECB would gain from a reserve coefficient of this order of magnitude would not be very large. If market interest rates are 8 per cent the ECB would earn about 2 billion ecu per annum on the 26 billion ecu of securities it can buy with the proceeds from the required reserves. For this reason the fiscal implications of required reserves are not stressed in this paper. For more details on this issue see Bruni (1990) and Gros (1990).

total amount available, commercial banks everywhere in the Community would tend to restrict their deposits because the interest rate on the federal funds market would rise. By limiting the total amount of federal funds that the ECB makes available to the system it would always be in a position to limit total liquidity creation.

This approach would be compatible with different operating procedures for the ECB. For example, it could choose an interest-rate target and restrict the supply of federal funds whenever the actual ecu or federal funds interest rate fell below the target and vice versa if interest rates go above the target. But it could also target the quantity of federal funds by not intervening in the federal funds market and letting the interest rate adjust to bring supply and demand into equilibrium.

Different operating procedures would presumably be appropriate for stages II and III, but the mechanism in itself would not have to be modified for the passage to stage III. The subsequent evolution of the system would then be gradual and could lead to a smooth passage to the final stage without additional substantial institutional changes.

After this presentation of the two possible ways in which reserve requirements could be used in stage II we now turn to a discussion of their advantages and disadvantages.[24]

12.4.3 A comparison of the two systems

A feature that is common to both systems is that they can only provide an *additional* anchor for the common monetary policy. In the present EMS the anchor is provided by a mixture of dominance of the strongest currency and informal coordination. The introduction of a system of required reserves can only put an upper limit on monetary expansion. It cannot become a constraint for any individual country (or even the average of all countries) wishing to implement a more restrictive policy.

One attraction – to the present authors – of the three-tier system is that it anticipates the hierarchical structure between the ECB and national central banks that will arise once full EMU has been reached. If the reserves are levied on the monetary base the reserve coefficient could be raised over time until it reaches 100 per cent. At this point national central banks would become the equivalent of wholly owned subsidiaries of the ECB (Bini-Smaghi (1990)).

A three-tier system would, however, have the disadvantage that it would not eliminate the under-reporting of the Community money supply that arises because national definitions of the main monetary aggregates often do not comprise foreign-currency deposits and almost never comprise cross-border deposits.[25] For

---

[24] Although it would not be impossible to combine the two systems it is useful to consider the problems that could arise if either system were implemented on its own. For more details see Gros (1990).

[25] The overall importance of under-reporting is difficult to estimate since no systematic data are available on the currency breakdown of foreign-currency deposits and of the country of origin of cross-border deposits. The scarce data available suggest that this phenomenon is not yet very important. However, it can only increase in importance with increasing integration in financial markets, becoming an important factor by the time stage II starts.

example, despite the Belgium–Luxembourg monetary union a deposit by a Belgian resident with a bank in Luxembourg is not counted in the Belgian monetary statistics because it is not with a Belgian bank, nor is such a deposit counted in Luxembourg because it is a deposit of a non-resident. Another example is the United Kingdom which uses explicitly the aggregate 'Sterling M4' excluding deposits in foreign currency. Imposing the reserve requirement directly on commercial banks could eliminate this issue and allow the ECB to control the total volume of liquid monetary assets that can be expected to finance expenditure within the Community.

A further disadvantage of a three-tier system (with reserves proportional to the national monetary base) is that it would have to deal with the implications of differences in national reserve requirements and thereby in national multipliers. This problem has two dimensions:

i) If there is a shift in the monetary base between countries with different multipliers the overall monetary aggregates would be affected: a shift from a country with a low multiplier (high reserve requirement) to a country with a high multiplier (low or no reserve requirement) would increase the total amount of deposits within the Community unless the ECB reacts to each such disturbance.

ii) National central banks could conduct an expansionary national monetary policy by reducing the domestic reserve requirements. In order to keep control over the Community total the ECB would again have to react to this development.

This suggests that a reserve requirement on the national monetary base would lead to difficulties unless national reserve requirements have already been harmonized. This is different under the two-tier system since the total of deposits in the entire Community cannot increase as long as the ECB does not increase its liabilities *vis-à-vis* commercial banks (i.e., as long as it does not supply more 'federal funds'). The two-tier system could therefore be implemented even before national reserve requirements have been harmonized.

The residual changes in exchange rates that are still possible in stage II are likely to pose another problem for a three-tier system because under this system the central bank of a currency that is depreciating would have excess reserves and would therefore be in a stronger position than the central bank of the currency that is appreciating.[26] This would not be a problem if one could rely on the emergence of a smoothly functioning market in these 'official reserve ecu'. But since central banks are not strictly profit maximizers and a small group among them would dominate this market it is not likely that a central bank that experiences an appreciation of its own currency would be able to buy the 'official reserve ecus' it needed.

In contrast, under the two-tier system, there would be a market among commercial banks that would redistribute the 'ecu federal funds' smoothly if exchange rates change (or if there is currency substitution).

---

[26] Gros (1991) shows that exchange-rate changes could also affect the overall demand of reserves because the ecu weights differ from the shares of the national monetary bases in the overall Community total. However, since this effect can be calculated mechanically it should not constitute a serious problem.

This market for the 'ecu federal funds' provides another argument for the two-tier system. Through its operations on this market the ECB would have, from the start, a direct contact with a Community-wide market working in ecu.[27] It would therefore immediately start to acquire the expertise that it will anyway need in stage III, when it acquires the exclusive responsibility for monetary policy, which will have to be executed in some Community-wide ecu market. The interest rate on the market for 'ecu federal funds' would also provide a convenient signal about the stance of the common monetary policy.

Finally, there seems to be no legal basis for the three-tier system. Art. 19 of the statute gives the ECB the power to impose reserve requirements on 'credit institutions' but not on national central banks. The ECB would therefore not be able to use sanctions to make sure that national central banks actually stay within the constraints imposed by the required reserves. In full EMU such compliance would anyway be assured by other means.

12.4.4 Concluding consideration about reserve requirements

This section has emphasized the potential usefulness of a system of reserve requirements to provide an anchor for the common monetary policy during the transition to full EMU. Since reserve requirements are a tax on deposits they are not the ideal instrument of monetary control in general, and, as the experience of countries without reserve requirements shows, this instrument is not indispensable for an effective monetary policy.[28] A sound monetary policy can also be based on the central bank's management of its supply of monetary base to meet demand from the public for cash and the demand from commercial banks for clearing balances with the central bank. However, this approach cannot be used as a base for a *common* monetary policy in stage II (probably even during stage III, i.e., before the introduction of a common currency) because cash would still be in national currency and because the clearing in national currencies would still be done at the national level so that clearing balances would be held with national central banks.

Imposing a small, uniform reserve requirement on all deposits held with commercial banks in the Community would give an emerging European monetary authority a convenient instrument with which it could always put an *upper limit* on total monetary expansion in the Community. The asymmetry in this system would provide a guarantee that it could never be used for a policy that is more expansionary than that of the most stability-orientated member.

Given the results at Maastricht with respect to the transition it is now obvious that reserve requirements are most unlikely to be applied in stage II, or in the early part of stage III, before introduction of the single currency when the instruments might also have made a useful contribution. With the 'indivisibility doctrine' of monetary policy

---

[27] See Steinherr (1990) for more suggestions about how to reinforce the role of the ecu in the transition.

[28] For survey see Bruni (1990).

accepted by a majority as the main guideline for the monetary control of stage II, the remaining case for using reserve requirements during the transition must clearly be reformulated. First, it must respect that the instrument could only be used by the EMI orchestrating voluntary and coordinated use by the national central banks; second, its eventual use must be based on forward-looking arguments, (to prepare through practical experience for stage III) rather than only on its capacity to contribute to better monetary coordination in the transition.

One of the central elements in the preparations for stage III – after Maastricht the main task for the EMI in the transition – will be to evaluate how the instrument of reserve requirements could be used after 1996 (or 1998). These reflections could hardly be pushed far without both the considerable reductions foreseen in the present divergent national use of the instrument *and* some experimentation as to how collective – though in stage II still necessary decentralized – use of the instrument could contribute to the evolution of a Community-wide Federal funds market in the future single currency. Such a market will be a cornerstone in a smooth start to stage III; without pushing it national money markets will retain their small peculiarities and a uniform policy will be hard to design early in stage III. This subject is taken up again in chapter 13.

Giving a spur to a Federal funds market in ecu through application of reserve requirements would also help the EMI discharge another task for which it has been given explicit responsibility: to promote the efficiency of cross-border payments (Art. 109 f (3)).

In summary, reasons remain why coordinated use of reserve requirements should still be considered part of the agenda for a stage II with a meaningful monetary content. The rationale is different from what the original proponents had anticipated and the application of the instrument will have to be voluntary rather than by a decision of the EMI Council.

12.5 The transition to stage III: how does stage II end?

The IGC on EMU had two principal tasks. The first was to define, as precisely as possible, how collective authority over economic policy will be exercised in the final stage. An elaborate legal and institutional framework for full monetary union and for the implementation of the non-monetary policies to accompany the irrevocable fixing of parities and subsequent rapid introduction of the single currency was the main result of Maastricht. The rationale for this part of the new Treaty on EMU was discussed in chapters 7 and 8: the former reviewed the main costs and benefits of monetary union while the latter looked at the case for mandatory constraints on excessive budget deficits, now incorporated in the new Treaty, as well as at the coordination of budgetary policies in EMU in general. Chapter 13 will review in some detail the structure, mandate and operations of the joint monetary institution, the ESCB, which will conduct the single monetary policy required in EMU.

The second task of the IGC was, however, no less essential: to clarify how a decision to end the transitional stage II could be taken. Having a fully worked-out blueprint for stage III is obviously important both in itself and as an inspiration during the transition. As already noted, once the final stage is clarified, national policy-makers should begin to behave voluntarily as if the provisions of the final stage were already in operation. But this view of the importance of the clarity and the attractiveness of stage III becomes overly idealistic if the timetable for arriving there is not well-defined. Prior to the final preparations for Maastricht there was no certainty at all about the timetable, and prominent officials admitted openly that full monetary union might be delayed indefinitely.

The transition from stage II to stage III had been the weak link in the procedure for arriving at EMU from the Delors Report onwards. The Report did not discuss any explicit time frame for the transition, but some of its recommendations for a gradual transfer of authority in stage II implied that stage II could be long and open-ended. The conclusions of the Rome European Council of October 1990, otherwise a bold attempt at upgrading the ambitions for beginning stage II early and at giving it a substantive monetary content, refrained from offering any guidance to the IGC as regards the procedures for putting an end to the transition. That work was only begun during the IGC, and the difficulties of reaching agreement between three different views of the road to monetary unification soon became apparent.

The first of these views, defended only by the United Kingdom, may be labelled *pragmatic*: monetary union may be desirable, but it is safer not to be committed to it, since much more experience needs to be accumulated to determine whether convergence has progressed sufficiently for it to become potentially desirable. This view could hardly be accommodated in a Treaty implying a passage to full EMU either by a fixed date or automatically on the fulfilment of pre-set criteria. It could only be accommodated by giving the country (or countries) subscribing to the pragmatic views the right to defer any decision on EMU. In this perspective, it is easy to understand the preference of the United Kingdom for the alternative procedure hinted at in the Delors Report (to make revisions to the EMU Treaty twice before entering into both stages II and III) rather than to make only one revision coupled with provisions enabling the European Council to decide on the second of these two moves.

An important part of the efforts at the IGC took the form of devising a procedure which could allow the United Kingdom to avoid commitment to EMU. Since no country wishes to be singled out for special treatment, but prefers to regard its own hesitations as being shared by others, the UK request was met in the text prepared by the Dutch Presidency in October 1991 by the inclusion of a generalized clause permitting all Member States only to opt into EMU when the conditions to enter the final stage and been found satisfactory by the European Council in late 1996. This general clause, however, proved unacceptable to a majority; in an ECOFIN meeting shortly before Maastricht, ten out of twelve Finance Ministers said their countries did not need it and wanted it removed from the Treaty itself. The United Kingdom (and Denmark) then had to accept that their concerns had to be dealt with in a separate Protocol, annexed to the Treaty.

The second identifiable view, defended in particular by Germany and the Netherlands, put the main emphasis on the conditions for entering full EMU. Provided tough criteria for nominal and real convergence, to be described below, can be met, this view admits a preference for going all the way to irrevocable locking of exchange rates and subsequently a single currency. But since it is not *a priori* possible to foresee when the convergence criteria will be met, this second view is opposed to a precise pre-set timetable for taking the decision to enter EMU. This German-Dutch view, which may be labelled *fundamentalist* because it stresses the importance of prior convergence of economic fundamentals, is consistent with the so-called 'economist' perception of the European integration process, articulated by the same two countries in the debate on the Werner Report of 1970, see Chapter 1.[29]

The third view was associated in the IGC with the position taken by Italy and, less forcefully, France. It emphasizes that convergence proceeds much faster once EMU has been achieved, or even planned with a definitive timetable. Market forces will then be harnessed to accelerate nominal convergence in goods markets as well as in financial markets, and the political readiness to take the tough adjustment measures required to meet the deadline will increase. This view, which may be labelled shock therapy or *telescopic*, because it relies on the catalytic effects of firm timetables, has recently also gained ground among many professional economists, earlier sceptical of rapid moves to monetary union. It is close to the so-called 'monetarist' perception of the European integration process, articulated in the early 1970s by the same two countries.

The outcome at Maastricht was a carefully constructed compromise between the second and the third view. The fundamentalist view found expression in the convergence criteria, the telescopic view the firm timetable for taking decisions to move to stage III, which has now made monetary union among some Member States of the Community a virtual certainty by the end of the present decade. A concession to the pragmatic view was finally made in the form of the separate Protocols which enable the United Kingdom and Denmark to defer their respective decisions on entering into full EMU until 1996. These three elements are reviewed below, beginning with the substance of the convergence criteria.

The Treaty lists in Article 109 j four criteria for evaluating convergence (see Appendix 1 to chapter 13): (1) a high degree of price stability; (2) sustainability of the government financial position; (3) observance of normal fluctuation margins in the EMS for a least two years without devaluation; and (4) evidence of durability of convergence reflected in long-term interest rates. Quantitative precision is given to all of these four criteria in a separate Protocol. The first criterion implies that a Member State has reached a rate of inflation, measured by consumer prices, over a period of one year before the examination at most 1.5 percentage points above, at most, the three best national performances. The formulation is not completely unequivocal, since it is not obvious whether the standard is the average of the best three performances or the inflation rate achieved by the third country in the ranking. The addition of the words 'at most' suggest that it will in normal circumstances be the latter interpretation that applies. The fourth criterion is defined similarly: to be ready for EMU a Member State

---

[29]. Some German observers have stressed that full monetary union should be seen as the crowning achievement of a long process of economic convergence. For an exposition of this 'coronation theory' see Kloten (1987).

should at most have an average long-term interest rate 200 basis points above the levels observed in, at most, the three countries with the best price performance (not with the three lowest interest rate levels).

The rationale for these two nominal criteria is straight-forward and they can be applied without entering into a broader political assessment of the national policies. The choice of figures is, however, unavoidably arbitrary; it is not possible to determine with precision what is the maximum inflation or interest-rate differential at entry to EMU which could quickly and without painful output and employment losses be squeezed out, once exchange rates are irrevocably fixed. Inflation differentials of 1–2 percentage points can be observed between regions of large Federal states for shorter periods of time and constitute no apparent threat to the cohesion of a currency area – provided the differentials do not persist over a long span of years. Interest-rate differentials between regions within a unified currency area obviously offer no similar point of reference. Anyway, this criterion of convergence, focusing on the longer-term credibility of inflation convergence and exchange-rate stability, must be seen as fairly loose; a country which is unable, on the eve of monetary union, to reduce the devaluation premium in its long-term interest rate below the maximum differential permitted would have a serious credibility problem. But perceptions in the financial markets as to the overall degree of preparedness for a country to enter EMU will play a major role in the importance of observed interest-rate differentials. A country which looks unlikely to have its credentials accepted in an overall assessment, notably because the ECOFIN Council may find its budget deficit 'excessive' will have an uphill fight in convincing financial markets to keep its long-term interest rate sufficiently in line. In this sense the criterion at the same time offers a strong incentive to a country to take its overall credentials beyond argument.[30]

The third criterion looks sensible at a time when the last realignment in the EMS before the Maastricht agreement is more than five years ago. Readiness to give, in the final two years prior to the entry into EMU, external consideration the highest priority in national monetary policy and to apply a judicious mixture of interventions, movements in the EMS fluctuation margins, and changes in short-term interest rates as agreed at Basle and Nyborg in 1987 would appear to offer a prediction of acceptance of a common monetary policy in stage III, particularly since that policy should be less painful to weaker currencies than during the transition. Although, as Kenen (1992) points out, past performance will not always be a good guide to future behaviour, since attitudes – and governments – may change, the exchange rate test seems well justified.

---

[30] The criterion of interest rate convergence could have been formulated in an analytically more satisfactory way by relying on the simple credibility test suggested by Svensson (1991), which takes into account the position of a currency in the EMS band. Assuming that the central rates towards the end of stage II will be the permanent exchange rates adopted for EMU, the position in the band implies a return to the centre of the band at the time of entry and hence expected appreciation and depreciation of particular currencies which should be taken into account in calculating open interest parity. Taking this as the starting point, probabilities of a realignment of a particular size, say corresponding to the width of the margins, can be calculated as a function of observed interest rate differentials. The exchange rate, or credibility, test would then say that only currencies for which that probability was below a very modest threshold would qualify for EMU.

The most controverisal criterion is the second one. The Delors Report was met with strong criticism for its insistence that mandatory upper limits should be imposed on measured national budget deficits of Member States participating in EMU. This criticism rested on economic analysis and political considerations. Most economists find such limits arbitrary and indefensible, once monetary union has been achieved, since participation in a single currency area will sharpen the perception of a long-term budget constraint for individual governments, no longer able to inflate their way out of large budget deficits and debt levels. Furthermore, some degree of national budget autonomy is seen by most economists as desirable in a monetary union in which some schocks may still affect individual Member States asymmetrically. These arguments were examined in chapter 8 which reached the conclusion that the substainability of a budgetary position is too difficult to assess theoretically and empirically – data inconsistencies appear to be very considerable – to justify the application of a precise quantitative criterion and the associated sanctions to assure compliance. At the same time upper limits to budget deficits are seen by most national policy-makers as a major infringement upon the decision-making process in national governments and parliaments[31], requiring a very precise justification and, even then, maximising the risk of conflict between collective judgments and the desire for national autonomy to as large an extent as possible, in accordance with the subsidiarity principle which is supposed to offer guidance to the degree of centralization to be aimed at in EMU. Finally, financial market specialists have argued that careful analysis by the financial institutions lending to sovereign debtors and by the credit-rating agencies on which they base their evaluation of creditworthiness, is well capable of enforcing the degree of prudent budgetary behaviour compatible with EMU. They have added, with support from economists, (see Begg *et al.* (1991)) that the necessary discipline might be reinforced by tightening prudential supervision, so that government debt is not automatically treated as safe assets in calculating the risk-weighted capital requirements of banks and other financial institutions under the new system of prudential control.

Despite this array of criticism of mandatory budgetary rules the new Treaty has incorporated a version of them which, taken at face value, is at least as strict as proposed in the Delors Rport. The Protocol on the convergence criteria states that criterion (2) is not met, if the Council has decided under Article 104c (6) that an 'excessive deficit' exists. Budgetary performance will be evaluated on the basis of reference values for the ratios of the planned (or actual) budget deficit, and of debt, to GDP; the values of these reference values are specified in a separate Protocol on the excessive deficit procedure as 3, respectively 60 per cent. With respect to both of these reference values, the decision (by qualified majority) of the ECOFIN Council remains judgemental, because the Council can decide that a deficit (or a debt level) which exceeds the reference value is not excessive, provided the deficit ratio has declined substantially and continuously to come close to the reference value, or is only exceptionally and temporarily in excess,

---

[31] By adopting a comprehensive definition of government, including regional and local authorities, the budgetary convergence criteria appear to oblige some central governments to tighten their controls over lower levels of government. This seems to be the case in Germany which has provided the Länder with an argument against the Treaty.

and the debt ratio is sufficiently diminishing and approaching the reference value at a satisfactory pace. The council will then decide after an overall assessment whether an excessive deficit exists.

Three elements appear particularly noteworthy in this elaborate formulation. The first is that **deficit** and *debt dynamics* will in practice be given greater weight than the levels. This brings the budgetary convergence criteria closer to what has been recommended by economists and financial market specialists. The second is that this criterion is the only one among the four for which a distinct overall judgement of the ECOFIN Council is required; with the other three criteria facts are assumed to be sufficiently clear to speak for themselves. The need for the Council to express itself explicitly on the excessiveness of a national budgetary deficit will, in the experience of the Community, imply a significant restraint on the number of occasions for this condition to be established. Third, the publication of the criteria by which budgetary performance are to be made will push private market participants into making an important part of the evaluation on behalf of the ECOFIN Council. If market opinion begins to regard a country as unlikely to meet the budgetary test the unfavourable evaluation will impinge on the performance of the country in question with respect to the three other, more objective, criteria: the national inflation rate will become more difficult to contain within the limits prescribed, tensions in the EMS are more likely to arise, and, above all, the differential of long-term interest rates will tend to rise.

It is an open question whether it is advisable for governments to leave to financial markets an evaluation which in part depends on information available only to governments, viz. the political readiness to accept countries in EMU before their credentials are established beyond doubt. It is, as Kenen (1992) argues, possible that the market view may be contaminated by biased forecasts about the intentions of governments, generating self-fulfilling prophecies out of these forecasts. But given the fact that governments have wanted to reserve judgement on a country's preparedness for EMU, the alternative to the Maastricht criteria would have been to leave the latter more open to a purely political evaluation; market participants would then have tried to interpret the likely outcome of the latter which could have been at least as destabilizing as the present situation in which there is at least an objective basis to start from.

Precision may still have been overdone in the reference values adopted, including the qualifications to them adopted at Maastricht. Any specific numerical value for the ratios of the deficits and debt to GDP may well be difficult to justify analytically, but the consequence of offering no quantitative precision whatsoever would have been to remove the strong incentive to aim for major improvement in budgetary performance now contained in the Treaty. The qualifications added to the reference values for the deficit and debt ratios at the same time assure that good progress in consolidation will be rewarded and temporary lapses will not be unduly punished. It is possible to see, for example, how the qualifying clauses could be made to fit, say, Belgium hopefully well into a process of debt reduction by 1995, but still a considerable distance from the 60 per cent ratio, or Germany in the present phase where the budget deficit has temporarily been allowed to rise above the 3 per cent level. As here interpreted, the essential purpose of the budgetary performance ratios is to give Member States maximum incentives for restoring budgetary prudence in the transition. Countries that have succeeded in this restoration will then have regained some budgetary autonomy for the final stage.

A discussion of how the present EC Member States are likely to come out of the examination based on the Maastricht criteria for convergence is postponed to chapter 14 which also presents a suggestive composite indicator, combining (1) and (2) and several other macroeconomic indicators, referred to more in passing in the new Treaty.

The demanding convergence criteria will form the basis for monitoring economic performance throughout stage II. From 1994 the EC Commission and the EMI will prepare regular reports to the ECOFIN Council on progress in convergence in terms of criteria (1)–(4). The reports will also monitor steps taken to make national central banks more independent, 'the development of the ecu, the results of the integration of markets, the situation and development of the balances of payments on current account and an examination of the development of unit labour costs and other price indices' (Art. 109 j (1)).

The ECOFIN Council shall then assess by a qualified majority vote on the basis of the two reports received, for each Member State whether the conditions for the adoption of a single currency are fulfilled and subsequently whether those who qualify constitute a (simple) majority of Member States. The recommendations of the ECOFIN Council will then be forwarded to the European Council.[32] Not later than 31 December 1996 – but conceivably before – the latter shall:

- decide, on the basis of the recommendation from the ECOFIN Council whether a majority of Member States fulfil the necessary conditions for the adoption of a single currency;
- decide whether it is appropriate for the Community to enter the third stage

and if so,

- set the date for the beginning of the third stage.

This agenda suggests that the European Council, even if a majority of countries are prepared, may find entry into the third stage premature. (If, for example, a minority of Member States are close to meeting the conditions and the majority wants to encourage them to sustain their efforts and catch up.) The European Council also has the option of setting a date well into the future. Despite these caveats it seems improbable that a starting date would not be set very soon after a positive verdict on the performance of a majority, if such a verdict were to be reached before the end of 1996.

An evaluation of the likely scenario in the light of the Maastricht compromise is further complicated by the difficulties of assessing what will be required to constitute a majority by 1996. By 1995 the Community is likely to have several new Member States. This would raise the simple majority from the present seven to at least eight by the time the decision to move to stage III has to be taken. The number required for a

---

[32] Or more correctly: 'the Council meeting in the composition of Heads of State or Government. The European Council includes the President of the EC Commission, and is not empowered to take decisions. Nevertheless, the shorter term 'European Council' is used in the following.

simple majority could rise further to nine, if Norway and Switzerland also decide to apply in the near future and in time to be admitted by 1995. It seems likely that this would ease the problem of finding a simple majority ready to enter into full EMU, since the degree of preparedness of the potential new members is currently higher than that of several present EC Member States.

The United Kingdom has chosen not to commit herself to entry into EMU, even if she proves economically ready to do so in the mid-90s. A separate Protocol makes it clear that the United Kingdom will only count in the number of Member States among which a majority is made up if a positive vote in the House of Commons has enabled the UK government to accept entry into stage III; such a vote has to take place before the discussion in the European Council, i.e. before the end of 1996. Denmark obtained in Maastricht a similar Protocol, recognizing that Denmark may need to hold a referendum prior to Danish participation in EMU; notification will have to be given, as in the UK case, prior to the decisive discussion in the European Council. Unless the notification is positive, Denmark too will not be included in the majority calculation. It is therefore possible that the majority will be reduced below the level referred to in the previous paragraph.

Whatever the estimate of the requirements for finding a majority, the new Treaty has added, following a last-minute initiative of France and Italy, a very significant procedural innovation which makes it a virtual certainty that some Member States, whether a majority is found or not, will enter the final stage of EMU not later than 1 January 1999. Article 109 j (4) foresees automatic participation on that date for Member States judged by a qualified majority in the European Council to have fulfilled the convergence criteria – provided, of course, that they have not explicitly reserved their position as the United Kingdom and Denmark may choose to continue to do. This second effort at determining which countries will be joining EMU – but no longer whether the latter should start or not – has to be made before 1 July 1998 in order to assure that the ECB will be fully operational and can take over from the EMI on 1 January 1999. The EMI will then be liquidated from the first day of stage III (Art. 109 l (2)). Countries that have not met the necessary conditions for participation by mid-1998 will be given a derogation, to be reviewed subsequently at least every two years. Chapter 13.4 returns to the status that these Member States would have in the ESCB and to the more general implications of variable geometry in EMU.

This modified procedure will viturally assure that full EMU starts, even if only a minority are ready for it. Theoretically it is conceivable that no country meets the budgetary criteria, but that would seem very unlikely. The other criteria are set in relative terms and hence could not exclude all countries. The formulation of the inflation and interest rate convergence criteria suggest that EMU might start with as few as three members, since the performance of the (at most) three most virtuous countries is taken as the benchmark. Although again this appears highly improbable, if the situation were to arise, Art. 109 l does not contain the general escape clause of Art. 109 j, permitting the European Council to find entry into EMU inappropriate.

The element of automaticity is accordingly very strong and the perception of this among policy-makers as well as market participants provides the main justification for the general conclusion above on the substance of stage II, viz. that the relative shortness of the transition and the virtual certainty of EMU for some by 1999 at the latest will necessarily cast a shadow over stage II and make it different and more ambitious than stage I.

This section has been careful in using the term 'virtual certainty' about the prospects for EMU, because it must be asked, despite the unambiguous language about the second effort at deciding on EMU, whether the whole project could still unfold. In principle, Member States could decide to renegotiate the EMU Treaty in 1996 when new or hitherto unresolved issues relating to political union presumably will anyway give rise to a new IGC. However, going back on the EMU Treaty so labouriously agreed at Maastricht would be a loss of momentum and prestige for European integration hard to imagine.

Recent German criticisms of the EMU Treaty have given rise to a more realistic type of fear, viz. that the German Bundestag and Bundesrat will only prove willing to ratify the present Treaty by entering conditions, which imply a new critical review of the EMU process in 1996. There is, however, a major difference between the present situation with hesitations on the part of German parliamentarians and the situation which would have existed if the admission of a general right of countries to defer their commitment to EMU had survived into the final text at Maastricht. German parliamentarians – and the Bundesbank – are now reminding their government that they will be looking attentively towards a rigorous application of the convergence criteria in 1996 (or 1998, at the latest), not that they will want to rewrite them. The Maastricht decisions were, as already noted, a careful compromise between the fundamentalist, convergence-first advocates and the proponents of a fixed timetable. It is not unnatural, and does not endanger the future process that each group attaches special importance to those elements in the compromise which most closely reflect their own position as long as there is no suggestion to upset the compromise itself.

The following chapter turns to an analysis of the central element to the final stage of EMU: the joint monetary policy and the institution which will implement it. Chapter 14 returns to a discussion of the transition and the complements to monetary union which critics, including he Bundesbank, regard as essential to make EMU work.

References

Begg, David et al (1991) Monitoring European Integration: the Making of Monetary Union, Centre for Economic Policy Research, London.

Batten, Dallas, Michael Blackwell, In-Su Kim, Simon Nocera and Yuzuru Ozeki (1990), 'The conduct of monetary policy in the major industrial countries: instruments and operating procedures', International Monetary Fund, Washington DC, Occasional Papers, 70, December.

Bini-Smaghi, Lorenzo (1990) 'Progressing towards European monetary unification: selected issues and proposals', Banca d'Italia, Rome, Temi di discussione del Servizio Studi, 133, April.

Bruni, Franco (1990) 'Il regime della riserva obbligatoria e l'integrazione Europea dei mercati finanziari', mimeo Univeristà Commerciale Luigi Bocconi, Milan, November.

Ciampi, Carlo (1989), 'An operational framework for an integrated monetary policy in Europe', in collection of papers annexed to Delors Report, 225–32.

Committee for the Monetary Union of Europe (1988), 'A programme for action', Crédit National, Paris.

Committee for the Monetary Union of Europe (1991), 'The economic and monetary union: the political dimension', Crédit National, Paris.

Committee for the Study of Economic and Monetary Union (1989), 'Report on Economic and Monetary Union in the European Community' (the Delors Report), Office of Publications of the European Communities, Luxembourg.

Conclusions of the Presidency, Rome, 28 October 1990.

Conference of the Representatives of the Governments of the Member States (1992), *Treaty on European Union*, CONF-UP-UEM 2002/92, Brussels ('Maastricht Treaty' signed on 7 February 1992).

De Larosière, Jacques (1989), 'First stages towards the creation of a European Reserve Bank – the creation of a European Reserve Fund', in collection of papers annexed to Delors Report, 177–84.

Giavazzi, Francesco and Luigi Spaventa (1990), 'The "new" EMS', chapter 4 in Paul De Grauwe and Lucas Papademos (eds.), *The European Monetary System in the 1990's*, Longman, 65–84.

Goodhart, Charles (1989), 'The Delors Report: was Lawson's reaction justifiable?'. Special paper 15, Financial Markets Group, London School of Economics.

Gros, Daniel (1990), 'The Ecu in the common monetary policy', *ECU Newsletter*, 32, April: 14–19.

Gros, Daniel (1991), 'Towards a common monetary policy in the transition: the role of the Ecu and required reserves', Centre for European Policy Studies, Brussels, *CEPS Working Document (Economic)*, 54.

HM Treasury (1989), 'An evolutionary approach to Economic and Monetary Union', London, November.

HM Treasury (1991), 'Economic and monetary union beyond stage I. Possible treaty provisions and statute for a European Monetary Fund', London, January.

Kenen, Peter B (1992), 'EMU after Maastricht', Group of Thirty, Washington D.C., Occasional Papers No. 36.

Kloten, Norbert (1987) 'Die Ecu: Perspektiven monetärer Integration in Europa', *Zeitschrift für Internationale Politik*, vol. 15, 451–66.

Kneeshaw, John T. and Paul van den Bergh (1989), 'Changes in central bank money market operating procedures in the 1980s', Bank for International Settlements, *Economic Papers*, 23, January.

Lamfalussy, Alexandre (1989), 'A proposal for stage two under which monetary policy operations would be centralized in a jointly-owned subsidiary', in collection of papers annexed to Delors Report, August: 213–19.

Leijonhufvud, Axel (1983), 'Constitutional constraints on the monetary powers of government', chapter 6 in James A. Dorn and Anna J. Schwartz (eds.), *In Search of Stable Money*, University of Chicago Press, Chicago, 129–43.

Matthes, Heinrich (1988), 'Entwicklung des EWS mit Blick auf 1992', in D. Duwendag (ed.), *Europa Banking*, Baden-Baden.

Ministerio de Economia y Hacienda (1991), 'The ECU and the ESCB during Stage II', Madrid, January.

Padoa-Schioppa, Tommaso (1988), 'The European Monetary System: a long-term view', chapter 12 in Francesco Giavazzi, Stefano Micossi and Marcus Miller (eds.), *The European Monetary System*, Banca d'Italia, Centro Interuniversitario di Studi Teorici per la Politica Economica and Centre for Economic Policy Research, Cambridge University Press, Cambridge, 369–83.

Pöhl, Karl Otto (1989), 'The Further Development of the European Monetary System', in collection of papers annexed to Delors Report, Office of Publications of the European Communities, Luxembourg, September: 131–55.

Russo, Massimo and Giuseppe Tullio (1988), 'Monetary policy coordination within the European Monetary System: is there a rule?', chapter 11 in Francesco Giavazzi, Stefano Micossi and Marcus Miller (eds.), *The European Monetary System*, Banca d'Italia, Centro Interuniversitario di Studi Teorici par la Politica Economica and Centre for Economic Policy Research, Cambridge University Press, Cambridge, 292–320.

Szasz, Andre (1990), Comment on paper 'Institutional development of the EMS', by Niels Thygesen, in Paul De Grauwe and Lucas Papademos (eds.), *The European Monetary System in the 1990's*, Longman, 26–8.

Steinherr, Alfred (1990), 'Roles for the ECU in the process of achieving European Monetary Union', mimeo, European Investment Bank, Luxembourg.

Thygesen, Niels (1989), 'A European central banking system – some analytical and operational considerations', in collection of papers annexed to Delors Report, Office of Publications of the European Communities, Luxembourg, September: 157–76.

Walters, Alan (1986), *Britain's Economic Renaissance*, Macmillan, London

CHAPTER 13

THE EUROPEAN SYSTEM OF CENTRAL BANKS AND PRICE STABILITY

This chapter describes the organizational structure of the institution that will be responsible for maintaining price stability for the Community once EMU has been reached. The Delors Report proposed to call this institution the 'European System of Central Banks'. This name seems indeed appropriate for a system that consists of a central institution (the European Central Bank) and the existing national central banks which will continue to operate as part of the system even after EMU has been reached.

The central bank governors agreed on most major points of a Draft Statute for the European System of Central Banks before the conference itself was officially opened in December 1990. This draft was subsequently endorsed at the political level and has since become a Protocol annexed to the new Treaty produced by the Intergovernmental Conference (IGC) on EMU, many of its provisions being also taken up in the revised Treaty text itself. This chapter therefore starts, in section 1 below, with a description of the statute of the European System of Central Banks, concentrating on its central component: the European Central Bank.

Aside from the necessary organizational details these statutes contain two crucial general prescriptions. The first is the requirement that the European System of Central Banks should aim at price stability and the second is that it should be independent. These two elements will determine the quality of the monetary policy of the Community, they are therefore important enough to merit some further discussion. This is done in sections 2 and 3.

Section 2 interprets the emphasis given to price stability not only as a political choice, but also as a theoretically optimal guideline for macroeconomic policy. Section 3 – besides discussing how price stability should be defined in practice – argues that independence is a necessary condition for a consistent and credible anti- inflationary monetary policy and discusses any potential conflict between independence and accountability. Finally, section 4 discusses briefly the status of those EC Member States that have not been ready or willing to join full EMU, i.e. 'variable geometry' in the final stage, and some issues relating to the introduction of the single currency as soon as possible after exchange rates among the participants have become irrevocably fixed.

Appendix 1 brings the text of those Articles in the revised Treaty which refer to EMU and to the ESCB. As in chapter 12 all references to the revised Treaty are to the text signed at Maastricht on 7 February 1992.

Appendix 2 to this chapter reproduces the Protocol on the Statute of the European System of Central Banks proposed by the Committee of Governors in November 1990, as revised and completed in minor ways in the course of the IGC.

Finally, Appendix 3 reproduces parts of the Protocol on the Statute of the European Monetary Institute, the tasks of which were reviewed in chapter 12.

13.1 The European System of Central Banks: organization and statutes

The Committee of EC Central Bank Governors submitted just prior to the opening of the Intergovernmental Conference on EMU in December 1990 an elaborate draft statute for the European System of Central Banks (henceforth ESCB).[1] The draft addresses only the final stage of EMU, hence leaving out the arrangements for the transitional stage, the proposals were discussed in chapter 12. The Governor of the Bank of England indicated that the UK authorities were unable to accept the imposition of a single currency and monetary policy; however, one may interpret the participation of the Governor in the preparation of this vital aspect of the final stage as indicating agreement that if there is, nevertheless, a political decision to move to full EMU by the United Kingdom in the mid-1990s, the Statute represents also the UK view as to how the common policy framework should be designed.[2]

The present chapter looks at four main elements:

(1) the organization and governing bodies of the ESCB, including the degree of centralization of operations,

(2) the mandate for monetary policy,

(3) the degree of independence *vis-à-vis* national and EC political authorities and

(4) the accountability of the ESCB to the European Council, the ECOFIN Council and the European Parliament.

In the following section we discuss the first point on the basis of the final Statute. We turn in sections 2 and 3 to some of the analytical and empirical issues relevant to an assessment of (2)–(4).

---

[1] See Committee of Governors of the Central Banks of the Member States of the European Economic Community (1990). The draft statute is the main example that the IGC on EMU was indeed convened following 'full and adequate' preparation, as requested by the Madrid European Council of June 1989.

[2] Annexing the full list of the Statute to the Treaty as a protocol gives the Statute the status of primary EC law and makes any future revision of it – with minor exceptions to retain minimal flexibility – subject to the complex process of Treaty revision according to Article 236.

13.1.1 Organization and governing bodies

The ESCB will consist of a central institution, the European Central Bank (ECB) and the national central banks of EC Member States who have joined the final stage (Art. 1). The Statute confirms the restrictive view of 'participation' of the Delors Report (para. 44), *viz.* that 'influence on the management of each set of arrangements would have to be related to the degree of participation by the member states'. Central Bankers from EC countries which have not entered the final stage of EMU will not take part in the joint decisions in the Governing Council of the ECB.[3] Art. 109k of the Treaty states, in case of non-qualification of some member states in the final stage of EMU, that voting rights for the representatives of the central bank governors concerned on the ESCB Council be suspended. They will, however, have a seat on the ECB General Council.

The ECB will have two governing bodies: the Executive Board and the Governing Council. The *Executive Board* will have six members: a President, a Vice President and four other members (Art. 11). The Board members will be nominated by the European Council for a period of eight years, not renewable, after the Council has given its opinion, and after consultations with the European Parliament and the Governing Council of the ECB.

The *Governing Council* (Art. 10) will comprise the six members constituting the Executive Board and the governors of the national central banks (Art. 10). The terms of office shall be no less than five years. (Art. 14.2). All members of Council will have one vote (Art. 10.2).[4]

These provisions are remarkable in several respects. Acceptance of the one-man-one-vote principle must be seen as an important concession by Germany (and to a smaller extent by other large member states). It has been obtained in return for the explicit mandate to preserve price stability and the high degree of independence for the ESCB to be discussed below. Together with assured long periods of tenure, and the proposal to consult the ECB Governing Council on nominations for the Executive Board the voting rule should assure that the decisive policy-making body develops a high degree of cohesiveness and collegiality. Weighted voting could have fostered the thinking that governors were primarily representing national interests and not equal members of a collegiate body charged with formulating a common policy. Alliances of a few large member states could then *de facto* have come to dominate decision-making; and it would have been difficult to assure a proper role for the European-nominated members of the Board in the deliberations of the Governing Council.

As regards the division of responsibilities between the Governing Council and the

---

[3] We saw in Chapter 1 that some EC Member States have at times participated in some aspects of the EMS, e.g. the ecu basket, transfer of reserves. However, as long as they do not participate in the exchange-rate mechanism (ERM) their representatives cannot take an active part in realignments. An additional issue that arises for the ESCB is whether nationals of those countries that do not participate in the final stage would be eligible for the Executive Board.

[4] This principle does not apply to voting on financial matters (distribution of profits and loss) for which a special key, based on objective criteria, will be set and revised every five or ten years (Art. 28).

Executive Board, the Statute vests the main authority in the former: 'The Governing Council shall formulate the monetary policy of the Community including, as appropriate, decisions relating to intermediate monetary objectives, key interest rates and the supply of reserves in the system, and shall establish the necessary guidelines for their implementation' (Art. 12.1). There was some disagreement as to the extention of operational responsibilities. The retained formulation, close to what had been proposed by the Bundesbank, is: 'The Executive Board shall implement monetary policy in accordance with the decisions and guidelines laid down by the Governing Council'; some other participants had preferred more limited and, in principle, revocable delegation. The difference may in practice be limited, since policy could hardly be set in sufficient detail by a Council likely to meet only on a monthly basis, like the present Committee of Central Bank Governors.

An intensive discussion did take place on the division of responsibilities for implementing policies between the ECB and the participating national central banks. The present formulation leaves no doubt as to the hierarchical nature of the system. The Executive Board implements policy 'including by giving the necessary instructions to national central banks' (Art. 12.1). But as regards the practical execution of policies:

> To the extent deemed possible and appropriate and without prejudice to the provisions of this Article (i.e. the capacity to give instructions), the ECB shall have recourse to the national central banks to carry out operations which form part of the tasks of the ESCB.

Some central banks had aimed for more decentralization than this wording suggests and an alternative proposal was for the ECB Executive Board to delegate to national central banks 'to the full extent possible'. It is important to discuss why this formulation was not adopted and why the drafters of the Statute in the end opted for a more centralized mode of operation. They were rightly concerned about the potential weakness of the central institution and its Executive Board, the members of which are clearly in a minority in the Council and its implications for the efficiency of operations. In this respect it is useful to refer to the experience of monetary policy execution in the two large federal countries – the United States and Germany – whose central banking legislation has, in a number of respects inspired the Statute.[5]

The ECB Board members will have six votes out of a total number of votes in the Governing Council of, initially, between thirteen (if only the minimal number of seven member states foreseen in the Treaty find themselves ready and willing to enter the final stage of EMU) and eighteen if all member states join the final stage. That latter number will rise further, as EC membership widens. This minority position resembles that of the Bundesbank Board (Direktorium) with seven members in its Council (Rat) of a

---

[5] Earlier publications by the present authors have analysed at greater length the experience of monetary policy formulation and execution in the United States and its potential lessons for Europe, see Thygesen (1989) and Gros and Thygesen (1988). Louis *et al.* (1989) contains a more detailed assessment of the division of responsibility in the Federal Reserved System.

total of eighteen members.[6] However, all significant monetary policy operations are centralized in Frankfurt which makes up for any perception of weakness at the centre.

In the United States, the Federal Open Market Committee (FOMC) which meets every five to six weeks has functions anologous to those envisaged for the ECB Governing Council in setting monetary objectives and in formulating guidelines for the main policy instrument, open market operations, to be undertaken through the Federal Reserve Bank of New York. The FOMC meetings are attended by the seven members of the Board of Governors, nominated by the President of the United States, subject to confirmation by the US Senate, and the twelve Presidents of the regional Federal Reserve Banks. Out of the latter only five have the right to vote at any one meeting, so the majority lies with the Board – provided they agree, obviously. The central position of the Board is further underlined by the attribution to it alone of two important policy instruments: discount rate changes and variations in reserve requirements. The Board of Governors accordingly has a dominant influence both on decisions and on implementation of policy.

A first comparison of the ESCB (as it is emerging from the drawing board) with either of the two main federal models – the Deutsche Bundesbank and the Federal Reserve System – in their present form must arrive at the conclusion that the ECB Executive Board is likely to have a relatively weaker position with respect to both decision-making and policy implementation than its German or US counterparts. The Board will be squeezed from one side by the Governing Council, the repository of all major policy-making authority, and from the other side by the participating national central banks, anxious to preserve as many operational tasks as possible, partly to retain influence for themselves, partly to defend the perceived interests of their employees. The national governors will argue, on the basis of the principle of subsidiarity, that they can implement policy at least as efficiently as a new and inexperienced operational centre at the ECB under the daily management of the Board. The degree of inexperience will be more evident the less the EMI is allowed to do in the transitional stage.

Since only a minimalist version of stage II, as discussed in chapter 12, is to be implemented, allowing only very limited direct contact with foreign exchange and domestic money markets in the participating countries prior to the start of the final stage, the governors may be able to argue convincingly that policy implementation should best be left in 'their' hands for some time after the start of the final stage.

Could an ambition to decentralize policy implementation 'to the full extent possible' become dangerous as long as decision-making remained centralized in the ECB Governing Council? It might not, but the experience of the Federal Reserve

---

[6] This was the position prior to enlargement when five new Länder joined. There is currently discussion in the Bundesbank and in German political circles whether some merging of Landeszentralbanken is advisable in view of the accession of the five Länder of the former German Democratic Republic. The German government has recently proposed that the sixteen members representing Länder be reduced to nine, going almost as far in merging representation as proposed by the Direktorium. It is presently unclear whether the government's proposal will be accepted by the Bundestag and the Bundesrat.

System in the first two decades of its existence suggests there are dangers inherent in such a formula.

When adopting the Federal Reserve Act in 1913, the US Congress aimed to give maximum emphasis to decentralization and flexibility. Illusions were no doubt more widespread in the United States at the time than is currently the case in the EMS countries, that it would be feasible, even within a single-currency area, to conduct a monetary policy with some elements of regional differentiation to allow for economic divergence. The role of the Board of Governors of the Federal Reserve System was initially to supervise the Reserve Banks and 'to review and determine' their discount rates and lending 'with a view to accommodating commerce and business'. The possibility that discount rates might differ between districts was envisaged, and the authority of the Board to impose a common level was ambiguous, though it was clarified in the course of the 1920s that the Board did have the decisive role. The Board was, in addition, weakened by the collective influence of the twelve Federal Reserve Bank presidents, meeting quarterly in an advisory capacity, and by the dominant international role assumed by the regional bank in the major financial centre, the New York Fed, under its first president, Benjamin Strong. It is not difficult to see fairly close analogies in this early US experience to what could happen in the early years of EMU, if a strong ambition to decentralize policy implementation prevails. The risks of indecision and slow, differentiated responses are magnified in the ESCB when it is recalled that the final stage of EMU will start without a single currency – it may take a few years to have the latter replace the national currencies – and from a long tradition of national monetary management by methods that are not closely harmonized and from the insistence, right up to the starting line of the final stage of EMU, on the notion of indivisibility of monetary authority which was critically reviewed in chapter 12.

In this perspective it becomes important to look for any detailed provisions in the ESCB Statute which could limit the potential for inefficiency and efforts at differentiation. Such provisions relate to possible financial and other incentives for the participating central banks to retain operations in their financial markets and/or to differentiate them from a joint policy and to manage their residual foreign exchange reserves with some independence.

The Statute, despite its detailed nature, is not sufficiently specific to permit a verdict. The requirement to draw up a consolidated balance sheet for the ESCB (Art. 26.3) and the presence of Art. 32, on the distribution of income of the ESCB among the shareholders, i.e., the national central banks, shows that the drafters were aware of the need to remove outright incentives for individual central banks to retain operating profits for themselves. All profits and losses which accrue in a year as a result of operations undertaken to implement a jointly decided policy will accrue to the ESCB and not to the individual national central bank performing the operations. It will make no difference to the total profits (or seigniorage) available at the year's end for distribution to the shareholders whether only, say, the Bank of England and the Bundesbank have been undertaking foreign exchange interventions in third currencies, whether they have been more widely decentralized or to some exent undertaken directly by the Board through the ECB. Incentives to retain operations in the national financial centres, arising from the desire to protect the employment of specialized staff in the central banks and to extend favours to the private financial institutions in a particular country, would remain. If these institutions can only keep accounts with the central bank of their own country of origin – in analogy to access to Federal Reserve credit only through the regional Reserve bank in one's own district – and the timing of additions to or withdrawals from bank reserves were left to some extent to the discretion of the individual central banks, risks of favouritism extended by the latter would arise, even if they had no financial consequences for the central bank concerned.

One could easily imagine that a national central bank anticipating a rise in interest rates in the area as a whole would advance the execution of a liquidity injection, for example through a one-month purchase/resale transaction with its commercial banks, hence effectively providing the latter cheaper credit than banks in other participating countries. Centralization of authority in the Executive Board to monitor and contain such departures from uniformity of policy is important in assuring the application of a homogeneous policy – 'the indivisibility of monetary authority', so strongly aspired to in the transition to EMU by many of the central bankers. Clarification of these potentially important operational issues may not come until the implementation of the final stage approaches and after some experience of harmonizing the methods of coordinating domestic money market operations on a voluntary basis has been gained.

It should be easier to gain acceptance for the view that both decision-making and implementation of policy should be centralized with respect to foreign exchange operations. In full EMU, even before the single currency has replaced national currencies, efficient markets will impose uniformity of movements vis-à-vis the dollar and other third currencies. It is usually seen as an important potential advantage of EMU to the participants that they will be able to manage with a much lower level of aggregate international reserves. They will no longer need to hold reserves in other EMS currencies or in ecu at all (or to have access to the Very Short Term Facility in the EMCF) because there will be no intra-EMU exchange rates to defend and collectively they should need fewer reserves to achieve any given result other than the sum of current individual holdings – provided of course that foreign exchange interventions are centralized in EMU.

A priori one might have thought that the full and definitive transfer of ownership of all international reserve assets, excluding holdings of EMS currencies and ecu, from the national level to the ECB would have been a logical step to take to mark the irrevocable nature of the final stage. A country which had transferred all means of defending its exchange rate to the ECB would clearly be seen as a credible member of EMU. This is at the same time an explanation why such a step is not contemplated; member states are not prepared to face the implications or to negotiate dissolution provisions in case one or more member states want to leave.[7]

---

[7] The Bank of England has objected to the transfer of ownership of reserves to the ECB and considers an agreement to put a predetermined amount of reserves at joint disposal as sufficient. A further complication in the UK – and some other cases – is that the central bank does not own international reserves assets, but would have to have ownership transferred to it from the government prior to participation in pooling.

There is also a more immediate reason why full pooling is unrealistic. The level and the composition of reserves both vary widely among the potential member states. Excluding gold (which can no longer be regarded as usable), IMF reserve positions and SDRs, foreign exchange reserves of the member states are currently (1991) somewhat in excess of ecu 200 billion. The shares of individual countries in this total do not always reflect their relative economic size as expressed, for example, by GDP weights in the Community. The reserve shares of Italy and Spain which have been facing very large capital inflows in the late 1980s are in excess of their GDP weights, those of Germany and the Benelux countries are below. Less information is publicly available on reserve composition, but the apparent similarity of behaviour of countries is, in this respect, even weaker. Germany holds reserves almost exclusively in non-EC currencies, while several others hold only 30–50 per cent in that form. For the EC as a whole non-EC foreign exchange reserves amounted to approximately ecu 120 billion (or 60 per cent of total currency reserves) in early 1990. If pooling in the ECB were to use the existing distribution of holdings of non-EC currencies, the contribution of Germany (and a few others) would be disproportionately high – far removed from GDP weights. This would be hard to reconcile with joint decision-making over the pooled reserves.

The Statute (Art. 30) therefore opts for a different model: national central banks are to endow the ECB with non-EC currency reserves up to ecu 50 billion; the key for contributions will be based on that for capital subscriptions, viz. weights determined equally by the national shares in EC population and GDP (Art.29.1). Capital subscriptions could then be made in the form of transferring international reserve assets. But the formula leaves two questions open: (1) How can the target level for reserves pooled in the ECB be set? (2) What constraints should be put on the use of reserves which remain in national hands?

How high must the target be set to assure the efficiency and credibility of the new system? That depends on the nature of the commitments entered into by the authorities of EMU *vis-à-vis* those responsible for managing the other main world currencies.[8] The less the reliance envisaged on interventions in the future international monetary regime, the smaller the need for reserves. The closer one moves to a system of target zones where interventions have to be relied upon at times, the higher the desired level of reserves. Present reserve levels, after several years of substantial net accumulation of dollars, during the long, though irregular, decline of the US currency *vis-à-vis* the EMS currencies, appear well above what could be required for interventions. But by how much?

In the absence of a concise answer from the perspective of the likely demand for reserves in EMU, one may approach the issue from the side of the supply constraint that will arise as member states are asked to transfer reserves to the ECB according to a key reflecting their relative size as measured by population and GDP. Assume for concreteness that GDP in 1989 is used as a key. One may then ask the question: how

---

[8] Note that the level of temporary transfers to the EMCF of 20 per cent of gold and dollar reserves of EMS participants was chosen in 1978 without analysis – probably the mobilization of gold reserves was the main motive – and should in any case, if it were to reflect reserves needed for intervention, have been revised during the life of the EMS to reflect larger potential capital flows.

high could the target for pooled reserves be set without obliging a member state to transfer more non-EC currency reserves to the ECB than its present reserve holdings? The calculations in table 13.1.1 suggest that such a figure would be around ecu 40 billion, or one third of present aggregate reserves in that form. At such a level French transfers of dollar and third currency reserves would roughly match France's currently held reserves, while other member states would still hold about ecu 80 billion in aggregate 'excess' dollar (and other non-EC currency) reserves, with a very uneven distribution between them; Germany would hold nearly half.

Table 13.1.1   Foreign Exchange Reserves in Non-EC Currencies: Actual and Hypothetical Pooling in ECB (bill ecu)

	Actual[a]	*Hypothetical pooling*[b]	*Memo GDP– weight, per cent*
Belgium/Luxembourg	3.6	1.3	3.16
Denmark	4.3	0.9	2.18
Germany	46.8	9.9	24.67
Greece	0.6	0.5	1.13
Spain	15.8	3.1	7.78
France	7.6	7.9	19.72
Ireland	1.5	0.3	0.70
Italy	10.3	7.2	17.90
Netherlands	7.0	1.9	4.66
Portugal	4.1	0.4	0.94
United Kingdom	17.4	6.9	17.16
Total	119.1	40.3	100.00

Notes:
[a] End of first quarter 1990.
[b] Assuming total pooling of ecu 40 billion based on 1989-GDP weights as indicated in column 3.

However, the second question posed becomes important if ecu 40 billion – not far below the maximum of the ecu 50 billion set in the ESCB Statute – were indeed to be adopted as the target for pooled reserves, because it meets any likely reserve use for interventions and observes the constraint that pooling should not first oblige one or more Member States first to acquire the reserves to be transferred. Should any rules be laid down for the disposal or conversion of the excess reserves in dollars? Article 31.2 states that operations in such assets 'shall be subject to approval by the ECB in order to ensure consistency with the exchange rate and monetary policies of the Community'. This may be a sufficiently clear guideline to avoid outright challenges to the authority of the new monetary institution. However, the greater visibility of the 'excess' reserves at the time of partial pooling into the ECB may make additional initiatives necessary. It should be made clear that these reserve assets are henceforth to be regarded as long-term investments in the currencies concerned rather than as an 'overhang', the disposal of which poses threats of instability and of downward pressure on non-EC currencies.

The EMS does not have a record of monitoring closely through the Committee of Governors the management of foreign reserves by its participants apart from outright interventions. The ECB Council will need to do better in an EMU in which, according to the present interpretation of the arrangements envisaged, as much as two thirds of international reserves will still be held nationally. As was the case for open market and other 'domestic' operations, the formulations in the Statute with respect to external operations suggest an insufficient centralization of authority in the ECB. The participants in EMU take risks by not going far enough in pooling their international reserves.

With respect to some important tasks to be performed by the ECB, and not strictly related to monetary policy, it is easier to reconcile the efficiency of operations and the ambition to decentralize. Art. 3 of the statute mentions as the final task of the ESCB that it should 'contribute to the smooth conduct of policies pursued by the competent authorities relating to the prudential supervision of credit institutions and the stability of the financial system'. National central banks start with a clear comparative advantage over the ECB and its Board with respect to familiarity with the financial institutions in their territory, particularly to the extent that they already exercise supervisory functions nationally. Not all do, however – in Belgium, Denmark and Germany supervisory authority is vested in a separate government agency and not in the central bank – and there is disagreement between, say, the UK and German authorities as to the desirable degree of responsibility for financial stability to be exercised by a central bank mandated to pursue a monetary policy oriented towards low inflation. A potential conflict between the execution of these two tasks exists if a central bank is seen to be generous in its efforts to prevent financial instability by injecting additional liquidity. Yet all potential participants exercise some lender-of-last-resort function and that could hardly be performed in a fully centralized way. Nor is that the case in existing Federal systems such as in the United States. Some discretion within pre-specified limits would have to be left with the individual participating central banks.

This discussion of the organizational and operational aspects of the proposed ESCB underlines a concern. Despite the, in most respects, clear and detailed provisions in the ESCB Statute, several ambiguities remain. Maybe it is not possible to clarify *a priori* working relationships between the Governing Council, the Executive Board and the participating national central banks. A formula of centralization of decision-making in the Council, delegation of implementation to the Board and some decentralization of operations to the national central banks is appealing as an application of the principle of subsidiarity. It reconciles wide participation in decisions and execution with operational efficiency. Yet some doubt may still be legitimate whether the former has been given too much emphasis relative to the latter. This concern is heightened when it is recalled that the model of the final stage is also the guideline for efforts in the transition.

With time the ESCB will no doubt become cohesive and centralized, as authority and operational experience gravitates towards the centre. It may not, given the high degree of financial integration which already exists in the area of the potential participants, take two decades or more, as was the case in the United States, to settle down to a system which is both representative of regional views and efficient.

There should be efficiency gains to be reaped from a process of centralization and specialization of central banking tasks. Some of these gains are related to the responsibility of the ESCB for fostering uniformity in money market conditions throughout the Community and in ensuring smooth payments and clearing systems at low cost. The Committee of Governors is already beginning to pay considerable attention to this area through a new sub-committee. These efficiency gains are integral parts of the benefits of establishing a single-currency area which was reviewed in chapter 7. But there should also be longer-term cost savings inherent in centralization for the central banks themselves.

The EC central banks currently have some 60,000 employees; the total wage and salary bill may be close to ecu 2 billion. Running Europe's monetary systems is a relatively labour-intensive industry; total employment in the Federal Reserve System which performs similar tasks, including supervisory and reporting functions, to those to be assigned to the ECB and the national central banks in a future EMU is less than half this number. Some European central banks operate in a highly decentralized way; both the Bundesbank and Banque de France have more than 200 branches or sub-offices. While private financial institutions undergo rapid restructuring, and mergers are common regardless of size of the partners, central banks appear to modify their operations much more slowly. Decentralization within countries has, as for local and regional public administrations, encountered resistance to change, particularly to the extent that employment is at stake.

National central banks are difficult to compare. Differences in geography, financial structure and historically inherited tasks can explain some of the striking differences in staffing. For example, some undertake extensive printing activities beyond those related to the note issue; others – of which the largest central bank, Banque de France, with 17,000 employers is the prime example – are heavily involved in the production of economic statistics, the analysis of company financial statements, etc. Some of these additional activities might be only marginally affected by the move to a single currency and the evolution of the ESCB. Yet the centralization of monetary authority provides an occasion for the governing bodies of the national central banks to look critically at their own use of resources and to break the inertia of their past practices. The ECB itself should avoid a repetition of the national experience of many of its participants of excessive decentralization of technical, labour-intensive functions, such as the distribution of means of payments and rediscount operations with localized collateral. The cost savings may be small in the overall picture of the implications of monetary union given in chapter 7, but they are not negligible.

The future performance of the ECB will not be determined primarily by its organizational structure and its mode of operation, however important these dimensions are. More essential is the general mandate for the monetary policy to be pursued by the new institution and the latter's relationship to the political authorities, summarized under the headings of independence and accountability. The next two sections take up these issues.

13.2 The cost of inflation: price stability as the primary objective

Art. 2 of the Statute states:

> In accordance with Article 105(1) of this Treaty, the primary objective of the ESCB shall be to maintain price stability. Without prejudice to the objective of price stability, it shall support the general economic policies in the Community with a view to contributing to the achievement of the objectives of the Community as laid down in Article 2 of this Treaty. The ESCB shall act in accordance with the principle of an open market economy with free competition, favouring an efficient allocation of resources, and in compliance with the principles set out in Article 3a of this Treaty.

This formulation is repeated in Art. 3a of the Maastricht Treaty. It is close to what was proposed as the mandate for the ESCB in the Delors Report (para. 32) and is remarkably clear as a political agreement. The wording is less ambiguous than that of the Bundesbank Act of 1957, which defines the main responsibility of the German central bank to be 'the safe-guarding of the value of the currency' (Art. 3), while 'the (Bundes)bank should support the economic policy of the government, but can not be subjected to instructions by the latter' (Art. 12). This leaves more room for interpretation than the ESCB Statute; other central banks in the Community, particularly those with statutes dating back to the 1930s or 1940s when the ambition to integrate monetary policy fully into government decision-making was at a peak, operate under legal mandates that are far less clear with respect to the ordering of macroeconomic objectives and more open to the imposition of the preferences of the government at any point in time.

It would be a mistake to attach exclusive importance to legal texts in predicting the future performance of the ESCB. Some national central banks with no special emphasis on price stability in their statutory obligations and little formal independence of their political authorities have nevertheless over an extended period proved able to pursue policies – e.g., through participation in the EMS – which implied these characteristics. Yet it is significant that governments – and not just central banks – in the Community now seem prepared to subscribe to a clear and permanent, almost lexicographical ordering of their preferences with respect to the objectives of their joint monetary policy. Why this conversion to a monetary orthodoxy which has not been feasible at the national level in most member states?

There are two main elements in the answer to this question. One focuses on political considerations and perceptions of the starting point for and of the build-up to EMU, the other is based on economic theory applied to past experiences with inflation.

13.2.1 Political considerations and perceptions

Chapters 3–5 attempted to show how perceptions as to how the EMS works have evolved over the past thirteen years among policy-makers and economists. The dominant perception among officials remains that the EMS has worked as a disciplinary mechanism constraining participants to convergence of national inflation rates towards the low level observed in Germany. In chapter 10 we further argued that in early 1988, around the time when it was decided to launch the study of EMU which resulted in the Delors Report, a political consensus began to emerge that to aim more permanently for low inflation was compatible with satisfactory growth in output and employment. The experience from 1986–7 onwards seemed to justify this view, as growth picked up, particularly in the Southern countries in the EMS. This change in perception modified significantly the context in which the move towards EMU and the feasibility of a permanently firm link to Germany was seen; the sacrifice of giving priority to low and stable inflation had already been made and there would be little additional cost to the real economy in sticking with this objective and making it fully explicit, given the starting point. Indeed, there would be additional benefits in such a strategy, since residual inflationary expectations could be squeezed out faster the tougher the commitment to price stability in the transition and in the final stage towards which the process of integration was heading. Since proponents of this dominant perception were aware that the price for German participation would anyway be a commitment of this nature, there was little hesitation in pushing ahead towards EMU and in accepting the mandate in the statute.

In chapter 4 we identified a rival, and more pessimistic vision of the recent workings of the EMS as a starting point. It may be more widespread among economists than among officials, though policy-makers in Germany occasionally express themselves in similar terms. It is the view, which we labelled 'the joint shock-absorption hypothesis', that the EMS has already become an interdependent and rather symmetrical system which serves to absorb, in the joint fashion imposed by rigid exchange rates and high-capital mobility, shocks from the rest of the world or from policy changes and other exogenous events, wherever they occur in the member states. While there could still be some asymmetries in the EMS due to the relative weight of the German economy, the main implication of this perception is that Germany, like other member states, has less control over its monetary developments and inflation rate today than in, say, the mid 1980s. The task in designing the mandate and other features of the ESCB and the transition leading towards the final stage then becomes more demanding: it is to reassert collective control over money creation and inflation that is already to some extent adrift. If one takes that view, it becomes more essential to put in place for the final stage a tough mandate to give maximum guidance to the transition. To assure that deviant inflationary behaviour in the group as a whole does not develop further becomes the top priority, once the potential sanctions fade, which can still be invoked in a system where foreign exchange crises and the associated large capital flows and current external imbalances remain visible.

These two perceptions are different, but they are often papered over in official documents such as the Delors Report; it may be considered impolite or politically risky to underline the potential instabilities of the present system. One should not be surprised that central bankers and other officials are reluctant to draw attention to weaknesses in the cooperative framework which they are charged with administering. But the two perceptions are not so far apart as to make agreement on the priority to the price stability mandate for the ESCB impossible. The first group would see that as the perpetuation of the present, fundamentally acceptable, working of the EMS; the second would see the mandate as the restoration of virtues which were more clearly in evidence in an earlier incarnation of the system. Both would agree that a visibly tight monetary regime in EMU is necessary to impress the financial markets and achieve a high degree of credibility.

The political perceptions which have made a consensus on the price stability mandate possible may also help to clarify why no possibility of overriding it has been included in the statute. An escape clause might have undermined the credibility of the new institution and effectively subjected it to the perpetual risk of political pressure to reorder priorities and to modify its operations. Independence of political instructions and hence autonomy in implementing policies has been seen as another cornerstone in understanding the role of the ECB in EMU. The following section illustrates how the Statute has proposed to assure central bank independence through the rules for the governing bodies and operational provisions for interaction with the political authorities. The literature on monetary constitutions has paid much attention to the importance of central bank independence for an effective pursuit of price stability.[9] There has been less attention to causation in the opposite direction.

It is difficult to imagine that an ESCB mandate to pursue a number of macroeconomic objectives in some unspecified order could have been made compatible with operational independence. If the ESCB Statute had indeed repeated the listing of objectives set for the Community in general,[10] regular political reassessments of the relative weight of the different objectives would have become legitimate. Such reassessments are essentially political decisions which could not be delegated to an institution outside the centre of the policy-making process. A simple and single-valued objective is arguably the only basis on which monetary policy could be delegated to the ESCB and subsequently monitored by the political authorities and the public.

To make delegation and monitoring transparent it would have been desirable to make the collective price objective more explicit. In discussing the selection of ultimate and intermediate objectives for stage II in chapter 12.2, it was argued that performance criteria in terms of specific price indices should be developed already in the transition towards EMU. With the ECB in full authority for monetary policy in the final stage, vagueness about which price index – or indices – the system aims to stabilize could complicate both the efficiency of policy and the accountability of the new institution.

---

[9] See, e.g., Neumann (1991).

[10] Article 2 of the Treaty lists the following objectives:
'to promote throughout the Community a harmonious and balanced development of economic activities, sustainable and non-inflationary growth respecting the environment, a high degree of convergence of economic performance, a high level of employment, and of social protection, the raising of the standard of living and quality of life, and economic and social cohesion and solidarity between Member States'.

Explicit performance criteria could hardly have been expected in the statute itself, even though that challenge has been taken up recently in central bank legislation in one industrial country.[11] They would need to be developed through careful statistical analysis and monetary experience in the transition to give more content to the mandate.

13.2.2 Economic theory and the optimal monetary policy regime

The agreement that the common monetary policy should aim at price stability as a primary objective is one of the cornerstones of the Statute of the ESCB. It is not just a political choice. It is also based on sound economic criteria because inflation has economic welfare costs. There exists already a vast literature on the costs of inflation,[12] the purpose of this section is therefore not to provide a survey of this literature, but merely to discuss the main arguments and present some empirical material that shows the effects of inflation in the Community. We do not discuss the link between inflation and monetary policy. There is a large empirical literature which shows that, in the long run, inflation can only persist if monetary policy allows it.

While there is general agreement among economists that inflation leads to substantial welfare costs it has not been possible to estimate these costs with any precision. The costs of inflation are as difficult to quantify as the benefits from a common currency. In both cases there is a small, but not insignificant, effect that can be quantified. However, this quantifiable part represents only the tip of an iceberg, the other effects that cannot be quantified are potentially much larger.

Another difficulty in determining the cost of inflation arises from the fact that the effects of inflation are quite different depending on whether it is anticipated or not.[13] The remainder of this subsection will therefore distinguish between anticipated and unanticipated inflation.[14]

---

[11] Goodhart (1991) discusses the Reserve Bank of New Zealand Act which defines a precise objective for inflation in terms of a range for the retail price index to be aimed for over a three-year period.

[12] For a survey see Cukierman (1991) or Fischer (1981).

[13] Fischer (1981) provides a concise summary of the difficulties in measuring the cost of inflation: 'It is well known that the costs of inflation depend on the sources of the inflation, on whether and when the inflation was anticipated, and on the institutional structure of the economy. There is, therefore, no short answer to the question of the costs of inflation. Further, since the inflation rate is not an exogenous variable to the economy, there is some logical difficulty in discussing the costs of inflation per se rather than the costs and benefits of alternative policy choices.'

[14] The remainder of this section draws heavily on the contribution of one of the authors to Emerson *et al.* (1991).

i)   The cost of anticipated inflation

Anticipated inflation has important micro- and macroeconomic effects. Since only the former can be quantified with some precision they will be discussed first although the macroeconomic effects, which are more uncertain are potentially much more important.

Microeconomic effects of anticipated inflation The main effect of *anticipated inflation* is that it leads the public to economize on holdings of money. This is socially wasteful because the social cost of producing money is equal to zero (the cost of printing additional bank notes is negligible). It follows that an economic optimum is attained only if the private cost of holding money is also equal to zero.

However, the private opportunity cost of holding money is in general not zero if there is inflation. For example, if the alternative to holding money is to buy storable consumption goods, the private opportunity cost of holding money is equal to the rate of inflation. If the alternative to holding money is holding bonds, or other 'near money' assets that yield interest, the private opportunity cost of holding money is equal to the rate of interest.

The optimum rate of inflation would therefore be zero if the alternative to holding money is buying durable goods. If the alternative is to hold interest bearing assets the optimum is attained when the nominal interest rate is equal to zero. A nominal interest rate of zero requires, however, negative inflation, at least as long as the real rate of interest is positive.[15] The difference between these two approaches is smaller than appears at first sight because the real rate of interest is usually taken to be small, in the vicinity of 2–4 per cent; there is therefore little difference between the prescription of absolute price stability or slight deflation. Positive inflation rates in the vicinity of or even above 5 per cent are clearly undesirable according to both approaches.

A precise estimate of the welfare cost of inflation for the Community is provided by Emerson *et al.* (1991) where it was found that under the approach that prescibes zero inflation an inflation rate of 10 per cent can lead to a welfare loss of between 0.1 and 0.3 per cent of GDP. This effect alone is of the same order of magnitude as the transactions costs that can be saved by a common currency and suggests that the advantages from a monetary union can quickly be lost if the common monetary policy does not ensure price stability.

The concept used so far of economic welfare loss from inflation is based on the assumption that inflation is the only distortion in the economy, which implies that the revenue the government obtains from inflation is not important. In other words it was assumed that the government can finance its expenditure through lump-sum taxes that do not distort any relative price. If this is not possible the inflation tax becomes just one among many other distorting taxes and should be used to some extent. This idea was already discussed in chapter 5 because it has sometimes been argued that the inflation tax was indeed an indispensable revenue source for some European countries which

---

[15] This is the well known result of Friedman (1969).

should therefore not participate in a low-inflation EMS. However, the assessment in chapter 5 has led us to the result that the inflation tax is not very important in practice. In our view the limited revenues that can be obtained through inflation do not outweigh the benefits of price stability. Moreover, the idea that inflation is a tax like any other has also been disputed on theoretical grounds (see Spaventa (1989) for a survey).

Macroeconomic effects of anticipated inflation The discussion so far has concentrated on the microeconomic effects of inflation that can be predicted and measured with some certainty. This is different at the macroeconomic level where it is less clear on theoretical grounds whether anticipated inflation should have any effects at all. It is therefore also much more difficult to estimate empirically the macroeconomic costs of inflation.

The dominant macroeconomic theories of the 1960s held that there was a stable relationship between inflation and unemployment (the so-called Phillips curve) so that the authorities could attain and maintain any desired level of employment by accepting the associated inflation rate. However, this view is no longer accepted on theoretical and empirical grounds. On theoretical grounds the main objection is that it assumes that economic agents never learn about inflation. On empirical grounds the 1970s, which had on average higher inflation and higher unemployment, showed that there was no stable trade-off between inflation and unemployment.

The observation that acceptance of higher inflation does not necessarily make lower unemployment possible is confirmed in Emerson *et al.* (1991) using observations for average inflation and unemployment rates for all twenty-three OECD countries over the fifteen years period 1970–85. On this cross-country basis (as opposed to the time series approach of the Phillips curve) there is a statistically significant *positive* association between inflation and unemployment.[16] This implies that, at least over the fifteen-year period considered, countries with higher inflation had also, on average, higher unemployment.

However, this cross-country evidence might not be relevant for a judgement of the effects of inflation in the Community because it includes countries with widely differing economic structures such as Iceland and Turkey. Some evidence was already presented in chapter 5 where it was shown that the Phillips curve seems to have shifted several times in most member countries over the 1970s and 1980s. Data for the Community averages also show that higher inflation does not lead to lower unemployment.

While the relationship between inflation and unemployment has been extensively researched in the literature less attention has been devoted to the impact of inflation on growth, which might be a more appropriate measure of the cost of inflation. Figure 13.2.1 therefore displays the relationship between inflation and real growth in the Community. Each point in that figure depicts the Community's average inflation rate

---

[16] This positive association between inflation and unemployment could be due to the efforts by countries with high unemployment to use expansionary policies, but the strength of the relationship suggests that these efforts have not been successful to say the least.

for the year indicated and the rate of growth of real GDP of the Community in the following year. The lag of one year was chosen because monetary policy is supposed to operate with 'long and variable lags' and because one might argue that the contemporaneous correlation between inflation and growth could be affected by the fact that the governments often react to lower growth with expansionary monetary policies.[17]

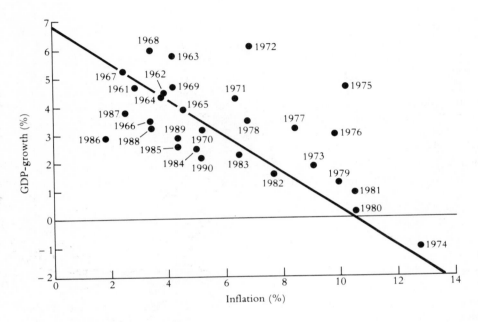

Figure 13.2.1 Inflation and growth in the EC.

This figure suggests strongly that there is a negative association between inflation and real growth. This negative association is statistically highly significant, as indicated by the regression line that is also depicted in figure 13.2.1.[18] This finding is corroborated by Emerson *et al.* (1991) which contains more cross-country analysis of the effects of inflation and confirms that inflation has only negative effects on macroeconomic performance in terms of growth or the level of per capita GDP.

The purpose of briefly discussing this empirical research is not to argue that the Phillips curve necessarily has a positive slope, i.e., that higher inflation reduces growth,

[17] The overall conclusions are not affected by this lag since the contemporaneous relationship between inflation and growth is also negative (and statistically significant).

[18] In a simple regression variations in inflation explain 40 per cent of the variations in real growth in the following year. The slope coefficient is equal to − 1.1 with a t-statistic of about 4, which is significant at less than 1 per cent.

since this is an old controversy in economics. But the data strongly suggest that, for the EC countries in the 1970s and 1980s, the effects of inflation on output were rather negative.

13.2.2 Inflation variability

Up to this point the discussion has focused on the effects of a steady rate of inflation that is entirely predictable. However, in reality inflation is never constant and therefore never entirely predictable. Moreover, economic theory suggests, that *surprise inflation* has much stronger economic effects than anticipated inflation. As already discussed in chapters 5 and 7 this is true, in particular at the macroeconomic level and for government revenues.

The potential welfare losses from a highly variable inflation rate are therefore larger than the losses that could result from a high, but stable inflation rate. Moreover, unanticipated inflation also tends to create variability in relative prices, which should have similar effects as the variability in exchange rates.[19]

The distinction between anticipated and unanticipated inflation might be somewhat artificial, however, since the available evidence suggests that there is a strong link between the level of inflation and its variability making high but stable inflation rates a very rare phenomenon.

This is confirmed by figure 13.2.2 which shows that there is a strong link between the level of inflation and its variability. This figure shows the relationship between the level and the variability of inflation in the Community by displaying the average and the standard deviation of inflation for all member countries over the six five-year periods between 1960 and 1990.[20] (Each point therefore represents the combination of average and standard deviation for one member country measured over one five year period.)

The link between the average and the variability of inflation has been demonstrated often in the economics literature. Emerson *et al.* (1991) documents it for a sample that includes all twenty-three OECD countries and a longer time period, and finds that, on average, a one percentage point increase in the average inflation is associated with a 1.3 percentage point increase in the standard deviation of inflation.[21]

As already discussed in chapter 5, modern macroeconomic theory holds that unanticipated inflation can temporarily increase output and employment above the equilibrium level (i.e., a short-run Phillips curve does exist). However, since the reverse

---

[19] See Cukierman (1981) for a detailed discussion of the various channels that link inflation, the variability of inflation and the variability in relative prices.

[20] It is clear that on a theoretical level variability and predictability are two separate concepts. However, as shown for example in Cukierman (1981), an increase in the variability of inflation is usually equivalent to a reduction in its predictability.

[21] For further references see Cukierman (1981).

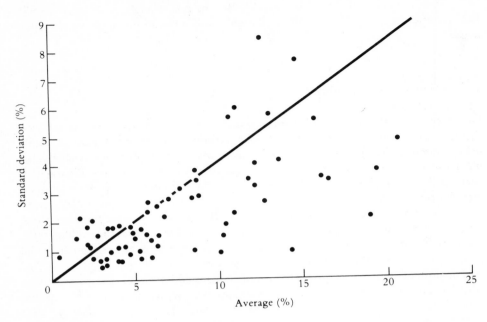

Figure 13.2.2. *Inflation and variability of inflation*

holds when inflation is lower than anticipated it follows immediately that a highly variable inflation rate keeps output continuously away from the equilibrium level.

This high correlation between average inflation and its variability should not be surprising since it should be seen as a consequence of the importance of unanticipated inflation. Governments that try to stimulate the economy through expansionary policies have to keep surprising the public. This is not possible with a high, but constant inflation rate. They therefore have to resort to stop-and-go policies that can only have negative overall effects in the long run.

13.3 Independence and the price stability mandate

The statutory mandate to aim at price stability will give the ESCB a clear direction for its policy. It was and remains a necessary element of the constitution of the ESCB. The purpose of this section is merely to clarify the precise meaning of price stability and to discuss what 'side conditions' are needed to enable the ESCB to persue this goal.

13.3.1 The concept of price stability

The discussion of the costs of unanticipated inflation in the previous section implies that price stability should not be taken to mean only an average inflation rate close to zero, but also that prices should remain predictable, i.e., inflation should vary as little as possible around the average value of zero. The task of the ESCB should therefore be not only to keep inflation at or close to zero in the medium run, but also to minimize its fluctuations in the short run.

In order to make the concept of price stability operational it is necessary to specify what price index is to be stabilized.[22] This choice is rarely made explicit even in countries where price stability is the main mandate for the central bank, probably because at the national level most prices move closely together. However, since prices can diverge much more at the European level than inside any member country, it would have been preferable to give some indication as to what price index it should look at. From a theoretical point of view the appropriate target index is the one that is most closely related to the source of the cost of inflation. For example, if one considers the main cost of inflation to be sub-optimal money holdings the appropriate index would be the consumer price index (CPI). But if the main cost of inflation is taken to derive from the variability in relative prices which leads to lower investment and production the appropriate price index to stabilize might be the producer price index. It is therefore difficult to decide on purely theoretical grounds what price index should be stabilized.

The main factors in this choice will therefore be availability and comparability across countries. The CPI has the advantage that it is published monthly everywhere, in contrast to wholesale and producer prices which are not available this frequently and usually only with a longer time lag. A further advantage of the CPI is that it is widely understood and used in wage negotiations.

13.3.2 Exchange-rate and debt management policies as a threat to price stability?

A statutory duty for price stability is, of course, effective only to the extent that the central bank does not have other policy goals besides price stability. The provisions that are most likely to make price stability difficult to achieve concern the exchange rate of the single currency *vis-à-vis* other major international currencies and the management of government debt.

It is apparent that if the central bank also has to support the exchange rate it may not be able to combat the imported inflation that results if the exchange rate is pegged to an inflationary currency. The ECB is, as we argued at some length in chapter 9, unlikely to be *obliged* to intervene in third currencies; few observers, official or academic, would expect a move in the foreseeable future to a system of mandatory interventions à la Bretton Woods. But occasional efforts to stabilize the dollar (or yen) exchange rate of

---

[22] It is assumed here that the variability of prices inside the union is not a cause for concern because these relative prices will just represent the effects of regional shifts in overall demand or other non-monetary factors. The ECB could therefore not be concerned with the lowest or highest regional inflation rate, but only with the average.

the European currency 'around current levels' along the pattern of the Louvre Accord of February 1987 is a more likely eventuality. How would such revisions of exchange-rate policy be decided and implemented in EMU? Could conflicts with the pursuit of the price stability objective be avoided?

The Treaty and the Statute are about as clear as one could realistically expect on this point. Among the tasks listed for the ESCB (Art. 3) one finds: 'to conduct foreign exchange operations consistent with the provisions of Art. 109 of this Treaty'. Art. 109 distinguishes two different types of situations regarding the exchange-rate regime. The ECOFIN Council may, if acting with *unanimity*, conclude *formal agreements* on an exchange-rate system for the ecu vis-à-vis non-EC currencies, though it must then have consulted the ECB 'in an endeavour to reach a consensus consistent with the objective of price stability'; the Council will also have to consult the European Parliament. The ECOFIN Council may then by a qualified majority 'adopt, adjust or abandon the central rates of the ecu within the exchange rate system'.

If there is no formal agreement with non-EC countries or international institutions, the ECOFIN Council may, by a qualified majority, 'formulate general orientations for exchange-rate policy ... without prejudice to the primary objective ... to maintain price stability'.

These provisions of the Treaty suggest that the ECB is unlikely for a long time to be obliged to intervene in exchange markets for non-EC currencies since unanimity in the ECOFIN Council to enter into explicit commitments in a Bretton Woods-like agreement with the United States, Japan and other nations seems a long way off. A non-publicized understanding of the type exemplified by the Louvre Accord would hardly be enough to pose a serious challenge to the emphasis given to price stability as the primary objective. Over the wide range of policies that stop short of 'formal agreements' the ECB is likely to retain the decisive influence over the external aspects of monetary policy in EMU. The Treaty goes further towards limiting political influence over the central bank than anologous institutional arrangements in the United States and Japan. In the two other main industrial countries authority for exchange-rate policy is effectively shared between the political authorities and the central bank.

In both the United States and Japan conflicts have occasionally arisen in the past over the desirability of influencing the exchange rate as well as over the appropriate means. There is little doubt that,[23] in such conflicts, the political authorities represented by the US or Japanese Minister of Finance or his Deputy have tended to have the upper hand on exchange-rate policy, even during the long span since 1973 when formal obligations in the international monetary system have been at a minimum. As regards giving discretion to the central bank in day-to-day interventions, the politically set constraints are also very visible in the United States and Japan, maybe because international reserves are in these countries owned by the Treasury which is accountable to Congress/the Diet for their management; some authors have used the term 'mutual veto', i.e., that the central bank and the Ministry of Finance can both exercise a veto on such

---

[23] As demonstrated for the US case by Destler and Henning (1989) and for Japan in Funabashi (1988).

operations.[24] Typically, this has implied fewer interventions (or other efforts at international coordination) than the central banks, with their concern about limiting short-run movements in the exchange rate, would have preferred, because the political authorities have tended to put a relatively greater weight on purely domestic objectives.

In EMU the relative preferences are more likely to be in the opposite direction. If the governing bodies of the ECB turn out to be as single-minded in their pursuit of price stability as the mandate suggests, the participants in ECOFIN – some of which are anyway quite sympathetic to more active management of the relationship to the dollar – will occasionally want more attention paid to exchange-rate stability. Within the more balanced relationship between the monetary and the political authorities foreseen in Europe, the Council majority will not, like their US and Japanese colleagues, simply impose a decision on a reluctant ESCB Council; they will need to persuade the central bankers in the ECB Council during the consultative procedure. It would be an illusion to believe that the Ministers would not, on some of these occasions, prevail, partly because appeal to external considerations will be their only formal way of overriding the views of the central bankers. Even though the ECB governing bodies would in such cases still have the authority to sterilize interventions and stick to an aggregate monetary objective, the pressure from external factors constitutes a residual, but weak threat to its ability to pursue its mandate at all times.

If anything, the remaining concern about the Treaty provisions for exchange-rate policy in EMU may be that the ECB will become so keen on demonstrating its authority over the exchange rate of the ecu that the EMU participants will find it difficult to participate in any efforts at international policy coordination in the G7 or elsewhere which imply some exchange-rate stabilization. Since the EMU participants will also be largely unable to commit to any significant measures of budgetary policy, because collective authority in this area is weak – partly for good reasons, as analysed in chapter 8 – they are likely to find themselves the most passive participants in global policy coordination. This in turn could cause conflicts with a majority of EC governments, some of which may still be taking part individually in the G7, and between the EMU participants and the two other main actors in the international monetary system. Furthermore, as the EMS has become more cohesive, fluctuations in the dollar no longer pose the threat of increasing internal pressures in the System; in full EMU this risk would, in principle, disappear completely. Increasing insensitivity to movements in the dollar could lead to wider fluctuations between the ecu and the dollar than those experienced since the Louvre Accord of 1987. Given the way in which it has now been set up, EMU is not a recipe for greater global currency stability.

The other route by which the independence of the ECB and its capacity to retain price stability as the primary objective could be eroded is through its participation in financing government deficits. If the ECB could occasionally be obliged to finance government deficits directly, the System might also be pushed into following a more expansionary policy than is compatible with stable prices. But on this point the ESCB

---

[24] Destler and Henning (1989), p. 88.

Statute is unequivocal in denying monetary financing (Art. 21.1); and a similar wording is used in Art. 104, 1 of the Treaty:

> Overdraft facilities or any other type of credit facility with the ECB or with the national central banks of the Member States (hereinafter referred to as 'national central banks') in favour of Community institutions or bodies, central governments, regional, local or other public authorities, other bodies governed by public law, or public undertakings of Member States shall be prohibited as shall the purchase directly from them by the ECB or national central banks of debt instruments.

The suppression of these two forms of direct monetary financing of public deficits is an extrapolation of a trend towards more effective separation of the power to spend from the power to create money, observable in most Community countries. The so-called 'divorce' of Banca d'Italia and the Ministry of the Treasury of 1981 is the most notable example. A central bank that is not obliged to, and may be not even permitted to, absorb the excess supply of government paper at issue is far less vulnerable to political influence.

Some critics, e.g., Branson (1990) and Goodhart (1991), have found that even these apparently firm operational constraints may prove illusory. Indirect financial support to governments through sizeable purchases of their securities in the secondary market, possibly shortly after issue, may convey as important a signal as more limited purchases at issue. It would be safer, according to this view, either to prescribe that ECB operations may take place only in government and other securities with the highest credit rating – this would eliminate pressure on the ECB to reduce risk premia on the securities of governments with high or rapidly rising debt – or to impose strict rules on the national composition of the system's open market portfolio. As an even more strict alternative one might envisage a reversal of the normal central bank practice to conduct open market operations only in government-backed paper by prescribing that they had to be confined to private securities. The Treaty has, however, refrained from constraining the scope for open market operations more than strictly necessary. The absence of the ECB from auctions of government securities, and the prospect that the significant method of influencing union-wide liquidity will become the system's operations in the evolving federal funds market described in chapter 12, should offer sufficient assurance that formal independence will also be real.

The Statute of the ESCB also contains the provision that the system should 'without prejudice to the objective of price stability support the general economic policies of the Community' (Art. 2.2).[25] However, given its subordinate rank this requirement could effectively be suspended if it conflicts with the need to pursue restrictive policies and should therefore not constitute a danger for price stability.

The requirement to support Community economic policies does not provide a direct channel through which the ECOFIN Council could affect monetary policy. In this sense it poses less of a danger to a consistent anti-inflationary policy than the other

---

[25] This is also the case at present in the Federal Republic of Germany (Bundesbank Act, Art. 12).

two provisions discussed so far. In the Community this requirement will anyway be difficult to interpret since the policy stance of different member states can be expected to diverge at times considerably even in EMU, and the Community itself would not be able to establish an overall fiscal policy stance because its budget would remain small relative to national budgets. For some time to come it will therefore be difficult to interpret what the policy stance of the Community is.

The conclusion is clearly that none of the three routes capable of eroding the independence of the ESCB and its commitment to price stability – political decisions on exchange-rate policy, participation in the financing of government deficits, and support of the general economic policies of the Community – are likely to modify the two main features of the ECB.

13.3.3 Independence and political accountability: necessary but also conflicting conditions for price stability?

All the provisions in the statutes that aim to assure price stability can, however, be effective only if the ECB is independent of other influences so that the public can be confident that price stability will be attained. The purpose of this section is to show that the more formal attributes of independence of the ECB established in its statute are crucial in assuring its anti-inflationary credibility.

Independence of the central bank is, of course, only a necessary condition for price stability. Other important factors that assure price stability in the long run are the aversion to inflation felt by the public and, more particularly, the behaviour of the representatives of employees and employers reflecting such an attitude. However, as these dimensions are, partly at least, also dependent on the behaviour of the central bank, this section concentrates on the role of central bank independence in assuring a credible anti-inflationary policy.

Even if a central bank has a formal statutory duty of price stability and the means to pursue this goal, it might not always be able to do so if it is not *politically independent*. There are strong theoretical reasons to believe that independence is a necessary condition for price stability.

The main reason is that, as shown above, unanticipated inflation has the potential to stimulate, even if only temporarily, economic activity (especially relevant to governments when facing short electoral time-tables) and to reduce the real value of public debt. Even well-intentioned policy-makers face the issue of how to convince the public that they will never succumb to the temptation to create surprise inflation. Since in democratic societies elected officials are in general free to determine economic policy at their discretion, it is very difficult for political bodies to acquire enough *credibility* to convince the public that inflation will always stay low. An independent central bank, however, does not face this temptation to create surprise inflation because, if its statutory duty is to safeguard price stability, it has no interest in temporarily increasing economic activity or lowering the value of public debt through surprise inflation.

Central bank independence can therefore, at least to some extent, solve the credibility problem.[26]

The degree to which a central bank is independent can never be established with precision. However, there are at least three objective factors that determine the degree to which a given central bank is politically independent:

i)   Independence of instructions from government bodies (in the EC this means versus the Community and the national level).

ii) Personal independence of Board and Council members.

iii) Legal rank of its statute.

(i)   The ESCB statute goes to great lengths in emphasizing this point: 'neither the ECB nor a national central bank nor any member of their decision-making bodies shall seek or take instructions from Community institutions or bodies, from any government of a Member State or from any other body' (Art. 7). This formulation, taken literally, would appear to preclude any possibility to override the way in which the governing bodies of the ECB interpret the pursuit of the general mandate for monetary policy. It is more explicit than existing national central bank legislation, though the Bundesbank Act (Art. 12) comes close: 'In exercising the powers conferred on it by this Act, it (the Bundesbank) is independent of instructions from the Federal Government.'

Freedom from instructions does appear indispensable for the credibility of the ECB. If it could receive instructions from the ECOFIN Council, or if individual members of the Governing Council could be obliged to vote in accordance with mandates from their respective national governments, suspicions that coalitions of political interests would impose their preferences, occasionally different from those embodied in the price stability mandate, would be unavoidable. The ECB needs formal attributes of independence more than existing national central banks.

In some European countries the central bank has developed considerable *de facto* independence despite being formally subject to instructions or to the risk of being reduced to insignificance by the activation of legislation enabling the government to implement major monetary decisions. For example, the Netherlands Bank can according to the Bank Act of 1948 (section 26) be subjected to instructions by the Minister of Finance, after consultations in a forum of representatives of industry, the labour market organizations and some independent experts, but the authority has remained unused throughout the post-war period. In the Dutch case the restraint by the political authorities is explained by the provision that disagreements between government and central bank would have to be made known to the public and debated in Parliament, see Eizenga (1987). In short, using its authority would entail risks for the government. Similar constitutional elements could not be built into a European

---

[26] The theoretical and empirical contributions concerning the issue of credibility always take as their point of departure countries where there is a political cycle with well defined dates at which national elections take place. This will not be the case in the Community and one could therefore argue that the issue of credibility and the political business cycle will be less important for the Community than for countries that have a central political authority which determines macroeconomic policies.

structure for the foreseeable future, because neither the ECOFIN Council nor any of its individual members would be faced with the threat of a parliamentary crisis in case there is open disagreement with the Governing Council of the ECB.

One could not count therefore on restraint with respect to the ECB, if an ability to override in exceptional circumstances existed, and there would hardly be time to await the slow-build up of a reputation for independence which would be underway as long as it was not used. Hence the pressure from those countries that have the most well-established traditions for central bank independence for assurance that the removal from national legislation of provisions for government instructions be underway already in the transitional stage towards EMU and be completed before embarking on the final stage (see chapter 12).

(ii) The personal independence of Board and Governing Council members is enhanced by appointing them for relatively long terms – eight years for Board members (Art. 11.2) and a minimum of five years for the national central bank governors (Art. 14.2) – and by assuring that a member can only be relieved from office on the grounds of 'serious misconduct' (Art. 11.4) or 'serious cause resting in his person' (Art. 14.2). Appointments will undoubtedly by politicized – as they are today in most countries, including those such as Germany and the United States which pride themselves on having an independent central bank. However, when there is security of tenure over a relatively long period, experience from these systems shows that members of the governing bodies develop substantial independence of the original environment from which they were nominated.[27]

(iii) The third formal determinant in assessing central bank independence is inherent in the conditions under which the statute can be changed. The more difficult this is, the more secure is the central bank; and the more easily will the confidence of the public be established that independence is permanent. The drafters of the Treaty and the ESCB Statute could not by the text itself generate such confidence. But there appears to have been early agreement in the IGC on EMU that the main structural features, including the mandate, should be written into the revised Treaty itself.[28] Since the Treaty can only be changed if all member states agree and ratify amendments, such features would have a special legal rank. Existing national central banks occasionally, though in practice rarely, see their legal framework modified, and national parliamentary bodies, if not governments, will be able to override the views of the

---

[27] Financial independence in the sense of being able to determine salaries and not being subject to normal governmental and politically controlled audit is another dimension which is a desirable complement to personal independence. As pointed out, e.g., in Louis *et al.* (1989) the experience of the Federal Reserve System is illustrative; the Fed is subject to a politically imposed ceiling on remuneration – this is thought to be one reason why it sometimes finds it difficult to retain the services of members of the Board of Governors and of top staff – and to government audit.

[28] Art. 106 of the revised Treaty opens up a simplified procedure for raising non-essential Articles in the ESCB statute.

central bank on the formulation of its general mandate or on other central issues.[29] In this sense, the ESCB will be more assured of an unchanged constitutional framework than are its national components.

We have stressed the three formal criteria for independence in addition to the more operational provisions, because they have been treated in a clear-cut way in the Statute and add further to the status of the ECB in the Community. But the three criteria also provide a link to the institutional literature on central banking history and to the limited number of efforts so far at testing empirically the relationship between central bank independence and price stability.

Recent research (see Alesina (1989) or Masciandaro, Grilli and Tabellini (1990)), using the three criteria discussed and combining them somewhat arbitrarily into an index of central bank independence, shows that there is a strong link between independence and performance in terms of low inflation. This link is evident in figure 13.3.1 which classifies the degree of independence on the base of an index that takes into account institutional provisions, such as the relationship between the central bank and the executive, and any rules that could force the central bank to accommodate fiscal deficits. This index, which ranges from one half to four is then plotted against the average inflation rate over the period 1973–86. The regression line in this figure shows the statistical association between independence and inflation performance. In particular the two most independent central banks in the industrialized world (in Germany and Switzerland) produced also the two lowest inflation rates. In terms of this formal approach the ECB would receive the same ranking as these two latter examples, or possibly an even lower one. This suggests that, from an institutional point of view, one should expect the monetary policy of the ECB to be at least as good in terms of price stability as that of the Bundesbank.

It is sometimes argued that there is conflict between the requirement that a central bank should be independent and the idea that it should also be accountable for its actions to a democratically elected body. However, this conflict might be more apparent than real. An effective statutory duty to aim at price stability and political independence appear to be necessary conditions for a consistent and credible anti-inflationary policy. However, these two elements alone are not sufficient to guarantee that the ECB will always pursue stable prices. Its task may become difficult if tensions in the labour market result in excessive increases in nominal wages because this would leave it the choice of accommodating the inflationary expectations or pursuing a restrictive policy with adverse consequences for employment.[30] Such a conflict is less likely to arise to the extent that the value of stable prices is generally recognized.

The general environment in which the ESCB operates is therefore an important element in determining to what extent it will be able to attain the goal of price stability.

---

[29] Amendments to the Federal Reserve Act or Congressional Resolutions containing monetary policy guidelines have been put forward and adopted in the US Congress on several occasions in the past two decades.

[30] Or if budget policy puts pressure on financial markets which is possible even in the absence of direct monetary financing of the deficit. See the discussion on binding guidelines for fiscal policy in chapter 8.

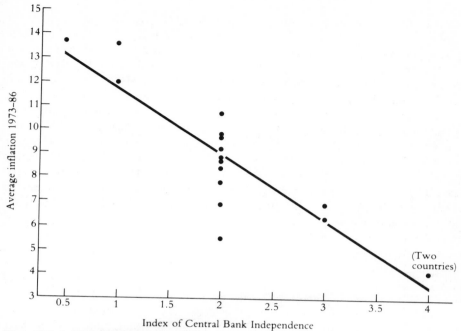

Figure 13.3.1 Central Bank Independence and Inflation
Source: Emerson *et al.* (1991).

Regular contacts between the Governing Council of the ECB and the constitutional national central banks – i.e. the entire system not just the centre and democratically elected institutions could increase public support for a policy aiming at price stability and and thus make it easier to achieve this target. In a number of countries an obligation for the central bank to report to a parliamentary body, to interpret what happens in financial markets, and to explain the purposes and achievements of monetary policy has been helpful in developing understanding of policy aims. The reports by the Chairman of the Board of Governors of the Federal Reserve System to specialized committees in the US Congress provide one such example. Accountability in this sense to a parliamentary body has not been in conflict with independence of the executive branch of government: it may have advanced the latter. Some degree of democratic accountability, for example in the form of regular reports to the European Parliament might therefore actually facilitate the task of achieving price stability.

13.4 The implications of variable geometry

In view of the informal nature of stage I and the continued reliance on ultimate national responsibility for policy in stage II the question of drawing any institutional implication from the fact that EC member states are proceeding towards monetary union at different speeds does not apply until the beginning of stage III. All Member States will participate fully in the European Monetary Institute (EMI) regardless of their degree of preparation for full EMU and of the constraints to which they have subjected their exchange-rate policy. The two countries which have explicitly reserved their position with respect to participation in full EMU – the United Kingdom and Denmark – will still take part in preparations for the latter in the Council of the EMI and in the ECOFIN Council, though with some exceptions in the UK case.

Once the decision to enter stage III has been taken it becomes unavoidable to distinguish institutionally between those Member States which have joined EMU (and have transferred all monetary sovereignty to the ESCB) and those Member States which have not (either because they have been found by a qualified majority in the Council not to be ready, or because they have themselves opted out). The Treaty expresses very clearly that non-participation in EMU implies exclusion from rights and obligations within the ESCB (Art. 109k (3) of the Treaty and Chapter IX of the ESCB Statutes) and suspension of voting rights in the ECOFIN Council with respect to a number of important provisions relating to EMU, notably efforts to assure compliance with recommendations on the reduction of 'excessive budget deficits' and decisions on recommendations ('general orientations') for exchange-rate policy. On these matters a qualified majority in the ECOFIN Council will be defined as two thirds of the votes of Member States without a derogation, i.e. the full participants (Art. 109k (5)).

The Treaty does not specify in great detail the institutional provisions for cooperation between participants and non-participants in EMU. Countries that have not met the convergence criteria, but are politically ready to join EMU will have their derogation examined at least every two years, but they may also request earlier examination (Art. 109k (2)). The United Kingdom and Denmark, if these two countries decide in the mid-1990s not to join but can be regarded as economically ready, may themselves take the initiative to have their derogation revoked at any time. The EMI in which all Member States participate with equal rights will be liquidated on the date of entry into stage III and its functions will be taken over by the ECB. Art. 44 of the ESCB Statute states, however, that the ECB will 'take over those tasks of EMI that because of the derogations of one or more Member States still have to be fulfilled ...', and the ECB will have an advisory role in lifting derogations.

For the purpose of discharging the tasks listed in Art. 44, viz. monetary coordination and preparation for the abrogation of derogations, and to continue cooperation in general with the non-participants, a third decision-making body of the ECB, the General Council, will be set up. It will be composed of the President and Vice President of the ECB – but not the other four members of its Executive Board – and the governors of the central banks of all Member States. The General Council has, like the EMI Council, advisory functions, but no obvious decision-making authority.

With the beginning of stage III the EMS agreement is implicitly abrogated among the countries that lock their exchange rates irrevocably. But the position of countries with a derogation is not clear. There is no explicit mention of intra-Community exchange-rate policy in the ESCB Statute. However, the regular examination of countries with a derogation and Art. 109m of the Treaty strongly suggest that an EMS-like arrangement will link the currencies of the non-participants to the common currency of the participants in full EMU. Art. 109m states that until the beginning of the third stage, or for as long as a Member State has a derogation, national exchange rate policy shall be treated as a matter of common interest. In so doing, Member States shall take account of the experience acquired in the EMS and in developing the ecu and shall respect existing powers in this field. Those provisions are clearly designed to constrain the centrifugal tendencies which might otherwise arise as some Member States join EMU whilst others do not. Depending obviously on the number of countries which are both economically ready and willing to join EMU, an EMS-like arrangement with the others will become very asymmetrical leaving very little influence for the non-participants. The most likely outcome is that the non-participants will *de facto* have to follow a one sided ecu-peg, similar to the policy followed by Sweden since 1991. The ECB could scarcely agree to potential intervention obligations to support the currencies of non-members without endangering its primary objective of price stability.

An important question, difficult to assess *a priori*, is whether the number of non-participants could have an impact on the speed with which the full EMU participants go beyond the permanent locking of exchange rates at the start of stage III to their introduction of the single currency. As discussed in Chapter 12.5 these two dates can be – and are likely to be – different; Art. 109 l only speaks of the 'rapid introduction' of the single currency after the start of stage III. Recent discussions in the Committee of Governors have again revealed some differences of opinion, both about the desirable and possible speed of moving from what in popular jargon may be called stage III a – irrevocably fixed rates – to stage III b in which the replacement of national currencies by the ecu occurs.

There would appear to be strong arguments for making stage III a as short as technically possible, regardless of the non-participation in EMU of some Member States. As discussed in Chapter 7 above the full benefits, but not the costs of EMU, are linked to the adoption of a single currency. Taking this final step early will also speed up the residual convergence to a common inflation rate and to a common level of interest rates relative to the situation in which national currencies continue in existence for an extended period. Finally stage IIIa could raise some difficult problems in giving concreteness to what is implied by the notion that 'the ecu will become a currency in its own right' (Art. 109 l (4)). A straightforward interpretation of this provision, viz. that the ecu would, from the first day of stage III become legal tender in all Member States which participate in EMU, appears to be resisted by some governments and central banks. Given this uncertainty about the operations in a phase in which the future single currency has been confirmed but is still treated as a foreign currency in participating Member States, inferior to national currencies within their territories, it would be preferable to move straight to the single currency as soon as the ECB is technically ready to issue it. Given the long lead time available until the earliest likely date for starting stage III – four to five years into the future – such a strategy would still seem entirely feasible, assuming the political will to prove it can be sustained.

References

Alesina, Alberto (1989), 'Political and business cycles in industrial democracies', *Economic Policy*, 8, April: 57–89.

Branson, William H. (1990), 'Financial market integration, macroeconomic policy and the EMS', in C. Bliss and Jorge Braga de Macedo (eds.), *Unity with Diversity in the European Economy: the Community's Southern Frontier*, Cambridge University Press, Cambridge, 124–30.

Committee of Governors of the Central Banks of the Member States of the European Economic Community (1990), 'Draft Statute of the European System of Central Banks and of the European Central Bank' (with Introductory Note and Commentary), Basle, 27 November.

Conference of the Representatives of the Governments of the Member States (1992), *Treaty on European Union*, CONF-UP-UEM 2002/92, Brussels ('Maastricht Treaty', signed on 7 February 1992).

Cukierman, Alex (1981), 'Interest rates during the cycle, inventories and monetary policy – a theoretical analysis', *Carnegie-Rochester Conference Series on Public Policy*, 15: 87–144.

Cukierman, Alex (1991), 'Central bank behaviour, credibility, accommodation and stabilization'.

Destler, Ian and Randall Henning (1989), *Dollar policies: exchange rate policymaking in the United States*, Institute for International Economics, Washington, DC.

Eizenga, Weitze (1987), 'The independence of the Deutsche Bundesbank and the Netherlands Bank with regard to monetary policy: a comparative study', *SUERF Papers on Monetary Policy and Financial Systems*, 2, Tilburg.

Emerson, Michael, Daniel Gros, Jean Pisani-Ferry, Alexander Italianer and Horst Reichenbach (1991), *One Market, One Money*, Oxford University Press, Oxford.

Fischer, Stanley (1981), 'Towards an understanding of the costs of inflation: II', *Carnegie-Rochester Conference Series on Public Policy*, 15: 5–42.

Friedman, Milton (1969), 'The optimum quantity of money', *The Optimum Quantity of Money and other Essays*, Macmillan, London, 1–50.

Funabashi, Yoichi (1988), *Managing the dollar: from the Plaza to the Louvre*, Institute for International Economics, Washington, DC.

Goodhart, Charles (1991), 'The Draft Statute of the European System of Central Banks: a commentary', *Special Paper*, 37, Financial Markets Group, London School of Economics, London.

Gros, Daniel (1988), 'The EMS and the determination of the European price level', Centre for European Policy Studies, Brussels, *CEPS Working Document (Economic)*, 34.

Gros, Daniel and Niels Thygesen (1988), 'The EMS: achievements, current issues and directions for the future', Centre for European Policy Studies, Brussels, *CEPS Paper*, 35.

Louis, Jean-Victor *et al.* (1989), **Vers un système Européen de banques centrales,** collection Etudes Européennes, Editions de l'Université de Bruxelles.

Masciandaro, Donato, Vittorio Grilli and Guido Tabellini (1990), 'Fiscal deficits and monetary institutions: a comparative analysis', in H. Cheng (ed.), *Challenges to monetary policy in the Pacific–Basin countries*, Kluwer Publishers.

Neumann, Manfred (1991), 'Central bank independence as a prerequisite of price stability', in *European Economy*, special issue, Commission of the European Communities, Brussels.

Spaventa, Luigi (1989), 'On seigniorage: old and new policy issues: introduction', *European Economic Review*, 33, 2–3, March: 557–63.

Thygesen, Niels (1989), 'Decentralization and accountability within the central bank: any lessons from the US experience for the potential organization of a European central banking institution?', in Paul De Grauwe and Theo Peeters (eds.), *The Ecu and European Monetary Integration*, Macmillan Press, London, 91–114.

APPENDIX I

Treaty on European Union[1]

Part One – Principles

Article 2

The Community shall have as its task, by establishing a common market and an economic and monetary union and by implementing the common policies or activities referred to in Articles 3 and 3a, to promote throughout the Community a harmonious and balanced development of economic activities, sustainable and non-inflationary growth respecting the environment, a high degree of convergence of economic performance, a high level of employment and of social protection, the raising of the standard of living and quality of life, and economic and social cohesion and solidarity among Member States.

Article 3 a

1   For the purposes set out in Article 2, the activities of the Member States and the Community shall include, as provided for in this Treaty and in accordance with the timetable set out therein, the adoption of an economic policy which is based on the close coordination of member States' economic policies, on the internal market and on the definition of common objectives, and which is concluded in accordance with the principle of an open market economy with free competition.

2   Concurrently with the foregoing, and as provided for in this Treaty and in accordance with the timetable and the procedures set out therein, these activities shall include the irrevocable fixing of exchange rates leading to the introduction of a single currency, the ECU, the definition and conduct of a single monetary policy and exchange rate policy the primary objective of both of which shall be to maintain price stability and, without prejudice to this objective, to support the general economic policies in the Community, in accordance with the principle of an open market economy with free competition.

3   These activities of the Member States and the Community shall entail compliance with the following guiding principles: stable prices, sound public finances and monetary conditions and a sustainable balance of payments.

Article 3 b

The Community shall act within the limits of the powers conferred upon it by this Treaty and of the objectives assigned to it therein.

In areas which do not fall within its exclusive competence, the Community shall take action, in accordance with the principle of subsidiarity, only if and in so far as the objectives of the proposed action cannot be sufficiently achieved by the Member States and can therefore, by reason of the scale or effects of the proposed action, be better achieved by the Community.

---

[1] Reproduced from CONF–UP–UEM 2002/92, Brussels, 1 February 1992; this is the final version of the Treaty agreed in the Conference of the Representatives of the Governments of the Member States (IGC) which was signed in Maastricht on 7 February 1992. Some Articles of the EMU Treaty not essential for the present purposes have been omitted.

Any action by the Community shall not go beyond what is necessary to achieve the objectives of this Treaty.

Article 4

1   The tasks entrusted to the Community shall be carried out by the following institutions:

  - a **European Parliament,**
  - a **Council,**
  - a **Commission,**
  - a **Court of Justice,**
  - a **Court of Auditors.**

Each institution shall act within the limits of the powers conferred upon it by this Treaty.

2   The Council and the Commission shall be assisted by an Economic and Social Committee and a Committee of the Regions acting in an advisory capacity.

Article 4 a

A European System of Central Banks (hereinafter referred to as 'ESCB') and the European Central Bank (hereinafter referred to as 'ECB') shall be established in accordance with the procedures laid down in this Treaty; they shall act within the limits of the powers conferred upon them by this Treaty and the Statute of the ESCB and the ECB (hereinafter referred to as 'Statute of the ESCB') annexed thereto.

Part Three – Community Policies

Chapter 4: Capital and Payments

Article 73 a

From 1 January 1994, Articles 67 to 73 shall be replaced by Articles 73 b, c, d, e, f and g.

Article 73 b

1   Within the framework of the provisions set out in this Chapter, all restrictions on the movement of capital between Member States and between Member States and third countries shall be prohibited.

2   Within the framework of the provisions set out in this Chapter, all payments between Member States and between Member States and third countries shall be free of restrictions.

Article 73 c

1   The provisions of Article 73b shall be without prejudice to the application to third countries of any restrictions which exist on 31 December 1993 under national or Community law adopted in respect of the movement of capital to or from third countries involving direct investment – including investment in real estate – establishment, the provision of financial services and the admission of securities to capital markets.

2   Whilst endeavouring to achieve the objective of free movement of capital between Member States and third countries to the greatest extent possible and without prejudice to the other Chapters of this Treaty, the Council may, acting by a qualified majority on a proposal from the Commission, adopt measures on the movement of capital to or from third countries involving direct investment – including investment in real estate-establishment, the provision of financial services and the admission of securities to capital markets. Unanimity shall be required for measures under this paragraph which constitute a step back in Community law as regards the liberalization of the movement of capital to or from third countries.

Article 73 d

1   The provisions of Article 73 b shall be without prejudice to the right of Member States:

   (a)   to apply the relevant provisions of their tax law which distinguish between tax-payers who are not in the same situation with regard to the place of residence or the place where their capital is invested;
   (b)   to take all requisite measures to prevent infringements of national law and regulations, in particular in the field of taxation and the prudential supervision of financial institutions, or to lay down procedures for the declaration of capital movements for purposes of administrative or statistical information, or to take measures which are justified on ground of public policy or public security.

2   The provisions of this Chapter shall be without prejudice to the applicability of restrictions on the right of establishment which are compatible with this Treaty.

3   The measures and procedures referred to in paragraphs 1 and 2 shall not constitute a means of arbitrary discrimination or a disguised restriction on the free movement of capital and payments as defined in Article 73 b.

Article 73 e

By derogation from Article 73 b, Member States which, on 31 December 1993, enjoy a derogation on the basis of existing Community law, shall be entitled to maintain, until 31 December 1995 at the latest, restrictions on movements of capital covered by such derogations as exist on that date.

Article 73 f

Where, in exceptional circumstances, movements of capital to or from third countries cause, or threaten to cause, serious difficulties for the operation of economic and monetary union, the Council, acting by a qualified majority on a proposal from the Commission and after consulting the ECB, may take safeguard measures with regard to countries for a period not exceeding six months if such measures are strictly necessary.

Article 73 g

1   If, in the cases envisaged in Article 228 a, action by the Community is deemed necessary, the Council may, in accordance with the procedure provided for in Article 228 a, take the necessary urgent measures on the movement of capital and on payments as regards the third countries concerned.

2   Without prejudice to Article 224 and as long as the Council has not taken measures pursuant to paragraph 1, a Member State may, for serious political reasons on grounds of urgency take unilateral measures against a third country with regard to capital movements and payments.

The Commission and the other Member States shall be informed of such measures by the date of their entry into force at the latest.

The Council may, acting by a qualified majority on a proposal from the Commission, decide that the Member State concerned shall amend or abolish the measures. The President of the Council shall inform the European Parliament about any such decision taken by the Council.

Article 73 h

Until 1 January 1994, the following provisions shall be applicable:

1   Each Member State undertakes to authorize, in the currency of the Member State in which the creditor or the beneficiary resides, any payments connected with the movement of goods, services or capital, and any transfers of capital and earnings, to the extent that the movement of goods, services, capital and persons between Member States has been liberalized pursuant to this Treaty.

The Member States declare their readiness to undertake the liberalization of payments beyond the extent provided in the preceding subparagraph, in so far as their economic situation in general and the state of their balance of payments in particular so permit.

2   In so far as movements of goods, services and capital are limited only by restrictions on payments connected therewith, these restrictions shall be progressively abolished by applying, mutatis mutandis, the provisions of this Chapter and the Chapters relating to the abolition of quantitative restrictions and to the liberalization of services.

3   Member States undertake not to introduce between themselves any new restrictions on transfers connected with the invisible transactions listed in Annex III to this Treaty.

The progressive abolition of existing restrictions shall be effected in accordance with the provisions of Articles 63 to 65, in so far as such abolition is not governed by the provisions contained in paragraphs 1 and 2 or by the other provisions of this Chapter.

4   If need be, Member States shall consult each other on the measures to be taken to enable the payments and transfers mentioned in this Article to be effected; such measures shall not prejudice the attainment of the objectives set out in this Treaty.

Title VI – Economic and Monetary Policy

Chapter 1: Economic Policy

Article 102 a

Member States shall conduct their economic policies with a view to contributing to the achievement of the objectives of the Community, as defined in Article 2 and in the context of the broad guidelines referred to in Article 103 (2). The Member States and the Community shall act in accordance with the principle of an open market economy with free competition, favouring an efficient allocation of resources, and in compliance with the principles set out in Article 3 a.

Article 103

1   Member States shall regard their economic policies as a matter of common concern and shall coordinate them within the Council, in accordance with the provisions of Article 102 a.

2   The Council shall, acting by a qualified majority on a recommendation from the Commission, formulate a draft for the broad guidelines of the economic policies of the Member States and of the Community, and shall report its findings to the European Council.

The European Council shall, acting on the basis of this report from the Council, discuss a conclusion on the broad guidelines of the economic policies of the Member States and of the Community.

On the basis of this conclusion, the Council shall, acting by qualified majority, adopt a recommendation setting out these broad guidelines. The Council shall inform the European Parliament of its recommendation.

3   In order to ensure closer coordination of economic policies and sustained convergence of the economic performances of the Member States, the Council shall, on the basis of reports submitted by the Commission, monitor the economic developments in each of the Member States and in the Community as well as consistency of economic policies with the broad guidelines referred to in paragraph 2, and regularly carry out an overall assessment.

For the purpose of this multilateral surveillance Member States shall forward information to the Commission about important measures taken in the field of their economic policy and such other information as they deem necessary.

4   Where it is established, under the procedure referred to in paragraph 3, that the economic policies of a Member State prove to be not consistent with the broad guidelines referred to in paragraph 2 or that they risk jeopardizing the proper functioning of economic and monetary union, the Council may, acting by a qualified majority on a recommendation from the Commission, make the necessary recommendations to the Member State concerned. The Council may, acting by a qualified majority on a proposal from the Commission, decide to make its recommendations public.

The President of the Council and the Commission shall report to the European Parliament on the results of multilateral surveillance. The President of the Council may be invited to appear before the competent Committee of the European Parliament if the Council has made its recommendations public.

5   The Council, acting in accordance with the procedure referred to in Article 189c may adopt detailed rules for the multilateral surveillance procedure referred to in paragraphs 3 and 4 of this Article.

Article 103 a

1   Without prejudice to any other procedures provided for in this Treaty, the Council may, acting unanimously on a proposal from the Commission, decide upon the measures appropriate to the economic situation, in particular if severe difficulties arise in the supply of certain products.

2   Where a Member State is in difficulties or is seriously threatened with severe difficulties caused by exceptional occurrences beyond its control, the Council may, acting unanimously on a proposal from the Commission, grant under certain conditions Community financial assistance to the Member State concerned. Where the severe difficulties are caused by natural disasters, the Council shall act by qualified majority. The President of the Council shall inform the European Parliament of the decision taken.

Article 104

1   Overdraft facilities or any other type of credit facility with ECB or with the national central banks of the Member States (hereinafter referred to as 'national central banks') in favour of Community institutions or bodies, central governments, regional local or other public

authorities, other bodies governed by public law, or public undertakings of Member States shall be prohibited as shall the purchase directly from them by the ECB or national central banks of debt instruments.

2 The provisions of paragraph 1 shall not apply to publicly-owned credit institutions, which in the context of the supply of reserves by central banks shall be given the same treatment by national central banks and the ECB as private credit institutions.

Article 104 a

1 Any measure, not based on prudential considerations, establishing privileged access by Community institutions or bodies, central governments, regional, local or other public authorities, other bodies governed by public law or public undertakings of Member States to financial institutions shall be prohibited.

2 The Council, acting in accordance with the procedure referred to in Article 189c, shall, before 1 January 1994, specify definitions for tha application of the prohibition referred to in paragraph 1.

Article 104 b

1 The Community shall not be liable for or assume the commitments of central governments, regional, local or other authorities, other bodies governed by public law, or public undertakings of any Member State, without prejudice to mutual financial guarantees for the joint execution of a specific project. A Member State shall not be liable for or assume the commitments of central governments, regional, local or other authorities, other bodies governed by public law or public undertakings of another Member State, without prejudice to mutual financial guarentees for the joint execution of a specific project.

2 If necessary, the Council, acting in accordance with the procedure referred to in Article 189c, may specify definitions for the application of the prohibitions referred to in Article 104 and in this Article.

Article 104 c

1 Member States shall avoid excessive government deficits.

2 The Commission shall monitor the development of the budgetary situation and of the stock of government debt in the Member States with a view to identifying gross errors. In particular it shall examine compliance with the budgetary discipline on the basis of the following two criteria:

(a) whether the ratio of the planned or actual government deficit to gross domestic product exceeds a reference value, unless

    — either the ratio has declined substantially and continuously and reached a level that comes close to the reference value;

    — or, alternatively, the excess over the reference value is only exceptional and temporary and the ratio remains close to the reference value;

(b) whether the ratio of government debt to gross domestic product exceeds a reference value, unless the ratio is sufficiently diminishing and approaching the reference value at a satisfactory pace.

The reference values are specified in the Protocol on the excessive deficit procedure annexed to this Treaty.

3   If a Member State does not fulfil the requirements under one or both of these criteria, the Commission shall prepare a report. The report of the Commission shall also take into account whether the government deficit exceeds the government investment expenditure and take into account all other relevant factors, including the medium term economic and budgetary position of the Member State.

     The Commission may also prepare a report if, notwithstanding the fulfilment of the requirements under the criteria, it is of the opinion that there is a risk of an excessive deficit in a Member State.

4   The Committee provided for in Article 109c shall formulate an opinion on the report of the Commission.

5   If the Commission considers that an excessive deficit in a Member State exists or may occur, the Commission shall address its opinion to the Council.

6   The Council shall, acting by a qualified majority on a recommendation from the Commission, and having considered any observations which the Member State concerned may wish to make, decide after an overall assessment whether an excessive deficit exists.

7   Where the existence of an excessive deficit is decided according to paragraph 6, the Council shall make recommendations to the Member State concerned with a view to bringing that situation to an end within a given period. Subject to the provisions of paragraph 8, these recommendations shall not be made public.

8   Where it establishes that there has been no effective action in response to its recommendations within the period laid down, the Council may make its recommendations public.

9   If a Member State persists in failing to put into practice the recommendations of the Council, the Council may decide to give notice to the Member State to take, within a specified time limit, measures for the deficit reduction which is judged necessary by the Council in order to remedy the situation.

     In such a case, the Council may request the Member State concerned to submit reports in accordance with a specific timetable in order to examine the adjustment efforts of that Member State.

10   The rights to bring actions provided for in Article 169 and 170 may not be exercised within the framework of paragraphs 1 to 9 of this Article.

11   As long as a Member State fails to comply with a decision taken in accordance with paragraph 9, the Council may decide to apply or, as the case may be, intensify one or more of the following measures:

- to require that the Member State concerned shall publish additional information, to be specified by the Council, before issuing bonds and securities;
- to invite the European Investment Bank to reconsider its lending policy towards the Member State concerned;
- to require that the Member State concerned makes a non- interest-bearing deposit of an appropriate size with the Community until the excessive deficit has, in the view of the Council, been corrected;
- to impose fines of an appropriate size.

The President of the Council shall inform the European Parliament about the decision taken.

12   The Council shall abrogate some or all of its decisions as referred to in paragraph 6 to 9 and 11 to the extent that the excessive deficit in the Member State concerned has, in the view of

the Council, been corrected. If the Council previously has made public recommendations, it will, as soon as the decision has been abrogated, make a public statement that an excessive deficit in the Member State concerned no longer exists.

13 When taking the Council decisions referred to in paragraphs 7 to 9, 11 and 12 the Council shall act on a recommendation from the Commission by a majority of two thirds of the weighted votes of its members weighted in accordance with Article 148(2) and excluding the votes of the representative of the Member State concerned.

14 Further provisions relating to the implementation of the procedure described in this Article are set out in the Protocol on the excessive deficit procedure annexed to this Treaty.

The Council shall acting unanimously on a proposal from the Commission and after consulting the European Parliament and the ECB, adopt the appropriate provisions which shall then replace the said Protocol.

Subject to the other provisions of this paragraph the Council shall, before 1 January 1994, acting by a qualified majority on a proposal from the Commission and after consulting the European Parliament, lay down detailed rules and definitions for the application of the provisions of the said Protocol.

Chapter 2 – Monetary Policy

Article 105

1 The primary objective of the ESCB shall be to maintain price stability. Without prejudice to the objective of price stability, the ESCB shall support the general economic policies in the Community with a view to contributing to the achievement of the objectives of the Community as laid down in Article 2. The ESCB shall act in accordance with the principle of an open market economy with free competition, favouring an efficient allocation of resources, and in compliance with the principles set out in Article 3a.

2 The basic tasks to be carried out through the ESCB shall be:

- to define and implement the monetary policy of the Community;
- to conduct foreign exchange operations consistent with the provisions of Article 109;
- to hold and manage the official foreign reserves of the Member States;
- to promote the smooth operation of payment systems.

3. The third indent of paragraph 2 shall be without prejudice to the holding and management by the governments of Member States of foreign exchange working balances.

4 The ECB shall be consulted:

- on any proposed Community act in its fields of competence;
- by national authorities regarding any draft legislative provision in its fields of competence, but within the limits and under the conditions set out by the Council in accordance with the procedure laid down in Article 106(6).

The ECB may submit opinions to the appropriate Community institutions or bodies or to national authorities on matters within its field of compentence.

5 The ESCB shall contribute to the smooth conduct of policies pursued by the competent authorities relating to the prudential supervision of credit institutions and the stability of the financial system.

6 The Council may, acting unanimously on a proposal from the Commission and after consulting the ECB and after receiving the assent of the European Parliament, confer upon

the ECB specific tasks concerning policies relating to the prudential supervision of credit institutions and other financial institutions with the exception of insurance undertakings.

Article 105a

1   The ECB shall have the exclusive right to authorize the issue of bank notes within the Community. The ECB and the national central banks may issue such notes. The bank notes issued by the ECB and the national central banks shall be the only such notes to have the status of legal tender within the Community.

2   Member States may issue coins subject to approval by the ECB of the volume of the issue. The Council may, acting in accordance with the procedure referred to in Article 189c and after consulting the ECB, adopt measures to harmonize the denominations and technical specifications of all coins intended for circulation to the extent necessary to permit their smooth circulation within the Community.

Article 106

1   The ESCB shall be composed of the ECB and of the national central banks.

2   The ECB shall have legal personality.

3   The ESCB shall be governed by the decision-making bodies of the ECB which shall be the Governing Council and the Executive Board.

4   The Statute of the ESCB is laid down in a Protocol annexed to this Treaty.

5   Articles 5.1, 5.2, 5.3, 17, 18, 19.1, 22, 23, 24, 26, 32.2, 32.3, 32.4, 32.6, 33.1(a) and 36 of the Statute of the ESCB may be amended by the Council, acting by a qualified majority on a recommendation from the ECB and after consulting the Commission or unanimously on a proposal from the Commission and after consulting the ECB. In either case, the assent of the European Parliament shall be required.

6   The Council, acting by a qualified majority either on a proposal from the Commission and after consulting the European Parliament and the ECB, or on a recommendation from the ECB and after consulting the European Parliament and the Commission, shall adopt the provisions referred to in Articles 4, 5.4, 19.2, 20, 28.1, 29.2, 30.4 and 34.3 of the Statute of the ESCB.

Article 107

When exercising the powers and carrying out the tasks and duties confered upon them by this Treaty and the Statute of the ESCB, neither the ECB, nor a national central bank, nor any member of their decision-making bodies shall seek or take instructions from Community institutions or bodies, from any government of a Member State or from any other body. The Community institutions and bodies and the governments of the Member States undertake to respect this principle and not to seek to influence the members of the decision-making bodies of the ECB or of the national central banks in the performance of their tasks.

Article 108

Each Member State shall ensure, at the latest at the date of the establishment of the ESCB, that its national legislation including the statutes of its national central bank is compatible with this Treaty and the Statute of the ESCB.

Article 108a

1   In order to carry out the tasks entrusted to the ESCB, the ECB shall, in accordance with the provisions of this Treaty and under the conditions laid down in the Statute of the ESCB:

   –   make regulations to the extent necessary to implement the tasks defined in Argicle 3.1, first indent, Articles 19.1, 22 or 25.2 of the Statute of the ESCB and in cases which shall be laid down in the acts of the Council referred to in Article 106(6);
   –   take decisions necessary for carrying out the tasks entrusted to the ESCB under this Treaty and the Statute of the ESCB;
   –   make recommendations and deliver opinions.

2   A regulation shall have general application. It shall be binding in its entirety and directly applicable in all Member States.
   Recommendations and opinions shall have no binding force.
   A decision shall be binding in its entirety upon those to whom it is addressed.
   Articles 190 to 192 shall apply to regulations and decisions adopted by the ECB.
   The ECB may decide to publish its decisions, recommendations and opinions.

3   Within the limits and under the conditions adopted by the Council under the procedure laid down in Article 106(6), the ECB shall be entitled to impose fines or periodic penalty payments on undertakings for failure to comply with obligations under its regulations and decisions.

Article 109

1   By way of derogation from Article 228, the Council may, acting unanimously on a recommendation from the ECB or from the Commission, and after consulting the ECB in an endeavour to reach a consensus consistent with the objective of price stability, after consulting the European Parliament, in accordance with the procedure in paragraph 3 for determining the arrangements, conclude formal agreements on an exchange rate system for the ECU in relation to non-Community currencies. The Council may, acting by a qualified majority on a recommendation from the ECB or from the Commission, and after consulting the ECB in an endeavour to reach a consensus consistent with the objective of price stability, adopt, adjust or abandon the central rates of the ECU within the exchange rate system. The President of the Council shall inform the European Parliament of the adoption, adjustment or abandonment of the ECU central rates.

2   In the absence of an exchange rate system in relation to one or more non-Community currencies as referred to in paragraph 1, the Council, acting by a qualified majority either on a recommendation from the Commission and after consulting the ECB, or on a recommendation from the ECB, may formulate general orientations for exchange rate policy in relation to these currencies. These general orientations shall be without prejudice to the primary objective of the ESCB to maintain price stability.

3   By way of derogation from Article 228, where agreements concerning monetary of foreign exchange regime matters need to be negotiated by the Community with one or more States or international organizations, the Council, acting by a qualified majority on a recommendation from the Commission and after consulting the ECB, shall decide the arrangements for the negotiation and for the conclusion of such agreements. These arrangements shall ensure that the Community expresses a single position. The Commission shall be fully associated with the negotiations.
   Agreements concluded in accordance with this paragraph shall be binding on the institutions of the Community, on the ECB and on Member States.

4   Subject to paragraph, the Council shall, on a proposal from the Commission and after

consulting the ECB, acting by a qualified majority decide on the position of the Community at international level as regards issues of particular relevance to economic and monetary union and, acting unanimously, decide its representation in compliance with the allocation of powers laid down in Articles 103 and 105.

5   Without prejudice to Community competence and Community agreements as regards Economic and Monetary Union, Member States may negotiate in international bodies and conclude international agreements.

Chapter 3 – Institutional Provisions

Article 109 a

1   The Governing Council of the ECB shall comprise the members of the Executive Board of the ECB and the Governors of the national central banks.

2   (a)   The Executive Board shall comprise the President, the Vice-President and four other members.

(b)   The President, the Vice-President and the other members of the Executive Board shall be appointed from among persons of recognized standing and professional experience in monetary or banking matters by common accord of the Governments of the Member States at the level of Heads of State or of Government, on a recommendation from the Council, after it has consulted the European Parliament and the Governing Council of the ECB.
Their term of office shall be eight years and shall not be renewable.
Only nationals of Member States may be members of the Executive Board.

Article 109 b

1   The President of the Council and a member of the Commission may participate, without having the right to vote, in meetings of the Governing Council of the ECB.
The President of the Council may submit a motion for deliberation to the Governing Council of the ECB.

2   The President of the ECB shall be invited to participate in Council meetings when the Council is discussing matters relating to the objectives and tasks of the ESCB.

3   The ECB shall address an annual report on the activities of the ESCB and on the monetary policy of both the previous and current year to the European Parliament, the Council and the Commission, and also to the European Council. The President of the ECB shall present this report to the Council and to the European Parliament, which may hold a general debate on that basis.
The President of the ECB and the other members of the Executive Board may, at the request of the European Parliament or on their own initiative, be heard by the competent Committees of the European Parliament.

Article 109 c

1   In order to promote coordination of the policies of Member States to the full extent needed for the functioning of the internal market, a Monetary Committee with advisory status is hereby set up.
It shall have the following tasks:

- to keep under review the monetary and financial situation of the Member States and of the Community and the general payments system of the Member States and to report regularly thereon to the Council and to the Commission;
- to deliver opinions at the request of the Council or of Commission or on its own initiative for submission to those institutions;
- without prejudice to Article 151, to contribute to the preparation of the work of the Council referred to in Articles 73f, 73g, 103(2), (3), (4) and 5, 103a, 104a, 104b, 104c, 109e(2), 109f(6), 109h, 109i, 109j(2) and 109k(1);
- to examine, at least once a year, the situation regarding the movement of capital and the freedom of payments, as they result from the application of this Treaty and of measures of the Council; the examination shall cover all measures relating to capital movements and payments; the Committee shall report to the Commission and to the Council on the outcome of this examination.

The Member States and the Commission shall each appoint two members of the Monetary Committee.

2   At the start of the third stage, an Economic and Financial Committee shall be set up. The Monetary Committee provided for in paragraph 1 of this Article shall be dissolved.
     The Economic and Financial Committee shall have the following tasks:

- to deliver opinions, at the request of the Council, or of the Commission, or on its own initiative for submission to those institutions;
- to keep under review the economic and financial situation of the Member States and of the Community and to report regularly thereon to the Council and to the Commission, in particular on financial relations with third countries and international institutions;
- without prejudice to Article 151, to contribute to the preparation of the work of the Council referred to in Articles 73f, 73g, 103(2), (3), (4) and (5), 103a, 104a, 104b, 104c, 105(6), 105a(2), 106(5) and (6), 109, 109h, 109i(2) and (3), 109k(2), 109l(4) and (5), and to carry ouy other advisory and preparatory tasks assigned to it by the Council;
- to examine, at least once a year, the situation regarding the movement of capital and the freedom of payments, as they result from the application of this Treaty and of measures adopted by the Council; the examination shall cover all measures relating to capital movements and payments; the Committee shall report to the Commission and to the Council on the outcome of this examination.

The Member States, the Commission and the ECB shall each appoint no more than two members of the Committee.

3   The Council shall, acting by a qualified majority on a proposal from the Commission and after consulting the ECB and the Committee referred to in this Article, lay down detailed provisions concerning the composition of the Economic and Financial Committee. The President of the Council shall inform the European Parliament of such a decision.

4   In addition to the tasks set out in paragraph 2, if and as long as there are Member States with a derogation as referred to in Article 109k and 109l, the Committee shall keep under review the monetary and financial situation and the general payments system of those Member States and report regularly thereon to the Council and to the Commission.

Article 109 d

For matters within the scope of Articles 103(4), 104c with the exception of paragraph 14, 109, 109j, 109k and 109l(4) and (5), the Council or a Member State may request the Commission to make a recommendation or a proposal, as appropriate. The Commission shall examine this request and submit its conclusions to the Council without delay.

Chapter 4: Transitional Provisions

Article 109 e

1   The second stage for achieving economic and monetary union shall begin on 1 January 1994.

2   Before that date.

(a)   each Member State shall:

adopt where necessary appropriate measures to comply with the prohibitions laid down in Article 73b, without prejudice to Article 73e, and in Articles 104 and 104a(1);

adopt, if necessary, with a view to permitting the assessment provided for in paragraph (b), multiannual programmes intended to ensure the lasting convergence necessary for the achievement of economic and monetary union, in particular with regard to price stability and sound public finances.

(b)   the Council shall, on the basis of a report from the Commission, assess the progress made with regard to economic and monetary convergence, in particular with regard to price stability and sound public finances, and the progress made with the implementation of Community law concerning the internal market.

3   The provisions of Articles 104, 104a(1), 104b(1) and 104with the exception of paragraphs 1, 9, 11 and 14 shall apply from the beginning of the second stage.
The provisions of Articles 103a(2), 104c(1), (9) and (11), 105, 105a, 107, 109, 109a, 109b and 109c(2) and (4) shall apply from the beginning of the third stage.

4   In the second stage of EMU Member States shall endeavour to avoid excessive government deficits.

5   During the second stage each Member State shall, as appropriate, start the process leading to the independence of its central bank, in accordance with the provisions of Article 108.

Article 109 f

1   At the start of the second stage, the European Monetary Institute (in this Treaty called 'EMI') shall be established and take up its duties; it shall have legal personality and be directed and managed by a Council, consisting of a President, a Vice-president and the Governors of the Central Banks of the Member States. The President shall be appointed by common accord of the Governments of the Member States at the level of Heads of State or of Government, on a recommendation from, as the case may be, the Committee of Governors or the Council of the EMI, and after consulting the Council and the European Parliament. The President shall be selected from among persons of recognised standing and professional experience in monetary or banking matters. Only nationals of Member States may be President of the EMI. The Council of the EMI shall appoint a Vice-President from among the Governors.

The Statute of the EMI is laid down in a Protocol annexed to this Treaty. The Committee of Governors of the Central Banks of the Member States shall be dissolved at the start of the second stage.

2   The EMI shall:

   −   strengthen cooperation between the national central banks;

   −   strengthen the coordination of the monetary policies of the Member States, with the aim of ensuring price stability;

   −   monitor the functioning of the European Monetary System;

- hold consultations concerning issued falling within the competence of the central banks and affecting the stability of financial institutions and markets;
- take over the tasks of the European Monetary Cooperation Fund, which shall be dissolved; the modalities of dissolution are laid down in the Statute of the EMI;
- facilitate the use of the ECU and oversea its development, including the smooth functioning of the ECU clearing system.

3   For the preparation of the third stage the EMI shall:

- prepare the instruments and the procedures necessary for carrying out a single monetary policy in the third stage;
- promote the harmonisation, where necessary, of the rules and practices governing the collection, compilation and distribution of statistics in the areas within its field of competence;
- prepare the rules for operations to be undertaken by the national central banks in the framework of the ESCB;
- promote the efficiency of cross-border payments;
- supervise the technical preparation of ECU bank-notes.

At the latest by 31 December 1996, the EMI shall specify the regulatory, organizational and logistical framework necessary for the ESCB to perform its tasks in the third stage. This framework shall be submitted for decision to the ECB at the date of its establishment.

4   The EMI, acting by a majority of two thirds of the members of its Council may:

- formulate opinions or recommendations on the overall orientation of monetary policy and exchange rate policy as well as on related measures introduced in each Member State;
- submit opinions or recommandations to Governments and to the Council on policies which might affect the internal or external monetary situation in the Community and, in particular, the functioning of the European Monetary System;
- make recommendations to the monetary authorities of the Member States concerning the conduct of their monetary policy.

5   The EMI, acting unanimously, may decide to publish its opinions and recommendations.

6   The EMI shall be consulted by the Council regarding any proposed Community act within its field of competence;
    Within the limits and under the conditions set out by the Council, acting by a qualified majority on a proposal from the Commission and after consulting the the European Parliament and the EMI, the EMI shall be consulted by the authorities of the Member States on any draft legislative provision within its field of competence.

7   The Council may, acting unanimously on a proposal from the Commission and after consulting the European Parliament and the EMI, confer upon the EMI other tasks for the preparation of the third stage.

8   Where this Treaty provides for a consultative role for the ECB, references to the ECB shall be read as referring to the EMI before the establishment of the ECB.
    Where this Treaty provides for a consultative role for the EMI, references to the EMI shall be read, before 1 January 1994, as referring to the Committee of the ECB.

9   During the second stage, the term 'ECB' used in Articles 173, 175, 176, 177, 180 and 215 shall be read as referring to the EMI.

Article 109 g

The currency composition of the ECU basket shall not be changed.

From the start of the third stage the value of the ECU shall be irrevocably fixed in accordance with Article 109 l(4).

Article 109 h

1   Where a Member State is in difficulties or is seriously threatened with difficulties as regards its balance of payments either as a result of an overall disequilibrium in its balance of payments, or as a result of the type of currency at its disposal, and where such difficulties are implementation of the common commercial policy, the Commission shall immediately investigate the position of the State in question and the action which, making use of all the means at its disposal, that State has taken or may take in accordance with the provisions of this Treaty. The Commission shall state what measures it recommends the State concerned to take.

     If the action taken by a Member State and the measures suggested by the Commission do not prove sufficient to overcome the difficulties which have arisen or which threaten, the Commission shall, after consulting the Committee referred to in Article 109c, recommend to the Council the granting of mutual assistance and appropriate methods therefore.

     The Commission shall keep the Council regularly informed of the situation and of how it is developing.

2   The Council, acting by a qualified majority, shall grant such mutual assistance; it shall adopt directives or decisions laying down the conditions and details of such assistance, which may take such forms as:

    (a)   a concerted approach to or within any other international organizations to which Member States may have recourse;

    (b)   measures needed to avoid deflection of trade where the State which is in difficulties maintains or reintroduces quantitative restrictions against third countries;

    (c)   the granting of limited credits by other Member States, subject to their agreement.

3   If the mutual assistance recommended by the Commission is not granted by the Council or if the mutual assistance granted and the measures taken are insufficient, the Commission shall authorize the State which is in difficulties to take protective measures, the conditions and details of which the Commission shall determine.

     Such authorization may be revoked and such conditions and details may be changed by the Council acting by a qualified majority.

4   Subject to Article 109k(6), this Article shall cease to apply from the beginning of the third stage.

Article 109 i

1   Where a sudden crisis in the balance of payments occurs and a decision within the meaning of Article 109h(2) is not immediately taken, the Member State concerned may, as a precaution, take the necessary protective measures. Such measures must cause the least possible disturbance in the functioning of the common market and must not be wider in scope than is strictly necessary to remedy the sudden dificulties which have arisen.

2   The Commission and other Member States shall be informed of such protective measures not later than when they enter into force. The Commission may recommend to the Council the granting of mutual assistance under Article 109h.

3   After the Commission has delivered an opinion and the Committee referred to in Article

109c has been consulted, the Council may, acting by a qualified majority, decide that the State concerned shall amend, suspend or abolish the protective measures referred to above.

4   Subject to Article 109k(6), this Article shall cease to apply from the beginning of the third stage.

Article 109 j

1   The Commission and the EMI shall report to the Council on the progress made in the fulfilment by the Member States of their obligations regarding the achievement of economic and monetary union. These reports shall include an examination of the compatibility between a Member State's national legislation, including the Statutes of its national central bank, and Articles 107 and 108 of this Treaty and the Statute of the ESCB. The reports shall also examine the achievement of a high degree of sustainable convergence by reference to the fulfilment of each Member State of the following criteria:

   –   the achievement of a high degree of price stability; this will be apparent from a rate of inflation which is close to that of, at most, the three best performing Member States in terms of price stability;

   –   the sustainability of the government financial position; this will be apparent from having achieved budgetary positions without a deficit that is excessive as determined in accordance with Article 104c(6);

   –   the observance of the normal fluctuation margins provided for by the Exchange Rate Mechanism of the European Monetary System, for at least two years, without devaluing against the currency of any other Member State;

   –   the durability of convergence achieved by the Member state and of its participation in the Exchange Rate Mechanism of the European Monetary System being reflected in the long-term interest rate levels.

   The four criteria mentioned in this paragraph and the relevant period over which they are to be respected are developed further in a Protocol annexed to this Treaty. The reports of the Commission and the EMI shall also take account of the development of the ECU, the results of the integration of markets, the situation and development of the balances of payments on current account and an examination of the development of unit labour costs and other price indices.

2   On the basis of these reports, the Council, acting by a qualified majority on a recommendation from the Commission, assess:

   –   for each Member State, whether it fulfils the necessary conditions for the adoption of a single currency;

   –   whether a majority of the Member States fulfil the necessary conditons for the adoption of a single currency;

   and recommend its findings to the Council, meeting in the composition of the Heads of State or of Government. The European Parliament shall be consulted and forward its opinion to the Council, meeting in the composition of the Heads of State or of Government.

3   Taking due account of the reports as referred to in Paragraph 1 and the opinion of the European Parliament referred to in paragraph 2, the Council, meeting in the composition of Heads of State or of Government, shall, acting by a qualified majority, not later than 31 December 1996:

   –   decide on the basis of the recommendations of the Council referred to in paragraph 2, whether a majority of the Member States fulfil the necessary conditions for the adoption of a single currency;

– decide whether it is appropriate for the Community to enter the third stage,

and if so,

– set the date for the beginning of the third stage.

4   If by the end of 1997 the date for the beginning of the third stage has not been set, the third stage will start on 1 January 1999. Before 1 July 1998, the Council, meeting in the composition of Heads of State or of Government, after a repetition of the procedure provided for in paragraphs 1 and 2, with the exception of the second indent of paragraph 2, taking into account the reports as referred to in paragraph 1 and the opinion of the European Parliament, shall, acting by a qualified majority and on the basis of the recommendations of the Council referred to in paragraph 2, confirm which Member States fulful the necessary conditions for the adoption of a single currency.

Article 109 k

1   If the decision has been taken to set the date in accordance with Article 109 f paragraph 3, the Council shall, on the basis of the recommendation from the Commission, decide whether any, and if so which, Member States shall have a derogation as defined in paragraph 3 of this Article. Such Member States shall in this Treaty be referred to as 'Member States with a derogation'.

If the Council has confirmed which Member States fulfil the necessary conditions for the adoption of a single currency, in accordance with Article 109j(4), those Member States which do not fulfil the conditions shall have a derogation as defined in paragraph 3 of this Article. Such Member States shall in this Treaty be referred to as 'Member States with a derogation'.

2   At least once every two years, or at the request of a Member State with a derogation, the Commission and the ECB shall report to the Council in accordance with the procedure laid down in Article 109j(1). After consulting the European Parliament and after discussion in the Council, meeting in the composition of the Heads of State or of Government, the Council shall, acting by a qualified majority on a proposal from the Commission, decide which Member States with a derogation fulfil the necessary conditions on the basis of the criteria set out in Article 109j(1), and abrogate the derogations of the Member States concerned.

3   A derogation as referred to in paragraph 1 shall entail that the following Articles do not apply to the Member State concerned: Articles 104c(9) and 11, 105(1), (2), (3) and (5), 105a, 108a, 109, and 109a(2)(b). The exclusion of such a Member State and its national central bank from rights and obligations within the ESCB is laid down in Chapter IX of the Statute of the ESCB.

4   In Articles 105(1), (2) and (3), 105a, 108a, 109 and 109a(2)(b), 'Member States' shall be read as 'Member States without a derogation'.

5   The voting rights of the Member States with a derogation shall be suspended for the Council decisions referred to in the Articles of this Treaty mentioned in paragraph 3. In that case, by way of derogation from Articles 148 and 189a(1), a qualified majority shall be defined as two thirds of the votes of the representatives of the Member States without a derogation weighted in accordance with Article 138(2), and unanimity of those Member States shall be required for an act requiring unanimity.

6   Articles 109h and 109i shall continue to apply to a Member State with a derogation.

Article 109 l

1 Immediately after the decision on the date for the beginning of the third stage has been taken in accordance with Article 109j(3), or, as the case may be, immediately after 1 July 1998:

- the Council shall adopt the provisions referred to in Article 106(6);
- the Governments of the Member States without a derogation shall appoint, in accordance with the procedure set out in Article 50 of the Statute of the ESCB, the President, the Vice-President and the other members of the Executive Board of the ECB. If there are Member States with a derogation, the number of members of the Executive Board may be smaller than provided for in Article 11.1 of the Statute of the ESCB, but in no circumstances shall it be less than four.

As soon as the Executive Board has been appointed, the ESCB and the ECB are established and shall prepare for their full operation as described in this Treaty and the Statute of the ESCB. The full exercise of their powers shall start from the first day of the third stage.

2 As soon as the ECB is established, it shall, if necessary, take over functions of the EMI. The EMI shall go into liquidation upon the establishment of the ECB; the modalities of liquidation are laid down in the Statute of the EMI.

3 If there are Member States with a derogation, and without prejudice to Article 106(3) of this Treaty, the General Council of the ECB referred to in Article 45 of the Statute of the ESCB shall be constituted as a third decision-making body of the ECB.

4 At the starting date of the third stage, the Council shall, acting with the unanimity of the Member States without a derogation, on a proposal from the Commission and after consulting the ECB, adopt the conversion rates at which their currencies shall be irrevocably fixes and at which irrevocably fixed rate the ECU shall be substituted for these currencies, and the ECU will become a currency in its own right. This measure shall by itself not modify the external value of the ECU. The Council shall, acting according to the same procedure, also take the other measures necessary for the rapid introduction of the ECU as the single currency of those Member States.

5 If it is decided, according to the procedure set out in Article 109m(2), to abrogate a derogation, The Council shall, acting with the unanimity of the Member States without derogation and the Member State concerned, on a proposal from the Commission and after consulting the ECB, adopt the rate at which the ECU shall be substituted for the currency of the Member State concerned, and take the other measures necessary for the introduction of the ECU as the single currency in the Member State concerned.

Article 109 m

1 Until the beginning of the third stage, each Member State shall treat its exchange rate policy as a matter of common interest. In so doing, Member States shall take account of the experience acquired in cooperation within the framework of the European Monetary System (EMS) and in developing the ECU, and shall respect existing powers in this field.

2 From the beginning of the third stage and for as long as a Member State has a derogation, paragraph 1 shall apply by analogy to the exchange rate policy of that Member State.

APPENDIX 2

Protocol on the Statute of the European System of Central Banks and of the Europan Central Bank

THE HIGH CONTRACTING PARTIES,

DESIRING to lay down the Statute of the European System of Central Banks and of the European Central Bank provided for in Article 4 a of the Treaty establishing the European Community,

HAVE AGREED upon the following provisions, which shall be annexed the Treaty establishing the European Community:

Chapter I – Constitution of the ESCB

Article 1 – The European System of Central Banks

1.1 The European System of Central Banks (ESCB) and the European Central Bank (ECB), shall be established in accordance with Article 4 a of this Treaty; they shall perform their functions and carry on their activities in accordance with the provisions of this Treaty and of this Statute.

1.2 In accordance with Article 106(1) of this Treaty, the ESCB shall be composed of the ECB and of the central banks of the Member States ('national central banks'). The Institut monétaire luxembourgeois will be the central bank of Luxembourg.

Chapter II – Objectives and Tasks of the ESCB

Article 2 – Objectives

In accordance with Article 105(1) of this Treaty, the primary objective of the ESCB shall be to maintain price stability. Without prejudice to the objective of price stability, it shall support the general economic policies in the Community with a view to contributing to the achievement of the objectives of the Community as laid down in Article 2 of this Treaty. The ESCB shall act in accordance with the principle of an open market economy with free competition, favouring an efficient allocation of resources, and in compliance with the principles set out in Article 3 a of this Treaty.

Article 3 – Tasks

3.1 In accordance with Article 105 (2) of this Treaty the basic tasks to be carried out through the ESCB shall be: – to define and implement the monetary policy of the Community;
   - to conduct foreign exchange operations consistent with the provisions of Article 109 of this Treaty;
   - to hold and manage the official foreign reserves of the Member States;
   - to promote the smooth operation of payment systems.

3.2 In accordance with Article 105 (3) of this Treaty, the third indent of Article 3.1 shall be without prejudice to the holding and management by the governments of Member States of foreign exchange working balances.

3.3 In accordance with Article 105 (5) of this Treaty, the ESCB shall contribute to the smooth conduct of policies pursued by the competent authorities relating to the prudential supervision of credit institutions and the stability of the financial system.

Article 4 – Advisory functions

4.1 In accordance with Article 105 (4) of this Treaty:

  (a) the ECB shall be consulted:

  − on any proposed Community act its fields of competence;
  − by national authorities regarding any draft legislative provision within its fields of competence but within the limits and under the conditions set out by the Council in accordance with the procedure of Article 42;

  (b) the ECB may submit opinions to the appropriate Community institutions or bodies or to national authorities on matters its fields of competence.

Article 5 – Collection of statistical information

5.1 In order to undertake the tasks of the ESCB, the ECB, assisted by the national central banks, shall collect the necessary statistical information either from the competent national authorities or directly from economic agents. For these purposes it shall co-operate with the Community institutions or bodies and with the competent authorities of the Member States or third countries and with international organisations.

5.2 The national central banks shall carry out, to the extent possible, the tasks described in Article 5.1.

5.3 The ECB shall contribute to the harmonisation, where necessary, of the rules and practices governing the collection, compilation and distribution of statistics in the areas within its field of competence.

5.4 The Council, in accordance with the procedure laid down in Article 42, shall define the natural and legal persons subject to reporting requirements, the confidentiality regime and the appropriate provisions for enforcement.

Article 6 – International co-operation

6.1 In the field of international co-operation involving the tasks entrusted to the ESCB, the ECB shall decide how the ESCB shall be represented.

6.2 The ECB and, subject to its approval, the national central banks may participate in international monetary institutions.

6.3 Article 6.1 and 6.2 shall be without prejudice to Article 109 (4) of this Treaty.

Chapter III – Organisation of the ESCB

Article 7 – Independence

In accordance with Article 107 of this Treaty, when exercising the powers and carrying out the tasks and duties conferred upon them by this Treaty and this Statute, neither the ECB, nor a national central bank, nor any member of their decision-making bodies shall seek or take instructions from Community institutions or bodies, from any government of a Member State or from any other body. The Community institutions and bodies and the governments of the Member States undertake to respect this principle and not to seek to influence the members of the decision-making bodies of the ECB and of the national central banks in the performance of their tasks.

Article 8 – General principle

The ESCB shall be governed by the decision-making bodies of the ECB.

Article 9 – The European Central Bank

9.1 The ECB which in accordance with Article 106 (2) of this Treaty shall have legal personality, shall enjoy in each of the Member States the most extensive legal capacity accorded to legal persons under their laws; it may, in particular, acquire or dispose of movable and immovable property and may be a party to legal proceedings.

9.2 The ECB shall ensure that the tasks conferred upon the ESCB under Article 3 are implemented either by the ECB's activities pursuant to this Statute or through the national central banks pursuant to Articles 12.1 and 14.

9.3 In accordance with Article 106 (3) of this Treaty, the decision-making bodies of the ECB are the Governing Council and the Executive Board.

Article 10 – The Governing Council

10.1 In accordance with Article 109a(1) of this Treaty, the Governing Council shall comprise the members of the Executive Board and the Governors of the national central banks.

10.2 Subject to Article 10.3, only members of the Governing Council present in person shall have the right to vote. By way of derogation from this principle the Rules of Procedure referred to in Article 12.3 may lay down that members of the Governing Council may cast their vote by means of teleconferencing. These rules shall also provide that a member of the Governing Council who is prevented from voting for a prolonged period may appoint an alternate as a member of the Governing Council.

Subject to Articles 10.3 and 11.3, each member of the Governing Council shall have one vote. Save as otherwise provided for in this Statute, the Governing Council shall act by a simple majority. In the event of a tie, the President shall have the casting vote.

In order for the Governing Council to vote, there shall be a quorum of two-thirds of the members. If the quorum is not met, the President may convoke an extraordinary meeting at which decisions may be taken without regard to the quorum.

10.3 For any decisions to be taken under Articles 28, 29, 30, 32 33 and 51, the votes in the Governing Council shall be weighted according to the national central banks' shares in the subscribed capital of the ECB. The weights of the votes of the members of the Executive Board shall be zero. A decision requiring a qualified majority shall be approved if the votes cast in favour represent at least two thirds of the subscribed capital of the ECB and represent at least half of the shareholders. If a Governor is unable to be present, he may nominate an alternate to cast his weighted vote.

10.4 The proceedings of the meetings shall be confidential. The Governing Council may decide to make the outcome of its deliberations public.

10.5 The Governing Council shall meet at least ten times a year.

Article 11 – The Executive Board

11.1 In accordance with Article 109a(2)(b) of this Treaty, the Executive Board shall comprise the President, the Vice-President and four other members.

The members shall perform their duties on a full-time basis. No member shall engage in any occupation, whether gainful or not, unless exemption is exceptionally granted by the Governing Council.

11.2 In accordance with Article 109a(2)(b) of this Treaty, the President, the Vice-President and the other Members of the Executive Board shall be appointed from among persons of recognized standing and professional experience in monetary or banking matters by common accord of the governments of the Member States at the level of the Heads of State or of Government, on a recommendation from the Council after it has consulted the European Parliament and the Governing Council.

Their term of office shall be 8 years and shall not be renewable.

Only nationals of Member States may be members of the Executive Board.

11.3 The terms and conditions of employment of the members of the Executive Board, in particular their salaries, pensions and other social security benefits shall be the subject of contracts with the ECB and shall be fixed by the Governing Council on a proposal of a Committee comprising three members appointed by the Governing Council and three members appointed by the Council. The members of the Executive Board shall not have the right to vote on matters referred to in this paragraph.

11.4 If a member of the Executive Board no longer fulfils the conditions required for the performance of his duties or if he has been guilty of serious misconduct, the Court of Justice may, on application by the Governing Council or the Executive Board, compulsorily retire him.

11.5 Each member of the Executive Board present in person shall have the right to vote and shall have, for that purpose, one vote. Save as otherwise provided, the Executive Board shall act by a simple majority of the votes cast. In the event of a tie the President shall have the casting vote. The voting arrangements will be specified in the Rules of Procedure refered to in Article 12.3.

11.6 The Executive Board shall be responsible for the current business of the ECB.

11.7 Any vacancy on the Executive Board shall be filled by the appointment of a new member in accordance with Article 11.2.

Article 12 – Responsibilities of the decision-making bodies

12.1 The Governing Council shall adopt the guidelines and take the decisions necessary to ensure the performance of the tasks entrusted to the ESCB under this Treaty and this Statute. The Governing Council shall formulate the monetary policy of the Community including, as appropriate, decisions relating to intermediate monetary objectives, key interest rates and the supply of reserves in the ESCB, and shall establish the necessary guidelines for their implementation.

The Executive Board shall implement monetary policy in accordance with the guidelines and decisions laid down by the Governing Council. In doing so the Executive Board shall give the necessary instructions to national central banks. In addition the Executive Board may have certain powers delegated to it where the Governing Council so decides.

To the extent deemed possible and appropriate and without prejudice to the provision of this Article, the ECB shall have recourse to the national central banks to carry out operations which form part of the tasks of the ESCB.

12.2 The Executive Board shall have responsibility for the preparation of Governing Council meetings.

12.3 The Governing Council shall adopt Rules of Procedure which determine the internal organisation of the ECB and its decision-making bodies.

12.4 The Governing Council shall exercise the advisory functions referred to in Article 4.

12.5 The Governing Council shall take the decisions referred to in Article 6.

Article 13 – The President

13.1 The President or, in his absence, the Vice-President shall chair the Governing Council and the Executive Board of the ECB.

13.2 Without prejudice to Article 39, the President or his nominee shall represent the ECB externally.

Article 14 – National central banks

14.1 In accordance with Article 108 of this Treaty, each Member State shall ensure, at the latest at the date of the establishment of the ESCB, that its national legislation, including the statutes of its national central bank, is compatible with this Treaty and this Statute.

14.2 The statutes of the national central banks shall, in particular, provide that the term of office of a Governor of a national central bank shall be no less than 5 years.

A Governor may be relieved from office only if he no longer fulfils the conditions required for the performance of his duties or if he has been guilty of serious misconduct. A decision to this effect may be referred to the Court of Justice by the Governor concerned or the Governing Council on grounds of infringement of this Treaty or of any rule of law relating to its application. Such proceedings shall be instituted within two months of the publication of the decision or of its notification to the plaintiff or, in the absence thereof, of the day on which it came to the knowledge of the latter, as the case may be.

14.3 The national central banks are an integral part of the ESCB and shall act in accordance with the guidelines and instructions of the ECB. The Governing Council shall take the necessary steps to ensure compliance with the guidelines and instructions of the ECB, and shall require that any necessary information be given to it.

14.4 National central banks may perform functions other than those specified in this Statute unless the Governing Council finds, by a majority of two thirds of the votes cast, that these interfere with the objectives and tasks of the ESCB. Such functions shall be performed on the responsibility and liability of national central banks and shall not be regarded as being part of the functions of the ESCB.

Article 15 – Reporting commitments

15.1 The ECB shall draw up and publish reports on the activities of the ESCB at least quarterly.

15.2 A consolidated financial statement of the ESCB shall be published each week.

15.3 In accordance with Article 109b(3) of this Treaty, the ECB shall address an annual report on the activities of the ESCB and on the monetary policy of both the previous and the current year to the European Parliament, the Council and the Commission, and also to the European Council.

15.4 The reports and statements referred to above shall be made available to interested parties free of charge.

Article 16 – Bank notes

In accordance with Article 105a(1) of this Treaty, the Governing Council shall have the exclusive right to authorize the issues of bank-notes within the Community. The ECB and the national central banks may issue such notes. The bank notes issued by the ECB and the national central banks shall be the only such notes to have the status of legal tender within the Community.

The ECB shall respect as far as possible existing practices regarding the issuing and design of bank-notes.

Chapter IV – Monetary Functions and Operations of the ESCB

Article 17 – Accounts with the ECB and the national central banks

In order to conduct their operations, the ECB and the national central banks may open accounts for credit institutions, public entities and other market participants and accept assets including book-entry securities as collateral.

Article 18 – Open market and credit operations

18.1 In order to achieve the objectives of the ESCB and to carry out its tasks, the ECB and the national central banks may:

  – operate in the financial markets by buying and selling outright (spot and forward) or under repurchase agreement, and by lending or borrowing claims and marketable instruments, whether in Community or in non-Community currencies, as well as precious metals:
  – conduct credit operations with credit institutions and other market participants, with lending being based on adequate collateral.

18.2 The ECB shall establish general principles for open market and credit operations carried out by itself or the national central banks including the announcement of conditions under which they stand ready to enter into such transactions.

Article 19 – Minimum reserves

19.1 Subject to Article 2, the ECB may require credit institutions established in Member States to hold minimum reserves on accounts with the ECB and national central banks in pursuance of monetary policy objectives. Regulations concerning the calculation and determination of the required minimum reserves may be stablished by the Governing Council. In cases of non-compliance the ECB shall be entitled to levy penalty interest and to impose other sanctions with comparable impact.

19.2 For the application of this Article, the Concil shall, in accordance with the procedure laid down in Article 42, define the basis for minimum reserves and the maximum permissible ratios between those reserves and their basis, as well as the appropriate sanctions in cases of non-compliance.

Article 20 – Other instruments of monetary control

The Governing Council may, by a majority of two-thirds of the votes cast, decide upon the use of such other operational methods of monetary control as it sees fit, respecting Article 2.

The Council shall, in accordance with the procedure laid down in Article 42, define the scope of such methods if they impose obligations on third parties.

Article 21 – Operations with public entities

21.1 In accordance with Article 104 of this Treaty, overdrafts or any other type of credit facility by the ECB or by the national central banks to Community institutions or bodies, Central Governments, regional or local authorities, public authorities, other bodies governed by public law, or public undertakings of Member States shall be prohibited, as shall the purchase directly from them by the ECB or national central banks of debt instruments.

21.2 The ECB and national central banks may act as fiscal agents for the entities referred to in Article 21.1.

21.3 The provisions of this Article shall not apply to publicly-owned credit institutions, which in the context of the supply of reserves by central banks shall be given the same treatment by national central banks and the ECB as private credit institutions.

Article 22 – Clearing and payment systems

The ECB and national central banks may provide facilities, and the ECB may make regulations to ensure efficient and sound clearing and payment systems within the Community and with other countries.

Article 23 – External operations

The ECB and the national central banks may:

–   establish relations with central banks and financial institutions in other countries and, where appropriate, with international organisations;
–   acquire and sell spot and forward all types of foreing exchange assets and precious metals; the term 'foreign exchange asset' shall include securities and all other assets in the currency of any country or units of account and in whatever form held;
–   hold and manage the assets defined above;
–   conduct all types of banking transactions in relations with third countries and international organisations, including borrowing and lending operations.

Article 24 – Other operations

In addition to operations arising from their tasks, the ECB and the national central banks may enter into operations for their administrative purposes or for their staff.

Chapter V – Prudential Supervision

Article 25 – Prudential supervision

25.1 The ECB may offer advice to and be consulted by the Council, the Commission and the competent authorities of the Member States on the scope and implementation of Community legislation relating to the prudential supervision of credit institutions and to the stability of the financial system.

25.2 In accordance with the Council decision under Article 105(6) of this Treaty, the ECB may perform specific tasks concerning policies relating to the prudential supervision of credit institutions and other financial institutions with the exception of insurance undertakings.

Chapter VI – Financial Provisions of the ESCB

Article 26 – Financial accounts

26.1 The financial year of the ECB and the national central banks shall begin on the first day of January and end on the last day of December.

26.2 The annual accounts of the ECB shall be drawn up by the Executive Board in accordance with the principles established by the Governing Council. The accounts shall be approved by the Governing Council and shall thereafter be published.

26.3 For analytical and operational purposes, the Executive Board shall draw up a consolidated balance sheet of the ESCB, comprising the assets and liabilities of the national central banks that fall within the ESCB.

26.4 For the applications of this Article, the Governing Council shall establish the necessary rules for standardizing the accounting and reporting of operations undertaken by the national central banks.

Article 27 – Auditing

27.1 The accounts of the ECB and the national central banks shall be audited by independent external auditors recommended by the Governing Council and approved by the Council. The auditors shall have full power to examine all books and accounts of the ECB and national central banks, and to be fully informed about their transactions.

27.2 The provisions of Article 188b of this Treaty shall only apply to an examination of the operational eficiency of the management of the ECB.

Article 28 – Capital of the ECB

28.1 The capital of the ECB, which shall become operational upon its establishment, shall be ECU 5.000 million. The capital may be increased by such amounts as may be decided by the Governing Council acting by the qualified majority provided for in Article 10.3, within the limits and under the conditions set by the Council under the procedure laid down in Article 42.

28.2 The national central banks shall be the sole subscribers to and holders of the capital of the ECB. The subscription of capital shall be according to the key established in accordance with Article 29.

28.3 The Governing Council, acting by the qualified majority provided for in Article 10.3, shall determine the extent to which and the form in which the capital shall be paid up.

28.4 Subject to Article 28.5, the shares of the national central banks in the subscribed capital of the ECB may not be transferred, pledged or attached.

28.5 If the key referred to in Article 29 is adjusted, the national central banks shall transfer among themselves capital shares to the extent necessary to ensure that the distribution of capital shares corresponds to the adjusted key. The Governing Council shall determine the terms and conditions of such transfers.

Article 29 – Key for capital subscription

29.1 When in accordance with the procedure mentioned in Article 109 l(1) of this Treaty the ESCB and the ECB have been established, the key for subscription of the ECB's capital shall be establised. Each national central bank shall be assigned a weighting in this key which shall be equal to the sum of:

- 50 % of the share of its respective Member State in the population of the Community in the penultimate year preceding the establishment of the ESCB;
- 50 % of the share of its respective Member State in the gross domestic product at market prices of the Community as recorded in the last five years preceding the penultimate year before the establishment of the ESCB;

The percentages shall be rounded up to the nearest multiple of 0.05 % points.

29.2 The statistical data to be used for the application of this Article shall be provided by the Commission in accordance with the rules adopted by the Council under the procedure provided for in Article 42.

29.3 The weightings assigned to the national central banks shall be adjusted every five years after the establishment of the ESCB by analogy with the provisions laid down in Article 29.1. The adjusted key shall apply with effect from the first day of the following year.

29.4 The Governing Council shall take all other measures necessary for the application of this Article.

Article 30 – Transfer of foreign reserve assets to the ECB

30.1 Without prejudice to the provisions of Article 28, the ECB shall be provided by the national central banks with foreign reserve assets, other than Member States' currencies, ECUs, IMF reserve positions and SDR's, up to an amount equivalent to ECU 50.000 million. The Governing Council shall decide upon the proportion to be called up by the ECB following its establishment and the amounts called up at later dates. The ECB shall have the full right to hold and manage the foreign reserves that are transferred to it and to use them for the purposes set out in this Statute.

30.2 The contributions of each national central bank shall be fixed in proportion to its share in the subscribed capital of the ECB.

30.3 Each national central bank shall be credited by the ECB with a claim equivalent to its contribution. The Governing Council shall determine the denomination and remuneration of such claims.

30.4 Further calls of foreign reserve assets beyond the limit set in Article 30.1 may be effected by the ECB, in accordance with Article 30.2, within the limits and under the conditions set by the Council in accordance with the procedure laid down in Article 42.

30.5 The ECB may hold and manage IMF reserve positions and SDRs and provide for the pooling of such assets.

30.6 The Governing Council shall take all other measures necessary for the application of this Article.

Article 31 – Foreign reserve assets held by national central banks

31.1 The national central banks shall be allowed to perform transactions in fulfilment of the obligations towards international organisations in accordance with Article 23.

31.2 All other operations in foreign reserve assets remaining with the national central banks after the transfers referred to in Article 30, and Member States' transactions with their foreign exchange working balances shall, above a certain limit to be established through Article 31.3, be subject to approval by the ECB in order to ensure consistency with the exchange rate and monetary policies of the Community.

31.3 The Governing Council shall issue guidelines with a view to facilitating such operations.

Article 32 – Allocation of monetary income of national central banks

32.1 The income accruing to the national central banks in the performance of the ESCB's monetary policy function (hereafter referred to as 'monetary income') shall be allocated at the end of each financial year in accordance with the provisions of this Article.

32.2 Subject to Article 32.3, the amount of each national central bank's monetary income shall be equal to its annual income derived from its assets held against notes in circulation and deposit liabilities vis-à-vis credit institutions. These assets shall be earmarked by national central banks in accordance with guidelines to be established by the Governing Council.

32.3 If, after the start of the third stage, the balance sheet structures of the national central banks do not, in the judgement of the Governing Council, permit the application of Article 32.2, the Governing Council, acting by a qualified majority, may decide that, by way of derogation to Article 32.2, monetary income shall be measured according to an alternative method for a period of not more than five years.

32.4 The amount of each national central bank's monetary income shall be reduced by an amount equivalent to any interest paid by that central bank on its deposit liabilities vis-à-vis credit institutions in accordance with Article 19.

The Governing Council may decide that national central banks shall be indemnified for cost incurred in connection with the issuance of bank notes or in exceptional circumstances for specific lossed arising from monetary policy operations undertaken for the ESCB. The indemnification shall be in a form deemed appropriate in the judgement of the Governing Council; these amounts may be offset against the national central banks' monetary income.

32.5 The sum of the national banks monetary income shall be allocated to the national central banks in proportion to their paid up shares in the capital of the ECB, subject to any decision taken by the Governing Council pursuant to Article 33.2.

32.6 The clearing and settlement of the balances arising from the allocation of monetary income shall be carried out by the ECB in accordance with the guidelines established by the Governing Council.

32.7 The Governing Council shall take all other measures necessary for the application of this Article.

Article 33 – Allocation of net profits and losses of the ECB

33.1 The net profit of the ECB shall be transferred in the following order:

(a) an amount to be determined by the Governing Council, which may not exceed 20 % of the net profit, shall be transferred to the general reserve fund subject to a limit equal to 100 % of the capital;

(b) the remaining net profit shall be distributed to the shareholders of ECB in proportion to their paid-up shares.

33.2 In the event of a loss incurred by the ECB, the shortfall may be offset against the general reserve fund of the ECB and, if necessary, following a decision by the Governing Council, against the monetary income of the relevant financial year concerned in proportion and up to the amounts allocated to the national central banks in accordance with Article 32.5.

(The remainder of the Articles – 34 to 53 – are not reproduced here, as they are of limited relevance to the analysis in the present chapter. These articles relate to various legal provisions, staff, provisions for amending the ESCB Statute, transitional provisions etc.)

APPENDIX 3

Protocol on the Statute of the European Monetary Institute

THE HIGH CONTRACTING PARTIES,

DESIRING to lay down the Statute of the European Monetary Institute,

HAVE AGREED upon the following provisions, which shall be annexed to the Treaty establishing the European Community:

Article 1 – Constitution and name

1.1 The European Monetary Institute (EMI) shall be established in accordance with Article 109f of this Treaty; it shall perform its functions and carry out its activities in accordance with the provisions of this Treaty and of this Statute.

1.2 The members of the EMI shall be the central banks of the Member States ('national central banks'). For the purposes of this Statute, the Institut monétaire luxembourgeois shall be regarded as the central bank of Luxembourg.

1.3 Pursuant to Article 109f of this Treaty, both the Committee of Governors and the European Monetary Cooperation Fund (EMCF) shall be dissolved. All assets and liabilities of the EMCF shall pass automatically to the EMI.

Article 2 – Objectives

The EMI shall contribute to the realization of the conditions necessary for the transition to the third stage of Economic and Monetary Union, in particular by

– strengthening the coordination of monetary policies with a view to ensuring price stability;
– making the preparations required for the establishment of the European System of Central

Banks (ESCB), and for the conduct of a single monetary policy and the creation of a single currency in the third stage;
— overseeing the development of the ECU.

Article 3 – General principles

3.1. The EMI shall carry out the tasks and functions conferred upon it by this Treaty and this Statute without prejudice to the responsibility of the competent authorities for the conduct of the monetary policy within the respective Member States.

3.2. The EMI shall act in accordance with the objectives and principles stated in Article 2 of the Statute of the ESCB.

Article 4 – Primary tasks

4.1 In accordance with Article 109f(2) of this Treaty, the EMI shall:

- strengthen cooperation between the national central banks;
- strengthen the coordination of the monetary policies of the Member States with the aim of ensuring price stability;
- monitor the functioning of the European Monetary System (EMS);
- hold consultations concerning issues falling within the competence of the national central banks and affecting the stability of financial institutions and markets;
- take over·the tasks of the EMCF; in particular it shall perform the functions referred to in Articles 6.1, 6.2 and 6.3;
- facilitate the use of the ECU and oversee its development, including the smooth functioning of the ECU clearing system.

The EMI shall also:

- hold regular consultations concerning the course of monetary policies and the use of monetary policy instruments;
- normally be consulted by the national monetary authorities before they take decisions on the course of monetary policy in the context of the common framework for ex ante coordination.

4.2 At the latest by 31 December 1996, the EMI shall specify the regulatory, organizational and logistical framework necessary for the ESCB to perform its tasks in the third stage, in accordance with the principle of an open market economy with free competition. This framework shall be submitted by the Council of the EMI for decision to the ECB at the date of its establishment.
   In accordance with Article 109f(3) of this Treaty, the EMI shall in particular:

- prepare the instruments and the procedures necessary for carrying out a single monetary policy in the third stage;
- promote the harmonization, where necessary, of the rules and practices governing the collection, compilation and distribution of statistics in the areas within its field of competence;
- prepare the rules for operations to be undertaken by the national central banks in the framework of the ESCB;
- promote the efficiency of cross-border payments;
- supervise the technical preparation of ECU bank notes.

Article 5 – Advisory functions

5.1. In accordance with Article 109f(4) of this Treaty, the Council of the EMI may formulate opinions or recommendations on the overall orientation of monetary policy and exchange rate policy as well as on related measures introduced in each Member State. The EMI may submit opinions or recommendations to governments and to the Council on policies which might affect the internal or external monetary situation in the Community and, in particular, the functioning of the EMS.

5.2 The Council of the EMI may also make recommendations to the monetary authorities of the Member States concerning the conduct of their monetary policy.

5.3 In accordance with Article 109f(6) of this Treaty, the EMI shall be consulted by the Council regarding any proposed Community act within its field of competence.

Within the limits and under the conditions set out by the Council acting by qualified majority on a proposal from the Commission and after consulting the European Parliament and the EMI, the EMI shall be consulted by the authorities of the Member States on any draft legislative provision within its field of competence, in particular with regard to Article 4.2.

5.4 In accordance with Article 109f(5) of this Treaty, the EMI may publish its opinions and its recommendations.

Article 6 – Operational and technical functions

6.1 The EMI shall:

- provide for the multilateralization of positions resulting from interventions by the national central banks in Community currencies and the multilateralization of intra-Community settlements;
- administer the very short-term financing mechanism provided for by the Agreement of 13 March 1979 between the central banks of the Member States of the European Economic Community laying down the operating procedures for the European Monetery System (hereinafter referred to as 'EMS Agreement') and the short-term monetary support mechanism provided for in the Agreement between the central banks of the Member States of the European Economic Community of 9 February 1970, as amended;
- perform the functions referred to in Article 11 of Council Regulation (EEC) No 1969/88 of 24 June 1988 establishing a single facility providing medium-term financial assistance for Member States' balances of payments.

6.2 The EMI may receive monetary reserves from the national central banks and issue ECUs against such assets for the purpose of implementing the EMS Agreement. These ECUs may be used by the EMI and the national central banks as a means of settlement and for transactions between them and the EMI. The EMI shall take the necessary administrative measures for the implementation of this paragraph.

6.3 The EMI may grant to the monetary authorities of third countries and to international monetary institutions the status of 'Other Holders' of ECUs and fix the terms and conditions under which such ECUs may be acquired, held or used by Other Holders.

6.4 The EMI shall be entitled to hold and manage foreign exchange reserves as an agent for and at the request of national central banks. Profits and losses regarding these reserves shall be for the account of the national central bank depositing the reserves. The EMI shall perform this function on the basis of bilateral contracts in accordance with rules laid down in a decision of the EMI. These rules shall ensure that transactions with these reserves shall not interfere with the monetary policy and exchange rate policy of the competent monetary authority of any Member State and shall be consistent with the objectives of the EMI and the proper functioning of the Exchange Rate Mechanism of the EMS.

Article 7 – Other tasks

7.1 Once a year the EMI shall address a report to the Council on the state of the preparations for the third stage. These reports shall include an assessment of the progress towards convergence in the Community, and cover in particular the adaptation of monetary policy instruments and the preparation of the procedures necessary for carrying out a single monetary policy in the third stage, as well as the statutory requirements to be fulfilled for national central banks to become an integral part of the ESCB.

7.2 In accordance with the Council decisions referred to in Article 109f(7) of this Treaty, the EMI may perform other tasks for the preparation of the third stage.

Article 8 – Independence

The members of the Council of the EMI who are the representatives of their institutions shall, with respect to their activities, act according to their own responsibilities. In exercising the powers and performing the tasks and duties conferred upon them by this Treaty and this Statute, the Council of the EMI may not seek or take any instructions from Community institutions or bodies or governments of Member States. The Community institutions and bodies as well as the governments of the Member States undertake to respect this principle and not to seek to influence the Council of the EMI in the performance of its tasks.

Article 9 – Administration

9.1 In accordance with Article 109f(1) of this Treaty, the EMI shall be directed and managed by the Council of the EMI.

9.2 The Council of the EMI shall consist of a President and the Governors of the national central banks, one of whom shall be Vice-President. If a Governor is prevented from attending a meeting, he may nominate another representative of his institution.

9.3 The President shall be appointed by common accord of the governments of the Member States at the level of Heads of State or of Government, on a recommendation from, as the case may be, the Committee of Governors or the Council of the EMI, and after consulting the European Parliament and the Council. The President shall be selected from among persons of recognized standing and professional experience in monetary or banking matters. Only nationals of Member States may be President of the EMI. The Council of the EMI shall appoint the Vice-President. The President and Vice-President shall be appointed for a period of three years.

9.4 The President shall perform his duties on a full-time basis. He shall not engage in any occupation, whether gainful or not, unless exemption is exceptionally granted by the Council of the EMI.

9.5 The President shall:

- prepare and chair the meetings of the Council of the EMI;
- without prejudice to Article 22, present the views of the EMI externally;
- be responsible for the day-to-day management of the EMI.

9.6 The terms and conditions of employment of the President, in particular his salary, pension and other social security benefits, shall be the subject of a contract with the EMI and shall be fixed by the Council of the EMI on a proposal from a Committee comprising three members appointed by the Committee of Governors or the Council of the EMI, as the case may be, and three members appointed by the Council. The President shall not have the right to vote on matters referred to in this paragraph.

9.7   If the President no longer fulfils the conditions required for the performance of his duties or if he has been guilty of serious misconduct, the Court of Justice may, on application by the Council of the EMI, compulsorily retire him.

9.8   The Rules of Procedure of the EMI shall be adopted by the Council of the EMI.

Article 10 – Meetings of the Council of the EMI and voting procedures

10.1 The Council of the EMI shall meet at least ten times a year. The proceedings of Council meetings shall be confidential. The Council of the EMI may, acting unanimously, decide to make the outcome of its deliberations public.

10.2 Each member of the Council of the EMI or his nominee shall have one vote.

10.3 Save as otherwise provided for in this Statute, the Council of the EMI shall act by a simple majority of its members.

10.4 Decisions to be taken in the context of Articles 4.2., 5.4., 6.2. and 6.3. shall require unanimity of the members of the Council of the EMI.
    The adoption of opinions and recommendations under Articles 5.1. and 5.2., the adoption of decisions under Articles 6.4, 16 and 23.6 and the adoption of guidelines under Article 15.3 shall require a qualified majority of two thirds of the members of the Council of the EMI.

Article 11 – Interinstitutional cooperation and reporting requirements

11.1 The President of the council and a member of the Commission may participate, without having the right to vote, in meetings of the Council of the EMI.

11.2 The President of the EMI shall be invited to participate in Council meetings when the Council is discussing matters relating to the objectives and tasks of the EMI.

11.3 At a date to be established in the Rules of Procedure, the EMI shall prepare an annual report on its activities and on monetary and financial conditions in the Community. The annual report, together with the annual accounts of the EMI, shall be addressed to the European Parliament, the Council and the Commission and also to the European Council.
    The President of the EMI may, at the request of the European Parliament or on his own initiative, be heard by the competent Committees of the European Parliament.

11.4 Reports published by the EMI shall be made available to interest parties free of charge.

Article 12 – Currency denomination

The operations of the EMI shall be expressed in ECU.

Article 13 – Seat

Before the end of 1992, the decision as to where the seat of the EMI will be established shall be taken by common accord of the governments of the Member States at the level of Heads of State or of Government.

(*The remainder of the Articles of the EMI Statute are not reproduced here, as they are of limited relevance to the analysis in chapter 12. These articles relate to legal provisions, accounts and auditing and liquidation..*)

CHAPTER 14

OUTLOOK

We discussed the events leading up to the launching of the two Intergovernmental Conferences in chapter 10 and analysed the operational and institutional aspects of EMU as agreed in the Maastricht Treaty in chapters 12 and 13. In this chapter we offer our personal conjecture of how the monetary integration process might proceed over the coming years, leading hopefully to the introduction of a common currency for a large majority of Members States well before the end of the decade.[1]

As a preliminary we start with a brief discussion of the linkage between political union and economic and monetary union that was introduced by Chancellor Kohl. We then turn to the issue of convergence. How much is needed in different countries and what does it require in terms of policy? Finally we present a personal assessment in the form of a timetable for the EMU process and conclude with a brief discussion of the reasons why the political, institutional and economic environment makes it likely that EMU will in our view be achieved by the end of the decade.

14.1 EMU and political union

What are the linkages between EMU and political union in the EC? When the subject of approaching EMU by stages was assigned to the Delors Committee in 1988 the inspiration was, as argued in chapter 10, two-fold: to improve on the EMS by creating the institutional framework for the exercise of joint monetary policy and to complement the creation of the Internal Market to be completed by end 1992.

The mandate given to the Delors Committee challenged it to give precision also to the economic aspects of EMU. The Delors Report obliged by providing a stringent definition of economic union, comprising some elements in addition to the completion of the 1992 programme for the Internal Market, of which the most controversial was

---

[1] We want to alert the reader that this discussion inevitably goes into arguments of a more general, political nature so that we are forced to go beyond economics, which is our own field of expertise.

the introduction in the final stage of EMU of binding guidelines for national budgetary deficits which we discuss in chapter 8. This was seen in the Report as assuring parallelism between the economic and monetary aspects of EMU.

The Delors Report did not go nearly as far as the Werner Report of 1970 in proposing a high degree of centralization of budgetary authority and a much larger role for the EC budget. Accordingly it did not follow the recommendation of its predecessor to create a centre of decision for economic policy. It found the existing institutions, supplemented by the proposed European System of Central Banks (ESCB), adequate to the tasks outlined. The Report does not refer to political union, not only because this was considered to be outside its mandate and competence, but also for substantive reasons, and it explicitly declined to point to existing federal experiences in Europe or elsewhere as a model:

> Even after attaining EMU, the Community would continue to consist of individual nations with differing economic, social, cultural and political characteristics. The existence and preservation of this *plurality* would require a degree of autonomy in economic decision-making to remain with individual member countries and a balance to be struck between national and Community competences. For this reason it would not be possible simply to follow the example of existing federal states; it would be necessary to develop an innovative and unique approach.[2]

Chapter 8 argued that the Delors Report may have overstated the case for binding guidelines for national budgetary policies. Both economic analysis and practical difficulties in defining operationally how such guidelines may be applied suggest that the ECOFIN Council is unlikely to be able to develop rules and procedures which clearly constrain in a permanent framework ultimate national authority over budget deficits, even if agreement could be reached to vest such powers in a Community institution. Attention in the Intergovernmental Conference has therefore focused on a graduated response by the ECOFIN Council to the persistence of 'excessive' deficits, ending possibly in fines imposed on the diverging country, and on the early application of some of these procedures – from some time in stage one – rather than only in the final stage. This change in perspective can also be explained by the recognition that the transition to EMU retains one powerful sanction which disappears, once the final stage has begun: the possibility of denying entry to a member state with diverging performance and policies. We find this change in emphasis desirable and make some simple suggestions in section 14.2 as to how the required convergence in the transition could be summarily evaluated.

If anything the increasing emphasis on the transition and the economic, practical and political difficulties of setting binding guidelines on budget deficits in a permanent way, has weakened the linkage from EMU to political union with a new division of responsibilities between Community institutions and national governments as seen in

---

[2] Delors Report (1989). para. 17; emphasis in original.

the Delors Report. The responsibility for reaching EMU and making it work has been placed more squarely in national hands than foreseen in 1989.

In the early discussion of EMU in the European Council no linkage was made to political union in any wider sense. However, following the joint initiative of Chancellor Helmut Kohl and President Francois Mitterrand in early 1990, the Dublin European Council in April 1990 decided to convene another Intergovernmental Conference (IGC) on political union, to proceed in parallel with the IGC on EMU. Both IGCs were completed in December 1991 under the Dutch EC Presidency and ratification of the new Treaty, incorporating the results of both conferences, should take place before the end of 1992.

It is not the task of this book, or of the present concluding chapter to it, to make any substantive comments on political union or its prospects for successful implementation. Our own view is that the substantive linkage between the two dimensions of unification remains tenuous. EMU in the form presently envisaged implies little more in terms of political union than already exists. The functioning of EMU could, for a long time span, be dissociated from the implementation of most of the proposals on political union which cover quite disparate areas: some of them introduce Community competences in new areas of the Treaty (notably foreign policy), whereas others extend the principle of majority voting beyond the areas provided for in the Single European Act of 1986. Finally there are some proposals which would modify the balance between existing Community institutions. An IGC of the Community scheduled for the mid 1990s is to reexamine many of the more far-reaching proposals for more political union.

We emphasized in chapter 5 that a tightly managed EMS without capital controls imposes similar constraints on macroeconomic policy-making as a monetary union. Since the present system has worked well within the existing assignment of competences to the Community and the existing distribution of power among its various bodies there is no urgent need to change the political structure of the Community. The present arrangements have kept monetary policy largely in the hands of central bankers and thus free of direct political interference, at least within the EMS. The absence of a powerful political Community institution preserves the present state of affairs. From the narrow viewpoint of safeguarding the independence of the ECB, less political union might therefore even be preferable. But, we recognize that this view has become irrelevant, because of the linkage made at the highest political level.

This linkage is the product of different priorities in the European integration process of Germany and of her partners. As the centre country in the EMS, Germany has tended to perceive that her interests were well guarded by the existing forms of policy coordination in the Community and that there would be more risks than additional opportunities in replacing it with the EMU, particularly if the safeguards for advance convergence of the participating economies seemed inadequate. At various points in this book, notably in chapters 5 and 12, this German view has been challenged; it is not obvious that the status quo is sustainable, nor that it would be in the German interest to attempt to make it so. Nevertheless it is a reality that German policy-makers show less of an interest in EMU than some of their partners. This has made them insist not only on tough entry conditions to EMU and on an institutional framework which assures as well as possible a continuation of what they see as the virtues of the EMS, but also on linkage to advances in political integration to which they attach greater importance. Such advances are seen, by Germany, as particularly desirable in the areas of an increasing role for the European Parliament and in extended scope for majority decisions in the Council. The perception among some of Germany's partners that Germany may over the next few years be more favourably disposed towards an integrated, even a federal, Europe than can be expected in the longer term when the unification of Germany has been completed, has advanced their readiness to respond favourably to German proposals for political union. The partner countries, who have increasingly come to share the German interpretation of the past achievements of the EMS, fear that a valuable opportunity for integrating the German economy into the Community might otherwise be lost. If a few years were allowed to lapse, Germany's option of developing its individual potential as Europe's main power and global spokesman may look more attractive than it apparently does at present to Chancellor Kohl's government.

Following the agreement in Maastricht criticism has continued in Germany of the balance struck in the Treaty between a fixed timetable which gives a certain automaticity to the process of moving to the final stage by the late 1990s. A statement by the Bundesbank Council of 7 February 1992 ends with a reminder to the German and other EC governments that

> It will be of prime significance for the overall success of the envisaged
> economic and monetary union that the Community decisions to be taken in
> 1996 and 1998 on the selection of the countries eligible for participation in
> EMU should by geared solely to their stability-policy performance. The
> fulfilment of the entry criteria on the convergence conditions must not be
> impaired by any dates set, (Bundesbank, 1992).

More significant in the present context than this general reminder is the Bundesbank Council's insistence earlier in the statement that even the best designed monetary policy can be undermined in EMU, as the value of money will also 'be crucially influenced by the economic and fiscal policies of and by the behaviour of management and labour in all the participating countries'. The Council recalled an earlier statement of September 1990 in which attention was drawn to the fact that 'a monetary union is an irrevocable joint commitment which, in the light of past experience, required a more far-reaching association, in the form of a comprehensive political union, if it is to prove durable'.

It is not clear from this statement what steps towards political union the Bundesbank Council would regard as essential, nor is it obvious to which past experience reference is made. The most visible steps towards political union advocated by the German government – a larger role for the European Parliament, European citizenship, intensified cooperation on immigration policy and, more generally, in the areas of foreign and security policy – have little immediate bearing on the viability of EMU. Similar comments could be made with respect to the inclusion in the Treaty of new policy areas and extensions of majority voting in the Council of Ministers.

A more transparent link exists between the viability of EMU with primary emphasis on monetary union as presently conceived and social and budgetary policy. If the Community had insisted on rapid development of an EC 'social dimension', i.e. moves towards common principles of regulation of labour markets, the experience of German monetary unification which implied the extension of the legislative and social framework of the Federal Republic to the former German Democratic Republic, and a rather rapid catching-up of wages in the ex-GDR with those in the West, might have been relevant. That experience has implied very substantial public transfers to the East, in particular in the form of unemployment benefits. But the operation of such a mechanism in which common social policies have to be underpinned by large budgetary transfers is, as already argued in our discussion of the relevance of German Economic, Monetary and Social Union for EMU in chapter 5, very far from being observable in the Community.

It is arguable, nevertheless, that the potentially constuctive role of budgetary policies in underpinning EMU and in advancing political union has been overshadowed in the Treaty by the – understandable – concern that strongly divergent national budgetary policies would need to be constrained. Such a constructive role could be assumed in two areas: (1) transfers to assure better cohesion in the Community, and (2) a mechanism to provide some minimum insurance against differentiated shocks.

The former purpose would be served by enlarging the allocations in the Community budget to structural funds. By providing larger resources for peripheral regions or countries to catch up faster with the average level of income in the Community cohesion – one of the aims of the Treaty (Art. 2) – would be advanced. There was an understanding that this issue would not be dealt with in the Maastricht Treaty itself, but that it would be addressed subsequently in the form of budgetary proposals. It is clear from the reactions to the EC Commission's proposals for the 1993–7 budget that there is strong resistance, particularly in Germany, to any significant extension of this redistributive function of the Community budget.

The second purpose appears more closely linked to the functioning of EMU. We reviewed in chapter 8 the claim, advanced most clearly in recent research by US economists, that the Community is far more vulnerable to differentiated shocks among its Member States than is the United States where important mechanisms for absorbing them exist in the form of a Federal income tax and Federally-supported unemployment benefits. Though on closer inspection the US system appears to be designed more with cohesion and redistribution in mind than with the absorption of regionally differentiated shocks, the fact remains that the Community almost totally lacks the latter mechanism for providing some insurance to Member States experiencing specific unfavourable shocks. This fact prompted the proposal in the McDougall Report (1977) for an EC-wide unemployment benefit scheme, but this proposal never found wide political support in the Community.

We believe that, if the Community were to desire a strengthening of political union as a complement to the present EMU project, the idea that merits the most serious consideration is the introduction of a carefully designed automatic fiscal transfer mechanism to protect Member States against transitory shocks to unemployment. Financial markets and *ad hoc* budgetary measures are both inadequate substitutes for serving this insurance function. Borrowing in financial markets by governments experiencing unfavourable shocks is discouraged by the emphasis on the measured budget deficit in the criteria for convergence during the transition and for prudent behaviour subsequently. *Ad hoc* budgetary measures decided upon in a discretionary way at Community level are likely to be inadequate, because they would take longer to negotiate amd might overburden the ECOFIN Council.

If carefully designed to absorb only *changes* in unemployment relative to the Community average, such a fiscal transfer mechanism would put very limited strain on the EC budget. There would, indeed, be no net costs in the long term and only very limited net transfers to particular Member States, yet the transfers could offset a considerable part of the fluctuations in unemployment benefits after the creation of EMU. Such a scheme is currently under study in a special working group set up by the EC Commission to study the applicability of this basic idea of the McDougall Report.

We are under no illusion that there will be early political support for an idea along these lines. However, this only shows that those elements of political union which come the closest to providing an underpinning for EMU meet with less political favour than do vaguer notions of political union with only tenuous links to EMU. The interest in more political union expressed by the Bundesbank Council and other German or EC critics who find the Maastricht Treaty inadequate is therefore difficult to rationalise with strictly economic arguments.

Monetary unification is a well-defined concept which requires a limited number of steps, finishing with the introduction of a single currency and the transfer of full monetary authority to a European System of Central Banks and its operating arm, the ECB. The previous chapters have, almost exclusively, been addressed to the analysis of past achievements in this area, of the benefits and costs of monetary unification and of the present state of preparations for taking a limited number of further steps. Economic union is already a much looser concept, a process that may never be completed, as demonstrated by the experience of existing national states, but which is greatly facilitated by monetary unification. Political union is even more of a process, rather than a well-defined state. Most national states continue to experiment in the assignment of competency to the regional levels of government. The basic challenge for the negotiations on political union as they relate to EMU is to agree on an institutional framework sufficiently flexible to permit the benefits of economic and monetary integration to be realized rather than attempting to prescribe over a large number of areas precise definitions of competence and procedures.

In this perspective it would be disappointing, if progress towards EMU which is the area where the case for joint policies and − especially in the monetary area − a joint institution is the clearest (and where preparations are also the most advanced) would be held back by failure to reach early agreement on policy areas where the case for a pooling of authority is much less obvious.

Does this perspective overstate the case for giving priority to monetary unification and EMU and overlook the momentum for political union which success in these areas would in itself bring? We do not think so, but the most obvious criticism of the view that EMU and political union may be dissociated needs to be addressed. It is that no monetary union has in the past survived without political union, and that, in the absence of well-established common political institutions to keep divergence in policy within bounds EMU could founder.

There are no clear historical parallels which can be used to assess whether or for how long monetary unification could survive without a central political authority for the currency area. Fixed exchange rates were established among most of the component states of Germany for a third of a century prior to the formation of the German Reich in 1871, but a common central bank was only established five years after that event.[3] Monetary unions among a number of sovereign states existed for about forty years prior to 1914 (the Latin Monetary Union, the Scandinavian Monetary Union), but without a joint monetary authority. These more informal unions only broke down because of the outbreak of World War I; among the potential participants in EMU political union has at least advanced sufficiently far to exclude any outbreak of armed hostilities! Existing monetary unions today are highly asymmetrical with a large country and one or more smaller participants, the latter operating their monetary affairs essentially according to the mechanical rules of a Currency Board.

These experiences do not assist in the evaluation of the prospects of survival of a single currency area in the Community, managed by a joint institution along the lines of the proposed ECB with a high degree of autonomy and with price stability as its main objective. These features will in themselves qualitatively distinguish EMU from earlier experience of allowing some form of monetary union to precede political union. The task of the ECB will not be to conduct an actively counter-cyclical policy, but to provide a stable nominal framework. About the former task, disagreements might quickly arise due to differences among EMU participants with respect to either economic trends or policy preferences. The ECB will be relatively robust to such differences, given its structure and mandate to concentrate on the latter task.

A more realistic issue in our view is whether the ECB can – or should – be robust, if policy preferences change among policy-makers in a majority of participating countries. Monetary policy can not be differentiated to suit different economic trends or preferences within the union, but it could, in principle, be adjusted in the aggregate, if the emphasis given in the ECB's mandate to price stability were felt by a majority of countries to be interpreted in an excessively restrictive way.

This issue was discussed more fully in chapter 13 which concluded that even in such a case EMU could only tamper with the priority of the price-stability objective at its own peril. The EMU project has become possible not only because of the relatively promising experiences with an increasingly tight EMS over the past decade, but also because earlier national efforts at counter-cyclical monetary policy were visibly unsuccessful. There is no reason to encourage any risk of repeating these experiences at the level of EMU, but monetary policy in the union has to be well explained.

What elements of political union, if any, are then required for monetary unification? In our view, the main requirements are that the ECB be obliged to report to the European Parliament and to coordinate with the ECOFIN Council. The former would help to give focus to the public debate, the latter would assure that there is full

---

[3] For a discussion of the Germany monetary unification process in the nineteenth century see Holtfrerich (1990).

exchange of information between the political and the monetary authorities. Both are well provided for in the Treaty, including the ESCB Statute. There seems to us to be no necessity based on economic arguments for introducing additional elements of political union in order to justify or sustain monetary union, beyond these features of accountability for the ECB.

14.2 Convergence: how and how much?

The Treaty has established, with some considerable emphasis, the need for a high degree of prior economic convergence as a precondition for the entry of each Member State into EMU. As discussed in detail in chapter 12 the provisions for the transition to EMU focus on four main criteria: a high degree of price stability; sustainability of the government financial position; observance of normal fluctuation margins in the EMS for at least two years without devaluation; and evidence of durability of convergence reflected in long-tern interest rates (Art. 109 j). These four main criteria are given quantitative precision in a separate Protocol on the convergence criteria. Although the EC Commission and the EMI which will have the task of reporting regularly to ECOFIN on compliance by the Member States are also encouraged in the said Article to look at other indicators, the legalistic approach coupled with the numerical precision leaves the initial impression that the whole procedure will be technocratic and almost mechanical – an impression actively encouraged by some governments.

Closer inspection of the formulations, of the procedure to be followed in the ECOFIN Council, and of the supplementary economic indicators proposed modify this interpretation. The two elements in the evaluation of government finances turn out to be qualified by references to the debt dynamics which downgrade the apparently decisive importance of the levels of the government deficit and debt, which could hardly be attained by all Member States by 1996. The fact that the ECOFIN Council will have to decide (by a qualified majority role) whether an 'excessive deficit' exists provides an additional illustration of judgemental elements in the procedure. Finally, the inclusion of supplementary economic indicators in the Commission and EMI reports is evidence that there will also be efforts to see the main convergence criteria in a broader macroeconomic framework. In this section we want to take these efforts further by suggesting an overall indicator of convergence which we find helpful in providing summary information about the macroeconomic environment. It starts from the inflation performance and the two dimensions of government financial performance referred to in the convergence criteria: the deficit and debt in relation to GDP. It uses the latter measure by asking what budgetary adjustment would be required to bring the debt ratio to the EC average over a period of ten years, which may still be ambitious, but not totally unrealistic. It then brings in two additional indicators, one referred to in the Treaty – the current account balance in relation to GDP – and one that is not – the unemployment percentage. It is hard to believe that the latter would not anyway play a major role in the assessment of macroeconomic performance both in relative and absolute terms and it would in our view have been desirable for the Maastricht Treaty to include it explicitly among the convergence criteria.

The main differences between using the overall indicator here proposed and the formal convergence criteria of the Treaty are two: (1) our indicator uses an absolute standard in all respects rather than the relative inflation measure stipulated in the first convergence criterion in the Treaty, and (2) by aggregating the various indicators extra creditable performance in one respect is allowed to compensate for deficient performance in other respects. In contrast the Treaty requires that all criteria be met, one by one. Anyway, our proposed indicator is not intended as a substitute for the individual criteria, but simply as a convenient summary. We now turn to a more detailed justification for it.

14.2.1 EMU indicator

The first component of our overall EMU indicator is the inflation rate. Rather than focus on differentials to the best performers, we take the emphasis on price stability to its logical conclusion, viz. that zero inflation is the objective in EMU rather than convergence towards some small number of good performers.

However, it is also clear that the current inflation rate cannot be the only indicator of convergence. A temporary fall in inflation that is achieved at the expense of high unemployment, for example because the anti-inflationary policy is not credible in labour markets, would thus not be a sufficient condition for a country to join EMU. This consideration seems particularly relevant at a time when the initial level of unemployment in the Community is high and concern is voiced that the convergence process outlined in the Maastricht Treaty would lead to competitive deflation and hence higher aggregate unemployment. We do not share this pessimistic view, but unemployment needs to be monitored – and it obviously will be, even if it has not been included in the formal convergence criteria. Nor would a situation in which a prospective participant found it impossible to maintain a satisfactory degree of utilization of domestic resources without a large budget deficit be reassuring. The discussion of the need to avoid 'excessive deficits' in the run up to EMU is an expression of this concern.

An additional consideration is the level of the real exchange at which to enter EMU. Although this is not an important factor in the long run, an excessively appreciated currency at entry (this could be the result of a deliberate policy aiming at achieving a rapid decline in inflation) would then result in strong deflationary pressures in the country in question, which, in turn, would make it more difficult for the ECB to maintain a strict anti-inflationary stance. Signs of an over-appreciated currency could show up in the external current account and, again, in the unemployment rate. The latter is included in our overall indicator as a measure of both the business cycle position and competitiveness. We also include the current account, even though it is less important as EMU approaches.

In short, convergence in inflation cannot be the only criterion especially if internal balance is attained at the expense of external balance. The overall indicator of convergence summarizes developments in the different areas in which adjustment might be required.

There is general agreement that convergence should aim at the best performance, rather than the average. The EMU indicator used here measures therefore the degree to which individual member countries are close to becoming 'virtuous' EMU candidates, characterized by stable prices, fiscal balance, full employment and external equilibrium. It takes into account five major macroeconomic variables which measure the health of an economy, namely, inflation, budget deficit, the level of public debt, unemployment and the external current account. The value of the EMU indicator is given by the sum of the following variables:[4]

i)   **Inflation**: annual rate of change of the consumer price index (CPI) in per cent.

ii) **Budget deficit**: public-sector deficit in per cent of GDP.

iii) **Public debt**: the surplus (in per cent of GDP) needed to bring the national debt to GDP ratio to the Community average currently close to the 60 per cent, listed as the reference value in the Treaty, within ten years.[5]

iv) **Unemployment:** the unemployment rate in per cent.

v)   **Current account**: the external current-account balance in per cent of GDP.

The weighting given by this indicator is obviously subjective. It gives a heavy weight to fiscal variables because of the strong emphasis in the Treaty on sound public finances. The weight given to inflation is larger than appears at first sight because the measured fiscal deficit is not adjusted for inflation although chapter 8 argued that, for some purposes, measured public deficits should be corrected for the effects of inflation on interest payments on the public debt. This is not done in the EMU indicator in order to increase (indirectly) the weight of inflation in the overall index.[6]

This EMU indicator, then, shows how far an individual country is from fitting into a 'virtuous' EMU characterized by price stability, a balanced budget, a public debt to GDP ratio equal to the present Community average, full employment and a balanced external current account. A high value of the EMU indicator indicates that the country needs a great deal of adjustment before it can join a 'virtuous' EMU. Table 14.2.1 gives the values of the variables used to calculate the EMU indicator.

Figure 14.2.1 shows the EMU indicator for 1991 to estimate the prospects for future convergence. This figure shows that there is a first group of five countries with an above-average performance, consisting of Germany, the Netherlands, France, Denmark and, implicitly, Luxembourg which is not shown explicitly in the figure because it would be in a class of its own on account of its large current account surplus and a

---

[4] These variables can be added because they are all dimensionless, i.e., they are all ratios or rates of change. The aggregate indicator was first discussed in DeGrauwe and Gros (1991).

[5] This is measured crudely by 1/10 times the difference between the national (public) debt to GDP ratio and the Community average for this variable.

[6] The components in the EMU indicator relating to the budget deficit and public debt could obviously be further refined by taking into account present differences in taxation especially in those areas in which large differences in taxes are unlikely to survive for long after the completion of the Internal Market. Countries which rely on exceptionally high corporate taxes, capital income taxation and indirect taxation, all of which will have to be brought closer to an EC average, would in a forward-looking revision of the indicator be assigned a higher value.

Table 14.2.1 An EMU indicator of economic performance

	Budget deficit	Debt indicator[a]	Inflation rate	Unemployment rate	Current account[b]	EMU indicator
Germany	3.2	− 2.3	4.5	6.0	1.4	12.8
France	1.5	− 2.2	3.0	9.5	0.7	12.5
Netherlands	4.4	0.9	3.2	7.2	− 4.1	11.6
Denmark	1.7	− 0.2	2.4	9.2	− 1.4	11.7
United Kingdom	1.9	− 2.5	6.5	8.4	2.1	16.4
Portugal	5.4	− 0.4	11.7	4.0	1.1	21.7
Belgium	6.4	6.0	3.2	8.6	− 1.0	23.2
Spain	3.9	− 2.3	5.8	15.8	3.1	26.2
Ireland	4.1	3.4	3.0	16.8	− 2.3	24.9
Italy	9.9	3.2	6.4	9.4	1.3	30.2
Greece	17.9	2.7	18.3	8.8	4.1	51.8

Notes: For Germany: Unemployment and inflation average rates for East and West Germany, weighted by GDP
[a] (National debt/GDP ratio minus the EC average)/10.
[b] A negative sign denotes a surplus.

Source: Commission of the European Communities, Annual Report, Special Edition 1991.

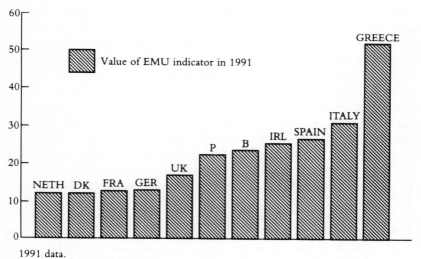

1991 data.
Germany's indicator is based on the average for West and East Germany.

Figure 14.2.1. The EMU indicator

debt/GDP ratio of only 10%. This group (if one excludes Luxembourg) is rather homogeneous in terms of the EMU indicator, which ranges from 11.6 for the Netherlands to 12.8 for Germany. Germany has the worst position in the group of best performers because unification has led to a large fiscal deficit, higher inflation and a current account deficit.

The United Kingdom, with a value of 16.4 seems to be close to the first group. Its position is not as bad as often assumed, because its relatively high inflation rate and external deficit are offset by the strength of its fiscal accounts.

The United Kingdon is followed by another, group of four countries, consisting of Portugal, Belgium, Ireland and Spain, with a slightly below-average performance. This group is not as homogeneous, in terms of the EMU indicator, as the first one. The relatively favourable position of Portugal, better than Belgium, Italy or Spain, is due to the improvement in its fiscal accounts and its low unemployment rate.

Italy, whose EMU value is 30.2, is not far from the group of slightly below-average performers, but it is clearly worse off than countries that are usually ranked higher, such as Belgium, Portugal and Spain. This is mainly due to its fiscal accounts, which confirms the discussion in chapters 5 and 8 where it was argued that Italy requires a radical fiscal adjustment.

Finally there is one obvious laggard: Greece which is by far the worst case, with a value of 51.8 in 1991.

The ranking of countries that emerges from figure 14.2.1 is in several cases somewhat surprising. Taking into account variables other than inflation alone (i.e. looking at overall macroeconomic performance) leads one to the conclusion that the United Kingdom might after all belong to the first tier and that Belgium, which is usually counted in the first tier, belongs to the second, in a rather similar position to that of Portugal and Spain, which are usually considered to be much farther from participation in EMU.

Although this indicator can be only suggestive it is useful in discussing the need for convergence in individual member countries. We therefore now turn to the implications of this assessment of convergence for the position of different member countries in the EMU process.

14.2.2 Convergence issues in individual member countries

At the political level there seems to be general agreement that there is a core group of six to seven countries that could proceed to EMU quite rapidly without requiring further substantial adjustment in macroeconomic terms. This group comprises Germany, France, the three Benelux countries, Denmark and possibly Ireland. Five[7] of these countries also belong to the best performers according to the EMU indicator presented above which suggests also that Ireland and Belgium would require adjustment, mainly in view of the large public debt burden these countries have accumulated.

---

[7] Luxembourg was not considered in the previous subsection since its fiscal and external accounts are so exceptional that it would belong in a separate category.

However, the additional adjustment required would seem to be minor if it is compared to the very substantial corrections of public sector deficits undertaken by these two countries in the early 1980s (even taking into account the uncertainty surrounding all estimates of the sustainability of fiscal positions that was documented in chapter 8). In other areas the adjustment seems almost complete since both countries have virtually eliminated their inflation differentials relative to Germany to less than 2 percentage points. Ireland and Belgium are also both close to current-account balance.

Italy still has an inflation differential, relative to Germany, that suggests that, if it persists, further realignments could become necessary. But if it were able to follow the example of France this differential could be almost eliminated within a couple of years and would then cease to be an obstacle. The second problem in the case of Italy is public finance. The debt-to-GDP ratio has now attained 104 per cent and is still rising. Moreover, the experience of the past years suggests that it might be difficult to service that debt because the political system is such that a large part of expenditures cannot be reduced and it is becoming increasingly difficult to raise additional tax revenues. Also because of the sheer size of its deficit (not far from the US deficit in absolute size), Italy is the prime candidate for major adjustment of fiscal policy. Chapter 5 estimated the required fiscal adjustment in Italy at about 4.5 per cent of GDP.

Spain has achieved about the same inflation performance as Italy and would therefore also not be far from being able to join a monetary union. The debt-to-GDP ratio is much lower than in Italy; hence its public finances are less of an obstacle. However, it might be unwise for Spain to enter into a monetary union before it is fully integrated into the European markets; since the exceptionally high unemployment rate could be taken as a sign that the Spanish economy has not yet finished the process of adjusting to foreign competition. This implies that there might be some merit to the argument (see Vinals (1990)) that it would be in the interest of Spain to wait until it is completely integrated into the internal market. This would also yield enough time to decide whether the external current-account deficit is just a result of an investment boom, and therefore can be financed, or whether it is the result of an expansionary fiscal policy and an overvalued exchange rate that needs to be adjusted. The time required for making this evaluation would not necessarily extend beyond the mid 1990s.

The EMU indicator suggests that in the case of the *United Kingdom*, which joined the EMS only in October 1990 with a wide band, the obstacles to an early participation in EMU are more political than economic. In terms of its fiscal accounts the UK belongs certainly in the first group; this implies that in terms of inflation differentials the adjustment required should not be difficult to achieve if one looks at the history of the EMS. The real issue in the case of UK participation might therefore be the question of when British trade unions and employers would be ready to accept the discipline of a monetary union. Only then would it be advisable for the UK to renounce permanently the further use of the exchange rate as an adjustment instrument.

Greece and Portugal are usually put into one category because substantial adjustments in almost all areas of economic policy would be required before they become candidates for monetary union. However, the EMU indicator reveals that there are significant differences between them. In terms of inflation, low unemployment and its fiscal accounts Portugal is in a much better starting position.

The problem that is common to both is that these countries would also have to face structural adjustment problems with the creation of the internal market which might require substantial changes in their real exchange rates. However, even this substantial adjustment programme need not push participation by these countries into the next century. If the necessary adjustment programmes were implemented now, most of the convergence required in macroeconomic terms could be achieved within less than a decade, certainly for Portugal. It may be recalled that, at least in terms of inflation, Italy achieved faster progress in the 1980s than would be required by these two countries.

14.2.3 How to achieve convergence?

The preceding section has indicated in a cursory manner how much additional convergence is needed in a number of member countries without indicating the means to achieve this. For those countries for which the main problem is in the fiscal area the required policy action is clear: only a combination of cuts in expenditure and increases in taxes can affect the deficit, and, over time, the debt.

However, in another area, namely inflation it is less clear how this convergence can be achieved. The basic issue, which has been debated for a long time, is whether inflation convergence can be achieved by fixing exchange rates or not. We do not wish to review this old debate, but one needs to go beyond the mere recommendation that inflation needs to be reduced.

One extreme view, also called the 'coronation theory', holds that inflation cannot be influenced by the exchange rate, and therefore it would be necessary to wait for a full convergence of inflation before it is advisable to go to monetary union by irrevocably locking exchange rates.[8] This view implies that the transition to monetary union should be rather long since it is clear that it would take some time to completely eradicate the existing inflation differentials.

The alternative view, also called 'monetarist', holds that a credible commitment not to accommodate inflationary pressures from excessive wage settlements would impose enough discipline on trade unions and employers to ensure a rapid convergence towards low inflation rates. An extreme form of this view says that at a certain point in time it would be preferable to introduce a common currency even if not all member countries have achieved full convergence in inflation. Through the adoption of the common currency inertia in inflationary expectations or trade union demands should be eliminated making rapid approximate convergence in inflation possible.

These two schools of thought were already prominent during the discussions surrounding the Werner Plan and the launching of the EMS. We do not pretend to solve this old debate here, but the experience with the EMS that was discussed in chapter 4 shows that a credible exchange rate commitment can indeed have a disciplinary effect. Moreover, in the EMS realignments are always possible, and in the

---

[8] See Kloten (1988) and Pöhl (1989) p. 131. This view was labelled 'economist' in the debate on EMU following the Werner Report of 1970.

early years were expected to occur with a certain frequency. This safety valve would no longer exist in a monetary union and one could therefore expect the disciplinary effect of participating in a monetary union to be much stronger than that of the EMS.

This implies that it would not be necessary to wait for a complete convergence of inflation before passing to the final stage of a common currency. The experience of the EMS suggests that in most countries the wage- and price-setting mechanism is sufficiently malleable to ensure that a residual inflation differential of 1–3 per cent could be eliminated very rapidly.[9]

14.3 Towards monetary union: a suggestive timetable

Many discussions about the desirable speed for the transition towards EMU remain vague because it is seldom spelt out in detail what constitutes 'fast' or 'slow' progress. The European Council of Maastricht brought some clarification because it decided on 1 January 1994 as the starting date for stage II. It further called for a decision on the move to the final stage and the subsequent introduction of a single common currency to be taken at the latest three years after that date, i.e., before the end of 1996 if a majority of member countries are willing and able to irrevocably lock exchange rates. However, these two dates alone are not sufficient to provide a clearer time table for the progress that remains to be achieved in many areas (e.g., disinflation, implementation of parts of the 1992 programme, establishment of common monetary policy procedures, etc.).

The purpose of this section is therefore to provide an overall picture of the progress that remains to be achieved. To do this we found it useful to draw up a formal time table.[10] This time table is definitely not meant to be a forecast of what will actually happen. However, it serves the purpose of clarifying what in our perspective – no doubt by many regarded as optimistic – is the minimum delay required before EMU can be achieved, taking into account the interrelations between the parallel processes of deepening and widening of the EC. It is optimistic in the sense that it assumes the Maastricht Treaty will be ratified by all member countries by the end of 1992 and that the momentum to implement the agreement will be maintained while enlarging the Community.

Discussing an explicit scenario has the advantage that it brings out the underlying assumptions regarding (1) the feasibility and speed of the movement towards EMU and (2) the interactions between four issues that will arise for the EC in the 1990s:

i)   Institutional/legal issues in the negotiation of Treaty revisions in the Intergovernmental Conferences and the subsequent ratification process:

---

[9] This requires, of course, that backward-looking indexation schemes be either abolished or suspended for the transition period. See chapter 5 and Emerson *et al.*, (1991) for a further discussion about the issues arising in the transition to EMU.

[10] The structure of the following is based on Gros and Pisani-Ferry (1990).

Table 14.3.1 A Suggested Scenario for EC Agenda towards EMU

	Institutional/ legal	Monetary policy, EMS/EMU	Individual country adjustments	Enlargements Associated Members
1989	Delors Report published;	capital markets liberalized in France; Spain joins EMS.		Austria applies for membership.
1990	Start of Stage I European Council launches IGCs on EMUand PU;	Italy goes to 2.25% margin and liberalizes capital; UK joins ERM.		German monetary union and political unification EC discussions with EFTA.
1991	IGCs finished with agreement on EMU and EPU Treaties;		Fiscal programmes in Italy, Greece and Portugal agreed;	Sweden applies for EC membership and links currency to ecu, as do Norway and Finland.
1992	EMU and PU Treaties ratified;	Portugal joins EMS Spain and UK go to 2.25% margin; Spain and Ireland liberalize capital.		Finland, Norway and Switzerland apply for EC membership
1993	Internal market program completed;	Final realignment? Reduction of margins to 1% except for Portugal (to 2.25%)		Enlargement negotiations with five EFTA-countries; Poland Czechoslovakia and Hungary associated members
1994	Start of stage II EMI set up	additional currencies from EFTA join stage II with margins of 1%.	Inflation differential with Germany reduced to ± 1% for Italy and Spain;	additional currencies from EFTA join stage II with margins of 1%
1995	Further IGC on reform of EC institutions start;		Fiscal deficits below 3% and debt declining in Italy and Spain;	Five EFTA-countries become members. En-largement negotiations with PL, H and CS
1996	Official report on convergence criteria.		Adjustment programmes for new Central European members.	
1997	Start of Stage III special status for new members from Central Europe;	irrevocable rates for all of enlarged EC (17?); preparations for common currency begin.	Fiscal adjustment completed in Greece	
1998-2000	Transition to common currency for EC16 + (?)			PL, H and CS become members, additional East European associated members?

ii) Convergence in monetary policies according to the gradualist vision of the Delors Report, focusing on the management of the exchange-rate mechanism and on the catching-up process of countries which have not yet achieved convergence in terms of inflation and public finances.

iii) Adjustment policies in countries with the presently highest inflation rates and/or public debt (Greece, Portugal, United Kingdom, Italy and Spain).

iv) Possible paths for enlargement of the Community, for present members of EFTA and for Central European countries.

Though these four issues may interact more continuously, we are interested primarily in the implications for the progress towards EMU. Here the framework of the Delors Report with fairly well-defined stages may be useful, since minimum progress required to pass to a subsequent stage puts all four issues into focus.

14.3.1 From stage I to stage II

Stage II will start January 1 1994, when the Committee of Governors becomes the European Monetary Institute (EMI) and economic convergence is reinforced. But one could also argue that the really inportant step will come only when this new institution becomes operative which is not likely to be the case since, as discussed in chapter 12, the insistence on the requirement that the 'ultimate responsibility' for monetary policy remain in national hands during stage II makes it difficult to give the EMI any real influence. However, from another point of view the start of stage II remains important as it signals the first institutional step towards EMU.

The maximum delay has been determined by the Conclusion of the European Council of Maastricht. What has to be achieved by 1994? The Intergovernmental Conferences on EMU and political union have to be completed and the Treaty Amendments ratified by all national parliaments.

The Intergovernmental Conference on EMU, although confined to a relatively technical agenda took the calendar year of 1991 to complete. The agenda for the Intergovernmental Conference on political union (PU) had a potentially more difficult agenda but since no sweeping transfers of power to the Community level were in the end agreed it was possible to finish this conference also in 1991. Ratification, of both Treaty Amendments, by national parliaments, possibly in some cases supplemented by a referendum, could take another year. The 1994 deadline does therefore not pose a particularly tight constraint on the political decision process. Moreover, it would come one year after the deadline for implementing the Internal Market by the end of 1992.

As regards the functioning of the EMS in the first stage the two main assumptions are that both the United Kingdom and Spain would find it possible to particpate with the normal fluctuation margins of ± 2.25 per cent in the course of 1992 and that Spain and Ireland would, at the latest by the end of 1992, be ready to remove capital controls. These are not radical assumptions; the Spanish authorities are already now recognizing that their capital controls have become so leaky that they are not very effective in limiting the capital inflows attracted by the high domestic interest rates.

No substantial economic policy adjustments are required during the first stage by those EMS members who have long observed the normal fluctuation margins. However, there are three countries, Italy, the United Kingdom and Spain, which need to undertake a substantial adjustment before they can participate in stage II. We discussed the convergence requirement in the previous subsection and found that they should succeed in qualifying for stage II, provided that Italy makes a sustained effort to reduce its budget deficit, that the UK succeeds in reducing inflation and that Spain contains its growing internal imbalance.

The new Convergence Directive would be used to monitor progress made by these countries. With nearly another two years to go until the second stage begins, the task of making policies in these three countries compatible with the requirements of tighter institutionalized cooperation is not unmanageable.

Portugal and Greece are, with some important differences among them, in a different category. It would not be realistic to expect Greece to be ready to participate fully in Stage II from 1994, but Portugal might just possibly succeed if a concentrated effort on the budget deficit is undertaken.

The EMU Treaty contains provisions for a transition period which imply some flexibility concerning the date and conditions on which some member countries join. These arrangements will therefore not prevent other member states from moving forward, as long as a consensus on the final objectives for the EC exists and has been confirmed by the Treaty revision.

An issue to be settled is whether the end of stage I (or the beginning of stage II) should be used for a final realignment among the EMS currencies aimed at establishing real exchange rates consistent with the perceived fundamentals. The institutional commitment to going well beyond the EMS towards a full EMU would provide a guarantee, or at least a major assurance, of stable nominal exchange rates for the future, hence the issue of undermining carefully built-up credibility would not arise in as acute a form as in the present system. The question of whether the peseta and the lira should be devalued was discussed in chapter 5 and it was argued that there are some indications that apparent overvaluation of these two currencies depends on fundamental factors. We therefore feel that there could hardly be scope for any major realignment, given the unavoidable tendency for national inflation rates to be driven apart by such a move.

Turning to the enlargement agenda the main issue is when the EC will be prepared to discuss association arrangements and membership with potential new members. Austria applied for membership in 1989 and Sweden in July 1991 and Finland in March 1992. Indeed, the very prospect of an acceleration of the move towards EMU has prompted reflections also in the remaining EFTA-countries that the 'acquis communautaire' may develop so fast that they have to reconsider their reluctance to aim for full membership now rather than later. Several countries in Central Europe – Hungary, Czechoslovakia and Poland – have expressed a long-term interest in membership and, in the shorter term, in association arrangement with the EC.

There is general agreement that these expressions of external interest do not justify any delay in the EMU process. Countries that have applied for membership and meet the basic conditions of full EMS participation – freedom of capital restrictions, readiness to accept the normal EMS margins and the principle of collective influence over their exchange-rate policy – have a justified expectation that they could participate soon in the Community's monetary arrangements at the stage to which they have developed at the entry date. Austria *de facto* already now fulfills the initial conditions. Norway, Sweden and Finland have shown, by linking their currencies tightly to the ecu, that they are in principle closer to being able to participate in stage I than some present EC member states. If these applications start to be discussed seriously in 1993, the EC could be under some pressure to give these countries a chance to participate as associate members in the EMS from early in stage II even before they become full members in the EC and thus participate fully in the subsequent EMU process.[11]

The time perspective for potential Central European members is obviously much longer, because the adjustments to be made are more fundamental. Their potential participation could arise only well beyond the completion of stage I as here envisaged. In any case a lengthy period of transition would be required.

14.3.2 From stage II to stage III

The decision to go to stage III will be preceded by an evaluation by the EC Commission and the EMI whether enough convergence has been achieved to make this step possible. It is also becoming increasingly clear that not all countries will be able and willing to participate at the same time in this move. In the previous section we outlined our assessment of the requirement for convergence which leads us to believe that, with one possible exception, a time horizon of nearly five years from now seems adequate to assume that the move to full EMU could encompass the present EC membership. An adjustment that cannot be done in five years may not be realistic within any time frame. Given this time perspective we believe that also Greece and Portugal could be ready for full participation with the others; however, given its track record and vey large adjustment requirement, Greece remains the only member for which early participation in stage III is unlikely. The EFTA countries that might have joined the Community by the mid-1990s would not require any large adjustment in macroeconomic terms and could therefore be expected to join immediately in the full EMU process even if they required transition periods in some other areas.

Finally, because of the political significance of a common currency, it would be desirable for this step to be taken by the entire Community at the same time. However,

---

[11] In 1990 Austria and Norway made informal soundings to explore what meaning could be given today to the status of having their currency associated to the EMS, but the response of the Community was not encouraging. This is why these two countries have not pursued this route, but have chosen other, more unilateral ways of assuring a stable exchange rate for their currencies *vis-à-vis* EMS participants. Sweden has recently made similar soundings and has so far met the same response.

once agreement on the final goal has been achieved, the economic equivalent of a common currency could be approached, if desired from the start of stage III, by a group of countries introducing zero margins and par clearing obligations for both central banks and private banks of the participating currencies. For the reasons we have developed in our analysis of the benefits of EMU we believe that there would be advantages to countries in accelerating the adoption of a common currency in order to keep the full benefits of monetary integration. A realistic time scale for the transition to a common currency could be at most two years after the irrevocable locking of exchange rates which constitutes the start of stage III.

14.4 Conclusions

We have assumed throughout this chapter that the EMU Treaty agreed upon at Maastricht will be implemented on schedule. Is this optimism justified? Sceptics would point to the failure of the Werner Plan of 1969/70, according to which monetary union was to be reached within one decade. The Werner Plan was not implemented, instead, as we saw in chapter 1, it was followed by an unprecedented increase in inflation and in exchange rate volatility. Another noteworthy example of failure in monetary integration is the second stage of the EMS which was foreseen for 1981, but never materialized. However, the present situation differs so much from that of the 1970s in political, institutional and economic terms that it seems to us highly likely that this time the goal will be attained.

The political factors are admittedly outside our own field of expertise. But it is apparent that the Community is now much more integrated in political terms than at the time of the Werner Plan. The majority voting introduced with the Single European Act and the agreement on Political Union achieved at Maastricht are two manifestations of this development. German unification, the collapse of socialism in Eastern Europe and the disintegration of the former Soviet Union have also contributed to push member countries to accept more and more transfers of powers to the Community. In this general context it becomes increasingly difficult for member countries to pursue independent monetary policies that are incompatible with the attainment of EMU.

The institutional factor is also important since, as argued in the summary of the lessons to be learned from the history of European monetary integration presented in chapter 1 of this book, a well functioning institution can affect the course of events in times of crises. The EMS has provided such a framework that is valued by all participants and has withstood the second oil price shock in its beginning and, more recently, the Gulf war and the economic consequences of German unification. It is therefore unlikely that outside shocks can disrupt progress along the lines fixed at Maastricht in the same way the break-down of the Bretton Woods system destroyed the Werner Plan.

Finally there are also economic factors at work which imply, as argued in chapter 7, that EMU is likely to bring more benefits than costs. The balance of costs and benefits might have been different at the time of the Werner Plans since, as documented in chapter 1, intra-Community trade is now much more important than in the early 1970s. Capital flows have also increased enormously during this period. Although this phenomenon is not limited to intra-Community flows the huge size of the international capital markets implies that in the absence of an institutional framework intra-Community exchange rates might be subject to the same fluctuations as the exchange rate of the US dollar or the yen. Asymmetric shocks, the main argument for exchange rate flexibility, are also less likely now than twenty years ago because the economies of the larger member states have now a more similar structure.

A further reason to be confident that the time-table fixed at Maastricht will not share the fate of the Werner Plan comes from the change in the philosophy underlying economic policy that has taken place in the meantime. In the 1960s and 1970s both monetary and fiscal policy were actively used to 'fine-tune' the economy, while it is now generally agreed that the main task of monetary policy is to ensure price stability. For national policy makers it is therefore now much easier to give up their influence over monetary policy if they can be confident that the European Central Bank will achieve this goal. This change in philosophy is also the reason why the present EMU project, unlike the Werner plan, does not call for a centralization of fiscal policy decisions. Limiting the direct competences of the Community to monetary policy, which does not impact the interest of national constituencies as directly as fiscal policy, is another element which makes it unlikely that strong national pressure groups can block progress towards EMU. In the longer term we regard some underpinning of EMU by fiscal transfer mechanisms as desirable; but the amounts involved need not be very large which may make agreement feasible.

The balance of costs and benefits in economic terms has thus also moved decisively in favour of EMU. Taken together with the new political environment in Europe there is therefore every reason to believe that economic and monetary union for the Community will be attained before the end of this decade and century.

References

Commission of the European Communities (1990), Annual Economic Report 1990–1, *European Economy*, 46, Brussels, December.

Committee for the Study of Economic and Monetary Union (1989), 'Report on Economic and Monetary Union in the European Community' (the Delors Report), Office of Publications of the European Communities, Luxembourg.

De Grauwe, Paul and Gros, Daniel (1991) 'Convergence and divergence in the Community's economy on the eve of Economic and Monetary Union' in Peter Ludlow (ed) *Setting EC Priorities*, Brussels and CEPS, London.

Deutsche Bundesbank (1992) 'The Maastricht decisions on European economic and monetary union' *Monthly Report of the Deutsche Bundesbank*, Frankfurt, February, 43–52.

Emerson, Michael, Daniel Gros, Jean Pisani-Ferry, Alexander Italianer and Horst Reichenbach (1991), *One Market, One Money*, Oxford University Press, Oxford.

Gros, Daniel and Jean Pisini-Ferry (1990), 'Toward EMU: fast track scenario', Centre for European Policy Studies, Brussels, mimeo, February.

Holtfrerich, Carl-Ludwig (1990), 'The monetary unification process in nineteenth-century Germany: relevance and lessons for Europe today', chapter 8 in Marcello De Cecco and Albert Giovannini (eds.), *A European Central Bank?*, Cambridge University Press, Cambridge, 216–45.

Pöhl, Karl Otto (1989), 'The further development of the European Monetary System', collection of papers annexed to the Delors Report, 129–55.

Vinals, José (1990), 'Spain and the "EC cum 1992" shock', chapter 7 in Christopher Bliss and Jorge Braga de Macedo (eds.), *Unity with diversity in the European Economy*, Centre for Policy Research, Cambridge University Press, Cambridge, 145–234.

INDEX